FREEDOM'S ORATOR

Robert Cohen

FREEDOM'S ORATOR

Mario Savio and the Radical Legacy of the 1960s

OXFORD
UNIVERSITY PRESS
2009

OXFORD
UNIVERSITY PRESS

Oxford University Press, Inc., publishes works that further
Oxford University's objective of excellence
in research, scholarship, and education.

Oxford   New York
Auckland   Cape Town   Dar es Salaam   Hong Kong   Karachi
Kuala Lumpur   Madrid   Melbourne   Mexico City   Nairobi
New Delhi   Shanghai   Taipei   Toronto

With offices in
Argentina   Austria   Brazil   Chile   Czech Republic   France   Greece
Guatemala   Hungary   Italy   Japan   Poland   Portugal   Singapore
South Korea   Switzerland   Thailand   Turkey   Ukraine   Vietnam

Copyright (c) 2009 by Oxford University Press, Inc.

Published by Oxford University Press, Inc.
198 Madison Avenue, New York, New York 10016

www.oup.com

Oxford is a registered trademark of Oxford University Press

Library of Congress Cataloging-in-Publication Data
Cohen, Robert, 1955–
Freedom's orator : Mario Savio and the radical legacy of the 1960s / Robert Cohen.
p.   cm.
Includes bibliographical references and index.
ISBN 978-0-19-518293-4
1. Savio, Mario.   2. Political activists—California—Biography.   3. Free Speech Movement
(Berkeley, Calif.)—History.   4. Student movements—California—Berkeley—History.
5. College students—California—Berkeley—Political activity—History.   6. University of
California, Berkeley—Students History.   I. Title.
LD760.C64 2009
378.1'9810979467—dc22   2009005312

Proceeds from *Freedom's Orator* will be used to support the Mario Savio Young Activist
Award and Memorial Lecture series. The award and lecture honor Savio's memory
by encouraging and recognizing young people engaged in the struggle to build a
more humane and just society. For more information on the Savio
Award and Lecture series, see www.savio.org.

Frontispiece image: Mario Savio speaking from the roof of the blockaded police car, Sproul Plaza,
October 1, 1964. Photo by Lon Wilson, Bancroft Library, University Archives.

1   3   5   7   9   8   6   4   2
Printed in the United States of America
on acid-free paper

IN MEMORY OF REGINALD E. ZELNIK
(1936–2004)

It was Mario Savio got me out here [to Berkeley]. I saw Mario on top
of that [police] car in Sproul Plaza and said "great google-bee I'm outta
here." I drove across the country. I wanted to go somewhere where it
looked like youth knew what time it was. Every other place, they were so
afraid. Out here, it was happening.
—Blues singer Taj Mahal

I am dreaming, and I want to do good. For the good you do is never
lost. Not even in dreams.
—Pedro Calderón de la Barca; Mario Savio inscribed these
words inside J. L. Austin's *Sense and Sensibilia*, which he carried in his
pocket during the Free Speech Movement

ACKNOWLEDGMENTS

I am indebted to all those friends and colleagues of Mario Savio who agreed to be interviewed for this book. On the pre-Berkeley years these included Arthur Gatti, Florence Feldman-Wood, and Nancy Scheper-Hughes. For sharing their memories of Savio in the Free Speech Movement and the rest of his Berkeley years, my thanks to Jack Weinberg, Jackie Goldberg, Suzanne Goldberg, Martin Roysher, Michael Rossman, Bettina Aptheker, Syd Stapleton, Brian Turner, Cheryl Stevenson, Leon Wofsy, Jack Radey, Kathleen Piper, Bernard Timberg, Sam Bader, Jeff Lustig, Reginald Zelnik, Clark Kerr, John Searle, Betty Garman Robinson, Walt Herbert, Lawrence W. Levine, and Adam Hochschild. Savio's fellow civil rights workers in Freedom Summer, Marshall Ganz, Robbie Osman, Ira Landess, Reebee Garofalo, and Jim Kates, were especially generous with their time. I owe a special debt to Cheryl Stevenson for saving Savio's Freedom Summer correspondence, and to Theresa Salazar at the University of California, Berkeley's Bancroft Library for making those letters available so quicky. On Savio's years at San Francisco State University, Oliver Johns and Geoff Marcy were especially helpful, as were Mette Adams, Victor Garlin, Ruben Armiñana, Donald Farish, Lowell Finley, Barbara Epstein, Jack Kurzweil, Elaine Sundberg, Andrea Granahan, and Nadav Savio on Mario's years at Sonoma State.

Art Gatti kindly provided his correspondence with Savio, the tape of a lost Savio speech, and a tour of the Queens neighborhood in which Mario grew up. My thanks to Suzanne Goldberg for providing me with a recording of a 1966 Savio speech. Linda Lye played a crucial role in helping me obtain the legal files from Savio's last political battle. For their assistance in the interviewing process, my thanks to Daniel Savio and David McDougal, who did excellent oral history work. I am grateful to my former student Ricky Gelber for his research into Mario Savio's impact on rock and folk music and to Gina Sartori for her editorial assistance. The students in my 1960s seminar in New York University's history department asked great questions about Savio, which influenced my thinking. My thanks to Patricia Oscategui, Jason Kok, Myra Cohen, and Hayan Chong for helping with the transcription of interviews, to Frank Pignatosi for translating the Italian news stories on Savio, to Lena Singh for her grant assistance, and to James Fernandez for his expert advice on Spanish translations.

The interviews that other scholars, journalists, and movement veterans have done with Savio have been great sources, and my thanks go to Max Heirich, Bret Eynon, Ronald Schatz, David Pickell, Marston Schultz, David Lance Goines, Jack Fincher, and Douglas Giles for these illuminating interviews. Filmmaker Mark Kitchell's interviews with Berkeley activists were extremely helpful, as was his classic documentary *Berkeley in the '60s*. Lisa Rubens's interviews with many Free Speech Movement veterans and Berkeley faculty have proven rich sources, and I can't say enough about her generosity in sharing the fine work she has done for the Free Speech Movement Oral History Project. The *Daily Californian*, Berkeley's student newspaper, and reporter Seth Rosenfeld opened a valuable source on Savio when, in 1982, they obtained the FBI files on him and the Free Speech Movement, and Rosenfeld's more recent reporting for the *San Francisco Chronicle* has further illuminated this important story. University of California archivist Kathryn M. Neal was of great assistance to me in researching the legal niceties of the border dispute over the Bancroft strip. Joan Malczewski and Ron Robin, colleagues at New York University, offered helpful advice on the final chapters. New York University travel funds and grants proved essential to completing this study.

I join with the publisher in gratefully acknowledging the generous contribution to this book provided by Stephen M. Silberstein, which made it possible to publish a selection of Savio's writings.

My interest in the Free Speech Movement originated in the twentieth-anniversary commemoration back in 1984, and so did my contact with Savio. The late Michael Rossman was the spark plug of those events. His passionate conviction that this history matters has proven contagious, and for that I am grateful. Bettina Aptheker offered a critical and insightful reading of the manuscript and generous encouragement.

The Organization of American Historians session on Savio and the Free Speech Movement that I organized with Lawrence W. Levine, Leon Litwack, Pedro Noguera, and Alan Brinkley proved an important event in the evolution of this study. I am grateful to them and to all the historians whose questions and comments enriched that session. The death of Larry Levine has been a tremendous loss; it leaves me all the more grateful that he shared his insights about Savio and Berkeley in the sixties at that session. Jesse Lemisch's sixties scholarship and support paved the way for this book.

The idea for this book originated with Lynne Hollander Savio. Her fabulous work in preserving Mario's speeches and papers generated the core historical materials for this study. If not for Lynne, this book simply would not have been possible.

My thanks to Susan Ferber and Niko Pfund at Oxford University Press for their faith in this project and for their patience and support, and to Ferber for her heroic efforts to slim down a very fat manuscript.

My wife, Rebecca Hyman, has been as eager as I to see Savio's story told, and her intellectual comradeship and love have made the years working on this project joyful, as has my son, Daniel, who by the time he got to high school had lived with Mario's words so long that he already knew the "bodies upon the gears" speech by heart.

This book is dedicated to the memory of Reginald E. Zelnik. When I agreed to take on this project I had hoped to sway Reggie into coauthoring it with me, stealing him away from Russian history, as I did in our prior book on the Free Speech Movement. The shock of his death almost led me to drop this project, since I could not imagine working on Berkeley and Savio without Reggie. A dear friend and brilliant historian, Reggie understood the Free Speech Movement and Berkeley in the sixties more deeply than any other scholar. In time I came to see that the best way to honor Reggie's memory was to complete this study and have it stand as a reminder of what is best about Berkeley. Reggie's scholarship, courageous battles on behalf of free speech from the 1960s through the early twenty-first century, teaching, and friendship embody Berkeley at its most inspiring.

CONTENTS

**IV In His Own Words: A Selection of Mario Savio's
Speeches and Writing**

FREEDOM'S ORATOR

INTRODUCTION

Few protest leaders have burst upon the American political scene more dramatically than did Mario Savio in fall 1964 when he was a twenty-one-year-old Berkeley student. The University of California (UC) had become the scene of nonviolent political warfare, with the administration enforcing and students defying a campus ban on political advocacy that closed down the free speech area at UC's busy southern entrance. Coming at a time when student civil rights activism was surging, the ban seemed an attack on the civil rights movement and a gross violation of the right to free speech, igniting protests in mid- and late September. This conflict escalated just before noon on October 1 as police drove a squad car to UC Berkeley's central thoroughfare, Sproul Plaza, to arrest civil rights organizer Jack Weinberg because he, like many free speech activists, was defying the ban by staffing a political advocacy table on the plaza. Before the police could complete the arrest, someone shouted, "Sit down!" Within moments a crowd of students surrounded the car in a nonviolent blockade that would last thirty-two hours. Shortly after the blockade began, Mario Savio, a leader of the civil rights group University Friends of SNCC (Student Non-Violent Coordinating Committee), removing his shoes so as not to damage the police car, climbed on top of it and into national headlines, using its roof as a podium to explain the protest and demand freedom of speech. From those first moments atop that car Savio emerged as the Berkeley rebellion's key spokesperson, symbolizing all that was daring, militant, and new about the Free Speech Movement (FSM).[1]

This was the first revolt of the 1960s to bring to a college campus the mass civil disobedience tactics pioneered in the civil rights movement. Those tactics, most notably the sit-in, would give students unprecedented leverage to make demands on university administrators, setting the stage for mass student protests against the Vietnam War. Savio's charismatic leadership in this new form of rebellion and his eloquence, highlighted in the press, made him seem larger than life. "Mario Savio, enigmatic to most, was everywhere," the *Daily Californian*, Berkeley's student newspaper, reported, "the messiah with waving hands...exhorting his followers from the police car's top."[2]

Savio was among the first media stars of America's New Left—the 1960s student movement "committed to redressing social and political inequalities of power," challenging cold war nationalism, and renewing "the atrophied institutions of American democracy" by creating "new institutions of popular participation to replace existing bureaucratic structures."[3] In 1964, when Students for a Democratic Society (SDS) had yet to attract the media coverage it would receive as the key New Left organization of the mid- and late 1960s, Savio was making headlines leading the largest, most disruptive campus rebellion in American history. He helped to define a new role for American college students, that of a dynamic youth leader igniting mass student protest.[4]

Savio's fame was closely linked to his oratory. Back in 1964 the press—with its cold warrior disdain for radicalism—hardly knew how to react to his militant yet popular oratory because it seemed so out of place on U.S. campuses, which had almost never witnessed mass protest (the only exception being the long-forgotten, left-led student movement of the 1930s).[5] *Time* magazine thus looked outside the States for comparisons, evoking Fidel Castro and attributing to Savio "an almost Latin American eloquence...a sense of demagoguery and a flair for martyrdom." Yet not even *Time*'s antiradical editors could miss the fact that Savio had prevailed over a university administration undermined by its "habit of vacillating between concessions and crackdowns."[6] The Bay Area press uncomfortably conceded his eloquence, hinting that its appeal was based on emotion rather than reason. "He harangues in rapid fire staccato," explained one San Francisco reporter, "shrill at times, emotionally charged always. He's a slender 6 foot 1, sloping at the shoulders, clad usually in baggy slacks and a heavy jacket, bushy hair...unkempt, his blue eyes sparkling and intense."[7]

Friends and foes alike recognized that Savio on the stump "cut an extraordinary figure," whose words and delivery made a lasting impression. Berkeley history professor Reginald Zelnik termed Savio "the most original public speaker I would ever hear." Zelnik saw in him the reflectiveness of a genuine intellectual, the questioning spirit of the most iconoclastic undergraduate, and an intense desire to inspire thought and dialogue. Berkeley immunology professor Leon Wofsy reflected, "He wasn't doing it for show. He wasn't doing it to provoke." When Savio argued on behalf of the FSM, as Wofsy put it, "he was speaking from his heart and from his head. There was a certain quality there. Not just his rhetoric, but there was a quality of sincerity and thoughtfulness that just lifted him above the others."[8]

It is Savio's speeches, not those of professors or campus officials, that have found their way into the histories of the 1960s. This was in part because during the FSM, as historian Henry May noted, students were the actors, making history through their protests, while faculty and administrators were merely reactors, trying to come to grips with this unprecedented outburst of activism and civil disobedience.[9] But it was more than simply Savio's insurgent status that made his words memorable. After all, many Berkeley protesters spoke up, but none of their words have proven so enduring, and none of these speakers could match Savio's passionate yet logical, accessible, democratic, and at times poetic oratory.

For Berkeley student activists, Savio's rhetoric—much like the FSM itself—transcended ordinary politics. It embodied a mass movement rooted in moral principle rather than in political calculation or opportunism, standing up for freedom despite the odds of succeeding against a powerful university administration. The cause was, in their view, so just and Savio's championship of it so principled that it elevated him and the movement to new heights of eloquence and political effectiveness. There seemed something almost miraculous about once-powerless students coming together to nonviolently blockade a police car, mount massive sit-ins, build a student strike, humble UC president Clark Kerr (the master builder of California's gargantuan state university system), and win the epic battle for student rights.

Savio did not have to be speaking from atop a police car for his words to be remembered. His most famous speech occurred two months after the police car blockade as he urged students outside Sproul Hall to join the FSM's culminating sit-in on December 2, 1964. He demanded that college youth heed their consciences and embrace activism. "There's a time," Savio exhorted his classmates,

> when the operation of the machine becomes so odious, makes you so sick at heart, that you can't take part. You can't even passively take part. And you've got to put your bodies upon the gears and upon the wheels, upon the levers, upon all the apparatus, and you've got to make it stop. And you've got to indicate to the people who run it, to the people who own it, that unless you're free the machine will be prevented from working at all![10]

This dramatic call to resist unjust authority embodied the youthful idealism and iconoclasm of the insurgent sixties. Well into our own century it continues to appear in feature films, documentaries, protest songs, and television shows that explore that decade and other times of revolt against oppression. The speech helped convince some thousand students to occupy Sproul Hall, paving the way for a mass sit-in, which for its time was the greatest act of mass civil disobedience (and provoked the largest mass arrest) on an American campus.

It is not surprising, then, that some FSMers used biblical imagery as they searched for ways to describe how politically Savio had helped to part the waters for the Berkeley rebels. In *Loose Change: Three Women of the Sixties*, Sara David-son, portraying Berkeley students whose lives were transformed by the sixties, recounts their initial reaction to his emergence in the movement's leadership:

> Mario...emerged from nowhere to become the spiritual leader of the Free Speech Movement. He stuttered badly but when he faced a crowd, words came in a silken flow. Jeff thought he was one fucking genius of a speaker. Susie thought he was a great man, a prophet. She heard kids compare him to Moses, who had also stuttered. "Mario could never lie.... He had this morality thing, right and wrong, no compromise on your principles." He inspired universal respect.[11]

Actually, even on campus Savio had his detractors. Administrators and fac-ulty who opposed the FSM saw him—much as the press did—as a dangerous demagogue undermining respect for authority. UC's graduate dean privately accused him of "speaking the language of the gutter."[12] Another high-ranking UC administrator grew so frustrated at the protests Savio helped ignite that he privately confessed a desire "to punch Mario Savio."[13] Critics charged that Savio preferred confrontation to negotiation and was more interested in mak-ing trouble than settling the free speech dispute. Since the Berkeley demonstra-tions were unprecedented in their size and disruptiveness, it was natural for those concerned with order to be critical of both the protests and Savio as a key leader of them.[14] Similar criticisms would be leveled at protest leaders on other campuses as the student movement of the 1960s spread. In turn, Savio was very critical of liberalism, since he was battling liberal administrators who he saw as behaving intolerantly. Examining him as a lightning rod of political controversy reveals the terms of political debate that loomed large as the decade progressed—the split between the Left and establishment liberalism, and the backlash against student unrest, which such conservative politicians as Ronald Reagan would ride to high office.[15]

Political labels, however, tend to simplify, and this was certainly true with respect to Savio. Radical as he was when it came to his socialist sensibility and willingness to use nonviolent civil disobedience to fight injustice, the causes Savio battled for in 1964, voting rights and free speech, were in accord with bedrock constitutional principles. It was not Savio but liberal UC officials who behaved illiberally when they clamped down on student rights. Savio was able to inspire his fellow students—most of whom were not radical—because he spoke the language of rights fluently, passionately, and convincingly to show that such establishment liberals as UC president Clark Kerr had constricted freedom of speech and compromised on principle for the sake of their own power. Critical as he was of liberalism, Savio was with regard to libertarian principles a better liberal than Kerr. Indeed, the greatest distinction between Savio's generation of student civil rights workers and such liberals as Kerr was not ideological; it was that these young radicals were far quicker to stand up—risking arrest and even their lives—for racial equality and to recognize that the struggle against Jim Crow was the defining moral issue of their time.

This makes Savio seem more like a reformer than a revolutionary. Actually, he was both. He had a revolutionary temperament, wanted immediate egalitarian change, disdained compromise, loathed bureaucracy, and worked for a total transformation of race relations and university life. Never a Marxist, he was as critical as a Marxist would be of American imperialism and capitalism's inequities. Savio's brand of radicalism was nonideological, a kind of moral inclination toward democratic socialism that was never systematized or carefully defined because of his aversion to grand political theories or dogma (which reminded him too much of Catholicism). His radicalism was hyperdemocratic, experimental, empirical; it was grounded in an ethic of fairness and compassion that was totally compatible with political crusades that today might be considered liberal reforms but which in the 1960s were well to the left of the liberal mainstream with regard to free speech, student rights, civil rights, and neocolonialism. He was enough of a realist to recognize that it was not dreamy rhetoric about socialism but immediate demands—what he called "consequential speech"—against oppression that offered the best prospect of major social change. Acts that might on the surface seem merely reformist had a deeper meaning for Savio. For example, the demand that a hotel stop racist hiring practices was for Savio an expression of moral economy, that human rights trumped property rights, so employers needed to practice fair hiring even if this hurt profit margins.[16]

Despite all the attention accorded to Savio's most famous speeches, remarkably little has been written about the person behind the oratory. It may be that because American students have been largely quiescent politically since the 1960s, the idea of portraying the avatar of student rebellion in the United States seems unappealing, even antiquarian. Perhaps the brevity of his time on the national political stage has contributed to this pattern of neglect by historians.[17] After all, at first glance he does seem like a shooting star who glowed brilliantly in fall 1964 but soon faded from view.

Savio's story is about far more, however, than a stormy semester at Berkeley. It illuminates not only the decade of the 1960s and its student dissidents but also political culture before and after that turbulent time. He grew up in the cold war era and was heavily influenced by the anti-Communist ethos of the 1950s, from which he struggled to break free.[18] He was hardly alone in this revolt against the cold war consensus. In this and other ways, his is also the story of his generation of sixties campus rebels who had lived through and become disillusioned with the tense age of the nuclear arms race, McCarthyism, and the surging consumerism of cold war America.[19]

Savio's rebelliousness evolved, however, in a distinctive milieu that separates him from affluent youths on cold war America's elite college campuses. Raised in an immigrant Italian Catholic working-class home in Queens, New York, his coming of age was painful in that it involved being pressured to jettison his Italian heritage in an assimilationist household, navigating the blue-collar version of the American dream, and breaking with the Catholic Church. How an altar boy en route to the priesthood became a student rebel tells us much about both Savio's times and the white ethnic working-class world into which he was born.[20]

By the time he got to Berkeley, Savio was a dissident ex-Catholic whose social justice ethos and political and educational trajectory were very much influenced by his religious sensibility. In a 1965 *Life* magazine interview he would remark: "I am not a political person. My involvement in the Free Speech Movement is religious and moral."[21] Much as he revolted against the Church and sought to escape its dogma through science, philosophy, the classics, and personal connections to Jewish teachers and friends, he remained as engaged as the most conscientious priest might be with questions of good and evil, battling injustice as if it were sin, striving for egalitarianism and community as if doing so were a biblical injunction for a kind of moral purity or grace.[22] Later in life he defined the political perspective he brought to the movement in a quasi-Catholic way, terming it "secularized liberation theology," referring to the Catholic radical tradition stressing a divine mission to liberate the poor. Savio considered that mission divine long after he had broken with the Church. Secular as he was, then, his political life was part of Catholic intellectual and political history—that is, if there is a place in that history for an agnostic radical whose politics were influenced by the egalitarian strand in Catholicism, with its critique of materialism and greed.[23]

The egalitarian sensibility that he had first imbibed in the Church led him to feel a powerful sense of solidarity with civil rights activists battling racism. His first experiences in mass protest were as part of the Bay Area civil rights movement. This was followed by his participation in the southern civil rights movement, as a volunteer in the Mississippi Freedom Summer campaign of 1964. Along with hundreds of volunteers from across the country, he risked his life registering African Americans to vote and teaching in Freedom Schools. The goal of that historic summer project, spearheaded by SNCC, the daring, predominantly black, youth-led civil rights organization, was to democratize race relations in the South's most violently racist state. Although bent on changing the South, Freedom Summer quickly transformed the volunteers themselves. They had come face-to-face with the evil of racism and the courage of black Mississippians in combating that evil, and returned home determined to purge America of its racism and to reject all compromise with social injustice. Although Savio ranked among the most famous Freedom Summer veterans to lead a protest movement outside the South, he was only one among many of these activists who bridged the democratic ethos of the southern civil rights movement and the rest of American society.[24] The civil rights movement inspired in him and others an antiauthoritarianism and a faith that mass protest movements from below could bring about democratic change even in the face of resistance by powerful social and political elites.

In Berkeley's Free Speech Movement Savio came to act on that faith, transitioning from rank-and-file member to leader. While the movement's public events are well known, the FSM's meaning for him both politically and personally has never been studied closely, in part because of Savio himself. His egalitarianism made it difficult for him to discuss his charismatic leadership and its pivotal role in the FSM's success. He and his fellow FSMers preferred to speak of the Berkeley rebellion as a grassroots movement whose leadership embodied its hyperdemocratic ethos, headed by elected and representative committees. Consequently, he was far more comfortable talking for and about the movement and its collective leadership, as opposed to discussing himself or the significance of his leadership. Thus it was not until three decades after the FSM that Savio admitted to the deeply personal way in which the Berkeley rebellion had liberated him. Never before had he discussed publicly the severe stutter he had suffered with and how he was able to shed his speech defect during the FSM and use his newfound oratorical skill to help lead the movement to victory.[25]

Savio's story and his observations about the movement reveal a dramatic shift in the FSM from spontaneous democracy (with on-the-spot decisions for immediate acts of civil disobedience) to the most deliberative form of democracy (a highly participatory, exhausting process of consensus decision making requiring marathon meetings and discussions before any action could be taken). His reflections on the FSM show he was powerfully influenced by Bob Moses and the hyperdemocratic ethos that this Freedom Summer leader and other SNCC activists pioneered in the South, which highlighted the responsibility of organizers to their constituents and experimented with a leadership style far less hierarchical than any found in mainstream politics. It would be difficult to imagine a movement and a leader that better embodied the New Left ideal of participatory democracy than the FSM and Savio.[26]

Those who envision FSMers as rebels shouting on the barricades will be startled to find Savio and his fellow Berkeley activists spending weeks during the FSM semester engaged in detailed, serious, and generally quite civil negotiations with faculty and administrators. He tended in the bulk of his FSM oratory to be at least as educational as agitational, and though always passionate about free speech and civil rights, he rarely displayed the level of anger visible in his "bodies upon the gears" speech. When seen within the FSM's complex history, his style of leadership, political ideas, and oratory seem more comprehensible, rational, and three-dimensional. This portrait also reveals his weaknesses, suggesting that not even the idealism of youth could always overcome problems caused by lack of leadership experience.

During Savio's life, his fellow FSM leaders, out of respect for his privacy and because they shared his democratic preference to discuss the movement's principles rather than its principals, did not comment much on his oratory and leadership.[27] But since his death, these FSM veterans have begun to open up about these issues, illuminating the nature of his leadership and clarifying how he operated both in public and at behind-the-scenes meetings.[28] It is now possible to see the way his leadership functioned in a movement that tended to think itself too democratic to rely on leaders.

In the FSM Savio and his fellow activists developed a critique of the modern American university that has only grown more relevant to the world of higher education. He worried that the university was becoming a service station for corporate America, the research and development arm of industry and the military. Preoccupied with service to the elite, the university, in Savio's view, neglected the welfare of those at the bottom of society and also seemed increasingly indifferent to the state of undergraduate education.[29] These ideas, along with his larger critique of corporate America and American liberalism, merit a fuller hearing than they have been accorded.

Savio's story also has implications for the debates that have raged among historians of the 1960s over the trajectory of the New Left and mass protest during that decade. Following the lead of former SDS president and sociologist Todd Gitlin, some historians have argued that as a child of the civil rights movement, the New Left was born democratic, nonviolent, undogmatic, and innovative in its approach to grassroots organizing, but was transformed as the Vietnam War and the black power movement evoked alienation, cynicism, and revolutionary fantasies. It imploded after aping the worst forms of Old Left dogmatism and embracing violence, in anticipation of a revolution that never came. A new generation of historians has challenged this view, arguing that even as SDS was torn apart by the sectarianism of its Weather and Progressive Labor factions, mass protest—much of it nonviolent—surged on the campuses, and new movements, such as women's liberation/second-wave feminism, were gaining ground in the late 1960s and early 1970s.[30] Savio's nonviolent approach to organizing and the success it bred will certainly strengthen partisans of Gitlin's perspective on the early New Left, as do Mario's loathing for sloganeering and vanguardism and his insistence that organizers respect the people they organize and communicate directly and unpretentiously with them. On the other hand, Savio, though never able to embrace ideology, was far more understanding of the late sixties New Left's shift to an Old Left style of thinking than was Gitlin, since Savio saw it as a logical response to the war and the need to come up with explanations for America's imperialistic behavior in Vietnam.[31]

The fact that even at the height of the late 1960s Savio never embraced violence says something that all too many histories of this period have missed. While violence, especially the torching of ROTC buildings, spread across America as the Vietnam War polarized the nation, the vast majority of student protesters of this era remained nonviolent. Savio was one of the millions of left-leaning dissidents in 1960s America whose stories do not conform to the SDS/Weather implosion narrative of militancy spinning out of control. Such nonviolent dissent was not merely more politically realistic and morally grounded than the Weather Underground's days of rage and bombings but also far more representative of sixties youth, and it ought to command greater attention from those who study this turbulent time.

Thinking seriously about Savio's role as a student leader and speaker means recognizing that the old debates about whether to valorize or demonize sixties campus rebels misses in some respects the deepest significance and irony of that troubled time. Thanks in part to the influence of Savio and the FSM, turbulence and crisis abounded on U.S. campuses in the Vietnam era—so much so that by the time of the Kent State massacre a majority of Americans saw campus unrest as the nation's number one problem. Yet out of this turbulence came an outpouring of ideas from the young about reforming and revolutionizing society. This is reflected in the *Norton Anthology of American Political Thought*, which includes a half dozen essays, platforms, and speeches by 1960s student and youth activists, Savio's among them. But in the post-sixties chapter on contemporary discourse not a single student entry appears.[32] As the campuses became less troubled places in late twentieth- and early twenty-first-century America their students generated little mass protest or memorable political discourse. So if the waves of protest and new political ideas on campus were defining features of the 1960s, and Savio's student days suggest they were, historians need to do more to uncover the keys to this political dynamism and why it proved so impossible for students to match in the past half century.

Biography, even political biography, is by definition personal. And in Savio's case the personal and the political are intimately linked. His sense of ethics, his political principles, and his personal problems combined to lead him to withdraw from leadership after the FSM. In a society where celebrity is a rare and desired commodity, it seems almost incomprehensible that someone would walk away from it, as he did. By making a star out of Savio, a person too democratic to believe in political stardom, the media made it difficult for him to comfortably stay connected to the growing antiwar movement—his celebrity kept getting in the way. The New Left, as Todd Gitlin has pointed out, was too ambivalent about leadership to come up with a viable strategy for coping with the ways that the media imposed instant celebrity on its key leaders. Savio was among the first student leaders to be burned by the media's glare.[33]

The complications of trying to build a democratic and nonhierarchical movement culture amidst media wedded to hierarchy and celebrity were only part of what drove Savio from leadership. At least as important were his psychological problems. He spent much of his adult life battling depression and panic attacks, which made it difficult for him to pursue either a career or a life of political activism—and even harder to pursue both simultaneously.[34] Nor did he see politics as a career path. His engagement with the civil rights movement and the FSM evolved out of moral commitments, not political ambition. Savio, a brilliant physics student, had hopes of working in science and—with the exception of a halfhearted run for the California state legislature on the underdog Peace and Freedom Party ticket—never pursued elected office.

As a result, Savio's political biography, so vibrant during his student years, has long gaps in it afterward. He was only intermittently active politically in the mid-1960s, and disappeared from the political stage during much of the 1970s. Savio was not, however, some burned-out sixties radical who became disillusioned with the Left or abandoned his egalitarian ideals. He was simply trying to make his own way, supporting his family, and coping with his psychological problems. When he had built a stronger and healthier foundation personally, he returned to the political stage in the 1980s and 1990s.[35]

It was during this late return to activism that I first met Savio. I was a graduate student at Berkeley and helped plan the campus commemoration of the Free Speech Movement's twentieth anniversary (FSM-20). It was the middle of the Reagan presidency, and the media assumed (incorrectly) that universities, like much of the country, were shifting rightward—having supposedly become the breeding ground for self-promoting and materialistic yuppies (young upwardly mobile professionals). The media made similar assumptions about sixties veterans, who had supposedly, like the much-hyped Jerry Rubin, learned the error of their radical ways and embraced the values of Wall Street.

Hollywood suggested in such films as *The Big Chill* that the sixties generation had outgrown the antiestablishment ethos of their college years. At FSM-20 Savio's keynote speech, delivered to a huge crowd on Sproul Plaza, shattered these stereotypes. He offered a scorching critique of Reaganism and beckoned America to embrace the victims of U.S.-backed violence in Central America the way his generation's young activists had embraced black Mississippians in the 1960s. His speech powerfully affirmed that the political idealism of the sixties generation was alive and well.[36]

For many who had never heard Savio before, it was not merely what he said but how he said it that was memorable. The speech was poetic, humorous, angry, and colloquial. It dealt with the excesses of capitalism and the imperialistic U.S. intervention in Central America without a hint of Marxist rhetoric or sloganizing. It invoked the spirit of the sixties, praising the interracial solidarity of SNCC, without falling into nostalgia.[37] It was delivered with only a glancing reference to notes, and soared like a jazz improvisation. Those of us raised on politicians who read canned lines from teleprompters could barely believe political speech could be so alive. It was surprising. Who expected Savio on the occasion of the FSM's commemoration to speak of the horror he experienced as a child when he first saw photos of the piles of bodies at the Nazi concentration camps?[38] Moving and original, his address bespoke a sensitivity and authenticity that had all but vanished from the American political stage.

During the commemoration I had the opportunity to interview Savio. He was reluctant to do interviews, but after much hesitation he agreed. It quickly became evident that he had retained detailed knowledge of the FSM because the struggle for free speech remained deeply meaningful to him. On the free speech issue he had a civil liberties lawyer's grasp of the complexities of campus regulations as well as a fierce determination that the free speech principles embodied in the December 8 resolutions (the Berkeley faculty's Academic Senate resolutions that settled the FSM crisis by barring the restriction of the content of speech on campus) not be abridged.[39] Equally striking was how quickly he connected to the struggles of student activists in the 1980s, having never forgotten what it was like to be a student and enter into negotiations with campus officials who refused to take student grievances seriously. Effortlessly, he dazzled 1980s student radicals as a kind of patron saint of free speech and student activism, proving eager and effective at passing the torch of sixties idealism to new generations of activists. It seemed ironic, then, that the news media focused on how old and gray he looked, while virtually ignoring how he thought and spoke.[40]

Thus it came as no surprise to me that at the time of Savio's death in 1996 he was in the midst of a battle against a fee hike at Sonoma State University, where he taught. He had become the champion of working-class students who could not afford the new fees. This battle occurred on the heels of his efforts to mobilize campus opinion against the California voter initiatives opposing affirmative action and immigrant rights. Some of Savio's friends and Lynne Hollander Savio, his widow, think that exhaustion from all of this activism—and especially the fee hike campaign—aggravated his health problems and contributed to his death from sudden cardiac arrest. Without depicting Savio as a martyr for political causes, it is evident that he kept faith with the politics of his youth, and that his last political battle, much like the one that made him famous, saw him use his talents as an orator to build a student movement.[41] So the later activist phase of his life is not merely a footnote to his famous Berkeley battles of the sixties; it is rather a reminder that no one has taken full measure of the impact that sixties veterans such as Savio had on America after that turbulent decade ended. This part of the Savio story suggests that the memory of the civil war of the 1960s inspired lifelong egalitarian activism and has been one of the key forces pushing back against the right wing's plutocratic agenda, imperialist ventures, and assault on minority rights and gender equity since the sixties.[42]

Of course, there was a difference between Savio's later struggles and those waged during the 1960s. While the whole world seemed to be watching the FSM in 1964, his battles in the 1980s and 1990s, even when they dealt with issues of national or international significance, had no comparable audience. In an America with a minuscule and moribund Left, and electoral politics moving rightward, voices like Savio's seemed to be heard less, to matter less, at least to the larger public. Indeed, through much of the 1980s and 1990s—and even to this day—conservative politicians and pundits have made much political hay by bashing the 1960s as a time of chaos, nihilistic rebellion, and hedonistic self-indulgence.[43]

Savio's political biography poses a challenge to those who write off the sixties generation's democratic idealism and judge the decade only by its excesses. He embodied that idealism and, alongside Martin Luther King Jr., Robert F. Kennedy, and Malcolm X, produced memorable oratory in behalf of social justice.[44] Unlike these martyrs, Savio lived to see the long-term impact that the reformist and radical waves of the 1960s had on late twentieth-century America. Savio's speeches in the 1980s and 1990s credited the sixties generation with making America a more just society, and refuted cultural critic Allan Bloom's claims that the New Left had closed the American mind and damaged the university. The social movements of the sixties had, in Savio's view, championed new freedoms, opening the American mind by pushing it into questioning the racism, sexism, homophobia, and imperialism that had predominated for so long.[45] His reading of the sixties' legacy was not uncritical, but it was upbeat and anticipated the recent work of historians Maurice Isserman, Michael Kazin, James

T. Patterson, Van Gosse, Beth Bailey, and Eric Foner, who depict the insurgencies of the sixties as giving birth to a rights revolution and a freer, more democratic political culture that endured in the United States, even after Nixon and Reagan shifted electoral politics rightward.[46]

Savio was acutely aware that Reagan and other conservatives rode to high office via a backlash against the social changes championed by the sixties Left—and it was his outrage over the imperialist, nativist, and racist implication of that backlash (which he termed "the new barbarism") that provoked his return to political activism in middle age during the 1980s and 1990s. Yet he believed that as powerful as that backlash was, it constituted the last stand of a tired old white politics of exclusion and chauvinism that was headed for extinction. He saw the increasing racial diversity of the university (via affirmative action), the rise of second-wave feminism (symbolized in the advent of feminist First Lady Hillary Rodham Clinton), and the surge in black political power (embodied in the emergence of Colin Powell as a presidential possibility) as a few of the many signs that the rights revolution his generation had launched was continuing. Savio believed that the panicky conservative mobilizations against such changes were signs of right-wing weakness, not strength, a perspective that to me seemed unduly optimistic until the Obama presidential victory in 2008 suggested that the new America he saw glimmerings of in the 1990s, and which the ferment of the sixties made possible, was no illusion.[47]

Defying stereotypes of his rebel generation, Savio was almost relentlessly nonviolent, committed to building a more democratic university—with a renewed emphasis on meaningful undergraduate education—and was among the most undoctrinaire and intellectually engaged students ever to set foot on a college campus. Characteristically, Savio viewed his contribution to American history more in communal than individual terms. He saw himself as a part of a generation of students that was determined to end racism by overturning Jim Crow in the South and challenging discrimination in the North. He took pride in being part of a movement that helped to make the university a freer place for political speech. Ultimately the University of California honored that achievement, naming the steps of Sproul Hall, from which he gave many of his FSM speeches, the Mario Savio Steps.[48]

For all his achievements, however, a lingering sense of disappointment about Savio is discernible among some who worked with him during the 1960s. His comrades on the left sometimes felt let down by his withdrawal from political leadership during the Vietnam era. Some believed that if he had stayed on the scene, his principled and charismatic leadership might have been a powerful force keeping the New Left from falling prey to the revolutionary adventurism of the late 1960s. Others simply thought that the antiwar movement and allied movements in the quest for social justice would have been stronger had they been able to draw on his gifts as an orator.[49]

It may be that these high expectations and sense of disappointment about Savio are a metaphor for the sixties itself. After all, this was a time when the sense of possibilities was expansive, when even someone as nonradical as Lyndon Johnson could speak of waging and winning a war on poverty, when expectations about social change were so high that nobody could have fulfilled them completely. To hear Savio speak was to believe that the world could be changed and that this was a person who could inspire such change. The reality was that Savio was not some political emblem or saint; he was a real person with serious problems and other interests, which, in spite of his powerful intellect and intense compassion, sometimes kept him from making use of his political gifts. Perhaps the sense of disappointment about Savio is the right note to sound in assessing his political life. On one level it attests to his humanity: even though he carried out heroic acts, he could not slay all of his personal demons. The disappointment is also a tribute to what he was and what he meant to people who admired him: he raised expectations so high that disappointment was almost inevitable. Mario Savio was that rare person in the political realm who challenges us to rise above ourselves and our daily lives, to dare to hope, and to work toward a better, more humane, and more democratic world. The story of his rise to leadership returns us to twentieth-century America during an era in which freedom of speech, civil rights, and antiwar agitation were on the rise; his life and work on behalf of those causes call us back, in Lincoln's words, to "the better angels of our nature."

Yet there is also a personal story within Savio's biography that, though intimately connected with the political, transcends it. In that realm the theme is not disappointment but persistence. This is the story of Savio's personal struggles, and of how his determination made it possible for him to challenge and sometimes overcome obstacles in his own life. Though few stammering children go on to become, as Savio did, powerful orators, many struggle, as he did, to shed a speech defect. The image of giving voice to those without power was no mere metaphor for someone with his personal history. Similarly, Savio, afflicted throughout his adult life with depression, and hurt as well by child abuse, managed to battle back, the former student radical reinventing himself as a caring teacher while again engaging in political organizing in the final decades of his life. One suspects that with Savio, personal hardships operated much as polio did with Franklin D. Roosevelt—enhancing his compassionate impulses, so that rather than permanently paralyzing him, these disabilities deepened his already strong ability to identify with and champion those enduring hardships at the hands of late twentieth-century America's inequitable social system. Savio was a unique combination of stunning abilities and formidable disabilities; his life of political and personal struggle attests that people can help themselves and others, and even make history, if they put their hearts and minds to it.

IN HIS OWN WORDS

Following the political biography is a section consisting of a dozen of Mario Savio's speeches and writings.* In the course of reading his papers I came upon the list he had made of the writings and speeches he planned to publish with his memoir.[50] What struck me about this list was that two-thirds of his selections came from *after* the 1960s. The selection is consistent with the way he viewed the 1960s: not as an era for nostalgia or reliving his most memorable moments of political triumph and celebrity, but rather as a moral touchstone for a life-long struggle to move America toward genuine democracy and to free it of its tendencies toward war, racism, sexism, and avarice.

Savio's writings and speeches in the 1980s and 1990s were informed by the radically egalitarian sensibility he developed in Mexico, Mississippi, and Berkeley in the 1960s, a sensibility shaped by his own ethical and spiritual drive as well as by the culture of the insurgent movements in which he participated. He did learn from some of the mistakes of the 1960s, but he never gave up on the idea that America could become a more just society and a less threatening world power if it heeded the voices of dissent raised by his generation's advocates of equality, free speech, and peace. While I have added three more selections (two of which Savio wrote after drafting the list of writings and speeches he planned to include in his memoir), this section reflects his own choices. His later writings and speeches enable us to see how deeply meaningful the social revolution of the sixties remained for Savio, as he took passionate stances on immigrant rights, affirmative action, and neocolonial war making, issues that continue to be contested today.

* Recordings of Mario Savio's speeches can be accessed online at http://www.savio.org/speeches_and_interviews.html.

PART I

The Education of an American Radical

1

CHILD OF WAR

Nothing in the political background of Mario Savio's family even hinted that he would emerge as a radical. Mario was born on December 8, 1942, the eldest son in a working-class Italian American family in New York City. Neither his father, Joseph, who had immigrated from Sicily in 1928, nor his mother, Dora, whose family came from northern Italy, was on the left politically. For the first three years of his life Mario's household was headed by an Italian Fascist, his maternal grandfather, Armando, while Joseph was serving in the U.S. Army during World War II.[1]

Those first few years as a "war baby" and child were for Mario a "golden time." He remembered his grandfather as a "very warm person." His mother and her sister Anne provided a loving home life.[2] Mario's earliest memory was as a three-year-old sitting by the open window of their third-floor Manhattan tenement with his mother, the two of them gazing at the stars. She told him the nursery rhyme about wishing upon a star, and he "imagined an angel like spirit up above in the sky," with the night sky seeming "a place of good magic." Mario was later somewhat wistful about his father's absence in these early years, and wondered "how many other anti-war activists...were born in tenement flats, whose missing fathers were off fighting the Second World War?"[3]

When Joseph returned from the military he resumed his place at the head of the household, but not without serious conflict with his father-in-law. This tension within the household spilled over into politics, as Joseph, a supporter of Franklin Roosevelt, had little patience for Armando's admiration of Benito Mussolini. Joseph and his antifascist views prevailed. But this hardly made Joseph a radical. During the 1950s Mario's father voted Republican, supporting Dwight Eisenhower for president on the grounds that the Democrats had been in power too long.[4]

Mario was, as one of his teachers put it, "a nervous child."[5] From elementary through high school he suffered from a speech defect. Mario related:

I…had a semi-paralytic speech blockage. Whenever I would reach a word or syllable on which I was going to block—and I often anticipated these dreaded places, trying to restructure my speech by circumlocution so as to avoid the boulder in my path—my entire vocal apparatus would simply freeze, and my head and neck and much of my body would buck in sympathetic spasm, while my eyes often rolled out of sight. The blocks could average one or two per sentence.…I occasionally had to abandon my effort to speak.[6]

Much as he tried to overcome it—through speech therapy and by taking on school activities that involved public speaking—the speech defect persisted. It became even worse on "those relatively rare occasions when I was challenging a figure in authority." Then he literally could not speak. In his unpublished memoir of his school days he described an incident when he wanted desperately to argue with an adult who was being insensitive but could not articulate the words to do so. "It is," Mario recalled, "painful just to describe the stammer; it was nightmarish to live through it."[7]

Ironically, this speech defect played an important role in preparing him to become a powerful orator. He developed an acute sensitivity to the tone and cadence of the spoken word, studying elocution and developing a love of language along with a poetic sensibility.[8] So when at last his stutter faded after high school he would approach oratory with the passion and thoughtfulness of one who had wanted to speak all his life and who had finally been freed to do so.

Mario's speech defect may have been triggered during his early childhood by the conflict in the Savio household between his father and grandfather. Some of that conflict was over Americanization and language issues. When Mario's father was away in the army, the language spoken at home was Italian. This was Mario's first language, and he spoke it fluently, without a stutter. But after his father returned and insisted that the family speak English, Mario developed the stammer that lasted beyond his adolescent years. There is no definitive cause for speech defects, but they can be triggered by psychological factors. In Mario's case the "struggle for family power" manifesting in "fierce" arguments between his father and grandfather, and culminating in his being pushed to embrace a new language, well may have set off his speech problem.[9]

This generational conflict affected his political development. He remembered thinking even as a child that his father's pro-FDR arguments were "basically sound" while his grandfather's defense of Mussolini was "unsound." But since he loved them both, he realized it would be simplistic to see their feuding in strictly ideological terms. "In those early conflicts," he later wrote, he "began to develop a mistrust of ideology and a predilection for looking beneath ideological posturing to the human and personal issues really at stake. I...began to develop a powerful interest...in insurgency and...reconciliation."[10]

Mario believed that his political development was influenced by an almost subconscious resentment of the Americanization process he had experienced when his father drove the Italian language from his home. His father "decided— I guess when he was...in the...U.S. Army that it was going to be an American family...and put our Italian past pretty much behind us. I guess he recognized...that that was the only way we were going to make it in America." But this forced shift to English was hard for Mario because before the return of his father he had been "raised in a different sort of a home," and he came away from it with a "drive to be part of America, but not really part of America (sort of in opposition to the way things are done)." His later embrace of dissident politics may have been related to being "lockstep assimilated into American culture, with a certain amount of denial of what my family was...So there's a kind of ambivalence, I think, which may have in part manifested itself in politics."[11]

When he entered school he experienced an incident that left him ashamed of his immigrant roots. Mario began his elementary education in Catholic school. One of the priests in that school sang his name in rhyme, "Maaaario Saaaavio," highlighting his ethnicity in front of the other children. When Mario's father learned of this incident he was, in Mario's words, "so ashamed that he had my name changed" to Bob (Robert was Mario's middle name). Thereafter at school Mario was known as Bob or Bobby. The lesson he learned from this was that "to be an American, and to be a democrat with a small *d* [as opposed to being a fascist] was not to be Italian, [and was] in fact to hide your Italian-ness." He was never totally comfortable with this name change. "I knew who I was. I was Mario okay, but nobody called me that thereafter" for the rest of his childhood and teenage years. It was only after he left for college that he would reject such assimilationism and change his name back.[12]

Among the institutions that shaped his childhood and adolescence, none was more important than the Catholic Church. Dora Savio was a devout Catholic, and two of her sisters were nuns. From them Mario inherited what he later termed "a somewhat dreamy religiosity."[13] After the family moved from lower Manhattan to Floral Park, Queens, he became an altar boy. Throughout his teenage years he gave a great deal of thought to entering the priesthood. "Churchly things...doctrinal things were very important" to Mario. While "other people were...concerning themselves with...more current and more real things" he "was thinking about what transubstantiation meant...mystery Catholic words that resonated with some deep meaning."[14]

The hold that the Church had on Mario as a child and early teen was nowhere more evident than in the ritual of confession where—like all devout Catholics—he would kneel behind the grille in a dark, narrow booth whispering his sins to the priest. This ritual left such a strong, painful impression that years later he would draft an article highly critical of it. He acknowledged that initially, when he was an eight-year-old, confession seemed "an exciting introduction to adult mystery." In his teens, however, confession became a dreaded event because "with adolescence came the rages of the flesh and a heightened sense of guilt and shame" over sexual thoughts and acts. The obligation to share this guilt through confession caused the ritual to become "a place of exquisite torment." At times he engaged in what he later termed "the guilty confession," being explicit about his sins so as to go through the "cleansing pain of a full and worthy accounting." But since this involved being admonished by the priest, he would sometimes engage in what he called the "commonsense confession," in which he understated his sins so as to avoid the humiliation of confessing to the priest, confessions rendered all the more difficult because of his speech impediment. Mario later scorned confession as a ritual that nurtured "fearfulness, cunning, and childish vanity," but in his youth he was quite absorbed in it.[15]

Growing up in Floral Park with his parents and his younger brother, Tom, Mario was a "good boy" who deferred to authority, whether it be to his parents, teachers, or priest. He focused much of his youthful energy on his studies so as to obtain the high grades that would do them proud. Neither of his parents could afford a college education, and both had professional aspirations that went unfulfilled. Mario's father, a very bright and articulate man who was a highly skilled machinist, had initially wanted to become a chemist and later pined for a degree in mechanical engineering. His mother had wanted to be an English teacher. Unable to realize their own dreams, they imparted to Mario the need to be at the top of his class so that he could go on to college. When he graduated from junior high school with a strong academic record but not as valedictorian, he got the message that his mother "was obviously disappointed in my second-best performance. And somehow I had promised myself that she would never have to endure that sort of 'humiliation' again." When he entered high school he strove for perfection. "While others developed real interests...I specialized in doing well in school."[16]

This quest for academic excellence paid off with respect to his grades. Mario took "only the most difficult courses, competing with the strongest students, and...earned the numerical equivalent of an A in every course." He was one of only two Martin Van Buren High School students—out of five thousand— selected for a National Science Foundation (NSF) Summer Science-Math Institute at Manhattan College in 1959, a Sputnik-inspired program designed to recruit top students into advanced science education as part of the cold war competition. His selection for the institute was considered such an impressive achievement that it made the local newspapers.[17]

By the end of his junior year in high school this pressing hard for grades and deferring to authority left Mario frustrated with his education. The quest for academic perfection rendered him "immensely weary of school as an endless round of competitive struggle." His deference to authority figures at school made him feel as if he did not have control over his own education.[18] This was evident in the pressure from his high school principal and his parents to enter the Westinghouse Science Talent Search.

Mario had never even heard of the prestigious Westinghouse competition until he was approached by the science department chair, who asked him whether he had begun preparing a project to enter it. Having a national finalist would enhance the school's academic reputation. Finalists were courted by leading universities with scholarship offers. But Mario already had a scholarship offer from Manhattan College and so strong an academic record that he saw no need to enter yet another competition. "I had," Mario recalled, "somehow nurtured the wholly unrealistic fantasy that the end of high school would mean the end of this hellish competition." So he told the science department chair that he had no plans to enter Westinghouse, which resulted in his being called down to the principal's office.[19]

The discussion with the principal, Paul Denn, proved difficult because of Mario's hesitation in challenging his elders. He remembered that "I tried as best I could to explain to Mr. Denn that I had no plans, no intention, no need to enter the Westinghouse Science Talent Search. I believe I stopped short of saying that I did not wish to enter the contest—wished *not* to enter, actually. That would have seemed rude, somehow. This attempt to avoid the contest, to convey my not needing to compete, was rendered all the more painful by" the stuttering. What Mario hadn't told the principal was that his reluctance to enter was linked to his exhaustion with school. For Mario "devoting serious attention to a science project meant sacrificing" what he thought of as his "real objective, to have only the highest grades." The contest represented an intensification of the pressures to perform academically since he would now have to attain high grades with less time to prepare.[20]

Denn refused to take no for an answer. He and the science department chair told Mario's mother that if he did not enter the Westinghouse competition, they "might not be able to send entirely favorable college recommendations" on her son's behalf. They also argued that "since the school had gone out of its way to accommodate" Mario's speech disability, he "owed the school a debt of gratitude" that he "ought to repay by entering Westinghouse." Mrs. Savio was persuaded by their arguments and with this additional pressure forced her son to enter the Westinghouse competition.[21]

Mario did very well on the written exam and was selected as one of the forty national finalists. He was dismayed by this news because even though it was a prestigious award, he got it in part as recognition for a science project he did in a halfhearted way. Worse yet, he had to present his project, which he felt was "a silly one," in Washington, D.C. This meant preparing charts for the public presentation, something Mario was so reluctant to do that his father ended up doing as much of the drawing as he did. Rather than feeling gratified, Mario "felt stupid and fraudulent because my father had to help me prepare the charts and because I knew my project was worthless." Nor did Mario have an adult in whom he could confide these feelings because his teachers were so enthused and his parents "seemed not to notice the valuelessness of the project." For Mario, presenting his project to leading scientists at the convocation was terribly embarrassing.[22]

Later Mario criticized the way the cold-war-era federal government and many foundations lured public school students into science so as to ensure that Americans kept pace with the Russians. Even at the time, he recalled, the Westinghouse convocation "was widely viewed as a facet of Cold War preparedness." At that event his sole form of dissent came when he was asked to make suggestions for future Westinghouse competitions. Mario "responded that perhaps among the scientists and politicians asked to speak at the concluding dinner, there might be included someone who could put the relentlessly celebratory shindig in some ethical context, a 'philosopher.'" He came to believe that holding generously funded youth summer institutes and competitions in the sciences but not in other fields drew teens into science before they really understood their own interests, and could prevent them from discovering that their real interests lay elsewhere: "There are no corresponding programs of which I am aware designed to ferret out future art historians for example. It appears that the very best fate that could possibly befall any high school student is to be 'discovered' as a future scientist! This sort of thing could be just right for some students. But it is also the sort of opportunity which can be exceptionally limiting." Mario reflected that in his own case his talent and deep interest in philosophy—as a high school student he was reading Kant—never attracted anything comparable to the courting he got over his scientific talents, and this seemed an uneven and distorted way of shaping education for young Americans.[23]

For Mario the deepest significance of the Westinghouse competition concerned not cold war politics or educational policy but his own state of mind. The reason he could not prepare those charts, he later realized, was because he "was already withdrawing into a shell of serious depression. But at that point" he knew only that he "felt very unhappy and always tired, and…wanted to hide."[24] Unable to express his disdain for academic competition, he internalized his dissent and bad feelings.

This susceptibility to depression seems connected to a disturbing chapter in Mario's boyhood. As a seven- or eight-year-old child he was sexually abused by a teenage uncle. Mario could later remember only one episode of abuse. But its psychological impact was such that he thought there might have been other episodes involving the uncle or someone else that he had blocked from his memory.[25] And it is almost certainly why in a letter to a childhood friend he referred to his youth as "traumatizing."[26] Although he never discussed the abuse publicly, he did so privately with close friends and relatives, as well as on an autobiographical tape in which he described the abuse incident as a crucial event in his childhood. In the late 1970s he confided to his friend and FSM comrade Bettina Aptheker about the sexual abuse, and in doing so "he put his hands out. And he said, 'One day you are right-handed and the next day you are left-handed and the world has changed.'...It was so poignant....I thought to myself that it was utterly remarkable that this was part of who he was."[27] Aptheker came to believe that though this abuse hurt Savio personally, its emotional scars left him a more sensitive person in ways that enhanced his egalitarianism in both politics and personal relationships and heightened his empathy with the suffering of powerless people. "I think because of Mario's childhood experiences he was much more sensitive to abuse of anybody. And he understood it in a way that many men didn't, the kind of experiences girls and women have" with powerlessness and abuse.[28]

Serious as the abuse was, it may have been less central to Mario's psychological problems than was his tense relationship with his father. Joe Savio was for young Mario a frightening and domineering figure. The battles his father had with his maternal grandfather terrified Mario, who as a small boy feared that his father "was going to come into his room and kill him, and so slept on his back so as not to be taken unawares."[29] Insecure because his machinist job was well below his abilities, Joe almost always felt the need to best others, including Mario. This parenting style "didn't leave much room for the kids"; for example, in card and board games Joe always had to win. At one point in his adolescence, Mario, tired of this domination, expressed his fury at his father for monopolizing the design of his brother's toy train sets by "smash[ing] the trains because his father couldn't let him do anything on his own." It is likely that having his father intrude into his science project—a project done only because of adult pressure—was yet another episode of paternal domination and contributed to his depression (which went undiagnosed in his youth).[30]

Despite his battle with depression, Mario completed high school as valedictorian of a class of twelve hundred, with the strongest academic record in the history of Martin Van Buren High School. Although this achievement qualified him to go to any top college or university, he began his higher education at nearby Manhattan College, a small Catholic school in the Bronx. The choice of this college was not Mario's; it was his parents', especially his father's. Manhattan, dazzled by Mario's science record, offered him a full scholarship. When Mario raised the idea of applying to Harvard, his father exploded, arguing that turning down Manhattan's scholarship offer would jeopardize his younger brother's education since the family could not afford to pay tuition for both of them. His father's arguments were, in Mario's words, made "at great volume and with intense emotion...How dare I?" Although he tried to counter his father's arguments, he conceded that during this "bitter shouting match...my defense was as disjointed and ineffectual as only a severe stammer could make it." Proving unable to stand up to his parents, he did not apply to another school. Thus the greatest student rebel of the early 1960s began his academic career in the most unrebellious fashion imaginable.[31]

Yet if the teenage Mario Savio was far from a political rebel or a disobedient son, he was on the intellectual and religious fronts already demonstrating iconoclastic tendencies and a social conscience. He was not merely an honors student who did well in school to impress his parents and teacher; he was intellectually intense, reading voraciously and with a questioning spirit. By his early teens he was grappling with the validity of religion, the inequities of capitalism, and the nature of communism.[32]

Catholicism was the earliest target of his increasingly critical view of the world. By the age of eleven or twelve he was expressing grave doubts about the historicity of Christianity. He took religion seriously and took his doubts seriously too. When he was about fourteen he had a long, polite, and embarrassed conversation with his priest about whether or not the Bible's miracles were genuine. He asked the priest to

> suppose that, back in gospel times, there was a group of people from a distant planet with a technically advanced civilization that had decided to perform a sort of historical and sociological experiment with the people of the Earth in which they wanted to see what the long range effect would be of beginning a new religion. So, because of their technical advancement, they were able to have their agent perform these miracles, and so forth.[33]

The conversation ended with the priest telling him not to worry about such doubts. But, as Mario recalled, "I continued to worry about it....I was on the lookout for some replacement in my life for the life of the Church." Still, he found the shelving of his spiritual aspirations an extraordinarily painful process, and he "oscillated daily between the wish to be a priest and the deadly guilt of a budding apostate."[34]

Mario's ambivalence about religion—increasingly sophisticated questioning of Catholicism while retaining his emotional ties to the Church—shaped his response to the NSF Math-Science Summer Institute in 1959, which he attended as a high school student. Since the institute was held at a Catholic institution, each class began with a brief nonsectarian prayer. This struck him as "quite special" but not offensive:

> The point of this prayer for me was to bring the realm of science, which till then I had thought of as Jewish or even relentless[ly] secular, under the sovereign lordship of God and Christ. The instructors, both secular and religious, obviously knew their science: by leading us in prayer they thereby acknowledged a divine order beyond science. To my mind this brief ritual seemed most appropriate, even inspiring, despite the fact that it actually resolved none of my corrosive religious doubts.[35]

As a high school junior he was already using his scientific education to test the validity of Catholic conceptions of the world. "The experimental basis of modern physics, constituting the reality behind the equations" he was learning seemed at odds with Catholic teaching. "Catholic Thomism had always insisted on the actual, not a merely hypothetical capacity of the mind to encompass being. But modern physics, it seemed, required a radically hypothetical standpoint just to get started."[36] At the NSF institute he delighted in the way physics challenged theology, but he also enjoyed playing "both sides of the philosophical fence" by exploring how some of what he was discovering in physics laboratories undermined scientific assumptions and created intellectual space for such theological conceptions as free will. Mario realized that "determinism was...[a] presupposition of the scientific method," and it clashed with the "religious position." In physics lab he did some experiments that on a philosophical level seemed to support the free will ideal as opposed to determinism:

> One day I made an observation, not one planned for us by the instructors, which convinced me—and does still—that this essential connection between macrophysics and microphysics also precludes strict determinism in both if in either....We had set up a scintillation recorder to...count nuclear disintegrations in a radioactive sample. According to quantum theory, such disintegrations are predictable only on a statistical basis. Therefore the number of instrument flashes within the next ten

minutes, say, is rather closely predictable: but the timing of the very next flash is quite unpredictable, not merely as a practical matter but as a matter of high principle. Now suppose we set someone up at the laboratory door with instructions to open the door when he sees the very next flash. In this way we have once again coupled a submicroscopic event with macroscopic human behavior. If the timing of the next flash is unpredictable, then, to that degree so is our human subject. While this fact does not, in any sense, prove free will, what it does is open a niche for free will. This physical indeterminacy of human behavior constitutes a necessary condition for human freedom.[37]

Mario's interest in science, then, was philosophical, an approach to understanding grand questions about the world, rather than merely technical—and was an expression of his desire to question the assumptions of his religious upbringing and other ways of knowing.

Even as he began on his long road away from Catholicism, Mario's religious sensibility and Catholic orientation led him toward a literature and mind-set that were at least implicitly critical of capitalism. He later saw this as connected to the Catholic Church's precapitalist origins. Writers and activists from "certain [reform-minded] parts of the Church," such as Emmanuel Mounier, Jacques Maritain, and leading contributors to Dorothy Day's *Catholic Worker*, influenced him. They emphasized the need for social justice and espoused a brand of anti-Communism that was of "a somewhat un-American sort" in that instead of demonizing the Left it credited Marxists for their concern about economic inequality. From this dissenting Catholic tradition the teenage Savio developed a "sense that the Communists or the Marxists, could teach the Church a lesson in terms of fervent commitment to social justice—but they'd gone off the tracks in some other respects."[38]

Near the center of his spiritual sensibility were elements of a kind of premature liberation theology. He identified with religious writers who were critical of materialism and who displayed compassion for those in poverty. As a teen he was inspired by the poem "At the Monastery of Acqua Fredda" in John L. Stoddard's *Rebuilding a Lost Faith*, which spoke of the church as a refuge from the "hate and greed" of the world: "So vain the world's poor tinselled show, / What wonder that some souls have need / To flee from all its sins and woe?"[39]

This same sensibility conditioned Mario's response to his earliest encounter with the ideas of Karl Marx. In a high school economics class he first learned about the famous Marxist slogan "From each according to his ability, to each according to his needs," admiring that phrase for having "a certain biblical purity...I knew that somehow it was wrong to think so, but there was something in this phrase that was more than elegant, beautiful actually."[40] Similarly, in 1956, the year of the Hungarian anti-Communist revolt, Mario read Milovan Djilas's *New Class* and found himself sympathetic not only to its critique of Communism but also to how its author "still identified himself as a socialist. So I was sort of primed for the kind of left movement in the Church marked by [the] Second Vatican Council."[41]

Mario was so taken by his initial encounter with the socialist ideal that he sought to discuss it with his parents. The egalitarian sentiment behind social-ism seemed so generous—and the beauty of the words "From each accord-ing to his ability, to each according to his needs" was so "astonishing"—that he "could imagine Jesus Christ himself speaking them in the Sermon on the Mount." How then, he wondered, could they have been said by Karl Marx, who was supposedly "the prince of devils, the anti-Christ, the ultimate generator of international communism?"[42] Since his mother shared his religious sensibility and love of poetry, he first tried to talk with her. But because, as he later put it, "this was long before Women's Liberation," she told him to discuss it with his father. When he did, his father told him a story about a Communist organizer who tried to convert Mario's great-grandfather Don Beppino in Sicily. The organizer told Don Beppino he believed all men should share their wealth equally. Don Beppino pretended to be interested, saying he would gladly give the organizer half his property. But then he asked the Red what would happen if after a year's time the Communist had squandered his share. The Commu-nist replied that "in that case we could need to divide the remaining property once again." Outraged, Don Beppino raised his cane over his head and bel-lowed at the organizer, "*Vattini via, prima che ti dugno 'na bastunata*" (Off with you, and be quick about it, before I hit you upside the head with this cane)."[43]

Though Mario tried to explain that he was talking not about the Commu-nist system but about the socialist "ideal for society," his father "wasn't listen-ing." Mario later realized that "in his own simple and powerful way" his father "exemplified the nature of political discussion in America. Alien ideas are con-sidered only for purposes of refutation." Joseph's "grandfather had said it, he believed [it], and that settled it." "I had," Mario recognized, "unwittingly played the Communist organizer, and I had given my father the opportunity to play his beloved grandfather." Mario regretted that his father "could never hear the poetry" in Marx's words about fulfilling human needs. But he expressed pride that years later his father realized that Mario's radicalism had indigenous roots: when a reporter asked Joe Savio where his son had learned his radical ideas, he said that Mario picked them up from a book he read at home. When the reporter inquired with some excitement as to what that book was, Joe showed him the family Bible, aware of the link between Mario's religious sensibility and his dissident politics.[44]

The parts of Christianity Mario identified with most strongly were those that spoke to the need to aid the impoverished and oppressed. Even decades later—long after he had ceased to be a Catholic—he was still moved by this aspect of his old faith. Describing a woodcut from a book of Peter Maurin's essays, which embodied this religiously based social conscience, Mario remarked:

> It showed...people on...a breadline. And one of the people had a halo around his head...that presumably no one else could see, representing Jesus Christ. And it's a very ancient idea. The Greeks had it too. In fact, it's present also in the Seder service...The person you let in may in fact be Elijah...It's an idea of...an absolute duty to embrace the rejected person. In fact it's very difficult for me to even mention it without...choking up a little bit.[45]

Throughout Mario's high school years his search, as he put it, for "some alternative to the suffocating narrowness of working class Catholicism" led him to develop close ties with Jewish students and teachers. Almost all of his friends were secular Jews. For him, theirs seemed to be "a freer culture...in which there was much more respect for critical thinking than in the Catholic culture that I was born into." His mentors at school were intellectually intense Jewish teachers who shared his reverence for the life of the mind.[46]

Connecting to adults more educated than his parents was important in fulfilling his need for "an alternative place to stand" instead of that of his blue-collar family.[47] Since Joseph Savio saw college as "only high powered vocational training if not plain pretense" and wanted Mario to get the engineering degree that had eluded him, Mario did not think his father could grasp his intellectual aspirations. He knew engineering "wasn't me...In that line of work I would have ended up as one of the white coated degree men with the imagination of a cabbage. But there was no way to explain to my father that I cared about poetry and philosophy, and perhaps physics as poetry and philosophy."[48]

Van Buren High School's top math teacher, Ira Ewen, a Harvard graduate, was among the adults who most contributed to his "development as an individual separate from [his own] family, class, and religion." Ewen taught the honors trigonometry course as "an unremitting exercise in critical thinking." Being invited by Ewen to visit his home was among the most memorable events of Mario's high school years. Even Ewen's living quarters seemed distinctive since he resided in a small apartment, unlike Mario's parents, who took such pride in owning their own (modest) home. He viewed Ewen and his wife as "free spirits who rejected comfort for the life of the spirit." He was also impressed that the apartment was crammed with books "covering the full range of culture." When Ewen urged his star student to apply to Harvard, Mario felt "not just flattered" but hopeful in a way that "I could not express even to myself that Harvard might be that alternative place to stand...outside and beyond my family and religion." Although Mario proved unable to persuade his father to let him apply, his longing was an early indication that he would not look upon higher education in the careerist way that his father did.[49]

Although Mario did not act on it in high school, he developed a student activist ideal well before he ever set foot on a college campus. This ideal came to him through his readings and the media, rather than through any personal contact with leftist activists. Mario recalled that as a teen he

> had...this romance about college...it must have been out of the television and the newspapers...Stories of students in other countries...involvement in radical politics...It really did appeal to me....It was very exciting. I never bothered to look into...what colleges were really like—I should have. I just had this feeling that [American campuses] were...naturally part of this tradition...and I was extremely disappointed [to find that they were not].[50]

In high school Mario tried to find his voice as a public speaker and leader. Despite his stammer he was elected student council president. He also agreed to speak at the school's graduation ceremony in June 1960.[51] The principal, aware of Mario's stutter, told him that even though, as valedictorian, he was entitled to give this speech, it was not a requirement. Yet Mario was determined to confront his speech impediment and told the principal he wanted to give the address. He worked practicing its delivery with the speech department chair. Mario "knew intuitively and precisely how every phrase should sound. After all I had been studying elocution informally for many years, but fruitlessly. No matter how deeply I wished, the stammer marred every effort I made, so that the valedictory, which I would not consider avoiding, seemed destined to be one more failure." But graduation day brought with it what Mario later termed a "miracle":

> It was my turn to speak. Everyone knew that I had this problem with speech, and everyone who had ever heard me knew exactly what to expect. My mother and father, my brother, my aunt and uncle were all there in this enormous sea [of faces]. At least my mother and aunt were praying for me. The hall was silent. I rose, walked to the lectern, and

stammered momentarily on the very first word. Even now, thirty five years later, to recall it is to sob and be flooded with feeling, for I did not stammer even once again throughout that speech. And, despite its conventionality, I managed to deliver it with a certain perfection of eloquence. The applause was truly thunderous....Mr. Denn [Van Buren's principal] remarked for all that it was the most stirring valedictory he had ever heard. If there is a God to thank, I freely give my thanks.[52]

He had demonstrated for the first time the ability to speak effectively in a large public forum.

This high school graduation speech is also significant in suggesting where he stood politically as the 1960s began. The Mario Savio of Van Buren High was much more willing than the Mario Savio of his Berkeley years to salute the flag and praise God. He opened his speech by declaring how "proud and grateful" he was to "call the United States...home," a land of "freedom and prosperity," attesting that "God has certainly looked kindly upon us." But he then spent the bulk of his speech exploring criticism of American life as excessively materialistic and of Americans as "hedonistic—lacking ideals, vision, and conviction." True to the spirit he had absorbed from the Catholic critique of materialism, he told the graduating class that "what is truly sad is that much evidence indicates that there is quite a bit of truth in such criticism." Linking the 1920s and 1950s, he noted that during eras of great prosperity "we seem to fall apart and lose sight of national goals." For Americans to realize their democratic ideals, "we must free ourselves from obsession with the material....Having once again become master of things...we must never again allow things to become our masters."[53]

The speech showed simultaneously Savio's dissent from the spirit of the 1950s and his recognition that the nuclear age had thrust unprecedented problems upon his generation. Ordinarily, it would be during times of stress that Americans would "unite to secure the national welfare." But the world had never seen such a period of stress as that bred by the cold war arms race. Instead of confronting those fears, Americans escaped into the marketplace, turning "our attention to the things we can grasp—the materials, the gadgets, the gimmicks."[54]

This was for its time a critical take on what Savio would later term cold war America's "consumer paradise of boredom and foreboding." It was a reaction to growing up in an era when "hydrogen bombs were exploded in the air" and "America's children...passed the decade crouching beneath our desks [in school drills preparing for nuclear catastrophe]..., never believing that those desks provided the slightest protection against a nuclear attack." Schools in the

1950s, Savio recalled, were "like the church—no place to discuss our fears" or to confront the contradictions of America—the pretense that there could be safety from nuclear attack, that one could ignore nuclear terror by getting absorbed in the world of consumption. This would promote such an air of unreality that one could believe "a new brand of laundry detergent was every bit as real and important as what President Eisenhower might be doing."[55]

Along with this critique, the speech conveyed an activist message. Savio urged his classmates to become involved politically and to take their roles as citizens seriously. With the threat of nuclear destruction, "now, more than ever before, we must face reality—with the intention of changing it." He acknowledged the sense of political impotence that the nuclear arms race induced, leaving the young convinced that there was nothing they could do to change world events. But the speech countered this political paralysis by "reaffirming our faith in the nobility of man and...that men have the power to shape events."[56]

Although this inclination to political action seems to link the teenage Savio to the Savio of Berkeley, the connection can be easily overstated, for in some respects this graduation speech, given in the closing year of the Eisenhower administration, was more a product of the decade that was ending than the one being launched. The kinds of activism he urged upon his classmates at Van Buren were exceedingly moderate, taking the form of letter writing and casting ballots on election day. There was no allusion to the civil rights movement and the sit-ins, even when he mentioned the attempt "to secure rights for minority groups." As of June 1960 he had not yet realized that the movement would play a transformative role for his generation.[57]

Later in life, when Savio began to look back upon his youth he reflected that it "was in reaction to the 1950s that we did the kind of things we did" in the 1960s. The foreign policy and larger political mood of 1950s militarized America, propagandized ordinary Americans to buy into a self-righteous vision of its anti-Communist mission, purged radicals via McCarthyism, and brought the world to the brink of nuclear annihilation: "The story we were taught about the world was painted in the whitest white of American purity and the satanic red of the world-wide Communist menace. We could do no wrong, they could do no right, and if necessary we would suffer the devastation of the planet to preserve our way of life." So eager was cold war America to "intimidate the Russians" that American leaders seemed indifferent to the fact that televised, open-air testing of nuclear weapons was "terrify[ing] the children of the United States."[58]

It is little wonder, then, that he chose to title his unpublished memoir "Beyond the Cold War: The Education of an American Radical." For Savio the cold war led Americans, including himself, to be unthinking about their nation's role in the world. As a young student, "the apolitical son of apolitical Italian immi-grants," he initially read J. Edgar Hoover's anti-Communist polemic, *Masters of Deceit*, as if it were gospel truth; he became more critical of it only after a liberal teacher clued him into its biases.[59] For him a central part of the meaning of the 1960s was awakening America to the flaws in its cold war assumptions, questioning why a nation that led the "free world" also fought colonial-style wars in such places as Vietnam. This meant freeing Americans from the pall of McCarthyism, giving dissenters the liberty to raise such questions without being Red-baited or accused of disloyalty or even treason. He did not think America could be free, did not think he could be free, until both pushed past the cold war and its simple-minded Manichean view of the world.[60]

Savio's reflections on the international scene of the 1950s were also shaped by World War II. He remembered his father's absence during that conflict, and for him the events of the 1940s were anything but ancient history. As a teen he found global conflicts terrifying because of the way he had processed images of the horrifying international events of the 1940s. "I was never deeply impressed by the belief some hold that human beings would never use these [nuclear] weapons in a real war. For the pictures of the destruction of Hiroshima and Nagasaki had a horrifying newness then."[61] The Holocaust added to his fore-boding, since "the human capacity for unlimited evil was borne to me vividly by the equally fresh photographs of Jewish bodies piled in heaps. Those pic-tures of the Holocaust...were and remain for me the granite-like reality against which every book or mere idea had to be tested."[62]

Being critical of cold war America involved more than just foreign policy. Savio looked back on this as the last "normal" era for the American bourgeoisie, a time when men dominated the family, whites monopolized power, and the white middle class—distracted by its orgy of consumerism—seemed unaware of racial injustice. For Savio, the 1960s were about challenging and freeing soci-ety of existing hierarchies of race, class, and gender.[63] This arc of liberation would connect with and reinforce Savio's personal liberation from a youth dominated by a hierarchical religion, a competitive school environment, and a serious speech impediment. While the 1950s had seemed grim, the 1960s held out at least the prospect of change, if he could find a way to move beyond the confining working-class world of his childhood.

2

THE MAKING OF A CIVIL RIGHTS ACTIVIST

Since Mario Savio's last act as a high school student was delivering a politically conscious speech, one might expect him to have emerged quickly as a college student activist. But this did not happen. He devoted his freshman year at Manhattan College in 1960–61 to his studies rather than to politics. The direction of his scholarship was, however, somewhat subversive. Although attending college on a science scholarship and majoring in physics, he focused on the classics, in effect using courses in ancient Greek history, philosophy, and literature to help distance himself from Catholicism. Savio "fell in love with the Greeks," who epitomized for him "a pre- and hence non-Christian culture . . . Greek literature and philosophy provided me a position to examine the Church critically. . . . Although hardly the intent" of the Christian Brothers who ran the college, Manhattan was, for Savio "an ideal setting in which he could "think my way out of the Church."[1] Thus while not yet a political activist, Savio was intellectually and spiritually, as he put it, a "sort of school rebel."[2]

Savio credited the Greeks with enabling him to develop a critical perspective not only on Catholicism but also on cold war nationalism—the latter of which came from a careful reading of Thucydides. Contradicting multicultural notions that classical education was narrow or Eurocentric, he looked back on the classics with great fondness:

There've been no plays written superior to the plays of Sophocles and Aeschylus and Euripides. We haven't had better philosophers [than the Greeks]; we've had other philosophers, all right? . . . And yet, the Church had, in some ways, attempted to assimilate that culture, and so it respected it . . . When I read the philosophers, especially . . . it

was...serious...because I was trying to do a personally serious thing....
I wasn't just cramming for exams. I was trying to find out what it all
meant to me, and whether or not I could leave the Church.[3]

This classical training, and especially the work it led him to do in logic and philosophy, served as a foundation for his work as a political leader and orator.

Savio struggled with his religious beliefs in the Church throughout his freshman year. He had stopped attending mass before entering college. His mother's
enthusiasm for Manhattan College derived from her hope that the Christian
Brothers would counter his wavering faith and, as Mario put it, "keep me in the
fold." When he first arrived at college, he had been—despite his doubts—"still
close to the Church—a Catholic unbeliever...celebrated on that campus as a
militant if polite non-Church goer." But by the end of the academic year he had
become fed up with the Church presence dominating the campus. For him the
most oppressively Catholic feature of the campus was the omnipresence of the
Christian Brothers, who

> were incapable of overcoming adolescence and entering adulthood, so the
> campus as whole was incapable of overcoming a medieval adolescence
> and entering into the mainstream of modern life. But I longed to breathe
> freely in modern, secular America. I felt stifled by that precious Catholic
> specialness. Even while I continued to sharpen my wits on Aristotelian
> and Thomistic debate, I yearned to risk it all for the daring simplicity—as
> I naively imagined—of the life of an agnostic outside the walls.[4]

Savio's intellectual independence had grown to the point where he had
managed to use his year at a Catholic college to further distance himself from
the Church.[5]

While his parents had felt elated about his attending this Catholic college,
and proud that he had earned a full scholarship there, Mario felt "just the reverse
of this. I was now deprived of my friends, mostly Jewish, who were all going
off to other colleges and universities in that secular mainstream from which
I was now excluded."[6] He was reminded of this isolation on an almost daily
basis when he passed by the campus of the Ethical Culture Fieldston School, a
liberal private high school, a few blocks away. His longing to escape his Catholic cloister, which also had a sexual dimension, was so strong that years later
he remembered observing the Fieldston girls "at a distance, walking to and
away from school, freely swaying in their mini-skirts, or pressing their books
against the front of their bodies as girls do, blissfully unaware that the body was
a principal 'occasion' of sin." His life at Manhattan College "was thus...tensely

drawn between two mythical poles: the Catholic repose of the thirteenth century…and the anything-but-Catholic unrepose of the Fieldston girls."[7]

Savio transferred from Manhattan to Queens College, spending his sophomore year at this tuition-free public institution, which had what he regarded as a more cosmopolitan intellectual and social milieu. With its predominantly Jewish student body and secular character, the school was an extension of the stimulating social and educational environment in which he had excelled at Van Buren. At Queens he took his first steps toward student activism. He went to Albany along with other Queens students to protest an attempt to raise fees at this low-cost municipal college. He witnessed his first civil rights demonstration, an antidiscrimination picket outside the Woolworth's store in his neighborhood. Savio briefly and spontaneously joined the line because he "felt an immediate rapport based on the justice of it." After reading the leaflet handed out by the picketers, he identified with them because he had been raised on "the basic Catholic ethical doctrine…: Do good and resist evil…this seemed to me to be a very clear-cut straightforward thing."[8]

While distancing himself from the Catholic Church and its rituals, Savio continued to connect with its social action wing. He still read Dorothy Day's *Catholic Worker*, sympathizing with its egalitarianism, but had qualms about it being too narrow in its Catholic identity. Nonetheless, Savio's most sustained political commitment at Queens came under Catholic auspices. He, along with some forty students from a variety of religious and secular backgrounds, joined a development project to assist impoverished Mexicans, organized by the college's Newman House in summer 1963. As part of the Queens College Mexican Volunteers, which he later likened to a private Peace Corps effort, he spent a memorable summer in Taxco, a town in Central Mexico, working to construct a laundry facility for that town's poor. The delegation member with the strongest grasp of Spanish (which his love of language enabled him to master in high school), he naturally fell into the role of translator for the Queens College group.[9]

The Taxco project added to his understanding of class conflict and inequality. Even though Taxco was "a center of tourism, a fabulously wealthy town," in "the hills up above surrounding the town" he observed desperate poverty, unlike any he had ever experienced. Savio saw "whole families (one with seven children) sleeping in one filthy bed…starved children, widespread dysentery." The idea for a laundry facility emerged from conversations with residents who complained that for half the year, when the local stream dried up, they had no place to wash their clothes. He was appalled by the refusal of the local Mexican elite, though Catholic, to cooperate with the Queens College Catholic student organization's efforts to raise funds for this project.[10]

In Mexico Savio got his first exposure to Third World nationalism and to the lasting resentment against U.S. expansionism. He learned that "when you

cross the border, things change. It's astonishing." More than a century after
the Mexican-American War, Mexicans remained angry at America for seizing
their territory, something about which Savio had learned nothing in school. He
observed "that it was a galling bone of...resentment sticking in the throat of
these people that...'wait, that used to be Mexico over there'...And so it was at
that point, actually I...started to wonder...about what the legitimacy of that
border [between the United States and Mexico] was."[11]

Savio's involvement in the Mexican project was his first political act to gar-
ner media coverage. The *Long Island Press* ran a story highlighting a letter he
sent from Mexico to his family. The fact that his parents shared this letter with
the press suggests that they were proud of his antipoverty work. Describing
Savio as a "young idealist," the article recorded his "reactions on everything
from politics to religion to social mores."[12] He expressed concern that the self-
ish, wealthy Mexicans who had refused to confront the problems of poverty
in their communities were "helping to bring Communism to Latin America."
Savio warned that "it may well be that Communism holds the key to social
justice here—I fervently hope that is not the case."[13] He took the Church to task
for its "ambiguous" role in the battle for social justice. On one hand, it "wants
to keep its old rich friends from the past, but at the same time is aware that the
socially unjust situation in Latin America is a sinful one."[14]

Indignation over Mexico's extreme inequality not only affected Savio's
social consciousness but also pushed him toward a new eloquence. Though
still afflicted with his speech defect in daily conversation, his anger enabled
him to transcend it temporarily. His fellow volunteers expressed surprise "at
Savio's transformation when he emerged, chrysalis-like, and seemingly overnight into an assertive and powerful speaker-organizer," at times shedding his
"bad stammer...standing up for a group of Indian-peasants and talking freely
to them...about liberation, democracy, and civil rights."[15]

Although it began as a summer project, Savio's interest in Mexican anti-
poverty work did not end that summer. He was among a small group of the
volunteers who made plans to follow up by building a school in Taxco. There
had been a half-built school structure close to the land where the Queens students sought to place the laundry facility, but there were no funds provided
by the government or local elite to complete it. "So we promised...that we'd
come back" to finish the school, Savio explained. He put some energy into raising funds for this school-building effort. Though he was unable to return to
Mexico the following summer, he remained in close contact with his childhood
friend Art Gatti, who did return to Taxco to build that school.[16]

While Savio was in Mexico his parents moved to Glendora, in southern California. He intended to follow them out west by moving on to his third college in

three years. He initially considered UCLA but found himself drawn to Berkeley, for reasons that were at least partially political. He had skimmed David Horowitz's *Student*, a highly laudatory account of the rise of campus activism at Berkeley, where since the late 1950s students had been expressing dissent against the arms race, the cold war, and the legacy of McCarthyism. Berkeley students made headlines protesting the appearance of the Red-baiting House Committee on Un-American Activities at San Francisco's city hall in 1960. The Horowitz book left Savio feeling drawn to Berkeley as "an exciting place."[17] UC would give him his first chance to be on his own at college—unlike Queens College, a commuter school, and Manhattan College, whose dormitories were closely policed by Christian Brother prefects. He was attracted by UC Berkeley's physical beauty, finding its groves, streams, and scenic overlooks of the bay "entrancing."[18]

Arriving at Berkeley in fall 1963, Savio did not immediately assume a political role. During the first month the young philosophy major was adjusting to his new environment and was "having a lot of personal problems." He "was still…growing up." He lived in an apartment he thought overpriced on Berkeley's north side with a "reactionary" business student with whom he had nothing in common. He was irritated by the constant noise of student housing and surrounded by undergraduates who "didn't seem to have any particular interests in any but the most shallow and…juvenile concerns." Although he acknowledged that there was a place for rowdy partying, "this was constant! Every night. And after a while you just can't take it…Very crowded, yet you really feel alone."[19] He was on the verge of dropping out.

About halfway through his first semester Savio connected with the student activist community, attending meetings of University Friends of SNCC, the solidarity organization that raised funds for SNCC, the predominantly African American student group battling racism in the deep South. He became involved in a tutoring project in West Berkeley, which University Friends of SNCC and the Campus CORE chapter helped to organize, teaching black high school and elementary school students.[20] This project gave him his first encounter with political repression and the fear that movements for social change evoked among conservatives. In December 1963 he wrote a friend that he and other tutors met with their students three times a week

in a room provided by the Mobilized Women of Berkeley (mobilized during W.W. I by Pres Wilson!). Recently Berkeley CORE began picketing on Shattuck Avenue near the University; some of the people on our tutorial are also in Berkeley CORE: Ergo the old (mobilized) women have evicted us for fear of contamination by the "radicals." We must now look for new lodgings.[21]

Although the tutorial project attested to Savio's evolving social conscience and did help some inner-city students, he was under no illusions about the project's overall impact. He soon realized it wasn't very successful, merely "a finger in the dike operation" that could not address the glaring social and educational inequities of inner-city children's lives. Even with the student who seemed responsive to his tutoring Savio "had the feeling that you weren't preparing him for anything at all, because as soon as he'd leave the session, he'd go to school where whatever curiosity had...been excited, would just as quickly be crushed...We seemed to be running just to keep where we were." When the tutoring project reached out to the schools, the activists found that those institutions weren't especially cooperative because the very existence of the project underscored the educational system's inadequacy. Far from disillusioning Savio, however, this experience left him searching for more daring ways to battle racial inequality. "It had the effect of convincing me that other more political means of attacking the problem were called for, rather than [merely] setting up tutorials."[22]

Savio was not yet the committed and militant civil rights activist that he would become over the course of the following spring and summer. He had never engaged in the daring form of protest involving civil disobedience, such as sitting-in. He did spontaneously join a picket line in Berkeley when, in October 1963, he happened upon a protest against the racially discriminatory hiring practices of Mel's drive-in restaurant.[23] Still, he remained a tactical moderate as late as February 1964, when he avoided participating in the antidiscrimination protest at Lucky's grocery stores because he viewed the "shop-in" tactic used by CORE—in which activists disrupted the store's operation by taking food off the shelves and leaving it at the checkout counter—as too "messy" and lacking "in self-restraint and dignity."[24]

By the end of the fall 1963 semester Savio was still unhappy. He wrote to his father explaining his plans to drop out of college. This letter was obviously painful to write since he knew that his father, who had never been able to afford to attend college, ardently desired that Mario complete his college degree. The letter also suggests that well before the FSM emerged and developed its critique of mass higher education, he was critical of the quality of undergraduate education at Berkeley. He complained of being bored with lectures in which "professors tell me commonplaces that I can—and do—easily figure out for myself." He disliked the mode of assessment that faculty used, contending that the tests did little other than force "memorizing of meaningless lists of information." Papers required such quick writing that they left students "saying glib things" rather than grappling with big questions in a meaningful way. He assured his father that he could "get a far better education by doing my own reading than by bowing to the meaningless ritual of taking courses."[25]

It is unclear why Savio decided to stay at UC, since he never wrote or spoke about how he came through this personal crisis. He explained to his father that the main reason he had returned to school for the spring semester was because "I felt certain that my completing college would make both you and mom happy, and it seemed that you two were about due for a little happiness."[26] But it seems likely that his increasing engagement with the activist community at Berkeley helped him to move beyond these doubts about staying in school. In the spring semester he began to develop friendships with campus civil right activists.[27]

For Savio the civil rights movement had a powerful appeal because it offered a new and serious role for students and connected with his passion for social justice. He viewed SNCC as "symbolic of...whatever is meaningful in American student life...You're just drawn like...a moth to a light." The kind of activism embodied by SNCC "most closely approximate[d] the rather romantic student notion" he had held before coming to college, that students could—as had been the case in Europe—become major agents of egalitarian change.[28]

The civil rights movement revealed that American society, which celebrated its affluence and freedom, was afflicted by poverty and oppression. Contrasting with the consumer paradise depicted on television commercials, "the civil rights movement burst on the national consciousness on the tube—people being hit over the head, holding one another against the fire hoses, and so forth—it's just such a contrast. That was so real, and what you'd been raised in was so unreal, that it was very attractive." Seeing those TV images of civil rights activists facing police dogs in Birmingham left Savio "both shamed and inspired"— shamed that America was so bigoted, and inspired to join the movement to battle racism.[29]

For Savio the religious dimension of this movement loomed large. The black freedom struggle, so rife with ministers, had "a quality of, for me—and it's hard for me to say this—sort of like God acting in history...Like God was going to trouble the water. It had a very deep meaning....I took it [to mean]...that: [since] people were really helping themselves and doing something good [in opposing the social sin of racism] then that would be itself a presence of God."[30] This sensibility left him inclined to identify with civil rights protesters on an emotional as well as a rational level, even before he read about the specific grievances that sparked the demonstration.

Savio found the Berkeley political milieu "amazing. And it got me just at the right time." Only a few years earlier he had been startled to encounter his first civil rights demonstration, and now at Berkeley it seemed as if there "were civil

rights demonstrations, massive ones, every week," targeting racially discriminatory employers in the Bay Area. "The country had changed very, very quickly;
I…found myself at the place which was at the cutting edge, absolutely the most
advanced of any place in the north or west."[31] It offered an appealing way of
seeing beyond the abstractions and academic tenor of his life as a philosophy
major because in the movement "there seemed to be a real wedding of thought
and action."[32]

His like-minded neighbors on Berkeley's north side were similarly ener-
gized by him. Berkeley students Sam Bader and Bernard Timberg, who lived
in his housing complex, recalled him as brilliant, vocal, and politically engaged.
Whether discussing science, philosophy, or civil rights, Savio was well informed
and had interesting things to say. Bader, a freshman from the Bronx, was
impressed with Savio's

> excitement and enthusiasm about not only the world of social upheaval…but
> also the world of science…Mario came to my apartment with two vol-
> umes…on mathematical biophysics and was totally swept away by the
> fact that the motion of an amoeba could be described by a set of differ-
> ential equations. This gives you [a]…sense of the breadth of his interests
> and enthusiasm toward the world around him. Mario became known…as
> something of a King Solomon. He was always on the moral and ethical side
> of the issue.[33]

Savio's initial civil rights activism in the Bay Area had an important social
dimension to it, especially in contrast with his lonely first semester. In the wake
of the Birmingham struggle, the March on Washington, and SNCC's initial
black voter registration work in Mississippi, civil rights organizers—though still
a minority of Berkeley's student body—forged a community of the campus's
most politically aware and compassionate activists. Savio was introduced to a
circle of activists who were serious about ideas and action. "It just seemed to
me" that these "would be the kind of people I'd like to get to know."[34] Through
this network he discovered that several students in his apartment building
had been involved in civil rights work before they came to Berkeley, and he
befriended and recruited them into University Friends of SNCC. Civil rights
activism helped draw Savio closer to his first girlfriend at Berkeley, Cheryl
Stevenson, a fellow ex-Catholic whom he had met in an ethics class.

Savio came to view the social dimension of activism as a testament to what
was so special and attractive about Berkeley in the early 1960s. Civil rights
"demonstrations had the moral cachet of the campus," and in the more socially
conscious student circles of the time one impressed a girl not by driving a fancy

car or being a football star but by acting on behalf of social justice. Part of the reason he attended the protest against discriminatory hiring at San Francisco's Sheraton Palace Hotel—a protest he learned about through a leaflet he picked up on the Bancroft-Telegraph strip on the campus's southern edge—was to impress Stevenson.[35] "I think it was actually a healthy thing. We were creating an alternative society, and in the alternative society, you impress people you want to go out with by doing things that are alternative, right?"[36]

Intellectually intense as he was, Savio was not some atomistic intellectual whose conscience led him to move from one protest to another as a lone individual. He was becoming part of a "subculture in the University community, which is what in part...attracted" him to Berkeley in the first place, but which had taken "a little bit of time to discover." Although he learned of the Sheraton Palace protest from a leaflet, he didn't decide to go until someone at a party raised it. Savio and two others decided on the spur of the moment to join, and with several Berkeley students they piled into a Volkswagen bus, driving to the Sheraton on March 6, 1964. It took a community to nurture Savio's activist impulse, a community in which he found himself increasingly and happily enmeshed.[37]

However much social relationships factored into his decision to go to the Sheraton Palace protest, Savio was clearly drawn by the issue of racial justice. With the Sheraton protest the demonstrators were trying "to communicate to a large number of people that there is something very seriously wrong" with the hiring practices of a hotel that employed few blacks and only in the most menial, low-paying jobs. He saw the protest as a way to show to the hotel's "management that unless they do something about this condition, they're not going to be able to keep on running a hotel." This meant, as Savio put it, nonviolent civil disobedience: disrupting the operation of the hotel, but "at the same time, not going around breaking things."[38]

Savio was powerfully influenced by the sense of community he experienced at the Sheraton Palace sit-in. Here he went through a radicalization process regarding mass protest. Earlier in the semester he had avoided militant tactics, but at the Sheraton his moderate sensibility dissolved: "Once you're in the hotel, something else takes over. Now there's a community" of protesters "inside the hotel, and it really is a community in a way quite different from and much greater than anything you are normally" accustomed to. It was certainly more of a community than any found at a big impersonal university such as Berkeley, because at the demonstration there were "all these people engaged in this common, worthwhile endeavor, able to sit down and talk to one another."[39] He was prepared to support more militant action than the sit-in in the hotel's lobby: "I was...in favor of going up to the upper floor and waking people up—not hurting anybody, but seeing to it that we really disturbed lots of people. It seemed to me that people in the hotel ought to be disturbed" about the hotel's discriminatory hiring practices.[40]

This was the first time in his life that Savio was Red-baited. He found himself denounced by a hotel guest who shouted at him to go back to Russia. Savio pointed out that he did not come from Russia, which drew the same refrain that he should go back to Russia, with the added comment, "You're a Communist." Mario replied, "My parents are from Italy."[41]

The Sheraton Palace protest represented a turning point in Savio's life. Hundreds from Berkeley's predominantly white student body joined black activists and students from other Bay Area campuses in the mass sit-in. For the first time in his life he was arrested—along with more than a hundred other Berkeley students—for nonviolently blockading an entrance to the hotel. Being jailed for civil disobedience represented an important rite of passage. Savio later compared this first arrest to the act of a Native American brave who brought home his first bear as a symbol of his "being initiated into manhood in his tribe."[42] Getting arrested in a civil rights protest in "the early 1960s was an event... It was proving that you really were committed, that it wasn't just a matter of words." For Savio this was "the initiation into... being part of the movement in the strongest sense," crossing "the line between being... a very sympathetic observer or being clearly and demonstrably part of the movement.[43] Even though the intent of the protest was to promote equal opportunity for an oppressed group of workers, taking risks on their behalf impacted Savio and other protesters as much as it did the blacks the demonstration was designed to help. This is what Savio meant when he spoke of the protest's surprisingly personal impact: "In the process of changing the things we saw, we were changing ourselves."[44]

Inspired as Savio was by the solidarity he had experienced at the Sheraton Palace, he was not uncritical of this protest. He noted that its organizers had not given sufficient thought to the decision-making process and communication between leaders and rank-and-file activists. He found it moderately distressing that the leaders did not do more to update the demonstrators on the state of negotiations with the hotel management. "There really was no provision made for mass decisions.... Attempt was made to put some matters to a vote... but very unsuccessfully, and I think somewhat half-heartedly."[45] These were mistakes Savio would strive to avoid in the FSM when he rose to leadership of a mass movement. The statement that he wrote for his attorney in the wake of the sit-in found him questioning some tactical decisions made by the protest's leadership. He thought it would have been more effective to have had all the protesters either block the hotel doors (thus courting arrest) or sleep in the hotel lobby, rather than having separate groups doing both things simultaneously. Indeed, it was in part to maximize the size and impact of the mass arrests that Savio, after some initial hesitation, decided to join the blockade and get arrested.[46]

The Sheraton Palace arrests changed Savio's view of the police. At first he considered the police to be "just doing their jobs.'" When a demonstrator had a seizure, the police exhorted the protesters to "go home before someone else got hurt" since they had already made their point. Savio thought this officer's remarks were "unmistakably patronizing... (a 'be good little boys and girls' quality)," but he still believed that the officer "was speaking, for the most part with sincerity." Just a few moments later, however, he was taken aback by the cop's "c[y]nicism and callousness... when... after giving his pretty little speech, he bent his fingers upward under the chin of one of the demonstrators, gouging the latter's throat violently in an effort to pull him away from his fellow demonstrators." In an attempt to cover up the violence, "two other policemen attempted, with fair success, to block the view of this brutality from the press photographers who were present."[47]

The protest proved effective. The hotel owners signed an agreement pledging to hire minority workers in the kinds of visible and higher-status jobs from which they had been barred not just at the Sheraton Palace but all over San Francisco. "The point was," according to Savio, "to hire black workers where you can see them,... in positions where they'd be paid the same kind of pay as white workers, on the average, and could be seen, not just as a scullery maid or a janitor."[48] Savio took pride in helping to push for this initial step toward fair hiring.[49] Making the victory even sweeter was his good fortune in being one of the arrestees to get a civil-liberties-oriented judge and to be acquitted for his role in the hotel sit-in. The lesson Savio drew was that bold action on behalf of social justice could yield quick and stunning victories.[50] It also sent a message to Bay Area employers that racist hiring practices would meet with serious resistance via pickets and civil disobedience.[51]

Savio's arrest at the Sheraton Palace caused him to miss classes in order to appear in court, leading to his first political encounter with the UC administration. He wrote to the dean of the College of Arts and Sciences, arguing that students should not be penalized academically for missing classes as a consequence of their acts of political conscience. Well before the FSM Savio was developing a strong position on student rights, arguing that "the University of California should not *ordinarily* interfere with its students acting in their role as citizens." Still idealistic about the university, he termed UC "a great and free institution of higher learning with a vital interest in the extension of democratic process," and urged that UC "*defend* the right" of its students "to use any *legal means* to secure civil rights...whenever these have been denied or abridged."[52]

The daring tactics of politically conscious students and community activists quickly began to rub off on Savio. One movement veteran whom he befriended was Jack Weinberg, who had dropped out of graduate school in math at Berkeley in spring 1963 to work full-time in the Bay Area civil rights movement as head of Campus CORE. Weinberg recalled the confrontational ethos of the movement when Savio became a civil rights activist:

> In the South the stakes were much higher, it was life and death; it was police dogs. In the North it was...provoking confrontation...where the powers that be would...rather paper everything over. So you would be looking for hooks that forced them to act. So forcing confrontation was part of the institutional culture of the civil rights movement. It was like we'd been living with this rotting corpse under the table and pretending it's not there for too long.... The only way you're going to change it is by creating confrontations that call attention to the problem.... The underlying logic is that what we're demanding is completely within the framework of the American tradition.... [I]t doesn't get addressed by avoiding it.... [I]f you create confrontation...you get the resolution you want even without overwhelming power.... The tactic was...confrontation leading to negotiation, leading to resolution based on a morally secure set of demands.[53]

Embracing disruptive civil disobedience was a radical step for Savio, but it was also a logical continuation of his political trajectory. At Berkeley he was accelerating his journey beyond the working-class liberalism of his parents. At the start of the 1960s Savio had hoped that John Kennedy might be for his generation what Franklin Roosevelt had been for his parents, a "people's president" who could prod America beyond its avarice and toward a more just and equitable social order. But he quickly lost faith in JFK, disappointed that the president allowed a private company instead of a public agency to run the Telstar communication satellites.[54] To Savio it seemed unreasonable for an international telecommunications system to be controlled by a single American firm. While this is not a part of the Kennedy record that most sixties radicals focus on when articulating their disillusionment with JFK, for Savio, with his strong interest in science, the commercialization of space left him convinced "that Kennedy was more flash than substance."[55] Later Savio would be critical—as most civil rights workers were—of Kennedy and the liberal establishment for often failing to use the force of the federal government to protect Deep South civil rights activists from racist violence.[56]

Losing confidence that a liberal president would effect reform left Savio open to the idea that egalitarian change would have to come from below, from mass protest of the kind he was being attracted to in the civil rights movement. Savio was coming to a view of this era similar to that Taylor Branch would adopt decades later in his Pulitzer Prize–winning biography of Martin Luther King Jr., when Branch spoke of the 1960s as not the Kennedy era or the Johnson era but the King era. Unlike Branch, Savio would see the civil rights movement itself, rather than King, setting the tone for this decade of social change, yet in both cases protesters rather than politicians were seen as doing the most to shape American history. As Savio put it: "The civil rights movement, it wasn't flash. It wasn't a fake. It wasn't fantasy land. Kennedy was...a mixed phenomenon....At crucial places, he failed to connect with reality....He was the official leader, but he wasn't leading. The civil rights movement was leading America."[57]

Savio's letters to his parents during his first year at Berkeley offer evidence that his civil rights activism was part of this steady shift leftward. In a letter to his father in January 1964 he wrote that he was "determined to be a conscientious objector in the event that I am drafted."[58] Five months later he informed his mother that he had joined the American Socialist Party, though he also assured her that it was "not—I repeat this is *not*—a subversive organization," and that some of its members worked for liberal Democratic candidates.[59] In subsequent interviews he indicated that his Socialist Party affiliation was a symbolic gesture, since he never attended any of its meetings or became active in it. But this affiliation did signal dissatisfaction with mainstream politics and growing self-identification as a radical.[60] He would also allude to his socialistic sensibility retrospectively when he highlighted the implicit anticapitalism of the civil rights protests, pointing out that the movement insisted that stores, hotels, and other commercial establishments elevate political morality above profitability, hiring minorities whether or not their presence might turn away prejudiced white customers.[61]

For all his radical tendencies, however, Savio came to Berkeley with a very limited knowledge of and no sustained connection with the Old Left or its youth organizations. When he first got involved in the student arm of the Bay Area's civil rights movement he did not understand the configuration of Old Left organizations or their role in the student movement. He had no familiarity with the two competing leftist organizations that played an important leadership role: the Ad Hoc Committee to End Discrimination (dominated by Communists and the campus group they led, the W. E. B. Du Bois Club) and Campus CORE (dominated by the non-Communist Left and especially by the Independent Socialists). Thus in the wake of the Sheraton Palace demonstrations when there was a mass meeting of the defendants and their lawyers, Savio was puzzled by the sectarian bickering. Du Bois Club members depicted the students who had raised questions about the legal defense strategy as disruptive "social democrats" who "had tried to break the meeting up," a charge that Savio knew "just plain wasn't true."[62]

Innocent of such factionalism, Savio only understood what was going on after speaking with Jack Weinberg, whom he had met in the minority tutoring project. Actually, Weinberg's knowledge of the Old Left was limited at this point, and from his perspective "I was like one inch ahead of Mario" in that knowledge. "I subsequently became more politically sophisticated but the only reason I was more sophisticated at that time was that" Savio "was very unsophisticated" about the organized Left.[63] This helps to account for the FBI's failure to prove Communist connections to or influence on Savio. He simply did not come out of the world of the organized Left, and so he began his campus activism in the dark about the history of and ongoing organizational tensions between radical groups on or off campus.

Savio's Catholic background had left him suspicious of grand systems of ideas on the left (or right), since their totalism and rigidity reminded him of Catholicism. He was in the process of freeing himself from that ism and had no desire to replace it with another grandiose worldview, including Marxism. He also thought that his not being "an ideological kind of person" was connected to his upbringing in cold war America, where "we'd been raised on a steady diet of…anti-Communism, anti-Socialism, anti-Marxism, anti-anything that was critical of society in a systematic way. I think that, frankly a lot of that stayed with me."[64] Thus for Savio one of the great attractions of the civil rights movement was that to join it and to fight for revolutionary democratic change in race relations, one did not have to adopt an ideology or "embrace grand schemes of a just order."[65] The movement enabled him to crusade as militantly for social justice as any of the Left's ideologues without having to become one. This was because the civil rights movement, in Savio's words, revealed

> injustice in palpable sorts of ways…You didn't need an ideology…because it was just sort of black and white. Very, "This is it. It's not just for a person not to have a certain job he's perfectly capable of handling because of the color of his skin. It's so unreasonable…." That…is how…it was able to draw me in.[66]

For Savio the pivotal event of his first year at Berkeley occurred not on campus but in jail, while he was being held following his Sheraton Palace arrest. John King, a fellow civil rights activist who was his cellmate, told him about the Mississippi Freedom Summer project, in which a thousand or so civil rights workers from the North and West were going to go to Mississippi to join a nonviolent campaign for racial justice in the Deep South's most violently racist state. Savio hadn't heard of the project before but, as an increasingly committed civil rights activist, he found himself instantly drawn to this battle for freedom in the heartland of American racism.[67]

3

FREEDOM SUMMER

For Savio the civil rights battle that the black-led student movement, headed by SNCC leader Bob Moses, waged in Mississippi was nothing less than heroic. Having rooted themselves in local black communities since 1961, these civil rights workers conducted voter registration campaigns that proved extremely dangerous because they challenged Mississippi's tradition of black disenfranchisement that dated back to the nineteenth century, antagonizing violent white supremacists. SNCC organizers had been beaten and shot, Freedom Houses bombed, and local black community members lost their lives when they allied themselves with the movement—among them Herbert Lee, gunned down in broad daylight by a segregationist state legislator.[1] Moses himself had demonstrated incredible courage, not only continuing his voter registration work after arrests by racist police and repeated beatings by white supremacists but pressing charges against one of his assailants even while still bleeding from the assault.[2] By 1964 Moses had become convinced that racist violence had gotten so out of hand that it threatened the survival of the Mississippi freedom movement. It was with this in mind that he launched the Freedom Summer Project, inviting college students from across the country to come to Mississippi in 1964 to assist the voter registration drive and teach in Freedom Schools. He hoped Freedom Summer would generate national publicity that could reduce racist violence. While white America had proven indifferent to the racial terror visited upon blacks in Mississippi, Moses believed that the nation would react differently if hundreds of white college students were involved in the movement.[3]

Even before the Freedom Summer idea had been announced, there were strong indications that Savio would end up in a SNCC-led civil rights crusade. Attracted to SNCC's daring brand of civil rights organizing, he had in his first semester at Berkeley become a member of University Friends of SNCC, a campus group that raised funds for the Mississippi campaign. Savio had been so moved by SNCC's selfless struggle against oppression that he used religious images to convey its appeal to him:

> Periodically...a SNCC worker would come, from the South, making a tour of campuses, raising money, and telling people what was going on in the South. Well, I mean, honest to God. This was like the sort of outlying church receiving some St. Paul's assistant or something.... There was...a tremendous cachet and glamour attached to the SNCC worker.[4]

Savio's well developed sense of social responsibility pushed him toward SNCC and Mississippi. His desire to help those at the bottom of society, an impulse linked to his religious sensibility, had carried him to Mexico in 1963, so it is not surprising that a similar impulse led him south in 1964. He thought that impulse more communal than individual, since being part of a group with a common enterprise on behalf of social justice created a sense of community, which was attractive to him. Although committing to such work was characteristic of only a small minority of his generation, Savio, because of the power of his own conscience, thought it quite ordinary, explaining that engaging in such activism, "identifying your efforts with people who very obviously were oppressed...just appeals to human beings."[5]

He was also drawn to the SNCC organizers for many of the same reasons he was attracted to the civil rights movement itself: they seemed to be waging the most admirable struggle for social justice in America, unsullied by self-interest, risking their lives for racial equality, and doing so without the ideological baggage of the Old Left. "The thing about the SNCC workers—and that's really what got to me, I think—it was radicalism without ideology. And I found it tremendously attractive because of my background," that one could work militantly for social change without having to buy into a rigid idea system.[6]

Freedom Summer represented a historic opportunity to change America, but one that demanded sacrifice since it involved unpaid and dangerous work. So when Savio learned of the project, his initial thoughts were that "it sounds very exciting," but also "Here I am in jail, right? Would I be willing to do it, or did I dare do it?" Joining the Mississippi crusade had so much to do with right and wrong that going South was a moral, almost religious imperative—which is why it meant so much to him to have his application accepted as a Freedom Summer volunteer. He knew that since the project was taking applications for volunteers nationally the organizers would be selective.[7]

Savio's Mississippi Summer application revealed that he was becoming a confident and committed activist. He thought his organizing experience qualified him, and he cited his work in the Berkeley tutoring program and highlighted his role in the Mexican summer community development project. He believed his experience in Mexico negotiating and explaining the group's antipoverty work to government officials and wealthy citizens, who displayed "considerable hostility toward our efforts," "was comparable though not as extreme as the situation in Mississippi." Savio concluded:

> I believe I could be successful in convincing Negro citizens of the importance of registering to vote, again on the basis of my work in Mexico last summer where I had to persuade the poor farmers in Taxco of the importance of helping us to help themselves; several of them expressed the belief that nothing could improve their situation, so desperate had become their situation.[8]

Malcolm Zaretsky, the civil rights activist who evaluated Savio's Freedom Summer application, had some reservations. He was critical of the short-lived tutorial project and saw Savio as a dedicated rank-and-filer with little leadership ability. Zaretsky's take on Savio was that he was "not a very creative guy altho he accepts responsibility and carries it through if you explain to him exactly what needs to be done." He wanted further references before making a final judgment. Ultimately Savio was "highly recommended" for the Mississippi project, though less for his leadership ability than for his "proper attitude" and his being "willing to do any type of work."[9]

The report's critical take reflected Zaretsky's bias against Savio's pragmatic and nonideological approach to organizing, which he misinterpreted as a lack of political imagination. Thus Zaretsky criticized Savio's eagerness to get "the thing [the tutorial for inner city students] into operation," as opposed to seeing the project in larger political terms. He criticized Savio for being oriented toward "helping the poor kids in the ghetto get through school easier, hardly my idea of why to establish tutorials and related programs."[10] After seeing this report years later, Savio thought it odd to question his political vision on the basis of his belief "that the main purpose of the tutorial was actually to help people learn some math—which I think wasn't that bad…come to think of it."[11] Zaretsky's assessment is a useful reminder that Savio's political experience to that point was limited. He had not yet demonstrated that he could lead a major political movement.

Savio was happy that his application had been approved, but he did have second thoughts about going south. In a letter to his mother in May 1964 he discussed his doubts, most of which were related to finances, since he needed to save up for his final year of school. He thought he could engage in any number of "worthwhile projects" in the Bay Area, apparently referring to local civil rights work, and wondered whether this would make more sense than venturing south. He had been active in Freedom House, a project in the Fillmore, attempting to mobilize San Francisco's black community against a redevelopment project that threatened to displace African American residents. Did it make sense to drop this important local work, which he was doing together with his girlfriend Cheryl Stevenson, and go off on his own to Mississippi? He even admitted that "I am not *perfectly sure* what my motives were in applying in the first place."[12]

Savio decided that the historic quest for racial justice in the South outweighed his hesitancy about leaving the Bay Area. That decision grew out of his conviction that he and his fellow Mississippi civil rights workers would be—as historian Howard Zinn later dubbed them—"the new abolitionists," striving to "finish unfinished business for America" with regard to racial equality. "We saw ourselves," Savio explained, "as going down [south] to make the Fourteenth Amendment mean something…Finish the business of the Civil War, not in a violent way, but rather to prevent violence, to overturn a violent order." Cheryl Stevenson was certain that "the pull of Mississippi was entirely moral for him."[13]

The racist violence of Mississippi posed such a threat to civil rights organizers that it dwarfed anything Savio had previously encountered. Violence and unprecedented publicity about it erupted in late June 1964 while Savio was en route to Mississippi. Word came back to the volunteers at the Oxford, Ohio, staging area for the final trek to Mississippi that three civil rights organizers working with the Freedom Summer Project—Michael Schwerner, James Chaney, and Andrew Goodman—had disappeared in Mississippi. Their bodies would be discovered later in the summer after a massive search by federal authorities.[14]

Both through this bad news and their Freedom Summer orientation Savio and his fellow volunteers received numerous reminders at Oxford of the dangers they would face in the South. They went through seminars "concerning the kinds of experience" they might have in Mississippi and "how to respond if you're attacked." It was "a lot to learn," as Savio put it, "in a very brief period of time." Most dramatic was Bob Moses's talk, shortly after the three went missing, in which he told the volunteers that they might want to reconsider their commitment to the Mississippi project. "People have been killed. You can decide to go back home, and no one will look down on you for doing it."[15]

This was Savio's first encounter with Moses's leadership style. He came away impressed by the latter's "evident sincerity," "intelligence," and "lack of guile." Two decades later, Savio recalled that "I wanted to be like Bob Moses. I wanted to *be* Bob Moses if I could do it."[16] Many Freedom Summer volunteers were similarly impressed, among them Robert Osman, who was with Mario in Oxford:

When Bob Moses spoke…everyone understood that this was a man speaking from the heart and…and being very careful about what he said. That…moment that we all remember, of Bob talking to us about the likelihood that the three were dead and the importance that we...not kid ourselves about it and feel free to make a genuine choice about it [spending the summer in Mississippi] as opposed to feeling a lot of group pressure.[17]

Moses's words carried all the more weight because he "had been horribly beaten...close to death," but nonetheless continued the battle for racial justice in Mississippi. "This was courage and...patience, and love and determination to come to real terms with the lives of people who had been made economic outcasts."[18]

The night after Moses's speech Savio stayed up late with Marshall Ganz, a fellow volunteer, discussing death and the odds "that we might not come back alive." The two talked about both the danger of continuing on to Mississippi and the Freedom Summer leadership's call for volunteers to work in the most dangerous, Klan-infested part of the state. "The issue was that in view of the killings, the movement leadership there felt it was important not to be scared off. And they wanted to maintain a presence...in all parts of the state that they formerly said they would."[19] Savio was still relatively new to the role of political activist, and the conversation with Ganz was among the most memorable in Savio's young life: "There was a very brief span of years, just two, three years all together, from the first picket line that I saw in New York to here I am in Oxford, Ohio, talking with this buddy I've just met about the possibility that in the next couple of weeks we would be killed. It's really hard to convey now."[20] The conversation ended with Savio and Ganz opting to stay with the Freedom Summer project and even volunteering to go to McComb, the most violent area.

Along with this willingness to take risks, Savio displayed an ability to reflect in a serious, self-critical way on his motives. As he explained shortly after volunteering at Oxford:

Dam[m]it I can't bear to sit safe at home while others are risking their lives. But I don't know why I feel this way. And I think that might be the reason for the hesitation I felt—the fact that I don't really understand why I have to take part. I know why *one* should take part and I can't stand to be safe while others are involved, but...we might die—I might die![21]

Southwest Mississippi—especially McComb—grew so violent and Klan activity so threatening that the Freedom Summer organizers delayed bringing the group of volunteers that Savio was with to that part of the state. Thus Savio spent the first weeks of Freedom Summer in Holmes County, a black-majority section in the Mississippi Delta. At first glance Holmes County seemed relatively safe. Back in the 1930s, the New Deal had redistributed some farmland to more than a hundred black families, making it possible for a largely self-sufficient leadership core to emerge. These local black leaders had begun the year before Freedom Summer to enlist SNCC's help in a local voter registration drive, and they were hospitable hosts for the volunteers.[22]

Yet even with this tradition of black landownership and leadership in Holmes County, danger and racist repression were still evident. As recently as 1960 there had been only 41 black voters out of a black population of 19,488. Attempting to register was difficult and dangerous since it meant that African Americans had to go into hostile territory: the courthouse in Lexington, a city patrolled by racist police and administered by segregationists. When in 1963 a local black minister working with SNCC sought to register to vote, death threats drove him out of the county. Another local leader of the voter registration movement had his house firebombed. When Moses sought to investigate this violence the police arrested him.[23]

The arrival of the summer volunteers in Holmes County was publicized in all the local papers, most of which, like the state's segregationist politicians, denounced these civil rights workers as alien "invaders."[24] Savio and his fellow volunteers had barely gotten settled in the abandoned farmhouse in which they would reside amidst Mileston's black community, when bomb threats started coming in: "Perhaps the worst night," Savio wrote in a letter home, "was the first night in Holmes County once we began living at the Freedom House. It was a night of veritable paranoia. We crawled about on hands and knees fearing to be caught before a window. We kept watch all night." Despite the threats, "the bomb never materialized." Subsequently the volunteers, as Savio noted, received reports that local whites were out "to break some heads."

> That night a car came by on the road near the place we were staying. It failed to give the proper signal with its horn. We turned on the flood lights in front and escaped out the back to the barn, where we climbed into the loft. On another occasion at the sign of possible danger we fled into the woods to a nearby friendly farm house. In both cases it was a false alarm.[25]

Savio quickly realized that his safety and that of his fellow volunteers was heavily dependent on a small but militant part of the local black community. Supportive black neighbors offered refuge, and they were armed and kept watch over the neighborhood. Although committed to nonviolence, Savio understood what an advantage it was to have black neighbors who "are not as nonviolent as we." He wrote in glowing terms about Hartman Turnbow, a local black farmer and movement leader who had fired back at racists—and apparently hit one—who attacked his house. And when his house was firebombed, Turnbow rebuilt his home "and became even stronger in the movement." The presence of black neighbors whom local whites knew to be armed proved a deterrent to assaults that might have otherwise been aimed at the house where the volunteers were staying. Savio noted, "If it were not very well known that the Negro farmers are not non-violent, I seriously doubt that a non-violent student movement would be possible in Mississippi." Nonetheless, with white supremacists and black farmers "armed to the teeth," as Savio put it, "Holmes County—as comparatively safe as it may appear—is the peaceful extension of a dangerously live volcano."[26]

The dangers of Mississippi did nothing to dampen the idealism that had brought Savio south. Being on the front lines of the struggle to reverse generations of racial oppression confirmed Savio's sense that the democratic goals of Freedom Summer were of epochal significance and well worth the risks. Virtually all of his letters from Mississippi, no matter how much racist violence they describe, evoke the liberating ideals of the freedom struggle. In his first letter from Holmes County he wrote: "It's wonderful...to be part of such a change for good that's sweeping across our country.... The history of the world is pivoting on the internal changes that are going on today in America—and we are in part the agent of that change. A breath of freedom."[27]

Savio came to view Mississippi as a society whose racism hurt whites as well as blacks. When he saw young whites he thought it tragic that their minds would be poisoned by bigotry. He wished there was a way to reach "the poor little white children whose hearts are not yet filled with fear and hate."[28] Yet his main focus was on black Mississippians. He hoped the movement's Freedom Schools could help "the poor little black children who've not yet learned to cringe and shuffle and bend their heads and say 'yasir' and 'nosir' to every white they see." Savio could not accept such deference, and felt badly that he found himself called "sir" by an eighty-year-old black woman whose age and experience should have made her the one to whom deference was due. Nor could he get used to the extreme poverty he encountered in the black community. "Only in Mexico have I seen it as bad. Rarely in Mexico did I see it worse."[29]

During his time in Holmes County Savio's civil rights work focused on voter registration. Most local blacks were either landless farmers or residents of local towns who depended on whites for their employment and feared that any attempt to register would antagonize their white bosses, costing them their jobs. "The town dwellers sometimes turn us away before we can even get in the door," reported Savio. "They have been warned by the whites not even to speak to the 'northern agitators.'" Even when admitted to black homes, the results were sometimes disappointing: "I have had the agonizing experience of . . . talking with a family for fully an hour without convincing them they should go down to the court house to . . . register to vote."[30]

The problem was that the risks were so clear and the benefits so uncertain. "After all, what can you tell these poor people," Savio asked, "when they say they may (or *will*) lose their jobs or have their welfare cut off if they agree to do what you ask? You can't even say they will become registered voters because Negroes are not permitted to pass the literacy test no matter how well they can read or write." That test required black applicants to interpret one or more of the state constitution's 285 sections to the satisfaction of racist registrars. "One never receives a paper back after the test."[31] About the only hope for black voter registration would be for the movement to document enough cases of blocked registration attempts to prod the Justice Department into finally taking legal action on voting rights violations. This left the volunteers with the difficult task of convincing vulnerable Mississippi blacks to "risk their lives and livelihoods because of a suit the federal government *may bring* if enough people register."[32]

Making matters worse was the role of the local police. During his first week in Mississippi Savio encountered police working closely with the segregationist white Citizens' Council in intimidating potential black voters. "While we were canvassing Negro homes in Tchula [a nearby town] the Deputy Sheriff and Citizens' Council radio trucks rode up and down the 'streets' past where we were working. The people at once clammed up for fear of being identified as 'uppity' Negroes."[33]

These difficulties made it all the more memorable when local African Americans braved the odds and agreed to try registering. During Savio's first week in Mississippi he was moved by how warmly he was received in one of the homes he canvassed: "Yesterday I spoke w/ one man who said he had been 'uplifted' by our visit. He gladly welcomed the coming freedom, and would work to hasten it. I too was 'uplifted.'" Two weeks later he concluded that in the registration effort "we make some progress, however slow."[34] The difficulties heightened Savio's determination to continue this grassroots organizing. He pondered staying in the South longer than he had planned in order to have time to overcome these obstacles: "With each person with whom I talk my desire to remain here past August increases. I'm ever more feeling this as a personal fight."[35]

Savio's growing confidence and skill as an organizer contributed to this progress. Approaching African Americans at their front doors, he would ask if they were registered or wanted to register. Their initial response was often negative. "Quite typically" the head of the household would "say in a very thick dialect, 'I work on this plantation,' or 'I'm a sharecropper.' He was working directly or indirectly for the boss. He would say 'if I go down and register to vote I'm gonna lose my work.'...'They'll kick me off this land.'..."I'm not going to be able to feed my family. May get beaten up.'"[36] Savio would acknowledge the dangers and admit that he and the other Freedom Summer volunteers would be gone after the summer so that they would not be facing those dangers with him. Then Savio would ask, "Did your father vote?" "No." 'Did his father vote?" "No." "Do you want your children to vote?" This last question, Savio later admitted, was nervy, an act of sheer chutzpah. "I don't know how I got the guts to say that." Nonetheless he found that the response to this final question was sometimes positive: "The person would say 'okay where do I go [to register]? There was a feeling...in the air, that this was the moment of change....The person coming to your door was an emissary from the change. Even if he was white! So then we'd arrange for a time when we'd come and pick the people up" to register to vote.[37]

The final step in the voter registration process was the most difficult, and for Savio the most memorable. This involved the prospective black voter going into hostile white territory downtown to register. Some of the blacks seeking to vote were elderly, and, in Savio's words, "it was very impressive and inspiring" to see them marching down to the courthouse. "The movement that had moved us so much had also been a kind of awakening for people who had been under the heel of an oppressive society for very long."[38]

The most powerful event he witnessed during Freedom Summer was "bringing an old man down to the courthouse in Lexington to attempt to register to vote." The elderly black farmer, who Savio had recruited, came into the registrar's office wearing "a hat...and was a bit stooped." He went up to the desk, and Savio waited by the door because Mississippi law required that the prospective registrant go through the registration process alone. The farmer "took his hat off very politely, with a kind of shuffling quality, held his hat...and then stood there." The registrar, who was the sheriff's wife, as Savio recalled,

started in on him: "What do you want, boy?" He was a man of sixty or seventy. We were just standing there. "What do you want, boy?"

"I want to redish, ma'm." It's part of the dialect. They say "redish." They turned register into a two syllable word, "redish." You get used to it. "I want to redish, ma'm." But in a very small voice.

"What's that you say, boy?"

"I want to redish, ma'm."

"What's redish? What are you talking about, boy?"..."We don't got no redish around here."...And on and on and on about the fact that he couldn't say [register], and she knew perfectly well, he knew perfectly well, what he was there for...to register to vote...He never gave up. She finally had to give him the form. But she made him eat shit for it. She humiliated him. She tried to. I was watching this....Here's somebody, who because of something I had done, was maybe risking his [life and his] family['s], facing that kind of humiliation. He must have been afraid. I know I was afraid. Yet he stood his ground.[39]

Forbidden to say anything during this process, Savio could only stand there. It was excruciating to watch as this black man was "treated like a dog—worse than a dog. And you[']r[e] powerless to do anything. It tears your insides."[40] Savio could not tell this story without choking up, awed by the quiet dignity this elderly farmer displayed, and pained at being barred from aiding him:

I died. In other words, I can't move. And let me tell you, the desire to move is very strong...I associate it in my mind with helpless[ness] like if my mother and father were there on opposite shoulders. My father used to say—he used the Latin word *tace*—"Be silent...Don't say a word." And my mother...saying "But don't forget one word...one thing that is happening!" The idea being that...I would need to do something with this [important memory].[41]

In the course of observing this event Savio felt he had become an adult, with a determination to stand up for freedom: "That man's courage changed my life."[42]

Less tense but hardly less memorable was the voter registration work he did on behalf of the Mississippi Freedom Democratic Party (MFDP). The idea behind the party was that since African Americans were disenfranchised and thus denied any voice in selecting the delegates to the Democratic Party's national convention, they would participate in an unofficial election in the state's black communities to elect convention delegates. At the national convention in Atlantic City these delegates would demand to be seated, challenging the seating of Mississippi's lily-white delegation. This was an effective organizing tool because it meant that volunteers could enlist blacks to vote in the MFDP election without having to go through the dangerous registration and voting process in Mississippi. Some eighty thousand black Mississippians participated in the MFDP elections, the state's largest black vote since Reconstruction.[43]

Savio was moved and inspired by the way local blacks responded to the MFDP election: "I've spoken to so many frightened, weary, nearly broken people who still had enough spirit left to light up when I explained the convention challenge to the party of the White Citizens' Council."[44] It was relatively easy to attract black support for the MFDP since its candidates were the only ones to "discuss the real issues of poverty and oppression."[45] The contrast between this integrated, pro-civil-rights party and the white, racist Democratic Party could not have been more stark.

For Savio the high point of the MFDP campaign came at a local convention in late July. This event left him so happy that he described it to Cheryl Stevenson as the embodiment of the Mississippi freedom struggle's democratic spirit: "People who had been denied the fundamental right of self-government for so long, who did not even have the most rudimentary education in the processes of democracy, were learning as they needed to, to elect representatives, pass resolutions, in short, to be free!"[46] At the convention's end the idealism of the event seemed almost overwhelming to Savio:

> Everyone joined hands to sing *We Shall Overcome*—and they shall! *we* shall! Someday white people will thank Negroes for saving America from the historical trashcan. Freedom and democracy are things to sing about, but what white northerner has not at some point felt uncomfortable when singing about freedom. I have felt that discomfort. Down here I do not.[47]

By the third week of July Freedom Summer's organizers decided it was time to bring the southwest Mississippi volunteers to McComb. So Savio headed there from Holmes County, stopping off in Jackson.[48] After lunch in a church, Savio and Robert Osman, a fellow Freedom Summer volunteer, met a local black teen who said he would lead them to the headquarters of the Council of Federated Organizations (COFO), which was coordinating civil rights work in the county. The three made an obvious target, black and white walking together through the streets of this segregated city. An old gray Chevy owned by a Klan member pulled up to the curb ahead of where they were walking. As Savio later told the FBI,

> Two white males sprang from the vehicle and both had brown wooden billy clubs. They came at us and we ran and they chased us. The Negro fellow...and I ran back toward the intersection....If the Negro fellow was struck I didn't see it. I was struck once or possibly twice as I was running. I was hit on the rear part of my left shoulder, but it was a glancing blow and I feel as though there is no permanent injury....When I turned around in the intersection...I could see Robert Osman being beaten on the back with a billy club. He was doubled up with his hands clasped over his head. The one who chased me ran back in the direction of the car and very shortly thereafter both of them fled in the vehicle.[49]

Since Osman was committed to nonviolence he did not use force to resist, instead protecting himself only by covering his head. He suffered injuries to his back, ribs, knee, and arm. And while neither Savio nor the black youth required medical attention, Osman did.[50]

During the assault Savio had the presence of mind to get the license plate number of the car used by their assailants and called the police. The Jackson police blamed the civil rights workers for the assault. In a letter written a week later, Savio angrily recounted the racist banter of the police at the crime scene.

"We don't call 'em 'Negroes' down here, they're 'niggers,'" and "go on back where you came from and stop causing all this trouble here, don't you have enough up there?" and "you'll get in a lot more trouble before you leave Mississippi," and "When did you take a bath last," and on and on. At one point both Rob and I fully expected the two cops to complete the job the attackers failed to do so well.[51]

Because of the national furor caused by the disappearance of the SNCC volunteers the FBI took an interest in the Jackson case. Savio was furious at the local FBI agents for covering up the police's misconduct. He and Osman spent the day after the attack "arguing with the FBI who refused to accept in our signed statements anything concerning the harassment by the police, but who insisted on including the willingness of the police to take Rob to the hospital."[52] The FBI did track down the Klansmen responsible for the assault and prosecuted one. Savio and Osman testified in the trial. This resulted in a conviction, a $100 fine, and a thirty-day jail sentence, a small but rare victory in a state that almost never convicted whites for attacking civil rights workers.[53]

For Savio the assault added to the tension of the summer in Mississippi. Even though he had responded in a level-headed fashion to the violence, he came away worried that if he slipped in even a routine task he could jeopardize the safety of his fellow civil rights workers. The anxiety is evident in his account of "driving a civil rights car in Jackson…an interracial group in the car…I managed to stall it repeatedly in a major intersection. I said 'O my God, what are you doing?'…It was like a nightmare."[54]

The threat of violence loomed large when Savio and Osman moved into the McComb Freedom House. Located in a black neighborhood, the house had been bombed shortly before they had gotten there, "so there had been a big hole in the front…that had been patched." Bombing was an imminent threat, "not an abstract possibility."[55] One of the responsibilities of civil rights workers who lived there was to patrol the sides of the house to make certain that no one was planting a bomb. For a reminder of how real this danger was, Savio had only to look

> to the wall across the room which is smashed at the corner from the last bomb attack. That wall is covered with what looks like a floral tapestry which covers the one-time picture window from which all the glass has been blasted out. It was that drapery which kept those sleeping in this room from being badly cut when the glass was shattered by the bomb blast.[56]

Savio wrote of taking the late shift, 3:00–6:00 A.M., and checking out every suspicious sound: "At first I was opening the door, but then I became fearful that I should be shot quite dead if I did that. But to look through the door around the curtain is not enough because I can't see to the sides where someone might be planting a bomb."[57] He worried about being caught in the lights of the house at night when armed night riders might be able to pick him off through the windows.[58]

During their first week in McComb, while Savio and Osman were on watch, a car pulled up in the dark and those inside shone flashlights on the house in what seemed preparation for an attack. The two of them hid behind some trees. Since Osman was closer to the house he

> ran back to the door of the house and woke everybody up. It was quite a scene. No one knew what to do. Someone swears that someone woke them up and said, "They're shooting, they're shooting," and someone swears they heard shots. There were not shots. One guy grabbed the tail of my shirt and had me pull him from room to room of the house just not knowing what to do. People were trying to hide behind refrigerators where there was no room to hide.[59]

It turned out to be a false alarm. Savio could see that the car had black men in it, who turned out to be part of the black community's police auxiliary. Nonetheless, in the charged atmosphere of Mississippi in 1964 pandemonium ensued in the volunteers' house.

When calm returned and Savio began his work in McComb he shifted from voter registration to teaching in a Freedom School. These schools had been created for black children to make up for the deficiencies of Mississippi's segregated schools, which expended on each black student only a little more than a quarter of what was spent on a white student. Freedom Schools offered subjects not covered in black schools, such as foreign languages, and taught students topics too controversial for the state-run schools, including African American history.[60]

While Savio was highly qualified to teach in a Freedom School, the voter registration work had been so meaningful to him that he had hoped to continue it in McComb. Within the project voter registration was considered more dangerous, and Savio worried that if he switched to teaching this would leave someone else doing that risky work in his place. He also admitted that "there was a certain attraction for the glamo[u]r of the reportedly more dangerous work." So he "told the Freedom School coordinator...that I'd changed my mind and had decided to continue doing VR [voter registration]." The Freedom School coordinator "seemed so let down" that Savio agreed to switch to teaching since "I could hardly feed my ego on the rich diet of the greater danger at the expense of starving the students here eager to eat up our instruction (to extend the figure into an all too hard to digest conceit)."[61]

With his intellectual versatility and enthusiasm, he proved an effective teacher. Ira Landess, who also taught in the McComb Freedom School, was struck by the fact that Savio, who stammered episodically in private conversations, seemed to lose the speech defect when he taught. He deemed Savio

an impassioned teacher. You saw that his kids adored him....Obviously everything's relative, since every teacher who was teaching there had a leg up on the basic teacher-student situation [because the teachers and students were there voluntarily. So] the motivation on both sides of the room was...sky high. But again he was singular in his capacity to engage the kids and really gain their love—and it was more than respect. You saw that they loved him....He was followed around by the kids as if he was the pied piper....That was Mario as a teacher.[62]

Savio taught English, Spanish, biology, "citizenship" (an activist-tinged version of civics), remedial arithmetic (which began as physics but quickly shifted to arithmetic because as Savio, explained: "I discovered that the 11th graders I was teaching did not know ratio and proportion"), and Negro history—which, as he noted, "I learn as I teach it." As the summer drew to a close this rewarding teaching experience added to his reluctance to leave: "They love it and I love it. They're really learning. In two and a half weeks the class will end—damn! So much to do, so little time."[63]

After learning black history he worried that a northern pullout following Freedom Summer might be as harmful to the cause of racial justice in the 1960s as had been the removal of Union Army troops after Radical Reconstruction in the previous century: "Just as the barbaric elements in the South waited until the troops were withdrawn in 1877...so they have been biding their time until the withdrawal of the *new reconstructionists*."[64] These fears were warranted. As the end of summer approached, there was an upsurge of cross burnings all over the state, shootings in Greenwood and Jackson, and a bombing not far from the house in McComb where the volunteers were staying. "The growing fear," Savio wrote in mid-August, "is that when large numbers of us leave, there will begin a period of blood letting as bad or worse than anything which has yet been seen." Only "the initial disaster," the disappearance of Chaney, Schwerner, and Goodman, and the subsequent federal attention on Mississippi had, in his view, made Freedom Summer "somewhat more peaceful than was originally anticipated." Once the spotlight was off the state there was "no indication that we have any reason to be hopeful" about the prospects for a decline of racist violence. As a Freedom School teacher, he was especially disturbed "that many of the crosses were burned on school property."[65]

Hoping to prove their resolve in the face of this upsurge of violence, the volunteers sponsored Freedom Days, consecutive days "of massive voter registration when large numbers of local [black] citizens go down to the courthouse to attempt to register to vote." The prior Freedom Days event had led to mass arrests. But the civil rights workers, including Savio, felt that this event had to be held so as to show the movement's violent foes "that we're not frightened to the point of being immobilized."[66]

Offsetting such fears were the powerful bonds of community that developed over the course of the summer. There was a sense of community among the volunteers and SNCC staffers, who felt that they were engaged in a historic democratic struggle that was well worth the risks they were taking. Savio likened this corps of volunteers to an army, albeit a nonviolent one, and even saw a parallel between the USO bringing aid to soldiers and folksinger Pete Seeger coming down to entertain the civil rights workers on the front lines of Mississippi.[67]

Black Mississippians added another dimension to this sense of community in that sizable numbers warmly embraced the Freedom Summer volunteers. They did so in a religiously tinged way that resonated with Savio, who retained elements of a religious sensibility despite his break with the Church. "You felt it in the black church especially. The singing. You really felt cradled. It's impossible to convey to someone who hasn't experienced it. As much as someone [could] who, by that time, was very much a secular person, you felt in the bosom of the Lord."[68]

Concerned about the freedom movement's fate, and growing increasingly confident as a civil rights worker and teacher, Savio considered staying on beyond the end of summer. He was "being considered as a desirable candidate for the permanent salaried staff" of the Mississippi movement.[69] Yet when he spoke with his parents about remaining in the South, their response was "violently negative." They argued that he needed to complete his college education, which he interpreted as "a little masked expression of fear for my own safety." He agreed to return to Berkeley at the end of the summer.[70]

Looking back on Freedom Summer, Savio credited the Mississippi crusade with helping to break down the racial, regional, and class barriers that for almost a century had kept white America from opposing racist violence and segregation in the South. Freedom Summer disrupted "the mechanism of isolation by which white and black America had been kept apart since the end of Reconstruction. It may come to be seen in retrospect as the most creative political enterprise in the twentieth-century history of the United States."[71] He thought it "incredibly creative" of SNCC to bring together privileged upper- and middle-class youths from northern campuses with the disenfranchised black community of Mississippi, since it raised awareness about the hateful, violent, segregationist regime in a country that prided itself on its democratic values: "It was the trigger for very deep change. Not just in the South," generating "as there had never been in America, a determination on the part of a significant number of young white Americans that racism had to go."[72] "We only realize in retrospect," Savio reflected,

> how many people it [Freedom Summer] touched, and how it caused the opposition to [Jim Crow] to grow in a way that it couldn't otherwise have. Until then, the people who'd gone South had been a fairly small group, who had a certain amount of political maturity and sophistication before they went down. The Mississippi Freedom Summer was a vehicle for bringing into the movement people with a high level of commitment, but with less political sophistication.... And it of course made an irreversible change in the South as well.[73]

For Savio it was not Martin Luther King Jr. and the March on Washington but Bob Moses and Freedom Summer that did the most to spark broader social change in the 1960s. Savio saw Freedom Summer as pivotal to the democratization of 1960s America, since it challenged the racist regime in the South and sparked campus activism nationally. Freedom Summer was, in Savio's words, "the event which more than any other created the white student movement" of the 1960s that would oppose the Vietnam War and disrupt the status quo both on campus and off, first on race and then on gender and other areas of inequity and discrimination.[74] After working with SNCC in Mississippi, Freedom

Summer veterans returned to their campuses and communities with organizing skills and a strong sense that if social injustice could be challenged in the Deep South, it could be targeted everywhere. So the volunteers became catalysts for egalitarian change all over America, having, as Savio put it, "a leavening effect on the whole country."[75]

This effect was made possible by a remarkable generation of dynamic, nonviolent organizers in SNCC. Their unassuming, hyperdemocratic approach to organizing—which stressed the need to communicate in jargon-free language with local residents and work with them so that they could lead their own movements for egalitarian change—made a big impression on Savio and helped him and other Freedom Summer volunteers to become effective protest leaders. Savio credited this organizing style to Bob Moses (actually, Moses picked it up from Ella Baker, a former aide to Martin Luther King Jr. who had become critical of King's hierarchical, preacher-centered style of leadership and so stressed community organizing from the bottom up). He thought that some of the most important lessons he learned in Mississippi came from SNCC's core of veteran African American civil rights organizers.[76] Savio later emphasized that his speaking and leadership style evolved out of his experience in the southern movement, shaped by Moses's example. Savio's self-image as a leader would be at least in part that of an emissary from the predominantly black southern freedom movement who brought to Berkeley the democratic style of leadership and oratory he had learned to love during Mississippi Summer.[77] He observed and absorbed the SNCC leadership style, which in Savio's words "was very much understated."[78] It was intended to empower each local black community to lead itself and not become dependent on outside leaders.

This egalitarian approach to organizing was reflected in the speaking style that Moses and other early SNCC leaders adopted. As Savio put it, "There'd be no harangues. People would talk to you in a conversational way.... It was a rhetoric of telling it like it was, a kind of a Will Rogers rhetoric" of "great concreteness" aimed at organizing the community for militant action on moderate constitutional demands, such as the right to vote.[79] Savio admired the way a "SNCC worker would describe for the [black church] congregation...what he just experienced," narrating the essential details of how they went to the courthouse to register a potential black voter:

> what the sheriff said, what the person who wanted to register to vote had said. All the time the anger would be building. Never would there be any general characterization of the sheriff as part of the ruling class, no reference to abstractions like the bourgeoisie.... and all the time a seething anger growing and growing out of a simple description of the

facts. OK, great militancy, very moderate demands, a rhetoric of extreme concreteness.[80]

Early SNCC oratory's stress on limited, concrete demands rather than on ideology reinforced Savio's own distaste for dogmatic or doctrinaire speech. He also noticed and emulated the use of politically tinged humor that grew out of this narrative style.[81]

Even before Savio left Mississippi he sensed that his experiences there were beginning to influence him in powerful ways. Near the end of Freedom Summer, he observed that "though I didn't plan it that way, there's no question but that this summer was more valuable for me than for Mississippi."[82] He had gained extensive experience registering black voters, enlisting support for the Mississippi Freedom Democratic Party, teaching in a Freedom School, standing up to white supremacists, even testifying against them in court. The fact that this was done in a climate made tense by the threat of racist violence was significant. Having defied the Klan in Mississippi, he was not going to be intimidated by campus officials in Berkeley. Cheryl Stevenson thought that he was more self-assured when he returned from Mississippi and stammered less.[83]

His sense of pride in his work in the South, along with a deepening political commitment, were present in the letters Savio had sent her from Mississippi. He wrote that even though he did

not want to die...there's no place else I'd have rather spent this summer—Knowing that the Negro people here daily live in this terror has only served to strengthen my commitment. Mississippi was an abstraction to me before. And I could only think of what some abstract "one" should do—namely to go to Mississippi to fight nonviolently—for freedom. But Mississippi is no longer abstract—the fight is mine.[84]

This political gravitas was connected to Savio's realization that the voter registration work he had done that summer was a far more serious and high-stakes form of activism than any he had experienced in his life. By encouraging these African Americans to vote, in counties where racist terror had dissuaded blacks from voting for generations, he was also inviting them to endanger themselves. The goal of all this was political equality and freedom. Savio understood that those who registered faced more long-term danger than he did, since they would remain in their communities amongst hostile and powerful segregationists long after he left. The burden of having placed black Mississippians at risk was not one that Savio bore easily. This was part of the reason he found himself so moved by the courage and dignity they displayed in seeking to register, and why he was so determined to keep faith with this struggle after he left the South.[85]

Although it is evident that Savio's work in Mississippi paved the way for his emergence as a central figure in the Berkeley rebellion, it is difficult to say how much Freedom Summer changed him politically, as opposed to simply confirming the direction in which he had already been headed. Freedom Summer was so dramatic that if we are not careful it can lead us—as it sometimes led others, even Savio himself decades later—to overdramatize its transformative power. Although that power was considerable, exaggerating it risks diminishing the importance of Savio's pre-Mississippi political activism and acumen. At his most candid, in one of his first interviews after the Free Speech Movement, Savio addressed in a contradictory manner the question of whether he came back from Mississippi any different from the person he was before that summer:

> Yeh, I guess so. Though I didn't realize how different until the FSM started. I'm not sure—I mean, I've been changing over a number of years, what with the time in Mexico and the Sheraton Palace and getting involved in civil rights activity around here [in the Bay Area], and in Mississippi—so that by the time I came back [from Freedom Summer] a long process had come to a kind of fruition.[86]

It is also debatable whether the experience in Mississippi radicalized him. At first glance the answer would seem to be yes, for example, with regard to his view of law enforcement. In Mississippi his encounters with the police and FBI left him convinced that they were on the wrong side of the battle for social justice, either indifferent or hostile to the rights of local blacks and Freedom Summer volunteers. After the FBI refused to record his statement on the racist behavior of Mississippi police he was critical of these officials. In a letter to Cheryl Stevenson he denounced the FBI agents as

> damned red-baiting bastards. I don't care who reads this—and, believe me, there's a good chance some one else will read this before you get it, Cheri. The FBI establishes a new office in Jackson and then releases its figures... "proving" that Mississippi has the lowest crime rate of any state. Murder of Negroes isn't a crime here. And what about crimes committed by the law itself[?][87]

This stinging indictment of the FBI was delivered with an anger that grew out of events in Mississippi. But Savio had begun to be critical of law enforcement officials in spring 1964 when he observed police misconduct at the Sheraton Palace demonstration. Nor did it take a summer in Mississippi for Savio to express anger at federal authorities for failing to protect civil rights workers from racist violence. He was outspoken on this issue before he ever set foot in Mississippi. Just prior to traveling to Mississippi, Savio and other Freedom Summer volunteers went to Washington, D.C., to lobby Congress and the Justice Department for federal protection of southern civil rights workers. The volunteers met with John Doar and Burke Marshall of the Justice Department's civil rights division; as Freedom Summer volunteer Jim Kates recounted, they presented these officials with several demands, including "federal marshals with every [Freedom Summer] project...and out-of-state FBI investigators to be used in civil rights cases." These demands were, as Kates put it, "generally—and rudely refused."[88] The volunteers responded by holding a press conference.

At this press conference a self-appointed spokesman for the volunteers who was politically well connected in Washington began, in the words of Freedom Summer delegation member Reebee Garofalo, by expressing gratitude "for the cooperation of the federal government." "The bullshit," Garofalo recalled, "was getting pretty high. And at one point in the press conference Mario just went 'bullshit' and grabbed the mike and started regaling these people with what was really going on in Mississippi and what the federal government wasn't doing" to protect movement activists there from racial terror. Garofalo remembered this vividly because up to that point he had thought of Savio as a shy person with a speech defect. But when Savio "grabbed the mike and started regaling people, the stutter disappeared. It's like people who lose their stutter when they sing. Mario lost his stutter when he was making an impassioned speech."[89] So in this case Mississippi seems less to have radicalized Savio than to have affirmed his already critical view of Washington's indifference to the violent attacks on the Mississippi civil rights community. Savio's remarks revealed that he was equally critical of the university. Kates, who was as startled as Garofalo at how Savio shed his stutter and "delivered an eloquent, fluent speech," noted that in his press conference speech Savio drew "a connection between economic interests in the North and southern politics," claiming that "Harvard University owned a controlling interest in Mississippi Power and Light and could, if it used its influence, bring segregation down."[90]

Savio's political trajectory was different from that of other Freedom Summer volunteers with respect to the Democratic Party. Some of his fellow activists had high hopes that the Mississippi Freedom Democratic Party could appeal to the conscience of the Democratic Party at its national convention in Atlantic City at summer's end, pressing President Johnson to replace the state's white segregationist representatives with the movement's MFDP delegation. Johnson's refusal to do so taught many activists the bitter lesson that the Democratic establishment would not jeopardize white votes for the sake of racial equality. But Savio, hard as he worked for the MFDP that summer, displayed a highly critical perspective on the national two-party system even before Atlantic City. Savio had mixed feelings about investing any trust at all in the Democratic Party because when it came to the two national political parties, "we don't have a 'good' party and a 'bad' but rather a 'bad' and a 'much worse.'"[91]

Well before Atlantic City, Savio saw the presidential race between Lyndon Johnson and Barry Goldwater as an exercise in evasion, since "neither will make civil rights a great issue." Savio felt that the liberal Johnson's unwillingness to take up "the cause of equality for all citizens" because he could more "easily win against Goldwater" by avoiding the controversial civil rights issue could "only be read as the beginning of a sell-out."[92] This is why Savio, though assisting with the MFDP challenge, privately fretted:

> To utter heresy, I'm not sure which would be better—that the FDP delega-
> tion be accepted or that it be rejected . . . [The MFDP challenge at Atlantic
> City is] the kind of thing you must fight for with all your strength. You
> can't gain anything if the opposition wins without a struggle on your
> side. But it's the sort of thing where you may gain more from a bravely
> fought defeat, than from a victory.[93]

Obviously Mississippi mattered profoundly to Savio and influenced his oratory and leadership style. But he was developing a distinctively democratic style of activism before he got to Mississippi. Thus Osman came away from his initial encounters with Savio, before they ever got to Mississippi, convinced that he was already a gifted organizer with inclinations toward a radically democratic politics and leadership, and far down the road toward the SNCC political style before he ever encountered SNCC:

> Mario was different. Mario was his own person. Mario came into that
> situation . . . already Mario. It didn't make him. SNCC didn't make him
> that. SNCC gave him the place to be that and I am sure it confirmed a lot
> in him. It's like a gay person who always knew they were gay and grows
> up in some place where it was denied that it could even be true, and you
> walk into a gay bar room.[94]

Osman thought that even before going to Mississippi, Savio was already a serious dissident thinker and activist who was "very focused, eyes on the prize" of social justice, "genuinely eyes on the prize . . . I saw that Mario was leadership stuff from word one."[95]

It may not be possible to determine precisely how much of what Savio had become by fall 1964 he owed to Mississippi and Bob Moses and how much to Mexico, the Sheraton Palace, the Berkeley political milieu, and his own roots in Catholic social action and ex-Catholic moral angst. Ironically, part of what makes such an assessment difficult is Savio's retrospective writings, which credit Mississippi and SNCC for so much of his political evolution. The Mississippi-centric account of his political development that appears in his autobiographical essays, however, seems more a reflection of his egalitarian idealism than an objective characterization of his political evolution. He selflessly made this part of his autobiography more about the movement and less about himself, placing SNCC's ultrademocratic politics rather than his personal story at the center of his narrative and crediting the Mississippi movement rather than himself for what was best in his politics. It was his way of sharing the spotlight with a movement he loved. If in the New Left the personal was political, in his perception of the New Left the personal merged with the political, making it difficult to disentangle Mario from Mississippi and Moses, Mario the rising leader from Mario the rank-and-file Freedom Summer activist.[96]

Savio's Mississippi memories challenge the white-centered popular understanding of Freedom Summer's place in the civil rights movement, which Hollywood promoted in its feature film *Mississippi Burning*. Satirizing this kind of whites-as-saviors mind-set, SNCC veteran Julian Bond summarized it as "Rosa [Parks] sat down. Martin [Luther King Jr.] stood up, and the white kids saved the day."[97] Savio's views were in accord with Bond's. Savio saw himself as a foot solider in an interracial movement whose leadership was black, bold, and brilliant, and whose allies in the local black community proved equally courageous. In Savio's Freedom Summer oral histories SNCC activists and black Mississippians were the heroes. He dwelled memorably and emotionally on the black farmer who defied his racist tormenters at the courthouse as he sought to register. Even though the farmer was not attacked physically, this scene got much more play than the actual physical assault Savio experienced at the hands of Klansmen in Jackson.[98]

Osman saw Savio's highlighting of the courthouse incident—as opposed to the assault on the two of them in Jackson—as true to Freedom Summer's mission. To have focused on the assault would have been to make it seem "heroic" by invoking the "mystique of having been attacked by the Klan." This would have meant "focusing on yourself rather than the people you" came to Mississippi to help. But, as Osman explained, "the whole mission was about...getting America to see" the racist realities of the deep South. "The whole thing was about *transfer*," prodding the nation to take its eyes off the white volunteers and to focus instead on the oppression endured and challenged by black Mississippians:

> America doesn't want to focus on those [black] people now or then.... The veterans of '64 Freedom Summer...came away...aware of how easy it would be for the whole purpose to be tripped up by letting it be about us.... So...to be true to that purpose you...make it a matter of discipline to keep the purpose of that transfer going.[99]

It would be misleading to suggest that there was anything preordained or predictable about Savio transforming himself from rank-and-file civil rights activist in Mississippi to student movement leader in Berkeley. Savio did not develop in Mississippi any ambitions to lead a mass movement. He deepened his commitment to the civil rights movement during Freedom Summer and planned to remain active in the movement when he returned to Berkeley, but as a grassroots organizer, not a leader.

Nor were Savio's goals for fall 1964 exclusively political. Several of his letters from Mississippi expressed concern about his academic work. His arrest at the Sheraton Palace and the ensuing trial had led him to miss classes back in spring 1964, which in turn ended in him being placed on academic probation—something he hoped to rectify quickly. He was keenly aware that Berkeley was the third institution of higher education that he had attended. He wanted to make up for the fact that these prior colleges had not worked out for him. Thus one goal that Savio planned to adopt for the fall was to buckle down and—as he wrote from Mississippi—"work harder in school."[100]

Savio did not, however, think about his studies in a narrowly careerist way. He had always wanted his academic work to be meaningful personally. In the past this had meant using the classics, science, and philosophy to construct for himself a secular, rationalist way of looking at the world as a replacement for the Catholic view he had inherited. During Freedom Summer Savio's thinking about his academic choices began to take on a more political coloration. "Mississippi has been making me do an awful lot of thinking about Mario Savio. Where do I fit in." Given the political crisis that surrounded him in Mississippi, he began to question his interest in science: "I believe that Physics...would be a form of escapism," and so he intended to "take some courses in Sociology and History."[101] He was unclear about what this meant in terms of the focus of his life's work, but for the first time he began to consider preparing himself at school "for some kind of public service, perhaps, even—tho I doubt it—politics. If there's one lesson to be learned in Mississippi it's that there is a crying need for honest men in the service of the common good."[102]

Along with trying to figure out where to focus his academic talents, Savio came though Freedom Summer grappling with spiritual concerns, still struggling to finally put his Catholic past behind him. Marshall Ganz, who roomed with Savio in the Holmes County Freedom House, recalled Mario initiating late-night discussions about spiritual issues: "What I remember was a kind of soulfulness, religious stuff. He was talking about his Catholicism." Ganz's father was a rabbi, and much like Savio, Ganz was "beating a path away from religion as fast as" he could. The moral issues that came out of these discussions had a special meaning in the context of Mississippi:

> Clearly he [Savio] was angry with the Church....But...it's like a disappointed lover. It's not indifference.... "It [the Church] has the promise of this but look [at what it actually does]." Clearly it was...really important to him....It was God questions. It was...about belief in the context of what we were doing [in Mississippi]....Losing faith, what does that mean?...What becomes of the moral ground on which you stand? Because clearly every day we were doing stuff that was morally rooted...in the middle of this good and evil...struggle...We weren't believers, yet we were creatures of belief. That's a lot to talk about, a lot to process.[103]

Savio's goals for the fall were at least as introspective as activist. He had discussed with Stevenson his struggle with the depression that had persisted since high school. She had gone through therapy herself and advised him to do the same. From Mississippi, Savio wrote her of his intention to follow that advice and "explore my motivations at great length with a psychiatrist." He felt that he was "finally strong enough" to confront those problems.[104]

Carrying such weighty academic, spiritual, and psychological burdens back to Berkeley, Savio never could have predicted that he would be leading a mass student movement in fall 1964. But when the need for such leadership emerged, his conscience led him to drop everything to heed the call—much as he had dropped everything to go south for Freedom Summer.

PART II
Avatar of Student Protest:
Leading the Free Speech Movement

4

FROM POLITE PROTEST TO
THE FIRST SIT-IN

Berkeley student politics was a strange amalgam of freedom and repression in the early 1960s. The repression came from university administrators, who adhered to hoary regulations barring political advocacy on campus. Those regulations dated back to the West Coast Red scare of the 1930s, provoked by the San Francisco general strike. They were reinforced by the cold-war-era Red scare, and kept in place by university officials who thought that the best way to curb radicalism and avoid antagonizing powerful legislators (who controlled the university's budget) was to keep the campus grounds politically neutral and closed to agitators. In 1964 UC's president, Clark Kerr, was still enforcing what he termed "the implicit contract of 1935," which allowed the university to maintain its autonomy from the legislature so long as UC "would not allow its facilities to be used as a 'platform for propaganda.'" In retrospect, Kerr admitted that this "contract," designed to keep UC "out of political controversy, lest such controversy disrupt...external political...relations," promoted an "antiseptic view of the university."[1]

For students UC's cramped view and restriction of free expression meant that political advocacy, rallies, and fund-raising could not occur on campus. These regulations, however, could not quell student activism or prevent Berkeley from becoming a center of militant civil rights agitation. In the wake of the civil rights movement's televised battles and triumphs—Birmingham, the March on Washington, Mississippi Freedom Summer—and in the midst of an unusually emotional and ideological presidential campaign, student interest in politics was sky high in fall 1964. That interest was translated into action by Berkeley student organizers via a political safety valve known as the Bancroft strip.

Thought to rest on city property, and thus not subject to UC's political restrictions, this twenty-six-foot-strip of brick sidewalk on Bancroft and Telegraph

Avenue had been the place where student activists raised money, recruited volunteers, and connected to the student body. For student activists of all political stripes—but in particular for civil rights organizers dependent on student volunteers and donations—this free speech area at the campus's busy southern entrance was considered holy ground. It was the place closest to the school where they could exercise their First Amendment rights and gather an audience. Berkeley activists from left to right made maximum use of this free space, converting it into a kind of political classroom without walls where, from card tables representing their civil rights, antiwar, and partisan organizations, they distributed leaflets, talked politics, and urged students to become involved in off-campus protest actions.[2] Thanks to all this activity on the Bancroft strip, students could hear radical, liberal, and conservative views on any number of issues.

In mid-September 1964 the Berkeley administration attempted to close down this free speech area. This action offended scores of activists who did their organizing there and thousands of students for whom learning about politics on the strip had become a vital, if informal, part of their Berkeley education.[3] Savio, much like other Berkeley activists, was shocked when he learned of the attempt to close down the free speech area. "It was a kind of amazement that they would be...so out of touch. *That* surprised me," he noted, as did the realization that UC's leaders

> weren't that smart. I figured...these are high powered administrators...[headed by] Clark Kerr....Absolutely it [the free speech ban] was very crude! And that was in our favor. It's almost as if intelligent people had been corrupted by the bureaucratic apparatus they were part of.... They behaved with...bureaucratic heavy handedness.[4]

Instead of welcoming Savio (and other antiracist crusaders) back to Berkeley, the university was making it impossible for new civil rights workers to be recruited, as he had been, from the Bancroft strip. For Savio this connection made the ban personal. He found out about the Sheraton Palace demonstration from somebody who gave him a leaflet in the Bancroft strip area. And it was while in jail for sitting in at the Sheraton he had learned of the Freedom Summer Project. "I had," Savio recalled, "been down to Mississippi...and here was one of the main outlets in the free part of the country...for recruiting people to go down there." It seemed outrageous "that the University would presume to cut this off...because...[the southern freedom struggle] was the most important thing going on in the country...It was a very personal thing. I could put it in terms of Negro farmer X whose home had been shot into—I mean, I had experienced those things."[5]

For Savio the ban transcended politics; it was about morality and ethics, right and wrong. This was in part because of the religiously tinged way he saw the civil rights movement. Despite his break with the Catholic Church, he thought of that movement as having a quality of "God...troubl[ing] the water" on behalf of justice. "The holy, for me...was right actions performed with great power. In that sense, the Civil Rights Movement was Holy."[6] To stand in the way of such a movement seemed to him evil.

"If the university could throttle politics on the campus, then in the spirit of 'Which Side Are You On?' they are saying...'we are on the same side as the state of Mississippi.'"[7] This was not a generous way of viewing such liberal UC administrators as Clark Kerr. And yet there was an undeniable moral power to Savio's position, since UC's administration was imposing free speech restrictions that hampered the student movement's civil rights work.

Solidarity and guilt were elements of Savio's response to the ban. Having spent the summer recruiting blacks to register in Klan-infested Mississippi, Savio understood that he had put them at risk. "To me it was a very clear question. Am I Judas? I'm going to betray the people whom I endangered now that I'm back home?"[8] He thought "it would be *shameful* not to stand up" against UC's attempt to disable the student arm of the civil rights movement. So there was "never hesitation...never any ambivalence" about protesting the ban. Such protest seemed easy compared to what he had experienced in Freedom Summer. "By comparison with the people we'd seen in Mississippi, who had to risk their livelihoods, and maybe their lives, just to register to vote, what was the risk here? This was nothing."[9] The administration, he concluded, had badly miscalculated. "They didn't realize the emotional depth of commitment of the students to the civil rights movement" and how that commitment would translate into determined resistance to their ban on political advocacy.[10]

Savio's strong feelings about the ban also evolved out of his history with regard to speech. Growing up with a stammer, "my *own* experience of repeatedly interrupted speech," left him very aware what a gift it was to speak freely.[11] Standing up against a free speech ban thus had this added personal dimension, for he knew as few others did how painful constricted speech was.[12] He linked this to the pain of witnessing black speech and voting rights blocked by Mississippi racists at the Lexington courthouse. This time, at UC, he finally had the chance—through protest—to stop those who would stifle speech. He was convinced that in terms of civil liberty the FSM was another phase of the struggle raging in the South.[13] Savio felt all of this so intimately that, in his words, "commitment to a free speech movement had never been an abstract or purely political matter for me."[14]

A final, powerful motivation for Savio and many fellow activists protesting the ban concerned the integrity of the university. They believed that UC officials lacked the courage and independence to preserve that integrity, caving in to outside pressures to quell dissident student politics, especially controversial civil rights protests. At least two different interpretations circulated among Berkeley activists as to why pressure was exerted on UC to close down the Bancroft strip. In one version it was the Bay Area employers (and their political allies) who set the repression in motion because student sit-ins against their racially discriminatory hiring practices disrupted their businesses and threatened profits. The mass sit-in and arrests at the Sheraton Palace were believed to have brought on the free speech ban. That sit-in had, according to Campus CORE leader Jack Weinberg, attracted headlines that called attention to Berkeley's emergence as an important base of support for the civil rights movement. Beginning with the Sheraton Palace sit-in and mass arrests, "forces in the community began to say to the University administration 'You've got to stop this thing. You cannot allow the campus to be used as a base for attacks on society.'... We saw it differently.... We saw that students were responding to [the civil rights movement's] appeals to do something to ... fight for a better society."[15]

The second version connected the Bancroft ban to the 1964 Republican convention in San Francisco, since Berkeley students had been prominent in demonstrating for the moderate Republican William Scranton and against the right-winger Barry Goldwater. Those demonstrations were said to have infuriated pro-Goldwater William Knowland, the powerful publisher of the *Oakland Tribune*. Knowland was also said to be livid about the demonstrations Berkeley students launched outside his newspaper's office protesting its racially discriminatory hiring policies. So Knowland, according to FSM leader Jackie Goldberg, "called up Clark Kerr and said 'you've got to stop these shenanigans. The students are making too much trouble in Berkeley and Oakland, and in San Francisco, and we really want this stopped so do something." That "something" was the free speech ban on the Bancroft strip.[16]

Savio had no way of knowing which of these versions—if either—was correct. It seemed to him that the administration wilted under pressure from the business community and so closed down the free speech area. He thought Knowland and the *Oakland Tribune* were involved in this, but he did not pretend to know whether "Knowland was angrier about the Scranton demonstrators" or about student antidiscrimination protests at the *Tribune* and other Bay Area employers.[17] Savio shared with Weinberg a sense that the UC administration, as part of the Bay Area power elite, could not tolerate students championing egalitarian change, especially very specific changes that protests might actually win, as had been the case in the Sheraton Palace.

> You walk in the lobby [of the hotel] and you don't see any black people
> working. But they *do have them* ... scrubbing the floors at night! ... This
> is the kind of fact [that once] you inform people of them they want to

do something about it. And...so that [is] the basic free speech right, and the most dangerous one in...the last analysis, because if the thing you tell people about is *bad enough* then it...leads immediately to advocacy, organization, and action....That was what...[the administration] had to stop![18]

Actually, it is more difficult than Savio suggested to sort out the genesis of the free speech ban. This is because during the Berkeley rebellion the movement battled not one administration but two—that of the UC Berkeley campus, headed by chancellor Edward Strong, and that of Clark Kerr, who presided over the nine-campus University of California system. Even among Berkeley's deans there was confusion as to whether Kerr or Strong called the shots during the FSM crisis. So it seems inevitable that those outside the administration, including Savio, would have trouble getting accurate information on who controlled UC policy making. Even decades later in their oral histories and memoirs Strong, Kerr, and their subordinates tended to blame each other for provoking and mismanaging the crisis.[19]

Kerr denied playing any role in initiating the free speech ban, contending that Knowland never pressured him to clamp down on student activists. Kerr stressed that over the summer when the ban was initiated he was traveling through Europe and Asia and was not consulted. Had he been consulted, Kerr claimed, he would have opposed the ban. Even campus administrators, however, were skeptical about Kerr's use of his Asian alibi to prove that he had played no role in the free speech ban. In fact, it evolved into a sort of catchphrase among UC officials: when asked about responsibility for errant policies they would reply, "Don't ask me—I was in Japan."[20]

Kerr thought that pressure from the *Oakland Tribune* contributed to the ban, but he saw that pressure as being directed toward the Berkeley campus administration rather than himself or the statewide university administration he headed. During the Republican convention the involvement of Berkeley students in anti-Goldwater demonstrations had yielded complaints that led *Oakland Tribune* reporter Carl Irving to research the student political scene at Berkeley. Irving asked UC public affairs officer Richard Hafner whether the recruiting of students to protest at the convention violated university regulations. Hafner initially thought no regulations had been violated since he assumed the recruiting occurred from city property, the Bancroft strip. But when Hafner checked he was surprised to discover that the tables from which students were doing their political organizing, "though appearing to be on public sidewalk, actually were located behind the plaques" marking the border of the campus with the city "and thus were on University property." This was an explosive discovery, since it led the Strong administration to conclude that the Bancroft strip was not—as the university and most activists assumed—city property and thus was not protected by the First Amendment, but was part of UC and therefore subject to campus regulations. This was worrisome to the campus administration, as Kerr recalled, because it meant potentially losing the support of the public and the Board of Regents "if the *Tribune* made this fact public or at least leaked it to some regents—that the campus could be accused of not applying university policy on university property."[21]

Kerr did not believe, however, that pressure from the *Tribune* started the Strong administration on the road to the free speech crisis. According to Kerr, "the campus [administration] wanted to close down this [free speech] area in any event, and Irving's inquiry gave it an excuse to go ahead."[22] Even before Irving's call to Hafner, Alex Sherriffs, UC Berkeley's vice chancellor for student affairs, longed to get rid of the free speech area. Sherriffs (who was on a rightward political trajectory, which ended with him becoming Ronald Reagan's education advisor) thought it terrible that the campus's busiest entrance was cluttered with unkempt and noisy radical agitators rallying students to make trouble in the community. Kerr thought it likely that Sherriffs and Strong were "apprehensive" that "the *Tribune* had the facts" about the Bancroft strip "and might choose to publish them" if the university did not push political agitators off this campus property.[23] Thus in Kerr's view this combination of internal conservatism and external pressure led to the free speech ban.

For Kerr, this version of events had the great virtue of letting him off the hook for the disastrous decisions that ignited the free speech crisis. And he had the airtight alibi of being out of the country when those decisions were made. This makes much of Savio's (and FSM) criticism of him seem wrongheaded, especially since Kerr later claimed that privately he thought the free speech ban was one of the biggest mistakes in UC's history.

What Kerr's memoir obscures, however, is how his stance on political advocacy set the stage for the free speech ban. What needs to be kept in mind is how controversial the civil rights movement seemed to much of white America in 1964. One of the movement's key tactics was civil disobedience. Even though civil rights sit-ins were nonviolent, they broke laws and provoked mass arrests. And in so doing, the movement generated political heat from critics who condemned its sit-ins as disorderly, lawless, and threatening to social stability. Given these negative perceptions, it would take a politically courageous university leader to stand up for the right of students to engage in civil rights activism and for campuses to serve as centers of such activism. Kerr, however, was much too cautious to take such a stand on behalf of student activism or the civil rights movement.

In the wake of the Sheraton Palace sit-in, which had generated 167 arrests, headlines, and controversy for UC, Kerr in May 1964 gave an address at UC Davis expressing great unease with civil disobedience. He criticized individuals who entered into such acts since "they may be paying merely lip service to democratic ideals while in actuality serving the cause of anarchy or some other cause." Kerr's rhetoric had Red-baiting overtones, since in the context of the cold war era, those who violated the law in the name of democracy while serving "some other cause" could be assumed to be Communist. The implication was that at least some of those engaged in unlawful civil rights protests had subversive motives. Kerr aligned UC with the forces of law and order by asserting that "the University deplores disrespect for the law on the part of any citizens, whatever their organizational ties."[24]

At Davis, Kerr sought to buffer UC from the controversy provoked by the student civil rights activists' unlawful tactics. He argued that UC students had no rights *as students* to engage in political advocacy but did have rights *as citizens* to do so as long as they did not use the campus as a base for such activism, since the university had to preserve its political neutrality. This position enabled Kerr to avoid pressure from right-wingers to expel the Sheraton Palace civil rights protesters but also distanced himself and UC from their acts of civil disobedience.[25]

This distancing of the university from its activist students and insistence on keeping the university free from political advocacy set the stage for the free speech crisis. Vice Chancellor Sherriffs believed that banning advocacy from the Bancroft strip was mandatory once it was clear that it was university property rather than city property. Sherriffs, in his oral history, lauded Kerr's Davis speech and said that his ordering the ban was meant to keep the campus in compliance with the policy defended in that speech—that UC must maintain its political neutrality.[26] Strong said that Kerr's principle of no political advocacy on campus was "the flag that had been nailed to the mast," symbolizing what the administration was fighting for in issuing and defending the free speech ban.[27] In this concrete sense Kerr was responsible for the ban—even if he was out of the country when it was formulated—for it was his Davis speech, his politics, and his stubborn adherence to archaic UC political restrictions dating back to 1935 that made the ban seem not merely viable but necessary. After all, the concern the Irving inquiry had raised was why the university policy against political advocacy was not being enforced on the strip—and that policy was Kerr's, forcefully articulated at Davis.

Even if Savio and other Berkeley protesters erred on the particulars—the idea of direct pressure from Knowland—there is no question that university sensitivity to outside political pressure had, as they suspected, contributed to the free speech ban. Kerr himself said that he had given the Davis speech as a response to the Sheraton Palace sit-in and the anger that it had provoked among conservative legislators.[28] So the student civil rights protests had yielded the Davis speech, and the student anti-Goldwater protests at the Republican convention had led to the Irving inquiry, both of which paved the way for the ban. The main error that Savio and other FSMers made in their analysis was that, in focusing on Kerr and outside pressure, they had not taken into account the internal pressure within the administration, especially from Sherriffs.

But the focus on Kerr was quite reasonable because once the free speech crisis began it was Kerr who—as Strong's boss—had the final word on university policy and who (much as Kerr tried to hide it) was actually calling the shots from his Berkeley office.[29]

The Berkeley revolt and Savio's role in it can be understood only if we recognize that this history consisted of far more than photogenic moments of mass protest and civil disobedience. Though those moments made the biggest splash with the media, actually the semester-long free speech campaign at Berkeley went through its quieter phases too, marked by petitioning and negotiations that rarely made the evening news.[30] In those less turbulent phases of the movement Savio was one among many leaders. Only when petitioning and negotiations failed, and the movement resorted to mass protest, did Savio's emerging skill as a brilliant, stirring orator shine forth, making him the Berkeley rebellion's most famous voice and most prominent leader.

The initial response to the ban was not open rebellion but polite petitioning. In mid-September 1964 students met with the campus administration, urging an end to its new prohibition on political advocacy at the Bancroft strip. At this early point Berkeley students did not know that it would take a mass protest movement to lift the ban, and the dissidents did not yet think of themselves as organizers of the Free Speech Movement—a name that would be adopted later—but instead called their coalition the United Front, referring to a coalition of campus political groups who were against the ban.

In this first, United Front phase of the free speech dispute, the key spokesperson for the student groups opposing the ban was not Savio but Jackie Goldberg, a veteran campus leader active in Women for Peace and her sorority. Goldberg and her brother Art, a leader of SLATE, the leftist-liberal student political party, initially called together the student political organizations to strategize about restoring the Bancroft strip as a free speech area. In her campus leadership roles Goldberg had interacted extensively with dean of students Katherine Towle, who had announced the elimination of the free speech area. Since she knew and trusted Towle, Goldberg set up a meeting, attended by Savio and the representatives of more than a dozen student organizations.[31]

Savio had only recently been elected head of a student organization, University Friends of SNCC. At the start of the Berkeley rebellion he was a virtual political unknown on campus.[32] He first learned of the ban when Towle's letter announcing it was read aloud at a Campus CORE meeting. Savio volunteered on the spot to join the student delegation to meet Towle to discuss the "unbelievable" and "totally absurd" ban.[33]

At that meeting with Towle, on September 17, Jackie Goldberg served as the delegation's official leader, but Savio debated the dean. In so doing he remembered pitting his training in linguistic philosophy against her sloppy argumentation. Savio told the dean, "Okay, I want to determine very clearly what are the grounds for saying we can't do these things on this strip of land. What's the basis for it?" Towle responded that the Bancroft strip—previously exempt from university political restrictions due to the mistaken notion that it was city property—was actually UC property and thus subject to university rules barring political advocacy. Savio recalled thinking

there's a clear distinction to be made between a reason and a fact.... A reason is something which determines an "ought" kind of situation, and a fact is just a fact. So I was saying "Okay, it's a fact that this is university property. There it is. I can see the plaques [on the Bancroft strip declaring it UC property]. But that has nothing at all to do with the decision whether or not these activities should take place there."...They said the only reason for the ban is that this is university property. But...I...pointed out... "That's not a reason. That's a fact."...I said... "Does the law require the University to forbid these tables here? Show that to us. Or does the law simply grant the University the *right* to forbid these tables here? Is this discretionary?"...She said, "Oh, it's discretionary. But that's our policy." I say, "Oh, so in other words, this is a matter of discretion and you've adopted this as a matter of policy. What's your justification for it? You need a reason. If you exercise discretion, you need a reason and we insist on getting a reason."[34]

Towle tried to come up with a reason for the ban, mentioning traffic and litter problems caused by the clusters of political tables on the Bancroft strip. But when the students offered to eliminate such problems, she dropped those explanations and simply reiterated once more that the ban was based on university policy and could not be lifted. She could not, as Savio put it, come up with a reason for the ban "that could really stand muster...So here's how the FSM [arose] in the simplest [terms]: We insisted on a reason." And the administration had none. "That was really decisive."[35]

This opening battle of the free speech conflict had been civil. In it Savio and his fellow protesters challenged the logic and justice of the ban. Insistent as they were in opposing the ban, none of them—including Savio—was hostile to the dean, whom he later called "a lovely person." They realized that it was not Towle but her superiors in the administration who had issued the ban, and that her clumsiness in defending it suggested that she might not even agree with it. (In fact she did not).[36] This amicability soon faded as the students—especially Savio—dealt with higher-ranking administrators who had the power to restore the free speech area but refused to do so.

The students requested a second meeting with Towle, which was held on September 21. She offered a compromise that the students found unacceptable: they would be allowed to set up their tables again on the Bancroft strip but only to distribute "informative" as opposed to "advocative" literature. This was a useless concession since the key activist organizations existed to advocate social action and political change.[37] Clearly the dissidents had to find new ways to protest the ban, and at this point they took to demonstrating on campus. Savio was among the hundred or so students who on September 21 participated in an all-night free speech vigil outside the administration building. A week later hundreds took part in an unauthorized campus rally. Signaling his emergence as a leader of the free speech cause, Savio spoke at this rally.[38]

Although the full text of this first Savio speech hasn't survived, in it he took on Kerr for misusing ancient history in his attacks on the student rebellion. Kerr had been quoted in the press arguing that techniques of political activism such as picketing and raising money for dissident groups "aren't high intellectual activity" and are not "necessary for the intellectual development of students. If that were so, why teach history? We can't live in ancient Greece."[39] Savio found Kerr's statement "preposterous" and argued that he had "no understanding of the need for student political activity" either as a means of addressing pressing social problems or as an educational enterprise that taught students truths about their society not covered in their classes.[40] Drawing upon his knowledge of ancient Greece, Savio accused Kerr of lacking "any understanding of the need for the study of history." He "mentioned specifically *the Peloponnesian Wars* of which Thucydides makes it clear in his writing that the future generation wouldn't be able to take part in the wars [but] may learn something from it [studying this history] in terms of the actions of war."[41]

Savio stressed in this speech that "rights students had exercised for years . . . had now been taken away." The latest administration concession—allowing students on campus to distribute literature for yes-or-no votes on propositions and electoral candidates, which the chancellor had announced that day—fell far short of full free speech rights because "what had been given back to us did not include the right to advocate specific off campus political and social action" and would leave student civil rights groups severely disabled.[42]

Though these early dissident acts broke no laws and made no headlines, they show Savio's analytic skills beginning to distinguish him well before his most daring acts of rebellion. Linguistic philosophy and ancient history were the first areas of his education he tapped into to express his dissent. Savio was a serious student who did not enter the free speech dispute in a rash manner. He and his fellow activists initially petitioned calmly for an end to the free speech ban, resorting to more heated rhetoric and civil disobedience only after it became evident that the administration was stonewalling.

Though not advocating anything unlawful, his speech nonetheless constituted a prohibited form of resistance to university authority because it was delivered at an "unauthorized rally" (i.e., one that the administration had not approved) and urged students to picket a university function—an outdoor meeting at which the chancellor was speaking. So during the rally Berkeley dean of men Arleigh Williams told Savio that his violation of campus regulations left him "no alternative but to initiate disciplinary action against him." According to Williams, Savio stood his ground, acknowledging that his conduct violated campus regulations but

> explain[ing] his actions in terms of his conviction that University policy violates the guarantees to free speech and equal protection under the law. He stated his belief that any person, student or non-student, inherently possesses the right to speak on any subject...at any time at any place on campus.[43]

In defending his actions Savio also drew on his readings in philosophy, offering the kind of abstract justification for defying unjust authority that could only come from a philosophy major. The dean, accustomed to students deferring to his orders, seemed taken aback by Savio's boldness, noting that

> Mr. Savio identified the "principle of double affect" as further justification for his actions. This principle appears to state that when one is seeking an end which is morally sound (quite apart from its legality or illegality), the selection of the means employed must be governed by the judgment that the probable good effects outweigh the potential bad effects which are inherent to the method under consideration. In his judgment, his actions had satisfied fully this philosophical requirement.[44]

Not persuaded by Savio's philosophical and constitutional arguments, the dean insisted that campus regulations had to be obeyed.

Initially Savio had more impact on students than he did on the deans. He loomed large in the movement's leadership as soon as his gifts as an orator became evident. Even in the first free speech rally students reported that Mario's speech was the most impressive since he spoke so powerfully "about the importance of the civil rights movement and of student involvement in the issues of the day."[45]

Savio's effectiveness in appealing to students became even clearer as the movement entered its mass civil disobedience phase, with the first sit-in at the administration building and the police car blockade. Here he emerged as the Berkeley revolt's most prominent figure, and his fame as an orator spread. He thought these days of escalation, when solidarity yielded spontaneous and mass resistance to authority, had "an almost magical quality." "This period of September 30–October 2 was in some ways the most radical period during which people were most easily prepared to do very fantastic things" to resist the ban, and did so with little or no advance planning.[46]

This crisis period was tailor-made for Savio, suiting his political skills, temperament, and intellect. The protesters needed someone who could distill the complexities of the issue and explain why the university's minor concessions were no substitute for eliminating UC's authority to police the content of speech on campus. Savio did this while affirming the anger and frustration students felt at UC's unwillingness to lift the ban despite weeks of petitioning, rallying, and lobbying. But he was not merely a master of logical argument; he was also an irate activist who would at several moments in these exhilarating but exhausting days of escalation let his anger get the better of him, using profanity and sarcasm to denounce the administration. In a contradictory mix of intellect and emotion Savio emerged as a kind of poet laureate of nonviolent resistance, citing Thoreau yet also biting a policeman's leg. The crisis called for brilliance, daring, eloquence, and anger—which Savio had in abundance—and first hundreds and later thousands of students rallied to the cause.

It would be misleading, however, to attribute the beginnings of this escalation to any single person, even Savio. By September 30 the protesters had grown more daring in their defiance of the ban. They moved their political advocacy tables from the periphery of the campus, at the Bancroft strip, right to its social center at Sproul Plaza and Sather Gate, reasoning that students ought to be free to advocate political action anywhere on campus so long as this did not disrupt classes or interfere with the other university business. The administration responded by taking the names of the first five activists caught staffing political advocacy tables in violation of campus rules and summoning them to appear at the dean's office later that day to face disciplinary procedures. As these students were cited other protesters took their places at their tables, demanding that they too be cited. Suddenly someone circulated a petition of complicity, which hundreds of students quickly signed, stating that they too had violated the ban. This stunning act of solidarity showed the administration that it could not disable the movement by singling out a few activists for punishment.[47]

Savio was prominent in these crucial events. The first student cited for violating the free speech ban on September 30 was his roommate, Brian Turner. When the deans came over to Turner he was unsure what to do in the face of their threat to discipline him if he did not leave. He asked Savio if he personally would stay there under similar circumstances. Mario told him he would. Then Turner asked whether students would support him if "he got in difficulty with the administration," and Savio responded "that as far as I was concerned and to the extent that I could [mobilize students] yes he would" be supported. Turner returned to the table and subjected himself to disciplinary action. Savio then stood up on a chair and urged students to sign the petition of complicity.[48]

As the deans began walking away after issuing five citations, Savio "called them back, saying that...others...wanted to sit at this table also and if...[the deans] stayed they could take down a hundred more names."[49] This group solidarity nullified the deans' intimidation tactics. These administrators "ran on back to the Dean's office" because they had "no intention of taking 50 or more names" of protesters willing to get cited. The students, Savio concluded, now had the upper hand in the free speech struggle, and in making this case, he drew on Thomas Aquinas, who "observed 700 years ago, that an unenforceable law is a mockery of law; and a law which no one will obey is obviously unenforceable. The deans realized this instinctively, and so made their hasty retreat."[50]

The movement displayed its solidarity that afternoon when hundreds of students marched to the dean's office with the five cited students. Before the day ended three more students prominent in the protests, including Savio, were suspended. He played so central a role in this march on Sproul Hall that the deans assumed he had organized the crowd. Arleigh Williams's account of this protest began with the assertion that "on September 30, 1964, Mr. Savio brought three hundred or more students to see me in my office."[51]

Actually, no single person coordinated this first march on Sproul Hall, which was a spontaneous response to UC's punitive actions. Even Savio's emergence as the protest's spokesperson simply happened in the heat of the moment. According to Savio:

We all marched into Sproul Hall and there we were...just a glob of people...And then there was Dean Williams...And so I just started talking for all these people...There was no formal legitimacy for my talking...in that fashion, but it was and continued to be clear that a lot of people were feeling what at the same time I was expressing and it was a very useful thing.[52]

Savio began to be conscious of his emerging skill as an orator, his "ability to put visceral reactions into words...To express the way a large number of people were feeling but no one had yet said they were feeling."[53]

When Williams told Savio that the five students cited for violating UC regulations should meet with the deans to discuss their disciplinary hearings, Savio presented him with the petition of complicity on behalf of the hundreds of students who claimed that they too had violated the ban and merited the same punishment. After the crowd and the cited students voted on the matter, he told the dean all were opposed to the cited students meeting alone with the deans. So the deans would have to talk with each one of the hundreds of students in the crowd if they wanted to talk to any of them.[54]

Williams found this unacceptable. Postponing the meetings with the cited students, he asked the protesters to leave the building. After the dean finished speaking, Savio responded on behalf of the demonstrators, declaring, according to Williams, that

1) equal protection under the laws was at stake;
2) that the group was prepared to leave only if I would guarantee that the same disciplinary action would follow each person in this group;
3) without such assurances he would urge everyone to remain where they were.[55]

The dean refused to meet these conditions, and again asked the protesters to "leave the building because they were interfering with the ability of the neighboring offices to continue their university work." According to Williams, "at the termination of my remarks Mr. Savio organized the sit down," which lasted until almost 3:00 a.m.[56]

Upon reading Williams's account of this demonstration, Savio humorously rebutted the dean's claim that he had orchestrated this protest. Actually, he said, "there was little to 'organize.' For students who had shown themselves to be well-apprised of their constitutional rights—and the attempted abrogation of these—the act of crossing one's legs and reclining was a relatively simple matter."[57] Savio was truthful, not merely modest, in claiming that he did not single-handedly organize the sit-in. The civil rights movement veterans involved in this protest were quite at home with civil disobedience and nonviolent confrontation.[58] There were at least twenty Campus CORE members at that demonstration who helped provide tactical leadership for the hundreds of students there who were new to such protests. Jack Weinberg recalled a group of trained civil rights organizers who knew how to convert the Sproul march into an extended sit-in:

> There was food. There were sleeping bags. Everything was ready to go because there was a group of people who had done [this before].... That summer we sat in at the Richmond Housing Authority,... the Oakland Welfare Department,... the U.S. Attorney's Office in San Francisco. And those are just the three I remember. There was a group of activists who were sitting in, getting carried out, getting arrested, picketing, who were doing it multiple times a week.[59]

While not alone in providing leadership, Savio was singular in dominating public speaking during this first sit-in—and two of his memorable speeches that evening were recorded. Shortly before midnight the graduate dean, Sanford Elberg, got up on a chair in the corridor of Sproul Hall and read a stern message from Chancellor Strong threatening disciplinary action and defending the ban, claiming that political advocacy on campus would endanger the university's "future as an independent institution."[60] When the dean finished reading Strong's statement, Savio stepped onto the chair and launched into a vigorous indictment of the administration for taking "arbitrary disciplinary action" against "certain students who thought they have a right to free expression at this University." He accused the administration of stripping students of the most critical part of their freedom of speech—the right to advocate "the taking of action on the various ideas that you discuss." In contrast to Strong's statement, which focused narrowly on UC's regulations, Savio's remarks set the dispute into a larger context, linking it to a battle against the technocratic vision of the university "as a factory; a knowledge factory" that Clark Kerr had articulated in his book *The Uses of the University*. He charged that Kerr's factory was infantilizing, dehumanizing, and narrowly vocational; it aimed to convert students into cogs in the corporate machine, stifling individuality and freedom. "Just like any factory," Kerr's knowledge factory manufactured "a certain product," and at Berkeley that product was conformist students. "They go in," Savio told the crowd,

> on one side as kind of rough-cut adolescents, and they come out the other side pretty smooth. When they enter the University they're dependent upon their parents.... Now, they're dependent upon the University. They're product. And they're prepared to leave the University, to go out and become members of other organizations—various businesses

usually...which they are then dependent on in the same way. And never, at any point, is provision made for their taking their places as free men![61]

Here Savio linked the personal and the political, an approach that would become a hallmark of the New Left. He thought the administration's political sins, cozying up with corporate interests and using the university to churn out unthinking managers for industry, hit students personally. It deprived them of a critical education which might involve questioning the social order and forced the most socially conscious among them into an existential crisis because this educational assembly line did not allow for dissent or meaningful work. The university, like the corporations it served, kept students from being, as Savio put it, "expressive of your individuality. You can't do that unless you have no intention of making it in society. You've gotta be part of a machine."[62] This rhetoric brought a leftist critique—pillorying the university for becoming a service station for big business—together with a psychological and philosophical sensibility that had larger generational appeal because it questioned the purposes of education, the way youths were rushed down career paths. Savio was stepping back—right in the midst of a sit-in—to reflect on what students were in school for in the first place, and in doing so he implied that his college generation's search for meaning was disrupted by a narrowly utilitarian administration.

Set against this context, disciplinary action represented the corporatized university's harsh underside, its managerial myopia and intolerance of dissent. Savio told the sit-in crowd:

Every now and then, the machine doesn't work. One of the parts breaks down. And in the case of a normal, regular machine, you throw that part out...and you replace it. Well, this machine, this factory here, this multiversity, its parts are human beings. And, sometimes, when *they* go out of commission, they don't simply break down, but they really gum up the whole works! That's what we're all doing here. We've kind of gone out of commission. We won't operate according to the way the parts of this machine should operate, and the machine started to go out of commission. But the remedy is the same! In the case of the regular machine, in the case of *this* machine, you throw the parts out! And that's what they decided to do. That's what the [chancellor's] statement says...an indefinite suspension...of those students who...weren't good enough parts, who didn't function well enough.[63]

Juxtaposed to this industrial metaphor of the university as an inhumane knowledge factory, Savio held up the dissidents, who put their own careers on

the line to defend freedom. In contrast to the anger he directed at the administration, his language here was warm, idealistic, even loving, as he described
the emerging community of dissenters: Thanks to the resistance to the free
speech ban,

> for one brief moment, there were...lots of students, whose imagina-
> tions were fired. Maybe we would not have to likewise be [machine]
> parts. Maybe somehow we could take our place as free men also! So
> those students said, "We're with you! We stand right with you! Not
> behind you. We're next to you! We're brothers!" They signed that sheet
> [the petition of complicity]! That sheet said, "We want you to treat us
> *all the same way*."[64]

The rapport between Savio and the demonstrators for whom he was speaking was strong and the relationship democratic. He expressed the spirit of the
crowd and the demands of the protesters with ease and humor. When he asked
the group if it backed the demand that all disciplinary actions be dropped
against the "individuals singled out by the administration," the protesters broke
into thunderous applause and cheers. He then evoked laughter by adding, "Are
there any abstentions?" He got the same response by challenging the chancellor—"none of these little guys, we're done with that"—to meet with them to
discuss their grievances.[65]

The interaction between Savio and the movement culture of the Berkeley
rebellion involved more than his speaking and others listening, his leading
and others following. His ideas and rhetoric were influenced by that culture.
In dwelling upon the flaws in Kerr's vision for the university, he reflected a
common desire on the part of movement activists for an explanation as to why
the administration constricted civil liberty and punished those who challenged
the ban. Early in the free speech crisis Savio, Weinberg, and other activists had
attended a talk by Hal Draper, a middle-aged radical intellectual and mentor
to one of Berkeley's socialist student groups, attacking Kerr's writings about
the university.[66] Savio did go beyond Draper's anticapitalist critique of Kerr by
dwelling upon its existential implications for students, but he was influenced
by Draper's critical discourse about the university as a knowledge factory. The
movement culture spotlighted Kerr's ideas and popularized a critique of them,
enabling Savio to place the administration's actions into the larger context of a
struggle to keep the university from becoming a soulless machine.

By the late evening, Savio was so established as the voice of the protesters
that when assistant dean Thomas Barnes finished a speech criticizing the sit-in,
the crowd chanted for Mario to speak in rebuttal—which he did. Barnes had

argued that the campus ban on political advocacy "does not seem to me...a restriction of free speech." By that he meant that students were free to discuss any political idea so long as they did not use the campus as "a forum for political action," since UC needed to maintain its political neutrality. Savio countered that University of California governance was overseen by the "Board of Regents...A pretty damned reactionary bunch of people." Big business representatives dominated it, while "Negroes—laborers usually"—had no representative on the board. Nor did students or faculty. Savio complained that "the only academic representative—and it's questionable in what sense he's an academic representative [on the board] is Clark Kerr." With such pillars of the status quo dominating the regents, it was clearly disingenuous to pretend that the university was politically neutral. Such claims of neutrality were, in Savio's words, "a lot of hogwash! It's...the most un-politically neutral organization that I've had personal contact with." Savio cited the university's role in the arms race—Berkeley scientists' work in "building newer and better atom bombs"— as further proof that UC was far from political neutrality.[67]

Democracy was central to Savio's critique of the university in this debate with Barnes. He linked UC's undemocratic governance to similar patterns in the larger polity and criticized both. Even though in 1964 the Vietnam conflict was still in a relatively early stage—before the massive U.S. escalation of the war—he pointed out that, in the wake of the Tonkin Gulf incident, the American people had no choice regarding the decision to wage war there. The Republican and Democratic presidential candidates had agreed not to make an issue of Vietnam since both were cold warriors, so voters had no meaningful choice since both major parties "have the same kind of foreign policy." UC supported this foreign policy by designing ever more powerful nuclear weapons—and neither students nor faculty had any say in choosing whether the university should in this way serve as a part of the cold war machine. Whether this university role in the arms race was "good or bad, don't you think," Savio asked, "in the spirit of political neutrality, either they should not be involved or there should be some democratic control over the way they're being involved?"[68]

Savio challenged the hierarchical nature of the university. He reminded the crowd that "the regents have taken a position that they have virtually unlimited power over the private property which is the University of California," and that this gave the administration the authority to ban political advocacy. Countering this conception of the university, Savio offered a democratic alternative: "Look at the university here not as the private property of Edward Carter [chair of the Board of Regents]....Let's...look on it as a little city" where free speech and due process were protected by the Bill of Rights. In that city restrictions on free speech, such as UC's rule requiring administration permission and seventy-two-hour notice for nonstudent speakers, would be voided as an "incredible violation of the First Amendment! Unbelievable violation of the 14th!...Anybody who wants to say anything on this campus, just like anybody on the city street, should have the right to do so—and no concessions by the bureaucracy should be acceded to by us...until they include complete freedom of speech!"[69]

Even in the midst of this rebellious act of sitting in, Savio conceded that the university had legitimate authority. The university had the right to distinguish students from nonstudents where "the distinction is very material: if, for example, you consider classrooms...perfectly reasonable, material distinction." But when the administration sought to distinguish nonstudents from students in political forums on campus so as to apply a seventy-two-hour waiting period limiting their right to speak, this amounted to an "arbitrary restriction." It had "no basis except harassment."[70]

Savio connected such harassment and restriction of free speech to the larger political world and the key issues that concerned him and his generation. Foremost was civil rights. The first example he used to underscore the injustice of the seventy-two-hour rule was from Mississippi:

> Let's say...and this touches me very deeply...that in McComb, Mississippi, some children are killed in the bombing of a church....That we have someone who's come up from Mississippi...and he wanted to speak here and he had to wait 72 hours to speak. And everybody will have completely forgotten about those little children because, you know, when you're black and in Mississippi, nobody gives a damn....72 hours later and the whole issue would have been dead.[71]

And foreign policy issues could not wait in the nuclear age either. If someone wanted to stop the war in Vietnam from imminent escalation and had to wait seventy-two hours to speak, "by that time it's all over...We could all be dead."[72]

After he spoke, others joined the debate with Barnes, essentially reiterating Savio's points. Savio had become so central that when Jack Weinberg addressed the crowd he praised Savio's rebuttal to the chancellor for articulating "a very clear, a very strong, a very moral position...[to which] we all responded...as one." Weinberg also relayed to the crowd "a request from Mario for every one of you" to continue sitting-in until "the groups involved reached a consensus" on how long to continue the sit-in and then the crowd could vote on the proposal.[73]

Savio, in both his response to Barnes and his rebuttal to the chancellor, exhibited a love of debate that was characteristic of him throughout the Berkeley rebellion. He believed, in Weinberg's words, that "a good argument can change...history....He was ultimately a rationalist....It's argument by itself, unrelated to power...[that] is sufficient [for democratic change]....That's...why he was a great spokesperson and a great symbol, because he believed so strongly...he was going to convince everybody."[74] Savio's eagerness to engage with critics of the Berkeley revolt meant that despite what Weinberg termed the movement's "bullheadedness" on its core free speech demand, it did not "just get itself isolated, smashed, and marginalized." Savio helped

> to create this broad chain of communication and keeping everybody in. Keeping the line open to the conservatives, debating with...the faculty. That was...part of the tradition of the civil rights movement, and maybe even a bit of a Gandhian-type thing. It's not quite "love your enemy."...It's part of the nonviolent [tradition], not...the left tradition, that you want to engage everybody all the time, and that your position is so right and so reasonable that [you can win people over] if you can just talk about it. So Mario['s]...ability to combine intransigence with explanation, dialogue, listening, responding to other inputs,...creating a broad consensus, maintaining a broad consensus, reflecting a broad consensus without compromising [was critical in building the movement].[75]

There was also an element of role reversal at work here, as the student taught teachers and campus administrators a thing or two about free speech in these debates. A brilliant philosophy major, Savio had an almost unlimited capacity to dissect an argument on his feet, find its weaknesses, and offer a powerful rebuttal, a fact that Berkeley's deans and other campus officials learned the hard way. How exhilarating it was for students to witness this is evident from the memoir of one FSM veteran, who recalled watching

> how with each day, a slick...UC Administrator would come out and explain how things were now OK. I saw the crowd waver. It was simply marvelous how day after day, with no opportunity for preparation, Mario Savio would...rebut the issues with a combination of eloquence and logic, adherence to principles, and empathy for his fellow students. In those early days, when the movement was so fragile it took his leadership to make the entire set of events at Cal...happen.[76]

Savio's approach to the decision-making process in the movement reflected his inclination to be "a different style of leader," embodying a far more participatory ethos than existed in mainstream politics. This can be seen in his discussion of one of the first major decisions of the Berkeley rebellion: resolving whether to continue the sit-in. This decision involved high stakes because the threat of arrests during the Sproul occupation seemed imminent.[77] Savio's democratic approach to such decisions was shaped in part by his Freedom Summer experience, when Bob Moses had invited the volunteers to deliberate carefully and consider the risks honestly before deciding to continue on to Mississippi.

Academics as well as activism mattered to Savio. His engagement with ethics, developed through his work in philosophy influenced his politics. In Savio's speech prefacing the vote over whether to continue this sit-in, he drew on Immanuel Kant. Here Savio stressed the need to respect individual conscience, arguing that each protester in making a judgment ought to do so on the basis of the best available information, including knowing how fellow demonstrators felt about leaving, but without feeling pressured by the crowd to violate his or her own ethical sense:

> How did I want them to hopefully decide? I told them, because I'd read this just a term before...Kant on morals—*Foundations and Metaphysics of Morals*...And it's here, therefore only one categorical imperative: it is to act only according to that maxim by which you can at the same time will that it should become universal law. And what that meant to me was don't do it just because you want to; do it because you recognize that you ought to do it in a sense that anybody who understands the situation and finds himself in a similar situation should do the same....I proposed...not [initially] a vote to determine what to do...but a vote that each individual should know what his fellows are thinking because that's relevant information. [I said,] "Let me make it very clear: Nobody who votes 'yes' is better than those who vote 'no' and vice versa."...I made it very clear. Why? Another form of the categorical imperative...Act so that you treat humanity, meaning the people in the room with you...whether in your own person or in that of another person always as an end and never as a means only.... We took that sort of thing very seriously...the kind of seriousness that only people fresh out of their teens could take it.[78]

This moral earnestness about voting connected to the early SNCC vision of grassroots organizing, with its focus on empowering rank-and-filers to build protest movements that were self-sustaining and deeply rooted in the community. This hyperdemocratic vision did not require or even desire famous or charismatic leaders. A key idea that Savio carried from Mississippi was that "the leader was on the same level as the people. The leader had more experience, had proven his commitment and so was entitled to lead, but that didn't make him a different type of person. In other words you might be a leader tomorrow."[79] Savio equated success in the FSM with building a broadly based movement on campus, yielding the kind of solidarity and community that had so moved him during Freedom Summer:

> A hallmark, both of the Civil Rights Movement and of the Free Speech Movement was solidarity. Not in the sense of a mass, as a block or something like this, but the human solidarity of a community. Brothers and sisters. When the Civil Rights people would give their talks, they'd speak of brothers and sisters... [as] in the black churches. That's very much the kind of feeling we wanted and that we worked to achieve [in the FSM].[80]

Similarly, the speaking style of SNCC organizers, which Savio admired and emulated, was neither flashy nor manipulative. That style of oratory, Savio stressed, was an exercise in community building, "conveying a lot of things to you not just by the content... but by the form." It reflected a high level of respect for the people being addressed, that they "weren't there to be persuaded against... [their] will... It was a style of leadership... that enhanced your individuality.... It encouraged you to be more critical. They didn't tell you what to think, but they told you a situation to think about."[81]

For Berkeley students drawn to the FSM, the idealism of Savio's speeches seemed central to their appeal. They equated those speeches with the moral high ground, characterizing his orations as expressions of "righteousness," giving "witness against oppression," standing up against injustice no matter the outcome. All of these bespoke a desire to take ethical action whether or not this resulted in victory.[82] This reflected Savio's conviction that the free speech dispute was a moral conflict, not a conventional political battle. He and most Berkeley free speech organizers were, as FSM leader Syd Stapleton pointed out, "full of moral issues, and we talked about them and confronted students with them and said, 'You know, everybody says they are for fairness and democracy. But what about this [free speech ban]?... What are you going to do about it?"[83] It was an appeal that drew its power from the democratic ideal itself: that students should have a say in governing their campus, that administrators ought not restrict student rights without consulting them. Savio's speeches challenged business as usual in university politics, with its remote decision making and bureaucratic unresponsiveness to the students whom the university was supposed to serve. This meant redefining the political in ways that tapped into the hopes and aspirations of the young for a more ethical approach to politics. As Savio explained,

> Berkeley students wanted to believe that we were right. Politics was so hypocritical. Politics and mendacity were the same things. And yet people craved politics. That's the promise of democracy, that people are going to participate in ruling themselves. So it's bad when to be political means being dishonest. So imagine what they would have felt if we were wrong. So they did want to believe us.[84]

As a Freedom Summer veteran, Savio had the credentials and moral authority to convince students that the dispute over UC's banning advocacy was far more than a minor squabble over campus rules. He embodied and articulated the link between Berkeley's free speech fight and the epochal struggle of the civil rights movement against racial oppression, elevating the Berkeley dispute to a matter of national, even global significance. Since many admired the civil rights movement, this connection helped to attract mainstream students to the free speech movement. Berkeley in 1964 "breathed the Civil Rights Movement. Those [students] who hadn't gone south literally had, many of them, been there vicariously—in spirit."[85] Having sat in against racism in San Francisco and risked his life in Mississippi battling for black voting rights, Savio was seen by many students as "conspicuously selfless…absolutely above question" in committing himself to democratic causes, including Berkeley's free speech fight.[86]

After extensive deliberation and votes, the decision was to end the sit-in a little after 2:00 A.M. Central to this decision were CORE activists, who had learned from one of their members' experiences with a prior but much smaller sit-in at the University of Chicago that a continuous indoor sit-in could exhaust protesters while isolating them from the larger student body. The United Front ended this sit-in but planned to continue defying the free speech ban the next afternoon out in the middle of the campus. This meant not only staffing their tables on Sproul Plaza again but also doing so in even more militant fashion, since this time the protesters agreed that if cited by the deans, they would refuse to identify themselves—courting further disciplinary action and possible arrest—and accompany this with a mass rally.[87] Thus the stage was set for escalation of the free speech crisis on October 1–2, yielding the most tumultuous thirty-two hours of student protest in American history, with Savio at the center of this storm.

5

THE POLICE CAR BLOCKADE

Aware that the free speech protests were about to escalate, the administration prepared for a confrontation on October 1. Kerr, Strong, and other top administrators met on the evening of the September 30 sit-in to discuss strategy and, referring to protest leaders, agreed that they should "pick off one at a time." While peeling away support for the movement, they considered it "important to get the opposition to a minimum as we build up the friends from students and faculty." To avoid alienating supporters in the academic community the administration decided to focus its repressive arm initially on those who were not official members of that community. The decision was "to avoid police action—except non-students. Right now have the police remove non-students" who violate the free speech ban.[1]

This decision to go after nonstudents quickly backfired because the attempt on October 1 to arrest Jack Weinberg—a nonstudent—on Sproul Plaza sparked the largest student protest the campus had ever experienced. Even though Weinberg was not enrolled at UC, he had been a math graduate student at Berkeley before dropping out to help lead Campus CORE and its civil rights protests. He was one of many protesters who had come to Sproul Plaza (with his organization's political table) to challenge the free speech ban. He had been one of the speakers at the sit-in the night before, and so was not an outsider who could be isolated from students.

The method used to arrest Weinberg could not have been more provocative. This veteran civil rights activist had gone limp after being threatened with arrest and refusing to identify himself at the Campus CORE table, and he had been dragged into a police car in the center of Sproul Plaza. It was the most crowded spot on campus and shortly before noon, the busiest time of the day. "We didn't expect the [police] car," Savio recalled. "That was [a]...fairly major level of stupidity.... I mean if they wanted to arrest Jack they could have arrested him anywhere," but instead they did so in front of the maximum number of students, where the potential for resistance was tremendous.[2]

That resistance took the form of a human blockade. As the police carried Weinberg to their car someone shouted, "Sit down!" Before the officer could start his engine students were sitting in around the car. Within moments dozens of students formed a nonviolent blockade that immobilized the car. "We were," Weinberg explained, "looking for a confrontation" to challenge the free speech ban, "something that was a good point of connection between our protest and the mass of students." His arrest provided that connection, as students outraged by the ban and the use of police power to enforce it joined the protest. "When I got arrested I...felt they had made a big mistake, and that made me feel good," recalled Weinberg, who had already been arrested repeatedly in nonviolent civil rights demonstrations. "It was exciting...the tremendous response we were getting...People were coming, sitting down around the car...More and more people were joining in."[3]

As the blockade began, Savio sat on the police car's hood. Then the thought formed in his mind to use that car as a podium from which to rally more supporters. So Savio, as he later described it, "pushed my shoes off, stood up on the car—on the hood—then I stood up on the top" of the car and began speaking. Initially the police objected and "tried to pull" his feet away, but soon they relented.[4] What had been planned as a free speech rally at the Sproul Hall steps instead turned into a marathon demonstration centered around the car, drawing thousands of students. For the next thirty-two hours—October 1–2, 1964—first Savio and then many others spoke from the car's roof.

Here was a police car, in Savio's words, "the symbol of the other side," which was supposed to have been used to cart a free speech protester to jail. Instead it had been paralyzed by demonstrators and used as a platform for protest. The image of the protester on top of the police car embodied the emerging antiauthoritarian spirit of the sixties—liberty over order. Of that historic moment when he climbed atop the car, Savio recalled:

When I do something I feel is a little bit questionable, a little bit risky, my heart beats faster. I wouldn't have been surprised if people had hooted me down....I had some feeling of embarrassment. I took my shoes off. I didn't want to hurt the car. But it...had a kind of poetic rightness to it. Sometimes you're just...gripped by the moment and you have a feel for what's poetically right....What was correct? Free speech or police taking away this person who was sitting at a table? It was a question of what thing would prevail. What deserved contempt and what praise? You somehow feel those things.[5]

For Savio, what mattered most was not his own daring in stepping atop the car or his emergence as the central figure in the rally as he spoke from that car. The most stirring thing was the solidarity of demonstrators that made this marathon protest possible. This spontaneous protest's meaning centered not on leaders but on every demonstrator who surrounded the car because, in Savio's words, every one

> was needed. And they were needed to stay there all night. They had a job to do...night and day—namely to keep this car. And so the beauty of that, of everybody [who] pulled together in this common work that they had to do [was that they created a community]. One of the things required for a sense of community is that they feel they're needed; not in any saccharin[e], trite way, but in terms of something— the importance of which touches the deepest part of you.... We felt a very personal responsibility for the well-being of all. That's something which must be described as beautiful.[6]

At the police car he and many other activists discovered "what's been missing" in their lives. "Suddenly a new world opens up and [there's] real community."[7] And it was community in a far deeper sense than people ordinarily experience, especially at a big, impersonal university, in Savio's view. Around the police car there were "all these people engaged in this common worthwhile endeavor," putting their careers on the line, and being "able to sit down and talk to one another...where you're close enough...so you can see the people who are doing it with you." Becoming part of this emerging community was so exhilarating that civil disobedience served not only as a means of demanding free speech and stopping Weinberg's arrest but also an end in itself. The sit-in could last thirty-two hours because it had worthwhile political goals *and* created a joyful sense of camaraderie. According to Savio:

> The act of sitting around the [police] car...of people getting up on the car and starting to speak—once this is done, once that hurdle is overcome, of physically structuring the possibility for a community...once all of these people are members of the community by having to act, then all of a sudden there is a...self-justifying factor to it. In a way, once it's been established, there might be other reasons for sitting around the car than keeping the car from moving—namely participating in the community....I have never experienced that [community ethos] anywhere nearly so strongly as around the police car.[8]

This community of protest was profoundly political, but it was more than political. It was a social community too. Within it students befriended one another, and some even fell in love, after being drawn together by a shared concern about free speech. Savio reflected that "many a romance bloomed on the picket line…I and the two women I married met as part of the Free Speech Movement. But also my most lasting friendships" came out of the Berkeley rebellion.[9] Many free speech activists established enduring friendships during those thirty-two hours of protest.

Savio quickly grasped, as did many protesters, that this nonviolent blockade was making history that resonated globally as well as locally:

I had a clear sense that this little place had become…one of the central places on the planet.…It wasn't a very puffed up, arrogant feeling. It was a good feeling…a feeling of exhilaration. But it was better than arrogant. It was real. The students of the University of Madrid sent a congratulatory telegram to the Berkeley movement. And I thought to myself, "…we've really arrived. These people living in this fascist state, there's probably more risk involved for them in sending us this telegram than there is in everything [we] were doing."…If you were in Berkeley that term…[and didn't participate in the rebellion] it was like not being…present at your own life.[10]

While the blockaders defied campus regulations and the law, such defiance was, in Savio's view, justified since it was undertaken in defense of liberty, a defense he thought should appeal to anyone who valued America's democratic traditions. Thus when California governor Edmund Brown spoke to Savio on the phone about the Berkeley revolt and criticized it from a law-and-order perspective, he took Brown back to the disorderly precedents set during America's own revolution, asking him, "Would you have opposed the Boston Tea Party?"[11]

When Savio looked back on the start of the police car blockade he saw an almost perfect democratic moment. It was a spontaneous political act from the bottom up, one that was, as Berkeley political scientist Michael Rogin put it, "expressive…rather than calculating."[12] This was for Savio the most amazing part of the revolt: protesters were not agonizing about tactical and strategic questions before acting, but instantly put their bodies on the line to stop injustice. "Who was running the police car [blockade]? Nobody was running it. It was running itself. People…who were part of the original United Front group would try to think of suggestions for things that could be done, but decisions were much more collective than that—and much more informal than anything like taking votes."[13] The police car blockade, Jackie Goldberg agreed, was "the only spontaneous act I've ever seen in my political career…Nobody directing, nobody calling instructions…People just sat down all around the car….Nobody knew…how long we were going to stay. We just sat down."[14]

This is not to say, however, that leadership was absent. Even though rank-and-filers launched the blockade and created the community of protest that he cherished, Savio fulfilled important leadership functions in this thirty-two-hour protest. He helped to set the tone of the event by using the car's roof to hold the marathon rally and by articulating the linkage among protest, democratic goals, and clear demands upon the administration. Thus from the top of the car his oratory was "immediately bringing it to the level of discussing issues like what does consent of the governed mean? Do rules have legitimacy unless the people they govern had a hand in framing them?"[15]

Humor, anger, and serious criticism of the administration all helped to make his opening speech of the car-top rally memorable. Savio began with a dose of sarcasm, crediting the administration's heavy-handed tactics with drawing the huge crowd: "We were going to hold a rally here at 12 o'clock. And we were going to have to shout our lungs out to get people. I'm so grateful to the administration of this wonderful university. They've done it for us. Let's give them a hand." Anger over the arrest of Weinberg led Savio to mock "these poor police-men here. They have a job to do." And when someone in the crowd shouted out, "Just like Eichmann," Savio welcomed this unkind analogy, agreeing that the arresting officer behaved like the Nazi leader, who "had a job to do. He fit into the machinery." Savio issued "a warning" and "threat to this administration" that direct action would not cease until there were "no arbitrary restrictions of any kind on free speech on this campus" and arbitrary punishment of protest-ers ceased.[16]

Savio attacked the administration for singling out protest leaders, depict-ing this as a crude intimidation tactic. He pointed out that only the eight most outspoken activists who challenged the free speech ban had been suspended, not the 409 students who signed the petition of complicity, so the disciplinary process was patently unfair. He turned to the wisdom of ancient Greece to show how old and predictable such bullying tactics were:

In one of the tales that Herodotus tells…about the Persian Wars…A person wanted to know, how can we take over a particular city or country in the most effective way, and the following…parable was told. "Have you ever seen a wheat field? You see how there are some stalks of wheat that stand above the others? It's very simple: don't cut them all down; just cut down the ones that stick out the highest. And you've won!" Well, that's precisely what they did. They're smart to that extent, at any rate. That's why they arrested him![17]

With Savio having set the tone for a rally whose oratory would be serious and passionate, much of the next day and a half around the police car witnessed unprecedented public discussion. It was the longest parade of speakers that anyone had ever experienced; speakers explored the meaning of freedom, democracy, and higher education as if their lives depended on it. And in a sense their lives, or at least their physical safety, were indeed at stake, given the threats from hecklers and later from the police. This was discourse with an edge of urgency rarely experienced in seminar rooms. Despite the risks, many of those present found the rally and its speeches extremely liberating. As Jack Weinberg described it:

> There were people getting on top of the car [to speak]. There was an open microphone on top of the police car. There were [by the second day] loudspeakers set up in the Plaza, and anybody...could sign up on a list and...had three minutes to say anything....Hour after hour people...who had never spoken before were orating and...inspiring each other. It was a wonderful thing.[18]

There is something extraordinarily poignant in Savio, who'd spent much of his youth struggling with a speech defect, helping others to find their voices in a movement for free speech. This brought him a joyful sense of liberation.[19]

The free speech conflict had for Savio a profoundly ironic quality, and almost a miraculous one. An administration enforcing regulations to discourage campus activism inadvertently inspired a once stammering student to become the most effective insurgent orator in the university's history. Speaking publicly for free speech somehow freed him from the remnants of his speech impediment. While his stammer had subsided since high school, it had not disappeared.[20] Even at a September meeting of the Independent Socialists (IS), Savio rose in the audience to comment but was unable to finish, and walked out in frustration. Weinberg believed he overcame his stammer because speaking for the movement was empowering, enabling him to cast off his inhibitions.

> When he was in his own personal capacity he was just paralyzed, because if the subject of the sentence is "I," "me," and the expression had to do with one's own will, one's own interests, one's own life, then what right do you have to even waste anybody's time making noise so that they should listen to you?...[But in the Berkeley rebellion] he was an agent of a cause...an agent of history. It was not his own ego that was being expressed. He was representative of something else...the Free Speech Movement..., [its] ideas [and] objectives. When...[speaking] in that capacity he was a very powerful person.[21]

To talk in the way Savio did involved being improvisational rather than formulaic. As Reginald Zelnik explained, "People when they listened to him...felt they were being invited to a forum. They weren't being harangued with dogma."[22] Above all, his speeches were fresh and original. Savio was not playing from some script; he was not an ideologue. He reasoned things out for himself, drawing on his wide-ranging knowledge of academic fields, the political world, and his experience in the civil rights movement. He might tell stories from or about Thoreau, Thucydides, Melville, Herodotus, or First Amendment scholarship, as he did all of this and more during the FSM semester. John Searle, Savio's philosophy professor and a leading supporter of the free speech protest (but later one of the Berkeley Left's harshest critics), aptly captured his quality of mind and how unusual it was in the political world, referring to Savio as a "remarkable integrated personality," an intellectual who mastered ideas from diverse disciplines and brought his learning to bear on Berkeley's political crisis.[23]

Savio's other key role in the police car blockade was as negotiator with the administration. He was the first of the protesters to take their demands to the chancellor. His initial encounter with Chancellor Strong occurred in the first hours of the sit-in, when Savio went to see him, together with UC's moderate student government president Charlie Powell, who opposed civil disobedience and hoped to mediate an end to the blockade. This meeting, attended by Vice Chancellor Sherriffs and several other campus officials in addition to Strong, proved a tense affair. Displaying no interest in negotiating, Strong reiterated that he "must insist on law and order and that students live within the rules." Strong claimed that "to talk of this as a free speech matter is to misrepresent the facts" since UC's free speech record was excellent and its rules regarding student rights had undergone a strong "trend toward liberalization." The ban was not negotiable since it was mandated by "the Regents' regulations and he did not have the power to change them should he wish to do so. He made it clear he did not wish to."[24]

Even if Strong had been inclined to compromise, this meeting likely could not have ended more successfully, because Savio was equally uncompromising. Viewing the free speech controversy as a moral issue, he saw his role in negotiating as one of carrying the movement's just demands to the administration, not cutting a deal to end the demonstration. This is reflected in the meeting's minutes, which, though taken by a member of the chancellor's staff who disliked Savio, evoke his contentiousness. He came in to the meeting and "announced his demands," which Strong rejected. Savio infuriated him by depicting his inflexibility as immoral and harmful to the university.[25]

Savio upset Vice Chancellor Sherriffs by charging that the administration "would be responsible for the trouble which came." Sherriffs replied that the fate of the crowd around the police car was in Savio's hands, not the administration's, and pointed out to Savio "his responsibility with the power that he assumed for the safety of others…and for the University too." The meeting ended on a sour note, with Savio expressing "irritation" that the chancellor's statement at the sit-in the previous night made it sound as if the protests were part of a conspiracy announced beforehand in an incendiary pamphlet.[26]

Savio's posture in the meeting with the chancellor did nothing to bring about progress in negotiations. The two sides simply antagonized each other. This was not solely because of their profound differences on the free speech issue. Administrators, with their heads still in the 1950s and accustomed to deference from students, were appalled by this militant student protest and its demanding representative. Strong told Kerr that "from my first conversation with" Savio "I had sized him up as an intractable fanatic." Kerr agreed, expressing regret that he was so unreasonable that he "could not be restrained or controlled."[27] Even decades later Kerr remained convinced, despite much evidence to the contrary, that Savio hated the university. Graduate dean Sanford Elberg scoffed at Savio as one who spoke "the language of the gutter."[28]

If these university officials were contemptuous of Savio, he in turn was far from fond of them. Unlike established student leaders on campus, he and other civil rights veterans had focused their activism on antiracist protests off campus and so had had little prior contact with UC administrators. The free speech ban came unexpectedly from officials they did not even know. As Weinberg recalled, "Somebody like Jackie" Goldberg, a longtime campus leader of her sorority and a student peace group, "had experienced these" campus officials, "had some idea how they thought; had some idea how you craft your argument in a way that comes half way or comes part way to their way of thinking. Mario didn't have that. I didn't have that. We couldn't comprehend their point of view, their way of thinking.[29]

Savio's disdain for Strong and Kerr reflected anger at what young civil rights activists took to be the political cowardice of establishment liberals. That anger was rooted in the civil rights movement's experience with Presidents Kennedy and Johnson's reluctance to use federal power to protect southern civil rights organizers. In summer 1964 Johnson had refused to seat the black-led Mississippi Freedom Democratic Party delegation in Atlantic City. UC's free speech ban seemed one more example of liberalism's moral bankruptcy.[30] Kerr and Strong had gained liberal reputations in the McCarthy era as critics of the faculty loyalty oath (an episode in which professors refusing to take an anti-Communist oath were purged from UC), but in Savio's eyes, they lacked the backbone to risk anything for justice, and so curbed student civil rights activism.

The contentious meeting with Strong convinced Savio that the chancellor's inflexibility could be ended only via escalation and more political pressure. So shortly after returning to the rally, Savio advocated opening a second front. "I suggested that we re-enter Sproul Hall and leave a group around the car.... We couldn't keep this up indefinitely, and the more trouble we could cause with the resources we had, the better."[31] So while some 500 students remained around the police car, another 150–400 went with Savio to the office of the dean of students at about two-thirty in the afternoon.

This Sproul Hall protest led to heated confrontations. The protest began calmly, with demonstrators sitting in the corridors and allowing business to continue. But tensions rose after police prevented Jackie Goldberg from entering the dean's office to make an appointment and threatened her with arrest. Goldberg responded angrily, yelling, "If you're not going to let us in, we're not going to let you out!" She asked students to block the doorways to the dean's office, which, after taking a vote Savio presided over, they did, in what came to be called the "pack-in."[32]

Things got even more physical at the entrance to Sproul Hall a few hours later when campus police attempted to seal the building. Protesters blocked the entryway, linking arms to prevent police from locking the doors. Police stepped on the protesters, ignoring both the cries of pain from those being stepped on and the crowd's demand that they take off their shoes. Students pulled one policeman down to take off his boots, and in the ensuing melee, Savio bit the policeman's leg.[33] He "apologized to him [the officer] personally...It wasn't right....If you're part of the leadership of the movement, your responsibility to the people you're leading is not to muddy the waters.... Now you're not arguing about free speech any more. So I felt ashamed."[34]

Savio noted that this was "the only time I remember it getting out of control in the whole three months" of the Berkeley rebellion.[35] But it would be a mistake to overlook this, since it speaks to an element of rage that helped to fire the rebellion. Not to justify this incident, but rather to explain it, Savio pointed out the pressures he was under in trying to lead a student movement whose scale and tactics were unprecedented—and doing so in the face of the opposition of a powerful university administration and police: "When you're shaking all the rules up, then you're shaking your own too....I mean, I'm not the type who goes around biting policemen's legs."[36] There were, then, in this new kind of insurgency moments when liberty yielded disorder, emotions surged, and even an activist as committed as Savio violated his nonviolent principles.

This incident suggests that there was a double-edged aspect to Savio's commitment to Berkeley's rebellion. That commitment made him a dedicated leader, but, as Weinberg noted, it also made him "strong-willed...to the point of maniacal strong will." There was a fine line between being driven on behalf of a noble cause and being so driven as to be out of control. And, as Weinberg explained, sometimes Savio crossed that line:

> We were true believers at an early point in our true belief careers. So...we were at the center of our universes, and this [free speech] issue was at the center of all universes as far as we were concerned....We were driven, with Mario particularly, but I was driven as well. So when you are driven you are not completely in control of yourself...See, when you're controlling yourself, your control just means controlling when the outbursts happen and how they happen—that had become more of a technique. You know it's still good to be driven. But if you're going to blow up, it's no good to let chance or somebody else determine when you're going to blow up.[37]

Having this "maniacal strong will" was often (but not always) a strength in the context of an insurgent student movement because it meant Savio would resist pressure to compromise on the movement's core free speech goals. Being on the edge of losing control of one's anger was also at times an asset because it helped to give him the daring quality that enabled him to step atop a police car to debate and defy campus officials with virtually no thought about its ramifications for his own future.

This explosiveness had verbal expressions as well, though almost never in his speeches, where Savio managed—even with very little time—to gather his thoughts and consider his words with care. It was only in actual confrontations in the heat of political battle that his anger got the better of him on several occasions. When the deans threatened students with suspension for violating the ban, Savio referred to such repressive officials as "animals" who were "shitting all over us." And when Strong issued a statement during the October 1 sit-in refusing to lift the ban and insisting on punishing its violators, Savio replied, "If you won't take this as an official statement of the group, I think they're [the administration] all a bunch of bastards."[38]

These moments when nonviolence gave way to harsher forms of confrontation, whether verbal or physical, can be seen as the kind of metaphor for the radical 1960s that conservatives love to use to denounce the social movements of this tumultuous decade. One must be careful not to make too much out of this with regard to Savio, since during the semester of protest he and the movement were almost relentlessly nonviolent. As Weinberg noted, "The amazing thing is how much control there was [considering] how this was an authentic youth movement."[39] But even so, this explosiveness and willingness to violate campus rules and laws were hallmarks of Savio and the Berkeley rebellion, and one that angered and frightened critics. Weinberg linked this explosiveness to an antiauthoritarian political ethos emerging in 1960s America:

> We were coming out of the fifties when everything in society had been so incredibly controlled, and the lid...popped off in the last year and things were exploding in the world and in ourselves. So these things were bubbling out of us. And I think it was so very important because without any theory of progress of history we [felt that we] represented truth and the future, and right.[40]

The tense confrontation where the biting incident occurred in Sproul culminated with the police withdrawing and the doors being left unlocked. The pack-in ended at 9:00 p.m. on October 1, when the protesters agreed to leave the building as a sign of good faith with a faculty group that had delivered on its promise to press Kerr to negotiate.[41]

The most serious threat of violence during the police car blockade came not from the protesters but from their critics, vocal fraternity members who viewed the demonstrators as lawless. Close to midnight, as more than a thousand students continued the blockade, fifty to a hundred angry fraternity members began heckling the protesters and hurling lighted cigarettes, eggs, fruit, and vegetables at them, demanding that they release the car.[42]

Savio's response to these provocations helped to prevent a riot. He appealed for calm from those who are "part of the demonstration for freedom of speech on this campus." Keeping his cool even while being threatened by hecklers and dodging the objects they hurled at him, Savio explained the protest to the counterdemonstrators, arguing that the blockade was part of a movement for free speech. But the heckling continued. Savio asked the fraternity boys what they wanted, and they shouted, "The car...give us the car." Savio replied, "It's not as simple as that," and proceeded to relate the blockade to a long, honorable history of nonviolent dissent in America.[43]

This was Savio at his best, showing that he was far more than an angry young man railing against university regulations; he was deeply engaged in exploring ideas about freedom, dissent, and the nature of the university. Here he acted as much a teacher as a rebel. Perhaps the most characteristic Savio moment of the Berkeley rebellion came as he stood atop the police car, explaining to this crowd of hostile frat boys the meaning of civil disobedience:

> I would like to explain—please, would the people here at least keep quiet—I would like to explain the principle...and see if you're willing to

accept it, on the basis of which we took action. Are you willing to listen? ["*Get off the car!*"]...Have you ever heard of a man named Thoreau? [*Loud jeers*] The man's name was Henry David Thoreau. Part of his life was during the time the United States engaged in a war with Mexico. At that time, there was no slavery in Mexico, and there was in the United States. This man believed that he could not in [good] conscience support a war to extend slavery into Mexico. And, so do you know what he did? He disobeyed the law! He refused to pay any taxes! He disobeyed the law! He believed that there were certain matters of conscience which exceeded any legal matters in importance. We likewise in this instance...believe that there are matters of conscience which greatly exceed the question of disobedience to law.[44]

Taken aback by this historical and philosophical argument, the fraternity crowd began chanting, "We want Thoreau!" Savio replied, "I wish I could give him to you!" And then he posed a question more appropriate for a seminar than a mob: "I'm asking you...this, if you would just keep quiet and think for a moment on the principle. Do you agree that there are times when questions of conscience exceed in importance questions of law? That's the question." Meanwhile, one of the hecklers threw an object that barely missed Savio, who appealed for calm and toward this end led the crowd in singing the civil rights anthem "We Shall Overcome." It took an impassioned speech by a priest urging nonviolence to finally defuse the situation and get the fraternity boys to leave.[45]

Looking back on this near riot, Savio credited not himself but the masses of free speech protesters for preventing bloodshed. He believed "the demonstrators had greater internal resources than those who were heckling us," and he linked this to the movement's sense of community. He thought the counter-demonstrators were motivated in part by envy, which he noted in the response of one of the hecklers: "Give us the car. But if you won't give it up, we want one too." He found this demand "fantastically poignant...We were the only people on campus who had this beautiful thing...that sense of community and importance and these people felt out of it. And the only way they could express it was by striking back."[46]

The threat of violence lingered on the second day of the blockade, but this time it came from the police. By the early evening of October 2 hundreds of cops gathered on campus in what appeared an imminent use of force to break up the protest. The only hope of avoiding violence was negotiation. Thanks to the intervention of the faculty and the governor, UC's administration had become willing to begin negotiations. This time the university would be represented by Kerr. It was a difficult situation for all the negotiators, especially Savio. As the movement's key spokesperson and leader, he felt a deep "sense of responsibility...I didn't want to have the campus bloodied. At the same time I could not get nothing [from these negotiations]....It would really have been shameful."[47]

Savio proved tough-minded in his interaction with Kerr. Confronting Kerr with the illogic and bias of the university's political regulations, Savio

> questioned Kerr on just what the University's position was...with regard to advocacy...I said "Well it's direct political and social action that you want to restrict. Let's see what that means. Let's say we have a poster which said "Hubert Humphrey to speak, Oakland Municipal Auditorium, Thursday 7:00 P.M."...Could we have such a sign be displayed on campus?" [Kerr said] "Yes." Then I asked "What if the sign said, 'Oakland Tribune to be picketed, Thursday, 7:00?' Could we have that sign?" [Kerr replied:] "No." So I said "They're both instances of legal [political] action. How do you distinguish between them?"...He didn't even answer that question.[48]

If it had been left to Savio alone, the pact of October 2, which ended the blockade and averted a police assault, might never have been signed. He came off as resenting having to meet with the authors of UC's restrictions on free speech, let alone compromise with them. When criticizing Kerr to his face for suppressing free speech, Savio was, by his own account, quite "sarcastic."[49] Savio's attitude toward these negotiations can be seen in the way he characterized activists who hung tough in this meeting with Kerr. He depicted himself and fellow protester Tom Miller as "the most belligerent at the meeting. Also good were Jo Freeman and Bob Wolfson." Here Savio classified a belligerent posture in negotiations as "good." Savio had, as he put it, "already developed a knack for being quite impolite" in negotiations, and was not uncritical of himself on this score—which is why he praised Wolfson for standing up for free speech principles in the meeting while being "more levelheaded and equable than I, and that seemed to be useful."[50]

This is not to say, however, that Savio was wrong or unsophisticated in his concern about the dangers of being too soft in the negotiations. The movement's United Front leadership was so inclusive that its negotiating team represented all shades on the political spectrum, from left to right. Though an avid supporter of participatory democracy, Savio came to believe that in this instance the movement's democratic idealism led it astray, assembling a negotiating team on the basis of its being highly representative without assessing the ability of these delegates to negotiate effectively.[51] In the midst of the negotiations a conservative student, Dan Rosenthal, broke ranks entirely, condemning civil disobedience and calling on the administration to punish those who engaged in illegal protests. Another conservative in the delegation quickly took issue with this statement and said that Rosenthal did not speak for conservative students. But this incident suggests that Savio had good reason to feel the need for more backbone on the negotiating team.[52] There were other factors pressing the negotiators to give ground, especially the need to stop the imminent police invasion. Kerr heightened this pressure by having his secretary come into the meeting reading out phone messages, supposedly from Sproul Plaza, that the use of force could not be held up much longer.

The most important split in the negotiating team was between Savio and Jackie Goldberg, who was eager to sign an agreement with Kerr. Savio wanted to hold out longer to see if the administration could be pressured further to meet the movement's demands. Goldberg, however, was very worried that police violence would ensue if an agreement was not signed. In her own words:

> I panicked, and I admit it quite freely, although at the time I was absolutely convinced that I was saving somebody's life....Around this police car...90 percent of the people had not even been in a demonstration before, and Oakland police had surrounded [them]...along with the highway patrol and the Berkeley police, and there's a phalanx of motorcycle cops ready to drive right through and liberate that car. I believed that [unless a negotiated settlement came quickly] someone was gonna die....I wasn't going to leave there until we signed an agreement. I didn't care how bad it was.[53]

She thought Savio and the other hard-liners in the negotiations were being unreasonable, even reckless. According to Goldberg, when the student negotiators were on their own for a few moments caucusing, "someone actually said...'Well, a martyr would probably move things along,'...and I became hysterical." While Goldberg understood that in revolutions "people will die," she did not believe that Berkeley's free speech protests constituted a revolution: "We're just protesting to get back [rights]...we already had. We are [nonviolent]....They have guns."[54]

Savio did not advocate martyrdom, but he was more willing than Goldberg to stare down the administration. He and the other hard-liners thought Kerr was bluffing about the use of mass police force. Their tactical sense was shaped by the civil rights movement, which had made gains by refusing to be intimidated by police violence. The hard-liners argued that "police dogs were let loose on people in the South but you don't back down." Goldberg countered that "everybody who was in the South" risking their lives in the civil rights movement "signed up to be there. These people" around the police car were in many cases political novices "who just came by and sat down. I would not have felt the same way . . . if they had been involved in something called the Free Speech Movement for a long time. It was more spontaneous than that."[55]

The tension between Savio and Goldberg was intense. Negotiating committee member Jo Freeman recalled that "when we met in a closed caucus to decide what to do Jackie and Mario almost came to blows."[56] After Dan Rosenthal left the caucus, Savio said, "I'm glad he left," and then asked if "anyone else wants to leave"—which Goldberg viewed as an attempt "to encourage me to get out of there."[57]

The split between Savio and Goldberg was not only about whether to come to a compromise agreement with Kerr but also about negotiating style. She believed that Savio and the other key hard-liner, Tom Miller, were too antagonistic. She later told Savio "that he had damn well better get used to the idea that there are all kinds of styles of negotiating, and one of them is not being rude."[58] Savio and Miller thought Goldberg too deferential toward the administration. Miller felt that Kerr "used Jackie Goldberg very effectively" during the negotiating session, as he "kept calling her by her first name, she kept on agreeing with him, she was a tool for him." A labor relations scholar and expert on negotiations, Kerr did, in Miller's view, what any crafty negotiator would—"pick out the weakest person and start calling him by his first name, and be very familiar, shoving out the other people. Then work through him to get his position accepted."[59] The sexist assumption that a female activist was likely to be weak and therefore proadministration seemed present in males on both sides of this dispute. Savio thought her a poor negotiator because "she more easily accepted a kind of paternalism." So when Kerr made his initial settlement offer, "she just wanted to take it out of his hand" and sign it.[60] In retrospect Goldberg admitted that on some key points she was "probably wrong." She came to feel that Savio had been right about holding out for a better settlement; "I think we should have held the car and we might have gotten things done a lot more quickly and people would have taken us more seriously earlier."[61]

In their assessment of the political dynamics influencing Kerr, Savio and Miller were also more perceptive than Goldberg. Understandably eager to avoid bloodshed, she could not grasp that Kerr shared that eagerness. Kerr, by threatening to send the police in, was responsible for her missing this, convincing her that an immediate settlement on his terms was the only way to avoid violence.

But what Goldberg missed was that police violence would have damaged his presidency. As Tom Miller explained,

> I knew those cops and what they were capable of, and figured that if they charged the crowd somebody would get killed. But Kerr *also* knew this. Kerr doesn't want a University of Mississippi any more than anybody else does. In fact, his whole image would have been ruined [if a bloody, Mississippi-style battle ensued]. That was a strong point on our side, when you have legitimate demands... It seemed to me that everybody was caving in there except Mario and me.[62]

Miller and Savio were right about Kerr's desire to avoid violence. Part of the reason he entered into negotiations with the protesters—after Strong had refused to do so—was because Governor Brown told Kerr he "feared there would be bloodshed" and "didn't want another Alabama or Mississippi."[63]

This meant that the student negotiators had some leverage, certainly more than Goldberg imagined. So when Savio pushed during the negotiations, Kerr could not simply walk out and call the police. This pushback occurred most notably when Savio rejected the initial phrasing of Kerr's proposed settlement: that students "promise to abide by legal processes in their protest of University regulations." Savio thought this phrasing was far too sweeping in barring civil disobedience, since it implied "that there shall be no more illegal protests about anything forever and ever." Initially Kerr made it sound as if any change in his language was unacceptable. But Savio insisted, and Goldberg came up with alternative language, inserting the word "desist" because the student leaders' "understanding of the word 'desist' [was that] it means to end, singularly, and...interpreted it to mean that we would desist [only] from our illegal protest...that was going on now." To Savio this singularity meant that the free speech activists were "not bound to avoid illegal protests in the future." Kerr accepted this new phrasing, but still interpreted it as barring the protesters from again engaging in civil disobedience.[64]

Although correct about both the possibility of getting Kerr to give some ground and on his bluffing about using police force imminently, Savio was almost certainly wrong in thinking that refusing to sign the Pact of October 2 would have brought major concessions. Kerr was not going to humiliate the campus administration by unilaterally dropping the eight suspensions, as the protesters demanded. Nor was he prepared to lift the ban on advocacy. Even decades later Kerr thought the ban did not violate free speech, since it prohibited only the mounting of political *action* from campus.[65] In retrospect this position seems absurd. Forbidding students to speak words of political advocacy was a

form of constricting speech. Nonetheless, Kerr clung stubbornly to this distinction, and was not about to let go of it in October 1964. It would take months of
conflict, more civil disobedience, and the administration's alienation of much
of the faculty to force Kerr to move on this free speech issue. Even in December
only the faculty's Academic Senate vote could impose a pro-free-speech policy
on an unwilling administration. None of this could have been won overnight,
as Savio was hoping, in the negotiations leading to the Pact of October 2.

It was fortunate for the student movement that Savio's militant inclinations
did not prevail in the negotiating committee's vote on the pact. Despite his best
efforts, he failed to win over to his hard-line position Goldberg and several of
her moderate allies on the negotiating team. Faced with this divided delegation,
he had little choice but to yield and sign the Pact of October 2. The democratic
character of the negotiating team and the fact that it included moderates as well
as militants tempered his hard-line inclinations. The risk of a bloody police
invasion was avoided when the negotiating team opted for the kind of strategic
retreat that Savio never would have come up with on his own.

The Pact of October 2 postponed most of the thorniest questions. The fate of
the eight suspended activists was to be submitted to a faculty committee. The free
speech ban would be discussed in hearings of a faculty-student-administration
committee charged with examining campus political regulations. Weinberg
was to be booked and released, and the university agreed not to press charges.
Kerr agreed to support the deeding of the Bancroft strip to the student government or the city of Berkeley.[66]

Savio never liked the Pact of October 2. He looked back on it as a testament
to Kerr's disingenuousness and considered it "a very bad document" that the
students signed under duress. According to Savio, in that agreement Kerr

> gave us a number of things and one of them was that the students cited
> would appear before this Academic Senate committee. There wasn't
> any [student conduct committee]. He knew that....It wasn't my busi-
> ness to know that.... We were told, we were threatened, if you don't sign
> this paper the cops will come in and break heads....It was a dishonest
> agreement.[67]

Since Kerr referred the suspensions to a nonexistent Academic Senate committee, Savio thought it a "kind of arrogance," where he would "tell the student[s]
anything...just as long as they get the signature on the paper...Kerr's attitude
was 'what the hell, we'll deal with it on Monday.'"[68]

Kerr didn't alienate only Savio. Jackie Goldberg came away offended that
during the negotiation session Kerr had threatened his own students with an

imminent police invasion of Sproul Plaza. She termed this "the most outrageous thing I'd ever seen." Bitterness over such tactics lingered for decades. As Goldberg explained, "It's one of the reasons why when they asked me [as a Los Angeles City Council member] to come to Kerr's funeral, I said, 'Are you kidding? Only to dance on his grave.'"[69]

For Savio it was not merely Kerr's negotiating positions but his whole attitude and demeanor that were objectionable. In the negotiating sessions, "you could feel that he didn't want to be there" dealing with the leadership of a rebellion that appalled him.[70] To Savio the mass protest meant that the lines of authority at the university had been shaken up, that students' views were going to have to be taken into account in campus decision-making, as never before. But in Kerr he found "an unwillingness to face the changed realities...the changed balance of forces."[71] Given that this was a high-stakes encounter between a top bureaucrat who came to power in the 1950s and a new kind of student rebel who heralded the rise of student power in the 1960s, it would have been surprising if they had seen eye to eye on anything.

Despite its problems, the Pact of October 2 represented a milestone of sorts. While the pact did not meet the protesters' goals for lifting the ban and suspensions, it put the movement in a far better place. Only the previous day Strong had refused to negotiate. Now Kerr was agreeing to have the ban and suspensions assessed by university committees and not to press charges against Weinberg. This was a form of recognition, conceding that student grievances had to be accorded a hearing.[72]

Although still in no mood to compromise, Savio realized that the pact was better than nothing, and that its meaning depended upon how it was interpreted—how well the protesters used it as a launching pad for a larger free speech movement. Despite its flaws, he thought the pact "had enough substance...that we could do something with it." Since it was all that they had and was the first negotiated agreement ever consummated between the administration and student protesters, the movement, as Savio explained, "made a lot of the Pact of October 2nd. We blew it all out of proportion to what it was.... We absolutely turned it into a Magna Carta."[73]

On the evening the pact was signed Savio spoke from atop the police car to explain the agreement and end the blockade. He may have been the only protest leader with the moral authority to do this. Given Savio's reservations about the pact, this could not have been an easy speech to give. Yet he insisted that he would be the one to read and explain the agreement to the demonstrators. He called for the crowd to pay "special attention" to the change in the phrasing of the agreement with regard to the "student demonstrators" promising to "abide by legal processes in their protest of University regulations." He said that as a representative of a civil rights organization, he along with others on the negotiating team "could not have accepted that provision." This drew applause. He explained the final wording about "desisting" from such protest "would not indefinitely bind anyone." This was Savio's way of ensuring that the protesters' view of the meaning of this change—not the administration's—would prevail.[74]

In describing the pact's other provisions, Savio did so in an antiadministration manner, not crediting Kerr for agreeing—as Strong had not—to negotiate. Savio stressed that the committee established to explore the political regulations on campus would be composed of "students—including leaders of the demonstration—faculty and administration." He trumpeted the fact that the cases of the suspended students were to be referred to a faculty committee, "not to the administration!" This drew applause, as did his statement that UC agreed not to press charges against Weinberg.[75]

On the free speech issue Savio was candid about what had and had not been won. The Bancroft strip would—if UC implemented the pact's provision deeding it to the city or the student government—be freed for political advocacy, and so, Savio said, "you will be able to do there...what had been done there for years." But he conceded that the fate of free speech on the rest of the campus, including its central space, Sproul Plaza, was unsettled and would be discussed by a university committee.[76]

Savio acknowledged that, due to the threat of violence, the negotiations had been flawed in terms of democratic process. "Until this time we have tried our best to submit all statements to a vote of those present." He asked the crowd to consider "what a vote means. A vote should be the result of an intellectual decision. Such a decision, if we have respect for our dignity as free men cannot, I believe, be made under the circumstances of a meeting of this sort, with the police present, as they are, with our knowing full well what they, or hecklers may do." The physical danger was so immediate—"the seriousness of the circumstances in which we find ourselves here and now" because of the presence of large numbers of police—that democratic deliberation was all but impossible. He proposed that a meeting be held at the start of the next school week to discuss the issues raised by the pact, claiming that "this will give adequate time for the free men involved to consider carefully the serious issues involved in this matter." Instead of calling for a vote on each provision of the pact, Savio asked that "those who have taken part in this protest...agree, by acclamation, to accepting this document, and as soon as they have done so to rise quietly and with dignity to walk home. May I please have that decision?" The crowd cheered its approval and then dispersed—ending the longest demonstration in Berkeley's history.[77]

This final speech of the police car blockade underscores some of the key reasons Savio's oratory had broad appeal on campus. First was its honesty and transparency. He made extensive use of narrative storytelling to communicate his lack of interest in obtaining personal power and his refusal to defer to those who held power. After meeting with university officials on October 2, Savio kept nothing secret or confidential. This became a hallmark of his oratory, which frequently included such phrases as "I was told the following by..." and then offered verbatim accounts of the administration arguments. Having established this link, Savio analyzed the narrative and how it fit into the ongoing free speech crisis, leaving listeners feeling that they had participated in a process by which evidence had been examined and rational conclusions reached.[78]

In this narrative style Savio was emulating what he admired about the SNCC organizers he had worked with in Mississippi. They respected the southern black community too much to manipulate people through inflated or self-aggrandizing rhetoric. Straight talk and directness were much preferred. Savio

had learned [in SNCC] great concreteness. [So] we didn't refer...to the faceless bureaucrats. Usually in speeches we talked about...the specific dean...would say "Dean Towle said thus and such and then Jackie said this," and...describe[d] in detail the way the meeting was proceeding, step by step—and then...that seething anger would be right beneath the surface, but it would be enmeshed with a clear and simple reporting of the facts. We'd learned that [in Mississippi] and we applied it...in a different context within the University of California.[79]

Students found this style profoundly democratic and inclusive. Another hallmark in these speeches was that Savio did not pretend to have all the answers, displaying his uncertainty in what Reginald Zelnik termed a dialogical style of oratory:

The way he attracted students and faculty and others who weren't political was that he argued with himself. He questioned himself in front of them. He could give a strong speech with a beginning, a middle, and an end, and keep everybody mesmerized and fascinated. But all the doubts that he had or questions or qualifications of the position he was trying to argue got incorporated into the speech and it gave students and listeners in general the sense that they were part of a dialogue. Obviously you can't have a real dialogue with 5,000...students so it's a little artificial, but in that setting...[no] public speaker...[was more] engaged in...back and forth with his audience... [than] Mario.... He had an ability to engage his listener at the visceral level, speaking to their own doubts and apprehensions. And ... students had lots of apprehensions and doubts that fall. And by feeling that the person addressing them shared them, his speeches became that much more powerful and persuasive.[80]

There was an aesthetic dimension to Savio's oratory. He had a poetic sense about language and a consciousness about the form as well as substance of political discourse. This is what the literary critic Wendy Lesser had in mind when she—while perhaps overstating Savio's uniqueness—termed him

the only political figure of my era for whom language truly mattered. He was the last American perhaps who believed that civil, expressive, precisely worded, emotionally truthful exhortation could bring about significant change. He was the only person I have ever seen or met who gave political speech the weight and subtlety of literature.... The sentences he spoke were complicated and detailed, with clauses and metaphors and little byways of digression that together added up to a coherent grammatical whole. When he spoke, he seemed inspired—literally so, as if he were breathing thought through language.[81]

All of this enhanced Savio's ability to reach out to nonradical students, which was critical, since most Berkeley students were not radical and had little or no history of activism. If the movement was to succeed, it needed to attract thousands of these students. The rebellion had begun with student groups from left to right seeking such support by banding together to protest the ban. That is why in its initial stages in September—before the insurgence named itself the Free Speech Movement—the coalition of student groups protesting the ban called itself the United Front. This wide base of support was one of the keys to the movement's success.[82]

Despite its broad support, the Berkeley rebellion's center of gravity was on the left. Even the term "United Front" comes out of the Left's history, denoting a coalition of diverse political groups led by leftists. Radicals from the student civil rights organizations, as well as the student branches of Old Left groups, loomed large in the rebellion. These activists had the most to lose if the ban endured, were the most skeptical about the motives of the top university administrators, had the most experience in civil disobedience, and were the most willing to employ such tactics on campus.

Savio came to the movement (and remained) an independent radical, with no formal affiliations with socialist or Marxist organizations on the campus and little experience with Old Left politics. Yet, having been involved in efforts at social change in Mexico and Mississippi, he had a well developed sense of class, experience with racial and class conflict, and a critical outlook on the inequities of capitalism, as well as the injustice and global violence bred by American imperialism. Zelnik, who grew close to Savio following the Berkeley revolt, attested that Mario was "not a Marxist, and I don't think that Socialism with a big 'S' was a central part of his identity, which was more of what some Russian Marxists used to call a 'radical democrat.'" In fall 1964 Savio told Zelnik that "he had recently discovered" the writings of Herbert Marcuse, the Marxist philosopher, and found them "really excellent." "Mario . . . never overcame his attraction to Marxism" because it grappled in a serious way with capitalism's flaws. "There was a level at which he really wished he could be a Marxist, but just couldn't, just like certain people who cannot [believe in God] still wish they could believe in God. . . . Like a lot of radicals his disdain of capitalism was a more powerful internal mechanism than his love of socialism." In terms of direct action, however, Savio was as least as militant as the historically leftist groups.[83]

Savio's radical sensibility enabled him to speak naturally and almost effortlessly for and to the campus Left. His speeches reflected the Left's indictment of cold war liberals' antiradicalism, the undemocratic governing structure of the university (with its Board of Regents dominated by big business), and Kerr's vision of the university servicing corporate America and the Pentagon while suppressing radical dissent.[84] Savio's effectiveness as an orator rested on his ability to speak for the campus's dynamic, action-oriented radical minority as well as Berkeley's nonradical majority.

This opening chapter of the Berkeley rebellion concluded with Savio playing a role that is virtually the opposite of the incendiary orator highlighted in books and films on the 1960s. Instead of rallying students to rebel, he was urging those who had rebelled to go home and end the police car blockade. Thus at first glance the Pact of October 2 does not seem to work well as a symbol for the decade that the Berkeley rebellion came to represent. Savio's willingness to deescalate, to sign that pact—albeit reluctantly—and give a speech ending the thirty-two-hour blockade may seem uncharacteristic for so famous a student rebel. It is possible to argue that since this strategic retreat proved temporary and was not Savio's idea— in fact, he initially opposed the pact—it is appropriate that this is not the part of the Berkeley rebellion for which he is remembered. But this misses the point. Savio was part of the leadership of a democratic movement, and when he was unable to win over the majority of the negotiating committee to his militant position, he did the democratic thing, giving in to the moderate majority. In this sense the pact did fit in with the spirit of the early New Left and the grassroots movements of the 1960s, since it was an agreement shaped by movement democracy.

We will never know whether in the absence of this pact Jackie Goldberg's fears of bloodshed would have been realized—as would occur later in the Vietnam era when panicky National Guard troops at Kent State and trigger-happy police at Jackson State turned their guns on college students. But the point is that the Berkeley movement's leadership chose not to take that chance, and the credit for that goes primarily to Goldberg, for insisting that a police invasion be avoided, and to Savio, for going along with a decision he had initially opposed, then honoring that majority decision by speaking on behalf of the pact from atop the police car. This may not quite make up for his having bitten the police officer's leg the previous day, but it does tip the balance quite decisively in favor of nonviolence.

Savio was not alone in this democratic sensibility. Jack Weinberg initially viewed the pact as a defeat, feeling that the demonstrators had given up the car without any promise that the movement's demand for an end to the campus ban on advocacy would be met. Nonetheless, he too acceded to the decision by the negotiating committee, and even agreed not to criticize the pact, out of solidarity with the movement. The same was true of the militant rank-and-file, some of whom were disappointed with the pact but nonetheless went along with it in the spirit of solidarity, recognizing that this was only the start of a growing student movement.[85]

Ironically, the most rebellious response to the Pact of October 2 came not from Savio or other militants but from the campus administration. Chancellor Strong, present yet mostly silent during the negotiations, read the pact but would not sign it. Strong had been far less willing to negotiate than Kerr was, and he was not happy to have the president of the university system presiding over negotiations on his campus and signing a pact with student rebels.[86] In this sense the movement's leadership, with its democratic sprit, proved more inclined to stand together than did the university administration, with its hierarchical and competing lines of authority.

The pact bought both sides more time, delaying a potentially disastrous battle with the police. This time would be used by the movement to get better organized, creating an inclusive representative system and leadership structure in the weekend following the blockade. It was then that the activists came up with the name Free Speech Movement for their insurgency. The movement continued to build a community of protest that proved amazingly energetic, dedicated, and enduring. This would provide Savio with the personal friendship and support, as well as the political inspiration, to function for the next two months as the preeminent orator of campus rebellion.

6

CONSOLIDATING THE MOVEMENT AND NEGOTIATING FOR FREE SPEECH

The Berkeley revolt departed dramatically from the conventions of American politics in many ways, the most obvious of which was its youthful leadership. In contrast to the middle-aged and senior politicians who dominated America's traditional party politics, a twenty-one-year-old undergraduate and a mass movement of students even younger took over Berkeley's political stage. With youth came an abundance of energy, drive, and idealism. Savio, like the movement he helped lead, was not bound by most of cold war America's old habits and prejudices; he could and did imagine new kinds of political arrangements, far more democratic than mainstream politics. His (and the FSM's) eagerness to involve the whole student community in the movement and its decision-making processes translated into a highly participatory organizational culture.[1] This style of politics helped make the movement attractive to students, as FSM organizer Robert Hurwitt recalled: "The continuing experiment in developing a workable form of representational democracy for the burgeoning, mostly unorganized masses of demonstrators was one of the most exciting day-to-day aspects of the FSM and one of its major contributions to the development of the movements that followed."[2] Savio and his fellow movement leaders rejected the exclusionary practices—the banning of Communists and the tendency toward Red-baiting—that marred cold war American politics. This enabled them to preside over a movement in which all kinds of radicals—who ordinarily were rivals—worked well together and built bridges to nonradicals.

Being new to the world of campus politics meant that Savio and the movement were not bound by the traditions of the university, freeing them to question its compromises with the political power structure and corporate America. In Savio the administration faced a bold militant who entered into negotiations with little deference toward constituted authority, insisting that students be treated as equals to high-ranking university officials. This contrasted with the faculty, which tended to be cautious and hesitant about challenging the administration; it also flew in the face of the trend over the course of the twentieth century for university administrations to have ever greater power and authority in higher education. In the Berkeley rebellion it would be youth, Savio and the student protesters, who challenged the faculty to restore the authority of teachers and learners over their educational institution by overruling an administration that gradually had discredited itself. This was a challenge that most faculty—with long memories of the McCarthy era's loyalty oath battle, which bred both support for Kerr and Strong and fear of the Regents' political intolerance—evaded until almost the semester's end.[3]

But though an asset in terms of iconoclasm and innovation, youth had its liabilities when it came to leadership experience. Savio had done intense and dangerous political work as a civil rights activist but had never led a large organization, let alone a mass movement. He had never wielded political power or experienced the clash of egos, competitiveness, internal dissent, and diverging political styles that sometimes make politics conflicted, complex, and difficult. Nor had he ever been forced to contend with a mass media eager to sensationalize his every move, and it would prove difficult for him to contend with his new celebrity status.

Even veteran leaders—most notably Clark Kerr and Edward Strong—found it difficult to navigate the political whirlwind that Berkeley became in fall 1964. So it is not surprising that in helping to lead the student movement Savio made mistakes. Savio's inexperience in political leadership and some of the very traits that made him a formidable foe of the administration, most notably his tendency to be uncompromising, at times led him to be unduly suspicious of advocates of compromise. Such failings existed side by side with his brilliance as a speaker and moral beacon within the movement. His leadership ultimately proved extremely effective but far from flawless.

In the aftermath of the police car blockade and the Pact of October 2 the Berkeley revolt went through a significant transition. The revolt had begun with a minimum of planning; its most important actions, the blockade and sit-ins, had been spontaneous. With the task of negotiating with the administration pending, the movement's leading activists—more than a hundred of whom gathered on the weekend following the blockade at the founding meeting of the new organization, which they named the Free Speech Movement (FSM)—elected leaders and adopted a democratic organizational structure. It consisted of a large Executive Committee representing student groups and unaffiliated students, which in turn elected to the top of the FSM leadership structure a smaller Steering Committee, whose nine (later eleven) members used a consensus decision-making process to guide the movement's daily tactics.[4] These committees would spend hours in meetings planning for every contingency. The FSM had no president or chair; its policies were made by committees and implemented not by a formal administrative apparatus overseen by a manager but by volunteers gathered into various "centrals," who carried out the phone calling, leafleting, and other nuts-and-bolts tasks essential to successful student mobilizations.[5]

Savio supported this shift toward a formal democratic leadership structure. He was elected to the Steering Committee when it first formed, and reelected throughout the lifetime of the FSM. While recognizing that formal organization was necessary to contend with a powerful university administration, he looked back with some regret on this need for structure. These new governing bodies planned everything, so in his view the movement "never recaptured the...magical quality" of those initial spontaneous acts of resistance.[6] At its start the revolt had been political only in the most idealistic sense, with protesters accepting "their role as citizens" and fulfilling their "duty" to protect liberty in their community. It quickly became political in, as Savio put it, the

pejorative sense where political means kind of calculating...seeing what particular public action will redound to one's advantage...Will the people be ready to do this [act of resistance?]...And how can we so structure the situation so people will understand the situation...[and] will do what we believe is required in the situation?[7]

Savio thought something had been lost in this transition. The newly elected FSM leadership had

certainly come of the people—it was certainly a government *for* the people, but it was no longer a government *by* the people...To some extent...the Civil Rights Movement has become a little bit that way too. And I think it's likely to become a little more that way...It may be inevitable in the nature of mass movements. I'm not sure. But it really makes me sad.[8]

There was in Savio almost an anarchist's love of spontaneous insurgency, and not even elected leadership and representative committees could quite measure up.

The movement's democratic governance and Savio's leadership style were starkly juxtaposed with the administration they battled. Kerr was hierarchical, sitting atop two layers of bureaucracy—the campus and statewide administrations of the university—and had as little direct connection with students as a corporate CEO had with assembly-line workers. Savio, on the other hand, approached leadership not from the corporate model of top-down management but from the civil rights movement and its participatory ethos. Even though the FSM's emergence and his leadership in it came as a surprise, he was not totally unprepared for this role given his immersion in the Mississippi movement's world of democratic leadership and oratory. So the Berkeley revolt pitted a free speech movement living (or at least aspiring to live) its democratic principles and staffed entirely by volunteers against professional administrators, who took orders from above in the UC hierarchy; it was democracy warring with bureaucracy.

Savio's belief in open and democratic leadership was also a by-product of growing up in cold war America. Even though he had never known any Communists in his youth he had always heard that their political style was "manipulative"— "people who would control the masses and so forth . . . That was clearly bad."[9] So while breaking with the cold war ethos in shedding antiradicalism and welcoming Communists into the movement, he rejected the Old Left vanguard style in which a small radical cadre made all the key decisions. It was in part to differentiate the FSM from this undemocratic tradition that Savio insisted that the movement be "*scrupulously* democratic" in its elections, as well as getting

> *direct feedback* from people . . . Though there were things wrong with it . . . it was . . . far above what passes for politics in the real world. . . . We . . . began to formulate *in concerto*, the meaning for us of the central New Left credo: "The people must participate in making the decisions that affect their lives."[10]

As this use of first-person plural implies, Savio's political ideas during the FSM were shaped by a collective process, a movement culture. When movement leaders veered away from this, they "got flak, got elected and dis-elected and re-elected."[11] As Weinberg explained, each leader "had lots of people that they were accountable to" and who fed them information and ideas.

> And the thing about it was, there was no politeness. I mean people would tell you if they didn't like what you were doing. And nobody had to demonstrate, nobody had to support us. We didn't have any credentials or office or anything. So the job of the Free Speech Movement leadership at every point was to do the right thing, to do the things that the mass of people . . . thought was going to be right. And that's how it worked.[12]

Savio himself held the leadership accountable for their actions. With his tough attitude toward the administration, he came away from the negotiations over the Pact of October 2 disdainful of Jackie Goldberg's negotiating style. He thought her too conciliatory, and brought this up during the vote forming the first Steering Committee, speaking out against her candidacy, implying that she had sold out. Goldberg recalled that "Mario denounces me and says, 'We cannot have Jackie in this [Steering Committee]. We don't trust her. She is ingratiating herself to the administration.'"[13] This charge infuriated Goldberg's brother Art, a leader of SLATE, the campus leftist-liberal political party. To avoid losing this important constituency, Savio backed down, and Jackie was elected to the Steering Committee. But her tenure proved brief. Within two weeks she had been voted off the committee, almost entirely because of Savio's outburst.

Goldberg never thought his charges against her had any validity. "I'm the one who [in the first Sproul Hall occupation] trapped Dean Towle in her office. That's kind of a bad sign for ingratiating yourself" with the administration.[14] Why, then, did Savio make such charges? His disdain for compromise played a role in this. When it came to negotiating with the administration, Savio, as Bettina Aptheker, a member of the Steering Committee, put it, had little "patience. He tended to see 'which side are you on?'... You were either on the side of the angels or you weren't." Aptheker thought that usually this characteristic "was a strength" since it gave Savio "a moral clarity" that "didn't let him in any way... get muddled or confused about what FSM was about. He stayed consistent. [But] it is a weakness when you are trying to negotiate."[15] Here it led to a misreading of Goldberg's diplomatic negotiating style and eagerness to avoid confrontation as signs of weakness and disloyalty.

There seems a generational aspect to Goldberg's removal from the movement's leadership. She was an established student leader, and to Savio and other civil rights activists new to campus politics, she and others who had experience working with the administration seemed too intimate with these repressive officials; they were an obstacle to more militant leadership. Goldberg, the spokesperson for the movement in its early, United Front stage, was pushed aside by Savio and other militants.[16] There is no evidence that this was done out of personal ambition or sexism, but it reflected—at least from Goldberg's perspective—a "more militant than thou" position:

I think part of what Mario did was because I was in a social sorority and the mind-set of people was that you couldn't possibly be okay if you were in a sorority.... You're suspect from the beginning.... The mind-set was [that] this is a militant organization and anybody who was not going to be militant at all times is not going to be in the leadership.[17]

The most one could say for Savio in this dispute was that he was correct about Goldberg often being less confrontational than he. She would initially oppose the FSM's final sit-in but joined it after hearing Savio's famous speech at Sproul Hall. So she had much in common with the mainstream students the movement sought to attract—which only adds to the dubiousness of his judgment in driving her off the Steering Committee. Looking back on this incident, Aptheker in 1965 recalled,

> Mario played a very bad role in that.... Mario really let out at Jackie, and said that she cracked up during negotiations with Kerr, and I don't think this was true. Even if she was a little nervous—which anybody might be—she sure as hell wasn't going to fink out on anybody.... Because I've known Jackie a long time... And I thought this was a really bad scene.[18]

This raises the question of why, if Savio misread Goldberg, he was able to carry the other FSM leaders with him in this turn against her. It is hard to avoid reading this as evidence that Savio, though generally too egalitarian to use it in so heavy-handed a manner as he did here, could on occasion draw on his prestige as the FSM's most eloquent spokesperson to dominate decision making. In an ordinary political group such influence by a key leader would not seem surprising or undemocratic, just a natural part of leadership selection. But in the FSM, which prided itself on its hyperdemocratic ethos, such influence by one individual led to self-criticism. Was this indeed a democratic movement led collectively? Or did it have at its helm a charismatic leader wielding power over the rest of its leadership? Aptheker had this in mind when, the year after the Berkeley revolt, she observed that

> you have to be very honest about this whole business, which is that there were many undemocratic features about the FSM. And in a certain sense, and very really, Mario was a charismatic leader, who when he was right was able to rally a lot of people around him. And this movement was based on that. Now the reason that it wasn't worse than it was was because of the content of the movement, which was for basic democratic rights.[19]

In a more recent interview Aptheker retracted this criticisms and would no longer argue that the FSM had many undemocratic tendencies or centered so much on Savio. She cited several times when he lost important Steering Committee votes, and so saw that committee as a collective.[20] Nonetheless, there were moments when his influence and charisma made him first among equals, and the Goldberg case was one.

To this day there are competing versions of the way the Steering Committee functioned. Such moderates as Jo Freeman, dissatisfied with the committee's strategic sense and mistrustful of its militancy, saw it as not a collective at all. She thought that by late October "all decisions were made by Mario and Jack [Weinberg]."[21] But she was never on the Steering Committee and had no first-hand experience of how it functioned. None of its members saw it as a rubber stamp for Savio and Weinberg. Syd Stapleton, Michael Rossman, Bettina Aptheker, and Weinberg emphasize that in their time on it the Steering Committee was collective and usually consensus-oriented. Yet it is also true that Savio and Weinberg were, as Weinberg himself concedes, often—though not always—its most influential members. According to Weinberg, Savio "was the dominant one on the big picture stuff...And there was not even a close second."[22]

Yet Weinberg insists that the collective style of the movement's leadership shaped how he and Savio functioned within the FSM. From the time that its organizational structure was established (and leaders elected) through the end of the revolt, politically "Mario stopped being an individual and I stopped being an individual and we created a Steering Committee that functioned as a leadership team. So no longer did Mario ever speak as Mario Savio; he was Mario Savio [spokesperson for] the Steering Committee."[23]

Savio still came up with his own speeches. The words he used in them and the style of discourse were his own, and when he knew in advance that he would be addressing a rally he prepared carefully for it. He did not write out a full text and seemed to work out the phrasing spontaneously, but he came in with notes for the speeches, handwritten "on small index cards (usually) in black in a carefully legible writing, each point designated by a hyphen." The themes his speeches highlighted were determined collectively in the Steering Committee, which, to avoid repetition between speakers at the rallies, assigned topics to each. Savio's leadership style centered on transparency and mass civil liberties education, which meant, in Aptheker's words, that the leaflets he coauthored and speeches he gave told "everyone everything," offering "details of the [negotiating] meetings, repeating over and over again the essential points about advocacy."[24]

Being a member of a collective leadership team meant that, despite all his celebrity and influence within that team, Savio was not treated by fellow movement leaders as a presidential figure whose time was uniquely valuable. Instead he was immersed with the rest of the Steering Committee in marathon meetings searching for consensus. "The older radicals came to the Steering Committee, but they couldn't stand it," Weinberg noted, "because Steering Committee would meet all day and all night until it reached consensus. So if somebody wanted to bring something up all over again you'd start all over again." This broke with conventional decision making on the left and in the American mainstream, where "you want to come to the meeting, have your point, have your vote, get it over with." By contrast, in the FSM, as Weinberg put it, "we would talk forever."[25] At times it featured almost twenty-four-hour-a-day talk-athons, leaving the movement's leaders with little time for sleep—hyperdemocracy as only the young could practice it. As Savio recalled, when the longest meetings were finally over the exhausted leaders would simply go to sleep at "whoever's house it was."[26]

Making it all the more demanding, in terms of time and energy, was that once the Steering Committee finally reached a consensus on policy it then needed to be brought to the Executive Committee, where a consensus was again worked out. Savio admitted that this was "not a style of politics" that could be used "without modification" on a long-term basis because of the time it took. But for a mass movement weathering one crisis after another over the course of a few months it proved a viable democratic process, and Savio afterward reflected that he was "glad that we did it that way."[27]

Even in the short term this consensus process did have its problems. Not only was it exhausting, but those lacking the time or dedication to sit through these sessions might not stay long enough to have a voice when decisions were finalized. A related problem, according to Mona Hutchins, the one Steering Committee member representing a conservative student organization (the University Society of Individualists), was that so many FSM leaders were radicals—since they were the most inclined to take time off from their studies for politics—and they tended to lean toward more militant tactics than would mainstream students. Hutchins thought the Steering Committee had

> a feeling of unreality about it...Sitting in a little room...for twelve hours at a time...Off in the clouds somewhere...without paying any attention to...what kind of support they could get...I never got a feeling of belonging. I could talk if I wanted to, and they would listen, but they wouldn't hear what I had to say. So I didn't talk.[28]

Although it had flaws, the FSM decision-making process often yielded a high degree of unity. The Steering and Executive Committees' protracted deliberations gave the FSM, as Weinberg put it,

> a nonmechanical way of maintaining discipline. If you have your vote, then the minority has to go along with the majority.... [This can create] real tensions. But if you have to talk it out till you have a consensus...then you can all go out and take responsibility. So each functions as a voice of the collective...Then you came out of it with a core of one

hundred activists who were united on a position.... We were much more
sophisticated on that than any of the organizations around us taught us.
I don't know how we figured that out by ourselves. I can't see any tradition that...taught us that, but we did it.[29]

This search for consensus between these two leadership committees meant
that the FSM had a "two-way" decision-making process that "wasn't just
[monopolized by] a small group," even if moderates and conservatives at times
regretted its militant tendencies.[30]

It was both fortunate and important to Savio that the Steering Committee
was so much of a team, so collective on many levels—intellectual, emotional,
political, and personal. Since he did not have to decide things alone, the pressures of leadership were mitigated in important ways. Decisions were mulled
over by a core of bright people who—because the cause was so inspiring and
the meetings so long—grew increasingly close. For Savio the Steering Committee served as a kind of support group, enabling him to function at a high level
during the FSM, unhindered by the bouts with depression that haunted him
through much of his life. It was on the Steering Committee that he grew close to
and fell in love with fellow committee member Suzanne Goldberg, an intellectually intense philosophy graduate student who would become his first wife.[31]

Politically, on the Steering Committee Savio's relationships with Weinberg
and Aptheker were the most important. Weinberg was, as Savio explained, the
movement's key tactician; he had "a consummate talent for determining what
the tactical possibilities in a given situation are—or enumerating them, analyzing them."[32] He conceded that at times Weinberg's passion for dissecting all the
tactical contingencies—the moves and countermoves by and against the administration—could go too far: "Sometimes he overdoes it" and "can see things
behind things to the point where the analysis is even more complex than the
reality. And that doesn't help." But to have someone with Weinberg's analytical
abilities helping to plan movement strategy was, in Savio's eyes, "essential."[33]

Weinberg, a math graduate student before dropping out of UC to work full-
time in the Bay Area civil rights movement, had been exposed to a type of game
theory in which the goal was to set up a situation so that

whatever move your opponent makes, you have another move; that will
then preserve the situation. That was the game I was playing [in the
FSM], trying to think through getting to where we wanted to get in a
situation where we never ended up in a cul-de-sac, where they make a
move and you can't respond to it, because the game ends because you
have no further moves.[34]

In Steering Committee meetings Weinberg would lay out potential situations: what the FSM might do, and how the administration might respond. Weinberg realized that "at times I drove people crazy," but his tactical judgment "would get tested" and often proved correct.[35]

Aptheker had political intelligence of a different kind, but one that Savio found as valuable as Weinberg's. She had a "very spirited, very pragmatic approach to politics. And very effective and balanced."[36] Aptheker was more inclined than either Savio or Weinberg to pull back from the most militant course of action when moderation seemed to hold the greatest promise of yielding political gains. This is what Savio meant when he contrasted her level-headedness with "Jack and I [who] tend to be a little bit unbalanced."[37] At first glance it may seem odd that Savio valued this trait in Aptheker when he had rejected Jackie Goldberg for her moderation. But Aptheker had such strong connections to the Left—coming as she did from a prominent Communist family—that Savio never questioned that her tactical advice was aimed at building the Berkeley revolt.[38]

Ironically, Aptheker's Communist background had an effect on Savio and the movement opposite to what the Red-baiting press imagined. Instead of pushing the FSM toward ultrarevolutionary positions, she rooted them in the larger, less militant world beyond the Berkeley student Left. She and most other effective Bay Area Communists emphasized the need to build coalitions between radicals and nonradicals. As Weinberg reflected:

> She was the connection for Mario both to broad forces on the campus and to people who were supportive of our interests....And the Communist Party was not particularly sectarian in those days, it was pretty defensive, it sort of merged with left-liberalism in an almost seamless way. And so she was a connection to [the] San Francisco liberal [community]...She...could articulate to Mario in a way I couldn't how this was being perceived outside by different forces....She was much more aware and capable than I was of the need to keep the thing broad and open.[39]

The mere presence of Aptheker, with her prominent Communist lineage, in the FSM's leadership encouraged its foes, including Kerr, to imply that the insurgency was not a genuine student movement with serious grievances but a conspiracy hatched by subversives. Within days of the police car blockade Kerr told a press conference that "the hard core of demonstrators contained...as much as 40 percent off campus elements. And within that off campus group, there were persons identified as being sympathetic with the Communist Party and Communist causes."[40] These were explosive charges in cold war America, made even more so by the press, which misquoted Kerr and so had him charging that "forty-nine percent of the [FSM's] hard core group are followers of the Castro-Mao line."[41] A leading San Francisco newspaper ran a three-part series claiming that the FSM was a Marxist-dominated revolt whose goal was not free speech but "draw[ing] young blood for the vampire which is international Communism."[42]

Such fears of subversion led to an FBI investigation of Savio and the FSM, a venture in guilt by association. Actually, his flight from Catholicism inoculated Savio against dogmatic thinking of any type; he never affiliated with any Marxist or Communist group. Savio's independence from the organized Left stood as a powerful refutation of Kerr's charges: the FSM's most prominent leader *was* a student and *not* an off-campus Maoist, Castroite, or ideologue in the orbit of the Communist Party.[43]

Berkeley did have Old Left student groups, and their members and sympathizers were active in the FSM Steering Committee, including Bettina Aptheker, of the Communist-led Du Bois Club; Syd Stapleton, of the Young Socialist Alliance (Trotskyist); and Jack Weinberg, who was close to the Independent Socialist Club. Through these and other connections the Steering Committee received advice from the most politically experienced activists on campus. But since these groups were all sympathetic to and well represented in the FSM, none dominated the Steering Committee or saw the need to do so. Old Left advice was as likely to be rejected as accepted by a student movement too rebellious to take orders from anyone. This was what Jack Weinberg meant in his much-quoted but little-understood remark: "Don't trust anyone over thirty." He was not spurning the entire older generation; rather, he was declaring that the student movement did its own thinking and was not a pawn of the aging Communists so feared by cold war America.[44]

Nor did the Left have a monopoly over the process by which the leadership got advice from outside its ranks. The Steering Committee was "the nerve center of a really dense network" of undergraduates, graduate students, and faculty offering advice and criticism. At the height of the FSM, the Steering Committee was flooded with communication from across the campus, so "taking in and processing inputs from other constituencies, reconciling...informational inputs," was a huge but very illuminating job. "It was amazing," Weinberg explained:

Suddenly—and we didn't plan it this way and I don't remember exactly how we coordinated it...—we were getting phone calls: "So-and-so works as a maid at professor so and so's house; there was a dinner party and they were talking about blah blah blah."...So suddenly we were...coming in to the Steering Committee with an absolute map of what everybody in Berkeley was saying...When a departmental meeting happened, we knew the outcome. When somebody had a conversation, we knew the outcome.[45]

With this overflowing information, endless discussions, organizing, rallies, and speeches, the FSM took over Savio's life from October through December 1964. His apartment became the FSM's headquarters. An avid reader throughout his life, he barely had a moment for books. Having been suspended by the administration, he could not have attended class even if he had had the time to do so. This does not mean, however, that his learning abated during the revolt; it occurred orally, since, as Weinberg explained,

> everybody wanted to talk to Mario...He was the guy everybody thought that "if I can talk to Mario I can change this."...Because he was a celebrity everybody wants to deal with a celebrity, because he was an intellectual everybody wants to deal with [him and his] influence, because he was changing the course of history and everybody wants to change it. So everybody wanted at Mario including the professors...He was willing to engage. That was partly his being a rationalist, partly his being young and therefore willing to take on in debate people with Ph.D.'s, leaders in their field and not even realize that [this was daring or unusual]. He was good at it.[46]

Despite his suspension Savio looked upon this semester of revolt as an amazing educational experience. He saw a connection between his major in philosophy and the issues raised in the FSM, leading one reporter to note that "no one can deny that Savio is getting experience in his chosen field, moral and ethical philosophy. 'I consider the Free Speech Movement and...[SNCC] are my workshop in applied philosophy,' he says." Savio made connections between the authors he had studied and the campus officials whose actions he was opposing. "Close to Savio's typewriter" was a copy of Camus's "*The Stranger* which he feels is the most relevant to the present conflict between the FSM and the University administration. 'We get inspiration from Kafka and Camus, what they wrote about an indifferent and incomprehensible bureaucracy is so much like what we are facing now.' "[47]

Although there was plenty of conflict with the administration over the course of the semester, and occasional disagreements within the FSM, generally the Steering Committee was a warm, comfortable place for Savio once its core members, a mostly like-minded group of radicals, settled in. It prepared him and the other leaders for their battles with the administration and their work convincing the Executive Committee and the FSM rank-and-file to support their strategic decisions. The Steering Committee's vocal members, as Weinberg put it,

> mainly played predictable roles…Mario would be the big picture guy and would articulate that—and not brook any deviation from that. He was…the visionary. I would be doing scenarios.…I would focus in on what happened and what's going to happen and how we're dealing with things.…Bettina was helping to soften and craft the message and put it more into a broader context. Mike Rossman was putting everything into [terms of] how it felt…and how you should feel and how you did feel.…The thing we fought about was what the [next] leaflet would say.…But it worked more as a team. And the long discussions were less over conflict and more over "I have another idea" or "What about this?" And sort of hashing it out…It meant…that when we got to the Executive Committee or…to the campus nothing took us by surprise. So there may have also been a way in which it was a bit of playacting. So when we got done and there was a decision we knew what it was. And so there was enough discussion so people felt confident that they could carry it.[48]

The contrast between this collective mode of leadership and what happened at the FSM's public events could not have been more stark. Even though multiple speakers addressed the crowds, Savio drew the most media attention because of his eloquence and the media's need for a movement spokesperson and symbol. There were advantages for the movement in this media stardom. Having a charismatic leader, famous almost overnight for his fiery oratory, attracted attention to the Berkeley revolt, leading Savio to hope that such publicity could spotlight the administration's abuse of student rights and win the movement valuable political leverage. His notoriety helped draw large crowds to the FSM rallies, though the organizing efforts of hundreds of volunteers, the leaflets, and the grievances themselves were far more important in facilitating these mobilizations.

In the long term the movement paid a price for this celebrity treatment. The FSM's democratic ethos was obscured in the press. Reporters made it seem as if Savio was "just sort of delivering edicts," although the movement "wasn't like that at all."[49]

Savio had mixed feelings about the media spotlight and eventually developed a negative view of it. To judge from his initially exuberant, idealistic quotes in the press, it seems that during the early stages of the revolt he enjoyed the attention. But this faded quickly, as he realized that he had to be careful in his interactions with the press. He came to see that "it's possible to become seduced by your own press image. It's like living in a house of mirrors. All you see is your own image." This put pressures on him that others in the leadership did not have to endure:

> If I'm going to be the person whom the press is going to ask, then I am representing the movement in a very special kind of sense.... What I say becomes very important, and how I say it becomes very important.... People are counting on me to say it well. So that inevitably pushes you into, in a sense, manipulating your own image. And that's not healthy.[50]

Before the FSM semester ended Savio had become openly critical of journalists. He felt so strongly that he told *New York Times* reporter A. H. Raskin he would not give him an interview unless it was held jointly with others in the leadership, warning that if the *Times* "intended to focus on him as *the* communicator for the FSM," it would "just perpetuate a misrepresentation that the press has already done too much to build up... This is not a cult of one personality...; it is a broadly based movement and I will not say anything unless it is made clear that the FSM is not any single individual." While he managed to get Raskin to do a joint interview, Savio's larger point was lost because the *New York Times Magazine* headlined Raskin's story "The Berkeley Affair: Mr. Kerr vs. Mr. Savio and Co."[51]

The problem, as Savio saw it, was that a democratic movement fired by idealism had to deal with a news media that had a top-down approach to political reporting, a bias against radicalism, a latent anti-intellectualism, and a penchant for sensationalism. Decades later, he bitterly recalled an encounter with a *San Francisco Examiner* reporter. He had just finished answering this reporter's questions, but, hearing none about the ideals motivating the protesters, told him "something that I'd like you to cover... the central civil liberties issue of the Free Speech Movement... namely that there should be no University regulation of the content of speech, and only that regulation of the time, place, and manner [of speech] necessary to the normal functioning of the University." But the bored reporter exited, telling Savio, "Ideas don't sell newspapers." Savio never forgot those words, which hit him "like a bullet."[52]

Such encounters led Savio to conclude that it "was impossible" to get "good press" from media that "said terrible things about us." The most they could hope for was "big press," because glaring headlines about the student revolt might embarrass and thereby put pressure on the UC administration. His mind-set was, "Okay, call us any names you want. But do it loud; do a lot of it. If it's the best we're going to get from you, okay, we'll take it." Though it was unpleasant being Red-baited and beatnik-baited, he came to accept this as inevitable given the media's bias. "I remember the words of the civil rights anthem...: 'We've been [re]buked and we've been scorned.' But so what? We were right. We can take a little 'buking and a little scorning" to win free speech.[53]

This top-down reportage ignored the way that hundreds of volunteers would appear—setting up various centrals working night and day—to take on the movement's nuts-and-bolts tasks, such as the printing and distributing thousands of leaflets and making large numbers of phone calls for political rallies. Although such grassroots activism made it possible to organize the huge campus, this went largely unreported by a news media more interested in confrontations and celebrity.[54]

This impacted Savio politically and psychologically. He found his sudden fame difficult to reconcile with his goal of building an egalitarian movement and trying to "be a different style of leader" in the Bob Moses hyperdemocratic mold. Savio, whose concept of leadership involved empowering people and not making them "feel dwarfed by it," had to contend with news coverage elevating him above his fellow students.

> Movements sometimes need powers of oratory. It's a resource. I had that particular ability. That fact in itself separates you from most people. And the press made it worse because the press tended to really glom onto me...I felt a certain shame....Let's say I'd make a speech. Others would, too. The speech I made would be most covered....So that would get featured in the press. It would be like I was some "maximum leader."...Then I would feel real shame in facing people in the movement.[55]

Despite Savio's growing closeness to his fellow Steering Committee members, he did not confide in them his distaste for his celebrity status, deeming it too self-indulgent. In this respect the FSM, coming so early in the history of the New Left, was not very advanced in recognizing the relationship between the personal and the political. Savio later reflected that if the FSM had come after the rebirth of the women's movement, "maybe there would have been the possibility of talking about those feelings." Movement events also unfolded so quickly, imposing so many demands upon him, that although "there was plenty of time to feel things" during the FSM, there was "not very much time to reflect about those feelings."[56]

While the media exacerbated Savio's difficulties, it did not create the inner turmoil he experienced over his leadership role. His own egalitarianism (and the New Left's) was at the root of this tension. On one hand, there was a hyperdemocratic movement whose ethos implied that the mass insurgencies should not rely on leaders. On the other hand, some people within the movement had talents that were of greater political value than others'. Trying to be highly egalitarian conflicted with the reality of this hierarchy of political skill levels within the movement. This left Savio "always apologetic about" his fame and was one reason why he, much like SNCC's Moses, would drop out of political leadership long before the 1960s ended.[57]

None of Savio's ambivalence about the spotlight was visible to the campus community during the FSM. From all outward appearances Savio seemed comfortable at center stage as the FSM emerged from its founding meetings following the police car blockade. The first crisis after the blockade concerned his right to speak on campus. In his final speech from atop the police car, he had announced that there would be a mass meeting to discuss the Pact of October 2 and the free speech crisis. Technically, however, UC regulations barred him from addressing this meeting, since he had been suspended, which meant that, like all nonstudents, he could only speak on campus if he got the administration's permission and waited seventy-two hours. An angry Chancellor Strong (with Kerr's concurrence) threatened to have Savio arrested if he spoke on campus. Neither Savio nor the FSM would back down on his right to speak. Concerned faculty intervened and convinced the administration to relent, at least for this first postblockade rally at Sproul Plaza on October 5.[58]

Savio prefaced his remarks on October 5 by discussing this controversy. "There was some question up until 20 minutes ago as to whether I should be permitted to speak here at all." He thanked the faculty who had gone "to bat for us" in obtaining permission for him to speak. He read Dean Towle's statement that the administration was "honoring the spirit of the President's agreement [the Pact of October 2] and therefore have granted a special waiver for this meeting today so that the leaders of the demonstration may discuss the written agreement of last Friday." Challenging Towle's statement about a one-time waiver, he insisted that the administration acknowledge his ongoing right to speak on campus.[59] He made this not as some personal appeal but as part of a larger argument about the Pact of October 2. He depicted that agreement as the product of negotiation between equal parties, whose implementation required that neither party take unto itself the role "of arbiter in specifying the interpretation of that agreement." By trying to ban him, he argued, the administration had inappropriately seized that role, punishing those it previously claimed to have negotiated with in good faith.[60]

Savio's speech suggested that the doubts he had held previously about the Pact of October 2 had been submerged following the discussions over the weekend during the FSM's founding. He told the crowd on Sproul Plaza that the pact represented "a substantial victory." Though the war for free speech had yet to be won, that agreement was evidence that the FSM had won "the biggest battle. It's the battle for jurisdictional recognition," and he compared the FSM's actions with those of a union signing a contract with an employer.[61] Anyone doubting the significance of this recognition, Savio commented, should remember that initially Strong had "said that absolutely under no circumstances would" he negotiate with the protesters. Yet on October 2 "they negotiated with us."[62]

In passionate but generally fair-minded terms Savio gave a blow-by-blow account of the negotiations leading to the pact, using neutral language to describe the administration's stance. While telling the crowd that "we obviously disagree very substantially" on free speech, he praised Kerr for displaying "a good deal of cool" and "a good deal of strength" during the negotiations. He thanked the faculty who had drafted the pact and submitted it to Kerr, crediting them with "a very wise act . . . to avoid violence."[63] Savio coupled these charitable comments with reminders that there was no moral equivalence between the two sides. The movement stood for freedom and nonviolence, while the administration suppressed free speech and interjected the threat of police violence. But the protesters had endured, and suspended their use of civil disobedience after winning "the right to further negotiations." Thus, Savio claimed, "we are now in the position of having acted with the utmost, and I would say of our side, the only one to have acted, with complete moral responsibility in that situation."[64]

As in his last speech atop the police car, Savio's advice to the crowd was the opposite of what one might expect from a sixties militant. Instead of calling upon students to again defy campus rules and the law, he urged restraint: "I really feel we should wait on any kind of provocative action and . . . negotiate completely in good faith."[65] Here he was speaking for the entire FSM leadership, which had decided to halt defiant tactics in order to promote free speech negotiations. Savio espoused such moderation even though only the day before—at the FSM's organizational meeting—he had voiced skepticism about the administration's willingness to lift the ban. "We have to be realistic" he said on October 4. "We won't get much from the negotiations. . . . The most we will get from them will be what publicity we give them. Everything must be completely public."[66] He did not speak in this skeptical way in the Sproul rally, however, since his militancy was held in check by deference to movement democracy.

Savio offered a startling critique of Kerr's vision of higher education, depicting it as subverting academic tradition and the FSM as defending it. Savio trumpeted the "conception of the university suggested by a classical Christian formulation," that the university "be in the world but not of the world," and he contrasted this idealistic vision—which allowed the university to maintain a healthy distance and critical perspective on society—with Kerr's crass knowledge factory. In Kerr's multiversity, academics would not critique the status quo but promote it by training its functionaries: "The conception of Clark Kerr...is that the university is part and parcel of this particular stage in the history of American society; it stands to serve the needs of industry; it is a factory that turns out a certain product needed by industry or government."[67]

There was a considerable continuity between Savio's speech at this first rally of the newly named Free Speech Movement and his prior criticism of the administration's hostility to free speech. He now added the idea of "consequential speech" to link this political repression more explicitly to Kerr's vision of the university as servant to corporate America. "Because speech does often have consequences which might alter this [Kerr's] perversion of higher education, the university must put itself in a position of censorship." The university, to preserve its tolerant and liberal self-image, allowed two types of speech: that which was inoffensive because it "encourages continuation of the status quo" and that which advocated change "so radical as [to] be irrelevant in the foreseeable future" (e.g., a Trotskyist advocating world revolution). What Kerr's university could not tolerate was "consequential speech," provoking immediate social change. "If someone advocates a sit-in to bring about changes in discriminatory hiring practices, this cannot be permitted because it goes against the status quo of which the university is part. And that is how the fight began here."[68]

This October 5 speech displayed a critical, historical understanding of Red-baiting. Kerr had implied publicly that the FSM's leadership was directed by Communists and sympathizers with Castro and Mao. Savio knew the Communist question would be controversial, and he told the crowd that though some people had urged him to avoid it, it had to be addressed in the interests of transparency: "We've insisted thus far on keeping all kinds of problems we've been having before all the students involved. I think we have to continue doing that."[69] He linked the Red-baiting of the FSM to other reform movements similarly tarred from the 1930s through the early 1960s.

It's kind of like this—30 years ago, just about, in that period of time, there were lots of people who in my opinion, and I'm sure there'll be people in the audience who disagree on this and I don't think that it affects the substance, but it's a good preface, a lot of people involved in trying to effect progressive change in the social and economic structure of the country. Now at that time and since then at various times, a great bogey man was raised. And this is the one of subversive infiltration and control of these activities.[70]

History was repeating itself in the sixties, as "we are now involved in another great movement...for political and social liberality and fairness...led at the present time by the negro people in their desire for freedom.... And again this same phantom is being raised."[71]

Adding a note of personal witness, Savio explained that when he was registering blacks to vote during Freedom Summer, "almost every day the Jackson papers had some article showing how the activities in which we were engaged...were designed, were being carried out in accordance with a long-standing [Communist] plan, according to one report, originally drafted in 1928...to infiltrate and subvert the United States." The same kind of Red-baiting was being used to attack the FSM. Students should be "on the look out for this kind of thing," since such slandering occurred because "no one wants to admit that...people are damn sick and fed up with the way things are."[72]

Although Savio voiced indignation that Kerr had stooped to Red-baiting the students of his own university, he proved judicious in examining Kerr's remarks. Had he been demagogic, he would have used against Kerr the most outrageous Red-baiting remarks the press attributed to him (that "forty-nine percent of the FSM's hard core group are followers of the Castro-Mao line"). Instead, he checked with Kerr's office and reported to the crowd that the UC president denied making the 49 percent charge but admitted to telling the press that "the hard core of demonstrators" contained at some points "as much as 40 percent off campus elements" among whom were sympathizers "with the Communist Party and Communist causes," and that some of the revolt's leaders "were impressed with the tactics of Fidel Castro and Mao Tse Tung." Since Kerr had cast the FSM as Communist-tinged, this legitimated Savio's attack on Red-baiting. But by publicly granting that only "the less provocative" of Kerr's quotes was accurate, Savio demonstrated a respect for the truth that is uncommon in political oratory. He told the crowd that the media might have concocted the worst of these Red-baiting quotes.[73]

In the weeks following this speech, FSM mobilizations and public speeches all but stopped, and negotiations began. Savio's role remained important but was not as central as it had been when the FSM was holding rallies. In this negotiating phase what was most striking about Savio was his impatience with the administration and the forceful way that he stood up for student rights. No other FSM leader proved quite so unwilling to defer to administrators, to challenge the legitimacy of their power, to demand that students be treated as equals, and to do so with an assertiveness that offended campus officials.

Administrators were taken aback by Savio's anger and lack of deference. A shocked secretary to Dean Towle wrote, for example, of an incident on October 6 where he came into the office demanding to meet with the dean. Informed that Towle was in a meeting, Savio "shouted" at the secretary, "demanding" that she go into Towle's meeting and get the dean. She told him that "I had no authority to go into that meeting." He "then shouted at me, demanding that I go, that if the building were on fire or something equally urgent was happening, I would rush in. He said 'I am on fire' and tried to order me in to go and get Dean Towle."[74] This encounter ended with Savio meeting the dean.

Actually, Savio was not a rude person or incapable of treating administrators respectfully. But the negotiating sessions he attended convinced him that there were compelling tactical and moral reasons to adopt a tough posture. His brashness intensified in the wake of the October 2 negotiations, as he believed that the administration had usurped powers that rightfully belonged to faculty and students. Although he restrained himself from angry outbursts in most negotiating sessions, as the FSM crisis dragged on he came to feel that the best way to battle a dictatorial administration was to undermine its authority, question its legitimacy, and assert student parity with the deans and chancellors as forcefully as possible. Savio learned that a degree of rudeness was sometimes necessary since the administration counted on deference and civility from student and faculty groups to maintain the hierarchical relationships that rendered the university so undemocratic.[75]

Savio's defiance was never more visible than during a tense meeting between the chancellors, deans, faculty, and the FSM Steering Committee on October 12. Here "Savio spoke in a critical manner of the way...the administration works, bringing up the Katz case," involving the UC administration's threat to dismiss a professor of German, Eli Katz, for refusing to discuss his allegedly Communist past. Savio declared that "Katz has been on a fishline for a year" but that the FSM would not respond the way the faculty's Academic Senate or the student government's ASUC Senate had. "We don't respond as children toward their parents; we respond as equals; this is a new situation and it should be dealt with in a new way." He insisted that the FSM's leaders "wanted to meet with the administration 'as equals' to see what the October 2 pact means."[76]

In this radical assertion of student power Savio cast the administration as abusing its authority. But to simply characterize his words as radical does not really explain why he was the only protest leader in this meeting to express such tough criticism. Berkeley historian Kenneth Stampp recalled the contrasting ways Savio and Aptheker acted in a joint meeting of the FSM Steering Committee and the Academic Freedom Committee of Berkeley's Academic Senate. Aptheker was calm and cordial, while Savio came off as impatient, tempestuous, and militant. "Savio was always sitting on the edge of his chair...ready to jump up and leave if things didn't go his way," though "he never did go actually." Aptheker, a student in Stampp's class, "got along best with" the committee and later came up to Stampp and "sort of apologized for Mario's behavior." Stampp attributed this difference to their political backgrounds, explaining that Aptheker, coming out of a Communist family, "knew something about political discipline," unlike Savio, a relative newcomer to activism, who "was a rather undisciplined free spirit."[77]

Stampp did have a point. For someone with Aptheker's Old Left background, who had grown up amidst waves of repression in the McCarthy era, just to be out of the political wilderness and negotiating with faculty and administration seemed quite an accomplishment, a form of recognition that was almost a victory in itself, while for Savio, new to the battle against political repression, such negotiations seemed far too protracted. Why should it take weeks and months to secure the self-evident right to freedom of speech? So being from the Old Left, with a long view of such struggles, helped to make Aptheker more patient in negotiations. Looking back on these negotiations, Aptheker agreed with this assessment, and noted that she and Savio "did balance...each other because I probably went too far accommodating. So I needed someone like Mario who wouldn't compromise and he needed someone who would."[78]

This contrast involved more than politics; other factors included personality, temperament, and the imprint of early educational experience. Looking back on his youth, Savio would have seemed anything but the "free spirit" Stampp described. He had been the altar boy, the stammering honor student uptight about his grades, the good boy who respected his elders and deferred to authority figures. The FSM was a respite from all of this pressure. Having been suspended from the student body for standing up for a noble cause, he could in good conscience dispense with the contest for grades, find his voice, question authority. Having waited all his academic life to confront authority and speak freely, when such opportunities finally appeared he proved eager to use them, and did so with a special vehemence.[79]

Although his negotiating style was especially hard-line and impatient, his critical outlook on the administration accorded with most of the FSM's leadership as the movement set aside its picket signs for the negotiating table in the weeks following the police car blockade. The Steering Committee quickly became convinced that Strong was not implementing the Pact of October 2 in good faith. The key points of contention concerned the committees that the chancellor empowered to implement the pact. Strong referred the disciplinary cases of the eight suspended FSM leaders to a faculty committee that he appointed rather than the Academic Senate Committee on Student Conduct, an independent faculty committee, which the pact had designated. Similarly, the FSM wanted the Academic Senate and the FSM, not just the chancellor, to have the power to appoint representatives to the Study Committee on Political Activity, the body charged with reviewing campus political regulation.[80]

At issue here was who ought to run the university. Strong naturally thought he should. But Savio argued that the days of top-down campus governance were over. The FSM had altered the political landscape, empowering students and faculty to govern their campus. The administration had, the FSM leadership contended, repeatedly abused its power, so it could not be trusted to implement fairly the Pact of October 2, accord due process to the suspended students, or explore alternatives to the restrictions it had placed on expression on campus. Thus the committee charged with these tasks needed to be freed from Strong's unilateral control. This represented a device for empowering the FSM and appealing to the faculty, reflecting the recognition by Savio and the movement that the free speech struggle would be won by the side enjoying the most faculty support.[81]

The entire FSM leadership and much of the rank-and-file stood firm in these initial negotiating demands, even as Strong resisted. At the first meeting of the Study Committee on Political Activity, on October 7, the Steering Committee demanded that it disband because it was "illegally constituted," and then walked out of the meeting.[82] The following week, at a Study Committee hearing, dozens of students made this same demand. The suspended students proved equally defiant of the administration-appointed disciplinary committee, declaring that they would only appear before an Academic Senate committee, as promised in the Pact of October 2. The FSM issued a deadline for resolving these disputes, threatening to unleash a new round of mass protest.[83]

Had it been left to Strong, the negotiating process might never have gotten off the ground, but here again Kerr intervened. He allowed the Academic Senate and the FSM to add two members to the Study Committee on Political Activity and created a new ad hoc Academic Senate committee to hear the cases of the eight suspended FSM leaders.[84] The FSM accepted Kerr's compromise, and the negotiation process began in earnest. At a rally on October 16 on Sproul Plaza, FSM speakers explained the dispute with the administration and the framework for negotiations.

Savio's speech on this occasion was far too complex to become a symbol of sixties youth defiance. The only account of it comes from the campus police, who recorded and transcribed it for the administration. As in his October 2 and 5 speeches, Savio was in at least one sense moderate, calling on students to avoid breaking the campus rules restricting free speech. "We're going to hold to the regulations exactly as set down," he announced.[85] Voicing relief that Kerr had made procedural concessions two hours before the FSM's deadline, he was proud that the FSM had stood tough on its demands, which had led to a fairer negotiating structure. The FSM had been effectively "practicing brinksman-ship," Savio argued, and he "was "glad...that we are still standing on the edge and have not gone over." He quipped that this Sproul rally would have been advertised as "One Hour Informational Meeting, Please Bring Sleeping Bags" (for a long sit-in), but "fortunately...we have not had to do it that way," since there could now be a moratorium on mass protest.[86]

Yet along with this moderation and openness to negotiations, he articulated a radical revision of the authority structure within the university. Elaborating upon his earlier argument that the FSM had enhanced the status of students in the university community, he claimed that this required partnership in deci-sion making regarding university policy as well as dispensing with the tradi-tional university role of *in loco parentis*.[87] The FSM, he insisted, was creating a new political reality in which university students had to be seen as citizens with rights rather than as children in need of guidance. Even though the con-flicts with the administration over the implementation of the Pact of October 2 might seem mere quibbles over process, they were actually a new recognition of student rights within university governance, which Savio characterized as an "extraordinary" step toward a more democratic university.[88]

While reaching out to the faculty, Savio also criticized their timidity. He told of debating professors who accused him of being unreasonable and urged capitulation, since the administration would never agree to more FSM repre-sentation on the committee reviewing Berkeley's political regulations. "Well, they judged wrong," Savio said, as had "a lot of people who have been giving us advice during the last three weeks." He reminded the faculty that the FSM had liberated them from an administration-dominated committee, for which he "hoped they will...be appropriately grateful."[89]

Savio was less celebratory than he had been a week earlier in discussing the Pact of October 2. This time he characterized it as "very loosely...and ambigu-ously worded." If the protestors had not been faced with the threat of police violence, he commented, "it's well known by now we'd never have agreed to it." Kerr, who Savio called a "wily negotiator," had intended the pact not as a device for addressing the causes of the free speech dispute but rather as "(1) a way to end a demonstration; (2) a way to get the students off his back; 3) a way to pretend that after all nothing special had occurred in the first place."[90] But by insisting on student and faculty rights in the implementation process, the FSM "turned what was a partial defeat [the Pact of October 2] into a very substantial victory, and we have gained a lot of experience in the art of bargaining from a position of weakness—and winning."[91]

His discussion of the committee rules that the FSM helped to establish for the implementation of the Pact of October 2 was thorough, covering issues of jurisdiction, due process, voting rights on the committee, and the need for frequent meetings (so that negotiations were not delayed).[92] The sophistication on these points was striking, reflecting the FSM leadership's negotiating savvy. Here the influence of the Bay Area civil rights movement made a difference. Prominent FSMers had learned the art of negotiation through CORE's fair-hiring movement. As Weinberg put it, "We came to the Free Speech Movement with a lot of confidence in our negotiating ability.... The ability to be intransigent and reasonable required self-confidence to negotiate in a public way without being put at a disadvantage."[93] This is what Savio alluded to when he described the FSM's team of

> disciplined negotiators—that means they will have a chairman; they will decide who talks when; they will have their policies set up; they will have the right to caucus; they will have student observers appointed by our executive committee who will caucus with us; we will have counsel present; and recordings will be taken in a way agreeable to the entire body.[94]

All of this talk of negotiating did not lead Savio to cast aside the protest tradition that the FSM had ignited. At the October 16 rally he warned students about becoming complacent. If student rights were abused or if the negotiating process broke down, "once again we will be out on the pavement with our sleeping bags. And if they are foolish enough to send a police car out," the events of October 1–2 would be repeated.[95] Savio coupled nonviolent threats against repressive administrators with lofty idealism about the freedom being sought, the more democratic university for which the FSM was struggling, and the dedicated activists who labored to win these important goals. Evoking a new birth of freedom, Savio grew lyrical near the end of his speech: "We have bent lovingly over the baby being born.... And by our courage... by dignity in the face of unprovoked violence, by the... principle[d protests] of the students on this campus... we've shown ourselves guilty of one thing—of passionately entering into a conspiracy to uphold the first and fourteenth amendments."[96]

For the next two weeks the FSM's Steering Committee converted itself into a negotiating team, participating in all seven sessions of the reconstituted Campus Committee on Political Activity (CCPA). Here the collective nature of the movement's leadership was most evident, as Bettina Aptheker and Syd Stapleton were very vocal, though Savio spoke the most for the FSM, particularly at the first and last sessions.[97]

Although the media largely neglected the CCPA hearings, those sessions constituted a startling chapter in the FSM's history. In the midst of the Berkeley revolt for two weeks both sides came together to talk about their differences over free speech, campus political regulations, and the laws govern-ing both.[98] Weinberg later contrasted this with the way New Left protesters in the late 1960s

> developed this non-negotiable demands [position,] "We never negotiate, we don't negotiate, we don't compromise," and all that kind of stuff. We didn't believe in compromising either. But we did believe in negotiat-ing... So what the movements of the [late] sixties end up not replicating [from the FSM] and being less successful in many cases because of [this], was our public posture, and in fact our practice, [which] was: "We're will-ing to talk to anybody"; "We're always ready to negotiate"; We're always looking for a solution"; "We want to convince anyone of the rightness of our position"; "We're willing to hear all points of view." And we were able to do that while being intransigent [on free speech] because that had been... the lesson... of... CORE.[99]

Savio's skills in logic and debate were displayed prominently in these hearings, and at crucial moments so was his impatience with protracted negotiations.[100]

These negotiations proved difficult because neither the administration nor the FSM was inclined to compromise. The FSM's only hope of winning free speech via the CCPA was to bring the faculty representatives over to its side. At best this was a slim hope, since these professors were not civil libertarians, and were reluctant to oppose Kerr. This became evident at the beginning of the CCPA process, when the faculty rejected the FSM's motion that for the dura-tion of the hearings the campus return to the pre–September 1964 status quo, with political advocacy permitted on the Bancroft strip.[101]

Given that most of the faculty on the CCPA were appointed by the adminis-tration (the FSM had won the Academic Senate the right to select two of the six faculty on this committee, while the other four were still appointed by Strong), it is remarkable that Savio's side made any impact at all on them. The professors gradually moved closer to the FSM position on free speech because during the course of the hearings some of the administration's anti-free-speech hairsplit-ting came across poorly. The administration entered the hearings insisting on upholding an implausible distinction between "advocacy" (promoting political causes, which was permissible) and "mounting" (using the campus as a staging area for off-campus political actions, which the administration insisted on ban-ning as a violation of the university's political neutrality). In one CCPA session Savio pushed Dean Towle into revealing the absurdity of the administration's position: she said that on-campus students could praise a particular picket line and say, "This is a worthy cause and I hope you go," but they would not be allowed to use the campus as a base from which to organize pickets, such as by informing students where and when to meet for the picket. The mounting/advocacy distinction died a quick death in the CCPA hearings.[102]

This was, however, far from a total victory for the FSM because the administrators took refuge in a new distinction that enabled them to carry the faculty to their position favoring order over liberty. This latest position permitted mounting political actions from campus, but *only if those actions were legal.* If students on campus advocated unlawful actions, the administration insisted it had the right to discipline them. The FSM rejected this position, for it would mean that students could be disciplined for urging participation in off-campus pickets that ended in arrests or in civil rights sit-ins. The students saw this as a form of double jeopardy (though technically it was not). If students violated the law, it was up to the civil authorities to deal with this in a court, where due process was guaranteed; students should not face the additional burden of fending off disciplinary action from officials of their state university, which lacked due process safeguards and the power to adjudicate legal disputes.[103]

As it became evident that administration and faculty on the CCPA were uniting on behalf of what for the FSM was an unacceptable prohibition on mounting illegal protests from campus, the negotiation process headed for a breakdown. The final CCPA sessions became contentious, ending in angry exchanges with administrators. The most revealing of these occurred on November 7, the last CCPA session, when vice chancellor Alan Searcy argued that the administration could be trusted to exercise the power to discipline students engaged in unlawful actions because campus officials "were men of good will who are concerned with the rights of students." Savio, as one of the students suspended without a hearing, disputed this claim: "Because of the kinds of external pressures to which the University is subject I doubt very gravely that the University would be capable of giving a fair hearing."[104]

Although the CCPA hearings never made the evening news, in one respect they were symbolic of the insurgent sixties. Here was a major role reversal, academic meetings in which students rather than faculty often directed the intellectual discussion. Savio, still an undergraduate, asked probing constitutional questions and even lectured a law professor (Sanford Kadish) on due process guarantees. FSM delegates challenged not only the faculty but even their own lawyers, whom they deemed naive in assuming that the university could conduct fair disciplinary hearings.[105]

Since the hearings ended with the faculty siding with the administration, it would be wrong to make too much of the students' effectiveness on the CCPA. Nonetheless, if names were omitted from the transcripts of the hearings, often it would be impossible to tell from the quality of argumentation that this was a debate between unequal sides, senior scholars versus a mostly undergraduate FSM contingent. For example, in questioning the administration about how it would ascertain whether an off-campus event was sufficiently unlawful to trigger disciplinary action against student activists, Savio asked what would happen

> where no one in fact is arrested but there was some action which has been judged by some persons to be unlawful. The second case is one for which committing the same acts...some of the participants are convicted but others are acquitted, in those two cases what would be the criterion by which unlawfulness would be decided?[106]

Dean Frank Kidner struggled none too successfully to handle this query and the equally challenging follow-up questions.

Although the CCPA hearings failed in their goal of ending the free speech crisis by revising UC's regulations in ways acceptable to both sides, the high quality of the CCPA debates and the cessation of mass protest for dialogue does say something significant about Savio and the FSM. Both were about more than confrontation; they were not power-tripping or looking for an excuse to take over another building. They had serious arguments to make on free speech and due process questions that addressed the core mission and moral and legal responsibilities of the university.

The CCPA process failed to resolve the free speech conflict because the FSM was the only party in the dispute that believed the university had no right to restrict the content of speech. This was a radical civil libertarian position that the CCPA's paternalistic faculty and administration could not accept. Making matters worse was the FSM's mistrust of an administration it thought autocratic and manipulative.

Barely held in check during the hearings, this mistrust exploded near the end of the CCPA's life when the FSM made public a "purloined" letter from Kerr. This letter, obtained by a student worker in his office, suggested that Kerr had not been negotiating in good faith—that he was recommending to the regents, even before the negotiations ended, campus rules barring advocacy of illegal off-campus political actions. Kerr denied having approved this letter, which was why the copy the FSM obtained had never been signed. But the fact that the FSM believed Kerr so deceptive and released this illicitly obtained letter shows how fragile the negotiating process was, and how easily that process could give way to a new round of protest and confrontation.[107]

Even before the last CCPA session, Savio and the other FSM leaders began predicting a return to confrontation. On November 6, he told a crowd of some four hundred on Sproul Plaza that unless the deadlock was broken in the CCPA meetings, mass demonstrations would return.[108]

At its November 7 meeting the CCPA again proved unable to resolve the "question of the authority of the University to discipline [students] for on-campus conduct that results in off-campus law violation."[109] On November 9 the FSM began demonstrating again, violating UC's ban on advocacy. Strong chastised the FSM for defying campus regulations, and on those grounds—with Kerr's blessing—he disbanded the CCPA. Savio called upon the administration to once again "enter into negotiations with us," but warned, "We will not pledge to end demonstrations until you can see the substance of our demands... that no institution except the courts has any competence to decide what constitutes abuse of political freedom."[110]

Savio's warnings proved well grounded. The FSM's return to mass protest carried the movement into its tumultuous final stage, which contrasted with the placid weeks of CCPA negotiations. This final period—in which Savio's oratory was featured prominently—would see the FSM riding a political roller coaster, alternating between prospects of dismal failure and smashing success.

7

"WE ALMOST LOST"

The FSM in Crisis

President Kerr viewed the deadlock and collapse of the CCPA negotiations with the FSM as good news. He thought it signaled a weakening of the influence that Savio's brand of militancy had on Berkeley student politics, and the beginning of the end for the FSM. In a November 10 meeting with Strong and university counsel Thomas Cunningham, Kerr asserted that the FSM "is breaking within its own ranks. The majority is still extremist but the moderates are gaining ground," and as proof cited the FSM Executive Committee's "28 to 17 vote the other night" endorsing the resumption of setting up tables on campus in defiance of the free speech ban.[1] Kerr's low opinion of Savio's political prospects was reinforced by reports from faculty with ties to moderate students, who disliked the direction that Savio and the Steering Committee were taking. One such professor, Seymour Martin Lipset, reported confidentially to the administration on November 11 that "Savio is giving thought to trying to seize the ASUC [student union] building. Savio is losing control, and is desperate to provoke his own arrest as a means of consolidating his followers."[2] On the basis of such dubious evidence Kerr became so convinced of Savio's and the FSM's decline that he decided against any concessions or further negotiations. Instead Kerr, in Strong's words, was "playing for time—and the isolation of the extremists."[3]

Given their political biases, it is not surprising that Kerr and Lipset took such a dim view of Savio's political prospects and those of his fellow FSM militants. Kerr had always thought Savio far too radical to attract support from mainstream students. Yet Savio was never in danger of being removed from the FSM's leadership, and Lipset's claim that he was seeking to provoke his own arrest was pure fantasy.

Kerr and Lipset were correct, however, in suggesting that the political road facing the FSM was not an easy one. With all formal power in the university on the side of the administration, and the faculty at the end of the CCPA negotiating process still refusing to back the movement's free speech demands, the FSM in early November needed to do something dramatic to sway the faculty. It was not at all clear whether such change was possible, especially when divisions within the movement and clever maneuvering by the UC administration (offering empty but confusing compromises) made it difficult to mobilize masses of students. "We almost lost," Savio recalled. "This is important...to understand...We worked our little hearts out...for a whole term...to mobilize students and to educate the faculty" about the complex civil liberties questions that were central to the FSM. "We had to work like crazy, disrupting the University, taking over buildings, having sit-ins, marches...just to have a real debate" about student rights. "We had argued it all beautifully: we presented all the facts, the arguments, the reasons, and the theories. We talked to everybody." Nonetheless, even toward the end of the semester, in late November, when "the FSM had almost run its course...things were still very touch and go."[4]

Victory seemed all the more unlikely as the FSM experienced major crises in mid- and late November. First it faced challenges in reigniting mass protest after weeks of negotiations. Moderate students resisted this transition back to insurgency, and one of their number, Jo Freeman, even tried to cut a separate deal with Kerr—planning to compromise the movement's free speech goals—without informing the FSM leadership.[5] Both the moderates' resistance to renewed FSM protest and Freeman's separate peace with Kerr failed. But new conflicts soon emerged as the FSM struggled in late November, without success, to launch an act of mass civil disobedience that could repeat the high level of mobilization it had achieved at the movement's birth. Instead the result was an aborted sit-in, the one failed protest in the movement's history.

What pulled the FSM out of this crisis was the administration's reversion to heavy-handed disciplinary actions, which angered students and enabled Savio and the FSM to reinvigorate Berkeley's mass protest movement in early December. He concluded that the administration "saved us" through its blunders, which were "luck, sheer luck. We knew how to take advantage of [these] luck[y]" mistakes.[6] It would take a combination of administration repression, FSM organization, Savio's oratory, and a reluctant faculty's intervention to put the FSM on the road to victory.

Neither Savio nor the rest of the FSM leadership did a great job of managing the shift from negotiation to confrontation in early November. For several weeks the Steering Committee had become so absorbed in the negotiations that it almost ceased to function as the leadership of a mass movement. The Steering Committee had discussed the CCPA deadlock at length with the FSM Executive Committee, but the Executive Committee had not taken a vote on the resumption of mass protest before Savio announced that such protest was imminent. The issues over which the CCPA talks stalled were complicated and had to be explained before a new round of protest could be launched successfully. As FSM organizer David Goines put it, these issues concerning advocacy, though "crystal clear to the Steering Committee negotiators," were "as clear as mud to...the FSM membership."[7]

Moderates began to express concern about Savio's political style as well. "A lot of us were pretty upset," explained FSMer Andy Wells, "about the way that Mario was conducting himself in the [final CCPA] meetings with the administration—yelling and screaming. You can be damned tough without having to do that sort of stuff."[8]

Some moderates, echoing the administration, even went so far as to charge that the Steering Committee had intentionally stalemated the negotiations because it was interested in generating mass protest rather than solving the free speech problem. Brian Turner, who had been Savio's roommate and a fellow activist in University Friends of SNCC, thought that Savio and the other Steering Committee militants were "short-circuiting the CCPA process" so as "to make the administration seem more odious than they were" in order "to manufacture a confrontation to restart the movement that was losing momentum."[9] Similarly, Jo Freeman of the Young Democrats claimed that she and other moderates believed that the "main interest" of radicals dominating the Steering committee was not free speech "but...action for the sake of action because of the mass mobilization it created regardless of results...They are continually and desperately looking for an excuse for a demonstration."[10]

The moderates' criticism, shaped as it was by their own biases, at times distorted political reality. For example, it was logical for Freeman, a Democrat oriented toward electoral politics and less comfortable with the politics of campus confrontation than Savio and other militant FSM leaders, to charge that they were interested in mass protest "for the sake of action." But actually these militants had spent almost a month holding off such action in order to facilitate negotiations. Indeed, some militants, such as Barbara Garson, the FSM newsletter editor, privately criticized Savio and the Steering Committee for having "bogged us down" in "a morass of negotiations...They are thrilled at the prospect of negotiating...in private with the administration." Worried that months of fruitless negotiations would bury the student movement because such talks were "complicated and boring," she characterized the front page of the FSM newsletter's second issue (which she edited) as "dull because the events of the week are intrinsically dull." Negotiations had become a poor substitute for "the good hard work it takes to really involve

the Rank and File at the current stage." So she eagerly awaited the turn from negotiating to mobilizing the "hundreds of students...willing to get arrested...and
thousands who have asked to help" with the struggle for free speech.[11]

Later Garson would use her literary skills in a more public way to mock the very
idea of negotiating with UC's shifty administration—and to poke fun at Savio for
having given any credence at all to such negotiations. Garson wrote a puppet show
pitting Mario Savio, "young and tousle-headed," against a Clark Kerr character,
called Dr. Kearl. The play begins with a speech by Savio that is interrupted by Kearl,
who offers to negotiate. The Savio puppet naively trusts in Kearl's good faith. But
then the wily Kearl outmaneuvers him in the negotiations. Kearl asks Savio what
he wants. Mario replies, "Freedom!" Kearl responds: "Uh-huh. And when do you
want it?" Savio answers, "Now." Kearl says to himself, "Roman numeral one: freedom. Roman numeral two: now." Then he tells Savio that though his demands
are "in conflict with the historic policy of the university," he will use his "personal
influence" to see that they "receive the careful consideration of the appropriate
authorities." After conferring with the authorities, Kearl proudly announces that
the university "is prepared to meet you people half way." He can't give them freedom since "the state constitution...forbids any freedom on this campus." But "as
to your second demand, which was, as I recall it, now, I am happy to say that I have
gotten the authorities to agree completely....So please disperse this mob...now.
According to our agreement, of course." Scandalized by this cynical response,
Savio threatens new protests, which Kearl undercuts though further negotiations.
Kearl reports back that "the highest authorities have agreed to establish a committee" to consider the students' demands. The ever-credulous Savio puppet expresses
delight—"A committee! We've won!"—only to learn later that, due to further
administration shell games, no meaningful negotiations occur.[12]

Whatever one makes of Garson's political stance, her criticism of the Steering Committee's delaying of mass mobilizations and her mockery of Savio's
naive faith in negotiations attest that Freeman and other moderates erred in
charging that the FSM leadership raced into confrontation. There was no such
race, but rather a deep division between the FSM leadership and the CCPA's
faculty and administration representatives over the right of the university to
limit on-campus political advocacy. Only after weeks of negotiations ended in
deadlock did the FSM resume political advocacy on campus in November.

The moderates' revolt raises important questions about the limits of hyperdemocratic politics among the FSM leadership. The consensus decision-making
process worked as long as all its participants shared the political goal of ending
campus restrictions on the content of speech. But what happens to this process
when the consensus over goals breaks down? Although the moderate revolt's
leaders did not publicly declare their willingness to compromise the FSM's

ambitious free speech goal, this willingness was implicit in their tactical position. After all, since the CCPA faculty and administration delegates opposed the FSM's position on unfettered free speech, then what was the point of continuing the already protracted negotiating process unless it was to turn those negotiations into a vehicle for compromising away the desired free speech rights? The moderates, as Weinberg put it, did not have "a different strategy for winning" free speech, but "felt we had to settle for less…and we were not willing to settle for less."[13] The question was how moderates were to be treated by the militant leaders of a movement whose raison d'être was to win that freedom.

The answer was that the militants were going to play political hardball. The moderates, led by Freeman, sought to hold an emergency meeting of the FSM Executive Committee on November 9, hoping to reverse the decision to resume the use of political advocacy tables on campus in defiance of UC regulations. Savio and most of the Steering Committee opposed convening such a meeting on the grounds that it would be seen as a sign of weakness if the FSM reversed its decision to defy those unjust regulations. Steering Committee aide David Goines undermined this meeting by taking phone lists out of the FSM office so that moderates could not use them.[14]

At first glance this seems a dramatic departure from the participatory democracy that the FSM claimed to embody. But Freeman, as she later conceded, was seeking to "pack" the Executive Committee with moderates and conservatives, some of whom had not been active in the FSM.[15] To FSM militants, Freeman appeared guilty of seeking to hijack the movement politically.[16] Weinberg recalled

a hostile move [made] by [moderate and conservative] organizations that were avowedly hostile to most of the [civil rights and leftist] organizations providing leadership in the FSM and were openly aligned with people on the faculty who were the main opponents of the Free Speech Movement. And they were doing an intervention aimed at disrupting it…She [Freeman] was never an important player in the FSM. She was an outsider who tried to destabilize it.[17]

Although the moderates' revolt failed, this dispute underscores how idealism rather than Machiavellianism guided the FSM's founding back in October. FSM leaders wanted the movement to be open and democratic, and so the FSM's structure was just that. Savio had taken pride in the movement's democratic ethos, its openness, the fact that one did not need a membership card or to pay dues to be considered an FSMer.

Through such looseness about membership, however, the FSM, as Weinberg noted, "opened itself up to this maneuver" by Freeman, enabling her to pack a key FSM meeting that might have changed the direction of a movement in which some of those voting with her had not even been participating. But by the FSM's own rules, Freeman was well within her rights to mount such a challenge.[18]

Had Savio, Weinberg, and the other FSM founders had more organizational experience, they might have taken steps that could have preempted this kind of attack. Weinberg admitted as much, suggesting that if he could have revisited the FSM's founding,

> I would have at the beginning of the Free Speech Movement secured agreement on a very brief statement of principles and that membership in the Executive Committee would have included both that you show up and you indicate that our organization subscribes to these principles....It means that if somebody comes in who is disruptive you have a legitimate line of defense. But we hadn't anticipated those problems.[19]

Consequently, the Steering Committee's response to the moderates' rebellion was abrupt, emotional, and in terms of democratic process little better than Freeman's own manipulative tactics. Weinberg defends the Steering Committee's behavior on the grounds of self-defense, protecting the movement from outsiders bent on disrupting it.[20]

The ambiguity in all this was the question of what constituted an "outsider." Freeman, after all, had been on the negotiating team that signed the Pact of October 2. So it seems unfair to cast her as an outsider bent on disrupting the FSM. Then again, she did enter into secret negotiations with President Kerr and was prepared to surrender the right of students on campus to advocate unlawful protests off campus.[21] Freeman's attempts to sign this separate peace with Kerr failed because he reneged on his promises to her. But the fact that she so dramatically broke ranks with the movement, violating the fundamental tenets of solidarity and loyalty to it, suggests that Weinberg's claims about the movement's need for, and right to, self-defense have merit.[22]

The moderates' revolt led the administration to underestimate Savio and the FSM leadership, thinking that delay and refusal to further negotiate would weaken a movement on the verge of imploding—when in fact the opposite was true.[23] The moderates lost in the November 9 Executive Committee vote and lost again as movement activists rallied to the FSM upon learning of Freeman's heretical attempt to cut a deal with Kerr. With the moderates routed, the movement united, and its leaders began the difficult work of reigniting mass student protest.[24]

The revolt is also important because the contrast between the moderates' conventional political thinking and the unconventional approach to campus politics taken by Savio and other FSM militants illuminates what was fresh, new, and daring about the movement. Freeman shared Savio's dislike of the restrictions the administration placed on political advocacy, but diverged from him in her willingness to compromise. Decades later, she admitted that Savio "was right" when he admonished her that "the difference between you and me is that you would settle for a drab victory, while I prefer a brilliant defeat."[25]

Schooled in conventional electoral politics, Freeman assumed that students lacked the power to overcome UC's powerful administration. Savio, on the other hand, thought it possible for the movement to prevail by using the powerful lever of civil disobedience. He was much more alert than Freeman (with her old-style faith in mainstream electoral politics) to the emerging realities of 1960s student politics: that campus sit-ins and other disruptive protests could serve as the great equalizer, giving students en masse the power to humble even the most recalcitrant administration. For Savio, defeat was well worth the risk, since an authentic democratic politics had to grow out of democratic principle rather than self-interested bargaining and unprincipled compromise.

Savio and Freeman also differed in their reading of campus political realities because of their relationship to cold war antiradicalism. She assumed that a movement headed by radicals, as the FSM was in its Steering Committee, could never win a major political victory in cold war America. In Freeman's words, at the start of the FSM "the steering committee consisted of two politically non-aligned, one Maoist (Art), one Trotskyist (Sid), one Stalinist, and one other Communist, and three independent socialists.... [So] our feeling was they weren't just leaving themselves open for red baiting—they were going out and asking for it." For her it seemed politically untenable that "the FSM Executive Committee was further left than the student body; the Steering Committee was further left than the Executive Committee; and the four who controlled [the] Steering Committee [in her view, Savio, Weinberg, Stapleton, and Aptheker] were further left than that."[26] Savio, however, thought that activists should be elected to the Steering Committee "for their own abilities not because of the organization they represented."[27] So he had no problem with the fact that radicals, often the most dedicated and able campus activists, won the lion's share of the elected positions on the Steering Committee. Where Freeman was "infuriated" that youth groups like hers, connected to the major political parties off campus, were relegated to a secondary role in the FSM, Savio saw no reason to elevate leaders based on such connections.[28]

The split between Savio and Freeman was emblematic of the rift between the New Left and the Democratic Party, which tore American liberalism apart in the late sixties. Having seen how the Democrats upheld segregation in the South and compromised with it during the Atlantic City convention, Savio had little patience for its campus representatives. When Freeman tried to get him to support the election of more moderates to the Steering Committee, he complained to the Executive Committee that he "was being badgered by the Democratic Party, and wasn't going to succumb to any threats or pressure...very...vituperative." And when she asked him to delay an FSM rally so as not to conflict with a speech by Democratic vice presidential candidate Hubert Humphrey, Savio replied, "No...what we ought to do is have our own meeting at noon and picket Humphrey's meeting...to keep people from going to it."[29] Freeman and Savio spoke past each other and looked at each other's world with little sympathy or comprehension: she was slow to see the new dawn in student politics wrought by mass protest, and he was unwilling to build bridges to the liberal establishment because he viewed it as morally bankrupt.

In their secret negotiations Kerr and Freeman had sounded similar in their assessments of Savio. Kerr depicted him as an out-of-control militant and, in Freeman's words, "wanted to know if we could put the clamp on Mario, and keep him from making such outlandish statements, harmful to everyone, as well as to act a little more rationally." Freeman replied that "we had absolutely no control over Mario or any of his henchmen" and that the only way to get the crisis settled was through a compromise "that we could convince the FSM to accept...despite Mario."[30] Freeman assumed, based on her conversation with political science professor Paul Seabury, that Kerr, as a fellow moderate, could more easily come to an agreement with her than with the militant Savio. Kerr, Seabury told her, "was willing to give in, but didn't want to give in to Mario, because that would cause him to lose too much face." Although to Freeman this seemed "very plausible," in fact Kerr offered her no more than the CCPA had offered Savio and the rest of the FSM leadership.[31] That offer had proven unacceptable to the FSM leadership because it did not include what for militant civil rights activists was the essential freedom: to advocate on campus for unlawful off-campus protest (i.e., civil disobedience).

The moderates' revolt may be the one moment in the FSM's history when its distinctly New Left political style was set aside and its politics took on an Old Left cast. Weinberg's view of this conflict, even decades later, presented it in Old Left political terms. The moderates were not moderate at all but either anti-Communist ideologues or their pawns. He saw that revolt as engineered by right-wing socialists, along with faculty mentors of this same political stripe, such as Lipset,

for whom anti-Communism was the defining feature...The Young Dems were a front group for the right-wing social democrats...Shactmanites, who considered the FSM illegitimate by virtue of the fact that there were

Communists in its leadership. Period, it's illegitimate...And if you go to the history of liberal politics in Berkeley, both the Communists and the right-wing socialists had a long history of packing meetings...That was not in the FSM tradition.[32]

Whether or not there actually was such a plot, the fact that Weinberg and others saw it that way, and responded in kind, represented a momentary resurrection of an Old Left mind-set, with one faction warring against another.

Savio was never comfortable with such politics. Engaging in factional combat only when forced to in this crisis, he regretted the need for it, and did not look back uncritically upon his role in this rift with the moderates. He regretted losing his temper with Brian Turner over the latter's role in the moderate revolt, having yelled at him on the phone. Not long after this blowup Savio was apologetic, bemoaning the fact that people were "getting paranoid about one another."[33] When a fellow Steering Committee member chided Savio for being "much too willing to forgive" Turner and argued that he ought not apologize for having yelled because Turner "deserved it" for "being totally obstinate," Savio replied that if Turner was being obstinate, "so was *I.*" Savio thought that there was "some question as to whether we were justified in taking that list [of Executive Committee] names [and phone numbers]."[34]

Savio was aware, however, that his anger had been sparked by the moderates' manipulative politicking. Trying to force an eleventh-hour meeting of the Executive Committee to consider whether the FSM should renew its defiance of the free speech ban seemed unreasonable, since "a lot of things...in the works," including a crucial mobilization of the teaching assistants, "would have been destroyed" if the moderates had had their way. He acknowledged that "it was somewhat unreasonable of us to insist on the letter...[of the FSM] Constitution," requiring that the moderates get a dozen Executive Committee names to convene that committee, "but it was unreasonable of them...to have tried to call a meeting" to reverse plans for new demonstrations that FSMers were already organizing. His angry phone call to Turner had been sparked by Turner and Freeman's claim that the Executive Committee wanted a special meeting, but when Savio asked Turner to name the twelve people on the Executive Committee who wanted such a meeting, Turner could not name them all. After one of the students named by Turner told Savio he had "absolutely not" endorsed the convening of such a meeting, Savio concluded that this demand for a meeting was "very fishy." Such suspicions were confirmed at the meeting itself, which, as Savio angrily recalled, was packed with people who were not activists.[35]

For Savio that Executive Committee meeting, and the manipulative politics that had led to it, served as a distasteful education in factionalism. He "learned at that meeting" that it was difficult to include in a mass movement's leadership students too conservative to support the protests needed to sustain that movement. Acknowledging that this was "very oversimplified," he nonetheless came to see it as highly problematic that "Democrats, social democrats, and other kinds of conservatives...only come to a meeting...to vote against the ongoing momentum of the movement...because it was too radical...and then they go back into their holes" and do nothing to help build the movement. These people, Savio considered, were the ones who went behind the backs of the FSM leaders in setting up their own meeting with Lipset and Kerr.[36]

Actually, as Savio himself sensed in speaking of his analysis as oversimplified, the moderates opposing the FSM's move back to confrontation were less monolithic than he and Weinberg implied.[37] Turner, for example, had not given up on the FSM's free speech goals but felt that the CCPA process still had potential. Turner disliked the existence of a militant-moderate split, with each side "having an interest in expanding their own side...and damning the other," and didn't see himself "at either end. I was on another axis which had to do with democratic process and taking care of the people we were with." He insisted that he "was never with Jo" in her move to negotiate a separate peace with Kerr.[38]

One area of agreement between Turner and Freeman was their conviction that the Steering Committee was less democratic than it claimed to be. Both saw the committee's endless talk and marathon meetings as manipulative rather than democratic. Turner asked, "How about an agenda, time limits on debate, speakers on each side, a vote with follow up assignments? It isn't really rocket science. And it doesn't take 17-hour meetings, where our sharp elbowed 'leaders' can hold their favorite agenda items til' the very end when—surprise!—only their buddies are left in the room."[39] Turner claimed he had been voted off the Steering Committee in one such late-night vote.

Freeman echoed this complaint, linking the moderates' defeat to the Steering Committee's use of "an old trick on the part of people who want to control something, you just wear everyone else out, and only those who are so enthused they have stamina to stay around are there."[40] But she also made the contradictory claim that the Steering Committee rushed in and "railroaded" policies through the Executive Committee. Since Savio and the other militants on the Steering Committee were "in this thing full time" and had time to plan for the Executive Committee meetings, they would come to those meetings "organized...knowing what they wanted, and push it through very simply. And we'd go in there unorganized, unconnected, not at all sure of what we wanted—not even knowing what was going to be brought up."[41] Freeman and Turner suggested that there was an Old Left style of disciplined cadre politics, a "vanguard orientation" on the part of the militants, whose behavior was, as Freeman put it, "a magnificent education in totalitarian politics. Now when I get to be dictator, I'll know exactly what to do."[42]

Such criticisms of the militants in the FSM leadership seem overstated. It is difficult not to see the intensity of the attacks as more a case of sour grapes by those on the losing end of a political power struggle than as an objective assessment. Their bitter critique of movement democracy is contradicted by the memories of many FSM activists, including Executive Committee member Jack Radey, who saw late evening decisions at the end of marathon meetings as a consequence of too much FSM democracy rather than too little:

> I stuck through most Ex Comm meetings, two in the morning wasn't unusual...The fact is that one could stay or leave, depending on one's sense of priorities and endurance. I really don't see it as a sinister plot to drive out everyone but the "buddies" of those with a proposal....I think it was the tendency to think democracy meant talk...and talk...and talk...and talk. But to confuse...unwillingness to restrict discussion with sinister plotting is a bit much.[43]

Exaggerated as they seem, these criticisms are meaningful as barometers of the emotional power of this internal FSM dispute. Such negative perceptions had consequences. The rift between Savio and Turner never healed; Turner recalled that it broke up his friendship with Mario.[44] Though Savio had come into the movement hoping to pioneer a new form of consensual democratic politics, and felt that for much of the FSM's life this hyperdemocratic politics yielded great results, it did break down here. This left some moderates convinced that such seemingly democratic aspirations masked undemocratic behavior, generating in them a bitterness that lingered long after the Berkeley revolt. Regardless of whether such bitterness was justifiable, it offers a sobering reminder that the FSM's victory was far from a smooth affair, that the movement's internal conflicts hurt feelings and bruised egos.

The moderates' revolt reveal two sides of Savio's political persona. He could be tough on his opponents, especially if he thought they were behaving unethically. When Freeman appeared at that crucial Executive Committee meeting with two conservatives who had not been attending FSM meetings—and whom she brought in to vote with her faction—with their "suits, ties, combed hair clipped short, both frat and YR [Young Republican] pins in their lapels," Savio turned to her and snarled, "Don't let anyone ever accuse *you* of being principled."[45] Yet Savio retained his desire to be inclusive and democratic. While Freeman, in her oral history, at times scorned Savio as dictatorial and intolerant of dissent, she also acknowledged that after she came to be seen as "a traitor...a sell-out and a spy" by some FSMers, who wanted to exclude her from the Executive Committee, he did not support that exclusion, implying that it was wrong to make pariahs of dissenters. And so the committee voted to keep Freeman on it.[46]

In contrast to the moderates' slightly hyperbolic charges of FSM violations of democratic process, Freeman's criticism of Savio regarding the off-campus political world had more substance. Freeman, who understood the arena of California electoral politics better than Savio, felt that he had been too quick to give up on the state's liberal Democratic establishment. Having connections to that establishment through her Democratic Party network, she felt it "would normally be sympathetic to our cause." Indeed, she insisted that those connections helped lead Governor Brown to press Kerr to negotiate with the protesters back in October. It was a mistake for "Mario and others" to depict their free speech battle as a conflict "between UC students and the whole power structure of California" and to be "sarcastically slurring the 'so-called' liberals." She concluded that he had not "mobilized support in the liberal community" of California; rather, "Mario said screw the liberal community."[47] He would have taken issue with Freeman's upbeat reading of California's liberal Democratic establishment, since these liberals authorized the mass arrest of Berkeley's free speech protesters and called for an FBI probe into the FSM's alleged Communist connections. Nonetheless, she certainly did have a better sense than he of how sad it was that the movement and the Democratic establishment became enemies. This rift between the Left and liberalism would benefit the Right and contribute to the rise of Ronald Reagan.

Savio was, however, far more prescient than the moderates in reading the campus political scene. They underestimated him while displaying a naiveté about the administration and anti-FSM faculty. Freeman claimed that "all Mario and co. had succeeded in doing was alienating everyone." But most of the alienated people she was talking about were those who had opposed student protest all along. For example, Freeman, a political science student, was upset that UC political science professors Robert Scalapino and Paul Seabury disdained the FSM. She blamed Savio for this, buying into Scalapino's claim that "Savio shitted all over him," when in fact he and Seabury had been impelled by their own antiradicalism and hierarchical approach to university politics to oppose the FSM.[48] Similarly, she thought Kerr would cut a deal with her to settle the free speech fight via compromise, but after leading her on, he never did. She assumed that FSM radicals were the main obstacle to serious negotiations, when in fact the administration's internal memos attest that Kerr was happy to end negotiations, since he thought that Savio's extremism was about to make the FSM implode.[49]

On the free speech issues itself, Savio and the Steering Committee grasped the legal as well as the political aspects of the controversy better than their moderate critics. Even Clark Kerr learned this as the FSM moved from negotiation to confrontation. Savio had publicly rejected UC's claiming the power to discipline students for speech that led to unlawful off-campus protest, arguing that it would lead to "prior restraint" of speech. Kerr soon found himself in "quite a debate" with the university's legal counsel, Thomas Cunningham, "on the position of the University concerning disciplinary action against students for their on-campus conduct in planning or initiating off-campus action." Though not mentioning Savio, Cunningham echoed him: "Tom mentioned that it was a prior restraint to threaten action to be taken at a subsequent time which at the time of its inception was lawful." Kerr's response to Cunningham also left no doubt that Savio had been correct in asserting that Kerr's attempt to ban campus advocacy of illegal political acts was motivated by a desire to punish students for disruptive civil rights protests. Kerr argued in his debate with Cunningham "that we have a responsibility to put people on notice on what becomes subsequently unlawful—we can't ignore it...For example [Sheraton] Palace Hotel incident."[50]

Although on the free speech issue Savio and the FSM leadership thought more deeply than their moderate critics, this intellectual strength was at times a political liability. The knowledge gap between the Steering Committee and the larger student body (and many faculty) made it difficult to mobilize large numbers of students in the days immediately following the CCPA's collapse. It was possible, after all, to view the CCPA negotiations as a partial victory in the struggle for free speech because the committee had endorsed a right that previously had been denied on campus—the right to political advocacy. In light of this gain, students had reason to be confused about why the FSM was dissatisfied, why the right to advocacy of legal political actions was insufficient, and why the FSM demanded the right to advocate illegal off-campus protest. The situation was complicated. The movement had won a new right, but the administration claimed a new power to police and punish speakers whose words led to unlawful off-campus protests. It is little wonder that the first rallies after the CCPA collapsed drew hundreds and not thousands.

At first glance, then, the moderates may have seemed correct in advising the FSM not to resume its defiance of campus regulations. It looked as if it would be difficult to mobilize students against what seemed a civil liberties technicality—far more difficult than the situation back in October, when all political advocacy had been banned from the campus. But if this discussion of new campus rules was confusing, the existing restrictions on student speech were, by contrast, crystal clear. When the FSM began defying those regulations on November 9, the protesters placed the administration in the role of dictator presiding over what Kerr himself later admitted was a "police state atmosphere." Savio proved correct in thinking the return to mass defiance would strengthen the FSM. Instead of alienating students and faculty, as the moderates feared, renewed protest exposed the weakness of the administration's position in restricting student rights, demonstrating how impossible it was to enforce those restrictions in the face of a growing resistance. Such defiance was militant, but it was defended in constitutional terms intended to appeal to mainstream students. Savio argued that owing to the administration's

> continuing acts of political oppression…the students have lifted the self-imposed moratorium on the exercise of their constitutionally guaranteed…rights…No institution except the courts has any competence to decide what constitutes the abuse of political freedom. The students shall not cease in the responsible exercise of their rights.[51]

As Savio spoke on Sproul Plaza at the start of this new stage in the movement, on November 9, students staffing tables for their political organizations were approached by two assistant deans. He interrupted his speech to note their presence: "I see a couple of deans coming, welcome gentlemen." The deans gave "the orator cursory nods and walked to the end of the tables and began taking the names of the students" staffing these tables, so as to subject them to disciplinary action.[52] The microphone was passed to the students being cited, so the crowd could witness the harassment of these free speech activists. A sample of the conversation:

DEAN: Are you manning this table?
STUDENT: Yes.
DEAN: Are you collecting money?
STUDENT: I'm accepting contributions.
DEAN: Do you have a permit?
STUDENT: No.
DEAN: Do you know that you are violating a school rule?
STUDENT: I know that school rule is unconstitutional.
DEAN: Will you cease this action?
STUDENT: No.[53]

By the time the rally was over, some seventy-five students had been cited for disciplinary action, and "though lines formed to replace the cited students at the tables, the deans retired [to their offices] refusing to take more names."[54]

The administration fared no better on the second day of protest, when campus officials gave up on citing students, apparently because the tables were staffed by graduate students employed as teaching assistants (TAs). Growing TA protest put the administration in an awkward position, since the university depended upon their instructional labor, and disciplining them might antagonize the faculty for whom they worked. This reluctance to cite TAs was viewed as a victory by the FSM. "The administration," Savio pointed out, "is on the horns of a real dilemma. They must take all of us or none of us."[55] UC counsel Cunningham "blew his top" in a meeting with Kerr, telling him that the administration had placed itself "in a ridiculous position" because they were "not being consistent," citing "the people manning the tables yesterday and not approaching them today for exactly the same violation."[56] More than two hundred TAs submitted a statement to the deans protesting the ban, affirming that they had violated it by staffing advocacy tables.[57]

Just days after the TAs demonstrated their support of the FSM, the administration suffered another setback, this time from the faculty, when the final report of the Academic Senate's ad hoc student conduct committee came out. Created by Kerr as part of the implementation of the Pact of October 2, this committee's job was to resolve the disciplinary cases of the suspended FSM leaders, including Savio. The report criticized the administration for due process violations: suspending students without a hearing, disciplining FSMers for violating rules that were vague, "gratuitously...singling out" protest leaders for heavy penalties "summarily imposed," using them "almost as hostages" "to "forestall further demonstrations." The committee, chaired by law professor Ira Michael Heyman, recommended negating and wiping from their records the suspensions of six of the eight suspended students and ending the suspension of Savio and Art Goldberg.[58]

Savio viewed the Heyman Committee report as a vindication of his critique of the administration, especially his charge that FSMers had been disciplined in an "arbitrary" fashion via "rules governing political activity [that] were obscure." The Heyman report proved too lenient for the administration to accept. Even decades later Kerr remained furious at the committee's verdict, complaining that if flagrant rule breaking by students was not punished, "then the only alternatives, given the...determined student opposition[,] seemed to be capitulation, or use of the external police, or continuing anarchy."[59]

Throughout mid-November, the administration found itself in a situation similar to that of southern police at the height of the civil rights movement, who could not keep up with the pace of protest. No sooner had they acted against one group of protesters than others appeared to take their place. The administration sent disciplinary letters to the seventy-five students cited on November

9 and then to TAs whose statement had affirmed their violation of the ban. But these were mild reprimands that would not be put in student records and merely warned that future rule violations "might lead to more serious penalties."[60] When on November 16 the FSM announced that the advocacy tables would be on Sproul all week, the administration did not respond with further citations.

In this period the FSM found itself in "a stalemate situation." It almost seemed as if, as Jack Weinberg put it, "we had won *de facto*...that you could win by just violating their ban...protesting, setting up its tables," since the administration "gave up on trying to enforce the...rules." But "the administration was holding out on the question of the right to discipline" students for advocating illegal protests."[61] Kerr was quoted on the front pages of the local papers warning that while the university had demonstrated "great patience with temporary violations of public conduct...this patience is not infinite."[62] There could be no decisive FSM victory until the administration abolished its restrictions on advocacy and agreed not to discipline campus speakers for the political content of their speech. To secure such changes the FSM appealed to the university's top governing body, the Board of Regents.

Organizing for the November 20 regents meeting became the FSM's top priority. This was the most impressive mobilization since the police car blockade. While the rallies of early November had attracted hundreds, the rally near the regents' meeting drew four thousand and involved no rule breaking.[63] The large crowd was drawn not only by the free speech cause and Savio but also by folksinger Joan Baez, who had recently played a sold-out concert at the university. At the rally she sang Bob Dylan's "The Times They Are a-Changin'" and civil rights freedom songs. Baez also made statements in support of free speech and the FSM, mocking the UC bureaucracy by singing "Let's Not Have a Sniffle, Let's Have a Bloody Good Cry." Following the rally, the protesters—all clad respectably, with Savio and other male leaders wearing jackets and ties and female leaders clad in skirts—marched silently, carrying only a free speech banner, toward University Hall, where the regents were meeting.[64]

For Savio this episode with the regents was a lesson in the arrogance of power. The regents refused to speak with protesters about their grievances. A delegation of five FSM leaders, including Savio, was allowed to attend the meeting, but only as observers. He was appalled by the regents' unwillingness to listen and by their refusal to engage the free speech and due process issues. This meeting seemed to embody the worst aspects of the multiversity, its "totally unresponsive bureaucracy."[65] He sat there in disgust while the regents rubber-stamped Kerr's recommendations. The board stood with Kerr in rejecting the Heyman report. The regents did this "with *no* discussion" and "voted unanimously" to authorize stiffer punishments of the protesters (though stopping short of mandating them). Savio was incensed that there was almost no discussion of Kerr's recommendation reserving to the university the right to discipline students who advocated unlawful off-campus political actions. The only dissent came from two regents who found Kerr's recommendations "too liberal." After these two spoke, "that was it." Kerr, in Savio's words, "concluded in ten minutes what we'd been working on for more than two months. And then he just sat down."[66]

The dismissive way that the regents responded to the FSM's grievances left Savio convinced that protests needed to escalate.

> We turned in all kinds of petitions, we'd been working with passion for two months to get our free speech...We'd made use of every official channel open to us. We followed the channels through to the very end. We'd opened up some new channels, the Committee on Campus Political Activity and the Heyman Committee..., those came out of the agreement we'd signed on October 2nd. We followed those channels through to their conclusion. All these channels proved fruitless, totally fruitless. All doors were closed to us.[67]

The question he pondered was no longer whether to organize a mass sit-in but when.

Savio was not alone in such feelings. Thousands of students on the lawn across the street from where the regents were meeting were disappointed when he described to them the rubber-stamping of Kerr's anti-FSM recommendations. "Students stood and sat in stunned silence and many of the co-eds burst into tears."[68] He told the crowd that he was "serving notice on them [the regents] now...We're not going to take this sitting down. If they try to enforce these unconstitutional regulations, they're going to suffer for it." FSM Steering Committee member Steve Weissman urged an immediate sit-in at University Hall to protest the regents' decisions, but Savio and others urged delay until the following week so as to allow for more deliberation. The crowd decided by a vote of more than ten to one to hold off on any civil disobedience.[69]

In the aftermath of the regents' decisions, the Steering Committee, pondering a response, held its longest meeting, which lasted some forty-eight hours. For the first time the Steering Committee itself was badly divided: a majority held that the timing was not right for civil disobedience, while Savio and three others wanted to sit in at the administration building on November 23. Aptheker, who usually sided with Savio, on this occasion disagreed with him. She opposed the sit-in "because I knew it wouldn't pull enough people. And then we'd get isolated, and then they could axe us" via arrest and expulsion.[70] She and the other opponents of the sit-in thought such defiance unwise since there had not been a clear provocation for mass civil disobedience. The problem was that the regents, though indifferent to the FSM's demands, had merely asserted their power over discipline and speech; they had disappointed free speech activists by backing Kerr but had not done anything dramatic. This made it difficult to justify risking mass arrests. The proposed sit-in would, Aptheker warned, have "no focal point. It was out of anguish rather than purpose."[71]

The pro-sit-in position did not, as Aptheker noted, make sense tactically. Savio later admitted that "the political considerations were really against us," and he had been "voting [his] visceral reaction." The logic was that "they screwed us after we had 4,000 people out there peacefully. What's the next thing to do?' Well...[the] gut reaction of alienated people—sit-in" even though most students "just weren't ready" for a new round of mass civil disobedience.[72] Weinberg termed this impulse to sit in "a plea,...an existential cry: 'Listen to my voice; you haven't heard me before; you ignore me. I came out in five thousand and you didn't recognize me....I sent in petitions; you didn't read them....I'm going to put myself in a position where I cannot be ignored.' "[73]

With the tactical arguments so weak, why the Steering Committee eventually voted (by a slim margin) for a sit-in may seem puzzling. Savio played a pivotal role here, refusing to budge from his pro-sit-in position during the marathon Steering Committee meeting. Had it not been for him, the vote against sitting in would have stood. Savio "ranted and raved and he said...'we have to sit-in, there's no other tactic in front of us.'" This went on "until 4:00 in the morning. Nobody would leave. In fact he insisted that he would sit-in all by himself."[74]

Savio's obstinacy might not have mattered had the Steering Committee a better alternative. Those opposing the sit-in were arguing to delay civil disobedience because the campus was not ready for it, but they could not say with any assurance that the movement would be in any stronger position later to mount a free speech sit-in. Aptheker conceded that, weak as Savio's pro-sit-in position was, her anti-sit-in position was almost equally weak:

> I kept saying "wait," and when I argued, Mario said, "Wait for what?" And I said, "Well, they're stupid; they're going to do something; they can't let it rest here. They don't have any solution; sooner or later we're going to violate something....Then let's move. But meanwhile, let's keep our rallies going...and continue exercising our political rights until they take some kind of action." But he wasn't so sure of that, and I admit that was a weak alternative to what we had.[75]

Neither side of the sit-in debate was totally sure of itself. Steering Committee member Michael Rossman, who favored the sit-in, thought it incorrect even to characterize this as a conflict over whether to protest the regents' decision: everyone on the committee wanted to protest the decision, but they were divided about how to do so.[76] Thus it took very little to change the vote. That change came when, during a meeting break, Marty Roysher picked up a copy of the *Daily Californian* and read its editorial denouncing the regents' recent decisions. If even this moderate student paper took such a position, Roysher reasoned, maybe many students would support the sit-in. This turned out to be wishful thinking, but Roysher's argument swung two additional votes, so a bare majority of the Steering Committee endorsed holding a Sproul sit-in on November 23.[77]

The democratic idealism of the FSM was never more evident than in the decision the Steering and Executive Committees made about the rally it would hold before the November 23 sit-in. Instead of pretending the leadership was united, the FSM opted to be candid about the lack of consensus, having pro- and anti-sit-in speakers address the crowd.[78] In practical terms this was a dubious decision, since getting contradictory messages from the movement's leadership could undermine the solidarity needed for an act of civil disobedience. This is why Aptheker looked back upon the rally as "awful. That's no way to give leadership, to have a public debate about it."[79]

The rally showed that the animating spirit of the movement was hyperdemocratic and genuinely committed to free speech, even for critics of the movement's tactics. Reginald Zelnik, a historian sympathetic to the FSM, asked if he could address the rally and urge students not to sit in. Even though Rossman was pro-sit-in, he, Savio, and the other Steering Committee members allowed Zelnik to speak, knowing full well that the remarks by this popular professor would strengthen the anti-sit-in forces.[80] FSM organizer Art Goldberg gave a middle-ground speech, calling for everyone to follow his or her conscience and respect those on the other side of the sit-in debate. The two sides generally behaved amicably toward each other. Thus Weinberg, while differing from Zelnik on the sit-in, spoke respectfully of the professor and praised him for rallying faculty support for the FSM. The other pro-sit-in speakers, including Savio and Rossman, were equally diplomatic in discussing the disagreement about sitting in. Weissman, in turn, coupled his anti-sit-in position with a call for solidarity, proposing that those not sitting in stay on the plaza ready to rally in case police stormed Sproul Hall.[81]

Since this protest proved a failure, drawing only a small crowd and lasting only a few hours, it came to be known as "the aborted sit-in." The debate-oriented rally leading up to the sit-in can be viewed as a mistake, confusing the crowd with pro- and anti-sit-in speakers right before the occupation of Sproul. Savio, however, did not see it that way. He thought it an act of political courage and candor not to pretend in public that the leadership all supported this pro-sit-in position. Leveling with the students in the plaza and sharing their own disagreements symbolized, in his view, that "we really were true to a certain set" of democratic ideals.[82]

Savio also saw in this rally echoes of something he'd learned in Mississippi: respect for individual conscience, especially when activists faced a decision on whether to put themselves at risk. By allowing both sides to debate the sit-in, the message to activists was: "If you don't go along, that's okay. It doesn't mean you're out of the movement....It's the decision we've come to. We are encouraging people to do this, but no one should feel beyond the pale if you don't do this."[83] For Savio, means mattered, not just ends, which is why he could seem proud of a political action that had failed when that action respected individual conscience, movement democracy, and free speech.

He also thought the type of sit-in planned was well calibrated to the student mood in that it was a relatively mild action that, as Savio told the crowd, would not "prevent passage" of campus officials or workers in the building. "We'll sit along the walls [of Sproul Hall] and wait" for the administration to listen to the movement's demands.[84]

This is not to say, however, that Savio lacked regrets about the aborted sit-in. But the way he thought about its failure was shaped by his democratic ethos. He rejected the Old Left leadership style and the Communist ideal of "democratic centralism," where a small radical elite shapes policy and presents a united face to the movement, covering up divisions within the leadership. He thought it unethical to "misrepresent publicly that you're unified when you're not." So the mistake was not the airing of this division but sitting in when the leadership was so divided. For him the lesson was "if a position can prevail only because of a vote taken within a tactical body, then you'd better start again...[because] you obviously haven't thought of the right thing to do."[85] The FSM should have come to a consensus before acting. Here Savio was criticizing himself and the movement, which had been so strikingly democratic in the November 23 rally, for not being even more democratic. If he had not been so eager to protest, he thought, he would have done better as a leader by choosing a course of action acceptable to all the movement's leaders.[86]

Given that the sit-in proved unsuccessful, it is not surprising that Savio's speech there has been largely forgotten. But this November 23 speech captures the spirit of the FSM and the distinctive character of his oratory. It focused on free speech and due process, and was complex and explanatory, not narrowly agitational. It was free of radical rhetoric or sloganeering. He outlined why the FSM rejected the administration's claim that it should have the right to discipline students for speech that led to unlawful off-campus protests. Here he raised the question of prior restraint and the chilling effect such university disciplinary authority would have on free speech:

> If I get up to speak I take into account the fact that I may be violating the law by speaking. But if I further have to take account of some action the administration may take depending upon some future action over which I perhaps have no control and in which I'm going to take no part then I don't know the extent to which my speech is abusive or not. I don't know if it is a violation of law or not. And the question of whether it violates the law or not is not the only criterion which determines whether I shall be disciplined. But likewise in an administrative hearing it's decided my language was abusive because the administration decides it was inappropriate. This is what we're against. Again they [Kerr and Strong] admit they want this right [to police political expression].[87]

Savio depicted the administration critically but three-dimensionally, conceding that "they're smart" and their strategy was "well planned. Their tactic from the beginning…has been…to confuse and by confusion to divide." On the key civil liberties sticking point, "they tried to obscure the issue by saying something is going to be decided by the courts," as if this meant that the administration would respect due process. But the courts would rule only whether the off-campus acts were lawful, not whether the campus advocacy leading to those acts justified disciplinary action against offending students. Here "the administration proposes to set up its own standards to decide if there has been an abuse of free speech."[88]

Questioning the administration's ability to oversee an impartial disciplinary process, Savio insisted in the heat of political battle that fairness mattered, that his conclusions derived not from political bias but from "past experience" about which "we have evidence." As evidence, he cited one thing the administration "said and one thing they did." On the former, he cited vice chancellor Alan Searcy,

> who repeatedly presented it, that the university is subject to external extralegal pressures, and that it must have some way of responding to these pressures so that it'd be protected. That means to me that the due process you get or consideration given the hearing by the Chancellor or both will vary roughly inversely with external pressures.

This was for Savio "totally unacceptable," since it meant student rights could be trampled whenever the administration felt pressured to do so.[89]

If this case of what they said was unacceptable, equally bad was what they did. Savio took aim at the administration's response to the Heyman Committee's lenient disciplinary report. This committee was not up to Savio's high standards since it did not extend to students the standard of proof demanded "in an ordinary criminal case, let alone a First Amendment case." Guilt was determined not "beyond a reasonable doubt and to a moral certainty," but by "the preponderance of the evidence." Though imperfect, this faculty committee's rulings were so sympathetic toward the FSM that the administration "couldn't accept its findings." Since administrators had absolute power on campus and had already proven their partisanship by rejecting this faculty committee's report, their record offered no reason to expect more judicious handling of disciplinary hearings for controversial speakers in the future: "We know the kind of things they've done in the past. We know the only reason they've given for wanting this power [to discipline advocates of illegal protests] is to respond to external pressure. Can we let them have this power? And can we let them take away *our rights*? I say 'No!'"[90]

Savio's speech took the administration to task for refusing to engage in genuine dialogue.[91] As evidence that a sit-in was needed, he cited Strong's statement on the day of the sit-in that he would not alter the free speech policy. Only through civil disobedience could Strong be pressured to listen to students. Airing frustration over the administration's stonewalling, Savio told the crowd:

> We're a little bit beyond anger, beyond tears now. It's a…moral protest…that I'm advocating. We don't have a voice.…We can't let the freakin' policy stand.…We want them to have to…look right into our eyes…after having told us that this policy which affects us, which affects the faculty, cannot change…, that we can't have the rights guaranteed by the Constitution.…It's that kind of moral…sit-in…that I am asking people to take part in.[92]

Passionate as Savio was in urging support for the sit-in, his speech nonetheless made it clear that both the pro- and anti-sit-in positions were legitimate, and he called on both sides of this debate to show understanding of each other. "If someone does take part in this sit-in…they will not consider those who have not taken part to be somehow out of the movement—just to have a different appraisal of the situation. And I would ask…that those who don't take part should at least recognize the legitimate feelings and judgment of those who do take part."[93]

Equally striking was Savio's insistence on speaking the truth to the crowd even when this undermined his own argument. This occurred when some militants mustered support for the sit-in by claiming that faculty endorsed it. Though aware that this claim might help his side sway moderate students to sit in, Savio insisted on the inconvenient truth, telling the crowd, "I don't know of any faculty members who support the sit-in now."[94]

The emotions from the split over the sit-in were so strong that they came close to overpowering Savio. On the day of the sit-in, his frustrations with these divisions, together with exhaustion, left him "quite literally...crying in the morning."[95] The divisions continued even during the sit-in, as the Steering Committee debated whether to have protesters leave before the building closed at five o'clock, and thus avoid arrests. The pressure of debating this under threat of arrest, with neither the time nor the atmosphere to arrive at a consensus, led Savio to the brink of rejecting the collective decision-making process that he usually supported so strongly. When "the Steering Committee met, eleven of us...on the second floor of Sproul Hall...we had a very intense meeting...very badly divided" over calling an end to the sit-in.[96]

Savio urged that the occupation continue after five o'clock, even though this would yield arrests in an action that had captured neither the attention nor the support of most of the campus. He "was adamant that we had to stay and it was like at all costs, and whoever was arrested, and go down in flames." Aptheker disagreed with him and urged that the protest end without arrests: "My reasoning was that the movement was much bigger than the few hundred of us that were in the building. And if we waited we could have a sit-in that was massive. I didn't really know that. It's just that I didn't want us to get slaughtered." The vote was 6–5 to end the sit-in; as she noted, it was "the closest and most divided we ever were in the movement."[97] During this meeting she rebuked Savio for his obstinacy, objecting to his suggestion the night before that he would sit in no matter what the Steering Committee decided. She "took after Mario very very strongly" for violating the group leadership ideal:

> "You threw a tantrum last night. You pouted...," and he did....What I blasted him for inside Sproul...was you don't have collective leadership and make collective decisions like that—we don't have a Steering Committee so you can go off and do as you damned well please....Maybe collectively we'll all get sunk....But...you ought to value the judgment of other people.[98]

This was the only time in what would be their lifelong friendship when, in Aptheker's words, "Mario was furious with me." After the vote to end the sit-in early, he turned to her and said, "Well, I'm leaving…you can tell everybody to leave. You do it; it's your idea." Then Savio left "in a big huff."[99] But he quickly realized that he'd erred in defying the majority will of the leadership, and that he had an obligation to help carry out the decision even though he disagreed with it. Thus he walked among the rank-and-file of students who were sitting in, asking them to "please at 5 p.m. please leave"—which almost all of them did, while singing "We Shall Overcome."[100]

This episode revealed that Savio's strengths as an insurgent leader—his ethical approach to politics, tactical boldness, and nerve—could at points be a liability, since these made him reluctant to hold off on militant action even when such action was impractical. Here he was less interested in whether sitting in was a winning strategy than whether it was moral. This led him to be the most persistent proponent of this sit-in, which proved the FSM's least successful protest. While being uncompromising proved an asset in fending off administration attempts to bargain away student rights, it was not helpful in this kind of internal dispute, when being headstrong perpetuated disunity. But such disputes were rare within the FSM.

It was easy for Savio to idealize the collective decision-making process when his views accorded with the rest of the leadership. But when consensus evaporated, he fell into an individualistic response. This was the flip side of the civil rights movement experience, which taught that, even in collective protest, acts of civil disobedience grew out of personal decisions, since ultimately it was the individual who risked arrest and physical harm in undertaking such protest. It was a sign of Savio's respect for the rights of the individual that he held that a protest movement cannot "bind anyone's conscience." Yet he recognized by the end of the sit-in that Aptheker was right about the need for solidarity, that a democratic movement whose leaders did not heed its decisions would crumble.[101]

The sit-in's failure left the FSM at its low point psychologically and politically. Even if its leaders were capable of reuniting, it was unclear what they would unite to do. The ill-timed protest suggested that masses of students might not again follow the FSM into political battle. With the chancellor cleverly boasting that the university had accepted the CCPA's "faculty recommendation of 'free expression within the limits of the law,'" the student body saw no pressing grievance, or at least none that yielded any eagerness for another round of civil disobedience.[102] Perhaps because he was so responsible for the aborted sit-in, Savio denied that the sit-in had damaged the movement, claiming that "we weren't demoralized by this particular event." Instead, he said, "we were demoralized by the general situation"—that is, administration stonewalling, and the difficulty of mobilizing students over the right to advocate civil disobedience.[103]

Actually, it seems more accurate to say that *both* the failed sit-in and the stone-walling by Strong and Kerr led to demoralization. Weinberg thought the sit-in's failure suggested that "the Movement was all over. I…was going to drop out…so was Mario."[104] Even if it was not over, the movement was, by Rossman's estimation, in a pause, because as the Thanksgiving holiday approached, "we didn't know what to do; as a matter of fact we recessed Steering Committee for a couple of days to give each other time to think. We said 'ok, things are done. We can pack up and go home…for the holidays.…There's nothing we can do now.'…We were that demoralized."[105] Aptheker was less glum. The night of the sit-in, the Steering Committee had, in her words, "one of these soul-searching meetings" to ponder why "the leadership failed" the movement. "But it was good because everyone understood the frustration we felt that day. And we didn't lose support."[106]

This nadir in the FSM's history offers powerful evidence that the movement's ultimate success ought not to be attributed merely to Savio's oratory or to the movement leadership's skills. The FSM had not achieved its overarching goal, and might never have attained it were it not for the blundering of the administration.

As the FSM drifted in the wake of the aborted sit-in, the administration made an enormous miscalculation over the Thanksgiving break, sending out letters initiating new disciplinary action against Savio and three other FSM organizers—Art Goldberg, Brian Turner, and Jackie Goldberg—an act that would enable the FSM to mobilize students on a scale not seen since early October. This was an example of Art Goldberg's "atrocity theory," which held that there was no reason for the movement to fret in its down periods, since all that was necessary was to wait for the administration to provoke the student body via another "atrocity" against student rights. In this sense the most effective protest organizers were not Savio and Weinberg but Kerr and Strong.[107]

In light of these Thanksgiving letters, Aptheker came to believe that the sit-in fiasco actually had a good effect on the movement. In her view, it led the administration to underestimate the FSM, to think it had "fallen apart…that the radicals had split themselves off," and that the time was ripe to pick off the movement's leaders via disciplinary action.[108] There is no evidence that the new disciplinary action was connected to the failed sit-in, but the fact that movement leaders viewed the administrators as bullies who struck when they thought the FSM was weak suggests how deeply alienated protest leaders had become from them.

Nor was it only protest leaders who displayed such alienation. The new disciplinary action looked vindictive to thousands of students. Unlike the free speech issue, with its technical language and political complexity, the disciplinary actions were clear, direct, and infuriating to mainstream students. The administration seemed to be singling out for punishment movement leaders for acts that many others also had committed. It appeared that Kerr and Strong could not let the free speech battle end "without punishing somebody and teaching a lesson [so] that something like this should never happen again."[109] This was precisely the kind of heavy-handed behavior—using disciplinary procedures to hold protest leaders "hostage" so as to decapitate the movement—that the Heyman Committee had criticized earlier in the semester. In fact, three of the four charges made against Savio in his new disciplinary letter were for acts that many others had committed—including encouraging "numerous demonstrators" to sit in around the police car on October 1–2.[110] The new disciplinary acts seemed a sign of bad faith in that the Pact of October 2 had assigned the responsibility for the disciplining of protesters to the faculty via the Heyman Committee. Rejecting that committee's recommendations, Strong and Kerr started a new round of disciplinary proceedings. It also seemed unfair to discipline Savio and Jackie Goldberg for the police car blockade when both had helped end that crisis by signing the Pact of October 2.

The FSM had a tradition of rallying against selective punishment that dated back to its first sit-in back in September. This was, as Weinberg explained, "a movement built on solidarity, and the 500 people who said 'If you're going to do it to them, you're going to do the same thing to us.' Now there were thousands of people saying 'Whatever happens to anybody, happens to all of us. We're in it together. You can't single anybody out.'"[111] The disciplinary letters were great for internal unity within the FSM, since they targeted not only Savio but less militant activists, including Jackie Goldberg.[112] The letters caused such moderates as Jo Freeman to align with FSM militants out of anger that the administration was "no longer arguing issues; they were attacking the students...a total violation of the agreements of October 2."[113]

In the wake of the failed sit-in, the entire FSM leadership and much of the rank-and-file were determined to take advantage of this opportunity to revive the movement, mobilizing students against the punitive administration actions and renewing the demands for free speech. So, while appalled by UC's attempt to punish Savio and the three others, they were delighted to have this new organizing tool. Aptheker recalled, "I rubbed my hands with glee" at the news of the Thanksgiving disciplinary letters "because I knew...that's what we were waiting for...[It was] the final atrocity."[114] Savio's "reaction was "a combination of outrage" and the pragmatic realization that such "bad acts" were good for the movement.[115]

This is not to say, however, that Savio simply abandoned negotiations. The Steering Committee tried to convince the administration to reconsider its disciplinary offensive. "We went to Strong's office," recalled Aptheker. "He wouldn't see us." On November 29 the FSM leadership made phone contact with UC vice president Earl Bolton, who instead of fostering negotiations threatened the protest leaders by repeatedly asking whether they knew they could be arrested for "criminal conspiracy" for planning the sit-in.[116]

The final attempt to reach the administration prior to the mass sit-in came on December 1, in a letter to Kerr that Savio wrote with fellow Steering Committee member Suzanne Goldberg. Although this letter failed to bring UC to the negotiating table, it is nonetheless a significant document in evoking the revolution in student politics that Savio was leading. The letter delivered an ultimatum to the administration: if three essential demands were not met within twenty-four hours, mass direct action would ensue. Displaying no deference, the letter cast student protesters as champions of the progress of freedom on campus and the administration as the obstacle against that progress: "Without the use of mass direct action we have been unable to make any substantial gains toward freedom for political activity at the University of California. The Administration has continued to act arbitrarily to repress that activity." The letter called for dropping the new disciplinary charges, an agreement that no further charges be lodged against students for violating UC regulations until a final settlement was reached between the administration and the FSM, and "no restrictions of on-campus advocacy."[117]

This was a striking assertion of student power. It proposed a mechanism for ensuring student rights that would end administration dominance of campus governance: "All regulations concerning the form of political expression on the campus" must be "determined, interpreted and enforced by a joint committee of faculty..., students, and administrators, chosen by their peers, each group having equal power on the committee, the judgments of which shall be final."[118] This embodied the FSM leadership's vision of an academic community in which faculty and students, teachers and learners, engaged in self-government rather than being dictated to by professional administrators. Unlike virtually all university committees, which only make recommendations to the administration, this one would have had the final say on UC policy regarding political expression. It would have turned the academic world upside down by making students equal partners.[119]

Since the administration refused to meet with the protesters—and Strong replied angrily to the Savio-Goldberg letter, insisting he would not submit to threats—the focus of the FSM's attention shifted to Sproul Plaza. For the FSM it was critical that the student body, which had stayed away from the aborted sit-in a little over a week earlier, come out this time en masse to oppose the disciplining of the movement's leaders. The initial signs were positive. Despite cold, windy weather, a thousand students attended a hastily called rally on Monday, November 30, to protest the disciplinary letters.[120] On the following day the rally was smaller, between three hundred and eight hundred students.

At this December 1 rally, Savio told the crowd of the letter the FSM had sent to Kerr with an ultimatum, which if not met would lead to a "provocative action," a sit-in on December 2. "I am not naive enough," he explained, "to believe the university will admit they're wrong." Savio predicted that Kerr would reject the demands, and implored students to support the FSM in the approaching confrontation to secure student rights, since only mass resistance could bring victory. "If you don't respond we're dead."[121] Savio also used some of the imagery that would become a part of his most famous speech the following day. "This factory [the university] does unjust things and we'll have to cause the wheels to grind to a halt....If we don't get our constitutional rights we won't let this machine operate."[122]

For Savio these industrial images were not new; he had used them in his speech in September at the dean's office, amidst the first sit-in. That imagery grew out of the FSM's critique of Kerr's vision of the multiversity as a knowledge industry. By adding imagery of machines and wheels in this knowledge factory, he highlighted not its modernity and efficiency but its lack of humanity and freedom. It is the university as an assembly line for conformity, serving the status quo, intolerant of dissent, doing "unjust things" to serve the interests of conservative clients and economic patrons.

There was some ambiguity as to whether Savio was indicting the entire university as a heartless machine or whether that indictment more narrowly focused on the university's bureaucracy. The FSM leaflet issued on December 2 suggested that it took his words as being focused on the administration rather than the larger university, using Savio's imagery in stating that "except to threaten and harm us, the machine of the administration ignores us. We will stop the machine."[123] It is not possible, however, to resolve this ambiguity, since Savio never did himself. For all his radicalism and his desire to see the university reconstituted as a community of teachers and learners with the administration's power diminished, he followed the administration's usage, in which the chancellor and president equated themselves with "the university." Thus when he said he doubted that "the university will admit they're wrong" on the free speech dispute, he used "university" as equivalent to the UC administration.[124] Judging from the context, this ambiguity reflected Savio's sense that the administration functioned as a callous bureaucracy, and that when the rest of the university allowed Kerr's cramped vision of student rights and vocational approach to education to prevail, both the university and its administration functioned as machines in a profit-driven knowledge factory.

In organizing the December 2 rally the FSM returned to its strategy of November 20, when it used folksinger Joan Baez's star power to help draw a crowd of some four thousand protesters outside the regents' meeting. The leaflet for the December 2 rally announced that Baez would be there and was explicit about the connection between this rally and civil disobedience. "The chancellor has taken his direct action. We must take ours.... Bring books, food, and sleeping bags."[125] Support for the FSM was solidifying, notably among TAs, who voted to go out on strike later in the week if the FSM's demands were not met. The stage was set for a confrontation that would rock the Berkeley campus.

8

SPEAKING OUT AND SITTING IN

The crowd at the noon Sproul Plaza rally on December 2 was huge, some six thousand students. Still, Savio had no idea how many students would find the movement's grievances sufficiently compelling to join him in sitting in at Sproul Hall after the rally. He and his fellow Steering Committee members had been on an emotional roller coaster in the week leading up to this rally. Only nine days earlier the FSM had held its most ineffective protest, the aborted sit-in. So with fresh memories of that fiasco, under whose weight the FSM had, as Weinberg put it, almost "disintegrated"—and having experienced "a feeling of defeat"—the movement reacted to the disciplinary letters that the administration recently sent to the FSM leadership with both anger and a hopeful sense that those letters (widely viewed as vindictive) presented "an opportunity to push the fight further." For the FSM leadership, the December 2 rally and sit-in offered a shot at redemption. The movement had "a lot at stake" that day. So "it was a very emotional moment," one when the FSM faced the question of whether it remained a genuinely popular movement capable of stirring the conscience of the campus. This context helps to account for almost "all the emotional energy" in Savio's famous speech, which he gave at this rally, seeking to persuade the crowd to sit in.[1]

The most widely quoted part of that brief speech (his entire speech lasted only a little more than seven minutes) finds Savio at his most lyrical and defiant:

> There's a time when the operation of the machine becomes so odious, makes you so sick at heart, that you can't take part. You can't even passively take part. And you've got to put your bodies upon the gears and upon the wheels, upon the levers, upon all the apparatus, and you've got to make it stop. And you've got to indicate to the people who run it, to the

people who own it, that unless you're free the machine will be prevented from working at all!²

These lines aptly, even beautifully captured the antiauthoritarianism of the 1960s, the democratic promise of the early New Left, and the willingness of student protesters to stand up to those more powerful (and older) than them on behalf of such causes as free speech, racial justice, and peace. Historian David Burner characterized those four Savio sentences as "poetry that combines the exaltation of the civil rights movement with the splendor of the existential vision…with no suggestion of violence, thinking of concrete change, its discourse as yet unthickened by dogmatic pseudo-revolutionary verbiage."³

Historians have made many attempts to deconstruct those famous Savio lines, almost as if doing so could account for the rebelliousness of 1960s youth. This may be why they have seen in this speech a dizzying array of influences—and perhaps, too, it is that his speech, like all true poetry, invites us to impose our own ideals, hopes, and assumptions on the words of the poet. Savio's words have been linked to the influence of Henry David Thoreau advocating civil disobedience, Walt Whitman promoting radical democracy and love of liberty, Mahatma Gandhi and Leo Tolstoy urging passive resistance and disdain for the machine, Charlie Chaplin's critical imagery of the machine in *Modern Times*, Martin Luther King Jr.'s "Letter from Birmingham Jail" defending direct action and protesters' use of their "very bodies" to appeal to the conscience of the community, C. Wright Mills urging a heroic role for dissident intellectuals, Herbert Marcuse's concept of repressive tolerance, and Albert Camus's existentialist gesture of self-identification (*acte gratuit*).⁴

In some respects, the "bodies upon the gears" speech represented a departure from Savio's prior FSM oratory. Most of his speeches "would have not aimed at getting…the student body to do something at that moment; they were not agitational in the sense of 'follow me into jeopardy,'" as was the case on December 2. They tended to be more educational: "This is what we are doing. This is why we are doing it. We can only do this with your support. You need to understand it. You need to be able to explain it to your professor. You need to be able to explain it to other students."⁵ Savio usually took great pains to explain the civil liberties issues at stake and also reviewed—as did the FSM newsletter and leaflets—"the strategic and tactical situation as of that day." Such speeches were essentially about community building, reporting back to the rank-and-file, and thereby serving what Weinberg termed "the need to maintain a committed base."⁶ The December 2 speech, by contrast, was at bottom a passionate moral summons to stop evil.

The anger in Savio's December 2 speech was so much stronger than in his other speeches that, though resonating with his fellow students, it made faculty—even allies of the FSM—uncomfortable. History professor Reginald Zelnik recalled that while Savio's most famous speech was "tremendously powerful and important," it

> should not be taken as typical of Mario's speeches. It was a certain conjuncture of circumstance and moment that brought out that particular speech and made it so effective. But if you did, as I did, spend lots of time listening to him talk on the plaza in the course of that fall I think you'll reach the conclusion that that speech alone would not have been so persuasive had it not been for the many...other slower,...more stammering, more considerate, more complex speeches that he'd made. I don't think thousands of students would have stood there applauding just anybody who got up there and made exactly that speech, and I certainly don't think a thousand students would have followed him into Sproul Hall at the risk of expulsion and arrest.[7]

Philosophy professor John Searle was far more critical, finding the speech's angry tone "dreadful. I thought that speech about throwing yourself on the machine was too damn rhetorical....Here [was] that most pampered generation of American history," and Savio talked as if they were "some Luddites being crushed" by machines. "But that wasn't typical Mario. That was a very atypical speech, and it is a shame that he is remembered...for that speech....A typical Mario speech...has a kind of freshness which combines an awareness of the problem that he can state in an ordinary, common-sense, nonintellectual level with a certain deep intellectual vision."[8]

The fame of the December 2 speech may seem problematic in the context of the FSM's history, since it can lead to judging Savio not by his long and illuminating civil liberties orations or his extensive periods of organizing and negotiating but instead by a moment of confrontation and less than a handful of his most irate yet eloquent lines. It seems pointless, however, to express regret that his best-known speech was in some ways uncharacteristic, since speeches are often remembered not for their typicality but for their distinctiveness. Here Savio was about to break university regulations and the law, asking thousands of others to put themselves at risk, as he was doing, in a daring act of civil disobedience sparked by what he viewed as a long train of abuses by the administration. The speech was a call to resistance and conscience, wedding thought with action and speaking out with sitting in. So while in emotional terms the speech was not typical of Savio and the FSM, it heralded a new form of defiant student oratory, one that would come to typify New Left student politics.[9]

To understand this speech it must be recognized that despite Savio's celebrity status he was not a soloist. The anger in his speech was an emotion developed and shared with others in the movement. All the FSM speeches at the December 2 rally were heated, their tone tough and their rhetoric at points harsh. For example, Steering Committee member Martin Roysher's speech charged that "this university is not a university at all. It's a travesty on that name. The administration has shown no commitment to the principles in which a university is based" and no courage to speak with student protesters. "And without courage and commitment there can't be any creativity or any dialogue." Responsive to improper outside pressure but not to their own campus community, these bureaucrats, Roysher concluded, "have no right to lead this university. This university is not a community of scholars; it's a stage full of puppets."[10]

Sociologist Max Heirich, suggested, in his pioneering study of the Berkeley rebellion, that the December 2 rally represented a retreat from reason and a break from the FSM's more moderate roots:

> The FSM rally of December 2 had a quality different from any which preceded it. Speakers were far more…strident and harsh…in striking contrast to…FSM rallies in the past. Previously some speakers may have been militant…but there had been an element of rational discourse…in most of the rallies. On December 2 this was gone.…The speakers made it clear that in their view anyone who did not enter Sproul Hall was deserting his fellow students, leaving them to the mercies of the police and an untrustworthy administration.[11]

Although Heirich was correct in noting that the December 2 speeches shared a fury at the administration, he erred in suggesting that this represented a retreat from reason. There were few moments in the rally where anger disrupted rational discourse. Heirich, like most social scientists in the early 1960s, assumed that in politics emotional expression was inherently irrational. More recent sociological scholarship, however, has challenged this assumption, suggesting instead that effective social movements "weave together a moral, cognitive, and emotional package of attitudes." And that was what occurred on the steps of Sproul on December 2. The emotion FSM speakers articulated was not a sudden or irrational response to unexpected stimuli, not an instinctual response, but a "higher-order" emotion, falling on "the more constructed, cognitive end" of the emotional dimension. This "indignation of perceived encroachment on traditional rights" was grounded in a series of events that occurred over the course of an entire semester, and translated into grievances carefully delineated by these speakers.[12]

Heated though they were, the FSM speeches preceding Savio's at the December 2 rally presented reasoned, evidence-based arguments indicting the administration for its abuses of power. Roysher and Michael Rossman provided extensive narratives on the FSM's struggle for student rights. The grievances Roysher discussed included the free speech ban, the phony reasons invoked to justify it, Red-baiting against the FSM, the rejection of the Heyman report, and a refusal "to respond to…the students or faculty." Instead, the administration took orders from reactionary "forces on the outside" who wanted to repress student protest. Rossman's speech framed the historical narrative in line with the "three things…we've been fighting for": (1) "a decent stand on advocacy" in which "only the courts can judge the content of speech"; (2) "an end to all the unnecessary restrictions on the way free speech is exercised," including the rules requiring seventy-two hours' notice for nonstudent speakers and the requirement of tenured faculty moderators at campus political forums; and (3) "an effective student voice in the regulations and policies which affect us." Instead, protest leaders were "getting the ax" from vindictive administrators, who used them as "hostages" in a crude attempt to crush the movement.[13]

These cogent narratives by the speakers who preceded him almost certainly influenced the character of Savio's remarks at the December 2 rally. The "bodies upon the gears" speech was one of the few he gave that did not explore the free speech or due process issues at the heart of the dispute. He did not even mention the disciplinary offensive that provoked the sit-in. Savio's previous speeches, together with FSM newsletters and leaflets, had brought out all these particulars. But the main reason he did not have to review them was that others had just done so. He was the last FSM leader to speak—preceded by Roysher and Rossman, Steve Weissman, and student body president Charles Powell, who compounded the anger at the rally by opposing the sit-in.[14]

Savio at once embodied and transcended the FSM political milieu. Part of the reason those four most famous sentences in his "bodies upon the gears" speech had such power was because they were so universalistic. Although these defiant lines were hurled at UC officials whose free speech and due process violations the FSM had been battling for months, they soared far above these particulars. Since Savio's call to resistance was expressed metaphorically in the clash of human bodies against an "odious" machine—without naming that machine—it was language that proved transferable to many other situations where people resisted oppressive forces, which is why musicians and filmmakers still quote it when evoking the spirit of social protest.[15] He had issued a classic cry for freedom, whose power was such that it long outlived the campus struggle and the decade that produced it. Although emotionally atypical of his oratory, it was consistent with Savio's ethical approach to politics, urging individuals to stand up for their rights no matter what the odds, and in this sense his most famous words capture his moral sensibility as well as any others he uttered in the 1960s or thereafter.

Seeking to rally support for the sit-in, Savio had no inkling that his words on December 2 were destined to constitute a classic in the history of dissenting oratory. This does not mean, however, that he simply blurted out his famous lines. The speech was not entirely spontaneous. A few days before this rally Savio and Aptheker had gone to see the movie *Becket*, which explored the religious conflict between the church leader Thomas à Becket and King Henry II of England. Savio admired that way the film dealt with the "principled position" that Becket was taking, and this inspired him to focus his speech on guiding principles rather than details: As Aptheker explained, "Mario got the idea for the classic argument for civil disobedience from the film. And we actually talked about it when we came out of the movie. He didn't have the language yet" for the speech, but he had decided to explain his thinking about the central ideas that justified defying unjust authority. "He said, 'That's what I'm going…to talk about.'"[16]

The most powerful image evoked in anger at the administration during the FSM's rally on December 2 was that depicting it as an inhumane machine. Since a similar image was used by Thoreau in his famous essay on civil disobedience it is possible—as some have claimed—that this was his inspiration. However, since Savio admired Thoreau and tended to cite classic thinkers when he borrowed from them in his speeches—and did not do so on December 2—the Thoreau connection remains speculative. It is just as likely that he opted for this image because of someone closer to home. Steering Committee member Michael Rossman was the first December 2 speaker to use that image of the administration at this FSM rally. But then again, Savio used the machine metaphor during the FSM rally on December 1, which seems to have put it back into circulation, since it immediately found its way into the FSM newsletter distributed to recruit students for the December 2 rally and sit-in.[17] The machine imagery may well be Savio's extension of the term "knowledge factory," used by Hal Draper, since in both cases industrial metaphors evoked oppression at the university. Perhaps Rossman's speech reminded Savio of this imagery's power and inclined him to use it again. This suggests that Savio was not a lone ranger but rather a creative part of a rich culture of dissent, which in turn fostered that creativity—and if he played a crucial role in inventing a new kind of political discourse, this happened with at least a little help from his friends at Berkeley, such as Draper and Rossman, along with inspiration from SNCC. Rossman's speech anticipated Savio's in its candor about the dangers students faced in confronting the machinelike university administration. Rossman's narrative attested that the administration had punished dissenters in the past, and suggested that such vindictiveness was possible, even likely, in the future:

The machinery of the administration seems to have no place in it for our protests, for these issues, for our needs.... If the machine wants to roll on we've got to stop the bloody machine. If you mess with the machine you may get hurt. The machine has already threatened the Executive Committee of the Free Speech Movement with criminal conspiracy charges if a sit-in occurs. If we walk into this building and disrupt the functioning nobody knows what's going to happen. There may be disciplinary action coming out of it, up to and including suspensions or expulsions. The police may come and take us away one-by-one. But by God if that machine is going to go on and not treat us as human beings, not listen to the 5,000 who were out in front of the Regents, not discuss any of the real issues then it's going to go on with some live human bodies sitting right inside its bowels![18]

Since most FSM speeches have been forgotten, it is not surprising that Rossman's should be among them. Still, his words were effective in warning students that they were taking on powerful forces and might well be punished for their rebelliousness. His speech had its eloquent moments, especially when appealing for solidarity with FSM leaders singled out in this latest round of disciplinary action—he reminded the crowd that they were suffering the consequences "not for what they have done but for what *we* have done."[19] But it is worth considering why this speech using the machine metaphor faded while Savio's resonated and became a famous symbol of the FSM.

The portion of Rossman's speech invoking the machine metaphor was twice as long but not half as elegant as Savio's. Rossman was inconsistent in the way he used the metaphor. Although a machine is by definition without a will of its own, he spoke of it as if it had historical agency, saying that the "machine wants to roll on." He told the crowd the machine had made threats against FSM leaders, something no piece of industrial apparatus could do. This problem was compounded near the end of his speech when he again blurred the line between machines and living beings by urging students to sit inside the machine's "bowels," a biological image that was not merely ill chosen regarding machinery but also unappealing. In contrast, Savio was precise in his use of language, consistent in employing the machine metaphor, using that imagery on two levels. The machine served first to contrast the inhumanity of the institution the FSM was battling with the humanity of the movement struggling for freedom. The second machine reference concerned its impact on the movement, on the consciences of the activists battling it. This was the inspiring part that paid tribute to the human spirit, noting that despite the risks, students took a stand against the "operation of the machine."[20]

This "bodies upon the gears" phrase might at first glance seem masochistic, setting up the rebels as martyrs to be crushed by the machine as they sought to stop it. But Savio's speech—unlike Rossman's—retained historical agency on both sides of the campus barricades. In the dramatic conclusion to his speech's most famous section, Savio made it clear that humans were in charge. The battle was targeted less at the machine itself than at "the people who run it...the people who own it." The movement had to demonstrate to them (in this case the Board of Regents, the governor, and their corporate benefactors) "that unless you're free the machine will be prevented from working at all"—that human resistance had the potential to overcome inhumane oppression.[21] So in the end this was a *human* battle, fought between people of conscience willing to take risks and a repressive elite, a battle that could only be won (though he never used the word "win" in his speech) through the solidarity of people insisting on their freedom.

He was urging an act of moral witness. It was more about doing right than about winning, which was consistent with Savio's view that politics ought to be about ethics rather than efficiency. He predicted neither success nor failure from the steps that day. It would have been irresponsible to have predicted either, since the FSM's history by then included both successful protests, such as the police car blockade, and failures, most notably the aborted sit-in. Since Rossman had just outlined the dangers of expulsion and arrest, Savio could not have papered over the risks, the possibility of failure, even had he wanted to.[22] And Savio, who admired and had been shaped by SNCC's tradition of factually grounded discourse, never would have wanted to mislead his fellow activists. He left it unsettled as to whether the machine would be stopped by bodies being crushed or by facing down the operators of the machine, as had occurred back on October 1 when the police turned the squad car off and submitted to the crowd surrounding it.

The closest Savio came in the December 2 speech to predicting success was when he said that "one thousand people sitting down someplace, not letting anybody by, not letting anything happen, can stop any machine, including this machine, and it will stop!"[23] But he did not pretend to know how long the sit-in could halt the UC machine or with what consequences for the protesters. There was no reason to doubt that an army of police would be called to campus, as it had been back in October. Savio implicitly acknowledged the danger, telling the crowd that the larger the number of people joining in the sit-in, "the safer they'll be and the more effective it will be."[24]

In discussing civil disobedience, Savio emphasized the difficult struggle that lay ahead. He explained the "two ways in which sit-ins and civil disobedience...can occur." The first way, the one with the greatest assurance of success, was "when a law exists, is promulgated which is totally unacceptable to people and they violate it again and again until it is rescinded, repealed." But in Berkeley the struggle was far broader than merely working to repeal a law, since the administration asserted not merely legal but intramural and institutional authority to restrict student rights—and could do so without according dissident students the due process protections that even criminals received in the courts. So students had to find "another way" to get justice. Thus Savio told the crowd that "sometimes the form of the law is such as to render impossible its effective violation as a method to have it repealed. Sometimes the grievances of people…extend…to more than just the law, extend to a whole mode of…arbitrary exercise of arbitrary power. And that's what we have here."[25] In response he urged students to occupy the administration building until those rights were restored.

The candor and open-endedness of the speech helped make it seem authentic, free of spin and pretense. Unlike the oratory of mainstream politicians, which tended to be triumphalist—promising great gains and easy victories and evoking American optimism—Savio's words set a different tone, foreshadowing a kind of David-and-Goliath struggle. He elevated moral conscience over brute force, choosing to do right regardless of the consequences. Having spent the summer battling Mississippi's segregationist power structure and the fall opposing UC's powerful administration, he knew what it meant to be an underdog, and spoke about it in a way that valorized the struggle while being realistic about the array of forces that stood in the way of its triumph.

It would be difficult to imagine a speech that could do more to motivate students to act boldly, even heroically. Some FSM veterans view his speech as crucial in inspiring them to occupy Sproul Hall, among them Michael Lerner, who though an FSM Executive Committee member "wasn't sure about going into Sproul Hall to risk arrest until Mario Savio gave his now famous speech [that] exhorted us to…stand up for our beliefs, to give witness against oppression." Jackie Goldberg, though threatened by one of the disciplinary letters, initially thought that sitting in was "the wrong idea…the wrong time…I was not going in there." But Savio's speech convinced her "that there were certain injustices that you didn't allow to happen. And it didn't matter…whether you really won or not…[Y]ou can resist, you can say 'no.'"[26]

In looking back on the December 2 protest, Goldberg said she wished she

had a dime for every person who walked into that building who had come to that rally not intending to sit in…people who went in who were only on their way to lunch when this happened but [decided to join]…because Mario had given that speech that just lifted us four or

five inches off the ground. And that whole business about my feet. I told
my feet "no" and they went in anyway. We all felt that way to some extent
or another.[27]

Not all FSMers went so far in crediting his speech for the success of the sit-
in. Michael Rossman, for example, though acknowledging that "Mario was vital
to us"—the FSM's "touchstone" and "moral rudder"—insisted that "I didn't
go into Sproul Hall because of Mario. Most of the people I know didn't go in
because of Mario. We would have been in without Mario."[28] Yet Rossman was
an FSM leader; he had already voted for the sit-in, as had his circle of friends
in the leadership, who were hardly typical of the thousand students who sat in.
As such, he was not in position to assess the impact that Savio's speech had in
convincing rank-and-filers to overcome their fears of arrest.

Still, Rossman made an important point in suggesting that most protesters
came to Sproul on December 2 because of their anger over UC's heavy-handed
actions against FSM leaders and the free speech violations. Had those concerns
not drawn six thousand protesters, Savio never would have had the opportunity to issue his historic appeal.[29] Those events and perceptions, more than
any speech, were keys to the sit-in's success. Savio was appealing to aggrieved
classmates, not manipulating them or thinking for them. This must be kept in
mind to avoid falling into the oversimplifications that the movement's detractors spread about his influence: As historian Lawrence Levine warned in his
memoir of Berkeley faculty politics:

We are often most satisfied with a crude picture of a simple world—leader
and led, preacher and convert, manipulator and manipulated. This alas
was the image too many faculty had of what was transpiring: Mario as a
rabble rouser mesmerizing gullible students. In fact, Mario was carrying
on a *dialogue* with students who came to listen to him *because* many of
them were already aroused.[30]

Ultimately one can never measure with complete precision the impact that a
speech has on a crowd of protesters. But Savio's speech was the only one at the
rally repeatedly interrupted by enthusiastic applause; his words helped, as Goldberg and Lerner attest, some demonstrators overcome their reservations about
sitting in, and the speech has long been remembered as the Berkeley revolt's
most eloquent oration. Even Kerr acknowledged that Savio "was obviously a
genius at understanding crowds, appealing to them, and handling situations
like that—and quite beyond the capacity of any of us in the administration."[31]
This suggests that his speech played an important—though not necessarily

decisive—role in the sit-in's success. One ought not fall into an either-or trap on this, that either the speech magically made the sit-in work or it did not matter at all. The reality was that in the wake of the movement's most notable failure, the aborted sit-in, the FSM needed to be at its best as it sought to reconnect to masses of students, and with Savio at his most eloquent and Joan Baez adding inspiring folk music and a touch of celebrity, the movement certainly did rise to the occasion on December 2.

The success of both the speech and the rally was due in part to a team effort by the FSM leadership. By recounting the movement's grievances, the first FSM speakers at the rally liberated Savio from the burden of detailing the sins of the administration, enabling him to explore radical themes and go to the root of the problem, the university's undemocratic governance, which he believed had led to all these abuses:

> We have an autocracy which...runs this university. It's managed! We were told the following: If President Kerr actually tried to get something more liberal out of the regents in his telephone conversation, why didn't he make some public statement to that effect? And the answer we received, from a well meaning liberal, was the following: He said, "Would you ever imagine the manager of a firm making a statement publicly in opposition to his board of directors?" That's the answer! Now I ask you to consider: If this is a firm, and if the board of regents are the board of directors, and if President Kerr in fact is the manager, then I'll tell you something, the faculty are a bunch of employees and we're the raw materials![32]

This was one of the most scathing indictments of an academic administration ever heard on a university campus. It was also a radical analysis delivered in a disarmingly undogmatic manner, a hybrid form of discourse, a combination of SNCC and Savio. It begins in the typical SNCC style with unadorned narrative (where he recounts the conversation with a "well meaning liberal") but moves from the empirical to the theoretical, using metaphors to evoke the undemocratic nature of university decision making. In this respect Savio— much as he liked to credit SNCC for his speaking style—was adding a whole other dimension of critical symbolism (in this case with a metaphor of the university as hierarchical corporation), transcending the narrative oratory he had imbibed in Mississippi. Even the way he draws conclusions has the ring of a philosophy student tracking down a formulation in logic ("if...if... if...then") rather than an ideologue making pronouncements. These Savio lines call to mind something John Searle noted about the "typical Mario speech" having "a kind of freshness which combines an awareness of the problem that he can state in an ordinary, commonsense, nonintellectual level with a certain deep intellectual vision."[33] Even though Searle, because he disliked its irate tone, did not think this speech fit his description, it really did. Savio was using the simple imagery of businesses, machines, and raw materials to relay some complex ideas about hierarchy and the university.

Read together with his other late FSM discourse, it becomes evident that although Savio's indictment of the university administration on December 2 was not explicitly anticapitalist—the word "capitalism" never appeared in the speech—it imparted an anticapitalist sensibility. The university was on the verge of dissolving as a community of scholars because it had taken on the characteristics of a business corporation, and he meant this in a negative sense, arguing that it had resulted in a tyrannical cadre of professional managers. Instead of maintaining an academic community dedicated to the pursuit of truth, Kerr "divides the university community into the managed and the managers. The managers are the administration and the managed is everybody else."[34] Kerr's corporate university led to dictatorship by the few (university administrators) over the many (students and faculty) in a way that paralleled nonunion factories, whose workers had no voice in their working lives.[35]

Savio thought it especially worrisome that those with absolute power over the university were administrators and regents, since he saw them as an external force lacking any genuine claim to membership in the university community. That community's mission was the pursuit of truth via teaching, learning, and research, intellectual activities undertaken by faculty and students, not by bureaucrats. The proper role of the administration was that of servant to the university, not dictator over it. So in university governance, Savio concluded, "the administration is to take an ancillary role, assistance...maintaining sidewalks clean, seeing that there are good building...But the important matters of educational policy and the regulation of speech and to its form, these are matters for the university community and not for the administration."[36] Administrators were the last people one would want presiding over decisions regarding free speech since, in Savio's words, they maintained "an intimate connection with the financial community" and conservative legislators—and so "can't tolerate" militant student activism that would "rock the boat."[37]

In calling for a university freed from the corruption of money, Savio looked not to some revolutionary future but to the preindustrial past. He claimed that when it came to the university ideal, "it turns out that we're the traditionalists," preserving freedom and a critical distance between campus and the business world, while Kerr, in seeking to convert the university into a knowledge factory, was the "revolutionist."[38] Both inside Sproul in his remarks during the FSM's final sit-in (later published as the essay "An End to History") and in his mid-December speech "The Berkeley Knowledge Factory," Savio declared that "our conception of the university, suggested by a classical Christian formulation, is that it be in the world but not of the world." This he contrasted to Kerr's conception of the university as something that "stands to serve the need of…industry."[39]

The university community should be self-governing, and to Savio this meant "those people who run the university are faculty, in consultation with and giving responsible voice to students." Faculty and students as teachers, learners, and researchers had the most direct stake in academic and political freedom on the campus. They thrived and depended on the free exchange of ideas, the lifeblood of the university. It was they who should be entrusted with decisions regarding freedom of speech.[40]

In accusing the UC knowledge factory of treating students like "a bunch of raw materials," Savio was harkening back to imagery he had used back at the first free speech sit-in on September 30.[41] Then he had criticized the knowledge factory as operating "just like any factory in any industry," processing products for the market, but in this case it was the students themselves who were manufactured into "a certain product…They go in on one side as kind of rough-cut adolescents, and they come out the other side pretty smooth…prepared to leave the university" and be absorbed by "various businesses." Whether the metaphor was "product" (September 30) or "raw materials" (December 2), Savio underscored the dehumanizing impact of an increasingly vocational and market-driven university, which was narrowing its role from education to mere training, stifling individuality and dissent.[42]

Students would not stand by while they were made into objects by that factory. On December 2 Savio defiantly predicted student insurgency: "we're a bunch of raw materials that don't mean to…have any process upon us, don't mean to be made into any product, don't mean…to end up being bought by some clients of the university, be they the government, be they industry, be they organized labor, be they anyone! We're human beings!"[43]

Savio's lines about stopping the machine are so dramatic that they have become equated in historical memory with the entire speech. While its most lyrical phrases have proven enduring, the bulk of the speech has not been widely quoted or remembered because it was too particularistic to transcend the Berkeley milieu.

In his opening Savio criticized the previous speaker, Charlie Powell, Berkeley's student government (ASUC) president, who so opposed the sit-in that he recruited strikebreakers in case the TAs walked out in support of the sit-in. Savio regarded Powell as a sell-out who typified the fraternity-dominated student government, which almost never took positions on off-campus political issues, instead specializing in childish "sandbox" pseudo-politics. The crowd jeered Powell after his anti-sit-in speech. Savio dispensed with Powell by challenging his legitimacy as a leader, terming him "the nominal head of an organization supposedly representative of undergraduates whereas in fact under the Kerr directives [UC's regulations regarding student government] it derives its...delegated power from the administration." Worse, because the administration had barred graduate students from voting in ASUC elections, Powell's student government was, in Savio's words, "totally unrepresentative of graduate students and TAs."[44]

Having questioned Powell's credibility, Savio did not dissect the ASUC leader's arguments, and failed to refute them with evidence, breaking with his usual style of political discourse. Instead, Savio let the anger of the moment get the better of him. Telling the crowd that he "didn't want to spend too much time" on Powell because his opinions were not "important enough" to merit extensive attention, Savio simply denounced him as "a strikebreaker and a fink."[45] This reflected his frustration with the ongoing problem of contending with a student government that refused to stand up to the administration. The lack of solidarity that traditional student institutions—both the ASUC and the campus newspaper, the *Daily Californian*—displayed toward the FSM meant that the movement had to create an alternative student voice. This situation had prevailed since the FSM's birth, but to have the ASUC president opposing the movement at this crucial moment infuriated Savio. Still, the irate and ad hominem manner in which he mocked Powell rendered his words ugly rather than inspiring, and made them as forgettable as Powell's own remarks. This was the one part of his speech where Heirich's conclusion about stridency interfering with rational discourse applied.

The Powell reference evokes not only Savio's anger but his sense that the FSM was institutionally isolated, even after months of protest. This sense of isolation applied not only to the student government but also to the labor movement and the press. Savio expressed regret that a local union had not responded to FSM calls to pull its painters out of Sproul for the sit-in. But for the sake of unity between the labor and student movements he insisted that these workers "not be heckled in any way."[46] He was less kind to the press, taking aim at the *San Francisco Examiner*, which had just finished running sensationalistic articles Red-baiting the FSM. Imagining how that paper would twist his words, he told the crowd that his language about stopping the machine "doesn't mean—and it will be interpreted to mean unfortunately by the bigots who run the *Examiner* for example—...that you have to break anything."[47]

Savio did not say much about the faculty in his famous speech, and what he did say was unflattering, embodying the movement's sense of disappointment over the professors' slowness to stand up for free speech. He contrasted the powerful "autocracy which runs this university" with the impotent faculty, reduced to "a bunch of employees." He was implicitly critical of the faculty for failing to initiate genuine learning, so the students who were sitting in would have to make up for this deficiency:

> We'll do something that hasn't occurred at this university in a good long time. We're going to have *real classes* up there. There are going to be freedom schools conducted up there. We're going to have classes on [the] First and Fourteenth Amendments! We're going to spend our time learning about the things this university is afraid that we know. We're going to learn about freedom up there. And we're going to learn by doing![48]

Here Savio was issuing a kind of declaration of independence—of dissenting students from a repressive administration and a timid, educationally ineffective faculty. The movement would provide students with its own model of liberation, prefiguring the kind of university it hoped to build. By sitting in they would stop the university machine and build something better: "We're going to…march up to the second floor of Sproul Hall. And we're going to conduct our lives for a while in the second floor of Sproul Hall." The protesters would show controversial movies that reactionaries had wanted to censor, discuss student rights in a way that the university had been afraid to, hold "*real classes*," and learn "about freedom up there" by exercising their rights—as he put it, they were going to "learn by doing."[49] Savio's speech evoked joy and idealism about students taking command of their lives, freeing themselves though an act of civil disobedience and educational revolution, teaching themselves about things that really mattered.

Savio ended his speech outside Sproul Hall by introducing Joan Baez. The popular folksinger sang freedom songs, including a reprise of a song she had sung at a previous rally, Bob Dylan's "The Times They Are a-Changin.'" The gender dynamics of these pivotal moments in the rally are striking. All the students who spoke at the rally were male, symbolizing the movement's prefeminist sexual politics. Though the FSM was egalitarian enough to include women in its leadership team, it lacked the feminist sensibility that would have made it obvious how unbalanced it was to have no female FSM leaders speak at this important rally. Baez's was the lone female voice at the rally. She played a role that accorded with her own pacifism but also with traditional gender roles: that is, after male speakers revved up the crowd's anger, so as to incite and justify mass civil disobedience, Baez gently calmed things down in the name of love.

After singing her first song, Baez told the crowd as they prepared to march into Sproul Hall:

> The only thing that occurs to me, seeing all you people there—I don't know how many of you intend to come inside with us—but that is that you muster up as much love as you possibly can, and as little hatred and as little violence, and as little "angries" as you can—although I know it's been exasperating. The more love you can feel, the more chance there is for it to be a success.[50]

As the rally ended, Savio too adopted this calmer tone, urging that students walk slowly into Sproul, which they did, giving the procession an almost religious solemnity—protesters not storming the building but entering in a dignified manner while singing "We Shall Overcome," following the amplified sound of Baez's angelic voice. Baez, Savio, and the other FSM speakers tapped into a powerful sense of idealism concerning freedom, democracy, and student rights, activated by a semester of grievances against the administration. More than a thousand protesters marched into Sproul Hall.[51]

Marching into Sproul was, in Rossman's words, "a proclamation, a petition, a solemn event." The rally was not spontaneous, and in this respect it was quite different from the police car blockade. As Rossman recalled, "We structured the rally" in such a way as to make it "the proper setting for a formal occasion. It *was* a formal occasion....Joan Baez was part of the proper framework" for this culminating protest, "like having the American flag there...Our muse sang a bit and walked in."[52]

The size of the sit-in exceeded Savio's expectations and those of the rest of the FSM leadership. Even while the threat of mass arrests loomed, the atmosphere of the sit-in was joyful, with films, singing, and dancing in the normally staid corridors of the administration building. A local newspaper referred to the sit-in as the Sproul Hall "hootenanny."[53]

Savio may have been, along with Joan Baez, the star of the rally preceding the sit-in, but once inside Sproul Hall he was just a part of the leadership team. The Steering Committee was overseeing about a thousand protesters on four floors of Sproul. The committee used monitors to keep the occupation orderly— ensuring that the crowds left aisles on each floor, arranging to make food accessible, opening communication (via walkie-talkies) with FSMers outside, and coordinating educational and social activities inside the building. Every few hours the FSM leaders would steal away to a secluded spot to meet and take stock of the protest.[54] All this organizational work impressed the *San Francisco Chronicle*, which noted that "with the sort of efficiency not often found in the military the demonstrators quickly designated the third and fourth floors as study areas. The second floor became the headquarters, the lobby a recreation room and first aid station. Eventually tables were set up in the lobby to feed the sit-in troops."[55]

Although the occupation was more a time for action than for words, Savio's oratory continued to resonate. Protesters jimmied open a window on the second-floor balcony so he could address the crowd outside, which according to the press was about a thousand strong. Appealing to the crowd to join the sit-in or help build the student-TA sympathy strike, he predicted that police likely would be sent in to break up the sit-in: "I want you to think about them taking (students) off campus in paddy wagons."[56]

The FSM helped spotlight the need for educational reform by following through on the promise in Savio's speech that the sit-in would set up Freedom Schools and hold "real classes." Sessions convened under the banner of the "Free University of California," with graduate students teaching sociology, literature, math, and Latin American history. Jack Weinberg led a session on civil disobedience, a local filmmaker lectured on the cinema as art, and San Francisco poet Gary Snyder taught about American poetry. Even the *San Francisco Examiner* grudgingly acknowledged this educational energy, running an editorial cartoon depicting a UC rebel standing on his classroom chair and interrupting his professor by insisting, "I'll do the teaching around here!"[57]

The electric atmosphere in Sproul impacted Savio. Despite the time involved in leading the sit-in, the chaotic environment, and the tensions of what seemed an inevitable police invasion, he managed to elaborate on his thinking about the university, history, and his generation in remarks that would later be published as his influential essay "An End to History."[58]

Savio began "An End to History" by finding new links between the civil rights movement and the FSM. Where in September he made this connection by stressing how the free speech ban was designed to disable the civil rights movement's student wing, now he stressed the parallels between blacks in the South and students at Berkeley. "The same rights are at stake in both places—the right to participate as citizens in a democratic society and the right to due process of law." Both movements were fighting "against the same enemy. In Mississippi an autocratic and powerful minority rules, through organized violence, to suppress the vast, virtually powerless majority. In California, the privileged minority...financial plutocrats...manipulates the University bureaucracy to suppress the students' political expression."[59]

To explain this administration behavior, he argued, "it is necessary to understand the bureaucratic mentality." He probed not bureaucratic thinking in general but the mind-set of the generation of administrators that the FSM had confronted. "An End to History" is arguably the only statement Savio made during the FSM that cast the conflict in generational terms: a clash between middle-aged bureaucrats wedded to the status quo and insurgent youth dedicated to social change (allied with the black community's struggle for justice). He described the university bureaucracy as dominated by the "end of ideology" perspective left over from the 1950s, which held that in affluent cold war America all major social questions had been settled and there would never again be serious ideological conflict. All that remained was to manage this consensual society and make adjustments for technical problems. "The conception that bureaucrats have is that history has in fact come to an end. No events can occur now that the second World War is over which can change American society substantially. We proceed by standard procedures as we are."[60]

Savio contended that students "were not about to accept this a-historical point of view" because it falsely implied that American society and its campuses had reached a "final state of perfection." Instead of perfection, the hierarchical nature of the university and the racially discriminatory character of American society left college youth and blacks in America "dispossessed." Students were thrust into activism for black voting rights in the South and free speech and due process rights on campus as they came to see that such rights—though they had "a deceptively quaint ring"—"are not being taken seriously in America today."[61] History, Savio insisted, had not ended. Students of the sixties would make history by challenging both racism and universities "autocratically run by unresponsive bureaucrats":

> After a long period of apathy during the fifties students have begun not only to question but, having arrived at answers, to act on those answers. This is part of a growing understanding...in America that history has not ended, that a better society is possible and that it is worth dying for....The most exciting things going on in America today are movements to change America.[62]

As if it were not enough to announce the coming of age of a new generation of student rebels, Savio concluded "An End to History" by defining the new form of alienation fueling this rebellion. Savio built on the analysis he had begun to articulate in the first Sproul sit-in about an existential crisis spreading on campus. "The university is well structured, well tooled," he complained, "to turn out people with all the sharp edges worn off...[to] suppress the most creative impulses that they have [since] this is a prior condition for being part of the system."[63] This was not humane education but dehumanizing training. It met only the narrow needs of corporate America, since to function well there, professionals such as "lawyers, ministers, businessmen, people in government...often must compromise those principles which were most dear to them." The university made conformists out of students who came to campus not yet having "learned to compromise, who...have come to the university to learn to question, to grow, to learn—all the standard things that sound like clichés because no one takes them seriously." This alienates many students, rendering them "strangers in their own lives," grooming them for hollow jobs in "intellectual and moral wastelands." Unless this educational system was changed, students would never have the opportunity to realize their most creative impulses. Instead they would "grow up to be well-behaved children" in a "chrome-plated consumers' paradise."[64]

Savio closed "An End to History" by saluting students who dissented from this system, "the important minority of men and women coming to the front today [who] have shown that they will die rather than be standardized, replaceable, and irrelevant."[65]

Savio had defined the ways the university left undergraduates deprived politically, psychologically, and even spiritually. He seconded anarchist Paul Goodman's claim that "students are the exploited class in America subjected to all the techniques of factory methods: tight scheduling, speed ups, rules of conduct they're expected to obey with little or no say-so." Others in the New Left would later extend this concept of oppression, depicting students as a new working class rushed into white-collar jobs that lacked meaning but who had great potential to replace the blue-collar proletariat as the primary agent of social change. The thinking was that students, treated as numbers in huge universities and trained for unrewarding jobs in corporate America, were psychologically oppressed, and that this oppression was sparking alienation, an existential crisis that could yield many Berkeley-type campus insurgencies.[66]

However one judges Savio's analysis, the fact that he could engage in such critical thinking about higher education within occupied Sproul Hall attested that even if the sit-in was chaotic, it was intellectually stimulating. Judging from Kerr's memoirs, the protesters also came close to their goal of pushing the administration into a dialogue. Kerr claimed that his initial response to the sit-in was to plan a face-to-face session to talk with the students in Sproul—and to do this on the morning of December 3 together with Governor Brown. Kerr recounts two telephone calls to the governor on the evening of December 2, in which Brown agreed to this diplomatic approach.[67]

Diplomacy would not prevail, however. There are conflicting accounts as to who convinced the governor to send in the police. Vice Chancellor Sherriffs and Chancellor Strong seem to have had a hand in this process—Sherriffs by reporting (inaccurately) to a Brown aide that the protesters were becoming violent, and Strong by urging the governor to overrule Kerr and send in the police.[68] Daniel O'Connell, a commander in the California Highway Patrol, called Brown from campus police headquarters, in Sproul Hall's basement, urging mass arrests to restore order and punish those causing anarchy. O'Connell had been incensed back in October when Kerr's negotiated settlement prevented the crushing of the police car blockade. He believed the failure to make mass arrests in October had emboldened the protesters and yielded further lawlessness, culminating in the December 2 sit-in. At Brown's request, O'Connell put Alameda County assistant district attorney Edwin Meese III on the phone. Meese seconded O'Connell's call for arrests, telling the governor that "temporizing would only make the eventual blowoff more dangerous." Brown responded by authorizing the police invasion so that "there will be no anarchy, and that is what has developed at the University of California." This resulted in massive use of police power: 200 Alameda County deputy sheriffs, 150 state highway patrol officers, 50 Berkeley police, and 37 campus police mobilized to clear Sproul Hall at three o'clock in the morning on December 3.[69]

Aware that arrests were imminent, Savio and the rest of the Steering Committee strove to keep the protest nonviolent, while also seeking to prolong the process of clearing the building as much as possible so that the arrests would extend into school hours, when students and faculty, en route to classes, would witness them. Thus FSM leaders urged protesters to go limp when the police sought to arrest them, but not to lock arms, since that would have placed them at risk of getting into shoving matches.[70]

Savio was not surprised that the police had been called in, but he was furious at Strong's statement preceding the arrests. Strong was legally obliged to announce that the sit-in was in violation of the law and to urge dispersal of the protest before arrests could be made. In doing so, he sought to absolve his administration of responsibility for the Sproul debacle, implicitly blaming the FSM for the breakdown of negotiations. He tried to project an air of sweet reasonableness by claiming that "the University is always ready to discuss [differences] with students." Savio viewed Strong's statement an expression of "gross hypocrisy" since the administration had not

shown itself over a period of the semester ready to discuss with any seriousness at all, matters of significance to it, in disagreement to its policies. As a matter of fact I followed the Chancellor, hoping that…he might look at me while he was reading the statement, and I thought it might be difficult for him to read that statement and look me right in the eye. He did not look at me.[71]

It took twelve hours to evict the eight hundred protesters, whom police began dragging off to jail at 3:30 a.m. Savio was among them. Students reported considerable roughness on the part of the police, as did journalists. The *New York Times* reported that the sheriff's deputies "bumped the buttocks of their male prisoners as they dragged them down the stairs" and then joked about it. "'There'll be some sore rumps in jail tonight,' one deputy said." Savio experienced some of this personally. As police seized him, they pushed him down a flight of stairs. Asked why he had gone limp when the police seized him, he explained "at that point part of my frame of mind which kept me on the floor was anger with regard to the fashion in which police…had been used to end what I believed was a legitimate demonstration…against University regulations…of free speech and political activity on campus."[72]

Although the arrests proved physically painful for many protesters, this police invasion strengthened the FSM by angering much of the UC community. Savio realized this immediately, and was quoted by the *Times* shouting gleefully as he was arrested: "This is wonderful.…We'll bring the university to our terms." Steering Committee member Art Goldberg was equally pleased, saying as the police took him away: "Good! The kids have learned more about democracy here than they could learn in 40 years of classes. This is a perfect example of how the State of California plays the game."[73] The mass arrests turned student opinion against the administration, ensuring that the TA strike and student boycott of classes would be effective.

For the media it was the FSM's sit-in rather than Savio's now famous words that were the big news. It represented the most massive act of civil disobedience ever seen on a university campus in the United States and resulted in the largest number of arrests in the history of American higher education. Photos of the police invading Sproul Hall and students being dragged out appeared in newspapers from coast to coast.

No leading paper included all of the lines for which Savio would become known. Though getting his point about preventing the machine from operating, they mangled his words. The *New York Times* reported him saying, "The time has come to put our bodies on the machine and stop it.…We will stay until the police remove us," sentences he never uttered.[74] Savio's eloquence was not initially captured by the mass media, except in a very truncated way via a TV sound bite.

More than a week after the sit-in, Savio's December 2 speech began attracting close attention. Alternative media played a critical role in spotlighting the speech and carrying it beyond the UC campus. Berkeley's listener-supported radio station, KPFA, broadcast the rally and aired a documentary on the FSM crisis. One of those who heard that documentary was Ralph J. Gleason, the *San Francisco Chronicle*'s eminent jazz critic and one of the few columnists sympathetic to the FSM. In his *Chronicle* column the week after the sit-in Gleason became the first print journalist to quote, with almost total accuracy, the most famous lines in the "bodies upon the gears" speech and to recognize their historical significance, pronouncing them "classic words of Mario Savio." Bemoaning the fact that Berkeley was the first "campus outside Mississippi to be taken over by the cops," Gleason predicted that Savio's "eloquent speech" and Joan Baez's appeal for loving protest would "remain the only rhetoric" of the Berkeley rebellion "that history will remember. Literature, poetry, and history are not made by a smooth jowl and a blue suit. They are made with sweat and passion and dedication to truth and honor."[75]

While Gleason's column did the most to call public attention to Savio's speech, the more truncated versions of Savio's words carried by the national news media played a role in making it possible for his speech to resonate beyond Berkeley. This speech and "An End to History" offered a critique of the university whose appeal would soon spread as New Left student protest became a major presence on campus, nationally and even internationally. It is worth considering, then, whether this dissident mode of viewing the academic world can stand up to critical analysis. Was its influence well deserved? Did its indictment of the university have merit in its own day and beyond?

Such questions would seem absurd to antiradical academics in 1964. The idea that serious criticism of the university could come from a militant student leader appeared far-fetched. Thus Henry May, chair of Berkeley's history department during the FSM, dismissed Savio's intellectual balance, terming him "always extreme but never sectarian, at times Messianic—and to adult ears—often skirting the edges of the ridiculous."[76]

At first glance May seems to have a point. The first criticism Savio raised about UC's governance in his speech—that "we have an autocracy which runs this university"—seems harsh. After all, Kerr, known for his moderation, had negotiated an end to the police car blockade. And Berkeley had a fairly strong system for faculty participation in university governance via its Academic Senate. Nonetheless, the administration behaved autocratically during the free speech crisis. The ban was imposed on the students unilaterally. The arrest of Weinberg came about minus faculty or student consultation with the administration. The same was true of the suspension of protest leaders in September. Plus the administration ignored the Heyman Committee's recommendations. The Thanksgiving disciplinary letters were yet another heavy-handed, unilateral administration action. Beyond Berkeley, the pattern in higher education by 1964 had been for professional administrators to dominate university governance with minimal student input. It would have been kinder to characterize the administration as unresponsive and bureaucratic rather than autocratic, but in light of all the dictatorial behavior in fall 1964 it is impossible to dismiss Savio's criticism as extreme.

The industrial images he used to characterize the university may seem overdrawn, since higher education concerns the life of the mind, unlike factories that process raw materials. However, in Berkeley the analogies between university and industry originated with Kerr, not Savio. Sounding very much like the economist that he was, Kerr had written in *Uses of the University*—his classic defense of the cold war research university—of the academic world as a central part of the "knowledge industry," celebrating the university's service to the corporate word. Decades after the FSM, Kerr insisted that Savio and Hal Draper (the socialist whose critique of Kerr influenced FSM leaders) had distorted his views, that "I never did refer to the university as a 'factory.'" Kerr objected to the image of him presented by Draper—and echoed by Savio—as the "Captain of the Bureaucracy" who had converted the university into a multiversity "parts-supply shop to the profit system and the Cold War Complex." Kerr claimed that he did not "support the development of the 'multiversity' in its entirety" but spoke out against the corporate university's "pathologies" and "tried to help correct some of them."[77]

Kerr is only half right. It is true that he never termed the university a "factory" in *Uses of the University*—and Savio erred in his September 30 speech in attributing that image to Kerr. But Kerr's "knowledge factory"/"knowledge industry" hairsplitting was a distinction without a difference, as *Uses of the University* speaks with approval, even awe, of the way the multiversity responded "to the expanding claims of national service; to merge its activities with industry as never before...By the end of this period, there will be a truly American university, an institution unique in world history, an institution not looking to other models but serving, itself, as a model for universities in other parts of the globe."[78] Kerr trumpeted the expansion of the knowledge industry as enthusiastically as an auto executive would boast about car sales, announcing in *Uses of the University* that "knowledge in all its forms is said to account for 29 percent of gross national product...and 'knowledge production' is growing at about twice the rate of the rest of the economy."[79] Kerr celebrated the university as an economic engine that made not only profits but history, transforming America's economy through knowledge production: "What the railroads did for the second half of the last century and the automobile for the first half of this century may be done for the second half of this century by the knowledge industry: that is to serve as the focal point of national growth. And the university is at the center of the knowledge process." On Kerr's pages the ivory tower was headed for extinction as "the university and segments of industry become more alike. As the university becomes tied to the world of work, the professor...takes on the characteristic of an entrepreneur....The two worlds are merging physically and psychologically."[80]

In light of Kerr's prophetic metanarrative of the university as the economic engine of this world-shaking "knowledge industry," Savio's images of the university as factory and machine seem eminently reasonable. The difference was that where Kerr saw the corporatization of the university as the realization of the American dream of prosperity, Savio saw it as an American nightmare, subordinating individuality, free speech, and the pursuit of truth to profit making—a university that served the elite and the corporate status quo instead of the disenfranchised and social justice.

Such concerns have not diminished since the 1960s. Criticism of universities morphing into corporations is made most eloquently in twenty-first-century America not by student rebels but by leading scholars of higher education, such as Sheila Slaughter and Gary Rhoades, who in *Academic Capitalism and the New Economy* (2004) argue that as "college and universities become more entrepreneurial in a postindustrial economy, they focus on knowledge less as a public good than as a commodity to be capitalized in profit-oriented activities."[81] They evoke the image of the university as processor of raw material, the same imagery Savio used on the steps of Sproul. At Berkeley the links between the corporate world and the twenty-first-century university have grown tighter and more remunerative than they were in the 1960s. In biotechnology and computer science those connections are so intimate that critics suggest that the university's research mission has been subordinated to the quest for profits. David L. Kirp, a leading scholar of that collaboration, saw the relevance of Savio's warnings about Berkeley becoming a servant of industry. "On a campus where the dean of the business school is now the 'Bank of America Dean,'" Kirp asked, "was Savio simply ahead of his time?"[82]

What distinguished Savio's critique from these other renderings of the corporate university is that he focused on the impact that this new, worldly, capitalistic multiversity had on undergraduates. Students, he feared, would be vocationally trained and politically tamed for the corporate world without ever having a chance to think for themselves or to reflect critically on corporate America and their place in it. Unless students resisted, the knowledge factory would reduce them to "product" (as Savio said on September 30) or "raw materials," (as he argued on December 2). He advocated such resistance as an affirmation of humanity: students "don't mean to be made into any product, don't mean...to end up being bought by some clients of the university...We're human beings!"[83]

Dramatic as it was, this call to rebellion had at its core a contradiction. If the university was a knowledge factory that stifled dissent, how was it that Savio and a powerful student movement had emerged from within its gates to mount such a rebellion? True, the Berkeley "knowledge factory" groomed many conformist students for the corporate marketplace, as he claimed. But it also created something Savio could not fit into his indictment of the university: the largest student rebellion in American history.

Savio's image of the university as a knowledge factory mass-producing conformists was also contradicted by his own educational experience at UC. He found great meaning in his humanities course work, majoring in philosophy and using his education in this area to crystallize his doubts about religion, enabling him to make his final break with Catholicism. His memoir even credited his Berkeley education with liberating him spiritually and spurring his political activism:

> I was a philosophy major and remained such until using my philosophical studies I had succeeded in moving completely beyond the Church. Part of the excitement of Berkeley for me was therefore the practical relevance of ideas to life—personally in my use of philosophy to free myself from religion and communally. Civil disobedience was studied in class in discussions of Socrates and Thoreau and acted out at Bay Area businesses in [civil rights] demonstrations that were frequent, massive, and successful.[84]

Savio was too clever a logician to get completely caught up in this kind of inconsistency. During the first Sproul sit-in, he initially told his fellow protesters that the "product" of the knowledge factory "is you." But he quickly corrected himself, saying that those products were "not really you. And not really me. The products are those...who wouldn't join our protest."[85] Those in the compliant student majority, not the dissenting minority, were the conformist "products" of the knowledge factory. But this still raises the question of how a university that was a soulless factory, grooming technocrats for the military-industrial complex, could produce such dissenters at all. The university has always produced pillars of the establishment, technocrats, *and* vocal critics of that same establishment, including Savio himself.

Even faculty friends of the FSM sensed the problems with Savio's negative portrayal of Berkeley education. Lawrence Levine, for example, of the Berkeley history department, commented on how in his famous Sproul speech

> Mario prophesied that when the FSM won its struggle "real teaching" would take place on the Berkeley campus for the "first time." Though

Mario with his parents
Dora and Joseph Savio,
1945.

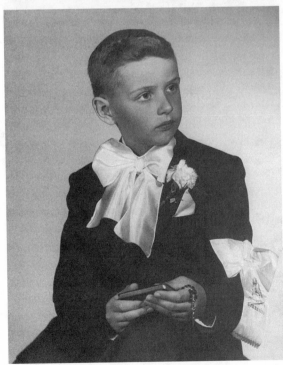

Savio at his first
communion, 1950.

Savio as a national finalist in the Westinghouse high school science competition, 1960.

Savio, the valedictorian of Van Buren High School, 1960.

Savio and Kevin Donnelan, members of Queens College volunteers doing anti-poverty work, Taxco, Mexico, summer 1963. (*Art Gatti*)

Savio in the Freedom House, Mileston, Mississippi, Freedom Summer, 1964. (*Matt Herron*)

Savio speaking from atop the police car, UC Berkeley's Sproul Plaza, Oct. 1, 1964. (*Steve Marcus, Bancroft Library collection*)

Students surrounding the police car as Savio speaks from its roof, Sproul Plaza, Oct. 1, 1964. (*L. Wilson, Bancroft Library collection*)

Committee on Campus Political Activity, left to right: Syd Stapleton, Suzanne Goldberg, Bettina Aptheker, Mario Savio, Charles Powell, Nov. 7, 1964. (*Steve Marcus, Bancroft Library collection*)

Marching through the Sather Gate en route to the Regents meeting. Savio (in coat and tie) is second from the right of the banner, Nov. 20, 1964. (*Don Kechely, Bancroft Library collection*)

Savio leading the protesters into Sproul Hall, FSM's culminating sit-in, Dec. 2, 1964. To his right, fellow FSM Steering Committee member Martin Roysher. (*Warren of SF Call, Bancroft Library collection*)

Savio with IBM card as FSM strike flyer, Dec. 1964. (*copyright Howard Harawitz*)

Police dragging Savio away from the podium at UC's Greek Theatre, Dec. 7, 1964. (*Nat Farbman, Time/Life: Getty Images*)

Savio and Jack Weinberg, 1964. (*Michael Rossman*)

Savio and Suzanne Goldberg on the their wedding day, May 1965.

Mario speaking with his oldest son Stefan, while younger son Nadav climbs over him, 1971. (*Lynne Hollander Savio*)

Mario, Suzanne, and Stefan, 1966.

Savio, as part of delegation of Campus Coalitions for Human Rights and Social Justice, marching against the California voter initiative (proposition 209) mandating the abolition of affirmative action, 1995. Barbara Epstein and Jack Kurzweil march to his left and right. (*Joseph Blum*)

Mario celebrating Chanukah with sons Nadav and Daniel, and Lynne Hollander Savio, 1995.

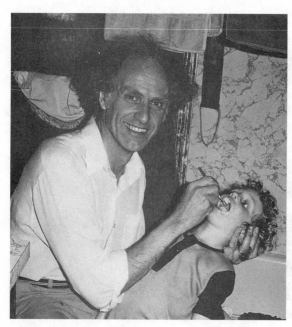

Mario with Daniel, 1985. (*Judy Mage*)

Savio with Jackie Goldberg, outside Sproul Hall during FSM Commemoration, 1994. (*Paul F. Knier*)

Mario and Lynne Hollander Savio, Belize, 1994. (*Daniel Savio*)

Savio at his office at Sonoma State University, in a press photo that ran with one of the stories about his new activism on behalf of affirmative action and immigrant rights, 1995. (*David Licht*)

I admired Savio as a leader and liked him as a person, I remember reacting negatively to...the irresponsible rhetoric of that assertion. Berkeley
had had its share of inspired teaching from the beginning, and I had not
the slightest doubt that "real teaching" went on in my classroom and
those of many of my colleagues.[86]

The indictment of the faculty is also inconsistent with Savio's own thinking
about the university ideal. He was idealistic about the faculty role in the university, arguing that professors and students—not the administration—ought
to govern the university, and in fact *were* the university. But if, as Savio put
it, the faculty had been cowed by the administration, reduced to an impotent
"bunch of employees," failing even to teach "real classes," then why should they
be entrusted with governing and defining the university?[87] Such contradictions
reflect the political milieu in which Savio gave this speech. Angry at the UC
administration for its abuses and the faculty for its diffidence, he was accentu-
ating the faculty's failings, not objectively assessing its academic performance
or political potential. And in fact, Savio's faculty friends, most notably Zelnik
and Searle, were gradually making progress in mobilizing professors on behalf
of the FSM's free speech demands.[88]

The history of the faculty's role in the free speech crisis is too complex to
be written off as a record of timidity by professors who had shrunken into "a
bunch of employees." Faculty had helped to press Kerr to negotiate with the free
speech protesters and had drafted the Pact of October 2. When Kerr and Strong
indicated that they were planning to have Savio arrested if he spoke on campus,
it was faculty who convinced the administration to back off.[89] A week before
the December 2 sit-in a professor sympathetic to the FSM brought the Levine
resolution, named for its key sponsor, Lawrence Levine, to Berkeley's Academic
Senate, asserting that

a great university, dedicated to freedom of thought and responsible citizenship, cannot deny its students the full exercise on campus of the rights
guaranteed...under the First and Fourteenth Amendments. The University's regulation of such activities should extend no further than is necessary to prevent undue interference with other University activities.[90]

The Levine resolution did not pass when it was first introduced in the Academic Senate in late November. This was because a majority of the faculty
were still too uncomfortable with the FSM's confrontational style to endorse
the movement's demands. The vote should not, however, be taken as a sign of
faculty timidity. The same Academic Senate meeting that rejected the Levine

resolution lashed out at the administration on the faculty academic freedom case of Eli Katz. The German department and the Academic Senate's Privilege and Tenure Committee had voted for Katz's promotion, but Strong refused to promote him because he would not cooperate with the House Committee on Un-American Activities. So the Academic Senate voted overwhelmingly, 267–79, to condemn the administration's "disregard of and contempt for the Academic Senate and its duly constituted committee system."[91]

While too dismissive of the faculty, Savio was not totally off base in the unflattering reference he made on December 2 to the politics of the Berkeley professoriate. True, senior faculty had stood up to the administration on the Katz case. But as Levine recalled, this "dichotomous behavior" of standing up for Katz and the faculty's freedom but not for student free speech was "evidence of the faculty myopia that…pervaded the campus: sensitivity to its own rights and insensitivity toward those of students." Regarding the FSM, the faculty had been less timid than Savio implied, since they were, as Levine recalled, "working behind the scenes with the Administration trying to carve out a compromise." But even the style of such well-intentioned intervention contributed to the crisis, for as Levine explained, "My senior colleagues were far more comfortable operating through the maze of administrative committee dialectics than openly and publicly. This *sub rosa* activity created a sense of drift and confusion."[92]

While Savio and most of the FSM leadership "craved faculty support" for their demands, they realized during the first months of the free speech crisis that such support was confined to a courageous but ineffective faculty minority. It would take the crisis that grew out of the culminating sit-in to mobilize the faculty at last—which coalesced thanks to the efforts of the dissident faculty "Committee of 200"—and align it with the FSM. But on the eve of that sit-in Savio's sense of disappointment with the faculty reflected their failure to take Kerr and Strong to task for restricting free speech. "The lack of an open faculty role," recalled Levine "made the massive sit-in…inevitable. If the faculty had become more involved openly and volubly they could have played a decisive role before we had to endure the agony of the sit-ins and the arrests." Levine seconded Savio's later reflection that "the saddest thing about" UC was "the continuing reluctance of faculty to defend the rights of students…Berkeley students have been forced to desperate acts because their professors repeatedly have failed them."[93]

Savio's indictment of the faculty's educational shortcomings, though one-sided, was far from groundless. Nor was his prediction that learning would be enhanced by the FSM and its efforts at educational reform. If we think back to Savio's pre-FSM alienation from his courses at Berkeley—expressed in his letter home during his first semester at UC—it is evident that his FSM rhetoric did correspond with the negative side of his academic experience. He had, back as a first-year student, felt so stultified by courses that seemed rushed and rote that he was on the verge of dropping out of Berkeley.[94] While Kerr celebrated the modern university's service to multiple constituencies—government, industry, the military, the alumni—Savio saw these new uses of the university as carrying it away from its obligation to students. Savio complained that faculty, concerned about their research contracts and projects, neglected undergraduate teaching. When prominent faculty did teach undergraduates, it was often in huge lecture halls where students would, as Savio put it, need "field glasses and some good luck...to glimpse that famous profile" and listen to "four- or five-year-old lectures."[95] Being given the runaround in a massive, impersonal institution of higher education by insensitive bureaucrats and distant faculty was alienating and dehumanizing. "At Cal," Savio concluded, "you're little more than an IBM card."[96]

A deep part of the FSM experience, then, for Savio was the evolving critique of the university. That critique had not created the FSM but grew with it as students became conscious first of the undemocratic governance of the university and then of the ways this lack of democracy connected with flaws in the academic side of campus life. He came to believe that too much of the curriculum "was organized around quantifiable lines," racing students through 120 units and scores of papers and exams with little time to think deeply.[97] Because of this emphasis on quantity rather than quality, "the undergraduate has become the new dispossessed; the heart has been taken out of his education."[98]

Through such criticism Savio and the FSM sparked a renewed interest in educational reform. First at Berkeley and then nationally, students, faculty, and even administrators began exploring ways to make student life less impersonal, consulting with students when the university made decisions and involving students in initiating courses. Reflecting on the way that Savio and the FSM spurred his own interest in educational reform, former Berkeley history professor Carl Schorske recalled being struck by something "Mario Savio said in an inspired moment...that had to do with flouting authority on educational grounds....That famous phrase: 'We're just a [IBM computer] card. Do not fold, spindle, or mutilate." Schorske thought that Savio's critique of the university was "vastly exaggerated," but also that it embodied a "basic truth. I felt it so personally that I thought I couldn't go on without addressing the university's impersonality towards students."[99] Similarly, Lawrence Levine credited the FSM with helping to make "the Berkeley campus...a freer, less hierarchical, more unpredictable, more diverse and far more interesting place than it had been at the beginning of the 1960s." He saw this educational impact among his own students:

One of the results of the FSM was...“academic activism” on the part of the students that helped to transform my own classroom with students actively questioning my assignments, wanting much looser deadlines, accusing me of being linear, etc. There were students who wanted to do posters rather than papers. I had a serious doctoral student who wanted to make a film rather than write a dissertation. I welcomed these interventions...as forms of involvement and debate about classroom procedures that turned my classrooms into far more dynamic places.[100]

Clark Kerr himself would admit that the Berkeley rebellion generated “a new urgency to efforts for educational and organizational reform, a new source of energy released to support those seeing new reforms, a new vitality.”[101] He had conceded in *Uses of the University* that “research, consulting, graduate instruction” were becoming “so absorbing that faculty efforts can no longer be concentrated on undergraduate instruction as they once were.” This meant that undergraduate education at Berkeley and other research universities was, as Kerr put it, “more likely to be acceptable than outstanding...The cruel paradox that a superior faculty results in an inferior concern with undergraduate teaching is one of our most pressing problems.”[102] Thus Savio was highlighting, if at times in an exaggerated way, flaws in the university and undergraduate education that even his foes began to take seriously. And given the priorities of the research university, Savio’s critique has a strikingly contemporary ring.

Savio’s indictment of the university raised issues that transcended the campus world, illuminating the ways modern bureaucracy, characterized by top-down decision making and repressive regulations, hampered genuine democracy. In “An End to History” he bemoaned the “depersonalized, unresponsive bureaucracy” that had emerged at UC as “the efficient enemy in a ‘Brave New World.’...We find it impossible to meet with anyone but...functionaries who cannot make policy but can only hide behind rules.” Although bureaucracies may “begin as legitimate...means to certain legitimate goals...they end up feeding their own existence.” Thus the university bureaucracy, even after an event as unprecedented as the thirty-two-hour blockade around the police car, refused to acknowledge that “something new had happened,” instead seeing this as just “something to be handled by normal University procedures.” The FSM found itself confronting what Savio termed “truly Kafkaesque” bureaucratic evasion and stonewalling.[103] Such antibureaucratic language would find echoes within a New Left fighting for equality and even in the New Right as it attacked the welfare state.

It would be a mistake to think of Savio as a consistent or corrosive critic of the university. He would not have taken as many risks or devoted so much time to changing the university unless he cared deeply about it. Both that concern and his aspirations for academia to serve as an engine for egalitarian change surfaced in "An End to History" when he momentarily dropped his portrait of the university as a knowledge factory and replaced it with an image of the university as a center of social criticism. "The university," he asserted, "is the place where people begin seriously to question the conditions of their existence and raise the issue of whether they can be committed to the society they have been born into."[104] It was inconsistent of him to offer even fleetingly this idealized view of the dissenting university on the same occasion when he indicted the university as the narrowest of trade schools, which stifles social criticism.

The segment of "An End to History" that was upbeat about the university's role as a center for social criticism was no slip; it was an expression of Savio's deepest hopes for higher education. The criticism of the university for which Savio is famed was fueled not by a hatred of the institution—which is what his nemesis Clark Kerr assumed based on a misreading of the "bodies upon the gears" speech—but by his vision of the university's potential to do good.[105] Weinberg recalled that within the Berkeley student movement there were "internal discussions of how…societies change" and of whether the university could be the locus of democratic reform. Weinberg was not optimistic about universities playing such a role, but Savio was. Through his involvement in the FSM, Savio was drawn to the view that you can change "the university to change society…The university trains trainers. It trains educators" who run "the educational system. Then by carrying out university reform and reform of the intellectual life of the country…changing the intellectual life of the country will change the environment and then the country will change as a result.[106]

Savio proved so scathing in denouncing university autocracy and corruption from the steps of Sproul on December 2 because he thought those failings interfered with the potential of students and the campus world to battle such social evils as racism. His anger with the university status quo was in this sense the flip side of his idealism about the university. And with the sit-in and the mass arrests creating a crisis of authority on campus, it began to seem in December 1964 that Berkeley might become a launching pad for criticism, change, even a revolution in higher education Some of the credit (or blame) for this educational ferment rests with Savio's oratory, which—whatever its flaws—raised profound questions about the university, capitalism, and freedom that still haunt American higher education.

9
"FREE SPEECH AT LAST"

The events of December 2–3, 1964, had proven that the FSM could generate mass protest, headlines, and new ideas about how the university should function. The sit-in had also shown that Savio—with his "bodies upon the gears" speech and "An End to History"—responded to the crisis at Berkeley by soaring to new heights in eloquent dissident oratory. But as Savio and his fellow protesters returned to campus after a night at the Santa Rita jail, the outcome of the free speech struggle was still uncertain. Neither Savio's famous speech, the mass sit-in, the arrests, nor the effective student strike (in which close to five thousand students and TAs picketed and at least twice that many boycotted classes to protest the Sproul Hall bust) had convinced Kerr to eliminate UC's restrictions on the content of speech. In fact, Kerr spent the days after the arrests searching for ways to deny the FSM its free speech goals. So even after all the tumult Savio and his fellow FSMers still had their work cut out for them if they were going to prevail.[1] Fortunately for the movement, Savio rose to the occasion. In terms of both political thought and action, he was at his most creative and daring during the crucial days following the sit-in.

The first campus rally Savio addressed when he got out of jail drew an immense crowd, estimated by one paper at six thousand and another at twelve thousand. The text of this speech has not survived, but its defiant tenor can been gleaned from a *San Francisco Chronicle* report that mocked Savio's "triumphant" return to Sproul Plaza, noting that "the voice was hoarse from a night of singing in jail, but it held the crowd…in its croaking spell." He was described as "unshaven, disheveled, but aflame as always with passion." Savio condemned the police invasion, which he characterized as "turning loose" on campus "people trained in sadism." He invoked the FSM ideal of a university run by teachers and students, not administrators, who should be relegated to such mundane tasks as seeing "that the sidewalks are swept." If this was accomplished, then "out of this long struggle, the University of California will be run by the University of California." Both the size of the crowd and the range of speakers—including three state legislators, faculty, and entertainers—suggested how rejuvenated the movement had become in the aftermath of the mass arrests.[2]

The arrests made their most important impact on the faculty, who were outraged that the administration had failed to end the crisis and then resorted to police action because of that failure. Some professors, including several previously indifferent to the FSM, responded by raising thousands of dollars and driving to Santa Rita to bail their students out of jail. Sympathetic faculty canceled classes on December 3, including Norman Jacobson of the political science department, who quoted Albert Camus ("by our own silence or by the stand we take, we too shall enter the fray") and told his students that after hours of witnessing "the astonishing scene at Sproul Hall" he was "incapable of violating the palpable air of protest which today surrounds every building on this campus."[3]

Sociologist Nathan Glazer canceled class so that his large lecture room in Wheeler Hall could be used for a hastily called faculty meeting. This gathering drew some eight hundred professors, probably more than had ever attended a UC faculty meeting. The administration was suddenly losing the confidence of the professoriate. Speakers at this meeting "used the word 'inept' over and over again" in criticizing Kerr and Strong's handling of the crisis. History department chair Henry May told his colleagues that "a series of provocations and reprisals...have resulted in disaster."[4] The assembled faculty, though not an official body, passed resolutions at odds with administration policy; they would have nullified the disciplinary letters that sparked the sit-in and ended all punishment for political advocacy. More than three hundred faculty signed a telegram to the governor condemning the arrests. Although there was no vote taken on it, applause greeted a call for Chancellor Strong's resignation.[5]

The administration's initial response to the arrests was hard-line. In contrast to Kerr's recent memoir, in which he casts himself as a peacemaker, his public posture in December 1964 was complete support for the mass arrests. On December 3 Kerr issued his harshest statement on the FSM, calling the sit-in an "attempt at anarchy."[6] He charged that during the sit-in protesters vandalized former UC president Robert Sproul's office, where "the files were opened and the contents were strewn about the room." Actually, as Sproul's secretary soon admitted, no such break-in occurred; Sproul simply kept a messy office.[7] Ignoring the movement's nonviolence and commitment to racial equality, Kerr likened the FSM's lawlessness to the Ku Klux Klan's. "This nation is devoted to freedom under the law, not to anarchy under a willful minority, whether that minority be radical students in the North or white supremacists in the South."

Rather than expressing regrets about the mass arrests, Kerr gloated about the punishment that awaited FSMers:

> The FSM and its leaders...are now finding that in their effort to escape the gentle discipline of the university they have thrown themselves into the arms of the less understanding discipline of the community at large. They have asked that they be subject only to external law and external courts. They are learning that the community is no more sympathetic with anarchy than the university they so violently condemn.[8]

Despite this tough talk, Kerr quickly found himself in a weakened position politically on campus. The large, irate faculty meeting of December 3 had rejected Strong's disciplinary actions and criticized restrictions on political advocacy on campus that Kerr himself had endorsed. Strong was in no position to defend himself, since he was physically and psychologically spent, and removed himself from the campus scene, claiming that he had taken ill with a gallbladder attack. Several groups of faculty, recognizing that a political vacuum had arisen, began pushing their own solutions to the crisis—and all of them backed some change in administration policy. Kerr aligned himself with the most moderate of these groups, the newly formed council of department chairmen, for even though it called for amnesty for the protesters, the chairs' proposed settlement would have preserved regulations barring on-campus advocacy of unlawful protests. Kerr was now, for the first time, facing a faculty revolt on top of the student revolt, and he hoped to keep a lid on it by governing via the department chairmen.[9]

Together with these department chairs, Kerr planned his answer to the TA/student strike. Like the insurgents, he proved willing to halt the university's academic work for his cause. He suspended morning and early afternoon classes on Monday, December 7 so thousands of students and faculty could attend a universitywide meeting in Berkeley's outdoor amphitheater, the Greek Theatre. This meeting was intended to defuse the campus crisis by imposing the department chairs' settlement. Once again Savio took center stage in one of the FSM's most dramatic confrontations.[10]

Instead of ending the free speech controversy, however, the Greek Theatre meeting generated a free speech crisis of its own over Savio's right to address it. Prior to this meeting, Savio approached Kerr, requesting permission to speak. An evasive Kerr told Savio that he lacked the authority to grant his request since "this meeting isn't being run by me but by the council of department chairmen." Savio objected that it "wasn't completely honest" to hold a meeting to discuss the free speech crisis while "excluding one of the parties in the dispute." But Kerr refused to budge, replying that if Savio wanted access to the podium, he had "to speak to the department chairmen."[11] So Savio appealed to Robert Scalapino, who headed the council of department chairmen. Scalapino, a critic of the FSM, turned him down. Savio would later see the humor in this exchange, and recounted it for an appreciative student audience:

> Professor Scalapino said "Well no, you see [you can't speak at this meeting]…"This will be a structured meeting not an open forum."…We argued with him.…He said, "… It is a faculty meeting. You're a student. It's really not appropriate for you to speak at that meeting." Well just then to my left was Professor John Leggett [an FSM sympathizer]…And he said to Scalapino, "I'm a faculty and I'd like to speak at the meeting. Can I speak at that meeting?" And…Scalapino said "It's a structured meeting not an open forum. It would really be inappropriate." [Laughter] The meeting was not an open forum. We were clear on that by then. [Laughter] We fought it out for a while [but Scalapino refused to reconsider].[12]

Savio challenged the authority of Scalapino and the other department chairs to make proposals without consulting the Academic Senate, implying that this represented an end run around that body and a slap at faculty self-government.[13] In retrospect it seems incredible that Kerr and Scalapino believed that after all the turmoil, mass arrests, and a student strike, they could impose a final settlement of the FSM crisis without consulting the FSM, or even convene a mass meeting on this crisis without including an FSM speaker. This was a recipe for disaster—at least for the administration—and what unfolded was a meeting that was, as columnist Ralph Gleason noted, appropriately housed in the Greek Theatre because it was a genuine tragedy.[14]

Kerr touted the event as designed "to inaugurate a new era of freedom under law," but he offered the fifteen thousand students and faculty gathered there little that was new.[15] He and the department chairs made only one concession to the FSM: withdrawing the Thanksgiving disciplinary letters. In the wake of the mass arrests, however, this did not amount to much since the FSM leaders targeted by these letters, along with hundreds of others arrested at Sproul, now faced the far more daunting prospect of paying for their free speech activism with fines or jail time as the sit-in case went to trial.

Since the department chairmen's proposed settlement would have maintained the restrictions on advocacy that the FSM had been battling, Scalapino and Kerr were at several points in their speeches loudly booed by the throngs of FSM supporters and sympathizers at the Greek Theatre. It did not help matters that Scalapino opened the meeting with a speech that oozed condescension toward the FSM. The political scientist was too angry to be gracious. Rather than conceding that the protesters had braved arrest for a cause that at least they found worthy, he depicted the movement's leaders as "fomenting a crisis merely for the sake of crisis—in the hope that continuing chaos will bring about a total revolution and their own particular concept of utopia."[16]

Even decades later, Kerr had bitter memories of the hostile way FSMers responded to him. Though Kerr proudly recalled his sympathizers in the audience giving him "a standing ovation," he was furious about the jeering. In his memoir he charged that this "unfriendly response" was part of a plot "coordinated by walkie-talkies from the leaders to their lieutenants scattered through the crowd. A very professional orchestration."[17] Actually, there was no such orchestration. None was needed, since the hundreds of students who had been dragged out of Sproul Hall and jailed were already enraged at Kerr over the policies that had led to their arrest.

The jeering proved to be the least of Kerr's problems that day. After a semester of fighting for the right to speak freely, Savio—along with fellow FSMers Aptheker and Tom Miller—refused to allow this universitywide meeting on student rights to end without a student voice being heard. As Kerr and Scalapino gave their speeches, Savio declared to Miller, "You know, I'm going to speak."[18] Savio, Aptheker, and Miller conferred from their seats in the Greek Theatre about how Savio could gain access to the podium.[19]

The fate of the FSM at this moment was, as Savio later conceded, "touch and go," since if Kerr succeeded in imposing the department chairs' solution, it would spell defeat for the free speech fight. He regarded Kerr's speech at the Greek Theatre as awful, "kind of half and half fabrication and platitude," and totally unresponsive "to any of the things that we had said" about the need for free speech. Kerr seemed concerned only with symptoms, ending the "campus chaos," while refusing to deal with the causes of that chaos, the restrictions the university had imposed upon advocacy.[20]

So it seemed crucial to challenge Kerr and his faculty allies. The Greek Theatre was a fabulous setting for this challenge since so many students and faculty were present, and because of the way authority was displayed there. Savio regarded the symbolism of the Greek Theatre gathering as "beautiful." Onstage they had "*baronial* chairs and sitting on them were the department heads. The chairs on the chairs...were like barons."[21]

Savio's initial thought was that after Kerr spoke and the official program ended he would race up to the microphone, having Miller "run interference with the faculty members on the stage," which meant that Miller would "leap up onto the platform, and get everyone around him while Mario got to the microphone."

Aptheker disapproved of this, thinking it would look too aggressive and "come over bad." Instead she told Savio, "You ought to see if you can get the people to *call* you to speak." She suggested he "walk up slowly'" to the podium just after the program ended, and since students would want him to speak and would call out to him, his taking the podium would seem a natural and logical act: "Just walk up to the microphone, No one's going to stop you. The crowd is going to wait; they're going to [want to] hear what you have to say. A little after somebody adjourns the meeting, just walk up there; I don't think anybody will move an inch."[22] All this was nervy, but it nonetheless constituted a modulated challenge to authority, since there would be no interference with faculty and administration speeches.

Savio heeded Aptheker's advice, and so walked up to the podium after Kerr's speech. Before he could utter a word, he was jumped by two campus police officers. According to the *New York Times* report, "one policeman put his arms around Mr. Savio's throat, forcing his head back, the other grabbed him in an arm lock. They forced Mr. Savio away from the microphone" and dragged his limp body toward a dressing room on the side of the stage.[23] This all happened in plain view of the fifteen thousand students and faculty in the audience, many of whom booed vigorously and chanted "We want Mario." Some FSMers were so outraged that they jumped up on the stage. Police tackled these protesters. It was pandemonium.[24]

Furious at this assault, Savio called out that those who barred him from speaking and used the police to gag him were "hypocrites" and "bastards." While detained in the dressing room, Savio demanded his release, telling the police, "Give me my rights! Arrest me or release me! You've got to let me out." He recalled trying to force the door open while the police "were holding me back, but I was making it plain to them that they were doing something that might get them into trouble. They were a little confused." It was such an intense moment that Savio turned to a policeman in the dressing room—one who he knew was of Italian descent—and "started talking to him in Italian...I'm in a different place, a different world....It was all very stirring."[25]

Nowhere was President Kerr's failed leadership in the FSM crisis more evident than on the stage after Savio's seizure by the police. Kerr, as the *Times* reporter observed, was "obviously astounded and unsettled" by the police action. But when, in an attempt to calm the crowd, Robert Beloof, the speech department chair, shouted at Kerr that Savio "must be allowed to speak," Kerr responded bureaucratically, telling Beloof this "would have to be arranged by Professor Scalapino."[26] Kerr could not act decisively or compassionately in a moment that cried out for both. Kerr later expressed regret that he had deferred to Scalapino: "Once again I was following university formalities. I should have gone with Savio, taking him by the arm...back to the stage to speak....And I should have explained to the audience what had happened [i.e., that the police overreacted and he'd not authorized them to seize Savio] and extended my apologies. But I did not."[27] Instead, Scalapino made a short speech explaining—to a chorus of boos—why in planning the meeting he had denied Savio's request to speak. Then he finally allowed Savio to address the meeting. Released by the police, Savio walked to the podium, urging the crowd to come to Sproul Plaza for an FSM rally: "Please leave here. Clear this disastrous scene and get down to discussing the issues."[28] Masses of students and some faculty heeded his call. The FSM rally following the Greek Theatre fiasco was the largest yet, drawing a crowd of some ten thousand.

The police assault had been an electrifying event, which, as the *New York Times* noted, "astounded almost everyone" present.[29] That assault, not the speeches, had the greatest impact on the audience and the mood of the campus. The symbolism could not have been more disastrous for Kerr, since right after he had spoken of the university supporting "the power of persuasion against the use of force, the application of decent means to decent ends, the constructive act as against the destructive blow," the police had used force to gag the most prominent leader of the Free Speech Movement.[30] As Kerr later admitted, "the crowd had seen Mario Savio dragged from the scene, and that was all it remembered. It was an accident that looked like fascism."[31] This image dominated the TV reports and was plastered on the front page of newspapers from coast to coast.[32] Upon seeing this photo in the San Francisco press, Dorothea Lange, the great documentary photographer, contended that that single photograph said more about the issues at stake in the FSM than all the hundreds of articles covering the crisis.[33]

The campus had fallen into a state of disarray. The chancellor was first politically and then physically impaired. Kerr's stepping in with the department chairs had led to nothing but chaos, which underscored all the more the sense of drift and failed leadership. This led faculty to wonder, as John Searle put it, "Who the hell was in charge? Nobody knew!"[34]

It seemed obvious by now that if the crisis was to be settled, the faculty would have to assert itself. The day after the Greek Theatre meeting that is precisely what happened. The FSM called off its strike so that the Academic Senate could meet in a calmer environment. The faculty supporters of the FSM's free speech agenda, known as the Committee of 200, had spent most of the semester as a bold but ineffective minority, unable to influence the Senate. The combination of faculty desire for an end to the chaos, sympathy with the arrestees and free speech, and anger at the administration's ineptitude and heavy-handedness suddenly empowered the Committee of 200, making its free speech positions seem no longer radical but reasonable. The Academic Senate meeting, attended by a record number of faculty, resolved the crisis. In an overwhelming 824–115 vote, on December 8 it endorsed the FSM's central free speech demand "that the content of speech or advocacy should not be restricted by the University."[35]

This was a stunning defeat for Kerr. He viewed it as a rejection of his leadership and believed the FSM's victory was engineered as much by a faculty revolt as by the student rebellion itself. Kerr was shocked that, in the wake of the Greek Theatre debacle, the department chairs lost their nerve, failing to present their solution to the crisis during the Academic Senate meeting—essentially refusing to compete with the pro-FSM resolution that ultimately passed. Kerr had, as he put it, "two very rough sessions with Scalapino on the morning of December 8—one in person and one on the phone…I insisted that the [original] agreement be kept—that the department chairmen present it and fight for it. This was refused. To me this was the central issue—one of good faith." Scalapino became so emotional about not reviving Kerr's now discredited solution to the crisis that he was, in Kerr's words, "crying at the end of the phone conversation."[36]

Savio and his fellow FSMers cried too on December 8, but theirs were tears of joy. Since only faculty could attend the Academic Senate meeting, thousands of students waited outside Wheeler Hall and listened to its deliberations broadcast over loudspeakers. As the meeting ended, with the Senate endorsing the FSM's free speech position, the faculty came walking out and the crowd of students, in gratitude to their professors for standing up for student rights, began, in Savio's words, "clapping and tears were just streaming down our faces."[37] Some faculty were also in tears, believing that the December 8 resolutions signaled a new birth of freedom on campus, undoing the damage inflicted by the McCarthy era and Berkeley's loyalty oath. There were, as Aptheker put it, "many among them and among us who finally came to believe that the repression of the 1950s was truly at an end."[38] And the tears reflected relief as well that the long, hard struggle to win over the faculty had at last succeeded. As Savio recalled,

To be on the Berkeley faculty you can't be that dumb. [Yet] it took us a very long time to explain to them the niceties of civil liberties issues where they could understand. But we didn't know even then [on December 8] whether they could understand. And we had done our all. If we'd lost it at that point it would have been gone.…It was a one person–one vote senate and they had a real debate. And that's really a side of the FSM which isn't understood. We had to work like crazy, disrupting the University, taking over buildings, having sit-ins, marches…just to open up a little space where people could have a real debate.…This is a free country…and [yet] you had to go crazy so we can have an actual, real debate that could really decide something. Astonishing! And they voted the right way.[39]

The next day Savio spoke at the FSM victory rally, joyful yet contemplative about what the December 8 resolutions signified. His speech conveyed his sense that a paradigm shift was occurring at Berkeley. The question would no longer be whether students had rights; they had established this. Nor would it be whether students would have power, since their movement had shown that they could unite and—when aligned with the faculty—become a force for change on campus. Now the question was whether students would use or abuse their rights and power. Savio, euphoric over the FSM's victory, approached this question in an upbeat way. The movement had finally won faculty endorsement of the FSM's position "that there be no restrictions on the content of speech save those provided by the courts." He reminded the crowd:

> That's an enormous amount of freedom; and people can say things within that area of freedom that are not responsible. We've finally gotten into a position where we have to consider being responsible because…now we've got the freedom within which to be responsible. And I'd like to say at this time I'm confident that the students, that the faculty, of the University of California will exercise their freedom with the same responsibility they've shown in winning their freedom.[40]

Critics of the Berkeley movement and the New Left nationally would disagree with Savio's sunny prediction about the way this new freedom would be exercised. In the mid- and late 1960s the student Left would be accused of abusing power, imposing a political monopoly on campus, demonstrating intolerance of antiradical voices.[41] Nonetheless, the way Savio framed this analysis was strikingly introspective. Instead of crowing about the rise of student power, he stressed the need to marry this hard-won freedom to a new adult awareness about exercising freedom and power responsibly.

He also made more explicit his idealism about the university as an engine of social change. Where a week earlier he had angrily denounced the "odious" autocratic tendencies of Kerr's corporatized university, he now calmly, happily, and hopefully held forth about the liberating potential of critical social thought generated by the university. The victory speech attested to Savio's love of the university as a place where free inquiry and imaginative social criticism could flourish—exploring "the question of what ought to be, not just what it is."[42] At the victory rally he also argued that

> the people—us, you know—who fought this fight are really maybe the most conservative people on this campus….Those who have been involved in the FSM are just exactly the students who have been most

concerned that this be a great university, that it have the things it needs—
full academic freedom—full...freedom of inquiry...and finally the University as a whole, faculty and students are squarely behind it.[43]

It surprised the crowd to hear him referring to the movement's stalwart supporters as conservative. In fact, the line evoked laughter, which was understand-
able since the FSM's key leaders were on the left, but Savio was dead serious.
He used the same language in subsequent speeches, accusing Kerr of ushering
in a brave new world of inhumane corporatized universities to which "we have
counterposed...a more traditional role of the university. It turns out that we're
the traditionalists and he's the revolutionist."[44] Rhetorically this was clever:
playing against type, refuting stereotypes in a startling fashion. But it was more
than just clever rhetoric. Savio had a strong sense of history and knew it was
possible to reach into the past for ideas to challenge current power structures
and belief systems. He had done the same thing as a freshman when he used
his study of ancient Greece, a pre-Christian culture, to facilitate his break with
Catholicism. There is in all this a strikingly original use of language, set in the
American vernacular: bringing in conventional terms to envision unconventional ideas. Savio was invoking academic tradition (the university before the
bureaucratic age had elevated administrators over faculty and students) to herald a new day, but in a reassuring way. There was a quaintness to his rhetoric at
the victory rally, which owed as much to 1776 as it did to the modern American
Left. Paying tribute to those arrested at Sproul, he termed them "800 patriots
here at the University...who risked their careers because they love...liberty."[45]

Despite Savio's use of language that was neither dogmatic nor ideological, the
press evoked images of him from the ideological left. The day after the FSM's
victory rally, a *San Francisco Chronicle* columnist referred to him as "Mario
(Fidel) Savio." That same paper, in covering the FSM victory rally, reported that
"the major speaker at yesterday's rally—and the movement's Patrick Henry or
Fidel Castro depending upon the point of view—was still Mario Savio."[46] Such
analogies were meant to be pejorative, inaccurately associating Savio with Communism and dictatorial leadership, both antithetical to his hyperdemocratic
politics. The Fidel label fell on Savio because Castro was then America's most
fear-inducing image of revolution. While he was no Castro, Savio certainly was
committed to sweeping social change and educational transformation.

The conflict at Berkeley in 1964, as in much of America during the 1960s, was
about loosening constraints, and Savio, having been involved in three liberation
movements—the civil rights movement in the Bay Area, Freedom Summer,

and the FSM—expressed this yearning for freedom and equality with a stirring eloquence that had ripple effects, ensuring that the Berkeley model of non-violent yet militant protest would be widely emulated on campuses nationally. This was evident in the crowds of enthusiastic students who in mid-December 1964 flocked to the speeches that Savio and other FSM leaders made in their triumphant tour of East Coast and midwestern campuses. The Berkeley revolt also drew enthusiastic support from such civil liberties groups as the ACLU, and locally the labor movement began with the FSM's strike to loan its support to student actions, with the Teamsters Union authorizing its members not to cross the picket line, and carpenters also walking out in solidarity. Strongest of all was the civil rights movement leadership, which realized that the FSM was deeply connected to its own freedom struggle. As CORE director James Farmer exclaimed shortly after the FSM's victory: "If anyone says he is for the negroes but against those students at UC he is a liar. There can be no separation of the battle."[47]

Although Savio and his oratory were admired and even loved by FSMers, this was not often the case beyond the world of social movements, the Left, and the campuses. Savio had his hands full mobilizing students and faculty and over-coming a powerful university administration. He could not give much thought to how he and the student movement were perceived by the general public and politicians. While his oratory helped build the movement on campus, it gained the FSM mostly opposition off campus, from both California's liberal governor and mainstream Californians. Polls showed that an overwhelming majority (74 percent) of the state's electorate did not approve of the FSM.[48]

To say that the public disapproved of Savio and the FSM is putting it mildly. In the days following the arrests at Sproul, thousands of Californians sent Governor Brown letters and telegrams hostile to the protesters. According to Brown, "of the 7,993 letters we received on the subject, only 351 supported the Academic Senate recommendations" on behalf of the FSM's free speech demands. The letters voiced overwhelming (six to one) approval of Brown's decision to use police to end the sit-in.[49]

Some of this backlash against the movement was directed at Savio. "If you watch that Mario Savio," complained a sixty-four-year-old San Jose woman, "you see Hitler all over. The way he raved and ranted."[50] Urging Brown to "meet force with force...to put this movement down," a World War II veteran suggested that the governor "have the FBI investigate this Mario Savio, for I fear that he could be another Harvey Lee Oswald [Lee Harvey Oswald, the assassin of President Kennedy]."[51] From San Francisco came a letter signed "Frightened Citizen," warning Brown of the need for stern action to halt the subversive activity of "Fidel" Savio. "For our country's sake, and as loyalty to the thousands who want no part of Savio's rebels, don't surrender! Expel all the rebels and make way for...decent boys and girls who are willing to obey the long established rules."[52] "Mario should go to jail," Josephine Southward of San Francisco wrote the governor, because "kicking, yelling, and wrecking property is not a civilized way of earning Free Speech or any other privilege."[53] "My solution to that bunch of 'Berkeley Beatniks,'" wrote "a disgusted taxpayer," is "expel the delayed adolescents, fire the Professors and draft Mr. Savio into the armed forces."[54]

Fear of disorder was a powerful motivating factor among these letter writers. "When you act in defiance of the law and resort to mobs taking over—they ought to crack some skulls a-plenty," wrote an Oakland housewife. She urged a hard line not only against Savio and the lawless FSM, but against "Civil Rights demonstrations too of which I am sick to death...As for police brutality give them plenty of it."[55] An irate businessman, warning against "appeasement," expressed concern that unless the Bay Area student and civil rights movements were halted, "your group of professional demonstrators...could call out their unwashed crew and close down my place of business, singing 'We Shall Overcome.'"[56]

Sounding themes that soon became standard fare on the right, the letters told of permissiveness yielding a breakdown of authority and paving the way for the rise of the FSM. "What kind of parents do they [Berkeley rebels] have," one critic asked Brown. "Failing to teach there [sic] young folks to Respect the laws and Rules of the school, city, counties, & state. There is too much...disrespect for people's property and homes."[57] Linking campus disorder to the "crime situation" in the community, one housewife blamed lax law enforcement, urging Brown to "get after the...judges who are just slapping wrists of criminals."[58] Complaints were directed at Brown for not acting sooner and more forcefully to suppress the Berkeley rebellion. A sarcastic critic asked Brown, "Since you have capitulated to...Mr. Savio why not appoint him as head of the University...of California? Or better yet, resign and allow him to be governor. On two occasions I have supported you for election: I will not err again in '66."[59]

Cold war imagery was almost universal among these FSM detractors. Not only did they view Mario as "Fidel" but they also deemed the movement's supporters subversives or dupes. A Southern California couple urged Brown to "clean out...Communist UC faculty...Taxpayers resent money for Communism, chaos."[60] A San Mateo housewife concluded: "There is only one way to handle these so called Free Speechers. Send them to Russia-Cuba."[61] A Canoga Park church leader wired the governor that "the 700 persons who worship with me each Sunday join in our petition that the students participating in the revolt at UC be immediately dismissed from the campus...[since] such brazen anarchy could only be fostered by Communism."[62] "If this keeps up," warned another foe of the FSM, "the Russians statement that they will bury us with out firing a shot is certainly more fact than fiction."[63]

Even though the FSM's key free speech goal was no more radical than the First Amendment, and the FSM's educational reform vision asked only that the university (faculty and students) become self-governing, which was a long way from Communism, the California electorate sensed that something radical was happening, and that Savio was the voice of an unwelcome revolution. The FSM was revolutionary, Strong contended, in the sense that "a revolution is the overturn of established authority [i.e., the university administration], and in its place the setting up of a new [student-faculty] authority."[64] John Searle too saw the FSM as "a kind of small scale revolution...that...overthrew a whole structure of authority."[65] The FSM's victory seemed to herald, in Searle's words, "a series of revolutionary expectations about the future of the university," convincing its jubilant supporters that "this is Day One of a new era! We can sit down and re-plan the whole structure of the university. If we want we can have the administrators busy just sweeping sidewalks. That was [thanks to Savio] a popular slogan in those days. We can have a completely different conception of education."[66] Though this revolt had occurred in a "knowledge factory," and though faculty/student self-government is far from incompatible with capitalism, it was easy for the electorate to see red, worrying that had this rebellion occurred in an industrial factory, the workers would be seizing control and displacing management in a Soviet-style revolution.[67]

The anti-Savio, anti-FSM animus on the part of a large segment of Californians focused more on means than ends. The electorate, echoing the press, was so fixated on the disruptiveness of the FSM that it barely paid attention to the civil liberties Savio and the movement were fighting for—and so made the Berkeley battle for free speech seem sinister and un-American. Carl Schorske recalled, "Those whose basic concern was with order...were always favored over those primarily concerned with freedom. It was much like the civil rights movement, where the protest marches were 'illegal,' but fundamental to the realization of new freedoms." The press and much of the public "focused on the worst student behavior, not the issues."[68]

The same held true for Governor Brown, whose statements defending the Sproul Hall arrests ignored the free speech issue and instead focused on the disruptiveness of the student rebels and their "violations of state law" through sit-ins, which he characterized as posing an "actual threat of anarchy." He blamed the FSM for throwing "the campus of one of the world's great universities" into "turmoil...for ten weeks."[69]

Despite Brown's use of the police to crush the sit-in and his harsh words about the FSM, California voters did not deem him tough enough on campus unrest. He had, after all, taken months to halt what the public regarded as campus anarchy. The electorate's anger at the lawlessness helped to fuel Ronald Reagan's campaign for the governorship in 1966, as Reagan promised to "clean up the mess" in Berkeley—and this melded seamlessly with Reagan's use of racially charged fears of disorder sparked by the Watts ghetto rebellion of 1965, presenting himself as the conservative cure to liberal permissiveness and lawlessness.[70] Thus ironically, even as the FSM won new freedoms and paved the way for a rising student Left on campus, the Berkeley crisis helped to push California toward the New Right.

Blaming any or all of this on Savio seems problematic, since the press was so hostile and may have made it impossible to turn back the wave of public opposition to the FSM. Nonetheless, Savio, emblematic of so much that made the student movement successful on campus, did nothing to prevent the movement's isolation from mainstream politics. With the notable exception of the faculty, the FSM was incapable of connecting with most adult liberals or conservatives, and this proved a limitation that would hinder the New Left through much of the 1960s.[71]

Might the results off campus have been any different had Savio's FSM oratory come off as less angry, less threatening to law and order? Is it reasonable to suggest that had Savio thought more about how his words were being received off campus, he might have found a way to appeal to students without alienating their elders? However valid his critique of liberal failures might be, his being based in the leftist-liberal world of Berkeley rendered him naive about the possibility that discrediting liberalism could open the doors of power to the Right.[72] Yet it seems odd to blame Savio for driving off public sympathy, since it was never there in the first place. In his earlier speeches, and in months of FSM press releases that he helped to shape, he offered detailed explanations of the free speech issues at stake in the conflict. Much of the public proved deaf to this civil liberties education, so it seems false to imply that calmer rhetoric would have attracted more Californians to the FSM's side. The irate correspondence FSM critics sent to Brown suggests that the divide separating the FSM's political culture from the off-campus world's was so enormous that Savio at his most even-tempered and eloquent could not have eliminated it, even if he had had the foresight to attempt it.

The FSM's ethos of direct and participatory democracy, its thousands assembled in mass meetings listening and debating themselves and their elders, was quite out of sync with the staid political culture of cold war America, which was suspicious of mass protest, frightened by disorder, and uncomfortable with insurgent oratory (equated with subversion and Communism). Savio, with his tributes to free speech and civil rights, and the FSM, with its pickets, nonviolent civil disobedience, strike, and solidarity with a sometimes disruptive civil rights movement, were simply too democratic to connect with establishment liberalism or the larger electorate.

There was deep, lasting bitterness toward Savio and the FSM on the part of faculty and administration critics. Paul Seabury accused the FSM of having "terribly damaged the university by politicizing it."[73] A Berkeley administrator privately complained that the movement, "led by Typhoid Mario," had pushed the university "in the direction of becoming Latin Americanized by beatniks [and] peaceniks."[74] UC chemistry professor George Pimentel thought that in the mid-1960s "we passed from addressing problems through rational behavior to addressing them through mob action."[75] The FSM had set dangerous precedents for mob rule on campus, according to Seymour Martin Lipset. Civil disobedience, Lipset argued, was justified only "if you don't have a democracy or if you have a severe evil, and an evil in which there were no democratic mechanisms to get rid of it. But that wasn't true" at Berkeley in 1964 since "the evil wasn't that great, and…there were other ways of trying to change it.[76] The FSM's tactics were, in Seabury's words, "extremely coercive and extremely disruptive," and when such tactics spread during the Vietnam era and made America's campuses a political battlefield, "our worst fears…were well borne out."[77]

Even two decades after the FSM, Robert Scalapino noted that the movement had "created serious cleavages in the faculty which have not wholly healed."[78] The FSM was held to have transformed Berkeley from a peaceful campus into a political war zone and countercultural zoo, and according to Searle, this "attracted to Berkeley the worst collection of kooks and nuts you've ever seen in your life." They had been drawn by the sensationalized television coverage of the FSM, which had led them to believe that "what you do is go to Berkeley and riot and you just have a great time. It's one big political, sexual drug feast."[79]

A great deal of disorder did, in fact, come to Berkeley in the wake of the FSM. In the mid- and late 1960s this included the controversial obscenity protests (the so-called Filthy Speech Movement), disruptive demonstrations against the Vietnam War, a violent Third World student strike, and the People's Park battle, which ended in military occupation, the shooting of demonstrators, and aerial tear gas bombardment of the campus. Some critics, who in their minds associated Savio with all of this chaos, considered the FSM leader an enemy of the university. This remained so even into the early 1990s, when Donald Farish, provost of Sonoma State University, was attending a dinner in connection with a science event at Berkeley. He brought up the fact that Savio was teaching on his campus. This caused quite a stir, evoking a bitter response from a science professor who had been a senior administrator at UC in the mid-sixties. The mere mention of Savio's name "all but caused him to have a stroke right there...He had...nothing good to say about Mario Savio. He blamed him for every ill" at Berkeley, including Clark Kerr's eventual loss of his job as president of UC.[80]

The contrast between such bitter memories and the fond way Savio is recalled by veterans of the student movement attests to the enduring division between those on opposite sides of the campus barricades of the 1960s. His words, leadership, and persona resonated with his generation of activists both during and after the sixties. Savio and the FSM—the two were sometimes separated but often discussed interchangeably—transformed the political consciousness of this generation. "I thank Mario for changing my life," wrote one FSM veteran. He encouraged her to believe that through activism and protest she "could have an impact...On the steps of Sproul Hall...my life was changed forever. I knew that my future was with my comrades, not with the frat boys I was dating who were throwing eggs at us." In the wake of the FSM, her "life has been one of living out" her "belief in social change."[81] "I was," recalled another FSMer, "one of the naive, working class students at Berkeley shocked to find that American Democracy had feet of clay....Mario helped me find the courage to act—a path that has shaped my life to this day....Mario...took the cork out of the bottle!"[82]

Some credited Savio with sparking their lifelong activism. One FSM veteran recalled that as a freshman in 1964 she had been "a middle class girl from West Los Angeles who was not so brave...I never got arrested, I always left when the police" were about to "start arresting people." But Savio's oratory and his "having the courage to stand up for what was right" had "a profound effect." She would "wake up" politically, joining the FSM, later marching against the Vietnam War, and ultimately working for a state legislator. "My sense of justice—and the part I could play in getting it—entered my consciousness...when I saw Mario stand up to be heard....Those few...weeks of Mario's influence...had a hand in creating the person I would become."[83] A similar political trajectory was detailed by another FSM veteran, who looked

> back to that fall of 1964 with one overarching memory: my moral and political self opened wide and began full flower one day in Sproul Plaza when...Mario got up on a car and spoke to us the truth as he knew it....My sense of justice and truth were inspired by Mario and the FSM....The inspiration ignited in me in 1964 carried me forward into the Vietnam Day Committee [Berkeley's militant antiwar group], the feminist movement, and ultimately to ministerial ordination and a higher degree in feminist theology.[84]

Savio was adept at appealing to students new to political protest, who recognized his interest in engaging them personally and appealing to their sense of fairness in a direct, unaffected manner, minus the condescension or frontline chauvinism that political veterans sometimes exude. This is why so many political journeys toward activism began via Savio speeches. Evoking this sense of engagement among politically inexperienced students, one FSM veteran wrote:

> In 1964 I was a first year graduate student at Berkeley from the Midwest. The political people, all so bright and sophisticated, frightened me. Hearing them speak at rallies...I felt smaller rather than bigger....There was only one person who seemed interested in sharing his knowledge rather than just showing it off, and that was [Savio]....He explained things I didn't understand....He enabled me and...many others to feel like we could be somebodies. He brought us into the struggle as partners; as empowered knowledgeable people.[85]

Unlike conventional politicians, who long to convince the electorate of their sterling character, Savio had no interest in self-promotion. He focused on the issues, free speech and democratic educational change, not himself. Nonetheless, his oratory was so personal and authentic, embodying a full range of emotion—from love to anger, leavened with wit and humor—that it conveyed who he was with such immediacy that many students came to feel that they knew, trusted, even loved him. Former FSM activist Kate Coleman evoked all this as she described an Executive Committee meeting before the final sit-in. Here an FSM organizer, in urging that Savio speak at the rally, said, "I don't believe in the cult of the personality...but if you've got one use him!" Savio's persona was accessible, attractive, and distinctive from that of the know-it-all radical cadre. As Coleman put it:

> God knows there were other orators, with big ideas on the FSM's Steering Committee, but it was Mario with his shy, warm persona—already such a departure from the graduate student "movement" heavies who were to dominate the landscape of the left for decades—who rose to the most passionate, articulate heights while preserving the common touch. Mario didn't believe in the cult of personality either, but...in the FSM battles...[he] emerged as a true leader, a visionary man of virtue and humility. God, I loved that man.[86]

Even taking into account the perils of nostalgia, it is impossible to avoid being impressed by how strongly these recollections emphasized Savio's moral appeal, character, and integrity—things his oratory conveyed and his charisma embodied. "What he mainly counted for," FSM veteran Jeff Lustig recounted, "was not just that acute intelligence or that strong, honest speaking, but a very particular presence. He helped us all get, and keep, our moral bearings. There are few people in any generation about whom that can be said. I can't think of another one in ours."[87] Playwright Barbara Garson, who as a young activist edited the FSM newsletter, observed that Savio's "contribution was a fierce insistence on honesty and democratic participation in decision making...and he set...the moral tone of the time...Outdoors before thousands of people, he gained the power to articulate their most idealistic yearnings."[88] A former graduate student during the FSM, later active in the antiwar movement and both the San Francisco State and People's Park rebellions, explained that "Mario gave *voice* to the *reason*, the *compassion*, and the moral integrity that were the very heart of the movement."[89] "He had a moral force that almost glowed...No one who was there can forget his hoarse, gangly, honorable presence. I thought...this must have been what Abe Lincoln was like," recalled journalist Jon Carroll, who first heard Savio speak atop the police car.[90]

Equating Savio with Lincoln may seem over the top—after all, Lincoln never bit a policeman on the leg—but the fact that Savio's oratory evoked such comparisons attests to its power to connect to the democratic faith of students. He made democracy seem real, immediate, and attainable, worth fighting for in one's own life—an ethos that one needed no prior political experience to understand and support. Meg O'Hara, who at the start of the FSM was a new Berkeley student, a "Wisconsin farm girl...my blond hair drawn into pig tails," found Savio easy to connect with because he was not invoking esoteric Marxist texts but bringing the Constitution to life. He

> had the strict logic and tight arguments of a philosophy major, and he applied them with passion to the Constitution...He believed that constitutional rights...applied to...UC Berkeley students. As his oratory entered my young head, and then my heart, and then my character, the Constitution became not some boring eighth grade text, but the "true North" of the compass that has guided my professional life.[91]

Savio's fellow activists also took pride in his oratory because they thought its intellectual quality attested to the seriousness of their movement. He showed that though the FSM's rhetoric was at times emotional, it conveyed dissent that was rational. This was what one FSM veteran had in mind when he termed Savio "the incarnation of the Free Speech Movement because the passion delineated the logic and the logic delineated the passion, neither subordinating the other."[92] Journalist Robert Scheer, a leader in Berkeley's antiwar movement in the mid-1960s, saw in Savio's intellectuality a powerful rebuttal to those "who denigrate the student activism of the 60s as...anti-intellectual"; they "inevitably stumble over the lanky figure of Savio in his sheepskin coat, ever serious, responsible...cerebral to a fault...and in all ways an American original."[93]

On one level the story of Savio and the FSM is local Berkeley history, since it was on that campus that they won free speech, revitalized educational reform, and strengthened the left subculture, drawing dissident students from across the United States and the globe to Berkeley as a center of insurgency and change.[94] But Savio's words and the FSM victory resonated beyond Berkeley, helping to build a dissident culture and a student movement that added to the sense that unjust authority could be effectively challenged—that David could defeat Goliath—through mass organization and protest. Savio and the FSM helped in this way to make the sixties a decade of campus, racial, gender, and antiwar insurgency. This is why veterans of the antiwar, feminist, gay and lesbian rights, and civil rights movements tend to look back on the FSM and Savio so fondly, and it is also why FSM veterans participated prominently in all those movements. "Like many in our generation," recalled a veteran of the student movement at Harvard,

> I loved and respected Mario before I knew him. His intelligence, eloquence, and courage set the standard that so many others used to motivate and guide their efforts to make the world a better place. I know this from personal experience because I was organizing political activities at Harvard in the '60s and we consciously measured ourselves by Mario's extraordinary example....Mario is responsible for countless lives well spent by people whose view of the world and whose expectations of themselves were shaped by his influence and...political activity....I meet these people all the time, and they represent an immense living legacy.[95]

It was not merely fellow activists who attested to Savio's national campus influence. University administrators and the FBI also were aware of that influence, and their antiradicalism left them unhappy about it. Only weeks after the FSM's free speech victory, the FBI received word from an informant that Ohio State University president Novice G. Fawcett was "concerned" that students organizing to change his university's speaker rules might invite Savio to speak. The FBI's Cincinnati office requested the help of the Bureau's San Francisco office, hoping to find "information relating to Savio which might connect him with any subversive groups...or any information of an adverse nature regarding Savio's character or morals. In addition, any derogatory information from public sources concerning Savio would be welcomed."[96]

This FBI attention reflected the fact that the Berkeley rebellion made Savio a political icon, an avatar of free speech and student rebellion. Since such rebellions helped to define 1960s America, his name became a symbol of those turbulent times. But the danger in reducing him to a symbol is that this can lead to losing track of his life story and humanity. While the FSM was, from the New Left's perspective, an enormous and unprecedented success politically, its impact on his life was mixed.

With the political gains would come personal setbacks. Historian David Farber has written that in the 1960s, activists "dared to dream grand dreams and they paid for it."[97] This held true, and with a vengeance, in Savio's case. Even an ordinary person might have difficulty resuming academic work after undergoing what he did in fall 1964. This was a semester in which he had been suspended from school, his apartment converted into the headquarters of a mass movement, and his name and picture plastered on newspapers across the country—making him a celebrity, the target of death threats by those regarding him as a dangerous subversive, and the recipient of adulation from movement activists who came to regard him as a political messiah. These pressures and distractions together with his lifelong problems with depression prevented him from returning to academic life at UC after the FSM. Not until the 1980s would he would earn a bachelor's degree.

This is why some of Savio's New York schoolmates as well as friends and classmates who knew him at Berkeley before the FSM viewed the Berkeley revolt more ambivalently than those who did not know him personally. These friends often thought of him as their most brilliant classmate, capable of phenomenal success in science—as one put it, she "expected to see him...in Stockholm accepting" a Nobel Prize.[98] So, though impressed by his effectiveness as a leader, they expressed privately a resentment of the FSM for disrupting his life and career.[99]

Savio never expressed such resentment himself, since he was not a careerist, and he was thrilled to be a part of the Berkeley revolt since it helped make the 1960s a time when students fought effectively for civil rights, free speech, and peace. Though critical of the excesses of the late 1960s Left, including dogmatism, violence, and vanguardism, he saw none of those as FSM legacies. Instead he reflected with pride that at the heart of the Berkeley rebellion was "a deep commitment to democratic objectives and to scrupulously democratic means of achieving those objectives." The FSM brought to campus the civil rights movement's political style, yielding a "sense of wonderment...Something new was being born in and through us, and we knew it was so."[100]

Merging the personal and the political, Savio reflected affectionately on "the intense and unique quality of loving and joyful solidarity which suffused the FSM," grateful to have made lifelong friends through the movement, among them the women he would later marry. In speaking on behalf of a free speech cause that so inspired him, his "stammer had essentially vanished." He came to feel that his leadership role was connected to the religious drive of his youth, for here "politics in a broad sense replaced the church," and he saw this role, freighted as it was with a strong moral component, as a partial fulfillment of his mother's wish for him to become a spiritual leader, a priest: "My role in the FSM had something of the sacerdotal about it. This was the closest I would ever come to leading a congregation. Instead of pleasing my mother, it frightened her."[101]

It is difficult to disentangle the joy of the FSM semester from the diverted dreams that followed. While Savio made history at Berkeley in 1964, in the process of doing so he unmade his own academic life, and this would contribute to his personal difficulties in the years ahead. Thus on the FSM's twentieth anniversary Savio reflected back on the Berkeley revolt by attesting that

> it affected my own life very deeply. Through two decades of some joy, but marked with much sadness and personal tragedy, it has remained for me a brilliant moment when...we were both moral and successful....This sense of the specialness, the beauty, and the personal and collective power of those days has been equally constant in the lives of those movement activists with whom I have remained in touch.[102]

PART III

After the Revolution: A Voice Lost and Found

10
DESCENDING FROM LEADERSHIP

In the aftermath of the FSM's victory on December 8 and in the opening months of the spring 1965 semester there were no outward signs that Savio's days as a political leader were numbered. His eloquent speech at the FSM's victory rally, celebrating the new birth of freedom at UC, was followed by a successful campus speaking tour, sharing the inside story of how Berkeley students pioneered new forms of campus activism.[1] The most important symbol of victory was Sproul Plaza itself, now a free political space and rallying point for many causes. Among those causes was the final local campaign of the Berkeley student movement in civil rights: demonstrations against racially discriminatory restaurants in Oakland's Jack London Square. Students rallied in solidarity with the freedom movement in Selma, Alabama, and Savio would participate in the second Selma march. Vietnam gradually emerged as the dominant issue, as students launched civil disobedience actions against the war—with Savio among those signing a pledge against military service in Vietnam.[2] For the remainder of the 1960s Berkeley would be known as one of the world's most politically engaged campuses.

But this victory came at a price for Savio and fellow FSM veterans. Soon after the celebrations ceased, he and all those arrested in the Sproul Hall sit-in faced prosecution. First legal preparations and then the trial took up much time and energy. Although he slightly exaggerated, *Daily Californian* columnist Eric Levine touched on an important truth in February 1965 when he noted that "the Free Speech Movement has become primarily a defendants' committee."[3]

In light of the lofty constitutional idealism of Savio's FSM speeches, there was an ironic quality to the FSM court case. Throughout the FSM he insisted that only the courts could be trusted to adjudicate free speech cases. He did not want campus officials wielding authority in such cases because their disciplinary hearings failed to protect student due process rights. He hoped the courts would uphold a higher standard of justice, based on his prior experience with a sympathetic judge in the Sheraton Palace prosecution. But in the FSM case the courts disappointed him. He found the focus of the prosecution "irrelevant and unfair," and so he initially refused to enter a plea at the pretrial hearing in February 1965. The court was focusing on the legal technicalities of trespassing instead of the larger First Amendment issues. As Savio told the press, "The issues discussed" in court are "obscure and minute points of law. The real issues are constitutional rights. Those who should be on trial are those who have been abridging constitutional rights such as Clark Kerr....It is unfair because we have been already tried in the press. We've been found guilty in the press through distortion and fabrication."[4]

The FSM trial opened on April 1, 1965, with the prosecutor, Alameda district attorney J. Frank Coakley, acting as if the student rebels had neither legitimate grievances nor support from the student body. Coakley denounced the FSM as a small, lawless, and "motley" group of student and nonstudent troublemakers, "seasoned agitators" who represented nobody except themselves. He mocked Savio as "either a good actor or egocentric personality" and a publicity hound who "blossomed...in the warm glow of...the limelight of this movement." Distorting Savio's academic record, he made it sound as if he had come to Berkeley in fall 1964 (when he had been a student there since fall 1963) and spent only a "short period" as a student before becoming "a dropout...on the fringe group" at Berkeley. During that period, Coakley charged, Savio "persisted in acting up and manifesting considerable arrogance and defiance of...the President, the Chancellor and other officials of the University."[5]

Savio grew especially disillusioned with the court on the issue of trial by jury. Judge Rupert Crittenden, to expedite the proceedings, brokered a deal in which the hundreds of defendants were tried en masse without a jury. Savio had reluctantly gone along with this because many of the protesters and their pro bono attorneys could not afford the time or expense of hundreds (or even dozens) of jury trials. He disliked this agreement since it denied the students their right to be tried by their peers.[6]

Savio's dissatisfaction erupted in court as he entered his plea. Judge Crittenden asked, "Do you understand that by waiving trial by jury you are giving up a right guaranteed you?" This question angered Savio, coming as it did from the judge who had presided over the deal that made the trial juryless. So he rebuked Judge Crittenden: "I understand fully the shameless hypocrisy to which this court has been reduced." This outburst led Crittenden to cite him for contempt and sentence him to two days in jail.[7]

Facing a trial and the possibility of jail time was bad enough, but even more infuriating to Savio were the signs that the Board of Regents might reverse the FSM's victory. In their first meeting since the faculty approved the December

8 resolutions, the regents chose not to endorse those resolutions, asserting that "authority in student discipline rests with the Regents and not with the faculty." Their language implied that the regents might impose new restrictions on political activity on campus. In response, Savio warned that the FSM "would take appropriate action against this horrendous decision."[8] This controversy was the first of several free speech disputes that riled Berkeley in 1965.

Despite the attention Savio devoted to defending student rights, there was one kind of violation of his own rights about which he was unaware. Law enforcement agencies had mounted spying and other covert actions against him as a consequence of his FSM leadership. The FBI opened an extensive Savio file, monitoring his politics through the end of the 1960s as part of its secret counterintelligence campaign against the New Left. FBI agents tailed him on his campus speaking tour, planting hostile questions in the press suggesting that the FSM had been Communist-led.[9]

Although Savio had no inkling of this covert FBI role, he had developed a very critical perspective on that agency. At a Sproul rally during the Selma crisis, protesting the brutal assaults on Alabama civil rights workers, he complained that the FBI had shirked its responsibility to protect them. The agent covering this rally reported in February 1965 that Savio told the crowd the "FBI does nothing except take notes" in the face of racist violence and the agents "have become a group of stenographers."[10] The FBI did not need to spy on him to elicit such criticisms since he offered them in person at the local FBI office in May 1965, when summoned in connection with a threatening letter he had been sent. He annoyed the agents by mocking the FBI as the "Federal Bureau of Inquisition," attacking "the Justice Department and the FBI for 'failure to make arrests…in the South where human rights are being violated every day.'"[11]

The Berkeley free speech issue that grabbed the most headlines in the 1965 spring semester was the obscenity debate. It erupted on March 3 after John Thomson, a self-described "confused street poet…, would-be author," and radical nonstudent, displayed a "fuck" sign on campus. This began as what Thomson himself termed a "prank."[12] He ran into Savio, who joked that "fuck was a versatile word in…English…—it could be a noun, verb, adverb, adjective, gerund." Thomson responded by changing his sign to read "fuck (verb)."[13] But what began as prank escalated into something more serious when police, upon seeing Thomson's sign, arrested him.

The next day protesters, including FSM leader Art Goldberg, held a campus rally (attended by only 150 students) objecting to the arrest on free speech grounds. They tested the limits on free speech by supporting Thomson's right to display his "fuck" sign and using the word "fuck" during their rally. Several students were arrested, one for displaying a sign that read "Fuck Defense Fund," and another for reading aloud passages of *Lady Chatterley's Lover*, to demonstrate that obscene words were part of Western culture and literature. A conservative student in solidarity announced that he was ordering a thousand "Fuck Communism" buttons.[14]

President Kerr denounced the obscenity protesters, charging them with "destructive degradation of freedom into license."[15] Several were brought up on disciplinary charges. Most faculty disdained the obscenity incident as childish, so the Academic Senate committees charged with handling free speech issues refused to consider this case. The administration appointed an ad hoc committee to do so.

Though the press and Kerr referred to the obscenity fight as the "Filthy Speech Movement" and tried to equate it with the FSM, so as to discredit both, the FSM leadership was initially divided on this dispute. Most within that leadership worried that Thomson's behavior would undermine the movement's hard-won free speech victory by making students seem licentious. The FSM Executive Committee rebuked the administration and the police for choosing "to escalate this issue and endanger campus peace," but also criticized the obscenity protesters for not having acted responsibly.[16] Yet several FSM leaders agreed with Goldberg that Thomson's act had taken the struggle for free speech to "the next logical step. It's fine to defend political speech, but what about artistic speech? Or meaningless speech?"[17]

Jack Weinberg was of two minds on the obscenity protest. His first response was "that I wanted to stop it," since he thought it detracted from the student movement's work for such serious causes as civil rights. But he soon realized that the obscenity controversy raised an important question of constitutional speech, and he presented this argument to the FSM Executive Committee.[18] Savio went through a thought process similar to Weinberg's on the obscenity flap. Savio's initial response had been to deny that the FSM had anything to do with this "indefensible" controversy.[19] But he soon came to see that student rights were at stake and that obscene speech might at times be a defensible form of social criticism. With the FSM divided on obscenity's merits as a free speech issue, he focused on the other student right jeopardized in this dispute, due process, objecting to the denial of fair hearings to the obscenity protesters. He condemned on free speech grounds the administration's next attack in this controversy, the banning from campus of the *Spider* (whose name was a rough acronym for "sex, politics, international Communism, drugs, extremism, and rock and roll"), a new countercultural literary magazine, over its use of a four-letter word.[20]

In a student-faculty panel discussion on the obscenity controversy on March 25, 1965, Savio displayed his characteristic candor, idealism about student rights, and criticism of authoritarian university governance. He acknowledged that though he supported the free speech rights of the students who published *Spider*, this controversy had "caused a lot of anguish in our Executive Committee." The right of students to publish and distribute this magazine needed to be defended not because of *Spider*'s content but rather because "if we did not we would be endorsing a precedent" undermining the free speech victory encoded in the December 8 resolutions.[21]

Perhaps the most striking aspect of Savio's remarks was his point that fairness, not winning politically, was at the heart of this matter. He disliked the process whereby the administration censored and threatened to punish students for speech, while the Academic Senate refused to intervene and had to be prodded by protests to reconsider. Such protests should not be necessary on a campus guided by fair rules judiciously applied: UC officials who "made the wrong decision under pressure of one side" might next "make the right decision under pressure of the other side. Well I don't consider that really better. It shouldn't be the case" that the university has "got to be pressured to make good decisions, and as a matter of fact we are not interested in winning every case. See…a corollary of believing that society can be run by rules is believing that sometimes when bad decisions are made in accordance with those rules, you've got to live with the bad decisions."[22] These are hardly the words of someone promoting campus chaos.

By raising the due process issue, he returned to a key FSM theme, that the university's "informal" disciplinary proceedings with "no rules of evidence" violated student rights. The treatment of the obscenity case seemed to Savio particularly egregious since instead of coming before an Academic Senate committee devoted to free speech issues it was sent to an ad hoc disciplinary committee—"a beer, sex, and cheating committee, that's the way its been referred to by many members of the faculty, the students, and the administration." He deemed it prejudicial that "only the good people go to the free speech committee and other people go to the beer, sex, and cheating committee. Well that's because good people neither drink nor confront ["confront" being the UC student euphemism for sexual intercourse] nor cheat." Here UC appeared guilty of offering a lower judicial standard than that found in the courts: "In the real world you have one set of courts and one set of laws." And it is "not the case that if you do intellectually justifiable crimes that you are in a good court and if you do reprehensible, mean, low, base crimes you're in another court with lower standards of due process. That's not the way it works in the real world, but I'm afraid that's the way it works in this world."[23] Conscious of how power functioned in the university, he argued that an adversarial proceeding, adhering to the highest standards of due process, was especially important since it could "minimize differences in power…between two adversaries," giving students a shot at a fair hearings from overbearing administrators.[24] The question was not whether one agreed with obscene expression but whether the university would handle such controversies fairly.[25]

Savio was under no illusions about the prospects of obtaining such justice in the "fuck" controversy. The administration was disinclined to give it, and the university community, offended by the obscenity issue, was not about to unite to demand fair hearings. This left him "fearful" of a "quasi-legal lynch," with punishment "railroaded" through the disciplinary committee, violating "the minimum standards of procedural justice...which are at the basis of...civilized society and civilized law."[26]

Although Savio, along with Jackie Goldberg and several other FSM leaders, tried to mobilize students on behalf of the obscenity protesters' rights, the campus proved unresponsive. A poll found that close to 80 percent of Berkeley students opposed the use of "filthy speech" in public.[27] Thus when the hearings ended with three students suspended and one (Art Goldberg) expelled, there was no effective response from the student movement. Savio and the FSM Executive Committee protested the decision and threatened civil disobedience if the punishments were not voided, but the support was simply not there for any such mobilization, and so the punishments stood.[28]

This outcome attests that Savio's eloquence alone was not enough to win political victories. His oratory could make a difference politically only if the Left and the larger campus community were open to his dissident message—and on "filthy speech" they were not. In looking back upon this controversy, Weinberg saw it as a movement failure, since despite Berkeley's reputation for radicalism, the campus proved unwilling to challenge the obscenity taboo. The first time the student movement at Berkeley

> was tested on a...free speech issue that was not popular it collapsed...The political leadership of all stripes really was furious at those "fuck" incidents....There would have been no way of reconstructing the Free Speech Movement to fight that battle. It would have been a...small isolated coalition....Mario was smart enough to understand all of those things....He didn't have...the support and it's hard now to understand how big that [obscenity] taboo was then because now that taboo has been pretty much shattered. But it was a big taboo then. And there was not the courage to take on that taboo. Or not the interest, or not...the strength. It was divisive; it was not what we wanted to be known for.[29]

The obscenity dispute left Savio worried that the administration would spend the whole spring 1965 semester attempting "to undermine...the principles of December 8."[30] His fears proved well grounded, and he was drawn into two other free speech disputes during that semester. One concerned the regents and the other the Berkeley administration. Back in December a regents committee headed by Thomas Meyer began codifying rules for speech on campus, and its proposals in April 1965 would have restricted outside political speakers, restrained student governments from taking positions on off-campus issues, and left open the possibility of disciplining students over the content of their political speech. Berkeley's new chancellor, Martin Meyerson (Strong had resigned after he and Kerr publicly feuded over how the FSM crisis was handled), had promulgated interim campus regulations that the FSM considered restrictive. Relations between the administration and FSMers grew contentious. Though there was not the mass civil disobedience of the previous fall, acts of defiance did occur. The FSM refused to get a permit for its political table and so police seized it. Savio, defying the campus requirement of a permit for nonstudent speakers, publicly shredded his permit and told a crowd of protesters that restrictive political rules would not be obeyed.[31]

Had he wanted to, Savio could have used these ongoing threats to free speech as a justification for continuing as Berkeley's leading activist. But before the spring semester ended he did something virtually unheard of in American politics: he walked away from his position of political authority and his own celebrity. On April 26, 1965, at the end of a Sproul Plaza speech, Savio announced his resignation from the FSM.[32]

The *San Francisco Examiner* featured a huge headline: "Savio Quits the FSM: Action Stuns His Followers."[33] The *San Francisco Chronicle* devoted its lead editorial to the resignation. Headed "A Revolutionary Bids Farewell," the *Chronicle* editorial noted, "Most of the things young Savio has said and stood for in the FSM...have struck the orthodox citizen and taxpayer as too defiant, too rudely insistent, too subversive of authority and discipline, too heartless." Yet even the *Chronicle* conceded his historical importance, noting that he had led a "student revolution...We are witnessing an upsurge of a whole student generation...The revolution of Mario Savio is still shaking the administrators, the Regents, the faculty, and the courts.[34]

The press offered contradictory accounts of why Savio stepped down. The *Berkeley Daily Gazette* claimed that he left the FSM because he was advocating moderate tactics, while the dominant FSM faction favored militancy. The *Daily Californian* suggested his militant tactics had isolated him from the FSM's dominant moderate faction.[35]

Neither of these interpretations was accurate. The timing of his departure was shaped by a collective decision by Savio and the remaining FSM leadership that since the organization had served its original purpose of winning student advocacy rights, it should dissolve itself.[36] Indeed, the day after he resigned, the FSM disbanded, replaced by a new organization, the Free Student Union, an innovative but unsuccessful attempt to build a student movement in the image of a labor union. This was the organizational initiative Savio alluded to when, in his open letter to the *Daily Californian* explaining his resignation, he pronounced himself "confident that this community is entirely capable of organizing itself into the powerful trade union form of organization that this 'knowledge factory' calls for."[37]

Savio's resignation was true to the hyperdemocratic approach to leadership he had learned in Mississippi, which held that protest movements ought to direct themselves from the grassroots and not become too dependent upon leaders. He believed Berkeley's student movement had become too dependent upon him. His speech disputed the notion that the movement needed him to stay on because other students "lacked competence," and he dismissed as undemocratic the idea that any leader was indispensable.[38]

Savio's words on democratic leadership were self-critical. His speech implied that he had become too powerful, even offering an unflattering historical parallel to his own leadership role to drive this point home. He told the crowd on Sproul Plaza that "if the kind of insurrection against educational tyranny— which would be required here among students and faculty—is not organized by *you* then it's not worth being organized. Accordingly…lest I feel that I'm deserving of the charge of Bonapartism—which I might be moved to accuse myself of—I'd like to wish you good luck and goodbye."[39]

His farewell speech coupled self-criticism with a scathing critique of the university. The tone of this speech was his bitterest to date. He implied that the administration's continuing abuse of power left him frustrated, contributing to his decision to step down. There was an air of exhaustion in the speech, a sense that the high hopes of a freer and more democratic university raised by the FSM's victory had been dashed. He told of his "great hope that all of the spirit of last semester, these rallies could be put away," that endless rounds of protest would no longer be necessary in the kind of reformed and democratic university the movement was establishing. But administration abuses and the faculty's failure to protect students from them meant that such a university had not emerged, and that only through protest could students protect their rights. Rather than glory in such turmoil, he expressed disappointment that protest continued to be necessary. If those who made and enforced campus rules "have no conscience then only the people *en masse* can do justice. But that's a dangerous kind of justice. I hope that we don't have to continue that kind of thing."[40]

Savio accused the Board of Regents of "pervasive corruption" and of operating arrogantly as a "kind of a model ruling class." The regents had disenfranchised UC's graduate students by barring them from participating in campus elections, nullifying a recent student vote endorsing such participation. By denying the student body "democratic access to legitimate power," the board kept UC in turmoil, since the lone "democratic channel" for redress of grievances remained mass protest. With the obscenity controversy in mind, he characterized the Board of Regents much as the courts "characterize hard core pornography, that is, unredeemed by any social value." Angry at the Meyer report's call for restrictions of free speech, he termed it "far worse to my ear than any four letter words I've heard" on campus.[41]

This denunciation of the regents was fiery but not groundless. Their interference had reached such a level during the obscenity uproar that Kerr became almost as furious at the regents as Savio was. Edward Carter, who chaired the Board of Regents, grew so angry at the obscenity protesters that on March 9, 1965, he ordered Berkeley's chancellor to "take instant action...by 5 P.M." or "he would call a special Board meeting and take control out of the hands of the chancellor." While sharing Carter's hostility toward the protesters, Kerr threatened that if Carter instigated direct regental control of the campus he would resign. Kerr publicly submitted his resignation, as did the chancellor. This dramatic move forced Carter to back down, but it alienated several regents and made it easier the following year for the new governor, Ronald Reagan, to fire Kerr.[42]

Savio's farewell speech voiced disappointment at the faculty's reluctance to stand up for student rights in the obscenity controversy. He implied that the faculty's moment of courage back in 1964 when it endorsed the FSM's free speech demands might have been an aberration, since it took mass student civil disobedience to shake the professoriate out of its apathy. Mocking both the faculty and himself, he argued:

> The only time that the [pro-student-rights] faculty here has been able to take significant action is when...they have been able to hold over the heads of their more conservative colleagues the threat of our gross irrationality. That's a very serious thing....If we have to have a standing army prepared to act irrationally in accord with—as *Tocsin* [a right-wing magazine] has put it—the psychotic leader [i.e., Savio] that they have, if that's what we need for the faculty to act rationally upon rational principles then we're in serious shape and they are too.[43]

This was a slender thread with which to protect student rights, since it was not possible to have students perpetually mobilized to disrupt the campus and wake up the faculty. Indeed, Savio acknowledged that student activists, himself included, were "very tired" and that "the same kinds of techniques [i.e., mass civil disobedience] appropriate last semester *aren't* appropriate this semester, that's a fact."[44]

Savio held out the hope that the faculty had largely untapped potential to better the university because, as he explained in a *Life* magazine interview, professors faced pressures not to become embroiled in campus controversies: "Most of the professors are very much concerned with their own areas of research, are frightened to speak out because they are not going to get their defense contract renewed or aren't going to get their tenure."[45] So he spoke to the faculty more in sadness than in anger, trying to prod them out of their lethargy, hoping that they might align themselves with students fighting for freedom and educational reform. He appealed to the faculty more elaborately in the open letter explaining his resignation:

> Perhaps the saddest thing about this community is the continuing reluctance of the faculty to defend the rights of students to self government, to due process, and to a full and liberal education as opposed to the factory training which we students have generally had to suffer. The Berkeley students have been forced to desperate acts because their professors repeatedly have failed them. I can only hope more faculty members may soon shoulder the responsibilities they have toward their students.[46]

This analysis of faculty politics proved only partially accurate. It *had* taken a semester of protest and the mass arrests to pave the way for the historic faculty action, the passage of the December 8 resolutions.[47] Compared with the student movement, much of the faculty was reluctant to serve as a vanguard expanding student rights. This was made evident by the faculty's alignment with the administration on the obscenity issue. However, the faculty, though unwilling to further expand those rights (to include obscenity), would for the rest of the 1960s show a deeper commitment to the December 8 resolutions than Savio's gloomy remarks implied. At several points faculty pressure halted administration violations of student rights, preventing a repeat of the painful confrontations that had occurred in 1964. The free speech framework won by the FSM would not, despite threats from regents and politicians, be undone.[48]

With regard to educational reform, Savio in his farewell speech aligned himself with the "Tussman plan" for an experimental college at Berkeley. This plan, named for its architect, Berkeley philosophy professor Joseph Tussman, took a "great books" approach to liberal arts education, emphasizing intensive study

of the classics in intimate seminars. Praising Tussman for "trying against fantastic odds, to set up an experimental curriculum," he noted that even though
Tussman's plan started small, reaching only 150 undergraduates out of a student body of 27,500, it still was not getting the resources it needed and deserved.
He criticized students for not championing Tussman's reform, claiming that
the denial of resources for this educational initiative boded "worse for us even
than the Meyer Report" and its threat to student rights. The student movement
needed to emulate Tussman in thinking deeply "about education. That's why
we're supposed to be *here*."[49] Savio expressed hope for change, praising curricular reform that today might seem educationally conservative and Eurocentric.

Coming amidst the FSM trial, the farewell speech reflected Savio's anger that
he and hundreds of others faced prosecution for making the university more
free. Reviewing the "catalogue of atrocities" whereby the administration abused
its power, calling "the police...twice on...a university campus," he denounced
the cops as "a helmeted, booted swarm of pests, insects, locusts, that's what they
were. It was disgusting." Savio wedded this furious rhetoric to an indictment of
liberalism, asking, "What is behind the liberal establishment? Organized violence. That's what's behind the liberal establishment in California anyway."[50]
Such rhetoric, sparked by a liberal governor's use of police against the movement, came just as a liberal president's war in Vietnam was heating up, and
heralded the break between the Left and liberalism, weakening both.[51]

In the tactics he urged upon the movement Savio was defiant but not reckless. Students should resist any restrictions of their political rights: "I don't
doubt for a moment that we can cause disruption on this campus" by defying such restrictions, "tearing...in two pieces those...permits" required to
set up advocacy tables on campus. "Then we go by our own regulations." But
he advised caution about sitting in, since "it's difficult to consider leading
people to do things which could result in their expulsion without some fair
knowledge beforehand that we will be able to support them in something
like a strike." Implying that he erred earlier in threatening mass civil disobedience if the obscenity punishments were not overturned, since support for
such action was lacking, Savio argued that activists should not be "ashamed"
to opt out of militant action if through it "they would lose more than it
would deliver."[52]

Near the end of his speech Savio aptly described the student movement's
evolution during his Berkeley years. The movement had begun as an adjunct of
the civil rights movement. In the FSM "we were demanding procedural rights
which we could then use to help others [blacks subjected to discrimination]
secure substantive rights outside." The FSM ended in a new awareness of how
students were oppressed politically and psychologically. What this

required of us is that we become aware of the victimization of *ourselves*. And that's much harder to do...to look inside and realize that by virtue of your very closest environment you are denied the minimum necessary to count as *human treatment* because to do that requires casting off the yoke which even parental obedience has placed on [us]...What we should be asking for is a digging into the deepest recesses of our own lives to see if we will longer accept...the subtle victimization which America has fashioned for white middle class youth.[53]

Although publicly explaining his exit from leadership in political terms, privately he acknowledged that his leaving had a personal dimension. He had recently become engaged to Suzanne Goldberg and wanted time to devote to their relationship. His role in the FSM had disrupted his academic career. He had not reenrolled since being suspended in the fall and needed to find a job. He felt positive about stepping down from the FSM because "I'll have time to attend to my own affairs as prospective husband, prospective father, and prospective physics student." Savio, the sixties radical, clung to a conventional dream of domestic bliss, with him and Suzanne "talking about the big, old house with five children running about which we'll one day have." He was "deeply in love" and soon alight with the "excitement and wonder" he shared with Suzanne as they looked forward to the birth of their first child, Stefan, late in 1965. Five years later they had a second son, Nadav.[54]

Savio was not forgetting about politics. His, after all, was a movement marriage, and he and Suzanne shared radical politics. In that same letter home articulating new hopes for his personal life, he expressed his hopes and fears about Berkeley—the dangers free speech faced from the Board of Regents and its Meyer Committee. But he felt good that "students and faculty are uniting in opposition" to that committee's "very oppressive report on discipline, political activities of students, and student government." To his parents the first reason he gave for ending his leadership was political: "The Movement had come to depend altogether too much upon my being its Leader—a very dangerous thing for any democratic movement."[55]

Savio turned out to be prescient when he told his parents that he was hopeful that resistance would stop new restrictions on student political expression. Determined student and faculty opposition pushed the regents to drop most of the Meyer restrictions, and the December 8 resolutions were left intact. The ferment at Berkeley forced the regents to change, though they did so grudgingly. Even back at their December 18 meeting the regents, in a statement overshadowed by their criticism of pro-FSM faculty, indicated that UC policies would not violate the First and Fourteenth Amendments, a position that would have been unthinkable without the FSM's impact. Free speech remained a contentious issue at Berkeley as UC officials periodically sought to use their regulatory powers to keep a lid on radical student politics, but they would never repudiate the December 8 resolutions.[56]

The final chapter in Savio's FSM history began in the courts and ended in jail. He served as a key defense witness, testifying that the sit-in had been the result not of lawlessness but of persistent violations of student rights. In this role he performed well. During almost a week of testimony he did not let his temper get the better of him, as he had earlier when he denounced judicial hypocrisy. But despite his testimony and the equally able testimony by other FSM leaders, the judge found most of the protesters guilty of trespassing. The leaders, including Savio, were also convicted of resisting arrest, a harsh verdict considering that they had just gone limp in the classic style of nonviolent civil disobedience and had not violently resisted the police. Where rank-and-filers received fines, the leaders received jail sentences, indicating that the judge had bought the prosecution's caricature of them as subversive troublemakers.[57]

Savio's last act of defiance in connection with the FSM came in July 1965, during the trial's sentencing stage, when his jail term was extended from three to four months because he refused to accept a probation agreement pledging not to get arrested for two years after his release from prison. He rejected (as did several other FSMers) the agreement because it would have barred him from engaging in civil disobedience, and that went against the beliefs that had led him into the FSM. No FSM defendant would receive a longer jail term—which he served two years later, once his legal appeals failed.[58]

Savio's most important and final speech in 1965 was at the mass antiwar teach-in late in May. This event drew tens of thousands of participants and featured prominent critics of the Vietnam War. The teach-in tactic had originated at Michigan, but the enormous size of the event at UC was a sign of Berkeley's emergence as a center of antiwar activism.[59] Savio, having left the political stage, had no role in organizing the teach-in, but as Berkeley's most famous activist, he was invited to speak at it.

The sight of Savio once more addressing a huge crowd of student activists might lead one to think that the antiwar cause was luring him back into political leadership. But his speech signaled something quite different: that his approach to politics and oratory, which had been ideally suited to the needs of the FSM, was not as appropriate for the emerging antiwar movement. Movement discourse was changing quickly and profoundly because of Vietnam. In the early 1960s, movement rhetoric, shaped by the early SNCC style of oratory, had been a plainspoken narrative of personal witness. But with Vietnam thousands of miles away, most speakers had never been to the war zone. Where in the civil rights movement and the FSM Savio had been able to offer first-person narrative, with Vietnam it was more complicated. "You had to talk about things like US imperialism," and this made it "difficult to express oneself in the...concrete sort of Jimmy Stewart...Will Rogers kind of way that we really tried for in the earlier time."[60] Uncomfortable with the "abstract quality" of the movement's increasingly Marxified discourse on the war, Savio had difficulty formulating his speech for that antiwar teach-in:

> I had just enormous discomfort about what I was asked to do, namely to give a speech against the Vietnam War. I was against the war. No problem. Enormous problem. I'd never been to Vietnam. I could not talk about Vietnam the way I had talked about the South. I certainly could not talk about Vietnam the way I talked about the dean [in the FSM]. See, I had no language in which to talk about Vietnam.[61]

This left Savio shying away from grand pronouncements and instead offering a speech that was "all questions. Why is our government doing this? In 1776 we were on the side of revolution. Now we're against it. Why is this so?" While most of the speakers offered an "instant analysis" of war and imperialism, he found himself offering "no answers."[62] He felt dissatisfied with both the ideologically bound analyses others provided and with his own lack of answers as to the nature of war and imperialism. This discomfort made it difficult for him to envision becoming an antiwar leader.[63]

His discomfort was also symptomatic of a larger gap opening between him and the increasingly ideological New Left. Savio's radicalism had been experimental, not ideological. He respected Marxists and praised them for offering a coherent analysis of American imperialism, but he could never embrace their fixed view of the world. As an ex-Catholic, he had expended too much time and energy freeing himself from one doctrinaire faith ever to embrace another.[64]

During the mid-1960s Savio's most forthright statement of his distrust of ideology came in a debate with socialist Hal Draper. Responding to Draper's criticism of the early New Left for lacking an ideology, he wrote that he was "scandalized" by Draper's view that radicals "require an ideology, that is a 'system of ideas about the transformation of society,' to determine 'this is wrong but not that' in our country's public practices and institutions."[65] Savio's approach, empirical and consistent with his scientific, rationalist cast of mind, centered on conclusions drawn from objective evidence—facts—rather than grand theories "It seems to me," Savio told Draper, that if some issue of *fact* about our society does not arouse deep feeling on its own merits, then either we are lacking in moral sensitivity, or the issue is unworthy of deep feeling...If we are correct in believing that the present social order is systematically...unjust, then we should be able to illustrate our belief by simply *pointing* to the *facts* of American life. If these facts do not support our theories, so much the worse for the theories.[66]

Thus Savio would not instantly echo the New Left's use of ideological explanations and Marxist terminology about capitalist expansionism and hegemony to account for the war.

Another obstacle to Savio's taking on leadership in the antiwar movement was his celebrity status. Through his FSM fame he "became a superstar," in Weinberg's words. "He was a name on the scene. In the [celebrity] tent if you named...young people who were famous, all the rest were rock musicians,...[the] Beatles and Bob Dylan—and Mario Savio was a celebrity of that caliber." His celebrity had come quickly and, as Weinberg noted, without "any infrastructural support. Usually celebrity status comes with money, comes with creating organizations to surround, to manage you, to help you organize. Suddenly you're that big. You need an interface with the world. Mario didn't have that. Didn't know how to have that. Didn't want to have that."[67]

Even had he wanted to use his celebrity to take on antiwar leadership, this would have been complicated, given how factionalized Berkeley's peace movement became. The movement divided on tactics, such as how confrontational its demonstrations should be, and whether to engage in electoral politics. These tactical questions did not have a single "rational answer...an ethical answer...a moral answer."[68] Weinberg recalled how such pressures bore on Savio and made antiwar movement leadership unappealing:

In any tactical debate...having Mario on your side would be very powerful. So that every time Mario came near the antiwar movement everyone wanted to convince him of their tactical position...And so...it was very difficult for him to approach the antiwar movement because as soon as he stepped his foot near any political thing...just making himself available became an event, he became an asset. Even if you saw—I saw—how this was tearing him apart.[69]

When movement organizers treated him as "a symbol, not a person," both his political principles and "his whole emotional makeup said that was wrong." "The glare of publicity," Weinberg concluded, not only "made it impossible for him to lead an ordinary life" but "also made it impossible for him to lead even a good movement life."[70]

Savio's discomfort with celebrity and with ideological discourse were expressions of the principled way he approached politics. He did not view political leadership as a career move. His role in the FSM had evolved organically out of his work in the civil rights movement, which gave him the moral authority to speak about that movement and defend its rights on campus. Lacking such authority with regard to Vietnam, he approached the war by sorting out his own position through reading and listening. He faced such fundamental questions as "Are you against the war because you are against all wars? Are you against this war because of some of its particularities? It's not as simple as being for or against free speech."[71] Feeling that he entered the Vietnam issue as a novice, Savio would not pretend otherwise, and this made it seem appropriate to approach the peace movement as a rank-and-filer rather than as a leader.

Satisfied that his moment of leadership had passed, he sought to return to his studies. Since it would have been impossible to resume his academic work at Berkeley, where he would be under pressure to lead protests, he opted to study abroad. In fall 1965 Savio and Suzanne Goldberg departed for England. His plan was to study physics at Oxford University, and with the help of Berkeley friends and faculty it was arranged for him to attend St. Catherine's College. Academically his Oxford time went poorly. Much as he loved physics, Savio was unable to focus on his work. By December 1965 he was thinking about going back to Berkeley. In 1966 he reapplied to UC.[72]

Politics—overtly and covertly—interfered with Savio's plans to return to his studies at Berkeley. Max Rafferty, a right-wing regent, told the press in summer 1966 that UC officials would be "nuts" if they allowed this troublemaker back into the student body. Regent John Canady proposed in October 1966 hearings to prevent his readmission. President Kerr refused to go along with such blatant politicization of the admissions process. But behind closed doors Berkeley's vice chancellor and the UC systemwide vice president and general counsel searched for ways to keep him out, even though the admissions office found that on the basis of academic performance he merited readmission.[73]

With this array of university leaders eager to bar Savio, he had little chance of gaining readmission. That slim chance evaporated thanks to his role in what he later dubbed the "Little Free Speech Movement." This movement emerged in fall 1966 in response to chancellor Roger Heyns's attempt to ban amplified rallies from Sproul Plaza. The chancellor sought to limit the influence of Berkeley radicals—especially the antiwar movement's militant wing—by forcing them to move their rallying site from the centrally located plaza area to a more secluded spot, the Lower Plaza, which students called "the pit." Students saw this as an attempt to take back the free speech victory of 1964 and demanded their right to rally on Sproul.[74] Passionate about protecting the free speech area, Savio briefly assumed a leadership role in the Little FSM. In the process he gave his first speech on campus since spring 1965, at the Save the Steps rally ("the steps" referring to the plaza rallying point, since speakers at demonstrations spoke from the steps of Sproul Hall) on November 4, 1966.[75]

The return of Savio to Sproul Plaza, reprising his historic role of rallying students for free speech, was a major event, drawing press coverage and a crowd of some five thousand. The first speaker at this rally, Brian O'Brien, head of the campus's TA union, left no doubt as to how important Savio's presence was for the Save the Steps cause. O'Brien promised the crowd he would keep his speech brief "since we have the distinguished and well-known...moral spokesman of the student movement with us here today and since most of you have come to hear him speak."[76] Accurate though they were, O'Brien's words were too leader-centered for another of the rally's organizers, Karen Lieberman, who, in the New Left egalitarian tradition, told the crowd: "Brian gave one slightly wrong impression" in presenting the demonstration as centered on Savio. "This isn't Mario's rally, and Mario will be the first to tell you that....It is *everybody's* rally," uniting all people who "strongly oppose the removal of the rallies from Sproul steps."[77]

Savio's speech at this rally has been largely forgotten, along with the Little FSM, ironically because of its success. The struggle ended without sit-ins and mass arrests. Savio's speech defending this free speech area, in Weinberg's estimation, gave the Save the Steps movement the stamp of FSM approval and was probably the decisive factor in establishing that the movement was not "just trying to make trouble" but was standing for cherished liberties.[78]

Having made history in 1964, Savio knew that the heart of his task in his speech at the Save the Steps rally in 1966 was to appeal to that history. Even before the rally, in a leaflet defending the Sproul free speech area, he stressed that he was not asking for anything radical or new, but defending freedoms already won, which was why he titled this leaflet "Our Traditional Liberties."[79] He opened his speech by directing his comments to professors "who were our allies once and who are unsure whether they should be our allies *today*," calling upon them to stand up for free speech as they had in 1964.[80] Savio told the faculty that even if they found the speeches in Sproul Plaza too radical, so long as they did not disrupt the university they must be allowed to continue, otherwise the administration would be violating the December 8 resolutions. At stake, he insisted, were free speech principles and the preservation of peace on campus. "I want those with *preponderant* power in this University, the faculty, to stand up for what once they thought was worth defending. If they do that, there will be no fight."[81]

Where Savio invoked history in an idealistic way regarding the faculty, he wielded it in a much tougher manner against administrators. Referring to how Chancellor Strong had lost his job after mishandling the FSM, he implied that UC officials were jeopardizing their own jobs in 1966 by igniting a new free speech movement over their proposed rally ban. Savio told the crowd, "I've expressed my *amazement*...[to] Vice Chancellor Boyd and Dean Arleigh Williams...that the Administration would *consider* such an outrageous [ban]....The University greatly benefited by the *purging* which it received, self-inflicted, during the Free Speech Movement. I seriously doubt it would survive a second showing. However, they may force it on us."[82]

The most dramatic part of this speech came when Savio's defiance moved from words to action. Here he turned from the plaza dispute and denounced the new university restrictions on nonstudent speech as "befitting more a *prison* than a university." Asking the crowd to watch, he violated the prohibition on nonstudents leafleting on campus by stepping away from the microphone to distribute his own free speech leaflet.[83]

Politically, Savio's speech and the Little FSM proved effective, but he paid a personal price for this activism. Not only the Berkeley Left but the faculty, traditional student groups—including the fraternities and sororities—and even the deans (privately) urged the chancellor to end his attempt to ban amplified rallies from Sproul Plaza. Heyns dropped the proposed ban by the end of the academic year.[84] However, Savio's defiance of campus regulations at the Save the Steps rally empowered his enemies in the administration. Using his public violation of campus regulations in that speech as a pretext, the administration denied his application for readmission. The chancellor's office was so eager to keep him out that it disregarded legal advice to hold a hearing before turning down his application, which at least would have given the appearance of due process. Savio's lawyer challenged the constitutionality of the rule barring nonstudents from leafleting on campus, but to no avail.[85] Savio refused to mobilize students to demand his reinstatement since he opposed the idea of mass movements promoting leaders. The orator who embodied the cause of free speech was banished from Berkeley's student body for distributing a free speech leaflet at a free speech rally.[86]

This banishment could not prevent Savio from undertaking one more defiant act on campus. In late November and early December 1966 he was prominent in antiwar protests at UC's student union. Since Naval ROTC recruiters had been allowed to set up a table in the student union building, antiwar activists staffed their own table nearby. When police removed the antiwar table, a sit-in ensued, but instead of arresting masses of students the police arrested only Savio and a few other nonstudent protesters. A brief but ineffective student strike ensued.[87]

The denial of Savio's readmission bid at Berkeley effectively ended his academic career for the remainder of the 1960s. He would never again in that decade attend college. Instead he worked part-time jobs, including bartending, clerking at Cody's Books near the campus, and doing warehouse and factory work.

Viewed in political terms, Savio looks very much like an academic martyr. He sacrificed a promising academic career for his free speech principles. Although such a conclusion has validity, it does not capture the personal side of Savio's academic and career problems, which are too complex to be seen as simply outcomes of political martyrdom. To some extent, he *chose* to abandon academia. He had a strong enough academic record to get him admitted to another university if he wished to continue his education. Had he been more concerned about his academic career, he could have rallied support for free speech in the Little FSM without brazenly defying campus regulations. That defiance seemed to reflect not just his fervent defense of free speech but also his ambivalence about resuming his student career, especially at UC, where activists would always be pressuring him to put down his books and pick up the microphone. It hardly seems possible that Savio, the emblem of student rebellion, could have matriculated quietly on any U.S. campus during the turbulent 1960s.[88]

Savio was not alone in experiencing this type of difficulty. Several black student movement leaders who launched the southern civil rights sit-ins and SNCC had similar problems returning to academic work after their tumultuous days in the civil rights movement.[89] Scholarly work requires a degree of concentration that can be difficult to find after the excitement and turmoil that comes with leading a mass movement. This may be a problem that has as much to do with the disruptiveness of politics as it does with the actions of any campus administration. Savio himself in 1969 hinted to a *Los Angeles Times* reporter that coming to the university in the turbulent 1960s had pushed him away from academic life. He told that reporter, "I think if I had been born at the right time I could have been a pretty good physicist."[90]

Rejecting an academic career may also have been a political statement. During the FSM he had denounced university officials for hypocrisy in claiming to stand for academic freedom while repressing student rights. During the Little FSM he had said that since the university refused to live up to the December 8 resolutions, it was unworthy of his attendance. Such statements led some of his professors to believe that he left the university because he was disillusioned with academia. They expressed regret that Savio, a "brilliant student," did not obtain a degree from Berkeley, finding it "tragic that the Free Speech Movement seemed to sour him on education."[91]

Yet to portray Savio's departure from the university in purely political terms is to miss its psychological dimension. While at Oxford, according to Suzanne Goldberg, he had fallen into a kind of "compulsive thinking." He would spend so much time analyzing questions unrelated to school or to "one small part of a problem" he was assigned that he would "never get to the others—so much so that even he was disturbed." While at some points in his life Savio's "desperate need to get to the truth of something" could lead to "brilliant insights," in other situations, as at Oxford, "this compulsiveness became crippling to him and kept him from being productive." Goldberg believed this psychological problem was an aftermath of "Mario's early childhood experiences, which were deeply disturbing and unresolved."[92] Even if UC had admitted him, it is possible that such problems would have blocked his academic success.

Whether its roots were primarily psychological or political, it is hard not to be struck by the pathos of Savio's work life in the mid-1960s. A brilliant student career had been short-circuited, and he would not again enjoy academic success until he returned to school in the late 1970s. Yet there may be a problem with this way of thinking about success, since it is premised on the notion that Savio approached his life, studies, and employment choices from a careerist perspective and that for him, going from being an honor student to a college dropout was a sign of failure. At Berkeley Savio was not a careerist, and he approached his education in a highly idealized way, as the final stage of a spiritual quest to sort out his moral universe through philosophy and science in the wake of his loss of faith in Catholicism. He was engaged, as he put it, in an effort "to save my soul."[93] He put ideas ahead of material considerations and viewed his willingness—and that of other student activists—to cast aside career ambitions as crucial to the success of the movement, since it meant they would risk their academic future for the causes they championed. The sixties radical ethos Savio came to support equated success less with high grades or top job prospects than with how free one could be politically and personally.

Connected to all this was the critique Savio began to articulate, at least privately, of the race for individual success. In a letter to Lynne Hollander in 1968, he cast full-time jobs as almost inherently oppressive, rat race work that stole too much of a person's freedom. In Savio's view back then,

> to be free of responsibilities for at least some time—after childhood— would be good for everyone...If you are...in a puzzle about what you want to get *involved in*, probably the worst thing to do is...work at all. Why tie up 40 hrs or more a week in something you only *may be* interested in? You only have to support one person, so...work not more than 20 hrs. a week at a job with minimal responsibilities....In your free time

do whatever comes in your head to do—provided it involves *no* entangl-
ing commitments. That is just what I've done. I'm now working at Cody's
Bookstore...30 hrs/week...I'm off 3 days a week, and on Sunday I start
work at noon. It's great.[94]

Savio may have developed this line of thought as a rationalization, making the best of a bad situation, presenting part-time work as desirable since he
could not handle a full-time career. But since this advice was given to a friend
about *her* life and not about his own, he may have been simply articulating
honestly his joy in the freedom of part-time work.

Although the antiwar movement surged nationally in 1967, this would not
be a very active political year for Savio. He faced the FSM prison sentence and
prosecution for his role in the anti-ROTC sit-in, neither of which was con-
ducive to movement leadership. He briefly maintained a link with Berkeley's
activist community by serving on the Council of Campus Organizations, but
he quickly lost patience with the political infighting and found that continued
campus activism conflicted with his need to support his family. His last speech
at Berkeley that year came in February when he criticized the administration
and students for doing too little to make their campus democratic and committed to educational reform.[95] He drew parallels between the situation on campus
and in the ghettoes, finding in both cases disorders caused by liberal official-
dom's unresponsiveness to the people's problems and complaints.

Savio also criticized the Muscatine report—UC's response to the FSM's
call for educational reform—for doing too little to change higher education.
This was a follow-up to an article he published in *Harper's* pronouncing the
Muscatine report timid, as it left intact the system of large, impersonal lecture courses and the "disproportionate emphasis on specialized education
and research" over undergraduate education.[96] The Muscatine report's failure
derived from the faculty's refusal to consider the FSM's call for more sweeping change—"instruction in small seminars and tutorials, with the quality of
students' work evaluated at length in writing rather than by the assignment
of a numerical or letter grade."[97] Savio thought meaningful reform impossible
without involving students committed to a more humane and personal form
of higher education.

This speech also dealt with Kerr and the Reaganite aftermath of the FSM.
In 1966 California's newly elected Governor Reagan fired Kerr. The shock on
campus over the firing led to talk of honoring Kerr by naming the student union
after him, an idea Savio denounced as "grotesque." A month prior to this speech
Savio responded gleefully to the first news of Kerr's firing, telling the press,
"Good riddance to bad rubbish." He quickly and publicly apologized for that

remark on the grounds that it had been "wrong to call any man 'rubbish,'" and later explained that the denunciation had been made in a moment of exhaustion, amidst the pressure of a court trial. In a letter cosigned by other activists who had initially endorsed the "rubbish" remark, Savio admitted that this attack on Kerr had been motivated "more than we would like to believe... [by] hatred."[98] Savio's bitterness toward his old nemesis made it impossible for him to go along with those who saw a need for campus radicals and administration liberals to unite in the face of a common enemy, the right-wing governor.[99] Although Savio's remarks about Kerr at the Sproul rally were not quite so bitter as those initial statements, they were still harsh. He urged students not to mourn Kerr's departure: he had opposed and Red-baited the FSM, and was neither a martyr nor a great educator. Savio conceded that Kerr lost his job because he had refused to be "the docile tool of the regents." Nonetheless, Savio proved unable (owing to his disdain for Kerr) to take the next logical step of denouncing Reagan for firing Kerr and setting a potentially dangerous precedent, which threatened to convert the UC president into the puppet of these powerful off-campus conservatives.[100]

After this Sproul speech Savio would not return to political action for another year. Since he had performed so brilliantly as the FSM's key orator, those who admired his political work hoped and expected him to continue leading the student movement during the mid-1960s. The natural place for him to provide such leadership would have been in the movement against the Vietnam War, which surged on campus after President Johnson escalated that conflict in spring 1965. Several key FSM leaders, including Weinberg and Aptheker, played important roles in the antiwar movement. Some Berkeley activists felt, as their first peace candidate for Congress, Robert Scheer, put it, "disappointed that Savio, whom I knew and admired, was not more prominent" in the antiwar movement.[101] Berkeley protest veteran Stew Albert likened Savio to Moses, who "did on occasion, surprise and shock his followers by rebelling against the power of his own charisma. He would periodically exile himself from the very student movement he helped so mightily to birth. Many of us... felt angry and let down by his political absence."[102]

Such expectations about Savio playing a prominent role in opposing the Vietnam War were consistent with his own interest in that conflict. The war loomed large in his political thought after the FSM. In fact, the titles he was considering for the chapter in his memoirs covering the mid-1960s all centered on Vietnam, including "Speaking Freely Against the War" and "We Take on the War Machine."[103] That the Vietnam conflict was escalating upset Savio, who rejected the cold warrior premises of the war and saw America's massive use of force there as trampling the Vietnamese people's right to self-determination.

He was very much affected by the "re-direction of energy" of the Berkeley student movement from civil rights struggle to antiwar protest, which, as he later explained, was sparked by "the rise of the Black Power Movement," which "increasingly made the older style of Black-and-white-together civil rights work untenable."[104]

Savio's reflections on the antiwar movement were characterized by an uneasy combination of pride and guilt. He was proud that the FSM had paved the way for Berkeley's emergence as a center of antiwar protest: "The free speech rights we had secured in the Fall of 1964 were put to work at once in the Spring of 1965," culminating in the huge, thirty-six-hour Berkeley teach-in against the war, which drew some thirty thousand people.[105] This event, along with similar if smaller teach-ins on campuses from coast to coast, helped to spark the growing student peace movement. Yet Savio looked back on the Vietnam era somewhat wistfully, regretting that he had, as Scheer and Albert suggested, not done more to build the antiwar movement.

Savio described his role in the antiwar movement as "a relatively minor part," "descending from the role of prominent movement leader to that of loyal foot soldier." He conceded that his political impact had declined from the FSM days, when he was "powerfully effective," to the point where he was "relatively marginal in the immediately succeeding era."[106] This was an unflattering way of looking at his political role, especially considering that despite personal problems—depression, family crises, economic constraints—he still participated and was arrested in a Berkeley anti-ROTC protest in 1966, worked to preserve the peace movement's access to the campus (in the Little FSM), and in 1968 ran as a third-party peace candidate for California's state senate.

This intermittent activism from 1965 to 1968 attests that even as Savio moved away from leadership he still did a considerable amount of political thinking and speaking. Were this a chapter in an average person's life, the politics in it would seem extensive, but Savio was not an average person, and so anything less than total commitment and full-time leadership seemed less than adequate. In this context his self-criticism about descending from leadership has considerable validity. Given his fame and the power of his oratory, he could have become a national leader in the struggle to stop a war he regarded as unjust. But he did not play that role, and this failure seemed so significant to Savio that he accorded it a prominent and gloomy place in the narrative he was planning for his memoir, which centered on the issue of speech—his own.[107]

In Savio's telling, his bumpy history regarding speech began with his painful stammer as a child and teenager, followed by liberation in the FSM, when he found his voice as an orator. But progress halted during the Vietnam era, with his inability to serve as a movement speaker in any sustained way. "My relative capacity or incapacity to say what was needed saying is a recurring theme," he wrote. His phrasing here—likening his limited role in the Vietnam period to the blocked speech of his childhood—suggests that he felt guilty about failing to do more to voice dissent when it was so badly needed.[108]

One ought not confuse guilt with envy. Savio had no love of the limelight and stepped out of it as quickly as he could. He did not begrudge the fame of his successors on the left, who came to prominence as the peace movement surged. He thought that movement a heroic attempt to confront "the ugly fact of US imperialism in Vietnam," and so displayed a deep solidarity with it.[109]

At the same time, however, he was never comfortable with the growing "influence of Marxist ideas and Leninist organization" within the mid- and late 1960s student Left, which eroded the experimental spirit of the early New Left. He found "Marxist analyses of difficult questions facile and reductionist." While aware that "ideological formulas and sweeping generalizations" used by radicals to explain the war were useful in provoking people to think about the roots of that conflict, he did not find the Marxist analysis persuasive. "It has often occurred to me that effectiveness in the struggle to end the War was sometimes in inverse ratio to thoughtfulness."[110] Thus while his retreat from leadership and personal problems made the Vietnam era a sad time, this was not a blank page in his political history. As a founder of the student movement of the sixties, but one who descended from leadership quickly, he was sympathetic with the evolving New Left, yet critical too—and thought this gave him a "unique perspective" on the Vietnam era movement.[111] Given the change in his role from leader to part-time activist, any account of Savio in the post-FSM 1960s must increasingly focus on his political *thought*, which was independent and insightful, and less on his political actions, which after spring 1965 first gradually and then greatly diminished.

This stepping away from leadership makes all the more ironic the FBI's covert decision in February 1967 to place Savio's "name on the security index" as an "increasingly involved" subversive and protest leader who threatened national security.[112] Actually, in 1967 Savio spent far more time paying for his past activism than engaging in political protest. After his appeal failed in the FSM case in July 1967, he began serving his four-month prison term.

Savio never published a word about his prison time. His letters from Santa Rita suggest that he used his jail time for personal and political reflection, and even enjoyed the respite prison offered from the pressures of life. He confided to a friend in mid-July that "prison, so far, has been good for me. I've long needed to be free of obligation, to be alone, to take stock. This place is a strange combination of monastery and boys' camp, and less regimented than the high school I went to. I've done a lot of reading, and more thinking about the present and the past."[113]

His prison letters document a continuing interest in politics, but also a sense that the time was not right for him to return to leadership. Savio thought he fit in neither with the politics of an increasingly ideological left nor with the bohemianism of the blossoming counterculture. "What we once called 'the Movement' has changed, it seems to me, quite out of existence," he wrote in August 1967. "People are really moving in different ways. Some people [in Progressive Labor, idolizing the proletariat] are talking about beginning political work in the factories again, others are moving in the direction, roughly, of the Haight Ashbury [hippie scene]. Neither direction is quite mine." He did hope that "in time something may develop on the political scene to which I can relate," and felt that as a veteran movement leader, he had "an obligation to help create that something. Yet I don't feel I'm ready to try." He thought overcoming his psychological problems had to take precedence over politics. To embrace a political role without first resolving those problems would be "to choose not to grow up, not to choose my own identity and some measure of deeper autonomy than I've known in the past."[114]

In his private writings Savio seemed to be arguing with himself, seeking to overcome his guilt about walking away from leadership amidst the crisis of a war-torn nation. He wrote of his worry that

I may be letting a need for stability and permanence push me away (or draw, seduce me away) from my political "duties." But we've always conceived our political "duties" in very personal terms. So I find it impossible to separate my political duties from my duties to myself. The other and more authentic side of it is, I get very suspicious whenever I feel the need to appeal to duty against desire![115]

Savio ended this internal debate by deciding that after he left prison, "politics can't be central—at least not at first." He planned to focus on finding "a way for" his family, which now included Suzanne and their son Stefan, "to settle into a sort of life which will permit more freedom than either S[uzanne] or I have ever known."[116]

Such writing leaves no doubt that Savio's family meant a great deal to him and that he hoped by removing himself at least temporarily from leadership he could build a happy personal life. It is ironic, then, that, due to the sexist political climate of the time, some of those disappointed by Savio's withdrawal from leadership made his wife a scapegoat for this unwelcome news. At its worst, as Suzanne Goldberg recalled, this scapegoating manifested itself in FSM veterans treating her as if

I was evil and the reason Mario stepped down had to do with my influence, and that's absolutely not true. It was completely Mario's decision....Mario had lots of problems, psychological problems, and I was blamed for everything without people...knowing what was really going on....I just wanted him to do what he wanted to do and...felt right about. I wasn't into telling him what to do.[117]

The Goldberg-bashing response to Savio's departure attests that the FSM, for all its egalitarianism, was a male-dominated movement, which displayed much of the same gender bias as the larger society. In the FSM women often had difficulty having their ideas taken seriously. Goldberg had already experienced this at FSM Executive Committee meetings, where she would speak and find that her ideas "would never be taken up. And a half hour later, either Jack or Mario would say exactly the same thing and the group would say 'Oh yeah, that's a great idea.'"[118] It is not surprising that some male movement veterans overlooked the fact that Goldberg was herself a committed activist (elected to the FSM Steering Committee because she was very bright, articulate, and one of the first graduate students to become involved in the free speech struggle) who had no desire to steer Savio away from any politics. They defined her only in terms of her relationship with him, and assumed the worst. This anticipated what happened later in the 1960s with Yoko Ono being scapegoated by rock fans for the breakup of the Beatles. In both cases a woman was blamed for interfering with the historic mission of a "great man": with Yoko it was John Lennon and his music, while with Suzanne it was Savio and his politics.

Neither she nor Savio had the language to critique sexism, which would only evolve later in the sixties as second-wave feminism hit its stride. Savio never implied that Goldberg hindered his political activism. The idea that he was a great man whose departure from the political stage was a tragedy requiring a scapegoat would have seemed preposterous to him, given his opposition to the notion that movements required great leaders. Temperamentally, Savio was disinclined to treat women or anyone in the movement condescendingly. Bettina Aptheker recalled that even though the absence of feminist discourse meant she could not articulate her complaints in gender terms, when during FSM meetings she asked Savio to help her get the floor, he would intervene on her behalf out of friendship and a sense of fairness. Recalling such intervention, she attributes it to his own experiences as a victim of child abuse, which made him "much more sensitive to abuse to anybody...He understood in a way that many men didn't the kind of experiences that girls and women have."[119]

In contrast to the gender issue, which still remained submerged, Savio, like other sixties radicals, tried to apply his egalitarian principles to child rearing.

He wrote from prison that he wanted his son Stefan—who had very serious developmental problems—to be raised in a way that made antiauthoritarian personal politics "central, since we will have to create a new society out of whole cloth." Thinking back to his own unhappy childhood, he expressed a desire to avoid "the extreme isolation of the 'nuclear family'" and "the concentration of authority which goes with such a family." The thought of his son being subject to overbearing authority left Savio "fearful to the point of panic." So he pondered working with Suzanne to create an "intentional community—an extended family by choice," which included others from their circle of friends.[120]

While Savio's prison letters tell us much about his political and family concerns, they say little about his relationships in jail across racial lines. But the stories told by fellow inmates indicate that he made a lasting impression. The most memorable of these stories was one told by Truston Davis. While Savio was in jail for an act of political conscience, Davis, as he later put it, was in Santa Rita because he was "a common criminal." Davis, a young black man, was mopping the floor in jail when Savio—whom he had never met before—came into the room. Annoyed, Davis yelled at him not to step on the floor. Savio paused and then replied, "What are my options? The walls, the ceiling…?" Though Savio had responded jovially, in the tense prison world Davis took this as an insult, and called on Savio to join him in the mop room. Savio followed him there, with Davis ready for a fight and Savio unaware that violence loomed. Savio asked him "a hundred questions," like whether the guards were allowed to walk on the wet floors (they were), and seemed such an empathetic and "special" person that Davis dropped the idea of fighting, especially after he realized who Mario was. Having grown up in Louisiana and with relatives in Mississippi, Davis appreciated Savio's work in the South. After the two talked they walked out onto the wet floor together. They became good friends. After their prison time, when Davis was homeless he would come to live with Savio, who convinced him to audit classes at Berkeley. When they lived together Savio consulted Davis about his writings, impressing Davis with his warmth, humor, and egalitarianism.[121]

After the end of his jail term, in fall 1967, Savio did not immediately reenter the political world. It was not until almost a year later that he returned to part-time political leadership, participating in launching the Peace and Freedom Party, a radical third party in California, on whose ticket he ran for state senate in 1968. That party's primary focus was opposing the Vietnam War. Savio knew that, as a third-party candidate, he had little chance of being elected, and so his campaign was an exercise in symbolic protest. His speeches denounced the war, racial discrimination, the two-party system, and poverty. He urged America off its path of imperialism and war, and advocated redistribution of wealth in a campaign that had a democratic socialist tinge.[122]

Although Savio articulated a serious radical critique of America, his campaign never made the kind of major impact he seemed to have envisioned initially. Making few speeches, he failed to pour much energy into the campaign. To his childhood friend Art Gatti, Savio confided that he was "running for State Senate…, but only nominally. My name is on the state ballot but I haven't been, and won't be campaigning." He explained this lack of energy primarily in psychological terms, writing Gatti that his failure to wage an intense campaign was "*mostly* due to my own tendency to fall apart from internal chaos. It finally caught up. I have had to declare a strict moratorium on all obligations, duties, responsibilities—except the minimum of food and shelter for my family."[123]

There was a political dimension to his failure to push harder in his third-party candidacy. Savio told Gatti the reason he wrote that his personal problems were "mostly" and not solely responsible for that failure was that "a good bit of the blame" rested "with my disagreement with the politics of the Peace and Freedom Party." Savio disliked the party's revolutionary posturing and sectarian tendencies. He "felt that that they [Peace and Freedom Party organizers] should be trying to build a broad-base opposition party. Instead they seem content—gleeful!—about confining their activities to addressing only the committed." While Savio was critical of the Democratic Party and of peace activists who remained in that party, he thought the Peace and Freedom Party carried this too far, displaying "contempt for the McCarthy people." He found his East Bay branch of the party "dominated by (very romantic) revolutionists—or so they imagine themselves to be," who lacked the inclination and ability to connect with the electorate and to become more than a small, isolated cadre of militants.[124]

Savio's reservations about the Peace and Freedom Party were linked to his discomfort with the political and intellectual rigidity of the late sixties New Left. Through his work with that party he "had the opportunity to observe…the increasingly Marxist orientation of the Movement," and how this led to poorly thought out political positions, which were often ultraradical and self-defeating. He thought the party erred by placing itself "under the lash of a troubled alliance with the [Black] Panthers," which led it to reflexively adopt "any and all 'third world' demands," making it impossible to build a party that could appeal to working-class whites.[125] Still committed to nonviolence, and distrustful of leader-centered politics, he looked critically on the Panthers, with their violent rhetoric and idealization of leaders. Thus at a March 1968 party meeting, Savio spoke up against a proposed resolution demanding the freeing of imprisoned Black Panther leader Huey Newton "by any means necessary." He told fellow Peace and Freedom Party members, "I don't think the revolution in America depends on burning down half the city of Oakland to free one man. Almost all are in jail unfairly."[126]

With his enthusiasm for campaigning dulled by his reservations about this third party and by his personal problems, Savio fared poorly on election day, receiving less than 12,000 votes to the Democratic candidate's 183,122.[127] Jack Weinberg, who helped direct the party's statewide effort, insists that Savio's poor showing in the election "was not his fault. The Peace and Freedom Party peaked with achieving ballot status, and all its campaigns were thin and ineffective afterthoughts."[128] The Peace and Freedom Party electoral initiative centered on raising the antiwar banner, since it lacked funds to compete with the major parties. Just getting on the state ballot in California, which required organizers to gather a hundred thousand signatures, represented a significant achievement for such a low-budget organization.[129]

After his candidacy, Savio rarely returned to the political limelight in the closing years of the Vietnam era. He briefly came back to UC in 1969 during the People's Park crisis to speak in support of the movement's demand to retain a community park on land the university owned and was seeking to take back.[130] He also occasionally spoke out against the war. In 1971 Savio and Goldberg filed to run jointly for mayor of Berkeley but withdrew before the race began.[131] There is no escaping the fact that he spent most of the mid- and late 1960s as a part-time activist rather than as a leader. In the early 1970s Savio's role in politics diminished further, and by the mid-1970s it had ceased entirely.

Since Savio's political stardom faded in the late 1960s and all but disappeared in the 1970s, it is not surprising that historians have said virtually nothing about him in this period. Nonetheless, he has much to teach about the New Left in these years, though more as an empathetic yet critical observer than as a leader. Because Savio knew the early New Left so well, helping invent its style of political discourse, he had a distinctive sensibility about how the student movement changed over the course of the decade. He reflected in bittersweet terms on the late 1960s crisis of the New Left. Where other early New Left veterans, such as Todd Gitlin, have been strongly, even harshly, critical of the late sixties Left, Savio was critical yet understanding. Calling for a balanced assessment, he thought those writing about the New Left should "not in retrospect presume to tell us how crazy we were—without also saying who and what made us crazy."[132]

Savio cast the radicals of the late New Left as well-intentioned yet flawed activists. They battled for peace, performing admirably in the face of tremendous political obstacles, but also adopted a flawed rhetorical and leadership style. In opposing the Vietnam War, the New Left had, in Savio's view, faced what was in some ways more difficult work than his age cohort had in their civil rights and free speech agitation of the early 1960s. Where the early New

Left had been able to grow while championing moderate demands for basic constitutional rights, the late New Left had to challenge cold war America's powerful anti-Communist consensus when opposing the crusade in Southeast Asia. The late sixties Left confronted the complicated task of popularizing what Savio termed "the most immoderate" demand imaginable—halting its war against a hated Communist foe. In articulating this demand the movement adopted an immoderate "rhetoric of opposition and disruption" to stop the war machine.[133]

In the hands of an increasingly ideological and dogmatic Left, this rhetoric of disruption evolved, much to Savio's regret, into sectarian political discourse that isolated radicals. This he contrasted with the coalition-building rhetoric of the early New Left, which had been a "rhetoric of communication."[134] As the movement's political posture became ever more revolutionary, radicals "no longer believed they could talk to ordinary Americans," yet they also believed "that revolution was just around the corner." Savio found incredibly contradictory this New Left dream of leading a revolution on behalf of people with whom it could not and would not communicate, and he criticized this as a brand of "fantasy thinking."[135]

Since he had such a fine-tuned ear for effective political discourse and a poetic sense of how to create such discourse, it is not surprising that he disliked the abstract, jargon-filled rhetoric of the late sixties Left. Savio had "a total mistrust of Marxist phrase mongering" and thought it bred oratory that was not merely unclear but actually incomprehensible.[136] He complained that in the late sixties

> people invented all sorts of neologisms like corporate liberalism....They didn't want to say capitalism because then people would stop listening....So they found all kinds of slippery neologisms...The rhetoric took on a[n]...abstract quality....It became increasingly difficult to know what the speakers were saying....I found it increasingly difficult in fact [to believe] that *the speakers* knew what they were saying.[137]

For Savio, not just the rhetoric but Marxist ideas themselves "often seemed simplistic and forced," suffering from "a strain of reductionism in which all questions were cast in monochrome," with class and economics explaining almost everything while overlooking race, religion, gender, and nationality.[138] He was equally put off by Marxist scholasticism. The Left's debates about the Soviet Union—whether it was a "deformed workers' state" or "a non-capitalist society called 'bureaucratic collectivism'"—reminded him of the Catholic Church's doctrinal hairsplitting.[139] The tone of the neo-Marxist sects, with

their competing political lines and certitude about their monopoly on historical truth—what they termed "correct positions"—seemed almost theological in the most negative sense: "For an apostate Catholic, shopping in the
dense...thicket of neo-Marxist sects was altogether too painfully like selecting
a Protestant denomination."[140] Their mechanistic view of how societies evolved
seemed naive to Savio: "With my background in Thomist and English language
philosophy, the neo-Hegelian talk of 'objective contradictions' was all a bit
much."[141] The Leninist concept of leadership, positing a leftist cadre leading the
way toward revolution, proved too elitist for Savio, with his distrust of leader-
centered politics. He planned to write a book (never completed) criticizing
the Marxifying of the New Left, while culling from Marxists any insights they
could offer on imperialism and inequality, and translating those "into ordinary
American English."[142]

It seemed to Savio that doctrinal purity led to a lack of balance on such
questions as the Arab-Israeli dispute: "Particularly unedifying (and ominous
for the future) was the way in which Jewish Marxist activists fell easily into
embracing the just cause of Palestinian national rights in disregard of the
competing claims of Jewish survival." He was particularly troubled by this,
since one of his formative political memories was the shock he had experienced as a child seeing the photos of the Jewish victims of Nazi concentration
camps. "Given the profound impact that the Holocaust had upon me," he
wrote, he was "astonished" at how ideology seemed to leave Jewish Marxists
ignoring the Middle East's Jewish minority and focusing exclusively on Arab
rights.[143]

Savio, however, tempered his criticism of the late sixties Left by taking into
account the difficult political environment in which it had to function. Much as
he disliked the confrontational rhetoric, he saw a justification for it in that "the
war effort needed to be impeded."[144] So there was a logic to using disruptive
rhetoric. The desperate need to end the killing in Vietnam meant that "there
was no way to have a decade to catch up to educate people so you could talk to
them about these things. In fact what was necessary was what the country got.
It got the best it could, given the time pressure."[145] In light of this very different
historical context, Savio thought it simplistic to indict the late sixties Left by
comparing it unfavorably with his own early New Left generation (even though
at points he had done just that). It was easier to communicate and to sound
uplifting during the early sixties since the work of aiding oppressed blacks was
a self-evident defense of human rights. Late sixties militancy had to be tied to
disruption of a war. "It's less sweet. I mean there is no way it could be otherwise.
It is an attack rather than a defense....That's what was needed because the war
had to be stopped."[146]

Trying not to hold himself above the late sixties Left, Savio argued that in some respects he and his successors in the New Left confronted similar obstacles, and responded in parallel ways. Both the FSM and the antiwar movement confronted a public that was too vehemently antiradical to give them a fair hearing. Savio found the media so biased against the FSM that he "drew a conclusion" similar to the one

> the antiwar movement drew…: that the Free Speech Movement could within the boundaries of the campus…communicate…deeply, clearly. But as far as the world outside was concerned we couldn't get good press, so what we had to get was big press. We had to make such a stink that they couldn't ignore us. And writ large the antiwar movement in some ways in its rhetorical approach to organizing people against the war did much the same.[147]

If Savio's writings and speeches about Marxism and late sixties radicalism seem conflicted, this reflected how his own politics, conscience, and upbringing pulled and pushed him on this issue. Having grown up in cold war America witnessing the way the anti-Communist crusade warped political discourse to a reflexive antiradicalism, he did not think it fair to simply condemn Marxism. He was willing to acknowledge that Marxism, for all its flaws, played an important and at times constructive role in the discourse of the late sixties Left. This was different from the early sixties, when, as Mario put it, "socialist or specifically Marxist ideas seemed to many activists to possess little relevance" to their civil rights work, and back then "the presence of Marxists in movement organizations was a curiosity if not an embarrassment."[148] But as the Vietnam War escalated, "the Movement needed ideas and ways of thinking about America's aggression in Southeast Asia. And only the Marxists were offering anything of particular relevance."[149] He found their economic critique of U.S. imperialism unsatisfactory but still more credible than the liberal explanation of the war as a mere mistake or historical accident, and so he was neither surprised nor outraged that Marxist influence grew on the campus Left.[150]

Savio was candid about the ways his own disaffection from capitalist, war-making America pushed him closer to the Old Left style of politics in the waning days of the 1960s. He came to believe that the demands for equality made by black America could not be met unless there was "radical reform of 'the system,'" and this gave the Marxist critique of American capitalism a certain resonance.[151] Although his worldview differed from that of the Marxists, he felt a bond with these radicals because they named and condemned U.S. imperialism at a time when it was waging an unjust war. The whole constellation of allies the antiwar movement now had on the left prodded him to become introspective about his relationship with the Communist world. Recognizing that in opposing the Vietnam War the antiwar movement had allied itself with "the National Liberation Front" (NLF, the Viet Cong) and thereby aligned itself with Communist Russia and China, Savio wondered: "Was this alignment a mere historical accident, or was there some deeper significance? How could our almost obsessively democratic movement now be fighting on the same side as the principal Communist powers?"[152]

On a more emotional level, Savio admired the determined resistance of the Viet Cong to the massive military might the United States employed in that "imperial adventure" in Vietnam. At antiwar demonstrations he "chanted on behalf of the NLF." Even in retrospect, he would say that he was "proud of" his "support for the national liberation struggle of Ho Chi Minh and the NLF." Ho seemed to him "a great man, an immeasurably finer person [than the]...endless succession of mindless puppets that [the] US kept supporting in Vietnam," despite the fact that Ho "was a Communist, a national Communist."[153] But Savio's civil libertarianism did not allow him to convert this admiration for NLF anti-imperialism into an uncritical reading of the Communist orientation of the Vietnamese revolution: "I could not discount 100% what I knew to be true of Communist government. I continued to believe that 'the most beautiful thing in the world is the freedom of speech.'"[154]

Despite his sympathy for the NLF, he shared none of the late New Left's illusions that the tide was turning toward world revolution. While romantic radicals saw evidence of such a tide in the uprising in France in May 1968, when students and workers united, he was far more sober, even somber. For Savio the most memorable event of 1968 was not France's student rebellion and the revolutionary hopes it raised but Czechoslovakia and the reforms the Soviet invasion crushed. He hoped that American Communists might find the courage and independence to emulate their Italian counterparts in adopting a brand of "Euro-communism," maintaining the socialist ideal while criticizing Soviet imperialism. Had American Communists shown such independence, Savio—who at this point in his life was as close to the organized Left as he would ever become, in part because he agreed with much of its radical critique of U.S. imperialism—might have joined the Communist Party (CP). Such an affiliation seemed possible only during that brief moment when a serious challenge to the Stalinist tradition was being mounted in the CP during the late sixties, and Savio had grounds for hoping that just as "a new generation was remaking the American political and social landscape a similar 'greening' might be taking place within the CPUSA." But when this revolt died and the CPUSA failed to criticize the invasion of Czechoslovakia, he gave up on this Old Left remnant, finding that its Russophilia made it incapable of building a viable, critically minded American Left.[155]

It seems odd that Savio would have even considered joining the CP given his democratic politics and distaste for the "elitist" character of Leninist organization, with its party hierarchy dictating key decisions, and the appalling Communist history regarding civil liberty. Almost as strange was the fact that in this same period the other Old Left group that he recalled feeling "a certain attraction toward" was "the Independent (then International) Socialists," an organization that was adamantly anti-Communist. So, as Savio later put it, he had been drawn to both the CP and the IS, "whose overall perspectives were the most divergent." The attraction seems a manifestation of Savio's sense of political isolation and ineffectiveness in the late 1960s, which made it possible for him to be impressed by "the *effectiveness* of 'disciplined' political work" of these two Old Left remnants. But Savio's politics had always centered on ethics rather than efficiency, and ultimately this and his dislike of ideology and sectarianism prevailed. He took it as "a clear danger signal" that he had been attracted by such opposites, realized that the attraction made little sense, and so "never applied to join either," concluding that the "*old left* in America had nothing to offer."[156]

While steering clear of the Old Left, Savio also had reservations about the mainstream antiwar movement, which he criticized for evading the truths exposed via radical terminology and radical questions about American war making. He scoffed at the movement for calling the national antiwar action a "*moratorium* instead of a *strike* because the idea of a *strike* might offend too many." And much as in its rhetoric, the movement, he felt, was in its analysis evasive on the connections between the Vietnam War and the broader, long-term pattern of U.S. imperialism, unwilling to explore such taboo questions as whether "Marx and Lenin, for all their deficiencies, were after all more right than wrong" about the links between capitalism and imperialism. He realized the difficulties in posing such questions, since "no weight of evidence will persuade one against one's will that father is a murderer," but he thought the movement needed to expose these hard truths.[157]

Savio's memoir of the late 1960s and early 1970s suggests that his thinking about politics was as experiential, honest, and iconoclastic as his oratory had been in 1964. Not tied down by the dogmas of the Old Left or late New Left, he never lost the intellectual openness of the early New Left. He viewed both sides of the cold war critically rather than falling into a romance with either side. But this does not mean he was balanced in his analysis. As he indicated in one of his final antiwar speeches of that era, "six long, frustrating years of anti-War protest" had pushed him toward an increasingly radical indictment of American imperialism and a sense that "the Communist states have been much more peace seeking" than the United States. Influenced by New Left diplomatic histories, he saw the cold war not as a post–World War II effort to contain Communist expansionism but as a capitalist offensive dating back to Western intervention in Siberia shortly after the Bolshevik Revolution. Though acknowledging the "oppressive character of the Russian government," he thought the Western powers bore a major part of the responsibility for this "lack of liberty," since their cold war kept the Soviets on a permanent war footing and in a state of siege.[158]

The leftist movement that Savio found the "most impressive and…inspiring" was Salvador Allende's Popular Unity government in Chile because it came to power democratically, implementing socialist reforms while respecting civil liberties. He was outraged that the United States destabilized this regime and "supported a blood coup" that resulted in Allende's death in 1973. This led him to "take a second look at Castro's Cuba." He wondered whether the civil liberties idealism that had led him to look down on the Cuban revolution had been realistic, for the coup in Chile suggested that any government in the Americas moving away from capitalism would be sabotaged by the United States, even if it was democratic. It became evident to Savio that it was precisely because Allende was democratic that he proved so vulnerable to the U.S. destabilization campaign. Cuba's lack of pluralism was "a policy which—at a high price to be sure—had permitted the survival of the Cuban experiment."[159] So we find him questioning both sides and then questioning himself, conceding that his love of free speech had left him with a perspective that may have been too provincial and idealistic to take into account the harsh choices Latin American revolutionaries faced because of the United States' violent counterrevolutionary policies.

Savio's open-mindedness was also evident in his response to the counterculture. He acknowledged major differences between the political and cultural rebels in the youth movement of the 1960s and noted that he "was more in sympathy with the style of the political radicals [since] that's what I was." Nonetheless, he credited the counterculture with creating "something real and meaningful…a counter-institutional movement." The cultural rebels led him to see "that it's possible to take yourself too seriously…Hippieness…was calling to all of us to be a little less staid, a little less proper and correct all the time." He saw the attraction in "the hippie theory of transforming the world. It was a theory of corruption of youth, happy corruption, to take people one at a time, and just sort of walk away from society and watch it crumble." This "happy defeatism" offered relief for political radicals who were tired because "we beat our head against the wall" but still found that society wasn't "going to listen." The counterculture provided the option of a "rest" from this losing crusade, along with a new, if more modest, hope for change by preaching that "we have to develop a new society within this one because we're not going to get this one to change."[160] He conceded that the cultural rebels had a more liberated lifestyle than his generation of political rebels.

> The political movement was a little more monochrome; we were passionate but single-minded. And that was correct; we accomplished what we could within the limits imposed on us. The hippie movement was more Technicolor...saying the whole shebang is just absolutely hopeless and going off and cultivating your own garden.[161]

Savio thought it would have been "dynamite" if the political and cultural rebels could have merged, and for one moment that had seemed possible. This came with the People's Park battle in 1969 as Berkeley radicals united with community activists—including some from the local countercultural scene—to protect a community park from being evicted by its UC landlord. This eventually proved to be only a rare moment of overlapping interests (when the Left's antiadministration agenda and the hippie desire for their own countercultural space coincided) rather than the start of a long-term alliance. Even Savio, whose background was in the straight political world, appeared on Berkeley's campus during the People's Park struggle in a different way. Having been banned from campus, he wore a Lone Ranger mask—given to him by a protest organizer—as he made his way to Sproul to give his speech. The next day, students also used a countercultural form to express their political solidarity, sporting masks from the Beatles cartoon movie *Yellow Submarine*.[162]

Savio saw merit in the counterculture's claim that "people need to be loosened up." It offered a way out of the social conformity that had gone hand in hand with the political regimentation of cold war America. "The hippies were saying we can eliminate that repression just like taking your coat off." This call to loosen up socially seemed more attractive than the new forms of political regimentation embraced by the Marxifying Left of the late 1960s. He concluded that though his political ideals prevented him from totally embracing the counterculture, "I felt less comfortable with the sectarian politicos than the hippies." To join the Marxist "sectarians...was like deciding to rejoin the Catholic Church. I could not stand that."[163]

Yet Savio maintained a critical perspective on the counterculture. He thought its message too escapist, which "would be bad if it became...simply a way for the privileged to ignore the less privileged." While admitting that a warm sense of community came with passing the pipe around, he regretted that under the counterculture's influence "a lot of people got blown away by

drugs."[164] The counterculture's emphasis on spontaneity and immediate grati-
fication was not compatible with political action, since movements for political
change "require planning, reason. There was something anti-intellectual about
hippieness." Being "too experimental with your life" in the countercultural
mode could leave a person too distracted to complete the kind of "planning
and coordination" necessary in politics. Ultimately he found the counterculture illusory because "hippies wanted to have a post-revolutionary life without
going through a revolution. I don't really think it's possible."[165]

Savio's ability to see both sides of complicated historical questions was
also evident in his assessment of the end of the 1960s and his consideration
of whether its protest movements went up in flames as the decade expired.
He did not allow the implosion of SDS to totally dominate his view of the late
1960s. While such New Left organizations collapsed, other organizations and
movements rooted in the 1960s thrived as America entered the 1970s, including the women's movement, gay and lesbian liberation, the environmental and
antinuclear movements, and the drive for alternatives to the two-party system.
In this sense, as Savio put it, "the Movement never died. The 1960s had been a
decade of relentless political, social, and cultural innovation. The Movement
was the mother of many movements."[166] Far from vanishing, the insurgent
spirit of the 1960s spread "the impulse for change" so far and so wide that in
the following decades it "reached the American majority." This impulse proved
powerful enough to reshape American politics and social life. He thought that
"the deepest result of the 1960s" came in the form of the women's liberation
movement and the related struggles for lesbian and gay rights, and their challenge to "the fundamental structural unit of the old society, the hierarchical
nuclear family."[167] This in turn bred a backlash (Reaganism) and conflict over
whether the social changes wrought by the 1960s would be reversed—a struggle
that dominated electoral politics in the United States through the late twentieth
century.[168]

While cheering this lasting impact of the 1960s, Savio was keenly aware that
key New Left organizations and the tradition of mass protest out in the streets
and on campuses declined dramatically in the 1970s. The progressive politics
that endured were "a quieter form." As to why the New Left declined, he thought
that "exhaustion was part of it." So were "the differing needs" that developed
in "the black [nationalist] and white [New Left] movements that precluded a
continuing cooperation." The New Left's revolutionary expectations led to disillusionment and demoralization when they could not be realized. "As political
hope receded…the movement dissolved in delusions of violence and chemical
euphoria, or for some in an inward migration." Beset with sectarian rivalries,
the Left lost its moral compass, leading Savio to reflect back on "the political

excesses in which a non-violent, anti-elitist, democratic movement now occasionally engaged in vilification, trashing or riot."[169]

Not all of the fault for the "chaos and quietism" of the New Left's final years was internal. Savio thought that the "world duopoly of the Cold War" meant that the New Left had to contend with immensely powerful international purveyors of violence, which, even after years of antiwar protest, proved unwilling to alter their imperialist policies. That duopoly "by its vicious behavior in Czechoslovakia and Chile (to cite only the most prominent cases) did its best to destroy our hope" for a more democratic and peaceful world.[170] Such events left Savio feeling grim about the prospects for change or even finding a mode of analysis that explained the movement's decline and its future:

> No existing theories seemed to fit the facts. A consistent moral stance appeared impossible to formulate w[ith]in the parameters of the Cold War. The murders at Kent State were not the only tragedies contributing to a widely shared experience of spiritual exhaustion and withered hope....We had free speech, but nothing left to say.[171]

For Savio the late 1960s and early 1970s were years of personal crises. His psychological problems, which by fall 1966 included "compulsive thinking" and "internal pressure," impaired his ability to function with any intellectual efficiency. He began to experience panic attacks, especially in work settings. He was frequently depressed, in part because of his inability to function well even in part-time jobs. Added to this was the stress of financial problems and coping with his handicapped son.[172]

In planning his memoirs Savio grappled with whether and how to discuss these problems publicly. Never comfortable with self-centered leaders, he wanted his memoir to illuminate larger political questions rather than to focus on his private life, so he did not plan to "include any lengthy purely personal narrative" exploring his psychological problems. But he thought "it would be less than candid to inquire whether" his "own difficulties" affected his political perceptions and his memories of the New Left's aftermath. He saw the need "to describe the process of withdrawal from explicit political struggle." So Savio planned to write briefly but candidly about the personal problems he would never address from a podium.[173]

In Savio's telling, past and present family problems led to his personal crisis. In one version of the introduction to his memoir he attributed that crisis to recent family troubles: "My first marriage...was falling apart. Our first child, born in a time of great shared optimism, was severely retarded. I became seriously depressed....When my marriage broke up [in November 1971], I did too. I spent a long time in a psychiatric hospital."[174] In another draft Savio, while linking his depression to the collapse of his marriage cited events dating back to his youth as contributing to his personal crisis. Only after the decline of the mass insurgency of the sixties did he "realize how unstable and inadequate" his "own formation of character had been. The deep division within my family...combined with a sharp severance from the church left me in real need for alternative structure."[175]

This second version is multidimensional and seems the more convincing; it suggests that the collapse of his marriage was a trigger for the onset of an identity crisis with roots in his childhood, centered, as he wrote, on the "deep division within my family." Here Savio seems to have been alluding to the battles between his father and grandfather that scarred him emotionally as a child. His ambivalent feelings about his father translated into resistance to the work he seemed destined for in the sciences, since Mario associated science and technology with Joseph Savio. Another aspect of the identity conflict had to do with his mother. In writing of the continuing price of his "sharp severance" with the church, Mario was referring to more than theology. He had been deeply affected by his mother's religiosity, never having forgotten her desire for him to become a priest or gotten over the disappointment he had caused her by his failure to fulfill that mission. He not only remained emotionally close to his mother but, he believed, never adequately separated from her, in part because of the strained relationship with his father, a dynamic that contributed to his psychological difficulties.[176]

Suzanne Goldberg tends to agree with this second version in that she sees Savio's emotional problems as having roots that stretched far earlier into his life than their married years. She views the ending of their marriage as a reflection of Savio's psychological crisis rather than the outcome of some flaw in their relationship. The marriage did not die because of quarreling or personal friction. It foundered, according to Goldberg, because Savio—beset by psychological problems—felt he was not an adequate role model for his sons and could no longer play the role of husband and father in a way of which he could feel proud.[177]

Savio's summary of what led to his breakdown may be as significant for what it excluded as what it included. There was no discussion of the sexual abuse he suffered as a child and how it factored into his psychological struggles. This may have been too painful and private for him to discuss in print, but it could have played a role in his crisis. Or it may be that he thought the abuse issue less responsible for his anguish than the birth family conflicts that he was planning to describe.

The memoir linked the timing of his personal crisis to events in the political world. "I, for one, had grown to rely upon the movement emotionally as well as intellectually and politically."[178] The movement's decline removed an important source of emotional support. The sense of community that Savio had praised so effusively when he wrote of his days in the civil rights movement and the FSM had played a major role in sustaining him psychologically as well as politically. In the FSM, Savio "functioned extremely well…because he was part of a movement and an ego-strengthening Steering Committee; he wasn't 'out there by himself.'"[179] And when, with the demise of the New Left, this community faded away, Savio, enveloped by personal problems, faded from the political scene too. Much like the student movement whose death he mourned, Savio, as he later put it, "had free speech, but nothing left to say." He would not find his political voice again until the 1980s.[180]

11

BATTLING BACK

Politically, the early and mid-1970s were fatal for the New Left and barren for Savio. The student movement went into a tailspin from which it would never recover. Although the massacre of students at Kent State by the National Guard in May 1970 sparked a record number of student demonstrations, by the following fall the memory of that tragedy as well as the bloodshed at Jackson State chilled the political atmosphere. Students now realized that death could be the price for antiwar protest. The winding down of U.S. ground troops' role in the war due to Nixon's Vietnamization program, followed finally by the Paris Peace Accords in 1973 and Saigon's fall to Communist forces in 1975, combined with the recession and the lack of radical leadership in the wake of the implosion of SDS to further impede campus activism.[1] At this time, when the declining New Left so badly needed leadership, it could not turn to Savio, one of the Left's most gifted leaders. He was in too much personal pain even to consider playing a political role. His bouts with depression worsened to the point where he spent extensive periods as an inpatient at a Los Angeles psychiatric institution.[2]

The low point of Savio's psychological crisis in the 1970s came with his mother's losing battle against cancer. He spent a great deal of time helping to care for her during her illness, and her death left him despondent, triggering his one attempt at suicide. He survived that attempt, but for the rest of his life he battled with symptoms of depression, high anxiety, panic attacks, obsessive thinking, and compulsive behavior, while always seeking to understand and resolve the conflicts that he believed responsible for them.[3]

The only window onto Savio's anguished state during this protracted psychological crisis in the 1970s comes through his unpublished poetry. Some of these poems make for painful reading: they are pervaded by despair and evoke the inpatient world of those burdened with mental illness. During one sleepless night, he wrote:

Right now it is in my room dark
  only worse
I scraped and clawed my
        self into this room
        awake...
        In every age
        fear invents what it needs.[4]

Other poems told of his room being "the best room, the prettiest room in hell," since he was in an institution where he confronted his own painful problems, and where other patients were in restraints and "on sleep dep" and "behavior mod." He wrote of feeling "the poison working in my soul," and having suicidal thoughts.[5]

How bad Savio felt about his life at this point is evident from a brief letter he sent to Art Gatti, his childhood friend. Savio let him know that Suzanne and their two sons were no longer living with him, adding, "I am 'living' for an indeterminate period—in a mental hospital." Yet he still managed a bit of humor, gently mocking Gatti over his interest in astrology, reminding Art that "I am afraid I still do not think much of astrology. But I don't think less of you for that. After all, I'm a little crazy too."[6]

Although beset by psychological problems Savio sought to battle back. His 1970s poetry at times expressed a more hopeful side. In one poem he pits hope against dread:

Blue and Red!
sky or bed
lie in dread...
No, you won't keep me
Sequestered...
"I fly —look, I fly!
I can, I do say...
Fly or dead!
I can   fly
look   look   I   am   not
pa   ral   I   z   d[7]

Several of his poems in the 1970s attest that he had not lost his political sensibility. Returning to a theme he first articulated during his teenage years as he was breaking with Catholicism, Savio criticized the materialism of Christmas:

See the toys in windows blaze…
legal tender cancels sin.
    Join the Christmas shopping craze![8]

He penned a tribute to the New Left's solidarity with the civil rights movement, imparting in his poem "Demonstrators" the idea that student protesters had to defy the disapproval of bigoted elders—who responded to the activists' chants with "antiphonal heckling":

Demonstrators
In a *dream* are
Brothers
(bum, bum, bum)
Traitors to their
Fathers and their
mothers
(bum, bum, bum)
Perfect whites have
joined the demon Brothers.
(bum, bum, bum)
Demonstrators
In a *dream* are
Brothers[9]

Even in these difficult times Savio shared his academic skills with those around him. He taught mathematics and English in the inpatient school for children and adolescents during the early 1970s. In the middle of the decade he continued teaching, first in a private school for learning-disabled students and later in a Venice, California, alternative private school. He took a college course in literature, which spurred his interest in writing poetry.[10]

Savio's psychological crisis has large implications for understanding his late political life. Its most obvious impact was disruptive, forcing his hiatus from the world of social protest. Recognizing the mountain of despair he had to climb in order to return to his studies and dissident politics gives new meaning to his resumed political and academic life from the late 1970s through the mid-1990s. This is where history and biography diverge. If viewed in a macrohistorical framework, Savio's political work during the 1980s and 1990s seems modest compared to what he did in 1964. But if considered in light of the hard times he endured in the 1970s, his political and career trajectories in the 1980s and 1990s seem a phoenixlike rise from the ashes. As Washington and Sacramento moved rightward during and after the Reagan revolution, Savio, having first struggled to regain his footing in academia, sailed against these political winds even when it was not in his personal self-interest to do so. He articulated the antiracist and antiwar principles of the sixties with an eloquence that honored his past and connected to the future.

Not until the late 1970s did Savio make enough progress psychologically to return to full-time academic study and also move on from his first marriage. In this period he deepened his relationship with Lynne Hollander, then a clinical psychologist, who had worked with and befriended him in the FSM and been involved in the Mississippi Freedom Democratic Party. In 1978 they moved in together in San Francisco, married, and had a son, Daniel, born in 1980.[11]

Savio's return as a matriculating college student began in fall 1978, when he entered San Francisco State University as a thirty-five-year-old physics major. Although his psychological symptoms never disappeared, he was—with the help of a therapist and Lynne as well as his own determination—able to control them enough to work his way toward his bachelor's degree. His progress was slow, especially since he was working part-time as a math and physics tutor, but his academic work "was all done absolutely perfectly." Earning his bachelor's degree in January 1984 and graduating summa cum laude required, as Hollander Savio recalled, "a tremendous effort on his part, one that few people" dealing with what he was "would have been able to make."[12]

At San Francisco State, Savio attracted attention as a brilliant physics student, but one whom faculty close to him knew to be troubled. Physics professor Oliver Johns recalled that Savio's struggle was never with the physics but with adjusting to academic deadlines. He "agonized over his work. It was really a trial and it was mostly psychological. His work was...excellent, but sometimes it would be late, because he just wouldn't be able to get himself to do it and we accommodated him on that because of the quality of what we got when we got it."[13] Savio developed a friendship with Johns, confiding in him about his emotional problems and how miraculous it was that with Lynne's help he had been able to return to academic work. "I got the impression," Johns recalled, "that he thought that she saved him.... He was not terribly optimistic about his own state. He was...enormously insecure....I got the feeling that he felt like this specter was there to grab him and it wasn't grabbing him right now, but it could."[14]

Johns was struck by how Savio, as a result of his personal problems and years away from the university, was initially so humble, even uncertain about his academic abilities that he enrolled in midlevel physics even though it was evident that his talents in science were extraordinary. As Johns put it, Savio was a dream student...that you would not get in a whole career...He had...friendships with a succession of professors because they would... fall in love with him...as an intellectual thing, not as a physical thing. He was just...wonderful...to teach. And he was a seeker...interested in the subject at the level you were interested in....You would think he would be a future academic....That was the obvious career path for him.[15]

As a physics graduate student he developed an original theorem in his classical mechanics class that held that "assuming only the laws of momentum and angular momentum and nothing else, one can prove that the forces of rigid body constraint do no virtual work." This was quite an achievement, since "in a course where most of the students struggled just to understand the text, Mario extended it with a truly ingenious idea." Johns was so impressed with this work that he dubbed it "Savio's Theorem" and included it in his quantum mechanics textbook.[16]

The conversations Johns had with him touched on philosophical issues that had always sparked Savio's curiosity, indicating that his interests in science transcended technical questions. Savio saw the connection between his religious upbringing and his passion for science, and the two of them discussed how a religious background can lead a child to focus on "cosmic or eternal things. It happens to be religion but still it is cosmic and eternal..., and this is...a predisposal to being interested in cosmic and eternal things as an adult, as a scientist."[17] In the scientific world, as in the political, Savio, still reacting against his Catholic upbringing, resisted rigid governing rules, so Johns found him "interested in the relationship between quantum mechanics and the question of free will." They would argue about the implications of quantum mechanics being indeterminant, or at least only statistically determinant. Johns thought this was a flaw, while Savio "thought this was a good thing." He "welcomed the indeterminism of quantum mechanics" because "he preferred an open universe to a closed one, a determined one."[18]

Another San Francisco State physics professor, Geoff Marcy, also got to know Savio well and could see explicit links between Mario's thought in science and politics. In Marcy's estimation, Savio

had a...brilliant physics mind...extraordinary acuity and insight in the physical processes, the equations, the subtleties of the physical universe. Everything from the mathematics to the concepts of physics came very easily and deeply to him, solving physics problems and understanding the world in a deep physical way...He was one of those rare people who could...understand the ticking clock of nature in the most profound ways on a microscopic,…macroscopic, and functional level, and put the math behind all of that, to come up with…objective…predictions about how nature would actually work.…He was gifted in a way that was almost unfathomable.…His…powers of concentration and perception and insight that allowed him to…do physics at an exquisite level [also]…allowed him to see the political realities of the world…so clearly,…to see all the layers…and…come up with a conclusion that is coldly sound, just as you do when you use physics equations.[19]

Marcy hired Savio as a research assistant (RA) on his astrophysics project, which in the 1980s pioneered a new method of searching for planets in other solar systems. This project would prove enormously successful, yielding the discovery of more than a hundred planets and earning Marcy international fame, but when he began this was hardly considered legitimate science by skeptical senior faculty, who thought "looking for planets was akin to looking for little green men."[20] This pioneering "work appealed to Mario…because…he enjoyed the idea of doing science that would open up a new door and a new path and a new subfield of science, and certainly the search for planets was in that realm." Marcy recalled that early in his RA work, Savio spoke to him about the project's prospects:

"Let me get this straight, you're going to use iodine gas to superimpose spectral lines on the star's spectrum and thereby measure the Doppler shift very precisely."…He…looked off to the side at an angle and…said, "This is going to work…your technique is going to be successful at finding planets." And I'll never forget it, because at that time…everybody…was not only skeptical, but also dismissive of our chances. But Mario had seen through the technique, and he was…optimistic and…conceded that it really was going to work.[21]

Savio shared with Marcy a questioning spirit and a willingness "to fight the established paradigm," which is what facilitates "the great breakthroughs" in science.[22]

Both Johns and Marcy noted that Savio was trying at San Francisco State to focus on science and gave little indication of a desire to return to politics. Even so, as Marcy discovered one night when he and Savio took one of their car rides to the observatory, the pull of politics was there. Savio discussed the U.S.-backed death squads in El Salvador and the contra war, funded by the Reagan administration, against Nicaragua's Sandinista regime. He was "very upset by all this and…indeed…he said, 'God, I hope this Central America thing doesn't get out of control because I may have no choice, but to…get involved to help address that issue.'" The better Marcy got to know him, the more he saw him as "someone who felt…moral dilemmas of the world so acutely that it made life hard for him…He was personally burdened, even where his health was affected, by the moral issues of the day."[23]

During another observatory trip with Marcy, Savio made a similar point about the 1960s and how politics pushed him away from his other intellectual pursuits, saying that while he loved both physics and philosophy and saw clear connections between the two,

> the events of 1964 entered in…He said…"I never wanted to be a political…leader." He felt very uncomfortable…being a leader. "But sometimes…this may happen in a person's life, at that juncture, I felt that I had no choice but to stand up for what was right."[24]

However Savio may have felt about returning to politics, his conscience would not permit him to remain silent. Well before graduating from San Francisco State, he took on an activist role. But his first return to politics, unlike the FSM period, was centered off campus. In 1980 he became engaged in the Citizens' Party, a new leftist-liberal third party headed by the environmentalist Barry Commoner.[25]

This move toward leftist electoral politics came as the United States shifted rightward, electing Ronald Reagan to the presidency. Savio loathed Reaganism, viewing it as aimed at reversing the historic gains made in the sixties on racial and gender equality while also escalating cold-war-style conflicts through proxy wars, yielding neocolonial bloodshed in Central America. Savio championed far greater egalitarianism than either major party would consider, including steps toward democratizing the economy, which was why he helped organize San Francisco's chapter of the Citizens' Party, serving on its steering committee and as a delegate to the party's national convention. While believing the party's "anti–big corporations, 'no nukes' platform" "limited though worthy," he wanted it "broadened to include strong concern for the aspirations of oppressed sexes, races and classes."[26] His socialist politics were evident in a proposal he drafted urging public ownership of the oil industry, which he hoped would encourage discussion of achieving "democratic socialization of the energy industry" and "partial, democratic structural reform of the American economy."[27]

While his oratory and reputation enabled him to become prominent in this new party, he felt self-conscious about returning to leadership so soon after his battles with depression. At the Citizens' Party national convention, after being nominated to its steering committee, Savio confided to fellow party activist Adam Hochschild,

"You know Adam I'm not really sure I should do this. I've had some trouble with mental illness. Don't you feel I should disclose this or say it might make me ineligible or something?"...I was moved and touched that he felt so conscientious about being honest...about this. I told him I thought it was not necessary for him to say that to people. It's not as if he was running for president or something, just to be a member of a party steering committee.[28]

Although the Citizens' Party provided an outlet through which to express his dissident politics, his experience with the party was not a happy one. Having come of age politically in participatory movements, he was disappointed that the Citizens' Party, "the would-be home for the populist conscience," proved itself "fatally flawed"—with a national office "hopelessly disorganized and incompetent," an autocratic national executive committee, and a "blatantly undemocratic" constitution.[29] Though he and other grassroots organizers opposed the constitution, the party's leadership pushed through its adoption in "a weirdly left wing rendition of Tammany Politics."[30] Disillusioned, he quickly ended this third-party work and returned to his focus on physics.

After graduating from San Francisco State in 1984, Savio stayed on to work on his master's degree in physics, which he would complete in 1989. He also taught there as a physics instructor. This assignment reflected the faculty's respect for his talent, since such teaching was usually reserved for doctoral candidates or those who had Ph.D.'s.[31]

Reagan's White House years, however, did so much to push America to the right that Savio's physics work periodically gave way to politics in the 1980s. Savio's activism centered on foreign policy, reflecting his concern that Reagan was reviving the worst aspects of cold war imperialism. He was especially disturbed about U.S. policy in Central America, which he thought brutal and counterrevolutionary, with Reagan backing undemocratic forces simply because they supported American capitalist interests. This policy fostered the growth of right-wing death squads in El Salvador and the contras' war against the Sandinista revolution in Nicaragua.[32]

The upsurge of liberation theology and its call for social justice in Latin America resonated with Savio, harking back to the Catholic egalitarianism that had led him to antipoverty work in Mexico in 1963.[33] He used this religious connection in mocking Reagan's attempts to demonize the Nicaraguan revolution. Stressing that several of that revolution's leaders were priests, Savio exclaimed: "It doesn't sound like godless, atheistic communism to me!"[34] He became increasingly involved in the anti-interventionist movement, which was especially active in California, mobilizing student, church, and labor groups.

Savio was so passionate about peace and social justice in Central America that in October 1984 he made this the focus of his first speech at Berkeley in more than a decade. Although the occasion for this speech was the twentieth anniversary of the Free Speech Movement (FSM-20), in his address he said not a word about the FSM. He was too worried about American imperialism in the 1980s to engage in nostalgia. This speech, made to a huge crowd of students and FSM veterans, proved that Savio had lost none of his eloquence. Beginning and ending with images from the Holocaust, the death camp photographs that had haunted him as a child, he called on America to halt Reagan's militarist policies in Central America. The speech was vintage Savio in that he still hesitated about pontificating on events he had not witnessed personally. He prefaced his remarks about Nicaragua by cautioning the audience, "Friends, I had trouble during the anti–Vietnam War days because it was hard for me to talk about something I had not seen. I have not been to Nicaragua, so what I say you need to check out. Check it!"[35]

This speech made use of the 1960s as a toolkit for resistance to Reaganism. He told the story of SNCC, Freedom Summer, and the social changes of the 1960s to illustrate the need for coalition building. He credited SNCC and the civil rights movement with inspiring oppressed groups toward insurgency, enabling African Americans, women, gays, Native Americans, and Latinos during and after the 1960s "to cast off…the definitions of inferiority by which society was keeping them powerless or poor." The sixties had in this sense built a "new majority" in America, one with the potential to dismantle old hierarchies of race, class, and gender. But this new majority threatened the old order, so the Right mobilized behind "the celluloid shield of an actor president" to defend "antiquated cultural values…very large corporations…[and] the Pentagon." He called upon students of the 1980s to reach out to Central Americans as his generation had reached out to black Mississippians. "Either we succeed in making it the Mississippi of this generation or it will be the Vietnam of this generation."[36]

Both in this speech and in the essay he published in the *Daily Californian* a day earlier, Savio went further than he had back in his FSM days in articulating a critique of the cold war and capitalism. Cold war America had been intolerant and undemocratic in seeking to force other nations to maintain capitalist economies, especially in Third World states "less wealthy than we" that had decided they could no longer "afford this dalliance with pure-as-possible capitalism." In Central America U.S.-backed regimes had often been dictatorial, as in Nicaragua, and so there was a democratic logic to a radical Central American response that "for us capitalism means life under Somoza—one Somoza or another! And we don't want it any more."[37] If the United States really cared about democratic principles, it would allow people outside its borders to choose their own political economy, even if Americans disagreed with their choices.

Rhetorically Savio was doing something quite original here: finding a way to talk about capitalism and imperialism as critically as a Marxist without getting bogged down in radical jargon or inaccessible theory. In fact, on Sproul Plaza he prefaced his critique of American capitalism by telling the crowd that "fortunately—it gives me a certain liberty—I am not a Marxist, and so I can say it. America, to accommodate the demands of the new majority, has to become a little bit less capitalist!" Aware that cold war ideologists made capitalism synonymous with democracy, he insisted on separating the two: "For us, becoming less capitalistic means we don't have to become less democratic, we can become more democratic."[38] Even more arresting than the message was the language in which it was expressed, an American vernacular that in plain English mocked the nation's timidity about even contemplating experimenting with noncapitalist forms. Such experiments were, as Savio told the crowd,

> not such a big deal. There are two, maybe three industrialized countries in all the world that don't have publicly financed, comprehensive health insurance. We are one of them!...Some element of moving in that direction is needed. It is sort of like the metric system: Come on, get off the dime America! Now this shift in our values...hey! Not a blueprint! Not jumping in the water before you can swim. A shift! This shift in our values means America is dominated less by production for private profit, less by production for war, and more by production to meet ordinary human needs![39]

The huge FSM-20 commemoration inspired student activism at Berkeley, which had been in a lull during the early Reagan era. The rally suggested to students that their campus still had the potential for mass protest. In the semesters that followed a new wave of student activism surged, centered on apartheid. Large student demonstrations, provoked by the bloody crisis in South Africa and antiapartheid demonstrations in Washington, D.C., spread from Columbia to Berkeley, demanding that universities end their investments in companies that did business with the apartheid regime. Delighted with this antiracist activism, Savio spoke at divestment rallies at Berkeley and San Francisco State. In the April 1985 antiapartheid sit-in at Sproul, which culminated in 158 arrests, the *Daily Californian*'s front-page coverage included a photo of Savio on campus urging students "to hold fast in their demands for UC divestment" of its holdings in South Africa.[40]

Although Savio found it inspiring that at Berkeley and other campuses divestment triumphed—despite Reagan administration opposition—and that ultimately apartheid fell, he noted the contrast with Central America. It was much easier to rally against apartheid than against the contra war because the former was not so closely tied in with cold war demonology. One could protest apartheid without being seen as pro-Communist, but the same was not true with regard to the contra war. For Savio this was one more reminder of how the cold war had poisoned American politics.[41]

Savio was concerned that Reagan blinded himself to the meaning of the worst U.S. foreign policy fiasco of the 1960s: the Vietnam War. Instead of reflecting on the limits of American power and the disaster sown by an imperialist policy opposing Third World revolution, Reagan spoke as if Vietnam-style interventions could work. This led Savio to see that "the lesson of Vietnam was equivocal. I and those who were really in resistance felt that our colonial war in Vietnam was not merely unwise but also morally wrong. But the government is pushing a different lesson: It was not wrong to fight, it was only wrong to lose."[42] This warped logic paved the way for Reagan's Central American adventure.

Having lived through the first cold war and the Vietnam debacle, Savio was determined to prevent Central America from becoming the Vietnam of the 1980s. So instead of allowing his distance from the war zone to make him feel removed from it—as had been the case with Vietnam—he acted to ensure he could speak from firsthand observation. Along with other antiwar activists, he visited Nicaragua and El Salvador, coming away "very impressed with Nicaragua" and its efforts to fight poverty, and viewing El Salvador as a U.S.-backed "police state."[43]

Savio became so engaged with the Central America crisis that he began planning, for the first time since the 1960s, to make extensive use of his oratory for a political cause: mobilizing opposition to the U.S.-backed contra war. Together with Lynne Hollander Savio he drew up a detailed project proposal for an international version of Freedom Summer. College volunteers, according to the proposal, would travel to Nicaragua to promote peace and reconstruction. He offered to undertake a national speaking tour to attract volunteers and funding for this "Nicaragua Summer of Peace."[44]

The Summer of Peace proposal showed that although it had been more than a decade since Savio last played a leadership role, he remained true to his 1960s political roots and drew upon them in a practical way. As with Freedom Summer, the goal was to use the news coverage that followed the college student volunteers to forge a bond of solidarity between mainstream America and those suffering from oppression and violence.[45] Drawing from another sixties initiative, Savio proposed that after returning from Nicaragua, Summer of

Peace veterans address campus teach-ins to maximize public awareness of the Central America crisis.[46]

This proposal reflected Savio's best thinking about what makes possible leaps in political consciousness. Ever the empiricist and scientist, he stressed drawing conclusions from facts; for him as a former Catholic, it was also about focusing on compelling moral questions. He wanted to provide for eighties-era youth a Central American version of what his generation had experienced in Mississippi, the opportunity for personal witness.[47] He thought U.S. imperialism in Central America, like Jim Crow, depended upon isolation, keeping Americans unaware of the legitimate aspirations of Nicaraguans and the way U.S.-sponsored violence was used to thwart them. As with Mississippi, Nicaragua transcended ordinary politics; its "claim on us is a manifestly moral one, especially so since a succession of U.S. governments bear the main responsibility for maintaining the…Somoza dictatorship in power."[48]

The other key parallels with Mississippi involved safety and sacrifice. Both the South in 1964 and Nicaragua in 1984 were dangerous places. Freedom Summer volunteers came south in part to help halt racist violence, since SNCC thought the presence of white students would make it more difficult for the Klan to continue attacking civil rights workers with little press attention or federal intervention. Savio thought the presence of U.S. students in Nicaragua would act as a shield discouraging the Reagan administration from bombing or invading that country. In both cases, student activists would put themselves in harm's way for the cause of human rights.[49]

Savio brought an empathetic yet critical spirit to his discussion of Nicaragua. While admiring the egalitarian thrust of their revolution, he was not proposing that the Peace Summer volunteers become apologists for the Sandinistas. The volunteers' orientation would include "political discussion focusing on the causes and continuing problems of the Nicaraguan revolution." This would include not only the economic and social initiatives that the American Left admired but also the thornier question of civil liberties.[50] In his speech at FSM-20 he called attention to the Nicaraguan government's political censorship, yet insisted that Americans consider their responsibility for this, blaming the censorship on "the state of emergency" caused by the "CIA-backed Contra armies attacking them on four sides."[51] He thought Nicaragua had established a "beachhead for human progress," crediting its leaders for trying "to avoid the mistakes of both Cuba and of Allende's Chile," while acknowledging that the Sandinista regime "made its own mistakes and will probably continue to do so."[52] The question Savio surely would have had the volunteers ponder—and the one that Allende's overthrow had raised for him—was how a revolution opposing U.S. imperialism could survive in the hemisphere with its civil liberties intact while U.S. dollars and arms were deployed in those countries to sabotage the democratic process.

In the process of seeking funds for his Nicaragua Peace Summer proposal Savio came east in November 1984 and gave a memorable speech at Columbia University on the Central American crisis. This speech had a title, a rarity for a Savio talk: "Beyond the Big Chill: Resistance and Survival." At first glance this reference seemed to challenge the theme of *The Big Chill*, a popular feature film that depicted a reunion of sixties radicals who as adults had moved away from their youthful activism, suggesting that Savio intended to show that his generation had not lost is political edge. Actually, Savio focused less on that "big chill" and more on the chill of the new cold war. He suggested that U.S. imperialism prevented him from being depoliticized like the characters in the film. Much as he might like to focus on physics and his family, the Central America crisis and the images of U.S.-backed forces killing children in the contra war shocked him into political action.[53]

Although his Columbia talk was not ideological, Savio's socialist sensibility was unmistakable. He spoke of how in Central America capitalism had enriched few and impoverished millions. He praised the Sandinistas for demonstrating— as Somoza, the U.S.-backed dictator had never done—passionate concern for the welfare of Nicaragua's impoverished majority, evidenced via lowered illiteracy and infant morality rates. Influenced by neo-Marxist analysis of Third World poverty, he drew physics-style models (minus the equations) on a blackboard to demonstrate how the international market and Central American elites sapped resources and hoarded wealth. He mentioned dependency theory not as some flawless guide but as a framework that made sense of the facts on the ground in Central America, and discussed it only at the end of his speech; it was, as always with Savio, facts first. He acknowledged that it would be an uphill battle to alter Reagan's policies, given his popularity and the failure of his Democratic rival, Walter Mondale, to take a principled position against the contra war. In a play on New Right rhetoric about the conservative Moral Majority, he called for an anti-imperialist "moral minority" to disrupt U.S. support of this war.[54]

The most personal part of the speech was its religious references. Savio urged the Columbia crowd to read about the Nicaraguan revolution, recommending to them *What Difference Could a Revolution Make?* The passage he read from this book spoke of Sandinista officials whose political "commitment was sparked in Catholic study groups where as teenagers they met to…reflect on the relevancy of Jesus' teachings in a society of gross injustice and misery…to live and work among the poor."[55] Savio's use of this passage implied that the Sandinista revolution embodied the kind of compassion and egalitarianism that had always moved him.

Much to his disappointment, the Nicaragua Peace Summer plan would never be implemented. He did enlist the ex-Yippie organizer Abbie Hoffman, who agreed to help with the project, in November 1984. But Hoffman proved difficult to work with, insisting that his administratively inexperienced protégé run the operation. The main reason the project never got off the ground was that none of the foundations and support organizations with connections to Nicaragua thought the country had the infrastructure to handle the large influx of volunteers—close to a thousand—that Savio was proposing.[56]

Although Savio's concern about the crisis in Central America had led him to champion the Peace Summer plan and to center his FSM-20 speech on Nicaragua, he still cared deeply about the rights the FSM had won on campus. This was evident during an FSM-20 panel discussion when a Berkeley free speech controversy connected to Central America came up: the disruption of Jeane Kirkpatrick's speech in 1983. Kirkpatrick, the U.S. ambassador to the United Nations and a key architect of Reagan's Central America policy, had been booed off the stage at Berkeley. A significant portion of the campus Left applauded this action out of a loathing for her support of authoritarian Latin American regimes. Some argued that disrupting her speech did not represent a First Amendment violation, since that amendment protected the people from government abuses rather than government officials—including Kirkpatrick—from the people.[57] Whatever the merits of such arguments, the disruption violated Berkeley's December 8 resolutions, which protected the "normal functions of the university," and one such function was presenting controversial speakers on campus. Despite Savio's loathing for Kirkpatrick's policies and his awareness that many in the audience at this panel supported the disruption, he defended her free speech rights: Making a distinction between heckling (raising tough questions in a robust manner) and disruption (drowning out or in some other way preventing the speaker from completing her remarks), he urged protesters "to stay on this side of the line that separates heckling from disruption."[58]

While his public speaking attested that Savio had lost none of the eloquence of his youth, middle age was catching up with him physically. In the early 1980s he began having episodes of illness related to a structural defect in his heart. He suffered from mitral valve prolapse, meaning that his heart's mitral valve did not fit securely. This "made him susceptible to bacterial infection in his heart...(endocarditis)." The first time he was struck by endocarditis was 1982. According to his wife, "there were at least two, possibly three" other episodes between 1982 and 1990, while they were living in San Francisco; "overall it was 5 or 6 times." The first three episodes required hospitalization, while with the last couple he was treated at home.[59]

Savio's health problems and his work as a college teacher prevented him from leading other ambitious international projects on the scale of Nicaragua Peace Summer. He did give a handful of talks in the 1980s and 1990s on college campuses and at his son Nadav's high school graduation, assessing the 1960s' legacy. While casting the sixties in positive terms, as a usable past offering insights for those working for social change, he did not deify the sixties insurgents. He conceded mistakes on the left. Still, he insisted that his generation had pushed the United States to become a freer, more self-critical society.[60]

He took issue with sixties-bashers such as Allan Bloom, who to appreciative audiences in the conservative 1980s denounced the New Left as "an unmitigated disaster for the university" that contributed to "the closing of the American mind" (the title of Bloom's best-seller on the decline of the university). In Savio's view, sixties insurgents had improved political and academic discourse in the United States by challenging "the myth of American perfection. Here the facts came to the rescue of young white Americans at least. And (thank you Professor Bloom) our minds swung open to receive the data and to assess the concrete experience of the Black struggle for Civil Rights and of America's war against Vietnam."[61] He conceded that the sixties generation had been better at awakening America to its problems than solving them.[62] Refusing to get lost in the past, he connected it to the present, arguing that the young had their work cut out for them if they were to prevent reactionaries from undoing the changes wrought by his generation and to make the United States a more just society and less of a threat to world peace.

In the 1980s Savio experienced an ethnic self-awakening, seeing that his identity was not the bland middle class of white America but working-class Italian. For many years he had said little about his Italian heritage. Much as he loved his grandfather, his fascist loyalties embarrassed Mario, who was also ashamed of Italy's role in World War II. On a trip to Italy, Savio had joined a parade in honor of the Italian antifascist resistance and began to reclaim a pride in his Italian heritage. He admired the Italian Marxist Antonio Gramsci, and traveled to Italy in the 1980s as a guest of the Italian Communist Party, giving speeches to radical audiences. Still, he never completely overcame his feelings that a part of his family had been linked to a shameful cause. In a journal he wrote during a trip to Italy, he noted that "some of us, I include myself have not as yet recovered from the Second World War. Let's please not have another."[63]

Since he keenly felt a tension in his life between his commitments to physics and politics and was making strides in science, his role in the FSM commemoration in 1984 had been initially a reluctant one. Passionate as he was about opposing war in Central America, he worried, as Hollander Savio recalled, that "if he did even one public political appearance he would be 'entrapped'" since his "own guilt or drive for justice" would pull him into full-time anti-war organizing, disrupting his graduate work.[64] He agreed to do the FSM-20 speech mainly because his wife "wanted him to very much." He "turned out to be right, as far as having to drop out of school that semester. He gave the [FSM-20] Central America speech, and that led to the idea of the [Peace Summer] project, and…[he] went to New York…to try to get [it] funded."[65] But after this flurry of activism and his bout with endocarditis, he returned to his graduate work.

Savio's physics scholarship at San Francisco State was so strong that the faculty expected him to go on to earn his doctorate and "become a theoretical physicist of the very first rank."[66] Yet because of the pressure this would have placed upon him while still struggling with emotional problems, he decided not to continue for a Ph.D.[67]

In reflecting on his student days at San Francisco State, faculty there were struck by Savio's intellect and how unassuming he was. He made no effort to call attention to his fame. Physics department chair Jerry Fischer witnessed this as students came to Savio, asking excitedly, "Are you Mario Savio?'" He replied, "Someone has to be." Fischer recalled that after it was announced that Savio would be honored at graduation as the outstanding master's student in science, a fellow graduate student surmised that Savio "would be asked to say something at graduation." A young student asked him whether he had ever spoken in front of a large group before. This question left Fischer with, as he put it, "a big grin on my face." Savio responded with a simple yes.[68]

His master's degree from San Francisco State qualified him to teach at the college level, the work he would do for the rest of his life. After working briefly as an instructor at a community college in Modesto, Savio was hired in 1990 as a lecturer at Sonoma State University (SSU). Initially he taught remedial math in the university's Intensive Learning Experience (ILE) division, which helped underprepared students (mostly students of color) attain college-level academic skills.[69]

Since he lacked a doctorate, Savio never would have the status, salary, or security of a tenure-track professor. His finances and intellectual interests led him to obtain additional teaching work in SSU's Hutchins School of Liberal Studies. With his background in philosophy and physics and his interest in poetry, literature, and politics, Savio was that rare academic who could teach well in both the sciences and the humanities. By 1993 he was teaching math in the ILE division, logic courses in the philosophy department, and interdisciplinary courses of his own design, "Discovery of Time" and "Science and

Poetry," in the Hutchins School.[70] He would also write his first academic article (later published in the *Notre Dame Journal of Formal Logic*).[71]

Since Savio was essentially working three different teaching jobs, cobbled together into a full-time position at SSU, he initially did not have time to play a major political role. Nor did he have the inclination to do so, since he was adjusting to his new status as a full-time faculty member. His lack of political visibility in the early 1990s led his colleagues—unaware of his work in the Citizens' Party and his speeches in the 1980s against U.S. policy in Central America and South Africa—to assume he had been politically inactive since the 1960s.[72]

Savio's work with students of color in the ILE division drew him into a dispute in spring 1991 that showed him how eager the press was to exploit his fame. One of Savio's math students and other black students had become livid that the *Star*, SSU's student newspaper, published a collage with a headline that had the word "nigger" in it. Although the paper was reprinting the title phrase from a 1967 manifesto, "Student as Nigger," used in a nonracist way to discuss student oppression, Sonoma's offended black students, fed up with hearing that epithet on campus, protested at the newspaper's office. The *Star*'s all-white staff proved unresponsive. They and Andrea Granahan, their faculty advisor, invoked their First Amendment right to freedom of the press and proved especially adamant because the prior semester black students, in protesting a racially charged cartoon, had burned copies of the *Star*. The black protests left the *Star*'s cartoon and collage designer feeling physically threatened. Such disputes were erupting nationally as campuses grappled with hate speech—an issue often resolved with the adoption of regulations curbing such speech, much to the alarm of civil libertarians. Drawn into this dispute by his students, Savio spoke to Granahan. According to Granahan and *Star* editor Benet Johnson, Savio urged the establishment of a "student board to exercise prior restraint before we went to press." Savio, however, claimed he was advocating "dialogue" between the paper's white staff and the protesting black students. He thought the *Star* could better handle such sensitive racial issues if its staff was desegregated and wondered "what forms of representativeness or oversight" by a more diverse editorial board would "constitute 'censorship' and what do not.'" Offended by his intervention, Granahan told the Santa Rosa *Press Democrat* Savio was championing "a censorship board." The *Press Democrat* found this story irresistible and echoed Granahan, reporting that he had sold out the FSM's legacy, shifting "from free speech to censorship."[73]

Savio's notes from this dispute indicate that he was quite aware that it involved a conflict of rights. "Is the freedom of the editors more important than a long-term commitment to undo the effects of historical racism? How to balance these claims? Can't we find a way to come together as a community?"[74] Savio found this case painful because, as he put it, "I love free speech and the First Amendment as much today as I did when I was twenty-two. But I also detest racism just as much today as I did then."[75] Viewing the "Student as Nigger" collage as "a particularly noxious piece of racial sensationalism," Savio wondered what faculty could do to help the students "put out a better newspaper. Editors really do need help to improve the *quality* of the newspaper." It is easy to see why Granahan, the paper's faculty advisor, felt offended by such questions, since they implied that she had poorly mentored the student journalists. But to this day she insists that Savio was advocating censorship.[76]

Savio refused to speak with the *Press Democrat*. He thought that faculty should resolve their own disputes, especially on sensitive racial issues, rather than sniping at each other in the press—as he felt Granahan had. He also thought that he had a right to shield his privacy from a newspaper interested in trading on his celebrity.[77] Instead of dealing with him in his present faculty role with its ethical responsibilities, the story's focus was on goading "Mario Savio, the former student firebrand," and misusing his name to make a headline. Savio resented this press coverage, especially since, in his view, the suggestions he made about improving the quality of SSU's student newspaper, "were complex and possibly wrong headed but not the simplistic nonsense that screamed" in the *Press Democrat*'s depiction of him as a censor.[78] Such resentment, his ongoing desire for privacy, and his workload led him to try to maintain a low profile politically.

Educational politics soon intruded, however, because of Savio's work in remedial courses for disadvantaged students. Programs to help such students did not have much support on Sonoma's overwhelmingly white, middle-class campus, and were placed at risk during an era of state budget cuts as California drifted rightward. The ascension of Ruben Armiñana to the SSU presidency in 1992 seemed to make matters worse. Armiñana's vision centered on conventional academic excellence, not equity, and this meant deemphasizing remedial education. He thought it his mission to push SSU to become "more academically rigorous," jettisoning its mediocre reputation as "Granola U and Frisbee U." The question was whether these changes had elitist implications, damaging SSU's accessibility to working-class students, especially students of color. Armiñana claimed that it was never his intent to diminish access, but he acknowledged that those influenced by "strong anti-elitism" on the campus Left thought otherwise.[79]

Savio noted with concern that Armiñana's "inaugural speech and slide show offered to consider eliminating the ILE," the center for remedial education.[80] He worried that the new president sought to purge SSU's links to its past as a campus drawing working-class, commuter, nonwhite, and older reentry students, and pushing it to become a "Public Ivy for the lighter" (that is, lighter-complexioned) "sons and daughters of the upper middle class." Victor Garlin, an SSU economics professor and leader of its faculty union, observed that SSU was "beginning to develop a reputation which it presently has right now as a 'safe' campus…[with] very few African Americans, very few Latinos…The campus is full of [white] middle- and upper-middle-class women from southern California whose parents come up and see a beautiful campus with no black or brown faces, or very few."[81]

This educational gentrification made it impossible for Savio to remain silent. "I was not always an activist on this campus. Before President Armiñana came here I was…*quiet*."[82] But as ILE director Elaine Sundberg recalled:

> When in 1993 our newly arrived president had put the ILE Program on the chopping block during one of our never-ending budget crises, Mario spoke up against its elimination at a large forum attended by the president. Mario's reasoned argument on behalf of under-prepared and disadvantaged students was heard and the ILE was saved. We have not been so lucky with other [remedial] programs our administration has selected to "downsize." Mario was distressed and vocal about changes to our Educational Opportunity and Summer Bridge Programs, in which he taught for two summers. These programs have been drastically changed and weakened, and this disheartened Mario.[83]

While this did not amount to full-time activism, it gave Savio a reputation at SSU as an eloquent champion of "the needs of students who had arrived with inadequate academic preparation and insufficient social and economic support." According to Garlin, "Mario helped organize statewide lobbying of the…board of trustees to oppose plans to eliminate remedial education."[84] Savio was emerging as the kind of politically engaged faculty member he had been asking UC faculty to become in 1964, caring enough about the campus and the world beyond it to raise his voice for equity and freedom.

Savio's other step toward activism came in labor relations. In his first two years at SSU, he attended few faculty union meetings, but in 1993–94 he became more involved. He believed that economically he and other non-tenure-track faculty were exploited. Employed by three different departments, he found it unfair that there was not one consistent pay rate—his compensation was higher in one department than in the others. So in consultation with the faculty union, Savio in 1993 wrote Armiñana asking for "a single rate of pay." Savio hoped his complaint would both raise his salary and set a precedent that could benefit other lecturers. But the administration proved unresponsive.[85] Savio went to the faculty union, whose focus had been on tenure-track faculty, to advocate more attention to the needs of lecturers. The vice president for lecturers of the statewide union, the California Faculty Association (CFA), Elizabeth Hoffman, recalled their meeting, where he advocated an organizing and negotiating strategy that better represented lecturers. As a result of Savio's urging, the Lecturer Council, which in a time of cutbacks had "felt dispirited and marginalized," demanded and attained greater representation in the union's collective bargaining team.[86] According to CFA leader Jack Kurzweil, this assertiveness inspired by Savio "had a lasting impact not only on CFA but…on lecturers nationally."[87]

Although Savio was still focusing on his teaching, his growing friendships with colleagues in the philosophy department added another inducement for him to explore political activism, but this time historically. At their invitation in April 1993 he gave his first talk on the SSU campus about his role in the student movement, "The Philosophy of a Young Activist."[88] While illuminating the sixties, the speech was most notable for what it revealed about Savio in the 1990s. He explained that he was trying to attain "some degree of distance" from his famous younger self. Toward this end, he had changed his name, adding a middle initial, so he was no longer history's famous youth rebel Mario Savio, but now Mario E. Savio. Yet even as he discussed this it was evident that his sixties past remained influential. Inspired by Bob Moses, who took his mother's maiden name when he stepped down from SNCC leadership, Mario had chosen to take on his own mother's middle initial.[89]

Much as Savio might have liked to move beyond his fame as a political leader, this proved impossible because of his concern with California's lurch to the right during Pete Wilson's governorship. Republicans poured money into a statewide ballot initiative in 1994 designed to deny educational and health benefits to undocumented immigrants (Proposition 187), and another one in 1996 barring affirmative action (Proposition 209). He saw these initiatives as right-wing demagoguery, scapegoating immigrants and other minorities for the state's economic problems, a West Coast version of the mean-spirited conservatism rising in Washington, led by House Speaker Newt Gingrich.[90]

Savio's decision to become active in opposing the new conservative offensive was in part a family affair. By this time his youngest son, Daniel, was in his teens. Daniel had been critical of Proposition 187, saying that he would not comply with its provisions, and this encouraged Mario to take a stand too. He exulted: "The fruit never falls far from the tree, thank God!"[91]

His return to activism connected as well to his disillusionment with President Bill Clinton. When Clinton caved in to conservatives and withdrew his nomination of Lani Guinier to head the Justice Department's civil rights division because she had been denounced for her pro-affirmative-action record and caricatured as the "quota queen," Savio lost faith in the president and would not vote in 1994. Savio's son Nadav prodded him, "Okay, I understand why you're not going to vote. But then you must do something else" to counter the rising tide of reaction. Nadav's words resonated. "When your son offers that sort of challenge," Savio explained, "it really gets the testosterone flowing. And that was the first indication to me that it was really necessary to do something."[92]

He responded to Nadav's challenge by becoming a campus orator and organizer again in 1994–95. By now comfortable and experienced in his role as a college teacher, he was better situated than he had been back in the early 1990s to take on an expanded political role. During the FSM's thirtieth-anniversary commemoration, he used most of his Sproul speech to discuss the threat from the Right, especially Proposition 187 and the upsurge of nativism. Savio denounced Proposition 187 as a "fascist solution: find a scapegoat...the poor, the Mexicans," so as to distract Californians from their economic malaise. "This latest so-called election [is] a shameful and shameless exercise in massive financing of...fearful propaganda of xenophobia and racism," he charged.[93] With an eye on history, Mario noted that Californians had special reasons to feel embarrassed by the "blame the Mexicans (Proposition 187)" approach to their economic problems. Americans, not Mexicans, were the true interlopers in California:

> Permit me to move rapidly from the ridiculous to the sublime: from Pete Wilson to brother Henry David Thoreau! Why...do we have an illegal alien problem?...It's because of the border, isn't it?...Thoreau went to jail as a tax refuser and a war resister because he could not, in good conscience, support a dirty war for the extension of slavery, a war which had as one of its consequences putting California outside of Mexico! And as a remote consequence, this cruel opportunist, Pete Wilson gets to make war on [undocumented Mexican immigrant] school children [denied an education under Prop. 187]! Give me a break! Give us all a break![94]

For Savio the solution to the moral problem posed by the passage of Proposition 187 was the same as it had been when the civil rights movement encountered the Jim Crow South's racist laws: nonviolent civil disobedience. He told the FSM-30 crowd that if court challenges to Proposition 187 proved ineffective, they ought to follow the example of his son Daniel, who pledged to defy the law by refusing to show proof of citizenship when he registered for school.

> The governor and the other opportunists who pushed for this vicious law do not have that strong a hand. For the effective enforcement of Proposition 187 they...require the...cooperation of many people who were and are against it: lawyers, doctors, social workers, teachers...It

should be possible to organize an "in your face" campaign of massive non-compliance.[95]

Savio's most introspective speech of the 1990s came at an FSM-30 panel discussion. Asked to speak about "spiritual values," he went beyond his earlier statements about the ways his Catholic background had inoculated him against Marxism. While admiring the poetic, utopian strain within Marxism and its call for equality, he deemed Marx a poor economist whose predictions about proletarianization had proved wrong and who had missed the class gradations within capitalist society. Contrary to what Marx had thought, "people would not end up in one boat against a class enemy." He also found Marx a poor guide to political history, noting that Germany, Europe's most advanced capitalist country, which Marxists had believed would "lead the western proletariat to success," had instead given rise to Nazism.[96]

Savio found Marxism underestimating "the importance of spiritual values," citing liberation theology and the Catholic Church's opposition to Proposition 187 as signs that religion could be a progressive force in a way Marx could not have fathomed. He urged radicals to begin speaking to working-class people in religious organizations. "There is probably no other institution" in the United States in which "there is a heavier representation of righteously working-class people" than in the Catholic Church. He urged the Left to get away from Marx's chiliastic expectations about capitalist crisis causing mass radicalization and leave behind the "message of immiseration," replacing it with a compassionate message that advocates "not everyone for himself, but all of us for the community." He thought of this as embodying "spiritual values," and by that he meant that "we as a community can feel something deeper than we are....Some sense of looking into the heart of things and being able to perceive which way is just."[97]

Candid as ever, Savio made no pretense that this struggle against the massive wave of intolerance would be easy. He told his Berkeley audience that countering the politics of resentment in a time of economic troubles would be "a very hard task. We need to educate on the basis of moral values, of what justice is."[98] Acknowledging that the influence of powerful politicians and wealthy contributors gave the Right a formidable political punch, he would make no predictions of success. Resistance to injustice was a moral imperative, even when the other side seemed to have the upper hand: "We are moving in a direction which one could call creeping barbarism. But if we do not have the benefit of belief that in the end we will win, we have to be prepared on the basis of our moral insight to struggle even if we do not know that we are going to win."[99]

After the commemoration Savio contacted Jack Kurzweil and then other sixties movement veterans about how to follow up these words with action. Despite repeated bouts of endocarditis, he spearheaded in 1995 the organization of the Campus Coalitions for Human Rights and Social Justice. This organization sought to unite activists from California's community colleges, California State University (CSU), and the University of California (UC) on behalf of an ambitious agenda initially centered on "preventing the implementation of Proposition 187."[100] The new organization defended affirmative action when it came under assault from the Right, which was championing a ballot initiative (later passed as Proposition 209) to outlaw affirmative action. The Coalitions articulated the need for an "end [to]…the disgrace of a massive underclass in a land of such phenomenal wealth and promise." Using the campuses as a base, the Coalitions sought to challenge "the prevalence of scapegoating, oversimplification of issues and political opportunism" that Savio believed had "come to characterize California and national elections."[101]

Creating such a coalition from diverse higher educational institutions was a radical idea. No one had managed to organize both faculty and students from the three largest public higher educational systems in California. This was because in public higher education there was a status hierarchy, with the community colleges at the bottom, CSU in the middle, and the UC system at the top, and neither students nor faculty interacted much with their counterparts in these other systems. Savio, out of both egalitarian idealism and practical considerations, sought to break down these status barriers, convinced that it was the only way the campuses could flex enough political muscle to "successfully resist the discriminatory aspects of 187 and later 209."[102]

Savio was not the first to conceive of the idea of organizing a progressive movement uniting activists across California's higher educational systems. Kurzweil of San Jose State and Barbara Epstein of UC Santa Cruz, two of the 1960s veterans with whom Savio worked most closely in organizing the Campus Coalitions for Human Rights and Social Justice, had sought to create a coalition in the early 1990s to unite faculty from the three systems against state budget cuts. This earlier effort "failed dismally," to use Kurzweil's words.[103] What Savio sought to do here was even more ambitious, uniting students and staff as well as faculty statewide.

Savio built on the contacts Kurzweil and Epstein had developed in their earlier organizing effort. But Kurzweil insisted that Savio's presence gave the new organization special momentum at its birth in 1995: "Mario was a unifying force" who "had the moral and intellectual authority and charisma" to draw people together. Recounting one of the Coalitions' early meetings, Kurzweil asked, "Who else could have gotten those 150 faculty into a room" for such a meeting?

> There was nobody but Mario who could have done it.... If Mario stepped onto the stage...*something* was going to happen.... These were all people who...were rooted in the 1960s or...close enough to the 1960s so it was a draw [that] Mario's back in action.... Structurally Mario was a lecturer at Sonoma State.... In the grand pecking order...in higher education the only place lower...is a lecturer in the community colleges. A meeting was called with an invitation from Mario and you have two dozen or more distinguished faculty from Berkeley and Santa Cruz,...faculty from the CSU and the community colleges.[104]

For Jeff Lustig, an FSM veteran who attended these initial Coalitions meetings, it was Savio's message that seemed so striking. He remembered thinking that even after decades away from political leadership Savio's handling of this early organizing work made it evident that he was a "natural leader," explaining the political situation "in a way that resonates with people." Elaborating on the way the Right was attacking immigrants and fueling bigotry, Savio challenged his colleagues: "We fought for these things in the sixties. If we don't fight for them [now], what do we count for?" Lustig also recalled being concerned about Savio's physical appearance. "He didn't look good. He was pale," which was worrisome since he knew Mario had a heart condition.[105]

Savio proved willing in February 1995 to use his celebrity to promote this new organization. Inaccurately announced by the *Press Democrat* as his "first interview in 30 years," the story was headlined "Free Speech Figure Savio Breaks Silence: SSU Teacher to Battle Conservative Wave."[106] The *Press Democrat* reported that "the lanky 52 year old with a graying pony tail" had spent the past four years laboring "in determined obscurity at Sonoma State University," shunning "public attention, preferring" teaching to politics, and speaking in his classes "about such esoterica as relationships between poetry and physics." Savio argued that "we are moving towards another moment in history in which people," as during the 1960s, "have to take sides." He described how he was helping to organize "teachers, students, and employees at a dozen campuses in Northern California" against Proposition 187 and the anti-affirmative-action initiative. "The public has only heard from the right on these issues. Someone must put forward an alternative vision...so that people will question whether they want to live their daily lives with resentment and contempt for others." Savio depicted such activism as a moral imperative in an increasingly inhumane political climate: "I don't know if we will succeed" in turning back this wave of intolerance, "but I don't want my children to ask me what the hell I was doing teaching logic while all this was going on…The last election demonstrated that the country has been taken over by barbarians."[107]

He carried this same message to the local ACLU chapter, giving a keynote speech to its annual meeting in Sebastopol. In its reflections on campus organizing, this speech was almost the opposite of nostalgic about the 1960s. Instead of holding up the New Left as an exemplar of political wisdom that ought to be emulated, he argued that the new insurgency was improving upon the sixties. "This is a movement grown up," which meant that it "can not be, will not be, a student movement, that this will be a movement in which the campuses are organized, that is, the faculty, the students, and the non-academic staff together." The 1990s movement would be more diverse than the New Left: "very multi-ethnic [with]…women and men leading in conditions of complete equality." Class boundaries would be crossed more than in the sixties campus movements, with community colleges being the most important part of the coalitions, since this was where the most students, the working class, went to college.[108] Here he was saying something significant about the nature of the university itself. Unlike the mostly "white, male, radical dominated" New Left of the 1960s, America's colleges and universities in the 1990s reflected the fact that "affirmative action has been working.…The campuses don't look that way [mostly white] anymore. Thank goodness." This progress meant that it was much easier than it had been in the 1960s to build a diverse movement.[109]

Although willing to acknowledge the limitations of the sixties Left, Savio in most of his nineties speeches credited the insurgent sixties with transforming American culture, making it more open and democratic. At UC Santa Cruz in 1995 he argued that success of sixties social movements in remaking American culture had sent the Right into a panic, and, along with the recession, spurred it into its offensive against affirmative action and immigrant rights. He made this point by opening his Santa Cruz talk with an illustration from an episode of the TV comedy *Roseanne*, which presented a "caricatured version of the 1950s" that captured, by way of contrast, all that the 1960s had changed. The episode revealed the 1950s as what Savio termed "the last normal decade." In that version of normalcy "the man thought he was in charge, the woman let him think that, while making certain decisions in the house (she took care of the kids, made sure they were all washed and went to school, everything went just right), and the only black man they knew was the one who came around collecting money for charity." But thanks to the feminist and civil rights movements, American culture no longer was captive to such "normalcy." Even a glance at the White House showed this to be the case: President Clinton was "not normal because after all he is married to Hillary, and Hillary," with her Yale law degree and feminist past, "is not normal, right?"[110]

What the Right had come to recognize and fear, in Savio's view, was that in the sixties "we began to break the whole idea of status down about everything. It was true about race. People who have dark skin in America were not regarded as normal. The norm was white male. That's no longer true anymore." Sixties activists had helped define a national agenda that resonated with the America's most democratic ideals. "The simple version" of that agenda was, as Savio put it, "anti-hierarchy...Anti-hierarchy in race, anti-hierarchy in gender, anti-hierarchy in class, anti-hierarchy in the environment. It's not one species *uber alles*. Anti-hierarchy in Empire, not one nation *uber alles*."[111]

Eager to restore the "normal" male-dominated family and white-dominated politics, conservatives sought to erase the changes wrought by the sixties. Why, Savio asked, was the Right "so gung ho for family values?" Factually this made no sense since "most of the families [in the nineties] aren't like those families in the fifties."[112] This was a drive to restore the patriarchal and prejudiced family lives of the "normal" 1950s:

> Where do we learn to obey and that some people are worse than others? You learn it in the family; [not] out of a book. You learn in the family that it's not what you do but who you are. If you have the wrong kind of genitalia then you are in one class. And if you have the right kind, you're in another class. Later on, you can transfer that kind of learning to other things, but it is very important lesson learned in the home and very early; that it's okay for whole classes of people to be above another on the basis of what they are not what they do.[113]

If the sixties legacy prevailed and prejudice broke down in the home, conservatives would knew they had "absolutely lost" their struggle against democratic social change.[114]

Translated into the political realm, this meant that the Right had to take power, using the courts, the state legislatures, ballot initiatives, Congress, and the White House to roll back the social revolution begun in the 1960s. Savio saw this as an attempt at the southernization of American politics. During the sixties the partisans of the racist status quo "lost in the South. We beat them." The same kind of reactionaries were, in Savio's view, "making a bid for national power" in the 1990s: "They are in an end game situation....I mean, where does Newt Gingrich come from? Where does Jesse Helms come from? Where does Phil Gramm come from? They don't come from Maine."[115]

As the right wing's attack on affirmative action grew, Mario and his son Nadav would coauthor a pamphlet for the Campus Coalitions, *In Defense of Affirmative Action: The Case Against Proposition 209*, which made the pro-affirmative-action argument accessible to the general public.[116]

Nadav had prodded Mario into activism by asking him what he was going to do about the right wing's resurgence. When Mario came to Nadav with the pamphlet project he told his son, "Look, you kind of instigated this [Mario's decision to return to political activism] a little bit…and we need some help. Would you be willing to do this [pamphlet]?" Nadav agreed, but only if Mario would coauthor it.[117] Since Nadav had not himself been "particularly politically active," he did not intentionally try to make Mario "feel guilty for not being politically active." He remembered that comment to Mario as being "a little bit flippant…a little bit off-hand in a way that was maybe a little bit atypical." Nonetheless, it struck a chord in Mario, who, as Nadav put it, "took it very seriously and thought about it and did some soul searching, and decided yes, he did have to be active."[118]

The pamphlet Mario wrote with Nadav was one in a number of Coalitions-related activities initiated to defend affirmative action as the Proposition 209 debate heated up in 1996. He spoke at forums, bringing to the affirmative action debate a historical perspective linking current struggles to those of the 1960s. He dubbed the ballot measure outlawing affirmative action "the Connerly-Wilson anti-civil-rights" initiative, a play on its formal name, the California Civil Rights Initiative. He justified this label on the grounds that the civil rights movement had pioneered forms of affirmative action as part of its drive to open "up opportunities in education and employment" across America by challenging racial inequity and discrimination. Affirmative action was a social contract promoting fairness in hiring and education without the disruptiveness of mass protest. Savio warned that its abolition could lead to a return to such protest.[119]

It was telling, however, that though Savio intended to give this warning to the Board of Regents, that body's time restrictions would not permit him to deliver his speech. In the end neither his eloquence nor the Coalitions' campus mobilizations could match the political power of the well-financed conservative movement, with its statewide media campaign. Proposition 209 would pass easily in 1996, an epochal defeat for affirmative action.[120]

Savio understood how long the odds were of overcoming the rich and powerful interests behind these conservative ballot initiatives. But it was not simply a matter of money. Struggles against Propositions 187 and 209 were tough because they required challenging widespread prejudice; as Savio put it, "it always requires a degree of genuine moral reeducation ('consciousness raising') to overcome those given fears and to encourage their replacement by truer feelings of empathy, human solidarity, and compassion."[121]

However valid this point, there was a larger strategic problem here. The strategy of using the campuses as a base for dissent was honorable, but in an age when mass student protest was just a memory it was simply not effective in influencing the larger polity. Indeed, some would question whether the campuses have exerted any influence at all on national politics since the 1960s, which is why critics such as Todd Gitlin have taken the late twentieth- and early twenty-first-century American Left to task for cloistering itself in academia—"marching on the English department while the Right took the White House."[122] Although the Campus Coalitions for Human Rights and Social Justice was an effort to break academics out of their cloister, it is an open question whether a campus-based political strategy could reasonably have challenged conservative forces in 1990s California unleashed by a faltering economy and a well-oiled Republican machine. The U.S. District Court, not the campuses, ultimately prevented Proposition 187's anti-immigrant provisions from being implemented, ruling them unconstitutional. But on Proposition 209 no such legal firewall emerged, and the lost battle to preserve affirmative action in 1996 has had a devastating impact on black enrollments at California's leading universities ever since. What is most significant here with regard to Savio, however, is not that he lost this battle for democratic rights but that, despite the longest of odds, he had chosen to fight it.[123]

12

DYING IN THE SADDLE

The final political battle of Mario Savio's life erupted at Sonoma State University in fall 1996. The issue was a proposed $300 fee hike that he believed regressive; sneaking in tuition under another name, it made the university too expensive for low-income students. This "differential fee," proposed by President Armiñana, would have to be approved by a referendum before it could be implemented. To Savio the process by which the administration promoted the fee proposal seemed unethical: the administration used its influence to discourage opposition and its resources to flood the campus with pro-fee-hike propaganda while failing to provide equal access to the fee's critics. He saw this as a free speech issue, since one side's views were privileged over the other's without a fair hearing, making a mockery of the democratic process.[1]

Although the fee fight was waged on one campus, it came in response to a larger educational crisis, raising issues (working-class and interracial access to college, conservative defunding of public education) that were of statewide and national significance. Critics suggested that the state budget slashing that caused SSU's fee battle was part of a right-wing drive to reverse public higher education's democratizing impact on late twentieth-century America, starving public universities just as they were becoming more racially diverse. In California this defunding proved so severe that within a three-year period in the 1990s "the state's four year public universities lost about a fifth of their per-student public support." It is little wonder, then, that Savio was drawn into the fee fight as a social justice issue as well as a free speech cause.[2]

While at first glance the fee fight may seem a minor matter compared to his prior work against Propositions 187 and 209, in some ways his anti-fee organizing was his most daring, selfless, stressful political activism since the sixties. Precisely because the battle was fought locally, its personal ramifications were large. The fee fight led Savio, an untenured lecturer, to become the SSU administration's most vocal faculty critic, forcing him into difficult conflicts with Armiñana and senior faculty. His organizing against Propositions 187 and 209 avoided such conflict because those were primarily off-campus issues focused on statewide elections. In Savio's 1995 ACLU speech heralding the birth of the Campus Coalitions for Human Rights and Social Justice he had been careful to speak respectfully of Armiñana, the first Cuban American to head a U.S. university.[3] But since the fee hike was Armiñana's initiative, there was no way to take it on without criticizing him.

This oppositional role was not one Savio sought or relished. In the early 1990s he had tried to carve out a space for his professional life as a teacher, which involved maintaining amicable relations with his university employer. Thus when he began to build the Campus Coalitions he went to see Armiñana, since, as Savio put it, "courtesy alone requires that" he meet with the president and tell him, "'We're going to be organizing on your campus.' So I...sat down and talked with him. It seemed the courteous thing to do, and, in fact, he was courteous in return."[4] Armiñana, aware that Savio was better known than he was, sought to avoid alienating him, and met with him several times after learning of his presence on campus. Even during the fee fight, Savio tried to avoid personalizing their political differences.[5]

Savio's handling of his relationship with Armiñana was quite different from his interactions with Berkeley administrators in 1964, when as a young radical he used sarcasm and even rudeness as a negotiating tool. In 1996 he was conscious of being a faculty member and coupled his dissent with personal civility in interacting with SSU officials. Even in the wake of their heated disagreement over the fees, Armiñana thought of Savio as "one of the most polite, civil, kind...respectful persons I have ever met."[6]

Armiñana's case for the fee hike rested on a quality-of-education argument. He claimed that because the state funded the university on a per-student basis, and SSU was one of the California State University system's smallest branches, it was perpetually in economic trouble. Even though it was the second most expensive campus in the system, the only way out was for student fees to rise. Most of this revenue would be "used to provide much-needed classroom equipment, enhanced class offerings, upgrade athletic fields, and improve and expand on-campus housing that will enhance students' residential life."[7]

Savio, however, connected this fee to Armiñana's earlier attempts to retrench academic programs assisting disadvantaged students. "This administration has a track record of hostility to needy students," he charged.[8] Attacks on remedial programs had hurt minority retention, and now this fee initiative could have a "discouragement effect" on low-income students: "It is part and parcel of...a *conscious* attempt to discourage the children of needy families...*poor folks*" from coming to Sonoma State.[9] He thought the fee initiative set a dangerous precedent for the entire CSU system. If fees upgraded only select campuses, this could yield a "commercial competition between" campuses for affluent students, and lead those who ran that system to forget that the CSU had been "set up for the poor and working class."[10]

Had the administration handled the fee referendum process judiciously, Savio might not have gotten so involved in this dispute. This process was, in his view, polluted by "a semi-shameless attempt by the administration to use the authority of the faculty to manipulate a student vote."[11] According to faculty union leader Victor Garlin, "the administration leaned on the deans to lean on the faculty to lean on the students to vote" for the fee hike, setting up a "phony organization called...the Partners of Excellence program...[which] students, faculty, and staff were pressured" to endorse.[12] Savio's outrage over the biased pamphlet prepared by an administration-dominated committee (and mailed to every student) launched him on the crusade against the fee hike. Instead of an even-handed voter education pamphlet, most of the pamphlet's fifteen pages featured fee endorsements, which came from the Academic Senate, senior faculty, department chairs, the President's Budget Advisory Committee, the student government, the alumni association, a leading fraternity, and a campus employee group. Buried in the back of the pamphlet—its last page and a half—were the only negative opinions of the fee.[13]

While admitting that the pamphlet was one-sided, Armiñana claimed this was unintentional: The fee critics were disorganized and had not submitted a sufficient number of anti-fee statements to make the pamphlet balanced.[14] But Mette Adams, a leader of the student anti-fee campaign, argued that the anti-fee statements that Savio and others submitted for that pamphlet were deliberately excluded. In Adams's words, the pro-free forces compiling the pamphlet "lied. They said they didn't get [these anti-fee statements] in time, but this was all submitted by e-mail, so we had the dates stamped."[15] She thought such manipulation occurred because the administration, championing an unprecedented "hefty fee hike," feared it "potentially would fail. And it also speaks to the type of administration that Ruben Armiñana run[s]...very heavy-handed."[16] The biased pamphlet so upset Savio that, in Garlin's words, he

> burst into my office waving the voters pamphlet produced by the fee advisory committee, and asking "Have you seen this?" "Yes I have," I said, with resignation. Mario could never be resigned about events that violated his sense of fairness. "The mendacity of it all!" he cried, sinking onto my sofa. And then he showed why people who worked with him on political matters loved him. "I have to fight this," he said. "But I have to remember to stick to the issues and not hurt anyone's feelings."[17]

Despite his hope that the fee battle could avoid personal antagonism, Savio knew from experience how heated campus conflicts could become. That was why at an Academic Senate meeting early in the conflict, Savio, in a "dignified" and "correct" manner, pleaded with Armiñana to postpone the fee referendum, a plea that the president turned down. Garlin recalled that when he "expressed" to Savio "an aggressive intent" in opposing the administration, Mario's attitude was "'Oh no, we can't go there.'... He was not pugnacious.... He didn't like the taste of blood in his mouth.... He was not relishing the battle. There was none of this 'Bring it on' stuff. None of that."[18]

Just as Savio feared, the conflict proved divisive. SSU's president framed the fee question "as a matter of survival of the mission of the university...a life-or-death issue for the character of the institution."[19] Even though Armiñana realized that the fee referendum process was flawed, he was too eager to win this new source of revenue to heed Savio's request that the election be postponed until the voter education process could be more even-handed.[20] From the other side, Savio proved equally inflexible. Communications studies department chair Jonah Raskin noted that "many" of Savio's "colleagues urged him not to make the fee increase a do-or-die issue, but he insisted on going ahead full steam."[21] Savio's position antagonized some of his colleagues. As Lynne Hollander Savio recalled, "A lot of the faculty felt, 'Oh, it's only $300 and the students have better cars than we have. They can afford it. And [without the fees] we'll have horrendous cuts.'"[22] Savio's prominent role in this battle and the resentment it evoked made him feel "uncomfortable," and he worried about how "we would begin as a community to heal" once the fee battle ended.[23]

Part of the reason his activism evoked resentment was that it was such an unusual role for a faculty member. Savio had come back to something approaching the intense activism of the FSM. He seemed to be everywhere, writing opinion pieces for the student newspaper, speaking to the off-campus press, appealing to the faculty union for support, mentoring the student opponents of the fees, consulting with a lawyer about a test case, addressing campus forums on the fee plan. Since he thought the administration guilty of virtually hijacking the fee referendum, he set out to counter this by nurturing a student movement allied with the faculty on behalf of accessible higher education, a sixties-style insurgency (minus the civil disobedience). This was so radical a departure from the conventional faculty role that it made some professors uncomfortable, all the more so because he pushed faculty to put their money where their mouths were by pledging to donate 1 percent of their salaries to ameliorating the budget crisis.[24] But Savio took little joy in this conflict, which grew so unpleasant that he considered leaving SSU.[25]

Coming from a working-class background, Savio, who had never had much money, "knew that $300 was a lot to many students, particularly... minorities."[26] The conflict tapped into his socialist sensibility regarding education: "A university education is as necessary to a decent life as a high school diploma was 75 years ago. What is necessary should be free....fees should be coming down not going up."[27]

Having spent the past year battling off-campus intolerance against immigrants and minorities (on the Proposition 187 and 209 initiatives), he seemed indignant at the idea that higher fees would reduce class and racial diversity on his campus. While publicly striving to remain civil, privately he fumed about the "administration puppeteers" and their "damnable" lies, likening their leadership in public education to "setting the fox to guard the chickens," bemoaning their alliance with "pampered tenured faculty."[28]

The small, dedicated group of students with whom he worked on the fee battle, the League of Student Voters—whose goal was "to delay the [fee] election for one term, or at least to get more information to the student body than the one-sided pro-fee rhetoric that was inundating our campus"—grew close to Savio, amazed by his deep commitment to battling for accessible higher education. As one student active in this work recalled, "Mario always made you feel significant and included. He showed the same respect for us that we had for him and that reflection was invaluable and altered many lives...Mario made sure that accomplishments and successes were shared by everyone."[29] Probably the only personal gain he took from the fee battle was the pleasure of seeing these students developing as political organizers. Lowell Finley, the attorney he consulted about a court challenge to the fee initiative, was struck by his egalitarian, enabling style of mentorship. He noticed that Savio saw himself as no more than "a catalyst for this group of students," and was determined that the emerging movement not "be dependent upon him."[30]

At SSU in 1996 Savio finally solved the press problem that had so troubled him back during his FSM days. At Berkeley in the sixties he had been almost overwhelmed by the media's conversion of him into a celebrity. Back then he tried to push back by insisting that the press do group interviews instead of stories spotlighting his role, a strategy that had mixed results at best. But at SSU, Savio, now more savvy about celebrity politics, developed an effective media strategy. He also displayed an ability to discuss the press problem with the student activists with whom he was working, in a way that was candid and empowering for them. Mette Adams characterized Savio's handling of the media as "really wonderful." He "would get the reporters to pay attention" to the fee opponents "because it was Mario Savio" calling them. The journalists would come to campus expecting to get their celebrity interview. "But then he would not be there when the reporters came," and the student anti-fee activists would be, so the coverage would focus on them.[31]

Offsetting this success with the media and his bonding with student activists were the increasingly unpleasant conflicts he endured with the administration and pro-fee faculty. The atmosphere on campus grew contentious as the fee debate wore on.

Adams recalled that when she and other students began to staff an anti-fee table on campus, "we had faculty members that came up...and screamed at us," reflecting the sense of urgency allies of the administration felt about the fiscal crisis.[32] Provost Donald Farish recalled that the administration mind-set was: "We're in the situation where we are pretty desperate for a few extra dollars and we know that we can make this thing [the fees] work. And all of a sudden Mario shows up and he's arguing principle. And we're saying, 'Principle be damned, we've got a [funding] problem here. We're going to have to solve it. No one is going to do it for us.'" At the start of the conflict the administration viewed Savio's leadership in the fee right as more of a nuisance than a threat. But as the debate heated up to the point where the opposition was even willing to go to court against the fees, the administration felt that Savio had gone "too far" and left the campus leadership "really terminally annoyed."[33]

The fee battle changed the way Farish viewed Savio, and in the provost's view it changed Savio himself. Before this battle, he saw Savio as "a very bright and engaging guy," "pretty mellow," a "reformed student radical," who had matured into a talented and responsible teacher. But with the fee battle, Farish saw the return of "the Mario of the Berkeley days. This very oratorical Mario, this person standing on the roof of the car Mario, this person that rallies the troops Mario...When there was an audience it was like the spotlight was on and he was like an actor on the stage...playing the part that he was meant to play."[34] Farish found this activist mind-set unappealing since Savio seemed to have become "very, very doctrinaire, very resistant to anything that would even speak of compromise."[35]

Actually, *both* sides in this debate proved uncompromising, since each saw itself as championing important educational principles. For Savio that principle was keeping higher education accessible to low-income students, while for Farish and Armiñana the goal was economic stability that could help realize their version of educational excellence. The administration wanted the fees for resources needed to make possible what Farish termed the "branding" of SSU as "a campus of choice" into which "people of some level of talent" came, moving into "the top tier in *U.S. News and World Reports*" ratings of colleges. Remaining affordable to low-income students was not a top priority because, as Farish put it, "We're not going to score any points by being open access."[36]

This dispute was not an amicable difference of opinion between equals but an increasingly personal dispute between powerful university officials and Savio, who as an untenured lecturer lacked institutional power or even security. Even worse for Savio were the antiradical assumptions of these officials, which yielded an air of condescension and impatience with his dissent. Farish, for example, regarded his earlier radical history as an unfortunate part of his past, which a "reformed" Savio needed to overcome. When looking back on Savio's return to activism, Farish thought it was "a little bit like watching...a reformed alcoholic saying, 'You know, life was more fun when I was a drunk. And I'm going to start indulging again.'"[37] This way of thinking made Savio fair game for caustic criticism, since he was viewed less as a colleague meriting respectful debate and more as a recidivist revolutionary. Farish implied that Savio was leading students toward pointless political martyrdom and sacrifice of their education. In rebuking Savio, he argued:

> "So you're asking the students basically to throw themselves on the barricades to make a point." And I was getting a little sharp...because I was frustrated at my inability to persuade him to my point of view....They were...sacrificing their lives for principle. And he agreed with that. He said, "That's right. If that's what we have to do, that's what we have to do." I said, "That's easy for you to say, Mario. You already have your education. These are kids that are trying to get their education. And you are a pied piper steering them down a different path. They're not going to understand...that they were deprived of a quality education...trying to save...a couple of bucks."[38]

This exchange was mild compared to those that occurred at a campus forum on November 1, 1996, just three weeks away from the fee vote. At several points this forum—which was supposed to be a panel discussion—turned into a heated debate between Savio and the fee hike's champions, including Armiñana and his faculty allies.[39]

Savio accused pro-fee officials of conflict of interest. He documented an alleged violation of academic freedom in the fee battle, distributing to the crowd and to Armiñana himself a letter from an SSU associate vice president, which "checks up [on]...the freshman seminar faculty to see that they are including...pro-fee information in their seminars."[40] In turn, a pro-fee faculty member angrily charged Savio with imagining political conspiracies—a charge he denied.[41]

Despite these heated exchanges, Armiñana remembered this November 1 fee forum differently than did those close to Savio. Armiñana did not experience this forum as a tense affair; he found the disagreements civil, and recalled that "Mario was very cool about it. Thoughtful about it." There were "not any harsh words exchanged." He even thought Savio relaxed at the forum's end and remembered engaging in friendly small talk while walking with him as they exited the forum.[42]

It was certainly not a relaxed affair for Savio. According to Hollander Savio, he came away from this forum, and his falling out with Armiñana and pro-fee faculty, "terribly, terribly upset."[43] Mette Addams recalled that on the way out of "that horrible debate one of our students" in the fee opposition "was hugging Mario and he was just trembling—he was so upset about what had happened there."[44] He seemed so shaken and frail that she and the other students leading the fee protest felt "after he left that night, 'Okay, we need to back this off a little bit with Mario, because we saw how upset he was. We know he has…a [heart] condition.'"[45]

On top of this stress Savio exhausted himself working feverishly to get a packet of documents on the fee battle to his lawyer, and moving with his family into their new house. On November 2 he finished that packet and drove down to the FedEx office in Santa Rosa, rushing because he thought the lawyer needed the papers by Monday. He got lost and frantic, but made it in time. Then he came home and went out to an art exhibit, where, according to his wife, Savio was "a little withdrawn and subdued—but if I noticed it at the time I probably chalked it up to fatigue…Then we went out again to take Daniel to a party, which is when Mario collapsed" while carrying a small amplifier out to the car. Savio went into sudden cardiac arrest, fell into a coma, and was rushed to the hospital. He died there four days later.[46]

Given Savio's history as a critic of higher education and his work to democratize America's universities, it is fitting that his final political act would be compiling materials documenting a campus administration's alleged abuse of power. These materials that Savio sent to his lawyer, Lowell Finley, enabled Finley to make the case that the courts should intervene to stop SSU from violating student rights in what had seemed to Savio an administration-manipulated electoral process.

The letter he enclosed in this packet to Finley was the last Mario ever wrote. Indicating the stress Savio was under, his letter noted that "Shakespeare, I believe, wrote that our troubles come in battalions." The letter ended with praise for a student activist, one of "the most articulate of the anti-fee student organizers" he had worked with over the past months. He thought that this student, Matthew Morgan, "might be interested in a legal internship," and gave him his "unqualified recommendation." In the closing line Savio wrote that Morgan had "a strong mind and a tremendous sense of both justice and compassion"—words that well describe their author.[47]

The students carried on the fee fight and ultimately prevailed. Finley recalled that though the students were "mourning losing him" and those closest to Savio clearly took it as a very "personal loss," they were "very firm and wanted to go ahead" with the legal case Savio initiated to halt the administration's abuse of power in the fee fight.[48] Their legal offensive gained traction when a superior court judge ruled that the university could not implement the fee without first coming back to a court "hearing on student complaints that the election was not open and fair."[49] But further legal steps proved unnecessary. On November 20–21, 1996, SSU's student body, in a record turnout, rejected the fee by an overwhelming 58 percent majority.[50]

Both sides in the fee dispute agree that Savio's death played a role in the surprisingly large vote rejecting the fee. But they disagree as to *how* his death had this impact. The administration, convinced that its views on the fee dispute were persuasive, believed that in an ordinary election its side would have prevailed. SSU officials saw Savio as "a kind of pied piper to these kids," whose death shortly before the vote created an emotional climate that changed the course of the election, leading the student body to see him as "a martyr to the cause. And what do you do with martyrs?" asked Farish.

> You rally behind them.... Ultimately this vote was not on the merits of the issue, but on the passions that were imbedded in the issue by virtue of the work that Mario did.... I think that the facts and the rational arguments were very much on our side, the emotion was very much on Mario's side—and in the end that's what won. And I don't say that out of a sense of bitterness... It's an interesting posthumous tribute to Mario that it worked the way it did.... In the end it was voted down, and I think that was all about Mario.[51]

Despite Farish's disclaimers about bitterness, there certainly were some lingering bad feelings about the referendum results. Having spent months making the case for the fees, SSU officials were annoyed that Savio's "martyrdom" undid this. Indeed, Armiñana went so far as to attribute the fee outcome to "the cult of personality that was created after his death."[52]

Unlike Farish and Armiñana, Savio's allies see the impact of his death on the fee referendum as enhancing rather than undercutting rational discourse. Mette Adams contended that most of her fellow students voting on the fees did not know Savio or how he died. His death impacted the election not because it directly altered the views of the voting masses of students but rather because of its impact on the activists leading the opposition to the fee. It led these activists to become even more determined to win the election, inspiring them to put in the long evening hours of organizing necessary to mobilize working-class commuter students, who took night courses, and who would come out in unprecedented numbers to vote the fee down. Adams explained that as a consequence of Savio's death, "our own group" felt "we have to win."

> In fact, Lynne said that to me in the hospital when I came to see [Savio].... "You've got to win this for him now because he wasn't going to be able to fight." And I would have laid my life down to make sure that happened because I knew in my heart that had this not happened at our school he'd still be alive. I didn't want his death to be in vain. And I wanted to make sure that this injustice was turned around. So...our small group of students..., the core of the opposition movement...just didn't go to class. We stayed at that table all day and till 11:00...at night till...we couldn't talk anymore. We were...going to talk to every person that walked by...day students, night students...We printed flyers, we...[posted] all over. And even though they got torn down, we went back the next day...It was a do or die situation for...all of us...We were committed before. But...when one of your mentors and...friends dies, as all of us knew...as a result of it [the fee fight],...we were in so much grief and shock that we...just [grew] even more...committed to the cause.[53]

Even in death, then, Savio in 1996 was provoking debate about a student protest movement, and the impact of his charisma upon it, similar to those he had sparked in his FSM days. For those hostile to student insurgency in both eras he was a "pied piper" whose oratory and charisma unleashed the emotions of the young, prodding them to reject authority irrationally. But for those who supported such student activism, Savio's impact came from a quite rational appeal that brought to life the democratic ideal, helping students to organize on behalf of it—which in this case meant inspiring activists to trust in their own abilities and redouble their efforts to explain to the student body why higher fees were untrue to the populist roots of public higher education.

The circumstances under which Savio died led some to speculate, much as Adams had, that he had sacrificed his life for his politics. At Savio's funeral Reginald Zelnik noted disapprovingly that such speculation kept "coming up over and over again in...private conversations," drawing political connections between his death and his life and finding meaning in his death since it could be linked to his intensity of purpose and his engagement up until the end in exhausting political action.[54] This line of reasoning held that since Savio had not been healthy to begin with and took on exhausting political battles, his politics caused his death, making him a political martyr. But Zelnik rejected this argument, as did FSM veteran Michael Rossman in a subsequent memorial speech. They knew that for quite a long time Savio's health had been fragile and that he had remained politically active nonetheless. His heart could have given out at any time. This is why Zelnik cautioned mourners about overinterpreting Savio's death, citing Susan Sontag's *Illness as Metaphor*, which "reminds us that putting too much metaphor into illness and death can be a dangerous thing," and remarking that he had died simply "because he had a chronic heart condition."[55] Rossman rejected a political reading of Savio's death as one final example of the "great man" myth that had distorted the FSM's history. "It's true, if you tell it that way, he's like a political hero who dies in the saddle of overcommitment. [But]...it's a sin, it's an injustice" to cast Mario's death as political martyrdom.[56]

Lynne Hollander Savio agreed with Zelnik and Rossman that Mario's politics did not directly cause his death and that he did not intentionally sacrifice his life to politics. But she thinks the stress and exhaustion from this final political battle took a terrible toll and contributed to his death: The fee fight was "tremendously stressful for him, physically and psychologically." He was so absorbed in that battle that "neither of us were paying great attention to his health," even though he had recently had a "bad episode of atrial fibrillation." Her feeling was "that semester at SSU killed him—the whole semester and then that weekend" following the debate with Armiñana: "The emotional stress, physical fatigue, and sheer preoccupation with the [fee] fight (to the exclusion of paying attention to his body) may have played a part in precipitating what happened, which of course had a physical 'health matter' cause."[57]

As history, the right or wrongs of the dispute over whether his political labors cost him his life are less significant than the fact that such a disagreement occurred at all. Even in death Savio was not merely a private person. He was a political figure who symbolized the egalitarian idealism of the 1960s, and who remained so true to it that he would die in the heat of political battle. Little wonder, then, that some accentuated his ongoing idealism by reading it—whether extravagantly or not—as leading to an act of martyrdom. Certainly Savio's resurgent activism, carried on exhaustingly up to the day of his fatal heart attack, offers a standing rebuke to the stereotype of the sixties radical who abandons youthful idealism and sells out to the establishment.

Savio's death came as a profound shock to his SSU students and faculty friends, who held a large memorial service to honor him. They paid tribute to him as a brilliant and compassionate teacher, an engaged and engaging intellectual, and a conscientious citizen of the university community. The California Faculty Association, SSU's faculty union, posthumously presented him with its

Equal Rights Award and by a unanimous vote changed the name of this annual honor to the Mario Savio Award.[58]

In life Savio had thundered against the corporatization of American higher education, and his death gave rise to one last challenge to the university. At the urging of the faculty union head, Lynne Hollander Savio filed a worker's compensation claim on behalf of Savio, arguing that since his fatal health crisis had been ignited by work-related stress, Sonoma State ought to provide some compensation to his family. The administration contested this compensation claim, denying that his death had been precipitated by his work as an SSU employee. The legal question seized upon by the university in this case, according to Victor Garlin, came down to whether Savio's death was "caused by what was required by the employer of the employee. That's the basic rule in worker's comp." For a tenured professor "the claim...would have been made that if you participate in the institutional life of the university that's in the course and scope of your employment because you're expected to do that, and in fact you're evaluated for promotion...in part of the basis of your service to the university." But a lecturer—which was Savio's job title—has less status than a professor and is "just paid for the teaching and...there's no expectation of...participation in the university life...If they want to do it, they can, but they don't have to. And that was the defense of the university."[59]

Ever the idealist, Savio had devoted enormous energy to serving the university, working to change it so as to render it true to his vision of a community of teachers and learners.[60] But the political realities were quite different, and the university remained a hierarchical corporation whose administration was disinclined to see Savio, its foremost critic and an untenured lecturer, compensated for his service as a dissident. Farish recalled that "within administration circles we were, oh, I guess a little cynical about the [worker's compensation] claim" because Savio had his fatal heart attack while "moving furniture [sic]...heavy lifting" at home rather than at his university workplace. "He died because he shouldn't have been lifting that heavy furniture."[61] Even if the stress from the fee battle set the stage for Savio's collapse, that form of oppositional service did not, from the administration's perspective, merit compensation since, as Farish put it, "He wasn't asked to do it. [I] tend to think he was asked not to do it [by the administration]."[62] Even in death, Savio was penalized for his politics. It is difficult to imagine the university aggressively contesting the compensation claim had he died in a campaign defending rather than criticizing the administration's fee initiative.

Although SSU prevailed in this case, the judge's ruling did not reflect agreement with the university's line of argument. The judge actually did see Savio's role in the fee fight as a form of work-related service. But the deciding legal fact was that his fatal malady did not strike when he was actively engaged in that service on campus, occurring instead on the weekend when he had been working on a lawsuit. The judge ruled that laboring on such a suit against the university could not be seen as service to the university—and so denied the Savio-Hollander family's compensation claim.[63]

Though largely ignored by the national news media—whose obituaries focused on Berkeley and the 1960s—Savio's 1990s activism reveals a good deal about him and the fate of sixties radicalism. His nineties organizing was an activism of defense: defense of affirmative action, immigrant rights, and low-cost public higher education. The Right had done so much to put the gains of the sixties at risk that the struggle now was to hold on to old freedoms rather than aspire to win new ones. What is also striking is that with the Reagan-Gingrich-Wilson political earthquake shifting the political ground in California, Savio's nineties activism was free of the attacks on liberalism that had been such a major element in 1960s New Left discourse. Savio's final political battle against the fee hikes called upon SSU to return to the California State University system's liberal tradition of making itself accessible to low-income students. That tradition, codified by California's master plan for higher education back in the 1960s, had as its primary author the leading liberal educational planner of his day, Clark Kerr.[64] The budget cuts conservatives implemented, constricting public higher education in 1990s California—which set the stage for SSU's fee initiative—provoked resistance, a call for democratic educational access that united liberals and radicals. In this moment, at least implicitly, the radical Mario Savio and the liberal Clark Kerr stood for once on common ground.[65]

Along with these novelties, the nineties activist years revealed striking continuities. The same powerful ethical drive that had taken Savio to Mississippi in 1964 and thrust him into the FSM's leadership pushed him out of the classroom to defend affirmative action, immigrant rights, and accessible public higher education in the 1990s. For Savio ethics trumped expediency, and this dictated activism in the face of injustice. It also meant that Savio, who insisted in 1964 that San Francisco's hotels stop their racist hiring practices even if this offended their white customers and cut their profit margins, would similarly insist that SSU prioritize minority access and remedial services, even if this burdened SSU's budget and stood in the way of higher rankings in *U.S. News and World Report*.

Another striking continuity was in Savio's political effectiveness. Though on a smaller political stage in the 1990s than in the 1960s, he still had that ability—whether in the Campus Coalitions for Human Rights and Social Justice, in the lecturer's caucus of the faculty union, or in the fee fight—to generate idealism and activism. Although Savio in the 1990s did not jump on a police car, make famous speeches, or lead a mass movement as he had during the FSM semester, his style of political organizing was still very much in the hyperdemocratic Bob Moses mold, and it appealed to students who encountered it in 1996, just as it had thirty-two years earlier. The memorials by SSU students display a spirit almost identical to those written by movement veterans who had worked with Savio at Berkeley in the sixties, evoking deepened political commitments and life trajectories changed in the direction of social justice.[66]

The Sonoma chapter tells us about the end of Savio's life, and also raises questions about another death, that of the insurgent sixties. The backlash politics Savio struggled against in his final years attests that the Right was dominating California and exerting great influence nationally. America had gone from liberalizing its immigration laws in the 1960s to voting to deny immigrants social services in the 1990s; it had gone from enacting historic civil rights legislation in the sixties to approving ballot initiatives outlawing affirmative action, and from expanding to cutting back on programs to make higher education accessible to the poor. Nor had mass movements arisen that could stop all of this. This string of conservative triumphs suggest that the sixties, which Savio helped to define as an era of egalitarian change, had passed into history. The New Left was dead. Or was it? After all, there was Savio, decades later, picking up where he had left off in the 1960s, doing all that he could to preserve the gains in racial, gender, and class equity that had been won by his generation. This involved not only political activism but also professional work, a 1990s counterpart to his labor in Mississippi Summer's Freedom Schools: teaching remedial math to low-income SSU students whose skills had been limited by a public school system riddled by class and racial inequity.

The kind of activism and educational work that Savio engaged in at the time of his death was not unique. Many New Left alumni were doing similar work, which is why conservatives in the 1990s railed against "tenured radicals" who made America's universities bulwarks of left-wing "political correctness."[67] There is an exaggerated quality to such charges, especially in an era when the university did far more to invigorate corporate America technologically than it did to renew America politically. Still, there is an element of truth here, and no denying that the university in the 1990s, and to this day, houses a more vigorous leftist subculture than does the off-campus world, in which the Left is pretty much invisible—just as Savio's SSU activism proved invisible to most reporters who wrote his obituaries.[68] His continuing activism and educational work, and that of other sixties veterans, helped to maintain the university as an outpost of liberal and radical dissent even as the political system drifted rightward. This academic Left of the 1990s was too weak to win national elections or build mass movements, but it was vigorous enough to win battles locally, as Savio had at SSU, and to keep the torch of sixties idealism from being extinguished in America's new Gilded Age.[69]

Savio's renewed activism in the 1980s and 1990s reflected not only important character traits—persistence and a deeply moral sensibility—but also the lessons he had learned from the 1960s. Having seen the cold war consensus challenged and cracked by the antiwar movement during the Vietnam era, Savio knew change was possible even after years of ideological stagnation. In the FSM he had witnessed how quickly even the longest of political odds could be overcome—that just as the Berkeley revolt seemed headed for defeat, administration blunders and movement mobilizations carried the insurgents to victory. This taught Savio that political obstacles, no matter how large or oppressive, could be surmounted, a valuable insight that steeled him to keep sailing against the winds of reaction in his final decades. The sixties gave Savio an ability to place the New Right in perspective since it led him to recognize that despite the Reaganite attempt at counterrevolution the clock had not been turned back to the 1950s; the sixties had mattered, and their egalitarian legacy needed to be preserved and extended. Indeed, in his last speech on the legacy of the 1960s Savio noted that the 1950s version of normalcy, a society dominated by white males, had been shattered forever by the upheavals of his youth. He saw this reflected in American culture and politics, from TV shows where white supremacy and sexism were mocked to politics where even the right-wing-run Republican Party came to the panicky realization that Colin Powell, an able and experienced African American leader, could be a serious contender for its presidential nomination. For Savio and so many others of his generation the 1960s was not a decade that ended but a seedbed for a lifelong commitment to a more democratic and egalitarian social vision and a nonviolent America.[70]

The month after Savio's death his family and FSM comrades held a large memorial service at UC Berkeley. It was broadcast on KPFA, the listener-supported radio station that in 1964 had covered his speeches and much of the Berkeley rebellion. This event took place on the anniversary of the FSM's final victory (also Savio's birthday), when the faculty passed its historic December 8 resolutions. Speakers included FSM veterans Bettina Aptheker, Jack Weinberg, Lynne Hollander Savio, Jackie Goldberg, and Michael Rossman. On the podium that day were people who had known Savio as a courageous Freedom Summer volunteer, a compassionate fellow inmate who served his FSM jail time, a star physics graduate student, an inspiring teacher at SSU, and an energetic 1990s activist working to preserve affirmative action and immigrant rights. The speakers spanned the generations, from senior faculty to Berkeley student government officials. None better summarized Savio's character, politics, and intellect than his old friend and FSM comrade Bettina Aptheker, who explained that

> Mario was appalled by injustice...personally appalled...Mario's great strength...was his absolute and transparent integrity....He never wavered from his bedrock principles of freedom of speech, justice, and equality. He was never beholden to any political party or ideology. He spoke from his own conscience....He was not interested in personal power....Mario's life was...a practicum in search of meaning, in search of wholeness, from politics to philosophy to logic to astronomy to healing...it was personal, it was political, it was spiritual...Mario saw the suffering, felt his own suffering and the suffering of the world. He believed that beyond this suffering was hope and beyond hope there was struggle, and beyond struggle there was community, and beyond community there was justice...redemption...freedom—a freedom that included the political, but went beyond it. It was a freedom of mind.[71]

Savio's own words were among the most memorable at this memorial. Here a tape was played from 1994, when he spontaneously spoke to an interviewer about the meaning of freedom of speech. He began by quoting Diogenes praising freedom of speech as "the most beautiful thing in the world." Then Savio said emphatically: "Those words are...burned into my soul, because for me freedom of speech...represents the very dignity of what a human being is. That's what marks us off from the stones and the stars. You can speak freely. It is almost impossible for me to describe. It is really the thing that marks us as just below the angels."[72] These words not only impart the depth of his passion about civil liberty, making evident why he was so effective a spokesperson for the FSM, but also add to the dialogue about free speech itself. As John Searle explained:

> Standard American accounts of free speech are all wrong. Free speech is justified because God gave it to us. Well, that's not much help nowadays. Or free speech is justified because it's got a utilitarian advantage. That's the John Stuart Mill account. Or what most Americans say, "Well, free speech is right because it's in the First Amendment." And that ends the discussion. But Mario saw something that I think is absolutely right. It's part of our essence as human beings, that we are speaking animals....And he had a very eloquent way of articulating [this idea]. I'd just [have] put it, "We're just speech-act performing animals who can't flourish [without freedom of speech]." But Mario, given his Catholic upbringing,...[draws upon religious imagery, and says that being able to speak freely is] what

puts us with the angels. That's very powerful. So it is this combination...
[of] deep intellectual grip together with a...common tack [that makes it
so memorable]. He understands what people need to hear.[73]

Equally powerful and simultaneously autobiographical and historical, telling his own story and late twentieth-century America's, were the words Savio
had written to his son Nadav in 1990, which Nadav read at the Berkeley memorial. Nadav had noted in his letter from Ecuador that that nation had both
injustice and a "cultural undercurrent of socialism," which carried with it "the
idea that there should be justice." In his reply, Mario recalled that in "the early
1960s...young people in the US began to notice injustice," but by the end of
the Reagan era this had changed. "We seem to have largely lost here" the ideal
of justice and so were politically impoverished "despite this great [economic]
wealth. Injustice is a negative, the name of a privation. Once a country has
lost the idea that there should be justice, and for most people in El Norte this
idea is lost, then it becomes almost impossible to notice injustice." Blending the
personal and the political, Mario—touching on lifelong themes, including his
concern about how to make a meaningful life for himself outside the Church,
finding his political voice in the 1960s, and losing it for a time afterward—in his
letter to Nadav reflected sadly on what had been missing since the days of his
youthful quest for meaning through religion and then through social protest:

Down to deeper feelings, I recently was wondering why I have had such
a hard time saying things to you, things that are important to me. One
of the reasons, believe it or not, is that I have never sufficiently recovered
from a lack (I distinguish it from a "loss") of religious faith. I have wanted
to see the world a[s] whole and beautiful with a deeper reality shining
through. At the beginning of the *Paradiso* Dante says "the glory of him
who moves all things penetrates throughout the universe and shines
forth." Some part of me really wished to be a priest. I would have wanted
to share such a mission with you. I have felt somehow speechless from the
lack of it. I tried to find some semblance of this in the "moral order." For
me the old Civil Rights Movement had a religious quality to it: The caring spirit working in the world. But beginning with Vietnam so much has
gone sour or bitter in politics and in society. Our best efforts—they were
our best—were as pearls before swine. This too has left me somehow
speechless.[74]

One could argue that these melancholy words, capturing a powerful orator
at a moment when he felt speechless, were out of place at a memorial designed

to pay tribute to the life and accomplishments of one of 1960s America's most famous student protest leaders. It would have been easier, and certainly more cheerful, to have focused only on all that he, the FSM, and the civil rights and peace movements achieved in their efforts to end Jim Crow, win black voting rights, expand free speech rights on campus, and stop an unjust war. But the quotes Nadav read were true to Mario's critical spirit, pushing the memorial service beyond nostalgia and toward an engagement with the ongoing struggle against America's greed, intolerance, and imperialism—much as Savio had helped to push the FSM twentieth- and thirtieth-anniversary commemorations in the same direction. The somber reflections that he had shared with Nadav in 1990 show he was well aware that in America's new Gilded Age, with its slashing of antipoverty programs and the resurgence of superpatriotism and militarism unleashed by Ronald Reagan, the reaction against the changes of the sixties had taken on ghastly dimensions, and this had added to his sense of paralysis, his feeling speechless. Savio was, in his own distinctive post-Catholic manner, grappling with the issue that many sixties radicals faced at the end of their most hopeful era: how to do good in the world without religious faith and without righteous social movements pushing, as the civil rights movement had in the 1960s, toward a more just society.

Savio, of course, did not remain speechless, and in the mid-1990s he had risen above such gloom to speak out against the tidal wave of reaction surging in California. His speeches on the radical legacy of the 1960s had tended to be far more hopeful than his 1990 letter to Nadav, stressing that American culture had been democratized, propelled beyond racism and sexism and away from an uncritical acceptance of imperialism. But his words from 1990 are an important reminder both of the contested legacy of the 1960s and of how Savio's iconoclasm extended even to himself. As much as he cherished that legacy, he did not shy away from raising questions about how much of a difference the human rights and antiwar protest movements of the sixties had made in changing the fundamental direction of America.

The memorial also, though inadvertently, raised questions about Savio's own legacy both personally and politically—at least among critics of the Berkeley Left. In attendance at the memorial, but not invited to speak, was John Searle, who had taught Savio in 1964 and had been one of the Berkeley faculty's most avid supporters of the FSM, but who subsequently had become disillusioned with the New Left. Searle felt that Savio's political activism had sidetracked him from a potentially distinguished academic career, and he considered Savio's life "a tragic failure." He "got a...degree from a second-rate place and he taught at a second-rate place. He's too good for those places.... The FSM was a total disaster for Mario Savio personally, because it derailed what could have been a brilliant career. And he died young, having achieved something, but nothing like what he was capable of achieving."[75] Searle found most of the Berkeley memorial

> embarrassing. And I'll put it very crudely: I thought, "This must be how religions get going. There are thousands of smelly losers in this room. They are the dregs of Berkeley." The people around me hadn't had a bath in a month and they were there for "Saint Mario." He...lent meaning to their stupid, meaningless existence. And this...may be the worse tragedy, that this is Mario's message, that he's a symbol of what exactly? That he's standing against the powers that be. For what end? That wasn't clear to me. I found the whole thing depressing.[76]

Most of those at the memorial came away from it with a far more positive reading about Savio's contributions to expanding freedom at the university and battling racial inequality. At the memorial there were calls for the university to rename Sproul Plaza for Savio or to find some other way to honor his memory. Although only one UC administrator addressed the Savio memorial, Berkeley chancellor Chang-Lin Tien sent Lynne Hollander Savio a letter stressing Mario Savio's contribution to the university, praising him as "a gifted leader whose passionate conviction and eloquence inspired a generation of students across America. His name is forever linked with one of our nation's most cherished freedoms—the right to freedom of expression. We are proud that he was part of the community at the University of California."[77]

In 1997 the administration acknowledged Savio's contribution to the university by naming the steps outside of Sproul Hall, from which he had so often spoken, the Mario Savio Steps. At the dedication of the Savio Steps Leon Litwack, who had taught history at Berkeley since 1964, told the crowd that Savio and the steps that now bore his name "stand most of all for the right of others to speak out on behalf of what we believe to be wrong, freedom for the speech that we find most distasteful and disturbing, freedom of speech for those with whom we are *least* comfortable." Citing Learned Hand, Litwack argued that " 'the spirit of liberty is the spirit which is not too sure that it is right.' That is the spirit in which I would dedicate the Savio Steps." Linking Savio to the most egalitarian and iconoclastic impulses of the 1960s, Litwack praised him for embracing

> the vision of a society that could be non-exploitative, a concept of democracy that would enable powerless groups to affect history and influence the decisions most directly affecting their lives...In naming

these...Savio Steps, we are celebrating the best qualities of a generation that Mario Savio came to symbolize:...that the highest loyalty to one's country and University often demands that its leaders be unmasked and its institutions, assumptions, and moral authority be subjected to critical scrutiny. Mario Savio cared deeply about his university and his country. That is why he fought so hard to compel them to become what they had long claimed to be. That is why he thought it imperative to stand up to irrational authority, whether in Mississippi in the Summer of 1964 or in Berkeley that Fall.[78]

One wonders what Savio would have thought of such tributes. Certainly he would have been struck by the irony of having part of Sproul Hall bear his name, honoring him for the same free speech activism that had led to his suspension from UC and his arrest in 1964. He never pursued and almost certainly would not have approved of such an individual tribute, owing to his democratic sensibility and ambivalence about celebrity. But he had long thought the university should honor the FSM. Back in 1990 he approved of the efforts FSM veterans made to convince the UC administration to allow for the creation of a monument to their movement. He came up with (but never submitted) a design for this monument, which would have included an inscription with an Athenian-style pledge: "We will never intentionally bring disgrace upon this our university. By our words and actions we will endeavor to honor the ideals of those who came before us, and to deepen and strengthen this community in which we are privileged to speak." And then, in the original Greek as well as in Swahili, Russian, English, and Chinese, representing "all inhabited continents," would appear words of Diogenes: "The most beautiful thing in the world is the freedom of speech." His proposed monument included none of his own words, but featured instead the faculty's endorsement of the FSM's free speech principles, displaying the Academic Senate's December 8, 1964, resolution barring the University from restricting the content of speech.[79] This design suggests that Savio would have preferred that UC honor the FSM rather than an FSM leader, the movement's free speech principles rather than its principal spokesperson.[80]

Tributes to Savio as the avatar of sixties radicalism tend to capture only the politics, not the person, and not the relationship between the two. Suzanne Goldberg, however, in her remarks at Savio's funeral, made these connections and reminded the attendees that he was more than a political symbol. He was "a very troubled person...damaged early in his life...And he struggled with demons his whole life. I think that's something we need to acknowledge." Goldberg suggested that Savio's psychological hardships contributed to his compassionate political sensibility: his "understanding of people who didn't make it into society who were on the outskirts…the castoffs," developed acutely "because he felt that in himself very deeply."[81]

There is no way to tell if Savio would have agreed with this assessment, since he cherished his privacy too much to have discussed publicly his struggles with depression or his subjection to child abuse. Had he lived long enough to read Bettina Aptheker's memoir, perhaps he would have joined her in seeing the abuse issue in political terms and view its open airing as a new way of battling oppression.[82] But he never did this and never wrote at any length about the impact that his emotional problems may have had on his politics. Still, the idea that Savio's psychological suffering contributed to his egalitarianism is consistent with what we know of Savio's other disability, his stammer, which helped to make him especially sensitive to the attempt of Mississippi racists to curtail the speech and extinguish the civil liberties of African Americans.[83] Here there certainly was a relationship between disability and ability, in which Savio transformed a personal disability into a heightened ability to identify with the political disabilities of others.

One must be wary, however, of pushing such psychologizing too far. The roots of Savio's politics were far too complex to be explained as simply or primarily a response to psychological problems. His working-class immigrant background played a role here—from Mario to Bob and back to Mario—as he forged a relationship to mainstream America that was often critical, ambivalent, and originating on the margins. Just as America had forced him to change as a child via assimilation—dropping Italian for English—he, in turn, wanted America to change, and pressed it to live up to the democratic ideals that were supposed to make it a society into which it was worth assimilating.

His empathetic political outlook was rooted as well in the religious sensibility he inherited from his mother and strengthened by his youthful immersion in the Catholic Left. Savio's political activism and oratory grew out of a moral impulse, powerful feelings about right and wrong. The need to do good and resist evil were moral absolutes from Savio's church upbringing that stayed with him long after he had rejected Catholicism. It helped to fire his oratory with a passion for social justice that resonated with the democratic yearnings of his generation. While Savio's aversion to dogma drove him from the Church, he had in his own way fulfilled him mother's priestly aspirations for him, emerging as a leader famed for his secular sermons on behalf of the American Left's moral crusades against war, poverty, and prejudice in the 1960s, 1980s and 1990s. Indeed, when Savio in 1994 spoke about the egalitarian community that radical activists had been building since the 1960s, he did so in the grammar of Catholicism, suggesting that it grew out of an almost Christ-like impulse to take on the suffering of others. It was a "community of compassion" that wanted "to relieve suffering *because we feel that suffering*."[84] More than a product of his background and personality, Savio's radicalism was nurtured by the political, social, and cultural environment he thrived in during the heady days of social protest when he came of age in the 1960s. Those times gave rise to the egalitarian community he came to love within the civil rights movement as well as the FSM. And his political idealism outlived that decade, sustained and deepened by his studies in philosophy, his decades of reading social criticism, his lifelong friendships with fellow radicals and civil libertarians, and his personal and political partnership with Lynne Hollander Savio.

Though Savio's political and personal life were disrupted by emotional travail in the late 1960s and 1970s, his battle back from depression says much about his character. It bespeaks a persistence, a quest for meaning, and a desire to use his talents to help others as well as himself. Although he said it in words shaped by grief and love, Michael Rossman's remarks at the memorial about Savio's personal struggles ought not be dismissed as mere sentimentalism. "If truth be told," Rossman explained, Savio "is a hero not for any reason that hit the public media. He struggled for years with great difficulty that disabled him in fair part. He and his wife, Lynne, are heroes because together they made a life, he came together as a functional person...out in the world."[85] The final chapters in Savio's biography offer much to support and even go beyond Rossman's words, since Mario was more than functional, and was again raising his political voice, with all its old eloquence.

Whether or not Savio's personal struggles are cast in heroic terms, it would be an exaggeration to claim that those struggles culminated triumphantly in a Hollywood-style happy ending. Though he had returned to political leadership and the university, where he emerged as a successful teacher, the internal struggle was never totally won; it was ongoing, which is why Nadav, in reflecting upon his reaction to his father's death, recalled it as "a conflicted time." He felt devastated to lose Mario, because "when you were with him things felt— the world felt—interesting and beautiful in a way that was particular to him, and...[with] the extinguishing of that feeling the world felt colder." But Nadav also knew that Mario "had struggled for a lot of his life...psychologically himself, and there's a part of me that...was almost happy for him to kind of put down his struggles and be able to rest."[86]

PART IV

In His Own Words:
A Selection of Mario Savio's
Speeches and Writings

VALEDICTORY

As the valedictorian of Martin Van Buren High School in Queens, New York, Mario Savio gave the class graduation speech in June 1960. Although not yet radicalized, Savio was already displaying an interest in progressive social change and criticizing American culture as excessively materialistic, as can be seen in this text. The delivery of this speech was fraught with tension for Savio because the severe stammer that afflicted him in his youth made public speaking difficult. But he managed to give the speech almost flawlessly.

Mr. Denn, honored guests, members of the faculty, friends and fellow graduates:

We who are assembled here today consider ourselves loyal Americans, proud and grateful to call the United States our home. This is as it should be, for God has certainly looked kindly upon us in giving us the freedom and prosperity we enjoy as Americans. And because this Providence-blest land is a precious gift, we must rise to meet the high responsibility we have to protect it—to keep it the land of high ideals that it has been.

With this purpose in mind, we might well consider recent criticisms: American life has been attacked as materialistic; Americans as hedonistic—lacking ideals, vision and conviction. And what is truly sad is that much evidence indicates that there is quite a bit of truth in this criticism. Let us today examine why and how such deplorable behavior has arisen among Americans and let us consider what we as individuals can do about it.

I believe such behavior exists—if it does—not because people in high places foster it, nor because Americans, as individuals, consciously want to be materialistic. Rather, it seems to be the spirit of the times, the attitude of the mass. The attitude that "If no one else concerns himself with ideals, why should I?"

This is the way America thought during the twenties and fifties; this is the way we think today. Somehow we seem to fall apart and lose sight of national goals during times of seeming prosperity. It is only during times of stress that we unite to secure the national welfare.

Never before in the history of the world has there been such a period of stress as exists today. It is, in fact, because crisis is so imminent and overpowering that we fail to grasp it. Indeed, this gives rise to a second and more deeply serious reason for today's complacency: today's crises have such fear-producing potential that we are actually trying to forget that they exist. Thus, we tend to turn our attention to the things we can grasp—the material, the gadgets, the gimmicks.

Now, more than ever before, we must face reality—with the intention of changing it; We must reaffirm our faith in the nobility of man—and in the belief that men have the power to shape events. Men are not pawns subject to irrational forces. They have reason and free choice. In the words of Hamlet:

What a piece of work is man
How noble in reason
How infinite in faculty
In action, how like an angel
In apprehension, how like a god.

Now let us get down to specifics. But, you will say, "What can we do to change events in the world—the world of missiles and atomic power?" We can do something. We can begin by realizing that we all have a purpose and a job to do. It is true that we may not be able to change the administration's policies directly. But we can vote intelligently, and get our neighbor to do so. We may not be able to control widespread inflation, but we can spend our own salaries wisely. We may not be able to change the policies of the American film industry directly, but we can and should write letters commending a fine production. We may not be able, as individuals, to secure rights for minority groups, but we can and should call attention to the valuable things these groups do. We cannot all go to summit conferences, but we can keep abreast of world affairs through intelligent reading and serious discussion. By such means as these, each can exert an influence which spreads rapidly indeed.

And certainly, in a group of this size some will surely become the leaders in government, education, industry, entertainment, and welfare. In fact, we might well consider each individual to be a single atom: Each atom is, of itself, insignificant, but one tiny spark can cause an explosive release of energy. So too, one tiny spark of purpose set loose among men can inflame the world in a chain reaction of fruitful activity. There is an organization called the Christophers whose motto we might well practice: "It is better to light one candle than curse the darkness."

What I have been stressing thus far is this: the actions of every individual—no matter how insignificant they may seem—can assume cosmic significance if only we have a purpose outside himself and faith in his ability to achieve that purpose. And our purpose must be spiritual. As President Eisenhower observed at the recent youth conference:

> We know that these [material] things are not the essence of civilization: for civilization is a matter of spirit; of conviction and belief; of self-reliance and acceptance of responsibility; of happiness in constructive work and service; of devotion to valued tradition.

If we would see the realization of our ideals for America, then we must be convinced that God has given men the power to achieve any reasonable goal that they set themselves. Further, we must free ourselves from obsession with the material. Finally, having once again become masters of things—using them to achieve our worthwhile purposes—we must never again allow things to become our masters.

I am confident that the class of June 1960 will make these principles working rules in their lives.

And now the time for farewells has come. The adjective "bittersweet" best describes our feelings. We are eager to meet new challenges but loath to leave Van Buren High. Our memories of Van Buren High School go deep and will be cherished always. In the name of the class, may I express our deepest gratitude to the administration and faculty for encouraging in us that spirit of participation which fosters leadership and self-development; that spirit of confidence which will help us to improve the world that we have inherited.

And personal gratitude. The very personal attention and encouragement that I have received have helped me to master in part and in part to accept an impediment that otherwise might well have obstructed my progress.

Thank you, Mr. Denn, for your wisdom and understanding. Thank you, teachers, not only for your instruction but especially for the inspiration that your dedication has been. Under your guidance we have grown mentally, emotionally, and spiritually.

And parents: you who have practically gone through high school with us, you who have shared both our triumphs and failures—thank you.

To all who have helped the class of June 1960: May God bless you and all your future endeavors. Be well assured that we will all try to live up to your highest expectations. Farewell!

BODIES UPON THE GEARS

This is the speech that established Savio's reputation as one of the great insurgent orators of the 1960s. He gave this speech outside Sproul Hall just before the FSM's final sit-in on December 2, 1964. It offers an emotionally and rhetorically powerful appeal to resist unjust authority via civil disobedience, as well as a scathing indictment of the political compromises and educational failings of the university.

You know, I just want to say one brief thing about something the previous speaker said. I didn't want to spend too much time on that because I don't think it's important enough. But one thing is worth considering. He's the... nominal head of an organization supposedly representative of the undergraduates, whereas in fact under the Kerr directives it derives its authority, its delegated power, from the administration. It's totally unrepresentative of the graduate students and TAs. But he made the following statement, I quote: "I would ask all those who are not definitely committed to the FSM cause to stay away from demonstration." All right, now, listen to this: "For all upper division students who are interested in alleviating the TA shortage problem, I would encourage you to offer your services to department chairmen and advisers." That has two things: a strikebreaker and a fink!

I'd like to say... one other thing about a union problem. Upstairs, you may have noticed already on the second floor of Sproul Hall, Locals 40 and 127 of the Painters' Union are painting the inside of the second floor of Sproul Hall. Now, apparently that action had been planned sometime in the past. I've tried to contact those unions. Unfortunately, and it tears my heart out, they're as bureaucratized as the administration—it's difficult to get through to anyone in authority there. Very sad. We're still... making an attempt. Those people up there have no desire to interfere with what we're doing. I would ask that they be considered and that they not be heckled in any way, and I think that...while there's unfortunately no sense of solidarity at this point between unions and students, there at least need be no...excessively hard feelings between the two groups.

Now, there are at least two ways in which sit-ins, and civil disobedience, and whatever, at least two major ways in which it can occur. One, when a law exists, is promulgated, which is totally unacceptable to people and they violate it again and again and again until it's rescinded, repealed. All right. But there's another way.

Sometimes the form of the law is such as to render impossible its effective violation as a method to have it repealed. Sometimes the grievances of people are more, extend...to more than just the law, extend to a whole mode of arbitrary power, a whole mode of arbitrary exercise of arbitrary power. And that's what we have here.

We have an autocracy which runs this university. It's managed! We were told the following: If President Kerr actually tried to get something more liberal out of the regents in his telephone conversation, why didn't he make some public statement to that effect? And the answer we received, from a well-meaning liberal, was the following. He said: "Would you ever imagine the manager of a firm making a statement publicly in opposition to his board of directors?" That's the answer! Now I ask you to consider: if this is a firm, and if the Board of Regents are the board of directors, and if President Kerr in fact is the manager, then I'll tell you something, the faculty are a bunch of employees, and we're the raw materials! But we're a bunch of raw materials that don't mean to...have any process upon us, don't mean to be made into any product, don't mean...to end up being bought by some clients of the university, be they the government, be they industry, be they organized labor, be they anyone! We're human beings!

And that...brings me to the second mode of civil disobedience. There's a time when the operation of the machine becomes so odious, makes you so sick at heart, that you can't take part; you can't even passively take part. And you've got to put your bodies upon the gears and upon the wheels, upon the levers, upon all the apparatus, and you've got to make it stop. And you've got to indicate to the people who run it, to the people who own it, that unless you're free, the machine will be prevented from working at all!

That doesn't mean—and it will be interpreted to mean, unfortunately, by the bigots who run the [San Francisco] Examiner, for example—...that you have to break anything. One thousand people sitting down someplace, not letting anybody by, not letting anything happen, can stop any machine, including this machine, and it will stop!

We're going to do the following, and the greater the number of people, the safer they'll be, and the more effective it will be. We're going, once again, to march up to the second floor of Sproul Hall. And we're going to conduct our lives for a while in the second floor of Sproul Hall. We'll show movies, for example. We tried to get *Un Chant d'amour*. Unfortunately, that's tied up in the courts because of a lot of squeamish moral mothers for a moral America and other people on the outside, the same people who get all their ideas out of the *San Francisco Examiner*. Sad, sad. But Mr. Landau...has gotten us some other films.

Likewise, we'll do something...that hasn't occurred at this university in a good long time. We're going to have real classes up there. There are going to be Freedom Schools conducted up there. We're going to have classes on [the] First and Fourteenth Amendments! We're going to spend our time learning about the things this university is afraid that we know. We're going to learn about freedom up there, and we're going to learn by doing!

Now, we've had some good long rallies. We've had some good long rallies, and I think I'm sicker of rallies than anyone else here. It's not going to be long. I'd like to introduce one last person...before we enter Sproul Hall. And the person is Joan Baez.

AN END TO HISTORY

This essay is an edited version of remarks Savio made inside Sproul Hall during the FSM's culminating sit-in on December 2, 1964. It embodies several key themes in his FSM oratory, including the link between the civil rights movement and the Berkeley student movement, the unresponsiveness of bureaucracies, and the need for students to convert universities from mere trade schools to centers of dissident thought and egalitarian social change. This essay initially appeared in the December 1964 issue of Humanity, a Berkeley magazine published by an interfaith editorial board.

Last summer I went to Mississippi to join the struggle there for civil rights. This fall I am engaged in another phase of the same struggle, this time in Berkeley. The two battlefields may seem quite different to some observers, but this is not the case. The same rights are at stake in both places—the right to participate as citizens in democratic society and the right to due process of law. Further, it is a struggle against the same enemy. In Mississippi an autocratic and powerful minority rules, through organized violence, to suppress the vast, virtually powerless majority. In California, the privileged minority manipulates the university bureaucracy to suppress the students' political expression. That "respectable" bureaucracy masks the financial plutocrats; that impersonal bureaucracy is the efficient enemy in a "brave new world."

In our free speech fight at the University of California, we have come up against what may emerge as the greatest problem of our nation—depersonalized, unresponsive bureaucracy. We have encountered the organized status quo in Mississippi, but it is the same in Berkeley. Here we find it impossible usually to meet with anyone but secretaries. Beyond that, we find functionaries who cannot make policy but can only hide behind the rules. We have discovered total lack of response on the part of the policy makers. To grasp a situation which is truly Kafkaesque, it is necessary to understand the bureaucratic mentality. And we have learned quite a bit about it this fall, more outside the classroom than in.

As bureaucrat, an administrator believes that nothing new happens. He occupies an ahistorical point of view. In September, to get the attention of this bureaucracy which had issued arbitrary edicts suppressing student political expression and refused to discuss its action, we held a sit-in on the campus. We sat around a police car and kept it immobilized for over thirty-two hours. At last, the administrative bureaucracy agreed to negotiate. But instead, on the following Monday, we discovered that a committee had been appointed, in accordance with usual regulations, to resolve the dispute. Our attempt to convince any of the administrators that an event had occurred, that something new had happened, failed. They saw this simply as something to be handled by normal university procedures.

The same is true of all bureaucracies. They begin as tools, means to certain legitimate goals, and they end up feeding their own existence. The conception that bureaucrats have is that history has in fact come to an end. No events can occur now that the Second World War is over which can change American society substantially. We proceed by standard procedures as we are.

The most crucial problems facing the United States today are the problem of automation and the problem of racial injustice. Most people who will be put out of jobs by machines will not accept an end to events, this historical plateau, as the point beyond which no change occurs. Negroes will not accept an end to history here. All of us must refuse to accept history's final judgment that in America there is no place in society for people whose skins are dark. On campus, students are not about to accept it as fact that the university has ceased evolving and is in its final state of perfection, that students and faculty are respectively raw material and employees, or that the university is to be autocratically run by unresponsive bureaucrats.

Here is the real contradiction: the bureaucrats hold history as ended. As a result, significant parts of the population both on campus and off are dispossessed, and these dispossessed are not about to accept this ahistorical point of view. It is out of this that the conflict has occurred with the university bureaucracy and will continue to occur until that bureaucracy becomes responsive or until it is clear the university cannot function.

The things we are asking for in our civil rights protests have a deceptively quaint ring. We are asking for the due process of law. We are asking for our actions to be judged by committees of our peers. We are asking that regulations ought to be considered as arrived at legitimately only from the consensus of the governed. These phrases are all pretty old, but they are not being taken seriously in America today, nor are they being taken seriously on the Berkeley campus.

I have just come from a meeting with the Dean of Students. She notified us that she was aware of certain violations of university regulations by certain organizations. University Friends of SNCC, which I represent, was one of these. We tried to draw from her some statement on these great principles: consent of the governed, jury of one's peers, due process. The best she could do was to evade or to present the administration party line. It is very hard to make any contact with the human being who is behind these organizations.

The university is the place where people begin seriously to question the conditions of their existence and raise the issue of whether they can be committed to the society they have been born into. After a long period of apathy during the fifties, students have begun not only to question but, having arrived at answers, to act on those answers. This is part of a growing understanding among many people in America that history has not ended, that a better society is possible, and that it is worth dying for.

This free speech fight points up a fascinating aspect of contemporary campus life. Students are permitted to talk all they want so long as their speech has no consequences.

One conception of the university, suggested by a classical Christian formulation, is that it be in the world but not of the world. The conception of Clark Kerr, by contrast, is that the university is part and parcel of this particular stage in the history of American society; it stands to serve the need of American industry, it is a factory that turns out a certain product needed by industry or government. Because speech does often have consequences which might alter this perversion of higher education, the university must put itself in a position of censorship. It can permit two kinds of speech: speech which encourages continuation of the status quo, and speech which advocates changes in it so radical as to be irrelevant in the foreseeable future. Someone may advocate radical change in all aspects of American society, and this I am sure he can do with impunity. But if someone advocates sit-ins to bring about changes in discriminatory hiring practices, this cannot be permitted because it goes against the status quo of which the university is a part. And that is how the fight began here. The administration of the Berkeley campus has admitted that external, extralegal groups have pressured the university not to permit students on campus to organize picket lines, not to permit on campus any speech with consequences. And the bureaucracy went along. Speech with consequences, speech in the area of civil rights, speech which some might regard as illegal, must stop.

Many students here at the university, many people in society, are wandering aimlessly about. Strangers in their own lives, there is no place for them. They are people who have not learned to compromise, who for example have come to the university to learn to question, to grow, to learn—all the standard things that sound like cliches because no one takes them seriously. And they find at one point or other that for them to become part of society, to become lawyers, ministers, businessmen, people in government, that very often they must compromise those principles which were most dear to them. They must suppress the most creative impulses that they have; this is a prior condition for being part of the system. The university is well structured, well tooled, to turn out people with all the sharp edges worn off, the well-rounded person. The university is well equipped to produce that sort of person, and this means that the best among the people who enter must for four years wander aimlessly much of the time questioning why they are on campus at all, doubting whether there is any point in what they are doing, and looking toward a very bleak existence afterward in a game in which all of the rules have been made up, which one cannot really amend.

It is a bleak scene, but it is all a lot of us have to look forward to. Society provides no challenge. American society in the standard conception it has of itself is simply no longer exciting. The most exciting things going on in America today are movements to change America. America is becoming evermore the Utopia of sterilized, automated contentment. The "futures" and "careers" for which American students now prepare are for the most part intellectual and moral wastelands. This chrome-plated consumers' paradise would have us grow up to be well-behaved children. But an important minority of men and women coming to the front today have shown that they will die rather than be standardized, replaceable, and irrelevant.

QUESTIONING THE VIETNAM WAR

As the war in Vietnam escalated in 1965 so did the antiwar movement, one of the earliest tactics of which was mass education about the Vietnam War via teach-ins held on university campuses. Though the teach-in idea was born at the University of Michigan, it was at Berkeley that the largest teach-in occurred, convened over a thirty-six-hour period on May 21–22, 1965, drawing tens of thousands of participants. As the most prominent leader of the Berkeley rebellion, Savio was invited to speak at the teach-in, where he drew parallels between the undemocratic behavior of liberal university administrators and the antidemocratic war-making of the liberals who dominated Washington in 1965.

This is going to be a very different style speech from the speeches which we've been listening to, because I don't have a very set idea just how history's going to turn out, nor what brought it to be the way it is right now, nor how we are going to change it, if we are going to. So, all I really have is a lot of questions, and I hope they are questions similar to ones that have been troubling other people who are here. Maybe if we can at least get our questions out in the open, we can begin to talk about the answers.

We have been handed down some famous dates with some famous events attached to them. Two important revolutions occurred in the era from 1776 to 1789. The United States got its start out of one of them, the French Republic out of the other. There was a spirit of enlightenment for which we remember the eighteenth century. Then, the nineteenth century—the whole age, a continuous age, of revolutions. Now I remember reading about them and reading about someone whom Isaac Deutscher mentioned, Metternich. I remember reading about the difference in spirit between Metternich on the one hand,

and the Paris Commune on the other. I remember last semester at one point some of us were trying to decide, "Should we have the sit-in in Sproul Hall or in the Student Union?" since the latter would be more in the spirit of the Paris Commune—we don't want anything you own, we want our things.

There was something exciting about those times, and I remember there was something exciting about the history that I read of those times. In some important way, what occurred around the turn of the century, and later in Russia, was a continuation of that spirit of revolution, that exciting period of the nineteenth century. But what happened when that moving conflagration reached the Soviet Union—what became the Soviet Union? What happened as we moved into the twentieth century? It seemed that the United States was on the other side, and it came to be more and more on the other side. Now, there were reasons. I don't think that they can be understood completely or adequately in terms borrowed from a great, if somewhat muddy, German philosopher, Hegel. But the important thing for me, and a cause of great sadness, was that somehow we seemed to be on the other side. And I have been trying to figure out why it is that we ended up on the other side.

I try to think of the bad things that our leaders say about those people who now are on the other side. One of the things they say is, "They don't believe in God. See, the Communists officially don't believe in God." And it seemed to me awfully peculiar that we should be in the situation of declared or undeclared war against people, at least in part, because they claim not to believe in God. I don't believe in God. A lot of the people here don't, I believe. I don't think that's the reason. Well, is it because they claim it's proper to organize their economies, their systems of production and distribution, goods and services, in a way different from the way we do here in this country? Well, I don't know if that's true either. Consider the University of California. I don't think we can call it a socialist enterprise, but it certainly is an instance of state capitalism of sorts. No, it can't be that, it can't be a technical matter, not exactly. In the continuing opposition to the descendants of our own period of revolution, the Viet Cong, I don't know what it is we're trying to protect them from in Asia. I really don't know.

Now, I don't think that the people who are formulating our foreign policy have asked the kinds of very naive questions that I've been asking here. I don't think that any of the perhaps naive solutions or suggestions which might come out of this meeting are going seriously to be considered by those formulators of policy. Let's consider a very radical suggestion. What if, for example, the president of the United States announced tomorrow that over a period of five years the United States would totally disarm? Not just nuclear weapons, but all weapons. Put them away slowly so as not to destroy the American economy. And the president would extend an invitation to the Russians and the Chinese to do likewise, but would indicate that whether they did or not, the United States would put these weapons away. Now, what effect could that have on the world? I don't have the vaguest idea. I don't know that the world would be worse off for it. It might be. I don't know that such a policy, as far-fetched as it sounds, would in the long run be any more dangerous, or less dangerous, than the policy we're following now. I don't think there is, in other words, any adequate, large-scale theory of historical causality. I don't think it's clear that if we put away all our weapons, Asia would stop being ruled in part by freedom-loving tyrants and would be ruled completely by tyrannical tyrants. I don't think that kind of change would necessarily follow if we put away all of our weapons.

But no solution such as this could be seriously considered or discussed by any of the responsible people formulating our foreign policy. Now that's a problem, because I don't think they know any more about historical causality than I do. That's not to say that I know a great deal, but rather there's not that much to be known. And that brings me to what I think is the important question. If an idea like that couldn't be seriously entertained before a responsible audience (and it cannot in the United States—only before students, not responsible audiences), an important question is raised, I think the most important question. If it's the case that such an idea, or ideas far less radical, cannot be entertained before responsible audiences, then in what sense is decision making in America democratic? In what sense? What about the consent of the governed? Does that mean that a very small group of people decide what the alternatives are, and then you either say yes or no to alternatives which fall within a common policy, which people on all sides of the question agree to? Is that what the consent of the governed means? I'd like to say some things about decision making in the United States, because I think this is the most important question with which we have to deal.

I have a naive belief in the generosity of our fellow countrymen. If they knew the facts, with even the incredible lack of clarity that we have, I believe they would move to affect their government in such a way as to change its policy. But they don't know the facts, and from our own experience we can see why. Consider something very close to home: what happened on campus last semester. And consider the way it was reported in the press. Consider that. Now I had never, before that, been able to compare an important historic event with the way it was reported, because I'd never been in on any important historic event, because I was only a citizen. But last semester I was engaged in causing important historic events. We all were. And we all had the opportunity to see just what those events were. And there was no comparison, or only a very slight comparison, which could be drawn between the reporting and the events.

And look again—personal experience—look at the incompetents, the twenty-four incompetents, who are put in charge of the University of California. These are the people who make fundamental policy which governs our lives. At the last regents' meeting, representatives of the students, of the Free Student Union, were present at the meeting of this governing board. They were not permitted to speak officially, and so one of them, in desperation and eloquence, said . . . :

> We have asked to be heard, you have refused. We have asked for justice. You have called it anarchy. We have asked for freedom. You have called it license. Rather than face the fear and hopelessness you have created, you have called it Communistic. You have accused us of failing to use legitimate channels. But you have closed those channels to us. You, and not us, have built a university based on distrust and dishonesty.

In the course of that speech, Governor Brown told Bob to shut up and called the police. That's one example of the body set up and a mechanism set up to make decisions in America.

Another example—very important. President Kennedy, who some of us felt, at the beginning in any case, offered some hope as a more responsible leader, sponsored and supported Comsat, or what has become Comsat, the Communications Satellite Corporation, a public and private corporation. Some people, including, I believe, Senator Morse, opposed this. And there was a liberal filibuster in the Senate. It didn't last very long. But President Kennedy supported Comsat. It has on its governing board some people representing the public and some representing private industry. Representing the public, on the whole governing board, according to Drew Pearson, are three people. Let me tell you who they are. Representing that part of the public which is business— this is in addition to those representing private corporations—is someone whose name I don't know from General Motors. He has come to virtually every meeting. Representing labor—all of labor (aren't many of those in America)— is Mr. Meany. Now that's like the Urban League representing the civil rights movement. Representing the public—that's those who are neither laborers nor businessmen (for example, students and housewives)—and, just listen, is Clark Kerr. He has, according to this report, not come to even one meeting. (That's right, we kept him busy.) That's the way decisions are made in America. This is a public and private corporation, public and private, and the public is represented . . . I'm very pessimistic, very pessimistic.

I'd like to speak, before I go on, a little bit about how decisions are made in the university. Regent Pauley, in an article in the *Oakland Tribune* of today, May

21, 1965, speaking about the Tussman Plan (a plan for about 150 undergraduates to get something a good deal better than what's normally handed out as undergraduate education), said that he would like to have letters from the teachers involved, certifying that they "believe in the capitalistic system," to reassure the state legislature.

Now I've talked about two things, about Comsat and about the Board of Regents. About how an international telecommunications satellite system is going to be governed. International—what incredible arrogance! Clark Kerr! And on the other hand, about the Board of Regents, how this university is governed by what can only be characterized as a committee of incredibly wealthy nincompoops!

And that brings me to the way I wanted to put it together. I really am exceedingly pessimistic about the possibilities for significant, for substantial, change. I don't think that we can hope for anything like substantial change in the foreseeable future. So we've got to ask for something less. Well, we've got to hope for something less. (You should never ask for less than you want. But we'll hope for something less.) What's that something less we maybe, maybe, can hope for in Vietnam? Well, I guess it would be the war ending by some kind of negotiations. So I'd like to say what I feel about the minimum kinds of negotiations which should be acceptable to people who have anything left of democratic ideals.

This is my feeling. There can't be the kind of negotiations that say, "If you stop fighting, well, then we'll give you all sorts of economic benefits." That's okay in the huckster world in which we live, but it's not okay in the kind of world in which I'd like to live. None of this buying people off. Well, now, what should we insist upon? Again, let's go back to our own personal experience of last semester. Consider the Committee on Campus Political Activity in its first form.* The administration appointed ten out of twelve people to a committee which was supposed to resolve the dispute. Now, the administration was one of the two parties to the dispute. It appointed ten out of twelve, without any consultation with the other side. And then people accused you of being unreasonable and doctrinaire because you refused to meet with them. Well, I don't know altogether that much about the National Liberation Front. I wish I knew a lot more about it than I do. But I know that in some ways—and this you can even get from the reports in the *Tribune*—in some ways, it's the counterpart of those dastardly FSM people last semester. That means to me, that if you have

---

* The Committee on Campus Political Activity (CCPA) was formed October 21, 1964, to attempt a solution to the free speech controversy. It dissolved November 7, 1964, without reaching a conclusion.

338   In His Own Words: A Selection of Mario Savio's Speeches and Writings

negotiations which take place between the United States and the Soviet Union and even Communist China, and possibly Hanoi, but leave out the National Liberation Front, that's like the CCPA without the FSM. Impossible! I tell you, if I were involved in such a revolution, I would rather die than get out under those circumstances.

All right. Who are the kinds of people who are proposing things like "If you stop fighting altogether, we'll give you a good payoff"? Well, you know they're the same kinds of people who opposed us here, when we fought on campus last semester. And right now I'm not talking about the reactionaries on the Board of Regents. I'm talking about some liberals, that's what I'm talking about. Who is one...of the architects of American foreign policy in Vietnam? Robert A. Scalapino. Who is it on December 7 (remember the Greek Theatre) who, with Clark Kerr, mouthed those magnificent generalities and hypocritical clichés which were supposed to end the crisis without letting the Academic Senate even have its say? It's the same people, the same ones. Those who want to make decisions by a kind of elite know-how here at the University of California are the same ones who will refuse repeatedly to let people, just little ordinary people, take part in decision making wherever there are decisions to be made.

BEYOND THE COLD WAR

This essay was published as part of a special issue of the Daily Californian (Berkeley's student newspaper) commemorating the Free Speech Movement's twentieth anniversary (FSM-20) on October 1, 1984. In it Savio offered his fullest critique of cold war America and assessed the radical challenge to its foreign and domestic policies by the New Left and the civil rights movement in the 1960s. This essay reflected his intense desire to move America beyond its cold warrior pattern of neocolonial wars abroad and deafness to critics of capitalism and its inequities at home. Savio was so convinced of the importance of challenging the cold war—that social progress was impossible while a cold warrior mind-set prevailed—that he planned to use this same title, "Beyond the Cold War," for the memoir he hoped to complete. He was especially critical here of the new cold war that the Reagan administration unleashed in Central America. Savio hoped that in the 1980s a new antiwar movement would do better than the sixties peace movement had in educating the public that capitalism and democracy were not synonymous, and that the United States actually sabotaged Latin American democracy when popularly elected socialists opposed capitalist interests, as in Allende's Chile. Savio would sound some of these same themes in his keynote address to thousands of students and movement veterans at the FSM-20 rally on the Berkeley campus the day after this essay's publication.

The student movement of the 1960s was largely a response of white youth to two great events in the world beyond the university: the domestic crisis brought on by the burgeoning civil rights movement, and the crisis in foreign policy caused by the U.S. colonial war in Vietnam. The lessons learned in these two arenas of struggle should have been mutually reinforcing, and they were for the most politically conscious participants. They could have led (and sometimes did) to a key political insight: recognition that the U.S. cold war establishment, with its ideology of reflexive "anti-Communism," is the principal obstacle to solution of America's chronic social problems, the principal reason for squandered national resources, both material and spiritual, and the principal cause of a U.S. propensity to fight or instigate colonial wars. In this view, the "cold war" in America is a complex of material and ideological institutions which shape and direct national public policy toward favoring profit making over meeting fundamental human needs (preventing "creeping socialism") and toward goals of "strength" and military "preparedness" over a credible policy of peaceful accommodation. If these beliefs about the cold war had become widespread within the broad opposition, then we would have sought quite directly to delegitimize the cold war ideology itself as a necessary step to achieving our objectives for fundamental reform.

These insights were arrived at (by those who did come to them) not through armchair theorizing, but in the course of active struggle in the civil rights and anti–Vietnam War movements. In the civil rights movement, we came repeatedly into conflict with various sectors of the United States political and business establishment. Locally there were massive, frequent, and often effective protests to force the hiring of black workers in decent jobs. (The Free Speech Movement, whose twentieth anniversary we are celebrating, was, essentially, a successful fight against the university's attempt to end on-campus organization of these demonstrations.) Regionally, there was an ultimately successful struggle to expand voting rights in the states of the Old South. Nationally, there were largely unsuccessful attempts to obtain acceptance by the Democratic Party of the antiracist, antiestablishment Mississippi Freedom Democrats and to obtain passage by Congress of "freedom budgets," designed to incorporate major community demands or the more substantial (and expensive) proposals of public commissions set up specifically to determine the causes of social unrest. In almost all such instances, the civil rights movement challenged the establishment to expand the public's role in the operation of the economy, either by allocating material resources to meet human needs—rather than to increase private profits—or by admitting the representatives of civil rights organizations or oppressed minority communities to positions of significant social power.

In brief, in the cause of eradicating racism, we began to assert—without always realizing that we were doing so—a right, however limited, to democratic social and economic planning. Such an assertion was implicit in every even purely local demand that a business hire black workers in good, visible jobs at prevailing white wages, whether or not this would be a profitable thing to do. Indeed, the basic thrust of the civil rights movement, with its steady insistence on the precedence of ethics over profitability, was inherently and decidedly non- or even anti-"business." The observation that this same alignment of protagonists (the movement vs. business) could be seen throughout the country led some to the key perception that the civil rights movement, if only implicitly, had a genuine anticapitalist potential.

This fact about the inherent thrust of the civil rights movement was recognized and exploited by its opponents to resist change or to severely limit its scope. In material terms, this resistance of reaction was quite successful. To this day, unemployed workers are black in highly disproportionate numbers and unemployment among black teenagers in our cities exceeds that for white workers in the worst years of the Great Depression. The principal achievements of the domestic struggles of the 1960s were thus not material gains but gains in consciousness. Following the lead of black Americans, one oppressed group after another cast off the definitions of inferiority by which American society had traditionally kept them powerless or poor. "Niggers" became black men and women, "wetbacks" and "spics" became Chicanos and Hispanics, Indians became Native Americans, "fags" and "dykes" became gay men and lesbians, girls became women. Extending well into the 1970s, this national drama of human dignity claimed was moving to behold. But the corollary demands for wealth and power commensurate with this newly won dignity were beyond the capacity of even the Johnson Great Society programs to satisfy. The limits of capitalist largesse had been reached, but even most civil rights activists failed to draw the obviously anticapitalist implication of their struggle. The attention of American society turned increasingly to war.

In the anti–Vietnam War movement, a similar counterpoint could be observed. By the latter days of the war, domestic opposition to the U.S. government's war policy had become, in every practical sense, allied with the government of North Vietnam and the National Liberation Front. That is, it was the practical objective of the antiwar movement (in its latter phase at least) to bring about the *defeat* of the U.S. policy in Southeast Asia. Nevertheless, only the most radical forces in the movement articulated this objective to mean the *military* defeat of the United States. For the majority of those opposed to the U.S. war policy, the implications of the movement's practical objective remained obscure, just as the implicit anticapitalism of civil rights demands had remained obscure. For it was always most comfortable—and more effective—to organize broad opposition on the perfectly valid, and also basically respectable, moral and ethical basis that our government was intervening in a civil war, in a region remote from any vital American interest, with little prospect of winning, and at seemingly limitless cost in treasure and lives. Hence, for many of the opponents of the U.S. policy, the full implication of the fact that the U.S. domestic opposition was allied with an anticapitalist revolution tended to be somewhat hidden.

But for the most thoughtful within the opposition, an alliance with the Communists of Vietnam (even a purely practical alliance) meant a decision that the triumph of Communism in Vietnam was preferable to the continued hegemony of the U.S. capitalism. This was a decision that the legitimate aspirations of a majority of the Vietnamese people, both for national independence and for economic improvement, could be better met through the leadership of national Communists than that of the local clients of U.S. and other Western corporations.

No doubt we were motivated in part by the stature of the North Vietnamese president, Ho Chi Minh, who in every moral dimension towered far above the succession of feeble U.S.-backed despots in the South. But, as I suggested above, we also were prepared to arrive at this watershed conclusion by our own direct experience in the civil rights movement of the preceding years. For many of us had learned the lesson that the principal cause of the repeated frustration of the legitimate aspirations of black Americans was the logic of economic decision making under capitalism, in which profitability in enterprises would almost always prevail in a contest with human need. The democratic traditions of America permitted us to link tightly the domestic struggle for economic justice with the fullest expansion of democratic rights. We now recognized, however, that, in the case of rebellion against the stranglehold of foreign (often U.S.) corporations in the developing countries, national economic development and independence might often be tied, for an indeterminate period, to the success of popular but authoritarian leftist regimes allied with the Soviet Union and other Communist states. The reason for this seemed obvious. Small and poor nations with anticapitalist governments would require both economic assistance and military protection against the re-imposition of authoritarian pro-capitalist regimes. Quite simply, anticapitalist rebels needed allies. The most stable and powerful—and the most consistently anticapitalist—allies to be found were the Soviet Union and the other so-called socialist states. Inevitably, it seemed, countries without strong democratic traditions of their own would come to resemble, in one degree or another, their Soviet mentors, especially so since only variants of the Soviet model appeared able to withstand the relentless hostility of the capitalist states and institutions, in particular, that of the U.S. government and corporations. And so there gradually emerged within our fiercely democratic American opposition movement a recognition that democracy and social justice are both goods to be fought for; but separable goods, which could be linked together only under rather favorable circumstances, such as we enjoy at the present time in the United States.

The foregoing conclusions were reached by only a small part of the antiwar movement, however, and were not advocated on a widespread basis. While such ideas would count as treasonable only on the dubious equation of America with capitalism, the advocates of the U.S. war policy tried to brand the entire movement as traitorous. The movement, and, increasingly, liberal segments of the press, rejected such charges as smear tactics. Opposition to the war was becoming the majority opinion in America; respectability was therefore of great importance. Those who insisted publicly on supporting the Vietnamese revolution per se risked losing the broadest possible appeal. Thus, some of us welcomed a certain ambiguity in the general perception of the movement's objectives for strategic reasons. For others who now supported the Vietnamese revolution as such, the desire for ambiguity reflected a genuine feeling of ambivalence toward a revolution which seemed at variance with our democratic ideals. Still others, having now declared themselves against capitalism, raced to join or organize a multitude of aggressively competitive neo-Marxist sects. By the end of the decade, those few voices raised against both capitalism and political theology were drowned in the general din. The press of events in a decade without speed limits effectively frustrated the sort of thoughtful consideration which alone could clarify an acceptable relationship of the movement toward anticapitalist revolution. Under the circumstances, given the wounding experience of U.S. anti-Communist hysteria of the 1950s and the extreme pressure in the latter 1960s to halt the war rapidly, we did the best we could. Nevertheless, we missed (perhaps unavoidably) the opportunity to educate ourselves and our society—while it was, for a change, listening—about the legitimacy of anticapitalist rebellions per se, and our right to assist or support them.

I am acutely aware that many who read this brief essay were born in the midst of the very developments I have been describing, and now move in a world very different from that of twenty years ago. These twists and turns in the development of movement consciousness may be of very little interest; their recounting a form of obscurantism, or personal idiosyncrasy akin to the telling of old war stories. According to *Time* magazine we now live in an era of national celebration and face, many believe, four more years of uninterrupted partying. But the celebration may be of shorter duration than the revelers imagine. For today our country is faced, *once again*, with the imminent prospect of colonial war—this time in Central America. Our previous failure to clarify, and then insist upon, our right to support (selected) anticapitalist revolutions now hampers our ability to resist our government's policy toward Nicaragua and El Salvador. Indeed, judging from public reaction to the U.S. "triumph" in Grenada, we must sadly conclude that for many the lesson of Vietnam is that fighting colonial wars is perfectly acceptable; what is unacceptable is losing them.

But some readers will soon find themselves in opposition to any such colonial war. For such potential activists I offer the suggestion that it will be insufficient merely to support the right of the people of Central America to national self-determination. The enemies of the Nicaraguan government, for example, hypocritically decry the least departure from exemplary democratic practice in the Sandinista government, citing blemishes which would have been obscured in the pervasive tyranny and bloodiness of the Somoza regime, which the U.S. established. They allege, moreover, that Nicaragua is by no means nationally independent, but is now merely a client of Cuba and the Soviet state. In responding to these claims, the antiwar opposition will need to do at least the following things:

(1) Establish its own credibility by honestly declaring that it disapproves unequivocally of the suppression of democratic rights in the strong, well-established "socialist" states and supports the struggles—for example, that of the Polish worker—for such rights

(2) Argue convincingly that in developing countries only a strong measure of anticapitalist public direction of the economy can achieve significant levels of economic development

(3) Show that it is the United States which prevents, in Central America, a path of development which is both unassailably democratic and sufficiently nationalist and anticapitalist to achieve the objective of balanced and rapid development

The opposition must assert therefore, that the people of Nicaragua (and of other developing counties in comparable circumstances) have an unqualified right:

(1) To make a specifically anticapitalist revolution

(2) To suppress opposition to a degree, if necessary, to prevent the manipulation of such opposition by the United States, as the latter seeks the restoration of capitalism

(3) To seek the assistance of any states, including the Soviet Union and Cuba in order to succeed in its revolutionary program

To accomplish the foregoing educational objective, a new antiwar movement will need to achieve a level of sophistication beyond that of the anti–Vietnam War movement of the 1960s. In seeking to achieve such sophistication, it would be helpful for movement activists to become familiar with the contrasting experience of two countries in particular: Cuba and Chile. The differing fates of the anticapitalist strategies of the popular movements in these two countries have had a profound effect on the left throughout Latin America, and deeply influence the policies of the present government of Nicaragua and the Marxist rebels of El Salvador. The policy of the United States toward the Popular Unity government of Chile in particular has been a sobering object lesson to all the people of Latin America and ought to be also for the people of the United States. The detailed history of that policy should receive the broadest dissemination possible. For it was in Chile that the Unidad Popular government led by Dr. Salvador Allende attempted an experiment exactly alternative to that in Cuba. Unidad Popular sought to achieve deep anticapitalist reform in an unassailably democratic manner, by means of elected government, and without the least suppression of the opposition. As should be made widely known, the government of the United States, after waging economic warfare against Chile through manipulation of the world market in copper, then instigated a bloody coup d'état, which brought to power the current procapitalist, pro-U.S. dictatorship. This history is well known in Central America; only if we can make it known here as well can we hope to win any broad measure of support in the United States for a cessation of the present U.S. policy in Central America.

In summary, any new movement must distinguish sharply the evils of capitalism from the benefits of democracy. For the main propaganda line of the cold war is that capitalism and democracy are inseparable. The truth is very different. It is often actually the hostility of capitalism toward its opponents that pushes those opponents to adopt undemocratic measures or to seek protection of undemocratic allies. But the people of the world, and our own county, have a clear right to seek to improve the conditions of their lives, whether or not corporations or governments permit them the opportunity to do so by fully democratic means.

If then, in the ways I have suggested, we manage to face the almost obviously anticapitalist implications of past movement experience, and if, during an opportunity opened up by crisis, we can succeed even partially in communicating to the American people at large the necessity for this redefinition of legitimate opposition, then we will have taken the first serious step toward defusing the cold war. For to the extent that our nation relaxes its reflexive opposition to anticapitalist movements and rebellions, to that same extent it should find the old enmity toward the Soviet Union reduced as well. Indeed, if the specifically anticapitalist character of Soviet society itself, as distinguished sharply from its undemocratic character, became more tolerable to the people of the United States, we should then probably recognize that the Soviet government was no longer necessarily our paramount enemy; no more so, perhaps, than certain other authoritarian regimes (e.g., the union of South Africa and the Philippines) which we now take as "free world" allies. Needless to say, with such a reduction of enmity our world would be a much safer place, and the lessened burden of armaments alone would at last permit us to address, practically and effectively a whole agenda of long-neglected human priorities.

RESISTING REAGANISM AND WAR
IN CENTRAL AMERICA

In his first speech on the Berkeley campus since the 1960s, on October 2, 1984, Savio used the occasion of the Free Speech Movement's twentieth anniversary to call for renewed activism against war and reaction, and for defense of the egalitarian changes won in the 1960s (under threat from the rising tide of Reaganism). Avoiding nostalgia, this speech commemorated the insurgent 1960s not via celebratory discourse but by juxtaposing the Holocaust and the civil rights movements—the former as a reminder of the great evil the modern world is capable of perpetrating if hypernationalism, imperialism, and prejudice go unchallenged, the latter as an example of the human progress that is possible when democratic activists struggle in a determined way and display solidarity with oppressed groups. He urged activists to show such solidarity in the 1980s toward the victims of U.S. imperialism in Central America, much as 1960s activists had aided oppressed African Americans in the Jim Crow South.

The thing in my childhood—which most people here have some familiarity with—that moved me the most deeply, were the pictures of the piles of bodies. I am not Jewish. Those were mostly Jewish bodies. There were a lot of children's bodies in those piles. There were people of all ages; they were very thin. I remember seeing those pictures as a very young child. I could not understand those pictures as a young child, and I do not understand those pictures now. And I got an idea that I got stuck with for a number of years. If people had really noticed the bodies, the piles of bodies, if they'd seen the pictures as I had, then they would have changed the way we lived with one another. But I could see that nothing all that much had been changed about the way we lived with one another.

The civil rights movement just burst on the United States right on the tube. We saw people afraid, not of pictures, afraid of things more frightening than any I'd had to face. They faced their fears. They held one another to face their fears. And that moved many of us in white America who had the privileges of at least a cultural middle class—after all, you know, I'm white, ethnic, working-class. I'm mostly Sicilian, actually. But we all felt, somehow, we were part of the "middle class." And I remember my parents saying things like: "You don't know how lucky you are. You haven't even had to work for it." And I don't say that to put them down. They did sometimes say that because they'd had to struggle. And so I saw the people on the tube and they had none of the privileges that I had and more to fear. They overcame their fear by holding one another, against the snarling and snapping dogs we saw, against the torrents of water from the fire hoses—and they held one another! And that got to the children of white America. And we threw ourselves ardently into their movement. We wanted to be part of them, because in America of the 1950s, a very boring and in some ways scary time, we had seen nothing of people holding one another. And that's what the black people showed us—that we could overcome our fears by holding one another.

One principal task of that movement was to bring together black and white. I remember a button that many of us cherished, a SNCC button, Student Nonviolent Coordinating Committee: two clasped hands, black and white—equality. That was a great achievement of the movement, an attempted, partial achievement, to bring about, within America, a solidarity of those who had privilege and subtle fear—fear that could not quite be named, with those who had to fear police dogs, those who had not enough to eat, those who had seen their own parents humiliated; seen, say, a sixty-year-old man called "boy" repeatedly—and who had to grow up with that. We attempted to bring together those two parts of America—the part that the Mississippi all around us wanted hidden—and our part—the "perfect" part. Those did come together, and there was established in those days a deep solidarity. It wasn't perfect.

Following the lead of black people—who, by some miracle that we will never understand with complete precision, managed to think their way and act their way out of a dungeon that they had been placed in—one group of oppressed people after another cast off, discarded, the definitions of inferiority by which society was keeping them powerless or poor. One group after another. It was black people first, they were "niggers" no more. It was "spics" who then were Hispanic Americans. It was "wetbacks," Chicanos; it was "redskins" or even "Indians" who became Native Americans. It was all women. It was—and this was really hard for that aging, white middle-class "perfection" to take—even "fags" and "dykes," and somehow we now had lesbians and gay men.

All of these people together are a numerical majority in America. We are the majority! Now let me say to you something that this means. The majority makes demands. The minority calls the majority "the interest groups." So now you have the struggle between the new majority to take control of our society—the democratic society. We are the majority. And on the other side is the aging, old establishment minority. We could break the bank for them, given the way in which they've got the pie split up. We discovered in the course of struggle that if the needs of each of these groups that formed a new majority were to be met—and they often were needs expressed very appropriately in demands on the public authorities—America would have to change direction. We discovered this especially in the seventies. America would need to change direction. How? I, fortunately—it gives me a certain liberty—am not a Marxist, and so I can say it. America, to accommodate the just demands of the new majority, has to become at least a little bit less capitalist!

That's not such a big deal. There are perhaps two, maybe three of the major industrialized countries in all the world that don't have publicly financed, comprehensive health insurance. We are one of them! So what I'm trying to say is that some element of moving in that direction is needed. It is sort of like the metric system: Come on, get off the dime, America! Now this shift in our values—and let me spell it out—not just a name. Hey, not a blueprint! Not jumping in the pool before you can swim. A shift! This shift in our values means America is dominated less by production for private profit, less by production for war, and more by production to meet ordinary, human needs!

And here is the clincher and what we need to say...to America. For us, becoming less capitalistic means we don't have to become less democratic; we can become more democratic!

But the understanding to bring this about is not something that matures overnight, and so there has been time for the reaction to take action. What does that mean? We are now confronted—behind the celluloid shield of an actor president—with the cold war in America in its last stand. What is it? Well, it has a cultural aspect; it has a military aspect; it has an economic aspect—and we only have a few minutes. It's antiquated cultural values. It is very large corporations. It is the Pentagon. We need to begin to confront it, directly naming it and moving beyond it, and why? Because it is too dangerous to do otherwise.

People outside our borders, less wealthy than we, have not been able to afford this dalliance with pure-as-possible capitalism. They have not been able to afford that. The people of Central America have said, "For us, capitalism means life under Somoza—one Somoza or another! And we don't want it anymore!"

They have succeeded in one place in making a revolution—Nicaragua. Now, my friends, I had trouble during the anti–Vietnam War days because it was hard for me to talk about something I had not seen. I have not been to Nicaragua, so what I say, you need to check. Check it! We know the names of lots of people in Nicaragua. We know the names of more people in Nicaragua than in any other Central American nation. We know Daniel Ortega. We know Miguel D'Escoto, a priest and a member of the cabinet. We know Ernesto Cardenal, another priest, a Jesuit, and his brother, Fernando Cardenal. They're both in the government; it doesn't sound like godless, atheistic Communism to me!

They write beautiful poems, and had I more time, I would have read one. Find out—Ernesto Cardenal is a published poet. Jocanda Belli, an Italian name, she's written some beautiful poems. This is Nicaragua! These are real people. I want to tell you about one other person, Melba Blandon. Very few people here, I'm sure, know the name Melba Blandon. She is the censor in Nicaragua. And they have censorship in Nicaragua because they have a state of emergency because the United States, the CIA-backed contras, are attacking them from four sides right now—in our name—with the money taken out of the school lunch program of our children! This is criminal!

They are afraid that our children will be sent to slaughter their children. They are afraid of those same kinds of images that frightened me! They are afraid of dead bodies! Our government is preparing a bloodbath in Central America, and we have a choice—we have a choice! Either we manage to prevent that by establishing some kind of bond of real solidarity between us and the people of Nicaragua, of El Salvador—of all of Central America—and therefore make it our Mississippi for this generation.

Either we succeed in making it the Mississippi of this generation, or it will be the Vietnam of this generation, and it will destroy their society and tear ours absolutely apart. The choice may be ours. I hope it is.

THE SECOND GENERATION

At his son Nadav's graduation from the Sidwell Friends School, Mario gave the major commencement speech on June 10, 1988. He took this occasion to rebut conservative critics of the New Left, most notably Allan Bloom, who in his sixties-bashing book—published during the Reagan era—charged that the student movement had severely damaged American higher education. Savio found that not only Bloom but much of mainstream America, including his own father, lacked the open-mindedness necessary to assess judiciously the insights that came from the Left. He voiced hope that the coming generation would be more open-minded and move beyond the narrow intellectual horizons of cold war America.

I would like to begin by acknowledging those of you, especially the students, who have made it possible for me to speak to you here today. Perhaps thanks would be more gracious than mere acknowledgment, but I am not at all sure how appropriate it would be to say thank you for the very stressful opportunity of speaking at the graduation of one's own son. Particularly so for me, since when someone calls "Mr. Savio" I still must suppress the reflex to look around to see if my father is somewhere in the room. Parents in recent times have grown used to being judged frankly—if not harshly—by their children, a practice which my own generation has had some hand in establishing as a dubious tradition. To rise quickly, then, at the opportunity to be judged in public by one's son and his friends is, in the Italian proverb, to skip happily into the mouth of the wolf.

You know, when I received the letter of invitation I was genuinely surprised—actually shocked. The terror set in only when I sat down to write the speech. I tend to have a sort of facetious sense of humor, and so the first thing that popped into my head was that this was some sly stratagem that my son had cooked up to ensure that I attend his graduation.

But surely only very special circumstances could cause a parent to miss this graduation. For the pride and the inevitable sadness in saying goodbye to childhood are deeply felt by all, not by the graduates only, but by the teachers and by the parents as well. This is an important moment.

I was surprised, but also pleased, by this invitation (for another reason also). Some of you may have read of the so-called Battle of the Books, raging now, according to the Sunday *New York Times*, on American university campuses, and others may have read Professor Allan Bloom's bestseller *The Closing of the American Mind:* Evidence, in both cases, that the impulse for deep reform, or radical change, which we correctly associate with the sixties, is still very much a focus of controversy. In his chapter on the sixties, Professor Bloom writes:

> About the sixties it is now fashionable to say that although there were indeed excesses, many good things resulted. But, so far as universities are concerned, I know of nothing positive coming from that period; it was an unmitigated disaster for them. I hear that the good things were "greater openness," "less rigidity," "freedom from authority," etc.—but these have no content and express no view of what is wanted from a university education.

Well, Professor Bloom's book is, as I said, a bestseller, and it is rather well written actually, displaying an impressive erudition. I recommend it to you as pre-college summer reading. But you can see then that, as one whom Professor Bloom might credit with having made a modest, personal contribution to the destruction of higher education in America, I could be pleasantly surprised by an invitation to address a graduating high school class, most, if not all, of whom will now be going on to those very colleges and universities which I and my ilk have presumably left in a shambles. I, of course, do not feel that any such great damage was done by the period of the sixties either to America or to American universities. On the contrary. And since it certainly is due to some fame or notoriety which I achieved in that era that you have invited me here as your commencement speaker, I know that you would feel cheated if I did not dwell upon what that time meant to me, and what it might mean to you. When you get to college you will be confronted, on the one hand, by those young professors who were students during the sixties, now achieving tenure, whose presence the [William] Bennetts and the Blooms decry, and, on the other hand, by Professor Bloom's conservative cohorts themselves, admonishing you to remain safely within the library's protective walls, lest premature contact with the world of causes and conflict result in the closing of your minds! In short, if you go to college at all, the question of your relationship to the generation of the sixties—to my generation—is one you will find it very difficult to avoid.

What, then, was so special about the sixties? And what was it like for me, a most apolitical son of apolitical Italian immigrants, prior to my departure from college? What was the nature of the alteration within my mind and spirit when, like you now, I was preparing myself to move beyond the influence and control of my teachers and my parents?

Life in the fifties—even the late fifties, despite rock and roll—was both more silent and more stark than what you have known. They used to test-explode nuclear weapons in the open air—and broadcast the results on the TV screen for all the world to see. America was undisputed top rooster in those days, and American policy makers evidently hoped to intimidate the Russians. The unintended outcome was to terrify the children of the United States. Frankly, I was never deeply impressed by the belief some hold that human beings would never use these weapons in a real war. For the pictures of the destruction of Hiroshima and Nagasaki had a horrifying newness then. And the human capacity for unlimited evil was borne to me vividly by the equally fresh photographs of Jewish bodies piled in heaps. Those pictures of the Holocaust—for some reason I will never quite understand—were and remain for me the granitelike reality against which every book or mere idea had to be tested.

There was another aspect to the starkness. The story we were taught about the world was painted in the whitest white of American purity and the satanic red of the worldwide Communist menace. Pink, of course, was a shade of red. We could do no wrong, they could do no right, and if necessary we would suffer the devastation of the planet to preserve our way of life. This is a caricature, surely, you will say. And you are right. But children may half believe what most adults will take with a grain of salt. So this is the first important thing to know about the generation of the sixties. We came of age with a powerful vested interest in proving that the previous generation's worldview was seriously in error. Because, given nuclear weapons, and given the recently demonstrated human capacity for evil, if they were right, we were doomed.

I have referred also to the silence of the times. I mean the pall of McCarthyism, of course. Few will have managed to graduate from this particular school without having gained at least some familiarity with the rigid conformity of mind which characterized (and accompanied) Senator Joseph McCarthy's obsessive search for Communists. But I was spared the full force of the intimidation of the time by my parents' lack of any real political sophistication. And, in any case, my father recognized McCarthy's televised hearings for the witch hunt they were. By the time I had gotten to where you are now, the Army-McCarthy hearings were already receding in memory, assuming the character of an aberration, an instance of excessive, if basically well-intentioned, zeal. It was even permissible (or necessary) to question Joseph McCarthy's personal good intentions. But America's motives—unlike those of the Soviet Union—were always presumed good. The rejection of anti-Communist hysteria thus marked the limit of responsible political debate. And in this sense, even I was affected. Let me share with you a personal story.

It was sometime during high school, and late on as it seems to me, that I took a one-semester course in economics. Part of the course was devoted to "other economic systems"—economic systems, that is, other than our own. I don't recall the context now, but in the textbook I encountered for the first time the following words (or perhaps it was the first time I had noticed them): "From each according to his ability; to each according to his need!"

I was a religious sort: I have two aunts who are nuns, and under other circumstances I might have become a priest. To my naive mind, the beauty of these words was astonishing. It still is. Now I was worried. For it seemed to me that these words possessed a biblical sort of purity. I could imagine Jesus Christ himself speaking them in the Sermon on the Mount. But these were the words of Karl Marx, the prince of devils, the Antichrist, the ultimate generator of international Communism. How evil could the Communists be to succeed in twisting an idea as touching as this? I discussed my problem with my mother, from whom I've inherited a love of poetry and the gift of gab. But this was long before women's liberation, and she felt that this was the sort of thing I needed to discuss with my father. So I did.

We had our discussion out in the lovely garden that my father had planted in our backyard in a working-class suburb in Queens, New York. Now, my father, Joseph, had an unfailing respect for his grandfather, also Joseph, Giuseppe, Don Beppino, whom he had left long before in the Sicilian mountain village of Santa Caterina. As my father told the story, one day a Communist organizer came to see my great-grandfather. Don Beppino was one of the most respected men in the village, and the organizer realized that if he succeeded in his audience with Don Beppino, he would have an easy in with the rest of the peasants. So my great-grandfather, baiting his trap, asked the organizer, "You believe, then, that all men should share their wealth equally?"

"That is exactly our belief, Don Beppino," the organizer is supposed to have said, taking the old man's bait.

"Well, I would gladly divide my property in half and give half to you."

"Ah, this is wonderful, Don Beppino."

"But let me ask you one thing more," my great-grandfather continued. "Suppose that after a year's time you have squandered your share. What are we to do then?"

"Oh, in that case, we would need to divide the remaining property once again." At which my great-grandfather is supposed to have raised his cane high above his head and bellowed at the organizer: "*Vattini via, prima che ti dungno 'na bastunata!* Off with you, and be quick about it, before I hit you upside the head with this cane."

This brief story may tell as much as many a learned treatise as to why Marxism never gained a foothold in southern Italy. Of course, I tried to continue the discussion with my father. "I had not meant Communism necessarily, and perhaps these words of Marx should be taken not as a sketch for legislation, but simply as a sort of ideal for society, etc., etc., blah, blah, blah...," but he wasn't listening. In his own simple and powerful way he exemplified the nature of political discussion in America. Alien ideas are considered only for purposes of refutation. His grandfather had said it, he believed, and that settled it. I had unwittingly played the Communist organizer, and I had given my father the opportunity to play his beloved grandfather. And now, you'll be thinking, I've had my revenge.

But there's more to my story. Don Beppino was, of course, right. In a society of enforced equality, as long as there is any scarcity at all, some will be workers and others will be parasites. Indeed, the new Soviet leadership of perestroika and glasnost appears to be beginning to acknowledge something like this right now. They are beginning, it seems, to acknowledge the truth in America's truth. Our leaders, however, have not as yet begun, publicly, to acknowledge any truth in Marx's truth. Jesse Jackson is an exception, of course. Consider his observation that the American eagle needs two wings to fly, a left wing as well as a right...

But back to my father. He was a wonderful gardener, as many Sicilians are. And his vegetable garden was, it must be said, the envy of the neighborhood. The tomatoes were beautiful, and one summer the beefsteak tomatoes were magnificent. This was with him genuine ability. A family could easily make a meal of one such tomato, and my father distributed them amongst the neighbors, much to my mother's consternation. He neither asked nor expected anything in return. He was also a first-rate layer of brick. The chiselers who had sold us the mortgage on the gimcracky cottages in that development had provided sad little concrete steps on which two could barely stand together. My father expertly replaced the concrete steps with a charming miniature porch of brick on which he eventually mounted a graceful trellis.

The neighbors wanted porches too. But few knew how even to start to make one. They asked my father, and he, again playing Don Beppino, showed them how. For the would-be junior management type, who seemed unable to learn which end to grasp the trowel by, my father all but built the porch himself. Again, he asked nothing. It was a simple case of one man's ability and another man's need.

But one day my father decided to turn the cottage into a proper house. To do this, he needed to raise the roof. To raise the roof, he reasoned, would take a large number of automobile jacks: once the roof was up on the jacks he could nail in the studs, put on the siding, and the job would be complete. He was a strategic thinker, and very resourceful. This job would take a lot of jacks and a lot of people to help with the work. Now my father was in need, if you will, and he went around to the neighbors, and they came with their automobile jacks. Out came the six-packs and up went the roof, and we had an old-fashioned all-American frontier house-raising right there in suburban Queens. "From each according to his ability, to each according to his need!"

My father could never hear the poetry in those words. But years later, when I had become notorious as a rouser of the college rabble, a reporter came to see my father. And the reporter asked him, "Where did your son learn all his radical ideas?" And my father, always eager to play Don Beppino, said, "He learned it all from a book he read at home. I still have it here." The reporter, my father tells me, was very excited. My father then showed him the family Bible.

Now let me step back and move more quickly. The young people who made the New Left of the 1960s had a deep vested interest in finding the flaw in the prevailing view of America and of America's role in the world. This, as I tried to show before, was a matter of elemental self-preservation. And it was character-istic of even those New Leftists, such as I, who were innocent of previous radical politics, to try to see the truth in Marx's truth. Think about it. How could one hope to prevent the final war without making a serious effort to listen to the truth of the national "enemy"?

But a key element was missing. There still remained the myth of Ameri-can perfection, the universal assumption of America's good intention. Here the facts came to the rescue of young white Americans at least. And (thank you, Professor Bloom) our minds swung open to receive the data and to assess the concrete experience of the black struggle for civil rights and of America's war against Vietnam. I will assume that your teachers have done their work. You know what the civil rights movement was. You know what the war in Vietnam was about. The conclusions we drew, however, may not all be your own. But we came to view America as a racist and imperialist power—covering its tracks with a beguiling opportunity for self-expression and conspicuous consumption for a considerable and privileged part of its population. Fortified by the peasant wisdom of my great-grandfather, perhaps, I never could become a thoroughgoing Marxist. But a socialist of sorts I became and remain.

What were we then? Something unique. Like immigrants in a new land, we were the most conscious part of the first generation of Americans to be raised from earliest childhood beneath the Damoclean threat of thermonuclear war. We fought for racial justice. We struggled to halt the crazed and cruel carnage that claimed more than fifty thousand American lives alone in Vietnam. We had a vision too, defined, if you will, by the unpremeditated and generous response of ability to need. It was the vision of a loving community. Let me quote for you part of a song of the sixties that tells well the temper of the time:

> Come on people
> Smile on your brother
> Everybody get together
> Gotta love one another
> Right now. (Repeat)

That's the authentic voice of the 1960s. Listen to the cadence: "Right now!" It was always "right now" in the sixties. Peace now! Freedom now! Why did we imagine that we needed to or could remake the world in the space of ten years or less? Did we not know that we would spoil the work by the way we dashed it off? Why were we in such a hurry? Because, in whatever we did, even perhaps while making love, we might suddenly become aware that the bombs could soon begin to fall.

We were the first generation of Americans to be raised from earliest childhood with the constant threat of thermonuclear war. It was common for us to accept that there might not be a second generation. We lived our lives as if we would never reach the ripe old age of thirty years. Even so, we did not put all our eggs in one basket. We bore children, daughters and sons. You are the second generation.

You are the second generation, and you must learn to live in the new land. Today we see only the dim outline of that new way of life:

- The weapons must be put away.
- The two systems, as the Soviet physicist Andrei Sakharov observed, must be permitted to converge, theirs becoming more free, ours more just.
- And the half of our common wealth that we now squander on our weapons must be put to work to build the loving community.

If you will learn how to pick up the trowel, if you take up this great work of construction, if you can advance the work, then you will be seen as first in the eyes of all the generations to come.

You are our children. We love you, we are proud of you, we are afraid for you, but like all parents, we have high hopes for you also. We are not yet moving from the stage. We still have our work to do, and perhaps we and you may have the opportunity to work together. I have described for you how I needed to define myself with respect to my father. My generation needed to define itself with respect to a previous generation of Americans, and you will have to do the same. We place in your hands our hopes and our dreams; we trust your generosity and your good judgment. Thank you. Good luck.

BUILDING A COMPASSIONATE
COMMUNITY

Although Savio was one of the most eloquent orators of his generation, he was never interviewed about how he prepared for his speeches. While Savio almost always seemed to do some advance planning about what he would say, his speeches had a strong element of spontaneity. Like the best jazz musicians, Savio soared through improvisation. He was almost never scripted, speaking his own words rather than reading from a text. This approach to oratory can be gleaned by comparing the two versions of Savio's speech, "Building a Compassionate Community." The first version is the one he actually delivered at the main rally on Sproul Plaza during Berkeley's commemoration of the thirtieth anniversary of the Free Speech Movement (FSM-30) on December 2, 1994. This speech expressed his deepening concern about the shift of American politics to the right, as reflected in the anti-immigrant and anti-affirmative-action ballot initiatives that would pass overwhelmingly in California. Savio saw the sixties generation's egalitarianism and its work building a compassionate community as offering a strong foundation to resist the wave of intolerance fostered by the Right. The speech displays Savio's own compassionate politics and his poetic sensibility as strongly as any he ever gave. This first version is followed by a shorter text, which is what he had written in advance and would have delivered at Sproul had he actually read his speech there.

VERSION I: SPEECH DELIVERED AT THE RALLY

I'd like to begin by calling attention to the newspaper because things are a little bit different today [than they were in 1964] because we got an editorial [praising the Free Speech Movement]....It says at the end, "Thirty years later we owe them a debt of gratitude and trust, however gray they may be." Well, okay, I can't tell you, "Trust me because the [*San Francisco*] *Chronicle* says so." So I won't...

My wife suggested how to begin this talk. She said, "You can say, 'I wish I was thirty years younger.'" Now, you know that's true. But she added, "You can also tell them your *wife* wishes you were thirty years younger." And I guess that's true too.

Thirty years ago—and I think we are closer to you now than we were then to the people who struggled during the [19]30s. But thirty years ago (a long time, one generation...a little bit more) we were awakened from *our* dogmatic slumber by a clarion that was sounding off the campus. It really was in response to and in participation in the civil rights movement that this all got started.

We had a lot of things to learn. We had to learn about race. We haven't learned that completely yet, have we? But we've made progress...We needed to learn about our relationship to the planet. We haven't learned that completely yet. But we've made a lot of progress. We needed to learn about gender. We haven't learned all of that yet. But I think we *have* made a lot of progress. Although I was at a meeting last night [and] there was a woman who got up to speak. I thought she was misguided. She was greeted by jeers and scorn. And those were the jeers and scorn of men, I have to say. So we haven't learned it all. But we've had a lot to learn—very deep lessons. And it's taken a long time. In fact, it's taken our community thirty years to mature....That's what's been happening.

They say, "Well, okay, the other side has won." Well, they'll get their squalid little footnote. Meanwhile, we're building a community, And it takes a long time because it's a community built on deepened consciousness, not mania and the fabrication of enemies. And that takes time. It's taken us thirty years. We had to do other things too. We had to learn how to make a living. I teach up at Sonoma State. Well, if you call college teaching work, I work. Now, we also had to raise children. It's one generation that's past. We had to find ways to do those things while exploiting our fellows as little as possible. It has been very, very difficult. Very difficult indeed. And those are hard lessons to learn.

I teach a course at Sonoma State: Science and Poetry. It's a seminar. And we were just coming to the end of "Burnt Norton." That's the first one of [T. S.] Eliot's "Four Quartets." And this is the passage. And I realized it could be about us:

Sudden in a shaft of sunlight
Even while the dust moves

There rises the hidden laughter
Of children in the foliage.

That was us. We were those children.

Quick now, here now, always—
Ridiculous the waste sad time
Stretching before and after.

One of the students said, "Well, you can't re-create the past." And I assumed he was talking to me personally.

So I hope you will feel that I am not completely insincere if I do try to redeem some of that time by noting that I once again hear a clarion off the campus. Once again I see a society in crisis. Okay. That crisis is a deep one. That crisis goes to the way people work and don't quite make it when they work. Our secretary of labor, or yours, or whoever it is, Robert Reich, described an "anxious class." Well, of course, he's talking about the working class... consisting of millions of Americans who no longer can count on having their jobs next year or next month. And whose wages have stagnated or even lost ground to inflation. They're afraid; they're frustrated; they're anxious. These are the people who voted in the last election.... Not mean people, people who are anxious, people who see their lives slip away, who work and don't see what they are working for—who are poorer than their parents were.

Why is this happening? There are a number of reasons. But I want to point to one that I think is very important because it is going to be with us for a long, long time. We as a nation are in competition with other nations which pay their workers much less than our workers are used to or have been used to receiving, That's good, my friends... because we want to spread the possibility of being wealthy very broadly over the entire planet. However, there will necessarily be a period of transition. That kind of competition inevitably exerts a very steady and harsh downward pressure on American incomes. The question is, *whose* incomes? Okay. That's the thing to think about. You know, we have those who have and never lose, and others who just barely make it. If you check the stats—and you can do it, okay, you can look it up, as they say—if you check the stats, you'll see that the rich have maintained their incomes. The middle class—so-called—the workers, in other words the rest of us, have gradually lost ground. That is going to continue because it's the whole world that's going to want to become wealthy, right? And therefore we're going to be in competition with that whole world for a long time.

So the question is: How do you spread the pain here in this land of wealth during this period of transition? Well, naturally...the wealthy don't want us to spread the pain to *them*. I mean, that makes sense, guys, okay? The wealthy do not want us to spread the pain to *them*.

Therefore they want us to enter into a coalition with them against the poor. We'll make the poor suffer! Then you know that you're not as bad off as they are. You won't feel so bad even though you're suffering a great deal yourselves. That kind of coalition, that's old. They try to do that all the time. But now they are getting somewhat desperate. And when in order to consolidate that coalition requires getting people to believe the unbelievable, not to turn and say, "Hey you [rich] guys have to suffer along with us," but "No, take it from them [the poor] and they have nothing." Right?

Under those circumstances the political class resorts to obscure, obscurantist, and finally very illogical arguments. And what is the nature of that argument? Find enemies...Circle the wagons. Who's inside? Inside are the normal Americans. The normal Americans are scrubbed white, 100 percent Christian, and mostly men. Those are the normal Americans. Outside whoever we can take it from, whoever we can shaft. Lots of enemies. If people are afraid of enemies, the aliens amongst us...they won't analyze the problem in its own realistic terms.

My friends...that is the problem with Proposition 187. It is *creeping fascism*....Don't get the wrong idea. This isn't exotic, pretentious, intellectual European fascism. This is American know-nothing fascism.

And they aren't all fascists. You have the Gingriches and the Helmses...[who are] crypto-fascists. But mind you...you have Pete Wilson. He's just an opportunist. But look at the opportunity he's taking. He's taking an opportunity based upon demonizing human beings in our midst in order to get first to Sacramento—second time—and then maybe to Washington. A very serious kind of opportunism. And *we need to stop it*.

Now, I want to tell you they don't have such a strong hand. They wouldn't be doing this if they had a strong hand....

Two days after the election my son [Daniel] says to me, quoting here from the [Santa Rosa] *Press Democrat*, he said, "Dad, I'm not going to back this law. I'm not supporting this law." And I'm thinking—a parent, right?—"What is he talking about? Is this kid crazy? What is this all about?" And he reads to me from the *Press Democrat*. It says, "All students registering for public school after January 1, 1995, must show proof of citizenship." And Daniel says to me, "Dad, I'm not going to do that. I'm not going to show that to them." They say the fruit never falls far from the tree, thank God!

It's not just my son. It's not just students. Here is why their hand is weak. This contemptible little law if it gets out of the courts depends for its effective enforcement on the willing and conscious cooperation of doctors, lawyers, social workers, teachers, librarians, and students. And most of those people were against it. And at least some of them can come over to an in-their-faces campaign of *systematic noncompliance.*

I suggest something...—if it [Proposition 187] comes out of the courts—...on the order of the old War Resisters League. Okay, you research, you find out how this law impinges directly on every class of people: on students, on workers, on teachers, everyone you can speak to. You offer them counseling. Don't tell them to break the law. Invite them to be counseled. Tell them what their options will be if they decide to break the law, that is, if they decide not to cooperate. *You* provide them with the lawyers. *You* provide them with the publicity. Don't let any act of *conscientious objection to class war*—which is what it is, my friends—don't let any act of conscientious objection—they're precious acts— go in secret. This is not hiding your light under a bushel. If the person has to go to work and say, "I won't cooperate," *go with that person.* Support every person who's willing to take a risk.

I just want to conclude by referring to two other poets. I love poets, guys. Love poets. Okay, two other poets. Yeats... Here's the situation. Yeats:

Everywhere the ceremony of innocence is drowned;
The best lack all conviction, while the worst
Are full of passionate intensity.

Don't let it be so! *Don't* let it be so! They don't have the passion. We have the passion. They have mania. Okay. We have the passion because our community is a community of *com*passion. We want to relieve suffering because we feel that suffering. The only thing they can do is make other people suffer. The second poet, José Martí:

Con los pobres de la tierra [with the poor of the earth]
quiero yo mi suerte echar [I want to cast my lot]

With the poor of the earth no matter what side of the border they're on— whether they're legal or illegal, just folks, folks whether they're black or brown, folks whether they're yellow or red, folks who wear pants, folks who wear dresses, folks who wear both, for God's sake!

We want to cast our lot with the people not with the bosses. We don't want to buy into that coalition against the poor. Do it! Do it!

VERSION II: SPEECH PREPARED IN ADVANCE

Welcome from the 1960s! Let me add at once that no one, so far as I know, ever made a speech during the 1960s with the opening line "Welcome from the 1930s!" That's a significant fact. The 1960s were remote from the thirties; the nineties are not remote from the sixties. The Second World War and the experience of the Great Depression separated us from that earlier generation of radicals. By contrast, the issues of race and gender and class and of the desecration of our natural environment unite us to a new generation of young people. I'll happily claim credit on behalf of my generation, that is, for establishing America's genuine current agenda—the agenda that so much of today's official leadership is running away from. But while we were very good indeed at identifying the real problems, we were less good at solving them. No one in the past thirty years has quite succeeded in solving these problems, although, certainly, some very good work has been accomplished. We cannot move on as a nation without the full solutions. And so these common problems—race, gender, class, the environment—unite us. And so I am not a sixties student radical retread; I am a parent and a professional person of the nineties who is still a political radical, not at all from nostalgia, but because my family and work commitments bring me every day into confrontation with problems that won't go away, and which only fester toward despair and violence because we, as a nation, have avoided for so long the great work of constructing comprehensive solutions.

Now, there's another important respect in which we are closer to the young people of today than were the remaining thirties radicals to us thirty years ago. There occurred, during the witch hunts of the late forties and the 1950s, a destruction of the natural link between radicals and radicalism on the one hand, and the majority of people and their common problems on the other. The American establishment either actively discredited its radical critics—shamelessly destroying lives if necessary—or else permitted the work to be accomplished by otherwise embarrassing extremists of the right such as Senator Joseph McCarthy. Radicalism was equated with Marxism, and Marxism with Communism; Communism was the name of the social and political system of Soviet Russia, and that, of course, needed no discrediting. The net effect of this demonization of dissenters was to make it difficult for us to learn anything from Old Leftists and from the experience of the Old Left. A great gulf existed between the Old Left, which popularly was seen as irrelevant or treasonous, and our New Left of the 1960s. And so our new radicalism had no history. But even those like me who never were and never became Marxists refused to permit the establishment to dictate whom we could talk to, whom we could learn from. And therefore, the New Left of the 1960s can fairly and proudly call itself the anti-anti-Communist Left. Ours was a great and noble refusal. As a generation, we refused to be turned either into traitors or into anti-Communist yahoos. That was the real beginning of the end of the cold war. We insisted on reestablishing the continuity of American radical history. We largely succeeded in accomplishing this task by focusing our attention on American problems—especially race—and by discussing those problems, not in accents borrowed from the experience of the European Left, but in plain American English. The measure of our success is this: that today's young people are willing to listen, cautiously but also eagerly, to our experiences. That is precisely what is happening right here during this reunion. Newt Gingrich and his ilk may wish, as he has averred, to eradicate the last vestiges of the counterculture of the 1960s, but the wish is vain. Here we are, Newt! Here we are! I affirm that twenty years from today, when the cryptofascist rantings of the Jesse Helmses and the Newt Gingriches have earned their squalid little footnotes, we will again gather, then to celebrate our fiftieth anniversary; and I have good reason to hope that that will also be a celebration of the triumph of our life-affirming values.

That celebration of life will not come without a further struggle. American society is not working well today, and in some important respects it is not working at all. As I said before, I am still a political radical, but not at all from nostalgia. Every day, as a working person and as a parent, I have to face a country whose major unfinished business festers toward despair and violence. Consider the case of our Proposition 187. Permit me to move rapidly from the ridiculous to the sublime: from Pete Wilson to brother Henry David Thoreau! Why, precisely, do we have an illegal alien problem? A "nanny" problem? It's because of the border, isn't it? Brother Thoreau went to jail as a tax refuser and a war resister because he could not, in good conscience, support a dirty war for the extension of slavery, a war which had as one of its consequences putting California outside of Mexico! And as a remote consequence, this cruel opportunist, Pete Wilson, gets to make war on schoolchildren! Give me a break! Give us all a break!

But there it is. A country unwilling to face its problems. America is now in direct and unavoidable economic competition with other countries that pay their workers much less than our workers are accustomed to receiving. Hence, a long-term downward pressure on American incomes. Hence, a recession that won't quite go away. Workers have had to trade good jobs for poor ones. There's widespread violence, in part because young men can't get decent jobs or the training to qualify. Many people are feeling tremendous insecurity. Solutions: build more jails (Proposition 184); blame the Mexicans (Proposition 187).

These are fascist solutions. Literally. Definitionally. The real culprits are the rich, the ones who make money no matter which side of the border the factories are built on. And they're running the country; and they're getting richer, while the rest of us are poorer than our parents were. Hence, the fascist solution: find a scapegoat, the criminals, the poor, the Mexicans. The rich don't want us to start thinking thoughts like these. Okay. So we're in long-term competition with poorer countries. For the foreseeable future people here in America are bound to suffer, but eventually things will be better for everybody in all the countries. Meanwhile, we ought to spread the suffering here in America, so everybody has to bear the burden, especially those who can bear most easily— the rich! The grip that a rich man has on his money is tighter, as my aunt used to love saying, than a crab's ass, and that's waterproof!

The fascist solution. "United we stand, America!" Fascism is a principle of social and national unity in which rich folks try to get the people in the middle strata of society to join with the rich against some imagined common enemy. Inevitably, that means to join against the poor and the weak, here and in other countries. This would be unnecessary if things were working well, if the pie were large enough to cut into decent-sized slices for everyone. But that is no longer possible and won't again be possible for a very long time. And so we are being asked to close ranks primarily against the poor. Naturally, under such circumstances you can't afford real elections. A real election is one in which the issues and the qualifications of the candidates are debated rationally. This latest so-called election was a shameful and shameless exercise in the massive financing of propaganda, the fearful propaganda of xenophobia and racism.

Please, do not let anybody persuade you that you are obliged to abide by the results. For now, Proposition 187 is in the courts. Let's hope it stays there. But don't count on it. Prepare to resist. The day after the election, my son Daniel is reading the [Santa Rosa] *Press Democrat*, and he says to me, "Dad, I'm not going to support this law." And, just like a parent, I'm thinking, "What the devil is he talking about now?" But he reads to me, "All students registering for public school after January 1, 1995, must show proof of citizenship." And then he says, "I'm not going to show any such proof." As the saying goes, the fruit never falls far from the tree.

In this game, the governor and the other opportunists who pushed this vicious law do not have that strong a hand. For the effective enforcement of Proposition 187 they absolutely require the conscious and willing cooperation of many people who were and are against it: lawyers, doctors, social workers, teachers. So while it may not be exactly a piece of cake, it should be possible to organize an "in your face" campaign of massive noncompliance. Students could play a significant part in such a campaign. First, it will be necessary to research in detail just how persons with various occupations would be affected by the law. Then a counseling organization could be set up roughly along the lines of the War Resisters League. While such an organization need not precisely advocate disobedience, it could offer advice to persons considering disobeying the law, and could make legal assistance available. As I said, students could take a significant role in such a campaign.

The Free Speech Movement was an outgrowth of the early struggle for civil rights. A crisis off campus led to the active political involvement of students. There is again a crisis in the off-campus community. Once again the powerful are victimizing the poor and the weak. The next stage in an ongoing struggle should again involve students as major participants. What you do, what we all do now, can help determine the sort of reunion we have twenty years from today. More importantly, what we do now can help shape the kind of world our children will inherit. The great issues rediscovered in the 1960s—race, gender, class, natural environment—call forth a long-term struggle between forces of hatred and fear and the values of life. Our willingness to continue to resist can help ensure that our countercommunity of life and affirmation will not merely survive but will in time prevail.

THEIR VALUES AND OURS

Asked to speak on spiritual values at an FSM-30 panel, Savio, an ex-Catholic, discussed how his religious background influenced his politics, which initially emerged as a secularized version of liberation theology. This December 3, 1994, speech offers his most extensive public discussion of Marxism and why the revulsion against dogma that led to his break with the Church also made it impossible for him to embrace Marxism, even though he admired Marx's compassionate and poetic sensibility. This speech initially appeared in the Threepenny Review in summer 1995.

It's kind of hard for me to do. This wasn't a problem thirty years ago. But, you know, I have to look at you, because it's a dialogue; I've got to look at the paper; and it's very difficult to do both at once. Maybe I should get bifocals: then I'll feel even more like Benjamin Franklin.

The assignment I was given was to talk about "spiritual values." Can you believe it? This is because, I guess, I have two aunts who are nuns. And in Italian Catholic families, there's the person who's chosen to be a priest, and I was going to be a priest. As a matter of fact, I wanted to do that, I realized only recently; I really did want to do it. And in fact the talk will be about that, believe it or not.

And so I'm going to begin by reading a parable from this book, *The Spotted Pony*, which is a collection of Hanukkah stories. This is the seventh night (is it the seventh now?—no, I think it's the seventh—yes, we celebrate it every year, guys, and we have to count up the presents, so . . .). I'd like to read this parable because this parable ties in, I think, with remarks that I want to make, and also sums up so clearly and simply (as Brother Albert Einstein said: make it all as simple as possible, but no simpler)—it sums up the difference, I think, between their values and ours.

Heaven and Hell

What is heaven like? In heaven, the righteous sit at a great banquet. The table is set with every imaginable delicacy. People in heaven have but to stretch out their arms to take whatever they desire. However, in heaven people's arms do not bend at the elbow.

What is hell like? In hell, the wicked sit at a great banquet. The table is set with every imaginable delicacy. People in hell have but to stretch out their arms to take whatever they desire. However, in hell people's arms also do not bend at the elbow.

So what is the difference between heaven and hell? People in heaven feed each other.

I think in order to do this—and this isn't my job. I know what my job has been, all these years. This isn't my job. But I'm going to try to do it anyway. And to do it, I'm going to have to tell you something about my background which I have generally not told people about, because that wasn't my job.

Okay. I'm not Jewish, I was not from a political family—no Marxists in my family. My father voted for "the man of the hour," Dwight D. Eisenhower, because he thought that the Democrats had been in power too long. But as good working-class people (and I'm from an Italian working-class family, both sides), my parents did vote, very faithfully, for Franklin Roosevelt, time after time after time, because "he was for the working man." And they voted for him. So that's as political as my family got. I take it back. There was one member of my family who was a fascist. I don't mean a fascist like Jesse Helms or like—no, no, this person had a uniform, and a card. *Fascista*, real *fascista*—it's an Italian word. So there were things in my family some of which, maybe, are best not discussed.

I went to a Catholic college for a year, Manhattan College, run by the Christian Brothers. I did not read Marx, but I did read, during the year before I came here, those people who most immediately formed my political education and helped me to understand what was going on. I read Thucydides and Plato. And those two people actually made the greatest contribution to my thinking, and helped me do things that I did. Strange. I also, that year, read a lot of physics and a lot of mathematics, and from the physics and mathematics I learned something very important: I learned the difference between evidence and opinion. And that's stood me very much in good stead, and it's an education I commend to people.

Okay. So how can I sum up, very briefly, the kind of perspective I came to the movement with those many years ago? Well, I can say it this way: it was secularized liberation theology. That's exactly it. I was the person who was going to be a priest in my family. I was influenced by the ferment in the Church around Second Vatican Council, deeply influenced. And I came to the movement from a perspective of secularized (because I didn't know whether there were spiritual beings—God, angels, and so forth) liberation theology.

I call to your attention, there have been movements, important movements, that have been very influenced by that perspective. And I in particular call to mind the recent Sandinista foreign minister (will somebody tell me his name?—yes, thank you) Miguel D'Escoto, Father Miguel D'Escoto. And Father Miguel D'Escoto said something I do need to say to you, and that is that no serious political person on the left in the late twentieth century can claim not to have been influenced by Marx and Marxism. Father D'Escoto said this. And so I think that I'd like to get into my remarks by explaining—because it is relevant to where we are and where we might go—both why it was important to me to define myself with respect to the Marxists I met, and also why, finally, I didn't turn out to be one.

When I came to the Berkeley campus, I became involved with the civil rights movement because it was just. Because the one moral principle that I took from my previous education was this: resist evil. And people persuaded me that there was evil to resist, that they were doing it, so that was the thing to do, given my previous religious education. I looked around, hooked up with people, and I found that the closer I got to people, the more people tried to persuade me that I should become a Marxist. It was not high pressure, guys; it was very loving. Especially, by the way, from the CP [Communist Party] people, who had a reputation for being unusually loving. It was very, very loving and very kind, and people who were their political enemies actually condemned them for being manipulative because they were, in this inclusive sense, loving. It's really true. I want you to understand.

But I wasn't buying. Because every time someone approached me that way, I would remember Brother Abdon Lewis—Brother Abdon Lewis at Manhattan College, a Christian Brother, who would be saying to me, in just this way, "But Mario, you need to get down on your knees; you are not humble enough. If you will just pray, you will believe." And I have to tell you, not with any disrespect for the people who helped me (I mean the Marxists who helped me): I did see Brother Lewis there too, and I wasn't prepared to do that.

Why was it important to define one's position with respect to Marx? First of all, because Marx is a poet. Even when I was very young, I heard, I remembered, I could not forget: "From each according to his ability, to each according to his need." It could come out of the Bible, it is so beautiful. And someone says, it did come out of the Bible, and of course, Marx must have known his Bible.

Those are burning words. Those words are in my soul. From each according to his ability, to each according to his need. And one other thing—again, Marx as poet, burning words that remain in my soul, from the opening passage of *The Eighteenth Brumaire of Louis Napoleon*. People will remember these words (and I may have mangled them somewhat, and someone will correct me): "The experience of all the dead generations weighs like a nightmare on the brain of the living." There's more; but that's the poetry. That's Marx rising to a pitch of poetry which is unusual in political writers. I want to repeat it, it's so beautiful. (I may have mangled it, but it's in essence that.) "The experience of all the dead generations weighs like a nightmare on the brain of the living." So it's hard not to be attracted to Marx if you have even a little feeling for poetry.

Second thing: it was quite plain to me that the imperatives of the black liberation struggle led to socialist conclusions—I don't say Marxist ones, but let me tell you what I mean. For me, at that time—and I still think it's true—here's how it goes. Suppose the people at the bottom of the stack want to be treated like everyone else, like real people. Now, there's a number of things you can do there. Of course, you can just shoot them. I mean, if they really get sort of vociferous, uppity, you can just find some way to suppress them. There are other possibilities. Someone further above, some group further above, will say, "Reasonable. We'll change places with you." You see, that doesn't really seem like it's going to happen. I could see that. Without much ideology, I could see that. Well then, you see, if you don't get rid of them, and you don't change places, then you have to think about eliminating the hierarchy. Right? You see, you can hardly think in any other terms. It's logical. It is very, very logical. I saw that then, and that moved me toward feeling I ought to check this out a little bit further.

Third thing: the most effective people in this struggle to resist evil whom I encountered were almost always Marxists, of one kind or another. That was telling. Many of them knew a lot more than I did, and were a lot smarter at strategizing what to do next. I like to be told where to go and what to do. (It's true.) So that was very, very impressive.

Unfortunately, because I did have a Catholic background, I had read Milovan Djilas's book *The New Class* the year it was translated. You may not like it, but you have to come to terms with it, okay? And so I was not such easy bait for this. It was attractive for the reasons I've stated. But it was something I couldn't quite go along with because, well, I'm not anywhere near a match for the people who put together those revolutions, and look where they ended up. I was aware of that.

Even so, I felt it was important to examine Marxism. And I'm not talking about Leninism, it's a subtler discussion; I'm not talking about Communism, it's a dead issue. I'm talking about Marxism. I felt it important to examine Marxism, and these are the two things it seemed to offer, finally. One: confidence. We can win because we will win. Okay? It's a question of how long it'll take, perhaps. Confidence. Second: strategy. That is, if the process of immiseration will result in the working class achieving an ever-deepening oppositional consciousness, then you have a basic strategy—namely, you can help them do it more quickly. But they're going to do it. The process of immiseration will bring that about.

Unfortunately, there were some problems. This process that would imbue you with confidence and would lead you to a strategy was based upon a kind of—I don't say deterministic inevitability, but a kind of at least strongly probabilistic inevitability about the development of society. Marx, even at his most poetic—that is, Marxism, even at its most poetic, is a kind of economism. There's no doubt about it. I don't mean it's simplistic economism, but a technologism, at least. The idea that there is, if not an inevitability, certainly a high degree of probability that the workings of the political economy will result in the kind of deepened oppositional consciousness, mostly due to this process of immiseration, and that one has something to work with then. One can help it along.

Then you look out at the world. Marxism had been in existence a long time. What did we have? We had in the world two camps, both armed with nuclear weapons. We had the experience of Nazism in the country that so many Marxists had believed would be the first country, the country to lead the western proletariat to success. Nazism giving rise to what? Nazism: it's not just exotic fascism. Nazism is to fascism as psychosis is to deep character disorder. We're talking about people who incinerated people. I have to tell you that, though I am not a Jew, those pictures had a deeper impact on me than anything else I ever, ever saw. Pictures of heaps of bodies. For me as a kid growing up, it was like some secret pictures you might find, say, in your uncle's drawer that show that he's really a child molester or something. This is heavy-duty, for a society to have this kind of experience.

Well, this leads you to think that with all that scientific understanding of society, if the successor state to capitalism in Germany could be this bizarre psychotic society, then we don't have a really effective predictive theory. That's very, very serious, guys.

I discussed, I remember, this kind of issue, though not in such graphic terms, with Hal Draper. Remember Hal Draper? (And bless his soul, I'm glad we had him.) And I remember Hal calling to my attention the historical writings of Marx and saying, "Look, it's so good," and I said, "What about the economics?" and he said, "Well, he's not as good as an economist." That's a very serious admission for a Marxist, is it not? Hal was honest about that, and you see, it was then hard for me to go along.

And I, unfortunately, in the midst of all that turmoil was also a student— I read the "protestants." That is, I read Eduard Bernstein, would you believe. I wanted to see what all the brouhaha was about. And I tell you, none of the comrades were suggesting that I read Bernstein. But I read Bernstein. And although, if I had been there to contend with him in meetings, I would have been on the other side, nevertheless he seemed to be somewhat better an economist, in many ways, than some of the Marxists that I also was coming into contact with.

And here's an interesting thing. Bernstein maintained, rightly or wrongly, that over the long run capitalism actually tends to differentiate the middle strata of society, so that there is a characteristic capitalist middle class—or middle strata, if you will—which is developed, which actually produces a condition of homeostasis. In other words, it is the very opposite of immiseration.

So you look out at society and boy, it looks that way in a lot of ways. And in fact—and here is, I think, the critical point—one thing that the Marxists insist you believe is that capital treats workers differently from other commodities. But this hierarchy, this (if you will) ladder of differential payment, means that capitalism is treating workers in some ways exactly like other commodities. It's exactly what you observe in the case of land and all those other things— namely, that the more productive gets more capital and the less productive gets less capital invested in it, by and large. That meant to me that the horror of capitalism was that it was not as good at producing a counterconsciousness as the Marxists needed to believe in order to sustain the confidence that they felt. The real operation of capitalism was such as to reduce people to the conditions of commodities precisely as other commodities were reduced, accepted, and dealt with—namely, a gradation. You go to the supermarket, what do you find? You find it's prime, choice, or whatever. And that is what capitalism was doing to people. And that was much harder to fight because people would not end up in one boat against the class enemy.

Okay. Let me say, we could see that our society was unstable. But unstable systems don't necessarily become nicer; they can become simply more stable. If you displace a system in equilibrium from equilibrium, something will happen; if time is involved, it may move. It may move to another state of equilibrium. It may go completely haywire. It's not just chaos theory that tells us that; Newton knew it. It's possible for systems to go haywire if they are in disequilibrium, even very, very close to equilibrium.

Keynes felt that it was possible for the system to achieve equilibrium with much less than full employment. Equilibrium—not just economic, but political—economic equilibrium. But let's say that it's really unstable. If it's really unstable, it'll change. But all we know then is that there will be a successor society. And this stuck with me, and it was a killer. Because the successor society obviously needed to be more collective, but how? It could be authoritarian collective; that's what we'd seen in so many places. If in fact the process of evolution of the society did not provide the opportunity for the development of a counterconsciousness adequate to change the society, then we might end up with stability under disastrous circumstances.

And so, having begun with the notion of either/or thinking, heaven or hell, I commend to you what was very important to me: a saying, a quote, that should have been Rosa Luxemburg's quote (Reggie [Zelnik] tells me it may have been [Henri] Barbusse—I don't know—it should have been Rosa's quote, okay?). And what it is, in brief, is this: "Socialism or barbarism."

"Socialism or barbarism" does not give you the same kind of optimism about what is going to happen. Right? We are moving right now in a direction which one could call creeping barbarism. But if we do not have the benefit of belief that in the end we win, then we have to be prepared on the basis of our moral insight to struggle even if we do not know that we are going to win.

I would like to conclude by bringing back the idea of the spiritual. One of the weaknesses of the Marxist tradition, which has been somewhat corrected late in the game, is to underestimate the importance of spiritual values. By spiritual values, I mean where we as a community can feel something deeper than we are: not that we as a community feel God is on our side, but in some sense that *we're* on *their* side. Some sense of looking down into the heart of things and being able to perceive which way is just, which way is not just. And that's what we have to convey to people. Not the message of immiseration—only temporarily does that work—but the message of commiseration. Not everyone for himself, but all of us for the community. And that means that we have a very hard task. We need to educate on the basis of moral values, of what justice is.

But, guys, people we would not expect to be on our side are. And I would like to conclude with reading to you an article—brief! brief!—from yesterday's [*San Francisco*] *Chronicle*:

"Archbishop Urges Circumventing Proposition 187"

We don't want to be to the right of the archbishop, yes?

Denouncing Proposition 187 as "a great wound to humanity," Archbishop John Quinn is urging Catholic clergy, hospitals, and schools to defend California's foreign-born population whether they are here legally or not.

That's the archbishop! I don't go to their meetings, guys, I haven't done it in a very long time. I'm not a mole for the archbishop; nothing like it.

In a pastoral letter this week to the 340,000 Catholics of the West Bay archdiocese, which includes Marin, San Mateo, and San Francisco counties, the prelate wrote: "A fruit of this growing hardness of heart"—

We need to talk in that language.

—"is the fear and humiliation in which so many immigrants amongst us are living. Sick people, women, children are frightened to seek medical help, and some have died."

Some have died, past tense.

Schools report drops in attendance by immigrant children because they are afraid.

And he's not a Johnny-come-lately.

Before the November election the prelate was one of many prominent California church leaders who spoke out against Proposition 187, which would deny state education, health, and social services to undocumented residents. Catholic bishop Philip Straling of San Bernardino has called the initiative "woefully unjust," and Quinn said it seems to turn people who "teach, heal, and counsel into informants."

Eh? That's the archbishop! He says,

" 'I ask our Catholic hospitals and clinics' "—

And it doesn't have to be Catholics, right? It can be the rest of us spiritual beings, okay?

—"to be even more attentive to the new and increasingly painful problems of immigrants." Quinn wrote, "I call on Catholic physicians, nurses, and lawyers to be imaginative and forthright in coming to the defense of immigrants. Catholic schools and charities in the archdiocese should be second to none in upholding the rights and dignities of immigrants."

It goes on. It's good, guys. The Church has stood for lots of bad things; this is not one of them.

And let me point something out: my last shot. There is probably no other institution in the United States in which there is a heavier representation of righteously working-class people than in those churches, in that Church. We ought to be talking to them as well as to one another. And in the years ahead, if we do it right, our values can—not will—can prevail. Thank you.

A MOMENT TO MOVE AGAINST
CLASS-RIDDEN BARBARISM

Savio's concern about the shift of California politics to the right, via ballot initiatives that appealed to and inflamed racial and anti-immigrant resentments, led to a renewed commitment to political activism. He spearheaded the formation of a new organization, the Campus Coalitions for Human Rights and Social Justice, which he hoped would convert California's community colleges, four-year colleges, and universities into bases for resistance to this rightward shift. In this speech, given at an ACLU dinner on February 24, 1995, in Sebastopol, California, Savio explained the work of this new organization and why the threat from the Right necessitated his playing a major political role again.

This is going to be a report: what caused things to change? Well, it was the appalling election. Everyone here found that election dreadful and appalling, and I was worrying, would it also be the case that it would be so daunting that it would result in a feeling of apathy and despair? But quite evidently that is not what has happened. I love voting. I have voted in almost every election that I could vote in, local, state, national. I did not vote in this election. I knew how it would turn out. I examined all of the things I could vote for, all of the positions and candidates, and I knew, I predicted this is the way it's all going to turn out, and it all turned out the way I knew it would.

Now I don't consider it to have been a real election. Let me say something about what to me a real election is...a real vote. I've attended many meetings. The kind of meetings I've attended go on interminably. A position is presented. Objections are raised. The position is refined. More objections are raised. People seem to have more objections than bases for agreement. The position is refined.

Finally, after all of the reasonable objections have been met and consensus has been arrived at, then you have the vote. And in fact, sometimes you have a straw vote ahead of time so that no one will feel bad. They'll know that they really had a chance to convince people one way or the other. Then you have the vote. And, hopefully, it's as unanimous as the Soviet-style vote I just saw the ACLU conduct right here tonight. [Laughter and applause]

Bless you. Please, please. That is not the kind of election we just went through. There was no real discussion. That was a sound-bite election. And the sound bites come at very great expense. Greater than anyone in this room can afford. That's not the way democratic elections should take place. All right, before that election, I had a chance to have dinner with my son, who's not here right now. It was a dinner to celebrate his birthday, a bit belated. Well, one does this sort of thing. And he was there, his girlfriend, Lynne Hollander, my wife, the four of us, we had dinner. And after a while, we got into discussing the election, and so I had to admit that I was leaning toward not voting, in fact leaning real hard toward not voting. And he said, "You can't do that." But we talked about it, and after a while he said, "Okay, I understand why you're not going to vote. But then you must do something else!"

Now when your son offers that sort of challenge, it really gets the testosterone flowing. And that was the first indication to me that it was really necessary to do something else. Then, and I talk personally about myself, many people have been involved in deciding that this is a moment to move. I talk personally about myself, and you can see how this may reflect upon experiences that you've had because many of us have come to that sort of decision.

Two days after the election, my other son, who is here, Daniel, reading in the *P.D.* [*Press Democrat*] about Proposition 187, which just overwhelmingly passed—I knew that it would—and he said, "Daddy, I'm not going to obey that law." I have no idea what he's talking about, so he reads to me and it says, well you see, if you go into school, you've got to prove that you are a citizen. He said, "I'm not going to present that proof." Oh, my God. Now you see, there really is a problem, and the problem is, I mean, I love my children. The problem is—that's not the problem. The problem is that sometimes you say something, but it's easier said than done. And I did have some notion, from having been through many of those interminable political meetings, I had some notion dimly as to what would be required to do something about it.

There's an Italian proverb, which I'm going to repeat to you a couple of times, and maybe we can look at it more closely toward the end. It's the Italian version of "Easier said than done." *Fra il dire e il fare, che il mezzo delle mare.* And that, in Italian, means, "Between the saying and the doing lies half the sea."

Half the sea. It's a little more colorful than the English version. What can I say? And I'd like to look a little later at just what it might mean. But you can imagine yourself in a boat out in the center of the sea. And of course then it's equally far to go in every direction and you have halfway to go, okay? We'll come back to it.

All right, so what happened? I and others started talking to others on the telephone, and, you know, ran up big phone bills. The person that I work most closely in that, Jack Kurzweil, is here. He teaches electrical engineering at San Jose State. And I'm very glad that he was on the other end of the telephone and we started talking and thinking of other people to call and so forth and started to think that maybe, maybe, we could pull something together.

Well, we talked to lots of people and they all, in a way, surprisingly, seemed ready to go. So we called meetings together. First meeting was about thirty people from about ten campuses. Then subsequently on the eleventh of February we had another meeting—both down in Berkeley—about 110 or 120, depending on who was doing the counting. People from a variety of California campuses, ready to do something.

That was a very interminable meeting, okay, and we didn't even succeed in selecting a name. We had twelve possibilities on the board. It's okay, fine, so I, for now refer to it, and I probably will always refer to it, as the movement. The word has a certain historical cachet, no? Look, it is actually the same movement grown up, all right? We've had to learn a lot of things, and I'll talk about some of them, and you know what they all are. And it took a long time to do that. It's easier to organize from the right because organizing from the right frequently involves no more than mobilizing on the basis of people's already existing prejudices, whereas organizing from the left always also requires a degree of genuine moral reeducation, so that people put aside their contempt for one another, which we are taught in this society, and learn that we are all brothers and have to pull together. That requires deep reeducation, and it's harder than what the other folks get to do.

Well, since this is a report, let me summarize very briefly the kinds of decisions we came to, important ones, at that meeting of February 11. We decided that we would take as our responsibility, you know, workplace organizing, organizing the campuses, that is, the public college and university campuses in California, the community college campuses, the CSU [California State University] level system, and the UC [University of California] system. I put them in that order because the community colleges will be the most important. That's where the folks are. And we have to really pull together.

Okay, and secondly, we decided, since this is a movement grown up, that this cannot be, will not be, a student movement, that this will be a movement in which the campuses are organized, that is, the faculty, the students, and the nonacademic staff together.

Third thing we decided that to the extent possible—it'll be a big extent, guys—to the extent possible, we will look like what we believe in. That is, leadership, people speaking, forums, whatever it happened to be, will be very multiethnic, and will have women and men leading, in conditions of complete equality.

Now, let me say that could not have happened thirty years ago. The movement thirty years ago on the campuses was more or less—not completely, but more or less—a white, male, radical-dominated movement. I say not completely, but more or less, more on some campuses, less on others.

Okay, but affirmative action has been working. It works. The campuses don't look that way anymore. Thank goodness. And, as a result, the meetings that we have been at have been multiethnic and, I think, multigendered meetings, as a matter of fact. And that is all to the good and it is the way we are gong to look, which means that white European, ethnic, immigrant types like me, right, I'm first generation actually, we're going to have to be somewhat more on the nature of tokens than we were in the past. That's all to the good. Okay.

We decided on a couple of other things. Number one, the issues that we would immediately tackle would be opposition to implementation of Proposition 187 on the campuses, and number two, because it's coming right up behind, we will resist the destruction of [affirmative action]. Finally—boy, this was a lot to accomplish, come to think of it, at that first meeting, to arrive at this kind of consensus, so maybe the fact that we weren't able to choose a name is not that bad after all. Finally, we decided—and this is really critical—that as we present these two issues and whatever other garbage they throw at us, we will...put those ideas within a broad political and social context. This is not going to be a single- or double-issue movement. We have matured. We know about a lot of things now, and let me tick them off. We have learned a lot about race, gender, class, the environment, and the empire. We've learned about those things and that is the context within which we have to put those positions we take on specific issues and why, for a very good reason, namely, the context has been set out now is one in which if we come and say, "I'm against Proposition 187," or "I'm in favor of affirmative action," it's [not] from left field. It doesn't make any sense within their context, within their Lockean context, that that government is best which doesn't exist.

Okay, so we do need, after all, to create an alternative voice, and that is our objective, that presents an alternative vision, an alternative context, within which it makes sense to be both intelligent and compassionate, in equal measure.

There's a problem for me, okay? What's the problem? I don't know about the whole universe, okay? And apparently you need to know something about the entire universe in order to, you know, begin acting politically here. I mean, it's really hard. Now, when Pete Wilson speaks, it's nonsense, but it doesn't matter. It doesn't matter. He gets away with ... you know, it started with Ronald Reagan, for God's sake, a real debasement, huh? of what one is entitled to expect from public speakers. I mean, you know, if the president of the United States can be a complete jerk, then it doesn't matter what anybody says. It just absolutely doesn't, and you don't have to listen or think and they don't want you to think at all. At all. All right, so we have to let ourselves a little bit off the hook, We need to be intelligent but not omniscient. Not omniscient. All right. Even so, you need to educate yourself, okay?

I had a gut feeling about Proposition 187—cruel and stupid. That was my gut feeling. But I don't know enough, frankly, about the intricacies of immigration policy, which a progressive society might adopt, so I have to learn. I'd like to recommend to you something that was helpful to me as a start.

It's a short book. I like short books. I assign long ones, but I like to read short ones. This is not a book with which I thoroughly agree, but it's a good book. It's a thoughtful book. It's by Roberto Suro. Sounds like the immigrant that he is—at least, from an immigrant family. It's called *Remembering the American Dream: Hispanic Immigration and National Policy*. And this is a book that is worth reading. Trust me. Read it.

Because one wants to be as clear as possible, not omniscient, but clear. When people say, "You're crazy, look at these scofflaws stealing from us, coming in, taking things, taking food out of the mouths of our children, and et cetera, et cetera," you need to be more knowledgeable than the yahoo who is confronting you.

I would like to say, by the way, I would like to acknowledge the person who gave me this book. I would like to thank President Ruben Armiñana of Sonoma State University. He's the person who gave me this book. He said it's a very thoughtful book.

You might not agree with everything in it. I read it. . . . I would like to tell you briefly how that happened. I thought, well, you know, Sonoma State University, we're going to be organizing on the campus, politeness, courtesy alone requires that someone sit down with the president and say, "You know, we're going to be organizing on your campus." So I decided to do it. And I went up and made an appointment and sat down and talked with him. It seemed the courteous thing to do, and, in fact, he was very courteous in return. His recommending this book is not an endorsement of what I am saying, and I wouldn't suggest that for a moment.

But what I am trying to point out is that whereas in the past the "us" was very small and the "them" very large, we have a potential today for an "us" that is somewhat larger. And let's not lose sight of that.

I would like, in terms of that context, briefly to suggest some things which I have been learning about and which we will be hearing more about. But briefly, the context on the immigration question: There are lots of reasons why people come to another country. Why people come, say, to the United States. And some I want to refer to, but not really deal with. There are cultural reasons, you know. We are spewing our culture over the whole world. In my father's hometown in Sicily, they all have TV sets. It's the Middle Ages except for the TV sets. And a lot of those programs on those TV sets are, you know—they know, what I'm trying to say is, more about *The Brady Bunch* than I do.

And the same thing is true throughout Latin America. So that there is a cultural attraction, and I'm using the word "culture" in a loose sense. There are other forces. There is an economic pull, and an economic push. What is the economic pull? It's not that there are just illegal immigrants; there are illegal jobs, okay? And there are lots of them in agriculture, in the garment industry, service industries. There are lots of illegal jobs, all right? So what does that mean? Somebody wants these folks to come, right? Pete Wilson, for example, in 1986, before he became governor, right? He was a senator. He, at the time that the immigration law changed, pushed for amnesty for agricultural workers, special agricultural worker amnesty so that the people who harvest the crops and keep the prices low and live in Third World conditions, driving down American wages, would not be excluded from our labor force, right? Pete Wilson. Then comes the election. Oh well, we have another problem—getting reelected. It's okay, we want their labor, but we don't want anybody to love them too much. In fact, if you hate them, you won't recognize that you ought to be directing some of your ire toward us.

And so we have then the whipping up of anti-Latino hysteria for opportunistic political purposes. Now 187 is in the courts. You know, when I see some of the buildings in some of our cities, I say, "Couldn't they have hired an architect?" And I think, here, "Couldn't these people have hired a real lawyer to put 187 together?" But I guess they didn't. It's in the courts. It may stay there. I hope it dies there. And Pete Wilson's agribusiness friends hope so too. So now that he's flipped, now he flops. Now Pete Wilson is in favor of a guest worker program. That's where you let them clean the floors, and then when you're done with them, you boot them out. I don't think that's the kind of society we ought to be building.

Okay, enough concerning the issue of pull. There's a question of push. We have an impact, we as a society that according to all figures, remember, [accounts for] 46 percent of the world's yearly consumption of raw materials and [only] 6 percent of the [world's] population. I forget the numbers, but you know some unbelievable Looney Tunes disproportion of use and waste.

We impact on the countries people come from. We contribute to maintaining dreadful conditions in their countries, so that they will be happy to try to sneak in here to work under dreadful conditions here, but not quite as dreadful. And I'm talking about things that we know about, the *maquiladoras*, right? On the border. The present Mexican interest rates—this is not to be believed—are now in excess of 50 percent. You put in a thousand dollars, you get back fifteen hundred. That is fantastic. But one would hate to be a worker under those conditions. We suffer at 8 percent. Imagine what it would be like at 50 percent! It's just now topped that.

Are they crazy? Don't they have economists in Mexico? Oh no, this wasn't the Mexicans' idea. This is part of the $20 billion bailout of Mexico that they need to jack these rates up. They can't be paying their workers too much.

Something else again, an impact that we have. Now I just throw these things out. It's really an outrageous event that recently occurred. There was a fellow working for the Chase Manhattan Bank. Let me read this to you. It's kind of astonishing. A fellow working for the Chase Manhattan Bank, his name is Riordan Roett. He was commissioned to write a report about what to do about Mexico, and that report was sent to potential investors. And the report contained the following words: "While Chiapas, in our opinion"— it's obviously the royal "our"—"while Chiapas, in our opinion, does not pose a fundamental threat to Mexican political stability, it is perceived to be so by many in the investment community. The government will need to eliminate the Zapatistas to demonstrate their effective control of the national territory and of security policy."

Now when they say "eliminate the Zapatistas," they do not mean "invite them to a party while we conduct business." Eliminate the Zapatistas means "Bang, bang, you're dead." Not long after that, President Zedillo and the government of Mexico did it, with helicopter gunships and search-and-destroy missions. They couldn't quite pull it off, they had to pull back. But they did, in fact, try to eliminate the Zapatistas.

Now I teach logic and so I have this problem here, you know, *post hoc, ergo propter hoc*. I do not claim that because the Chase Manhattan Bank sent this report out, which they later said was only Mr. Roett's "private opinion," mind you, but they sent it out. I do not claim that because they sent it out and because subsequently the government of Mexico tried to destroy the Zapatistas, bang bang—I'm not claiming that there was a causal relationship, but don't you think we ought to check it out? We ought to check that out! We ought to check that out.

And if there are journalists here, which there are, there is a Pulitzer Prize in the making. Let's get all the details, folks, let's get it out. Let's see, did it have some impact on the conditions of the $20 billion loan guarantee? We don't know. Check it out. Please. We want to know. Check it out, please. We want to know. We want to know.

So we have a situation of pull—come and take these cheap jobs, illegal jobs, we want you to do that—and push—we're going to create conditions in your country so horrible if you try to get uppity about it and change them, we'll wipe you out. That sort of thing. So there's the push. But then they come and someone wants to get reelected and so he demonizes them. Now this is sick. This is actually sick. One needs an immigration policy. One wants in a respectful way to be able to integrate the people to whom one offers entry. That immigration policy cannot be, cannot be a piece of architecture which is presented to us by the very people most interested in exploiting these immigrants. That cannot be. We have to have a share in deciding what that immigration policy should be, and this particular proposition is not part of it. And we cannot cooperate in having it implemented in this country, in this state.

Now I would like to say something about the other one of our two main issues. It hasn't happened yet, but is about to happen. I will be brief, because I think the issues are actually for me anyway simpler although they're not that simple. Affirmative action.

First of all, we have our marching orders. I hate to say it that way. Rosa Parks just a few days ago made a speech at San Francisco State University, and she said, "Guys, you've got to protect it." And she, as far as I am concerned, is the mother of us all.

I know that affirmative action needs fine-tuning. But, my friends, I want it fine-tuned by people who hate racism. We can do that job. The first time that I was arrested—there were not a lot, I was not a compulsive arrestee, we had some, okay? But the first time I was arrested was at the Sheraton Palace Hotel in San Francisco, and the issue was decent jobs in visible locations for black workers. That was before affirmative action got its name. And this is something that I will go to the wire [on] and I hope that we all will. This is something that we cannot yield on.

Now, what does that mean? Consider these two things together: Proposition 187, disrespect, cruelty towards immigrant fellow humans, gutting affirmative action, disrespect, rejection in most cases, I guess in all cases of fellow citizens, be they black, be they women, if you're a male or whatever it happened to be.

Affirmative action is not in the nature of a universal right. In a good society you wouldn't need it. But we're not close, my friends, we're not close. Fine-tuning, yes, but we are a long way from the kind of society where you don't need to have an institutional preference for those who have been repeatedly rejected, disrespected, suppressed.

Now I want to say just one thing about it. If you consider these two issues, then a larger context begins to emerge. In both cases, white males are appealed to, against the others. The others, many of whom have fallen into what is called the urban underclass. It is respectable to say "underclass." It is not respectable, for example, to say "working class." Now my family happens to have been working-class. And I consider myself still part of that particularly presently invisible group. But it is respectable to say "underclass." Now the word "underclass" has an interesting connotation. It's sort of a portmanteau word, isn't it? It's "under-world" and "working class," okay?

These are the criminal workers, these are the workers so desperate, so stupid, so benighted, you don't want to fall in with them. This is the rhetoric of a word. The rhetoric of a word. Now why in this wealthy country do we have an under-class? You see, it's not obvious that . . . one would need to have an underclass; it's not that totally obvious. I don't think that we need to have an underclass.

However, in order to eliminate the underclass, therefore, in order to show respect to our newly arrived fellow workers, in order to show respect to those who have been here a long time—women, African Americans, Latino citizens, and so forth—and in order to do it in such a way that you don't start a race war with white males in order to do that, in order, in other words, to avoid the tra-ditional American error because the American error is to divide and conquer the people by means of intergroup and especially interethnic rivalries of the worst sorts.

So how do you do that? I've thought about it hard. I can only see one way. We need more money. And there's only one place to get it. You have got to really be clear on this, okay? You can't have a society in which you cut education programs, cut health programs, in which you eliminate libraries, you can't have that sort of society and also eliminate the underclass. You see, it can't be done. So we have a very, very tough row to hoe. Because I cannot—I've thought about it real hard because this is not the kind of way you want to go. This is hard row-ing. This is not the way you want to go. This is hard rowing. But I don't see any way—let me say this as clearly as I can—to accommodate the people who have so long been disrespected, and also not to start a war with white male workers, without a significant redistribution of power and wealth downward, the direc-tion opposite to the direction it has been going.

I said—it was quoted in the [Santa Rosa] *Press Democrat*; I don't think it's exactly the way I said it—"The barbarians have taken over." They are trying, I think I put it in the progressive tense, but I'm not sure. They are taking over. It is a rising tide of barbarism. I mean, he's not Phil Gramm, after all. All right, you've got to make, if you're going to do this intelligently, you have to make subtle distinctions. I was told I need to refer to Newt Gingrich as a "principled conservative ideologue"; even my conservative friend put it that way. But let's see what they're doing and then we judge what they are. The school lunch program. Out. Now it's going to go down to the states, and they can decide what to feed the kids. And let me tell you, it's not [haute] cuisine.

School lunch program. Well, meanwhile nowadays, junior high school children stick up other junior high school children for their lunch money. And that is a serious state of affairs. And I claim that there is a connection between the kind of lack of empathy and cruelty that could consider eliminating the school lunch program and the corresponding feeling of community which our young people feel today. I think there is a connection. "Social pork," that is a coinage of Phil Gramm. He would like to become president. "Social pork" was coined in reference to nighttime basketball. When I heard it, you know, it just makes your skin crawl. I have been trying to adopt certain Buddhistic ways, but there is a level of anger, there is a level of anger that is hard for me to completely eliminate from my repertoire. Social pork. Now my favorite Jesus Christ quote: "From the fullness of the heart, the mouth speaketh." And I do not like to contemplate what is in that man's heart that he could refer with such contempt and gleeful contempt toward people trying to put a basketball in a kid's hand rather than waiting until that kid has picked up a gun.

Why do I call them barbarians? I will tell you why. To me, barbarism means coarseness, coarseness. These are people who are incapable of recognizing a problem until it has achieved the level of guns and bloodshed. And then they are incapable of conceiving a solution other than in those very terms. So that these are people with a law enforcement approach to every social problem. That is their way. And we need to offer an alternative way to that.

I'm going to conclude by returning briefly to that Italian proverb. I feel I'm entitled to interpret Italian proverbs. So let me repeat it to you. *Fra il dire e il fare*—that is, between the saying and the doing—*che il mezzo delle mare*—there lies before you half the sea. We are trying to start something. There is a lot of hard rowing in that boat between here and port, a lot of hard rowing.

Right now certain people have their hands firmly on the tiller. We are supposed to do the rowing. I will not row unless I get a chance to contribute to steering the boat. And let me say, if you can bear a pun, if you want to take the boat to port, you have to steer left.

CALIFORNIA AT THE CROSSROADS: SOCIAL STRIFE OR SOCIAL UNITY?

Pamphlet coauthored with Nadav Savio,
Jeff Lustig, and Dick Walker

This was the founding publication of the Campus Coalitions for Human Rights and Social Justice, the organization, whose creation Savio spearheaded to resist the politics of resentment that wrought statewide anti-immigrant and anti-affirmative-action ballot initiatives. The primary authors of the pamphlet— published in May 1995—were Mario and his son Nadav, with Jeff Lustig and Dick Walker writing its "Fortress California" section.

WHO WE ARE

Prompted by deep concern over the conduct and results of the 1994 California and national elections, a group of women and men of diverse racial and ethnic backgrounds—students, faculty members and non-academic staff of the California Community Colleges, the California State University and the University of California—has come together on a basis of full equality to form the Campus Coalitions for Human Rights and Social Justice.

We are committed to preventing the implementation of Proposition 187 on our campuses, to reversing Proposition 184, to defending affirmative action, and to working for adequate funding for higher education in California. It is our hope that through the Campus Coalitions we will be able to assist and coordinate the efforts of so many in our communities who are already working to achieve one or more of these objectives.

As individuals and as an organization, we choose an end to the disgrace of a massive "underclass" in a land of such phenomenal wealth and promise; we want a population that is healthy, well educated and gainfully employed; we envision a country where race and gender no longer keep people apart. And we see no route to these reasonable objectives without a significant increase in social investment for medical care, public education, and job creation. These goals will be achieved neither quickly nor effortlessly, but will require creative struggle, sophisticated organization and personal commitment. If you share our goals, we welcome you to join us....

CALIFORNIA AT A CROSSROADS

In these economic hard times, California voters must either choose opportunities for all—and social peace; *or* deepening struggle between competing groups—and continued and growing violence. Public policy and recent and proposed ballot initiatives show that Californians are making the *wrong choice.*

- Proposition 184, by mandating permanent imprisonment for third time felons irrespective of the nature of their offenses, promises a massive increase in California's law enforcement budget at the inevitable expense of desperately-needed funding for education.
- Proposition 187 scapegoats undocumented immigrants rather than offering a rational and compassionate immigration policy. 187 completely fails to deal with the causes of illegal immigration and inflicts its severest penalties on children, depriving them of health care and education.
- The so-called California Civil Rights Initiative (CCRI) proposed for the 1996 ballot, seeks to halt a generation of slow but significant progress towards the full inclusion of women and minorities in the benefits of our society. CCRI blindly denies that there are continuing social problems caused by racism and sexism.

Chronic tuition increases and cuts in financial aid threaten access to higher education and quality employment for all but the privileged few, while crippling

California as a global economic competitor in a period of rapid technological innovation.

The 1994 election highlighted a choice which must now be made between two paths for California and the nation. One leads to a society whose people are healthy, well-educated and gainfully employed; the other, to a society whose men and women, whose ethnic and racial groups are trapped in endless struggle over dwindling resources. One alternative will address the real needs of the people for medical care, education and jobs; the other will continue to fan the flames of prejudice and resentment, promising to maintain order only through a growing law enforcement apparatus. The 1994 elections suggest that we are making the *wrong choice.* Even as Americans seem to have lost the ability to imagine any sort of truly hopeful future, they appear to be rushing headlong toward condemning so many of their children—our children—to live in an anti-Utopia of poverty and despair.

In 1994, California's voters defeated a plan for universal health care but approved Proposition 187, a simplistic response to the subtleties of illegal immigration. Voters also adopted Proposition 184, which mandates costly life sentences for all third-time felons, no matter what the character of the felony, violent or not, thus threatening to bankrupt the state for years to come. In the state and the nation, politicians won elections by promising both to slash welfare, health care, and education budgets, and to boost spending for police and prisons. The so-called California Civil Rights Initiative, an anti-affirmative-action measure, is shaping up to be the most divisive issue of the 1996 statewide and national elections. In the following pages, we will examine these political developments in the light of the two alternative future paths between which citizens must now decide.

SUNSET ON THE CALIFORNIA DREAM

By 1990, following years of booming economic growth, California had surpassed most countries in income and output, with a gross domestic product of $700 billion. From 1979 to 1988, the state added 2.6 million jobs. Average income per capita rose 18 percent in real terms from 1980 to 1990. California had taken over as the principal engine of U.S. economic development. Indeed, the state's electronics and aerospace industries were trumpeted as a source of national renewal and a sign of American innovation and entrepreneurship at their best.

However, weakened by fiscal mismanagement and political gridlock, and devastated by the base closings and military contract reductions which followed the end of the cold war, the state economy came crashing to its knees in the recession of 1991–1994. Over the last four years, virtually all of the key functions of state government have been cut back by one-fourth to one-third. California has plummeted from among the highest ranked states in the United States in per pupil spending in public schools to 38th. It now has the largest average class size of any state, and a school maintenance backlog 45 times the national average. Job loss amounted to almost 1.5 million from 1990 to 1992: 900,000 in wholesale and retail trade; 200,000 in manufacturing; 150,000 in construction; 70,000 in agriculture. Unemployment was the worst since the 1930s, peaking at over 9 percent in 1993.[1] The official poverty rate skyrocketed from 12.5 percent in 1990 to 18.2 percent by 1993, putting California among the poorest ten states in this most poverty-ridden of wealthy nations.

While the United States as a whole has fared slightly better than California, an increasingly globalized economy can only accelerate the flow of investment abroad. International trade agreements such as NAFTA and GATT, designed primarily to benefit business, will lure investors in search of rock-bottom wages, relaxed environmental regulations, minimal consumer protections and little or no worker organization. In response, the United States will increasingly be pressured to lower domestic operating costs, as has already begun in the House Republicans' Contract with America, which would, among many other provisions, sharply curtail corporate liability for unsafe products. The future is not bright. While U.S. technological innovation has generated a significant number of high-wage jobs, both job loss and population growth have exceeded job creation. Moreover, to keep such high-skill, high-wage jobs, U.S. workers require education and vocational retraining, neither of which has been an investment priority for policy makers. The logical response to the country's economic situation would seem to be investment in education at the secondary, post-secondary and vocational levels to give workers the skills to compete effectively in a global economy in which many foreign workers can work for much lower wages. But in California, as in the nation generally, investment in education is declining.

One result of the combination of California's ongoing recession and misguided spending priorities is a growing income gap between the state's wealthy few and working many. In the Bay Area, despite the current slump, the number of million-dollar executive paychecks has jumped from 5 to 54 in ten years.[2] This

1. Figures from the California Employment Development Department, cited in the *San Francisco Examiner*, November 4, 1992, p. C1.

2. *San Francisco Chronicle*, "Annual Report on Executive Compensation," May 23, 1994, p. B1. As reported in *The Nation* (Andrew Shapiro, "We're Number One," April 27, 1992, p. 552), the U.S. has the highest average salaries of CEOs and the lowest productivity gains since 1980.

disparity has been exacerbated by the wholesale cutting of the social welfare programs in place since the middle of the century. The result has been a growing pool of low-skilled and unskilled workers competing for an ever shrinking number of jobs. Along with a worsening economic situation and grim future prospects for an increasing number of Californians, the state has seen an increase in problems of deep poverty and despair: homelessness, crime, drug use.

However, instead of striving to create opportunities for all citizens, policy makers have simply found ways to misdirect the growing insecurity and frustration of working men and women, most recently championing the alleged interests of white workers against the supposed incursions of minorities. This has worked for the politicians since, for example, in the 1992 California election whites provided 83 per cent of the voters even though they made up only 53 per cent of the population.[3] It is not surprising, therefore, that those most often blamed for California's economic woes are African-Americans, Asian-Americans and Latinos.

The foregoing rather harsh facts of electoral life have given rise to a politically coherent right-wing platform in California. This platform is most notably apparent in Propositions 184 and 187, and the proposed CCRI anti-affirmative-action measure (as well as in extreme cuts in higher-education budgets). All of these measures place blame for decreasing opportunity on those groups seen as competing with white males (African-Americans, Asian-Americans, Latinos and women). In so doing, such initiatives deflect anger and resentment away from the small number of people and corporations controlling far more than their share of wealth in a time when most families must struggle for financial survival. Together, these initiatives promote mutual resentment as well as conflict among underprivileged groups over a severely and unnecessarily limited pool of resources and opportunities.

Chicanos and Latinos, for example, have felt more affected than others by Proposition 187 and have been the most consistently mobilized against it. They in turn have watched a strong majority of whites, and substantial minorities of African-Americans and Asian-Americans, display support for the measure's restriction on public expenditures for undocumented immigrants. Meanwhile, polls indicate that the "three strikes" initiative has gotten much more support from Latinos and whites than from Blacks. In contrast, the attack on affirmative action threatens a whole new set of divisive realignments.

While each one of the foregoing policies has the power to divide the people of California, setting competing groups against one another, taken together they

3. *San Francisco Chronicle*, September 22, 1994.

form a unified, cohesive political position. They answer a cold and resounding "No!" to the crucial question: "Is California a society in which all the people are welcome to enjoy the benefits their work has helped to create?"

PROPOSITION 187: FORTRESS CALIFORNIA?

Proposition 187—passed by 60 per cent of the voters in 1994—would deny illegal immigrants access to a broad range of government-provided social services, such as child immunization, pre-natal health care for pregnant women and all levels of public education. The proposition, currently suspended under temporary injunctions, would also force public educators and health care workers to act as auxiliary INS agents, required by law to report all those whom they suspect of being in this country illegally. Contrary to American tradition, this would tend to force persons merely suspected of wrongdoing to bear the burden of proving their right to remain in the country. Proposition 187 is obviously a draconian law. A wise and workable immigration policy would take fully into account the complex circumstances which combine to encourage families in large numbers to uproot themselves and come to the United States.

Why, then, do foreign nationals come here as immigrants, especially given the difficulties of immigration (legal as well as illegal)? As an explanation, the oft-repeated assumption underlying Proposition 187 is far from obvious: that people from impoverished countries leave their homes, risking deportation and death, simply for the superior social welfare programs of the United States. Beyond the cultural attractiveness of the United States, as tantalizingly portrayed in American movies and television programs, and except for those cases where severe political oppression drives people from their native countries, the principal causes of immigration are economic. There are essentially two such causes: a push out of the home country and a pull into the United States.

It is well known that in less wealthy, less industrialized countries, workers endure *far worse* working conditions than in even the lowest-level U.S. jobs. They face not only lower wages and few benefits, but poor protection against job-related injuries, limited collective-bargaining rights, and little or no job security. Advocates of Proposition 187 have argued that the United States cannot continue to be a haven for economic refugees from these poor countries. But this position ignores the fact that in many cases U.S. investors and government officials actually pursue policies designed to maintain such dreadful conditions which, up to a point, increase the profitability of investment. A single current example may suffice. The extreme austerity measures now being implemented in Mexico by the Zedillo government have been undertaken directly at the behest of U.S. (and European) investors as an absolute requirement for the $20 billion Peso-stabilizing loan guarantee program engineered by the Clinton administration. This program has met widespread opposition from both left and right in Mexico. It has already propelled Mexican bench-mark interest rates well beyond 50 percent. The Mexican austerity program will obviously create a mighty push out of Mexico which can only make the problem of illegal immigration far more severe in the years immediately ahead. Nonetheless, many of the same politicians who helped generate this current wave of anti-immigrant hysteria, which led to the massive vote for Proposition 187, have also supported the Peso bailout, with its built-in impoverishment of Mexican workers.

On the other hand, an economic pull into the United States is also exerted by American, especially California, business interests, which offer illegal jobs to undocumented workers at below the U.S. minimum wage but at wages far above those they could earn in their own countries. It is the prospect of such jobs, rather than the attractiveness of U.S. welfare benefits, that makes people from poor countries risk deportation and death to come to the United States. Indeed, U.S. businesses provide enough such illegal jobs to maintain an undocumented immigrant population of almost 4 million.[4] By filling jobs with undocumented workers at lower than minimum wage, employers are able to maintain abnormally low prices for American products. Moreover, these ultra-low wage, no benefits jobs further serve business by exerting a strong downward pressure on the minimum wage of citizen workers. In a range of California industries, from seasonal agriculture work and the garment industry to Silicon Valley assembly work, employers are only too willing to ignore their workers' immigrant status in exchange for also being able to ignore laws setting standards for wages, benefits and working conditions. Illegal immigrants, afraid of deportation or jailing, make for the most easily-exploited of workers.

While the pivotal 1986 Immigration Reform and Control Act (IRCA) included sanctions against illegal employers, such regulations have been little enforced to this day. In fact, both national and state economies rely heavily on undocumented workers, especially in agriculture. For generations, workers, both documented and undocumented, have moved in regular seasonal and geographic patterns from towns in Mexico up through the valleys of California following seasonal crops. These patterns have been encouraged by California politicians

---

4. U.S. General Accounting Office, Illegal Aliens; Despite Data Limitations, Current Methods Provide Better Population Estimates, Report PEMD-93–25, Washington, DC, 1993. Cited in Roberto Suro, *Remembering the American Dream*, The Twentieth Century Fund Press, New York, 1994, p. 14.

in the past because they guaranteed cheap seasonal work with a minimum of employer or social obligations to the workers. For example, *Senator* Pete Wilson was criticized for fighting to ease immigration restrictions on seasonal agricultural workers in 1986. In 1994, behind in the polls, Governor Pete Wilson flip-flopped on to the Proposition 187 bandwagon. Since the passage of 187, Wilson has flip-flopped once again and now wants a so-called "guest worker" program.

Given the relative economic bounty of the United States, it is no surprise that there are many people who make the attempt to immigrate illegally. As we have argued, however, U.S. investors and government officials actually pursue policies which result in driving many workers from their home countries—and into the United States. Moreover, U.S. businesses and consumers also benefit substantially from the exploitation of illegal workers.[5] Under these circumstances, it is only justice to attempt to integrate these immigrants fully into society, guaranteeing them the full range of worker advantages now enjoyed by citizens. It is certainly unethical to blame such undocumented workers for our own domestic economic and social failings.

Free social services or none, people will continue to immigrate to the United States in search of economic opportunity. They will continue to work not only for their own benefit but for the benefit of the whole country. They and their children should not also be vilified, scapegoated and, confined to a permanent and inescapable underclass. California and the nation are ill-served by the simplicities of the current spate of anti-immigrant hysteria typified by Proposition 187. On the contrary, we need a compassionate, intelligent and comprehensive immigration policy which takes into account all of the following factors: the U.S. role in stimulating illegal immigration, the country's legitimate needs for immigrant labor, our responsibilities to any persons resident in the United States, and the realistic social, economic and environmental limitations on the capacity of the United States to welcome and integrate new immigrants.

CIVIL RIGHTS IN REVERSE GEAR

Hand in hand with Proposition 187's scapegoating of immigrants for domestic economic woes, a proposed amendment to the state constitution pits white males against those who would share diminished opportunities. The California Civil Rights Initiative (CCRI) seeks to dismantle all affirmative-action programs

---

5. Suro, p. 94.

in state-funded institutions including, among many others, the entire UC, CSU and Community College systems. Despite the effects of centuries of racism and sexism, proponents argue that a single generation of affirmative action has been more than enough, and that any prolongation of such programs amounts to unfair "reverse discrimination" against white males. U.S. pundits and policy makers take a high moral tone against apartheid in South Africa or bride-burning in India, but, of course, this country is no stranger to sexism and racism. Slavery in the United States is quite recent history, and racism has been a part of the national character beginning with the European settlers' first contacts with Native Americans. Similarly, sexism has always been pervasive in American culture. It can easily be argued that women, who have been the principal beneficiaries of affirmative action, would be the principal victims of its elimination.

Prejudice is more than just a matter of unfair attitudes and hurt feelings. It has lasting and very tangible effects. For example, in 1939, Federal Housing Authority (FHA) lending guidelines specified that loans not be made that might "disrupt the racial integrity" of a neighborhood. Based on the avowed goal of segregation, the FHA made it next to impossible for blacks to get the low-rate loans granted to whites. Thus, between 1946 and 1960, 350,000 new homes were built in Northern California of which fewer than 100 went to African-Americans. The significance of these facts to the discussion of affirmative action is that, today, the greatest financial difference between blacks and whites is in their net worth, overwhelmingly a result of the disparity in value of their equity in housing stock. In 1991, the median net worth of white households ($43,279) was more than 10 times that of African-American households ($4,169). This is the lasting effect of a racist government policy. Affirmative action seeks to redress precisely this sort of injustice.[6]

When, beginning one generation ago, the nation decided to try to undo hundreds of years of injustice by adopting affirmative action, it was expected to be a temporary measure. One day, the programs would make themselves unnecessary because the playing field would be level; women and minorities would be fully integrated into society. To argue, as the drafters of CCRI do, that affirmative action should be dismantled because it gives unfair advantages to underrepresented groups is to claim that the playing field is now already level. In truth, affirmative action has had significant success, most notably in colleges and universities, where the representation of women and minorities has significantly expanded over the past twenty years.[7] Despite sizeable gains,

---

6. Troy Duster, "The Advantages of White Males," *San Francisco Chronicle*, January 19, 1995, p. A21.

7. From 1980 to 1990, for example, African-American enrollment at UC Berkeley doubled and Latino enrollment saw a more than three-fold increase, as reported in *The Diversity Project*, Institute for the Study of Social Change, University of California, Berkeley, November 1991, p. 2.

however, much remains to be done, as recent reports on "the glass ceiling" make evident. The opponents of affirmative action mistake what is still an effective and essential *corrective* measure for a *punitive* one.

Ironically, other opponents, including some African-American conservatives, have argued that affirmative action may actually damage the self-esteem of members of under-represented groups and lead to increased feelings of personal inferiority. Even the most cursory understanding of this country's history, however, leads one to recognize that women and people of color have always been considered by society to be intellectually or morally inferior to white men. It is the lasting social and material effects of precisely such historic and current prejudice which make affirmative action necessary. No imagined injury due to employment under allegedly clouded circumstances could compare with the inevitable diminishment of self-esteem caused by a denial of suitable employment in the first place.

Even so, affirmative-action policies are far from perfect. Few would argue, for example, that the daughter of a Latino law professor should be given preference in college admission over the son of a white sharecropper. And no one would wish to encourage black contractors to seek preferential government awards of business for the eventual benefit of white investors. Affirmative action may sometimes require fine-tuning, but such adjustment, when necessary, should be undertaken only by people fully committed to the goals of gender and ethnic equality, not by those who deny the persistence of prejudice.

Opponents of affirmative action play on the fears of white males that hordes of undeserving women and minorities are going to take an unfair share of the limited number of jobs. However, the very notion that there are such large groups of undeserving women and minorities is itself eloquent testimony to the persistence of racism and sexism in our society. There is thus plenty of evidence of prejudice; but there is no scientific evidence for any general lack of merit among women and minorities. The traditionally privileged position of the one supposedly deserving group (white males) is therefore unwarranted. However, the proponents of CCRI, by playing on white male fears, may nevertheless hope to protect this unwarranted privilege in the face of diminishing employment opportunities and diminishing earnings.[8]

The American tendency to locate the source of inequality in the supposed lack of individual merit of women and minorities really serves to mask a social

---

8. Secretary of Labor Robert Reich noted in November 1994 that nearly three out of four working men—those who lack College degrees—have suffered a twelve percent decline in average real income since 1979. Quoted by Cynthia Tucker, *San Francisco Chronicle*, March 24th, 1995, p. A23.

problem: a systematically racist and sexist society confronted with severely and unnecessarily restricted resources and opportunities. This social problem calls for a social solution: the only way to avoid increased societal fragmentation and conflict while preserving the civil rights gains of the past 30 years is to greatly increase social investment so as to expand the pool of resources and jobs.

PROPOSITION 184: THREE STRIKES AND WE'RE BANKRUPT

Both Proposition 187 (a reactionary response to the complex pressures of immigration) and the CCRI (a simplistic attack on affirmative action) show the failure in creativity of conservative policies. This lack of creativity is even more obvious in Proposition 184, the so-called "3 strikes and you're out" measure.

The non-debate preceding passage of this measure completely excluded any reference to the significant fact that the United States has higher rates of violent crime and incarcerates more criminals than any other comparably wealthy industrialized society. This is an extraordinary state of affairs. To accept this fact must surely lead us to seek its causes and to attempt to prevent crime, to the extent possible, rather than merely to punish criminals. Proposition 184 not only fails to address the root causes of crime but actually contributes to them by taking limited funds away from education, job training and other critical social programs.

Between 1984 and 1994, the California Department of Corrections hired 25,864 new employees while the number of higher education personnel actually decreased by 8,082.[9] In 1984, the State of California still spent more than two and one-half times as much on higher education as on prisons. For 1995, however, the rates of expenditure are about equal. It is unusual by world standards, and a dangerous sign of future social breakdown, that *California now spends as much annually on incarceration as on higher education.*

In Governor Wilson's budget for 1994–95, higher education staffing decreased by 968 persons, but corrections increased 7.5 percent, by 2,879. For the cost of imprisoning one person for one year we could educate ten Community College students or five CSU students or two UC students.[10] To sentence a third-strike burglar to 40 years in prison is to forego educating 200 two-year community

---

9. Center on Juvenile and Criminal Justice, 1622 Folsom St. 2nd Floor, SF 94103.
10. This analysis was done by the Graduate Student policy consortium at the University of California, Berkeley.

college students. If just one of those 200 denied affordable education turns to crime, the massive cost of incarcerating one prisoner will have had no effect whatsoever on the crime rate.

In October 1994, just about a month before the elections that would approve Proposition 184, the Rand Corporation published its own analysis of the comparative costs of incarceration strategies. The publication was entitled *Three Strikes and You're Out: Estimated Benefits and Costs of California's New Mandatory Sentencing Law.* This analysis is important because Rand placed estimates of the costs of building more prisons in the context of the state's broader budget alternatives. In just seven years, by the year 2002, the new legislation will require the proportion of the state's budget marked for corrections to double, from its current nine percent to 18 per cent. *The important fact is that this then reduces some other part of the state budget by that same amount.*

The Rand analysis points out that this cannot come from K-12, because the state constitution was amended several years ago to set minimum levels for K-12 education. Nor can more than a small fraction of the money come from reductions in the health and welfare segment of the budget. For the last quarter-century, there has been a steady increase in the proportion of the state budget devoted to health and welfare, and it is now seven per cent higher than in 1969. Since the number of beneficiaries and legitimate claimants will grow in the next seven years at a rate faster than the state's population, budgetary increases in this segment seem unavoidable.

We come therefore to higher education. In the last 25 years, higher education's share of the state budget has fallen from 17 per cent in 1969 to 12 per cent in 1994. More cuts will come as the effect of Proposition 184 becomes felt in the next two years. *Rand predicts that higher education and the remaining government services segment will have to be cut by forty per cent in the next seven years to accommodate Proposition 184 provisions.*[11]

POST-SECONDARY EDUCATION

In this era of economic globalization and rapid technical innovation, the new jobs being created in the United States require an increasingly high degree

---

11. The remainder of the budget covers a range of services, from workplace safety to parks, from pollution control to the regulation of insurance. Since 1980, the percentage of the budget absorbed by this segment has fallen from 12 to 9.

of specialized training. Such training must obviously take place at the post-secondary level, including community colleges and vocational schools. Therefore the wisest investment in the future and in a continued high standard of living for our state and nation would be to increase our vocational school, college and university budgets, to reduce tuition, and to expand the availability of financial aid for all students who wish to attend. At present, we are doing precisely the opposite. Term after term, tuition in our public colleges has increased and the availability of financial aid has diminished, hence enrollment has steadily declined. In such a diverse and wealthy nation, there should be sufficient educational opportunity for all qualified persons regardless of gender, ethnic group or social class. Just as working people should not have to compete with each other for an artificially limited number of jobs, prospective students should not be forced to fight, one group against another, for a shrinking number of positions in our vocational schools and colleges

CONCLUSION: EMBRACING HOPE

The idea behind Proposition 187 is to deny our dependence on immigrants so as to avoid taking responsibility for including them fully in our society. The idea behind the proposed CCRI is to deny the legitimacy of the claims of long-disrespected groups so as to avoid extending social benefits to them. Finally, the idea behind Proposition 184 is to deny the social causes of crime so as to avoid having to provide opportunities for people before they become criminals.

Embracing the immigrants upon whom we depend, investing in and honoring those groups so long denied and disrespected, opening up the kinds of opportunities that might prevent criminality will all require a great increase in social expenditure and public services, the very reverse of the policies we are currently pursuing. In a country as wealthy as ours, it should not be necessary, for example, to withhold jobs from white men so that others can work, or to deny working people the chance to send their children to college. The American problem appears to be less a matter of limited resources than of the maldistribution of wealth and of the social disutility of great wealth. If the so-called free market system is incapable of generating sufficient health care, education and employment to meet the needs of all the people, then we must not hesitate to modify that system intelligently and boldly.

IN DEFENSE OF AFFIRMATIVE ACTION: THE CASE AGAINST PROPOSITION 209

Coauthored with Nadav Savio

As a civil rights movement veteran, Savio viewed the attack on affirmative action as an attempt to reverse the gains for racial justice and equal opportunity that he and many others had fought so hard to win in the 1960s. In fact, he came to view the first civil rights demonstration at which he was arrested, at San Francisco's Sheraton Palace Hotel in 1964, as an early affirmative action effort, to force nondiscriminatory hiring. In this sense his last major publication returned him to his roots. And it is also fitting that this last publication, which appeared in October 1996, should involve two Savios, father and son, since it was Nadav whose challenge to Mario to do more than complain about the new politics of resentment helped prod Mario to renewed activism and the founding of the Campus Coalitions for Human Right and Social Justice.

In order to get beyond racism we must first take account of race. There is no other way. And in order to treat some persons equally, we must treat them differently. We cannot—we dare not—let the Equal Protection Clause perpetrate racial supremacy.—Dissent of Justice Harry A. Blackmun, *Regents of University of California v. Bakke*, 1978

INTRODUCTION

Affirmative action is under attack in California. Proposition 209, on California's November ballot, is one of the most important measures that state voters will ever be called upon to decide. This proposition, misleadingly referred to as the California Civil Rights Initiative (CCRI), would end all affirmative action in state government hiring, contracting and college admissions. Its deceptive clause (c) would seriously erode legal protections for women. If passed, this initiative could set back the cause of equality to a time when people's only legal recourse was mass demonstrations.

Extremes of inequality stubbornly persist. People's real needs are not being addressed and, in fact, call for complex and sophisticated solutions. Real political leaders should now be educating the public concerning the need to improve rather than abandon affirmative action. This would permit continuation of the peaceful progress that affirmative action has already accomplished. Instead, opportunistic right-wing politicians, such as Pete Wilson and Bob Dole, are attempting to advance their careers by promoting wedge issues which incite the voting public against the supposed beneficiaries of "reverse discrimination."

To accomplish their ends, these politicians have created a vocabulary of deception. *Discrimination, reverse discrimination, preferences, quotas.* All these words are used to prey upon the insecurity that many Californians, especially white males, feel in this era of rapid and bewildering social change. Ever since the famous 1978 Supreme Court decision in *Regents of University of California v. Bakke*, quotas have been permissible only if court-ordered. Hence, the affirmative action programs which CCRI would eliminate involve no quotas. Nor are affirmative action programs designed to perpetuate a government preference for certain pampered groups. On the contrary. If affirmative action involves a preference, it is merely a preference for the traditionally excluded, a preference, that is, to right a wrong. And, to right this wrong, it is essential to differentiate those who are harmed by prejudice from those who, even unknowingly, may benefit from it. Discriminating in this sense, in other words "distinguishing," is a good and necessary act. When opportunist politicians appeal to "angry white males" by condemning affirmative action as *reverse discrimination*, they are attempting to confuse the good sort of discriminating with the bad.

Californians—majority and minorities, male and female—need to resist inflammatory rhetoric and to carefully consider what affirmative action is and what Proposition 209 would undo. Because it employs specific, positive mechanisms for overcoming society's pervasive prejudice, affirmative action also makes the profound statement that our nation will no longer tolerate racial and gender bias. If Proposition 209 passes, and those affirmative mechanisms are dismantled, California voters will have made the opposite statement: that bias is once again acceptable. We hope that voters come to feel, as we do, that it is essential for the good of both our state and nation that this extremist measure be defeated. It is encouraging to note recent polls which demonstrate that, when California voters actually understand what CCRI would do, they are far less likely to support it. Hence, we have tried to present the facts of the case and also some analysis of the economic and social causes for the current attack on affirmative action.

WHAT IS THE CCRI (PROPOSITION 209)?

The substantive clauses of the California Civil Rights Initiative (CCRI) are as follows:

"(a) The state shall not discriminate against, or grant preferential treatment to, any individual or group on the basis of race, sex, color, ethnicity, or national origin in the operation of public employment, public education, or public contracting.

"(c) Nothing in this section shall be interpreted as prohibiting bona fide qualifications based on sex which are reasonably necessary to the normal operation of public employment, public education, or public contracting."

If passed, the CCRI would:[1]

- Abolish all goals and timetables for increasing the number of women and minorities in public jobs, colleges and universities and government contracts.

Under affirmative action, such goals and timetables enable institutions to assess their own progress. Without such guidelines, no measurable determination of improvement would be possible.

- Eliminate outreach programs designed merely to increase the number of women and minority applicants.

A variety of significant obstacles impede the entry of women and minorities into fields and positions from which they have traditionally been excluded.

---

1. "Fight Attacks on Affirmative Action," National Lawyers Guild Training Manual, National Lawyers Guild, 558 Capp Street, SF, CA 94110, especially pp. 59–62.

Proactive recruitment of applicants is a necessary first step to overcoming these barriers.

- Outlaw elementary and secondary school math and science programs for girls.

Traditionally, girls have been discouraged from pursuing careers in such fields. Many educators believe that only programs specifically targeting girls can successfully counteract this traditional tracking.

- Eliminate Women's Resource Centers on college campuses.

These centers educate students on topics such as rape prevention and sexual harassment.

- Expand the opportunities for employers and educational institutions to discriminate based on gender.

Under the California Constitution, discrimination based on gender is only allowed if it can be shown to be necessary to achieve a compelling government purpose. The CCRI language in clause (c), allowing any discrimination which is "reasonably necessary to the normal operation" of public employment, education or contracting, is far weaker. Under the CCRI, for example, an employer could refuse to hire a woman with a child because it was "reasonably necessary" to the business for employees to work long hours. Pro-CCRI forces are counting on their ability to miscast Proposition 209 as a solely racial issue. But white women have benefited more than any other group from affirmative action policies and stand to lose the most if CCRI becomes law.

- Eliminate race and gender as acceptable non-academic criteria, while retaining such "qualifications" as athletic ability and relation to alumni or large donors.

Most educators recognize that consideration of some non-academic criteria is necessary to assure an appropriately diverse student body. CCRI would single out only race and gender for elimination, while retaining academically irrelevant criteria such as relation to alumni or large donors. Given this society's past and continuing discrimination based on race and gender, it is striking that politicians would select precisely these factors as inappropriate. Indeed, race and gender are the very criteria we should most be seeking to emphasize if we wish to heal society's wounds.

BACKGROUND

The idea that affirmative action unfairly discriminates against individual white males is central to the case made for CCRI. Proponents argue that all hiring, promotion and admissions decisions should be determined solely by objective criteria, with white male applicants and all others facing one another as equals on a level playing field. While on the surface this may seem compelling, it completely ignores the context in which such decisions take place. The contenders are not equal and the playing field is not level. For the weight of past discriminatory practice bears heavily on and limits all present options.

Even the most zealous opponents of affirmative action recognize that, *in the past*, certain groups of people have been subjected to severe injustice, including uncountable individual injuries ranging from repeated insult to the violence of lynching and rape. Equally damaging have been racist and sexist institutions (unequal legal status, forced segregation, slavery). It would seem unnecessary to remind US citizens of the present relevance of our country's history of prejudice. But even presidential candidate Bob Dole recently dismissed the current impact of slavery because "that was a long time ago."[2] Thus a reminder of US history and its bearing on the present seems appropriate.

Racism in the United States began in 1619, when the first African was brought to Virginia in chains. Of the subsequent 377 years, for 245 the country permitted slavery. For the next 100, legal discrimination was the rule, accompanied by frequent acts of terror such as lynchings and church burnings. The burnings haven't stopped. Not until the Civil Rights Act of 1964 did our nation formally resolve to overcome the damage done over the previous 350 years. For only about 30 years has the US, as a whole, undertaken positive action to heal its centuries-old racial wounds.[3] It is offensive to suggest, as CCRI proponents do, that a single generation of affirmative action has remedied such a long, sustained history of abuse.

---

2. Cited in Duster, Troy, "Individual Fairness, Group Preferences and the California Strategy," University of California unpublished manuscript, p. 5.

3. Wilkins, Roger, "Racism Has Its Privileges," *The Nation*, March 27, 1995, p. 412.

Women, too, have endured a long history of oppression. Until the end of the last century, women had no legal property rights in the United States, only gained the vote in 1920 and have faced blatantly discriminatory property, marriage and divorce laws to the present. More shockingly, as recently as 1991 it was generally legal, in 30 US states, for men to rape their wives.[4] It remains extremely difficult for women to escape violent marriages or to gain redress for widespread sexual harassment in the workplace.

It is in the nature of sexism, however, that among the most damaging barriers to women's equality are cultural biases. Such biases, held for generations, consider women fit only for certain limiting occupations. "Women's work" is generally an extension of traditional domestic chores, involving service, caretaking or the performance of repetitive, menial tasks. Thus, women have generally staffed low-status or subordinate occupations such as typing, cleaning, sewing, nursing and teaching young children. Indeed, sexist bias permeates our culture. Parents and teachers often dissuade girls from pursuing non-traditional careers such as science or firefighting. Employers frequently discriminate against women. And women are effectively excluded from the highest managerial positions ("the glass ceiling").

Similar injustice based on race and ethnicity has been perpetrated against many other groups. Consider the confinement of over 100,000 Japanese-Americans to internment camps during the Second World War or the segregation faced by Mexican-Americans through much of this century. Or consider the beginnings of this "land of equality."[5] In 1492, when Christopher Columbus landed in North America, there were between 1 and 2 million Native Americans. By the beginning of the twentieth century, following 400 years of massacres, unheeded treaties and forced dislocation, the native population had dropped to 300,000.[6] As the *Columbia Encyclopedia* complacently notes, "Indians [have] settled into a life dominated by poverty, poor education, unemployment, and gradual dispersal."[7]

Even so, despite this dismal history, can't we just start over? We can't. The present cannot be considered apart from the past, as the following example makes painfully obvious.

Current disparities between white and black academic performance can only be understood in light of past government-sanctioned segregation. In 1939, three generations ago, Federal Housing Authority (FHA) guidelines specified

4. Faludi, Susan, *Backlash*, 1991: Crown, New York, p. xiv.

5. Freeman, et al., *Who Built America*, American Social History Project, CUNY, 1992: Pantheon Books, New York, pp. 243, 289, 448.

6. Zinn, Howard, *A People's History of the United States*, 1980: Harper & Row, New York, p. 514.

7. *The Concise Columbia Encyclopedia*, 1983: Avon, New York, pp. 609–10.

that loans not be made that might "disrupt the racial integrity" of a neighborhood. Based on that avowed goal of segregation, the FHA made it next to impossible for blacks to get the low-rate loans routinely granted to whites. Thus, between 1946 and 1960, 350,000 new homes were built in Northern California of which fewer than 100 went to African-Americans. This policy (and others like it) had two results directly pertinent to the discussion of affirmative action. First, it reinforced and lent government authority to the racial segregation in effect since slavery. Second, the greatest financial difference between blacks and whites today is in their net worth, overwhelmingly a result of the disparity in value of their equity in housing stock. In 1991, the median net worth of white households (143,279) was more than 10 times that of African-American households ($4,169).[8] In other words, overtly racist government policy led not only to separate, but to poorer black neighborhoods.

In turn, this housing disparity must be considered in light of two facts about public education in the US: that school attendance is largely local (despite attempts at busing), and that funding for public schools comes primarily from property taxes. Hence, the relative poverty of black neighborhoods led directly to a relative inferiority of black neighborhood schools. Indeed, the recognition that school funding out of property taxes results in such glaring inequities prompted the California Supreme Court to decide in 1971 (*Serrano v. Priest*) that the state government must guarantee a minimum level of school funding per student in every school district. Since then, funding of California public schools has grown gradually more equitable, although significant disparities remain.

Thus a conscious government policy of maintaining segregated neighborhoods led to blacks living in much poorer neighborhoods than whites; and the relative poverty of black neighborhoods has condemned three generations of black children to attending inferior schools. It entails no exaggeration, therefore, to assert that *current* disparities between white and black academic performance are, in large part, the result of *past* history of government sanctioned segregation.

INSTITUTIONAL BIAS

Since disparities in current educational attainment are substantially attributable to past discrimination, otherwise objective criteria, such as standardized test

---

8. Duster, Troy, "The Advantages of White Males," *San Francisco Chronicle*, January 19, 1995, p. A21.

scores, are often unfair. The playing field is clearly *not* level. To grasp such subtle bias requires an understanding of the interplay between *overt* bias and less obvious *institutional* discrimination. For example, when an African-American is forced to the back of a bus, we know this is racism. When a woman is denied a promotion because the employer thinks men will refuse to take orders from a woman, we know this is sexism. These are examples of outright or overt discrimination. *Institutional* bias arises when apparently neutral practices, such as minimum job qualifications, are applied on what is a significantly uneven playing field. While themselves objective, such practices can have quite unfair consequences because of past or continuing overt bias. Indeed, technically fair institutional practices can be, and often are, manipulated as an expression of overt bias. Thus, until the Supreme Court outlawed it in 1966, the seemingly impartial poll tax was routinely used to deny blacks and poor whites the right to vote.[9]

Because the practices which constitute institutional bias are, in themselves, neutral, they can easily be overlooked. It is worthwhile, then, to examine the most common forms in greater detail.

Standardized "Merit-Based" admissions

As discussed above, neighborhood poverty may lead to inferior educational attainment. For example, a student attending an inferior neighborhood school may excel within that school. Even so, his or her performance on a standardized achievement test may fall well short of the performance of another student of equal or even lesser ability who had the benefit of superior schooling. Nor is educational attainment a function of formal schooling alone. Children of well educated parents growing up in safe, prosperous neighborhoods will obviously enjoy immense academic advantages, for they will be able to focus their attention on learning, free from the dangers and distractions endemic to poorer neighborhoods. Therefore, any student who excels under the adverse conditions imposed by poverty and racial exclusion may fairly be assumed to have special strengths which no standardized test of academic achievement could possibly measure.

Hiring by word of mouth

It is widely taken for granted (as evidenced in the popular wisdom "It's not what you know, but who you know") that the vast majority of hirings result

---

9. Ezorsky, Gertrude, *Racism & Justice*, 1991: Cornell University Press, Ithaca, NY, p. 10.

from word of mouth referrals. Most new jobs are garnered through personal networks of friends, relatives or acquaintances. This occurs for a variety of reasons and is, in itself, unbiased. For example, it is cheaper and easier for employers to rely on contacts instead of advertising when seeking candidates. Hiring through personal connections also contributes to the feeling that the employer is getting a "known quantity."

But because our society is so rigidly segregated by race, people of color are excluded from the informal relationships through which mostly white employers find new hires. Schools, no longer segregated by law, and neighborhoods, no longer kept racially homogeneous through codified policy, generally remain so in practice. Thus, in their families, social circles and neighborhoods, people of color "tend to be isolated from the networks in which connections to desirable employment—where whites predominate—are forged."[10]

It is crucial to note that this process occurs at all levels of employment. Whites tend to occupy not just the best jobs overall, but the best of any given level of jobs. For instance, not only are whites more likely than blacks to hold executive positions in a given company, but they are also more likely to be factory managers or crew foremen. What's more, since workers tend to hear of jobs at their own level, and since blacks tend to occupy the lowest paid and least prestigious jobs, blacks will generally only be able to refer their friends, family, and so on, to similar jobs, both ensuring that blacks remain predominant in lower status positions and simultaneously reinforcing the stereotype that they belong there.[11]

Qualifications for admissions and hiring

Minimum standard qualifications, while in themselves completely impartial, may also unfairly discriminate against certain groups of applicants because of past or present prejudice. Test scores, for example, do not take into account unequal educational backgrounds resulting from years of segregated and underfunded schooling. Furthermore, many standard measures of aptitude fail to accurately predict future performance.[12] Of course, some minimum qualifications are necessary for determining the ability of applicants to perform a given job. But to avoid discriminatory impact, such qualifications must correlate closely with actual on-the-job success. In this regard, the facts surrounding the *Bakke* case are most enlightening.

---

10. Ezorsky, p. l5.
11. Ezorsky, pp. 15–18.
12. Ezorsky, p. 22.

Allan Bakke successfully sued the University of California for having been passed over as a medical school applicant in favor of African-Americans with lower test scores. While Bakke went on to a part-time anesthesiology practice in Rochester, Minnesota, Patrick Chavis, one of the lower-scoring African-American applicants admitted ahead of Bakke, has a thriving OB/GYN practice in a low-income, mostly minority community in the Los Angeles area. If Chavis had been denied admission to medical school, it is hardly likely that any "better-qualified" white obstetrician would presently serve the patients that he does. Although Allan Bakke had higher test scores than Patrick Chavis, it would seem that those scores did not predict who would make a more dedicated physician.

Seniority

Basing promotions and layoffs rigidly or inflexibly on seniority ensures that even if long-excluded people are hired, they will be the first fired during times of economic hardship and the last to be promoted. Also, many seniority systems hold only within a given department or job classification, so that if the employee moves to a new, potentially more desirable, position, all seniority is lost. Fearful of losing their seniority, women and ethnic minorities will therefore tend to remain segregated in the lowest-paying, least desirable positions—those into which they were originally hired.

It is important to note that the barriers to women and people of color, while often the same, also diverge somewhat. For example, as a result of racial segregation, hiring by word of mouth affects minorities much more acutely than white women, who have greater access to the social networks which lead to good jobs. In a different way, the qualification, often cited by male managers, that managerial positions require an aggressive, dynamic style works to exclude women from those positions.

WHAT IS AFFIRMATIVE ACTION?

Because the playing field society presents—to whites, to ethnic minorities, to women—is significantly uneven, it is not enough merely to declare sexism and racism problems of the past, enforce antidiscrimination laws and be done with it, as conservative critics have argued. Permitting redress only when an alleged victim claims discrimination (the so-called "complaint remedy") is utterly inadequate in dealing with either overt *or* institutional racism. In the former case, victims of discrimination are often too intimidated to seek redress. In the latter, it is extremely difficult or impossible to prove wrongdoing. Where is the culprit, for instance, in the case of a job for which a black woman never applied because she didn't know it existed? To call merely for an end to discrimination demonstrates willful ignorance of current conditions if not outright malice.[13] Affirmative action was designed—and is still necessary—to overcome both overt discrimination and the severely unjust impact of institutional bias.[14]

To remedy the effects of both institutional and overt discrimination, a variety of affirmative action policies can be employed. Below, we describe the affirmative action admissions and hiring policies currently in effect in the California State University (CSU) system.

Recruitment, retention and graduation

A three-stage process is employed in the CSU system to extend the opportunity of a college degree to formerly excluded students. Potential students are actively recruited by admissions officers who cultivate relationships with teachers and guidance counselors in high schools throughout the state. The overwhelming majority of students admitted are regularly qualified to attend. A much smaller group of "special admits" accommodates students who show unusual promise despite lower standardized test scores. Once admitted, the most disadvantaged students may be invited to participate in a Summer Bridge Program which helps them make the social and academic transition from their neighborhoods and schools to the collegiate environment. Students whose academic background includes deficiencies in language or mathematics will attend developmental classes until those deficiencies are remedied. Students who find the transition to college life especially difficult have the opportunity to work one-on-one with special Educational Opportunity Program counselors.

Affirmative action officer oversees faculty hiring

Each campus employs an affirmative action officer, charged with researching comparable institutions and providing feedback to departments so they can accurately and fairly assess their progress towards unbiased hiring.

---

13. Ezorsky, pp. 28–33.
14. From author interviews with a CSU Affirmative Action officer and a CSU Remedial Education instructor.

Advertising faculty positions

To address the problem of hiring by word of mouth, each position that opens must be advertised widely with adequate time for applicants to submit necessary materials. Advertisements must appear in a variety of places, especially where they are likely to be seen by potential affirmative action applicants. For example, if a law school is hiring, it would typically advertise in a black law journal. Finally, once the hiring department (or other entity) has chosen the qualified applicants for interview, the campus affirmative action officer reviews the candidate pool. If the pool is found significantly lacking in diversity in comparison with the range of candidates available to similar institutions, the affirmative action officer may require the department to reopen the application process. This simple step of requiring fair advertisement of each position elegantly ensures that, even if many candidates learn of positions by word of mouth, at least a much wider range of applicants will also be included in the hiring process.

Qualifying job criteria

In order to minimize the impact both of impartial job qualifications which nevertheless discriminate and of the biased use of qualifications to keep out unwanted applicants, CSU affirmative action requires that departments demonstrate that their qualifications are truly relevant. It is not the case that such a requirement allows unqualified hires. On the contrary, there is evidence that forcing employers to devise more predictive qualification criteria has actually improved job performance.[15]

Standardized interviewing

To reduce partiality or outright bias in the interview process, several affirmative action policies work in concert. First, the department must agree on a standard set of questions to be used in the interview. These questions are then reviewed by the campus affirmative action officer; they must be sensitive and appropriate for any potential applicant. The final set of questions must be asked in its entirety of each candidate, and no other questions may be asked.

---

15. Ezorsky, pp. 88–89.

In other words, each candidate is asked exactly the same questions. It is not permissible to ask a woman applicant if she plans to have children or to ask an unwanted candidate only a few cursory questions. Finally, the interviewing panel must be as diverse a group as possible given the limitations of past hiring. If the department is made up of five white men, a Latina and a black man, neither of the latter two should be routinely excluded from departmental interview panels.

It should be noted that CSU policies do not specify any "quota" of minority or women candidates which must be hired. Since the 1978 *Bakke* decision, it has been illegal to set aside a specific number of spots for affirmative action candidates. The term "quota," was originally applied to the racist practice of *limiting* opportunities and excluding a specific group (Jews). Critics of affirmative action have employed this term to vilify programs which actually aim at *increasing* opportunities and *including* those groups which have long been excluded. The term "reverse discrimination" has been similarly misused to cast affirmative action policies in a discriminatory light. But the numbers are instructive here: according to the Department of Labor, from 1990 to 1994, of more than 3,000 discrimination cases, only 100 alleged "reverse discrimination." Of those 100, all but 6 were thrown out for lack of merit.[16] Even so, popular criticisms of affirmative action should be answered. What follows, in the form of a series of questions, are the major criticisms leveled at affirmative action.

CRITICISMS OF AFFIRMATIVE ACTION

- Has affirmative action worked?

Some critics suggest that affirmative action has worked well and is therefore no longer necessary. Such a view is not borne out by the hard facts of current social and economic reality; obvious examples of continuing discrimination can be found in every sector of US society, public and private. Others argue that affirmative action is ineffective and that any gains made in the past 25 years by minorities and women have come about for other reasons. On the contrary, there is clear evidence that affirmative action programs have been quite effective in advancing the status of women and people of color. From 1971 to 1991,

16. Cited in "Questions and Answers about Affirmative Action," CrossRoads, PO Box 2809, Oakland, CA 94609.

the number of women receiving doctorates in the US more than doubled.[17] Similarly, under a program of aggressive affirmative action, Black and Hispanic enrollment at UC Berkeley rose from 11.6 to 29.4 percent of incoming students from 1981 to 1988. During this period, it should be noted, the average combined Berkeley SAT score rose from 1130 to 1185.[18]

- Does affirmative action reduce hiring and admissions standards?

As should be clear from the example of CSU policies given above, affirmative action guidelines do not promote unqualified hires or admissions; they merely assure that qualifications actually are necessary for job or school success. Moreover, by forcing institutions to develop qualification measures that accurately reflect future performance, affirmative action has been demonstrated to raise competence levels. Indeed, people selected under affirmative action may often be more qualified than those, such as employers' relatives or friends, who have benefited from more traditional preferences. Finally, hiring and admissions have not traditionally been based on abstract merit alone. For example, both public and private universities have always insisted on recruiting a diverse student body, taking into consideration such non-academic qualities as athletic ability, musical talent, place of origin and relation to alumni or large donors. CCRI would single out only race and gender for elimination, while retaining academically irrelevant "qualifications" such as relation to alumni or large donors.[19]

- Does affirmative action damage its beneficiaries' self-esteem?

Women and people of color have always been considered by society to be intellectually or morally inferior to white men. This social falsehood has long been the basis for denial of appropriate employment and is the principal cause of any damaged self-esteem. No imagined injury due to employment under allegedly clouded circumstances could compare with the inevitable diminishment of self-esteem caused by a denial of suitable employment in the first place.[20] It should be noted, moreover, that beneficiaries of other forms of

---

17. Lawyer's Guild Booklet, p. 80, note 23.
18. Karabel, Jerome, *Freshman Admissions at Berkeley, A Policy for the 1990's and Beyond*, University of California-Berkeley, pp. 17–18.
19. Ezorsky, pp. 61–62, 89 n. 22, 91–93.
20. *California at a Crossroads: Social Strife or Social Unity?* Campus Coalitions for Human Rights and Social Justice, p. 9.

affirmative action (such as athletes or the children of alumni) haven't seemed to suffer from reduced self-esteem.[21]

- Does affirmative action only help those who are already relatively well off?

This is not true. Although affirmative action is of no direct benefit to those too disadvantaged to compete, it has helped many women and people of color across the wage continuum and has facilitated social mobility. Some of those who have benefited from affirmative action (like Dr. Patrick Chavis, mentioned above) have been of indirect help to others by acquiring skills of use to their communities.[22]

- Should affirmative action be based on income instead of race and gender?

Affirmative action should be based on income as well as *race* and *gender*. The two are by no means mutually exclusive. But to insist on strictly income-based affirmative action is to deny the persistence of racial and gender inequality. Limiting affirmative action to income would benefit all poor people to some degree. But because of prejudice, people of color and women would still receive less than their share. We need both increased opportunity *and* more equality.

In a related criticism, it is often lamented that a wealthy person of color or recent immigrant might receive affirmative action preference over a poor white applicant. This would generally be unfair and would rightly be avoided in any hiring or admissions process based on income in addition to race and gender. But this is hardly reason to abandon affirmative action, which should take into account a variety of pertinent factors and can easily be amended to do so.[23]

- Why do blacks need affirmative action if other minority groups have succeeded without it?

First of all, many arriving Europeans, although denied full acceptance into the majority community, were nonetheless deemed more worthy than blacks and were permitted to displace black workers. These immigrants actually benefited

---

21. Ezorsky, p. 61.
22. Ezorsky, pp. 63–72.
23. Ezorsky, pp. 65–72, esp. 70–72.

from racism. Other immigrants (European and non-European) arrived in the US with the social-class advantages of wealth and education. Contrary to stereotype, however, some recent poorer immigrants from Asia and Latin America have fared much less well, and, like many black workers, currently work for low pay with little hope of advancement.[24]

- If we enforce antidiscrimination laws, why do we need affirmative action?

The "complaint remedy" (as discussed above) is not a practical solution to discrimination. First of all, in the case of much institutional bias, there is no specific perpetrator. Even for cases of obvious prejudice, victims are often reluctant to bring a complaint for fear of retaliation; and even when validly made, such allegations are very difficult to prove.[25]

- If our goal is equality, should we have discriminatory policies?

To eliminate discrimination will require remedies which *differentiate* those who are harmed by prejudice from those who benefit from it even unknowingly. Such differentiation cannot possibly be color or gender neutral. Thus, we require law which is color and gender conscious in the short run to produce a society which in the long run is color and gender blind.

- Is it unfair for affirmative action to single out certain individuals to pay for past discrimination committed by others?

At the heart of CCRI's attractiveness is this feeling of the unfairness of programs which place the burden for redressing past discrimination on the shoulders of specific individuals (often white males). Even if only a small number are subject to such adverse effects, this moral argument can neither be ignored nor callously dismissed as "white males getting their just desserts." For there is certainly some element of injustice if anyone other than the specific perpetrator of a wrong is singled out to suffer. Ideally, then, the burden of redressing past and present discrimination should be shared by all who have benefited, whether directly or indirectly. But present US society is far from ideal. In no other industrial democracy is the gap in income and wealth between the rich

---

24. Ezorsky, pp. 57–59.
25. Ezorsky, pp. 28–29.

and the poor as great as it is in this country.[26] Hence, the availability of benefits and resources in the US is unnecessarily restricted. It should not be necessary to harm white men so that others may share equally in society's opportunities, and it would not be if those opportunities were divided fairly. This points not to the injustice of affirmative action, but to the injustice of a society in which so many are forced to compete for so little while the wealthy few enjoy so much.

WHY AFFIRMATIVE ACTION IS NOW UNDER ATTACK

So why is the assault on affirmative action taking place now? Have the past thirty years of positive remedies erased the effects of 300 years of racism and 3,000 years of sexism? No, inequity and bias still abound. But relatively recent economic and political changes and the opportunism of politicians such as Pete Wilson have combined to make affirmative action the critical issue of the 1996 election.

Recent political developments are best understood in contrast with the situation thirty years ago. Affirmative action programs were first designed in the mid-sixties in response to mass civil disobedience and the social disruption of ghetto uprisings. But the civil rights movement and the ghetto rebellions occurred at the height of a period of sustained and unprecedented economic growth which helped to produce a climate of rising expectations. Today, however, following years of economic contraction, there is less hopefulness and only muted popular resistance.

This is not to say that people are complacent. On the contrary, there is widespread dissatisfaction. But the sources of the country's problems are much more difficult to identify now than at the height of the civil rights movement. In the former era of general prosperity and confidence, overt acts of racism seemed to stand out as obvious and limited problems, suggesting straightforward solutions. Now, in economic hard times, racism and sexism are but two of myriad social ills. Moreover, institutional bias is inherently more difficult both to identify and to remedy than overt racism ever was.

Aggravating this already tragic situation is a recurrence of our country's periodic weakness for indulging racist pseudo-science. *The Bell Curve*, a recent bestseller, now thoroughly refuted, is the latest attempt to locate the source of

---

26. Hartman, Carl, AP, "Rich Getting Richer, Poor Getting Poorer," *San Francisco Chronicle*, 10-28-95, p. B3.

racial disparities in the alleged inferiority of the real victims of economic and social injustice.[27] In this climate of near-hysteria, and in the face of numerous seemingly intractable social and economic problems, what our country most needs is wise political leadership and serious analysis.

For the actual causes of our current troubles are immensely complex. They include economic globalization, domestic downsizing and disinvestment in training and education, unprecedented technical innovation and rapid cultural change. Analyzing and solving any one of these problems would require a national mobilization of resolve, resources, expertise and wisdom.

Instead, opportunistic politicians have bombarded us with a succession of numbingly simple-minded quick-fixes, each designed to scapegoat a different group. Proposition 184 targets criminals but discounts the social causes of crime. Proposition 187 targets immigrants but ignores the economic forces which drive immigration. The campaign for Proposition 209 targets people of color but denies the injustices under which people of color and women (the majority of the population) are forced to compete.

The reality these false solutions mask is a growing gap between the wealthy few and working many. As multiple studies have shown, the difference in wealth and income between rich and poor is larger in the US than in any comparable country. And the gap has continued to grow.[28] This disparity has been exacerbated by the wholesale cutting of social welfare programs, most recently in President Clinton's approval of a law eliminating funds for the Federal safety net. The result of such short-sighted and cruel spending priorities will be an increasing pool of low-skilled and unskilled workers competing for the country's ever shrinking number of entry-level jobs. And even those who do find work must face the likelihood that they will never enjoy their parents' standard of economic security and must anticipate that their children will be even worse off.

In this erosion of "the American Dream," many politicians only see an opportunity for electoral gain. Much as Nixon positioned affirmative action as a wedge issue to fracture the traditional Democratic coalition of Blacks and white workers in the 1970s, Republicans, led by Pete Wilson, Newt Gingrich and now Bob Dole, are pursuing exactly the same strategy in the 1990s.[29] The

---

27. Marshall, Jonathan, "New Work Refutes Conclusions of The Bell Curve," *San Francisco Chronicle*, Mon. 8-12-96, p. B1.

28. In 1987, for example, the wealthiest 10 percent made at least 5.9 times more than those in the poorest 10 percent. Hartman, Carl, AP, "Rich Getting Richer, Poor Getting Poorer," *San Francisco Chronicle*, 10-28-95, p. B3.

29. Lemann, Nicholas, "What Happened to the Case for Affirmative Action," *New York Times Magazine*, 6-11-95, p. 54.

Republican party is far and away the largest contributor to the CCRI campaign, donating nearly $500,000 since January.[30]

Appealing to the alleged group interest of white males, CCRI proponents seek to divide Californians. We who oppose CCRI hope Californians will unite on the basis of a broader social interest. The present crisis affords us an opportunity to identify and confront the root causes of injustice in our state and nation. As we have tried to demonstrate, the major barrier to the success of affirmative action is that available resources have been needlessly limited. This is so because wealth and income in our country is unequally divided to a degree exceeding that in any other industrial democracy. In other words, the rich get so much that the rest of us have too little to share. As a result, white males and others are pitted against each other in an unduly harsh competition. Excessive greed on the part of the rich leaves job seekers—white, minority, male, female—to fight one another when we should be working together.

But as we have also noted, because affirmative action sets in place specific positive mechanisms for eliminating discrimination, it makes a profound statement of genuine commitment that our nation will no longer tolerate racial or gender bias. Those who are urging us to vote for CCRI apparently want us to believe that the social costs of eliminating any further bias are simply too high.

Each voter will need to decide this issue for himself or herself. Is the cost of justice *really* too high? It is because the richest 1 percent of the population owns 40 percent of privately held wealth, that we are forced to determine so carefully which Californians (white males or others) will benefit and which must suffer?[31]

Is this fair? Is this wise? The 1996 election highlights a choice which must now be made between two paths for California and the nation. One leads to a society whose people are healthy, well-educated and gainfully employed; the other, to a society whose men and women, whose ethnic and racial groups are trapped in endless struggle over dwindling resources. Each voter's decision on the California Civil Rights Initiative, pro or con, will help decide which path we take.

---

30. Chart, *San Francisco Examiner*, Sunday, 9-1-96, p. A5.
31. Chart compiled by Campaign for America's Future, *The Nation*, Aug. 26/Sept. 2, 1996, p. 18.

NOTES

Introduction

1. Robert Cohen and Reginald E. Zelnik, eds., *The Free Speech Movement: Reflections on Berkeley in the 1960s* (Berkeley: University of California Press, 2002).

2. *Daily Californian*, October 2, 1964.

3. Doug Rossinow, "The New Left: Democratic Reformers or Left-wing Revolutionaries?" in David Farber and Beth Bailey, eds., *The Columbia Guide to America in the 1960s* (New York: Columbia University Press, 2001), 91; Stanley Aronowitz, *The Decline and Rebirth of American Radicalism* (New York: Routledge, 1996), 32. The question of whether Savio was the first New Left media star can be answered differently depending upon how one defines the New Left. If the New Left is defined as the predominantly white campus-based student movement of the 1960s, then Savio was certainly its first media star; but if defined more broadly to include the predominantly black student wing of the civil rights movement—most notably SNCC and CORE's young militants—then Bob Moses, the Freedom Riders, and the Freedom Summer martyrs would qualify as the first sixties radical protesters spotlighted in the press. I lean toward this more inclusive definition since SNCC set the tone for so much of the sixties Left, and that predominantly black student movement's politics in the early sixties, neither Old Left nor liberal, constituted a new form of nonideological radicalism. On this more inclusive definition of the New Left, see Van Gosse, *Rethinking the New Left: An Interpretive History* (New York: Palgrave, 2005), 1–8. On the traditional definition of a white New Left, see Rossinow, "The New Left: Democratic Reformers or Left-wing Revolutionaries?" 91; Todd Gitlin, *The Sixties: Years of Hope, Days of Rage* (New York: Bantam, 1993), 4. On the Freedom Riders, see Raymond Arsenault, *Freedom Riders: 1961 and the Struggle for Racial Justice* (New York: Oxford University Press, 2006); Eric Etheridge, *Breach of Peace: Portraits of the 1961 Mississippi Freedom Riders* (New York: Atlas, 2008); on Bob Moses and Freedom Summer, see Eric R. Burner, *And Gently Shall He Lead Them: Robert Parris Moses and Civil Rights in Mississippi* (New York: New York University Press, 1994), 1–168.

4. The mass media only began to spotlight SDS in March 1965, almost a half a year after Savio had become a media star for his role in leading the Berkeley rebellion. On the emergence of SDS as a media topic, see Todd Gitlin, *The Whole World Is Watching: Mass Media in the Making and Unmaking of the New Left* (Berkeley: University of California Press, 1980), 26–27, 32–40. Savio's relationship to the media is discussed

briefly (177–78) in Gitlin's SDS-centered account of the media's impact on the New Left. For a summary of news coverage of the FSM, see several of the essays in Cohen and Zelnik, eds., *The Free Speech Movement*, including Robert Cohen, "The Many Meanings of the FSM," 25–26, Martin Roysher, "Recollections of the FSM," 143, and Henry Mayer, "A View from the South: The Idea of a State University," 165; Colin Miller, "The Press and the Student Revolt," in Michael Miller and Susan Gilmore, eds., *Revolution at Berkeley: The Crisis in American Education* (New York: Dial Press, 1965), 313–48; Ray Colvig, *Turning Points and Ironies: Issues and Events, Berkeley 1959–1967* (Berkeley: Berkeley Public Policy Press, 2004), 59–112. On press use of doctored photography to Red-bait the FSM, see David Lance Goines, *The Free Speech Movement: Coming of Age in the 1960s* (Berkeley: Ten Speed Press, 1993), 174–75. For the FBI's role in fostering hostile press coverage of Savio and the FSM, see *Daily Californian*, June 1, 1982. For a discussion of "the Berkeley invention," the new style of militant politics pioneered by Savio and the FSM, see *Report of the President's Commission on Campus Unrest* (Washington, D.C.: U.S. Government Printing Office, 1970), 22–23.

5. Robert Cohen, *When the Old Left Was Young: Student Radicals and America's First Mass Student Movement, 1929–1941* (New York: Oxford University Press, 1993), xiii–xx.

6. "Students: Where and When to Speak," *Time*, December 18, 1964, 68.

7. *San Francisco News-Call Bulletin*, December 3, 1964.

8. Reginald E. Zelnik, "Mario Savio: Avatar of Free Speech," in Cohen and Zelnik, eds., *The Free Speech Movement*, 569–70; Leon Wofsy, interview by author, August 26, 2004, Berkeley, 3.

9. Henry May, "The Student Movement at Berkeley: Some Impressions," in Seymour Martin Lipset and Sheldon S. Wolin, eds., *The Berkeley Student Revolt: Facts and Interpretations* (Garden City, N.Y.: Doubleday, 1965), 454.

10. Ted Widmer, ed., *American Speeches: Political Oratory from Abraham Lincoln to Bill Clinton* (New York: Library of America, 2006), 617. Often the speech is reprinted with a minor error, as if Savio started his most famous lines with the words "There is a time" when in fact he said "There's a time" and emphasized the word *time*. For the best narration of the most famous lines in the speech, see Greil Marcus, "On Mario Savio," in Cohen and Zelnik, eds., *The Free Speech Movement*, 567. The speech is reprinted in part IV of *Freedom's Orator*.

11. Sara Davidson, *Loose Change: Three Women of the Sixties* (Berkeley: University of California Press, 1997), 78.

12. Leon Wofsy, "When the FSM Disturbed the Faculty Peace," in Cohen and Zelnik, eds., *The Free Speech Movement*, 347; Leon Wofsy oral history, Regional Oral History Office, Berkeley, 26; Wofsy interview, 6–7.

13. Wofsy interview, 6.

14. After the mass arrests at the FSM's culminating sit-in, more than seven thousand letters criticizing the protesters and especially Savio came pouring in to California governor Edmund Brown. See L. Robbes to Brown, December 8, 1964, and "Frightened Citizen" to Brown and Kerr, December 11, 1964, Edmund G. Brown papers, Bancroft Library, UC Berkeley.

15. On Reagan and the conservative backlash against the Berkeley revolt, see Gerard J. De Groot, "Ronald Reagan and Student Unrest in California, 1966–1970,"

Pacific Historical Review 65, 1 (1996): 107–29; W. J. Rorabaugh, "The FSM, Berkeley Politics, and Ronald Reagan," in Cohen and Zelnik, eds., *The Free Speech Movement*, 511–18; Matthew Dallek, *The Right Moment: Ronald Reagan's First Victory and the Decisive Turning Point in American Politics* (New York: Free Press, 2000), 189–96; Michael Flamm, *Law and Order: Street Crime, Civil Unrest, and the Crisis of Liberalism* (New York: Columbia University Press, 2005), 72–74. On the crisis of liberalism and the New Left, see Rick Perlstein, "Who Owns the Sixties? The Opening of a Scholarly Generation Gap," *Lingua Franca*, May-June 1996, 30–37; Allen J. Matusow, *The Unraveling of America: A History of Liberalism in the 1960s* (New York: Harper and Row, 1984). Also see Michael W. Flamm and David Steigerwald, *Debating the 1960s: Liberal, Conservative, and Radical Perspectives* (Lanham, Md.: Rowman & Littlefield, 2008), 1–98.

16. Mario Savio, "Resisting Reaganism and War in Central America" (speech at FSM twentieth-anniversary commemoration [hereafter FSM-20], October 2, 1984, Berkeley), in Robert Cohen, ed., "The FSM and Beyond: Berkeley Student Protest and Social Change in the 1960s" (unpublished anthology, 1994, in author's possession), 53–55 (the full text of this speech can be found in part IV of *Freedom's Orator*); Goines, *The Free Speech Movement*, 237; Mario Savio, "Beyond the Cold War," *Daily Californian*, October 1, 1984; Mario Savio, "Beyond the Cold War: An Education in Politics" (unpublished memoir outline, copy in author's possession), 31–40. Doug Rossinow makes an important point in finding that historians sympathetic to the New Left who wrote in the conservative 1980s and 1990s sought to valorize sixties radicalism by depicting New Leftists as not revolutionaries but reformers who "simply wanted to improve American society, not destroy it," ignoring the revolutionary rhetoric and self-identification of the New Left itself (Rossinow, "The New Left: Democratic Reformers or Left-Wing Revolutionaries?" 94–95). In Savio's case it seems simplistic to argue for an either/or frame of reform or revolution since his fame derived from his work in radical-led movements that championed major reforms—civil rights off campus, free speech on campus—but the tactics and implications of those movements were viewed as revolutionary, especially by their critics. Savio's radically egalitarian vision for America was a form of democratic socialism, which in a capitalist society does qualify as revolutionary. It is only if one defines revolution as involving violence and adherence to Marxist-Leninism that Savio would certainly not qualify.

17. With so little biographical work on Savio, most retrospective writing on him is in the form of memorials published shortly after his death. See Arthur Gatti, "Mario Savio's Religious Influences and Origins," *Radical History Review* 71 (1998): 122–32; Mike Parker, "Mario Savio, 1942–1996," *Against the Current*, January-February 1997, 49–50; Louise Dunlap, "'Carry It On' for Mario Savio, 1942–1996," *Peacework*, February 1997, 12–13; "Remembering Mario Savio," *Tikkun*, January/February 1997, 27–30; Barbara Garson, "Me and Mario down by the Schoolyard," *Progressive*, January 1997, 24–25. Also see the historical essays and memoirs on Savio in Cohen and Zelnik, eds., *The Free Speech Movement*, 449–84, 519–70, and the excellent oral history by Bret Eynon, "Community in Motion: The Free Speech Movement, Civil Rights, and the Roots of the New Left," *Oral History Review* 17, 1 (1989): 39–69.

18. Mario Savio, "Beyond the Cold War: The Education of an American Radical" unpublished memoir outline, copy in author's possession; Savio, "Beyond the Cold War: An Education in Politics." Note that these two sources are similar outlines for

the memoir that Savio intended to write. Both are undated but appear to have been prepared sometime around 1985. Also see Mario Savio, "FSM Leader: Beyond the Cold War," *Daily Californian*, October 1, 1984 (reprinted in part IV of *Freedom's Orator*).

19. John Downton Hazlet, *My Generation: Collective Autobiography and Identity Politics* (Madison: University of Wisconsin Press, 1998), 37–150; Gitlin, *The Sixties*, 11–126.

20. Savio, "Beyond the Cold War: An Education in Politics," 4–14.

21. "The University Has Become a Factory" (excerpts of Jack Fincher's interview of Mario Savio), *Life*, February 22, 1965, 100; Art Gatti, interview by author, October 1, 2004, New York, transcript in author's possession, 1–6.

22. Mario Savio, telephone interview by Ronald Schatz, August 13, 1996, transcript in author's possession, 15.

23. Mario Savio, "Speech for an Anniversary," *Threepenny Review*, Summer 1995, 2, available online at http://www.threepennyreview.com/samples/savio_su95 .html (reprinted in part IV of *Freedom's Orator*); Mario Savio, "Thirty Years Later: Reflections on the FSM," in Cohen and Zelnik, eds., *The Free Speech Movement*, 59; Gatti, "Mario Savio's Religious Influences and Origins," 122–32. On other connections between Catholicism and Left activism in this era, see James R. Barrett, "The Blessed Virgin Made Me a Socialist: An Experiment in Catholic Autobiography and the Historical Understanding of Race and Class," in Nick Salvatore, ed., *Faith and the Historian: Catholic Perspectives* (Urbana: University of Illinois Press 2007), 117–47.

24. Doug McAdam, *Freedom Summer* (New York: Oxford University Press, 1988), 161–240.

25. Mario Savio and Michael Rossman, interview by Doug Giles, December 1994, Berkeley, transcript in author's possession, 7.

26. Savio used the term *hyperdemocracy* to describe the intensely democratic ethos that he imbibed as part of the Freedom Summer Project and which the FSM embodied. This was a form of self-government that went way beyond mainstream politics in seeking to ensure full participation in decision making and leadership and to empower community members as activists rather than to reduce them to passive constituents. In the FSM this led to a consensus mode of decision making, which was thought to be more inclusive than mere majority rule since it would avoid having a losing minority coerced by majority will. Other examples of hyperdemocracy include a structure based on committees rather than a single president leading the group; the explicit emphasis that no one should feel themselves to be out of the movement even if they disagreed with the tactical decisions that were made; and a strong interest in maximizing student participation in the movement, so that both other student organizations and students unaffiliated with any campus group would be represented on the FSM's executive committee. This was part of the New Left political tradition that historians have referred to as *participatory democracy*, but in this book I use Savio's term, *hyperdemocracy*, because it better captures the intensity of this democratic faith, how distinctive it was from conventional democratic forms, and how exhausting and exhilarating it could be in practice. See Mario Savio interview by Brett Eynon, San Francisco, March 5, 1985, 55–57, transcript in author's possession; Mario Savio interview by Robert Cohen and David Pickell, Berkeley, September 29, 1984, 5–7, transcript in author's possession. On the New Left tradition of participatory democracy, see James Miller, *Democracy Is in the Streets: From Port Huron to the Siege*

of Chicago (Cambridge: Harvard University Press, 1994); Francesca Polleta, *Freedom Is an Endless Meeting: Democracy in American Social Movements* (Chicago: University of Chicago Press, 2004), 120–48.

27. The long historical silence about leadership was the legacy of what Tom Hayden terms the New Left's "anti-leader," anti-bureaucratic organizational model, which made life difficult for sixties student protest leaders. See Tom Hayden, *Reunion: A Memoir* (New York: Collier, 1988), 44–45. On the limits of New Left thought about leadership, which left the movement ill-prepared to handle the complexities of dealing with the media, see Gitlin, *The Whole World Is Watching*, 146–78.

28. Michael Rossman, remarks at memorial service for Mario Savio, UC Berkeley, December 8, 1996, transcript in author's possession, 15. Memorials to Savio were held on the Berkeley campus, at Sonoma State University (where he had worked as a lecturer), and in his hometown of New York City.

29. Mario Savio, "The Berkeley Knowledge Factory," *New Politics*, Summer 2005, 75–81. Note that this radical critique of education was a minority view on the Berkeley campus and that the critique grew out of the student rebellion but did not cause it. See Robert Cohen, "This Was *Their* Fight and *They* Had to Fight It: The FSM's Non-radical Rank and File," in Cohen and Zelnik, eds., *The Free Speech Movement*, 260–61.

30. Perlstein, "Who Owns the Sixties?" 32–37. On the violent wing of the late New Left, see Jeremy Varon, *Bringing the War Home: The Weather Underground and the Red Army Faction, and Revolutionary Violence in the Sixties and Seventies* (Berkeley: University of California Press, 2004).

31. Mario Savio, "The Free Speech Movement and the Rhetoric of the Student Movement of the 1960s" (speech at SUNY New Paltz, November 14, 1985, transcript in author's possession), 7–10.

32. Isaac Kramnick and Theodore J. Lowi, eds., *American Political Thought: A Norton Anthology* (New York: W. W. Norton, 2009), 1281–523. Writings selected from the student Left of the 1960s for this anthology included SDS' Port Huron Statement, Savio's "An End to History," SNCC's Statement of Purpose, Stokely Carmichael's "Toward Black Liberation," and Jerry Rubin's "A Yippie Manifesto." From the student right of the sixties the Sharon Statement was included. This is not to say, however, that student activism became extinct after the 1960s; rather, it never came close to the scale of the sixties either politically or intellectually. On post-sixties activism, see Philip G. Altbach and Robert Cohen, "American Student Activism: The Post-Sixties Transformation," in Philip G. Altbach, ed., *Student Political Activism: An International Reference Handbook* (New York: Greenwood Press, 1989), 463–70; David Yamane, *Student Movements for Multiculturalism: Challenging the Curricular Color Line in Higher Education* (Baltimore: Johns Hopkins University Press, 2001); Robert A. Rhoads, *Freedom's Web: Student Activism in the Age of Cultural Diversity* (Baltimore: Johns Hopkins University Press, 1998).

33. Gitlin, *The Whole World Is Watching*, 177–78.

34. Suzanne Goldberg, "Mario: Personal and Political," in Cohen and Zelnik, eds., *The Free Speech Movement*, 557–62; Suzanne Goldberg, interview by author, May 7, 2004, New York City.

35. Lynne Hollander Savio, interview by author, June 13, 2005, New York City, 1–7.

36. Savio, "Resisting Reaganism," 53–55. On American student politics in the Reagan era, see Altbach and Cohen, "American Student Activism: The Post-Sixties Transformation," 463–70. For evidence suggesting that Savio and the other FSM

veterans resembled many activists of their generation in maintaining their egalitarian political views well into the 1980s, see Jack Whalen and Richard Flacks, *Beyond the Barricades: The Sixties Generation Grows Up* (Philadelphia: Temple University Press, 1989), 112–283; Doug McAdam, *Freedom Summer* (New York: Oxford University Press, 1988), 199–240.

37. Savio, "Resisting Reaganism," 54–55.

38. Ibid., 53–54.

39. Mario Savio, interview by Robert Cohen and David Pickell, September 29, 1984, Berkeley, transcript in author's possession, 16–19.

40. *San Francisco Chronicle*, October 3, 1984; *Time*, October 15, 1984, 87.

41. Reginald Zelnik, remarks at Mario Savio's funeral, November 9, 1996, 9–10, Sebastopol, California, transcript in author's possession; Lynne Hollander Savio, e-mail to author, March 10, 2004; Jonah Raskin, "Mario Savio's Second Act: The 1990s," in Cohen and Zelnik, eds., *The Free Speech Movement*, 519–30.

42. On the idea that 1960s America experienced the political and cultural equivalent of a civil war, with contending sides sometimes viewing each other as enemies deserving of punishment, even violent repression, see Maurice Isserman and Michael Kazin, *America Divided: The Civil War of the 1960s* (New York: Oxford University Press, 2000), 1–5.

43. Probably the most widely circulated of these attacks on the sixties rebellions—and their impact on campus—was made in Allan Bloom's bestseller, *The Closing of the American Mind* (New York: Simon and Schuster, 1987), 313–35. For Savio's rebuttal to Bloom, see Mario Savio, "The Second Generation" (Sidwell Friends School graduation speech, Washington, D.C., June 10, 1988, copy in author's possession), 2–12. The full text of this speech appears in part IV of *Freedom's Orator*.

44. The political crises and mass protest movement of the 1960s made this a decade that towered over the preceding and succeeding decades in generating memorable dissident oratory. This can be seen in a recent collection of historic speeches, which included three dissident speeches from the 1950s and one from the 1970s, but ten from the 1960s—including five by Martin Luther King Jr., two by Robert F. Kennedy, one by Malcolm X, and one by Mario Savio. See Widmer, *American Speeches: Political Oratory from Abraham Lincoln to Bill Clinton*, xiv–xv.

45. Savio, "The Second Generation."

46. Maurice Isserman and Michael Kazin, "The Failure and Success of the New Radicalism," in Steve Fraser and Gary Gerstle, eds., *The Rise and Fall of the New Deal Order, 1930–1980* (Princeton: Princeton University Press, 1990), 214–15; Isserman and Kazin, *America Divided*, 294–300; James T. Patterson, "The Rise of Rights and Rights Consciousness, 1930s–1970s," in Bryon E. Shafer and Anthony J. Badger, eds., *Contesting Democracy: Substance and Structure in American Political History, 1775–2000* (Lawrence: University of Kansas Press, 2001), 210–19; James T. Patterson, *Grand Expectations: The United States, 1945–1974* (New York: Oxford University Press, 1996), 787–90; Van Gosse, "Post-Modern America: A New Democratic Order in the Second Gilded Age," in Van Gosse and Richard Moser, eds., *The World the Sixties Made: Politics and Culture in Recent America* (Philadelphia: Temple University Press, 2003), 13–15, 24–33; Beth Bailey, "The Sexual Revolution: Was It Revolutionary?" in David Farber and Beth Bailey, *The Columbia Guide to the 1960s* (New York: Columbia University Press, 2001), 134–41; Eric Foner, *The Story of American Freedom* (New York: W. W. Norton, 1998), 275–305.

Some historians, most notably Arthur Marwick in *The Sixties: Cultural Revolution in Great Britain, France Italy, and the United States* (Oxford: Oxford University Press, 1998), have divided politics and culture into separate spheres, arguing that this turbulent era failed to change the structure of political or economic power but instead yielded a cultural revolution in lifestyles, the family, and individual freedom. While the sixties' impact on culture was massive, as Marwick stresses, this view underestimates political change wrought by the rights revolution. The Civil Rights Act and the Voting Rights Act spelled an end to Jim Crow, yielding unprecedented black political participation—a political revolution without which Obama's rise to the White House would not have been possible. For an international history that does more to connect the cultural and political changes wrought by the sixties, see Gerd-Rainer Horn, *The Spirit of '68: Rebellions in Western Europe and North America, 1956–1976* (New York: Oxford University Press, 2007).

47. Savio, "Thirty Years Later," 58–59.

48. Savio, "The Free Speech Movement and the Rhetoric of the Student Movement," 2–10; Leon Litwack, "On the Dedication of the Mario Savio Steps" (speech at UC Berkeley, December 3, 1997, transcript in author's possession).

49. Stew Albert, "Remembering Mario," *Tikkun*, January–February 1997, 29; Marshall Ganz, interview by author, September 30, 2005, Cambridge, Mass., 13; Jack Weinberg, interview by author, May 19, 2005, Chicago, 4, 28–29; Barbara Garson, "Me and Mario Down by the Schoolyard: Reflections of the Free Speech Movement," *Progressive*, January 1997, 25; Robert Scheer, "The Man Who Stopped the Machine," *Los Angeles Times*, November 12, 1996.

50. Mario Savio, "The Activist's Dream" (memoir outline, 1995, copy in author's possession).

Chapter 1

1. Mario Savio, "Beyond the Cold War: An Education in Politics" (memoir outline, n.d., copy in author's possession), 5.

2. Savio, "Thirty Years Later," 57; Savio interview by Schatz, 3; Hollander Savio interview, 1.

3. Mario Savio, "Starlight," unpublished autobiographical fragment, c. 1990, copy in author's possession; Savio, "The Activist's Dream"; Mario Savio, journal kept in Italy, May 1995.

4. Mario Savio, "Beyond the Cold War: The Education of an American Radical," 1. Mario Savio, interview by Bret Eynon, March 5, 1985, San Francisco, copy of transcript in author's possession, 15.

5. Mario Savio, undated outline for memoir (possibly c. 1985), 3. This is a shorter version of the two handwritten "Beyond the Cold War" memoir outlines.

6. Mario Savio, interview by Doug Giles, 7; Mario Savio, "Sadness on Leaving Home" (chapter from unpublished autobiography, c. 1994), 10–11; Art Gatti, interview by author, October 1, 2004, New York, 2.

7. Savio, "Sadness on Leaving Home," 11. Savio recalled: "I waged war on this disability [the stammer] taking every opportunity in school for public speaking." Savio, "Beyond the Cold War: The Education of an American Radical," 3.

8. Savio, "Sadness on Leaving Home," 11; Savio, "Beyond the Cold War: The Education of an American Radical," 3; Hollander Savio interview, 4.

9. Savio, "Beyond the Cold War: The Education of an American Radical," 1. The latest research indicates that stutterers are physiologically inclined to have speech problems. But speech researchers and speech therapists believe that psychological factors can activate speech defects among children who are physiologically disposed to have such problems. See Neil Gordon, "Stuttering: Incidence and Causes," *Developmental Medicine and Child Neurology* 44 (2002): 278–82.

10. Savio, "Beyond the Cold War: An Education in Politics," 7.

11. Savio interview by Eynon, 2–4.

12. Mario Savio, speech at Dividing Line Conference, September 1996, transcript in author's possession, 1; Mario Savio, autobiographical notes for ACLU speech, February 24, 1995. Savio changed his name back from Bob to Mario when he had to register for the draft, and found that his birth certificate had his first name as Mario. See Savio, "The Berkeley Knowledge Factory," 75.

13. Savio, "Sadness on Leaving Home," 7; also see Gatti, "Mario Savio's Religious Influences and Origins," 122–32.

14. Savio interview by Schatz, 5–6.

15. Mario Savio, "The Varieties of Confession: A Look Backward," unpublished essay, c. 1990 (copy in author's possession), 1–3.

16. Savio, "Sadness on Leaving Home," 10.

17. *Bee Line* (Martin Van Buren High School newspaper), May 9, 1960; Savio, "Sadness on Leaving Home," 5–10; Florence Feldman-Wood, interview by author, August 24, 2005, Boston, 2, 5.

18. Savio, "Sadness on Leaving Home," 10.

19. Ibid., 10–13. Manhattan would sweeten Savio's scholarship offer, converting the partial scholarship offered him after the NSF Math-Science Institute into a full scholarship after he became a Westinghouse finalist.

20. Savio, "Sadness on Leaving Home," 10.

21. Ibid., 10–12.

22. Ibid., 12–13.

23. Ibid., 7–8, 13; Savio interview by Schatz, 12.

24. Savio, "Sadness on Leaving Home," 11.

25. Hollander Savio interview, 2–3. The documentation on this abuse is not extensive since Savio never spoke or wrote publicly about it. But from what he told Suzanne Goldberg, his first wife, and, Lynne Hollander Savio, his second wife, there is no question that the abuse incident occurred and that Mario reported it to his parents at the time. So this is not a case of recovered memory—i.e., recalling an incident of child abuse that trauma blocked until adulthood. Mario's only issue with memory concerned whether there were more episodes of abuse than the one that he remembered so clearly; he suspected that there were (Lynne Hollander Savio, e-mail to author, January 14, 2009; Suzanne Goldberg e-mail to the author, March 18 and 24, 2009). The one public speech in which Savio touched on child abuse was his talk "Their Values and Ours," at the FSM's thirtieth-anniversary commemoration, Berkeley, December 2, 1994 (henceforth FSM-30). Even here he did not mention his own victimization, but used abuse as a metaphor, comparing the horrific pictures of Jews murdered by the Nazis to the unspeakable crime of child molesting: "For me as a kid growing up it was like some secret pictures you might find, say, in your uncle's drawer that show that he's really a child molester or something. This is heavy-duty" (Savio, "Speech for an Anniversary," reprinted in part IV of *Freedom's Orator*). Note

that Mario's vulnerability to depression may have had biological roots as well, since his mother also suffered from this malady (Lynne Hollander Savio, e-mail to author, February 14, 2009).

26. Mario Savio to Art Gatti, c. 1965, copy in author's possession.

27. The autobiographical tape Savio made, in which he described the abuse incident, was recorded in Berkeley in the late 1960s, intended for the memoir he was planning to write; Goldberg e-mail to the author, March 18 and 24, 2009 (tape in possession of Suzanne Goldberg); Bettina Aptheker, interview by author, Santa Cruz, California, October 9, 2004, 27–28.

According to Suzanne Goldberg, Savio kept this abuse issue private, telling only his therapist and her about it during the years they were married. Thus while we tend to depict the 1960s as a time of expanding freedom of speech—and Savio was a symbol of that freedom—even he did not feel free to discuss this difficult and painful subject openly (Goldberg e-mail to author, March 27, 2009).

28. Aptheker interview by author, 27–28.

29. Lynne Hollander Savio, e-mail to author, May 18, 2008. His father's "dominance and hostility" left Mario feeling "always under foot, in my father's way," beset by "fears" and a "crushing" social "impotence," Savio to Cheryl Stevenson, August 12, 1964, copy in author's possession and also available at UC Berkeley's Bancroft Library.

30. Hollander Savio interview, 1–2.

31. Savio, "Sadness on Leaving Home," 14.

32. Savio, "Beyond the Cold War: An Education in Politics," 13; Savio interview by Eynon, 3–9; Savio, "Thirty Years Later," 59.

33. Savio interview by Eynon, 9.

34. Savio, "Sadness on Leaving Home," 3; Savio interview by Schatz, 9–11.

35. Savio, "Sadness on Leaving Home," 7.

36. Ibid., 8–9.

37. Ibid., 9.

38. Savio, "Thirty Years Later," 59; Savio interview by Schatz, 6.

39. "Sadness on Leaving Home," 2.

40. Savio, "Beyond the Cold War: An Education in Politics," 13–14.

41. Savio interview by Schatz, 7–8. On Vatican II and the reform impulse in American Catholicism, see Philip Gleason, "Catholicism and Cultural Change in the 1960s," in Ronald Weber, ed., *America in Change: Reflections on the 60s and 70s* (Notre Dame, Ind.: University of Notre Dame Press, 1972), 91–107; Patrick Allitt, *Catholic Intellectuals and Conservative Politics in America, 1950–1985* (Ithaca: Cornell University Press, 1993), 122–60.

42. Savio, "The Second Generation," 6.

43. Ibid.

44. Ibid., 7.

45. Savio interview by Schatz, 21–22.

46. Savio interview by Eynon, 5–6; Savio, "Sadness on Leaving Home," 4. Savio's favorite high school days were Jewish holidays because few students attended but most teachers he admired did, including Jewish ones. It was then that he "got to experience…non-working-class adults in…the same relaxed way in which their own children must have experienced them." He was "on the lookout" for opportunities to meet teachers "out of role," connecting to adults more educated than his parents, "an

alternative place to stand" from that of his blue-collar family and his domineering father.

47. Savio, "Sadness on Leaving Home," 4.

48. Ibid., 2 This search for alternative mentors persisted. During the 1990s, as he became closer to Leon Wofsy, a senior professor at Berkeley with Old Left roots, Savio told him "that he never had a relationship with his father" and asked Wofsy if he would be his godfather (Wofsy interview, 7).

49. Savio, "Sadness on Leaving Home," 5–7.

50. Mario Savio, interview by Max Heirich, June 8, 1865, Berkeley, transcript in author's possession, 13, 15–16.

51. Savio, "Sadness on Leaving Home," 11.

52. Ibid., 16.

53. [Mario] Robert Savio, "Valedictory," graduation speech at Martin Van Buren High School, 1960, in author's possession, 1–3. The full text of the speech appears in part IV of *Freedom's Orator*.

54. Ibid., 1–2.

55. Savio, "Beyond the Cold War: An Education in Politics," 8, 11; Savio interview by Eynon, 12.

56. Savio, "Valedictory," 2.

57. Ibid, 2; Savio, "Thirty Years Later," 61–62; Savio interview by Eynon, 12.

58. Savio, "Thirty Years Later," 57; Savio, "Beyond the Cold War: An Education in Politics," 10–12; Savio, "The Second Generation," 4.

59. Savio interview by Eynon, 7–8.

60. Savio, "Beyond the Cold War: An Education in Politics," 36–45.

61. Savio, "The Second Generation," 4.

62. Ibid.

63. Savio, "Thirty Years Later," 57–72.

Chapter 2

1. Savio, "Beyond the Cold War: The Education of an American Radical," 3; Savio, "Beyond the Cold War: An Education in Politics," 16.

2. Savio interview by Schatz, 13.

3. Savio interview by Eynon, 10. This study of the ancient world had such an impact on Mario that he titled the chapter on Manhattan College that he wrote for his memoir "A Year with the Greeks" (n.d., copy in author's possession).

4. Mario Savio, "Why I Left Manhattan College" (unpublished essay, n.d., copy in author's possession). This is almost certainly an outline for the later "A Year with the Greeks." Savio summarized his estrangement from the Church and the pain it caused him by noting that he was "not receiving the sacraments nor even attending mass. Masturbation and guilt about everything" ("The Activist's Dream," 3).

5. Savio, "Why I Left Manhattan College."

6. Savio, "Sadness on Leaving Home," 16.

7. Savio, "A Year with the Greeks," 1.

8. Savio interview by Schatz, 15, 17; Art Gatti, speech at memorial service for Mario Savio, New York City, December 8, 1996, videotape in author's possession.

Some Queens College movement veterans claim that Savio in his year as a student there participated in a brief strike protesting a campus ban on Communist speakers. See Seth Cagin and Philip Dray, *We Are Not Afraid: The Story of Goodman, Schwerner, and Chaney and the Civil Rights Campaign of Mississippi* (New York: Macmillan, 1983), 103–4. But Savio never mentioned participating in this Queens protest, even when he returned to Queens in 1964 to deliver a speech on the struggle for free speech at Berkeley, so that strike seems not to have played any role in his political development.

9. Savio interview by Eynon, 5; Savio interview by Heirich, 6–10; Gatti, "Mario Savio's Religious Influences and Origins," 129–30; Savio interview by Schatz, 18–20; [Mario] Bob Savio to Art Gatti, July 4, 1963, copy in author's possession.

10. "LI Volunteers Find Elation and Deflation in Mexico," *Long Island Press*, clipping summer 1963, copy in author's possession; Savio interview by Schatz, 18–19; Savio interview by Heirich, 6. Also see Nancy Scheper-Hughes, "Taxco, Mexico, Summer 1963: Queens College Mexico Volunteers—A Few Scattered Memories," copy in author's possession.

11. Savio interview by Schatz, 20–21.

12. "LI Volunteers Find Elation and Deflation in Mexico"; "Our Collegians in Mexico," *Long Island Sunday Press*, August 25, 1963.

13. "LI Volunteers Find Elation and Deflation in Mexico."

14. Ibid.; Gatti, "Mario Savio's Religious Influences and Origins," 130.

15. Scheper-Hughes, "Taxco Mexico, Summer 1963," 5. Savio learned in Mexico that when he spoke Spanish he could do so without the stammer that afflicted him in English (Art Gatti, interview by author, February 13, 2009, New York).

16. Savio interview by Heirich, 9–10; Gatti interview by author, October 1, 2004, New York, 5–8; Gatti, "Mario Savio's Religious Influences and Origins," 129–30; [Mario] Bob Savio to Art Gatti, August 26, 1963, copy in author's possession.

17. Savio interview by Eynon, 10–11; Savio, "Beyond the Cold War: An Education in Politics," 17–18.

18. Savio to Gatti, August 26, 1963; Savio interview by Heirich, 5–6, 13.

19. Savio interview by Heirich, 40–41.

20. Ibid., 29–36.

21. [Mario] Bob Savio to Art Gatti, December 20, 1963, copy in author's possession.

22. Savio interview by Heirich, 36.

23. Ibid., 32–33.

24. Ibid., 35.

25. Your son [Mario Savio] to Dad, January 10, 1964, copy in author's possession. As Mario transitioned from using Bob to Mario as his first name, he signed his letter to his parents "Your son." In this letter to his father Mario noted, "I've felt it necessary to be true to myself, without really ever knowing who Mario (Robert? Bob?) Savio really is."

26. Ibid.

27. Savio interview by Heirich, 29–30, 34, 40–43; Savio, "Thirty Years Later," 63–64.

28. Savio interview by Heirich, 29–30, 34. Mario's brother, Tom, believed that there were maternal roots to Mario's concern about racial justice, since during the World War II era Dora had protested when she discovered that a fellow worker in the dime store in which she was employed was paid less than her simply because she was black. Yet Mario never told this story, and expressed surprise when he learned well after the

1960s that his mother was disappointed that the Catholic Church had not been more "in the forefront of the civil rights movement. I didn't even know that she'd noticed these things." This suggests that Mario was unaware of her sympathy with the civil rights struggle and did not trace his involvement in the movement to her influence. Tom Savio, remarks at Mario Savio's funeral, November 9, 1996, 12; Savio interview by Eynon, 26.

29. Savio interview by Eynon, 12; Savio interview by Giles, 4.

30. Savio interview by Schatz, 33.

31. Savio interview by Eynon, 18–19; Savio, "Thirty Years Later," 61–63; Savio interview by Cohen and Pickell, 2, 8, 12.

32. Savio interview by Heirich, 45.

33. Sam Bader, interview by David McDougal, October 10, 2004, Berkeley, transcript in author's possession, 1; also see Bernard Timberg, interview by author, April 11, 2005, New York.

34. Savio interview by Heirich, 40.

35. Ibid., 46–47; Savio, "Thirty Years Later," 64. Of their shared religious background, Stevenson recalled that when she and Mario drove to San Francisco for civil rights work, "we would sing the Mass the whole way in Latin. That was both of our pasts." She, like Savio, was a philosophy major when they first met. Cheryl Stevenson, telephone interview by author, December 19, 2005, 1–2.

36. Savio, "Thirty Years Later," 64.

37. Savio interview by Heirich, 40–46.

38. Ibid., 49.

39. Ibid.

40. Ibid., 47, 49.

41. Savio, "Thirty Years Later," 64.

42. Savio interview by Heirich, 52.

43. Savio interview by Eynon, 21.

44. Ibid.

45. Savio interview by Heirich, 47.

46. Ibid.; Mario Savio, "Defendant Statement," March 1964, copy in author's possession.

47. Savio, "Defendant Statement."

48. Savio interview by Eynon, 21.

49. Savio speech at the Dividing Line conference, San Francisco, September 1996, 1.

50. Savio, "Thirty Years Later," 63; Jo Freeman, "From 'Freedom Now' to Free Speech: The FSM's Roots in the Bay Area Civil Rights Movement," in Cohen and Zelnik, eds., The Free Speech Movement, 79–82.

51. Weinberg interview by author, 6–8.

52. Mario Savio to dean of the College of Letters and Sciences, May 20, 1964, Chancellor's Papers, University Archives, Bancroft Library, UC Berkeley (hereafter Chancellor's Papers).

53. Weinberg interview by author, 8.

54. Savio interview by Eynon, 16–17; We Accuse (Berkeley: Diablo Press, 1965), 34.

55. Savio interview by Eynon, 16–17.

56. Ibid., 18.

57. Ibid.; Taylor Branch, *Parting the Waters: America in the King Years, 1954–1963* (New York: Simon and Schuster, 1988).

58. Mario Savio to Joseph Savio, January 10, 1964.

59. Your son [Mario Savio] to Dora Savio, May 26, 1964, copy in author's possession.

60. Mario Savio, interview by Mark Kitchell (c. 1984), copy of transcript in author's possession; Robin Dellabough, "A Conversation with Mario Savio and Bettina Aptheker," *California Monthly*, December 1984, 18, 20. Mario was not consistent in his retrospective characterizations of his political orientation in 1963–64, telling Dellabough he had been merely a "small d" democrat, but later telling his colleagues he'd been a "libertarian socialist" in these early Berkeley days (Mario Savio, notes for a speech to the Sonoma State University Philosophy Club, April 20, 1993). This likely signifies that, though not ideological, he had by 1964 developed a moral critique of capitalism, a system whose hierarchies and class inequities offended his democratic sensibilities. That would explain his becoming a member—though an inactive one—of the Socialist Party. As to why he seemed to shy away from the socialist label back then, it is likely due to both his fear of being Red-baited and having his democratic, libertarian socialist inclinations mistaken for ideological politics. It would take a non-ideological movement, the civil rights struggle, to draw Savio into deep and sustained activism, since this spoke to him in a way that a Left political party or ideological group never could.

61. Mario Savio, "FSM Leader: Beyond the Cold War," *Daily Californian*, October 1, 1984, reprinted in Part IV of *Freedom's Orator*.

62. Savio interview by Heirich, 57–58.

63. Ibid.; Weinberg interview by author, 19.

64. Savio interview by Eynon, 22.

65. Ibid.

66. Ibid., 23.

67. Ibid., 24–25; Savio, "Beyond the Cold War: An Education in Politics," 18–19; Savio, "Beyond the Cold War: The Education of an American Radical," 5–6.

Chapter 3

1. Savio interview by Cohen and Pickell, 35; Clayborne Carson, *In Struggle: SNCC and the Black Awakening of the 1960s* (Cambridge: Harvard University Press, 1981), 48–49. Louis Allen, the black witness to this killing, was also murdered before he could testify against Lee's killer.

2. Taylor Branch, *Pillar of Fire: America in the King Years, 1963–1965* (New York: Simon and Schuster, 1998), 50–51; Mary King, *Freedom Song: A Personal Story of the 1960 Civil Rights Movement* (New York: William Morrow, 1987), 144, 146, 152.

3. On the decisive role that the need to combat racial terror played in Moses's decision to launch the Freedom Summer Project, see Branch, *Pillar of Fire*, 223. On the voter registration goals for the project, see Aaron Henry and Constance Curry, *Aaron Henry, The Fire Ever Burning* (Jackson: University Press of Mississippi, 2000), 164–65; Fred Powledge, *Free at Last? The Civil Rights Movement and the People Who Made It* (New York: Harper, 1991), 563. Freedom Summer was a crucial chapter, but

only part of the larger history of the freedom struggle in Mississippi. SNCC-led organizing efforts both before and after that summer—together with the Voting Rights Act and mobilizations by local African Americans—had a major impact in securing political rights and a degree of power for black Mississippians. By 1971 black voter registration surged to 68 percent of the eligible black population in Mississippi, after almost a century of disenfranchisement. In Holmes County, where Savio did his voter registration work, black registration, a miniscule 20 in 1964, surged to 6,300 by 1967—more than 70 percent of the black voting-age population of that county. Savio and his fellow southwest Mississippi volunteers contributed to "the rebirth of the movement in McComb," which "in the face of the most violent and sustained campaign of intimidation and terror in the state…was a major achievement of the summer project," as John Dittmer notes in *Local People: The Struggle for Civil Rights in Mississippi* (Urbana: University of Illinois Press, 1995), 270–71. See also Mary Aickin Rothschild, *A Case of Black and White: Northern Volunteers and the Southern Freedom Summers, 1964–1965* (Westport, Conn.: Greenwood Press, 1982), 174–75; Kenneth T. Andrews, *Freedom Is a Constant Struggle: The Mississippi Civil Rights Movement and Its Legacy* (Chicago: University of Chicago Press, 2004), 85; Youth of the Rural Organizing and Cultural Center, *Minds Stayed on Freedom: The Civil Rights Struggle in the Rural South, an Oral History* (Boulder: Westview Press, 1991), 16–17; Charles M. Payne, *I've Got the Light of Freedom: The Organizing Tradition and the Mississippi Freedom Struggle* (Berkeley: University of California Press, 1995).

4. Savio interview by Schatz, 27.

5. Savio interview by Heirich, 10. In emphasizing his desire for community Savio was not alone. This was a major theme among student activists in 1960s America. See Paul Goodman, *Growing Up Absurd* (New York: Vintage, 1960), 216–36; Kenneth Kenniston, *Young Radicals: Notes on Committed Youth* (New York: Harcourt, Brace, and World, 1968), 143–46; Doug Rossinow, *The Politics of Authenticity: Liberalism, Christianity, and the New Left in America* (New York: Columbia University Press, 1998), 72, 78, 82.

6. Savio interview by Schatz, 27.

7. Savio interview by Eynon, 25.

8. Mario Savio application for Mississippi Summer Project, c. spring 1964, copy in author's possession.

9. SNCC evaluation of Mario Savio application for Mississippi Summer Project, c. spring 1964, copy in author's possession.

10. Ibid.

11. Ibid.; Savio interview by Schatz, 29–30.

12. Mario Savio to Dora Savio, May 26, 1964, copy in author's possession.

13. Savio interview by Eynon, 28; Stevenson interview, 4; Howard Zinn, *SNCC: The New Abolitionists* (Boston: Beacon Press, 1965).

14. Savio, "Beyond the Cold War: An Education in Politics," 20; Mario Savio to Cheryl Stevenson, July 3, 1964 (Mario Savio's correspondence from Mississippi to Cheryl Stevenson, recently donated by Stevenson to UC Berkeley's Bancroft Library, is the most complete documentation of his Freedom Summer experience; all citations to Savio-Stevenson letters come from this collection); Sally Belfrage, *Freedom Summer* (University of Virginia Press, 1999), 9–10; Robert Osman, interview by author, August 24 and October 7, 2004, Oakland, California; Ganz interview, 2. Goodman had been

part of the first group of about three hundred civil rights workers who came to Oxford, Ohio on June 15, 1964. After their orientation there to the summer project he, together with veteran civil rights workers Michael Schwerner and James Chaney, traveled to Mississippi. Savio was part of the second group, which came to Oxford a week later and journeyed to Mississippi in late June. See Len Holt, *The Summer That Didn't End* (New York: William Morrow, 1965), 43; Burner, *And Gently He Shall Lead Them*, 156. Also see Howard Ball, *Murder in Mississippi: United States v. Price and the Struggle for Civil Rights* (Lawrence, University of Kansas Press, 2004); William Bradford Huie, *Three Lives for Mississippi* (New York: WCC Press, 1965).

15. Savio interview by Eynon, 28, Burner, *And Gently He Shall Lead Them*, 156–57; Elizabeth Sutherland Martinez, ed., *Letters from Mississippi: Personal Reports from Civil Rights Volunteers of the 1964 Freedom Summer* (Brookline, Mass.: Zephyr Press, 2006), 38; *New York Times*, June 23, 1964.

16. Savio interview by Schatz, 31; Mario Savio, "Beyond the Big Chill: Resistance and Survival" (speech at Columbia University, November 13, 1984, tape in author's possession).

17. Osman interview.

18. Ibid.; Burner, *And Gently He Shall Lead Them*, 51–52.

19. Savio interview by Eynon, 29; Savio interview by Schatz, 31.

20. Savio interview by Eynon, 29.

21. Mario Savio to Cheryl Stevenson, July 3, 1964; Savio interview by Eynon, 30.

22. Andrews, *Freedom Is a Constant Struggle*, 78–80; Ganz interview, 1–2.

23. Andrews, *Freedom Is a Constant Struggle*, 80, 115–16; Payne, *I've Got the Light of Freedom*, 278–80.

24. *Jackson Clarion-Ledger*, June 30, July 9, 21, 22, 24, and 30, 1964; Jeff Woods, *Black Struggle Red Scare: Segregation and Anti-Communism* (Baton Rouge: Louisiana State University Press, 2004), 200; Holt, *The Summer That Didn't End*, 38; *Lexington (Miss.) Advertiser*, July 2 and 30, 1964; *New York Times*, June 29, 1964. After Hazel Brannon, Smith, the editor of Holmes County's *Lexington Advertiser*, criticized the hostile reception the Freedom Summer volunteers received from local white supremacists, the office of the newspaper she owned in Jackson was bombed. See *Lexington Advertiser*, September 3, 1964. On white hostility toward the Freedom Summer volunteers, also see Lee, *For Freedom's Sake*, 77–78, 114; Yasuhiro Katagiri, *The Mississippi Sovereignty Commission: Civil Rights and States' Rights* (Jackson: University Press of Mississippi, 2001), 163–67; Joseph Crespino, *In Search of Another Country: Mississippi and the Conservative Counterrevolution* (Princeton: Princeton University Press, 2007), 120–21.

25. Mario Savio to Cheryl Stevenson, July 5 and 25, 1964.

26. Savio to Cheryl Stevenson, July 25, 1964. On Turnbow, see Payne, *Light of Freedom*, 279; Youth of the Rural Organizing and Cultural Center, *Minds Stayed on Freedom*, 25–26. Savio maintained his commitment to nonviolence, but with racist violence a constant threat, he was not totally consistent on this: he took some comfort in the fact that on occasion the violent white supremacists got a taste of their own medicine. See Savio to Cheryl Stevenson, August 16, 1964.

27. Savio to Cheryl Stevenson, July 3, 1964. Savio was keenly aware, however, of the obstacles to peace and social justice. In the sentence after his lyrical tribute to the "breath of freedom" that the civil rights movement represented (in his July 3 letter to Stevenson), he went on to ask: "But what about Vietnam?"

28. Savio to Cheryl Stevenson, July 25, 1964.

29. Ibid.

30. Ibid.

31. Ibid.

32. Savio to Cheryl Stevenson, July 5 and 25, 1964.

33. Savio to Cheryl Stevenson, July 7, 1964. On the background of this segregationist group, see Neil R. McMillen, *The Citizens' Council: Organized Resistance to the Second Reconstruction* (Urbana: University of Illinois Press, 1994).

34. Savio to Cheryl Stevenson, July 7 and 25, 1964.

35. Savio to Cheryl Stevenson, July 7, 1964.

36. Savio interview by Kitchell, 2; Savio interview by Eynon, 42.

37. Savio interview by Eynon, 42.

38. Savio interview by Kitchell, 3. See "That Long Walk to the Courthouse," in Martinez, ed., *Letters from Mississippi*, 75–101.

39. Savio interview by Eynon, 43; Savio interview by Kitchell, 3. On the use of the word *redish* by blacks attempting to register and the way whites used that mispronunciation to mock them as they sought to disrupt their registration, also see Youth of the Rural Organizing and Cultural Center, *Minds Stayed on Freedom*, 48–49.

40. Savio to Cheryl Stevenson, July 25, 1964.

41. Savio interview by Schatz, 36.

42. Savio interview by Eynon, 43. Also see Savio, "Beyond the Cold War: An Education in Politics," 21.

43. Carson, *In Struggle*, 117. The relative ease of registering black voters for the MFDP's unofficial election as compared to using the official registration process controlled by hostile whites is reflected in the statistics Carson provides: 80,000 registered for the MFDP versus 17,000 who went to the courthouses seeking to register in the general election—and of these 17,000, only 1,600 could actually register during Freedom Summer.

44. Savio to Cheryl Stevenson, July 25, 1964.

45. Ibid.

46. Savio to Cheryl Stevenson, August 1, 1964.

47. Ibid.

48. Savio to Cheryl Stevenson, July 25, 1964; Mario Savio statement to the FBI, July 23, 1964, FBI file 44-2300, report by Joseph B. McAleer and Harold F. Good, Savio FBI files, copy in author's possession.

49. Savio statement to the FBI, July 23, 1964.

50. Robert David Osman statement to the FBI, July 23, 1964, FBI file 44-2300, report by Joseph B. McAleer and Harold F. Good, Savio FBI files.

51. Savio to Cheryl Stevenson, July 25, 1964.

52. Ibid.

53. Savio to Cheryl Stevenson, August 16, 1964. The FBI tracked down this assailant by tracing his license plate number (which Savio had taken down during the assault), identifying him as a Ku Klux Klan member. See SAC Jackson to FBI Director, August 18, 1964, JN-44-68, Savio FBI files. On appeal, the prosecution, hoping to avoid a jury trial, reduced the sentence to a $50 fine plus court costs. See Horace Beckwith FBI field office report 44-68, Jackson, October 15, 1964, FBI file 44-26027.

54. Savio interview by Eynon, 37–38.

55. Osman interview. On the bombing of the Freedom House, also see *New York Times*, July 9, 1964. On the other racist violence in McComb in summer 1964, see David Harris, *Dreams Die Hard: Three Men's Journey Through the Sixties* (New York: St. Martin's Press, 1982), 62–67; Dittmer, *Local People*, 265–71.

56. Savio to Cheryl Stevenson, July 25, 1964.

57. Ibid.

58. Savio interview by Eynon, 39.

59. Osman interview.

60. Savio to Cheryl Stevenson, August 1, 1964. For Savio the racism of McComb reached its most absurd heights in its having a "home for the *blind* with separate entrances for white and colored!" (Savio to Cheryl Stevenson, August 1, 1964). On the Freedom Schools in Mississippi, see Payne, *Light of Freedom*, 301–5; McAdam, *Freedom Summer*, 83–86; Sandra E. Adickes, *The Legacy of a Freedom School* (New York: Palgrave, 2005); Howard Zinn, *Howard Zinn on History* (New York: Seven Stories Press, 2001), 189–201; Wesley Hogan, *Many Minds, One Heart: SNCC's Dream for a New America* (Chapel Hill: University of North Carolina Press, 2007), 63, 57, 167–68, 352, 354.

61. Savio to Cheryl Stevenson, August 1, 1964. There may well have been gendered implications to this reluctance to switch from voter registration work to teaching. Freedom School teaching, as historian Charles Payne explained, "always had relatively low status value…within the movement.…because women did much of the Freedom School work and because it wasn't as dangerous as…Voter Registration [which] was the prestige assignment." Payne, reflecting on the importance of education for black youths in a state that had so neglected them, thought it "tragic" that within the movement teaching "was accorded relatively little respect" (Payne, *Light of Freedom*, 305; McAdam, *Freedom Summer*, 108–9). Though not immune to the male bravado that went with this preference for voter registration work—which is why he hesitated initially to make that switch—Savio quickly transcended it when he agreed to teach, and so was not a captive of this form of sexism. On gender relations, movement sexism, and the roots of second-wave feminism, see Sara Evans, *Personal Politics: The Roots of Women's Liberation in the Civil Right Movement and the New Left* (New York: Vintage, 1980), 3–82. On the McComb Freedom School, see Adickes, *Legacy*, 126–27.

62. Ira Landess, interview by author, October 11, 2007, New York City.

63. Savio to Cheryl Stevenson, August 1 and 4, 1964. On the positive student response to Savio as a teacher in the Freedom School, also see Rothschild, *A Case of Black and White*, 172.

64. Savio to Cheryl Stevenson, August 16, 1964.

65. Ibid.

66. Ibid.

67. Savio interview by Eynon, 39. Pete Seeger visited the McComb Freedom School and, having recently returned from Africa, taught Savio's students South African freedom songs. See Mario Savio to Cheryl Stevenson, August 4, 1964.

68. Savio interview by Eynon, 40. Savio dwelled on this kind of interracial warmth over the summer—the Mississippi black community's embrace of the Freedom Summer volunteers—rather than on tensions between the white movement volunteers and SNCC staffers. On the importance of such unity, see Payne, *I've Got the Light of Freedom*, 306–15. Marshall Ganz confirms Savio's as an accurate representation of the southwest Mississippi group of Freedom Summer volunteers, to which they both

belonged. There was little, if any, tension between this group's black leadership and white volunteers because those leaders, Hollis Watkins and Curtis Hayes, were highly talented and experienced, and headed an especially dedicated core of activists, who had signed up to work in the most dangerous part of the state (Ganz interview, 8–9); David Harris notes that "SNCC's personnel rule was, the more volatile the place, the better the people who ought to be sent; under that logic, assignment to McComb was the highest rating a volunteer could have. McComb had the reputation of a rabid dog. Before the summer was over, two-thirds of the state's 70-odd racial bombings would happen within a half-hour's drive of the place" (Harris, *Dreams Die Hard*, 61). See John Lewis with Michael D'Orso, *Walking with the Wind: A Memoir of the Movement* (New York: Simon and Schuster, 1998), 243, 246. On Hollis Watkins, see Cheryl Lynn Greenberg, ed., *A Circle of Trust: Remembering SNCC* (New Brunswick, Rutgers University Press, 1998), 61–66. On black-white divisions in the movement in parts of the state that were less dangerous, see Paul Cowan, *The Making of an Un-American: A Dialogue with Experience* (New York: Viking Press, 1970), 40.

69. Mario Savio to Cheryl Stevenson, August 16, 1964.

70. Ibid.

71. Savio, "Beyond the Cold War, 21.

72. Savio interview by Eynon, 40, 44–45.

73. Ibid, 27.

74. Mario Savio, "Beyond the Cold War: An Education in Politics," 21. On Freedom Summer's significance, also see McAdam, *Freedom Summer*; Lewis, *Walking with the Wind*, 273; Stokely Carmichael, *Ready for Revolution* (New York: Scribner, 2003), 384–85; Sally Belfrage, *Freedom Summer* (New York: Viking Press, 1965); Huie, *Three Lives for Mississippi*; Martinez, ed., *Letters from Mississippi*; Barbara Ramsby, *Ella Baker and the Black Freedom Movement: A Radical Democratic Vision* (Chapel Hill: University of North Carolina Press, 2003), 299–329; Chana Kai Lee, *For Freedom's Sake: The Life of Fannie Lou Hamer* (Urbana: University of Illinois Press), 74.

75. Savio interview by Cohen and Pickell, 35. For equally upbeat assessments of Freedom Summer's national impact, see Carmichael, *Ready for Revolution*, 384–85; Lewis, *Walking with the Wind*, 273. But for a more critical view of Freedom Summer's impact on SNCC, see King, *Freedom Song*, 523; Forman, *The Making of Black Revolutionaries*, 372.

76. On Ella Baker's influence on Moses and early SNCC, see Robert P. Moses and Charles E. Cobb, Jr., *Radical Equations: Civil Rights from Mississippi to the Algebra Project* (Boston: Beacon Press, 2001), 32–40.

77. Savio, "Beyond the Cold War: The Education of an American Radical," 4; Mario Savio, "The Free Speech Movement and the Rhetoric of the Student Movement," 1, 3.

78. Savio interview by Eynon, 51.

79. Ibid.; Savio, "Free Speech Movement and the Rhetoric of the Student Movement," 3.

80. Savio, "Free Speech Movement and the Rhetoric of the Student Movement," 3.

81. Savio, "Beyond the Cold War: An Education in Politics," 26.

82. Savio to Cheryl Stevenson, August 16, 1964.

83. Stevenson interview by author, 5, 7. Through Freedom Summer Savio's stammer was still strong—so much so that Marshall Ganz characterized it as "defining" and was amazed to learn that so shortly after leaving Mississippi Savio had

overcome his speech defect and become a famous orator (Ganz interview, 3). Even in September 1964, shortly before the FSM emerged, Savio still was afflicted with the stammer (Weinberg interview by author, 27). This does mean Stevenson was wrong about his stammer diminishing, but rather that it had not completely vanished, even after Mississippi. A friend of Savio's recalled him telling her in the mid-1960s that he lost his stammer while fleeing from the police (though he probably said from the Klan) in Mississippi (Florence Feldman-Wood, interview by author, August 24, 2005, Boston, 9).

84. Savio to Cheryl Stevenson, July 25, 1964.

85. Savio, "Thirty Years Later," 65.

86. Savio interview by Heirich, 61. In their brief portraits of Savio, Jo Freeman and Doug McAdam argue that his summer in Mississippi gave him the confidence and single-mindedness to lead the FSM (Jo Freeman, *At Berkeley in the Sixties: The Education of an Activist* [Bloomington: University of Indiana Press, 2004], 156; McAdam, *Freedom Summer*, 165–66). While this is not untrue, both Freeman and McAdam exaggerate the difference between Savio pre- and post-Mississippi. Freeman states that "when he returned [from Mississippi] he was no longer a cautious, inquisitive, do gooder." But Savio pre-Mississippi was *not* cautious; he dropped out of his Catholic college, jettisoned his religious faith, journeyed to Mexico for a summer to do anti-poverty work, and got arrested at a civil rights sit-in. McAdam suggests that Savio was a "pretty shy guy" before the Mississippi trip, when in fact Savio had been president of his student body in high school, done door-to-door organizing in San Francisco's black community, tutored minority students, dominated political discussions among the students who dined together near his Berkeley apartment, and pressed the UC administration not to penalize students who missed classes because of their Sheraton Palace arrest.

87. Savio to Cheryl Stevenson, July 25, 1964. For an argument about how Freedom Summer—and especially the federal government's refusal to stand up to racist terror—radicalized many of the volunteers, see McAdam, *Freedom Summer*, 126–32. Savio's criticism of the FBI for its rosy statements about Mississippi and crime had a firm factual foundation. The FBI report issued that summer termed Mississippi "the most law abiding state in the nation" (*Jackson Clarion-Ledger*, July 21, 1964).

88. Jim Kates, "June 1964," unpublished essay on Freedom Summer, 2007, copy in author's possession, 6.

89. Reebee Garofalo, interview by author, October 1, 2005, Somerville, Mass., 1.

90. Kates, "June 1964," 6. Kates, much like Garofalo, expressed surprise that Savio suddenly overcame his speech defect to deliver an eloquent speech.

91. Savio to Cheryl Stevenson, August 4, 1964. Savio had planned to attend the Democratic Party Convention in Atlantic City to help with the MFDP attempt to get seated there, but his limited finances made this impossible. See Savio to Cheryl Stevenson, August 1, 1964. Note that despite Savio's misgivings about the Democrats, he earnestly lobbied California's Democratic governor, Edmund Brown, on the seating of the MFDP delegation at Atlantic City. From McComb he wrote Brown an impassioned letter asking him to "help free Mississippi!" by supporting the MFDP. Savio was diplomatic, even praising Brown's civil rights record. See Mario Savio to Edmund G. Brown, July 24, 1964, Edmund G. Brown Papers, Bancroft Library. Brown proved a disappointment, lining up with LBJ in advocating a "compromise" on MFDP's right to

be seated at the convention. See Ethan Rarick, *California Rising: The Life and Times of Pat Brown* (Berkeley: University of California Press, 2005), 296.

92. Savio to Cheryl Stevenson, July 25, 1964. Savio was referring in this letter to "the recent tete-tete between Goldwater and Johnson to the effect that neither will make civil rights a great issue" in the presidential race. In this July 1964 meeting, held in the wake of the East Coast ghetto riots, both candidates agreed to avoid inflaming racial passions during the presidential race. See Robert Dallek, *Flawed Giant: Lyndon Johnson and His Times, 1961–1973* (New York: Oxford University Press, 1998), 134–35; *Jackson Clarion-Ledger*, July 21 and 25, 1964.

93. Savio to Cheryl Stevenson, August 4, 1964. Here Savio indicated that he had earlier felt ambivalent back in Berkeley about working with the Democratic Party even on the laudable goal of fair housing.

94. Osman interview.

95. Ibid.

96. Savio, "Beyond the Cold War: The Education of an American Radical," 4; Savio, "The Free Speech Movement and the Rhetoric of the Student Movement," 3–5. On at least one occasion, Savio hedged a bit, giving himself a little of the credit while paying homage to SNCC and the civil rights movement's influence: "*To some degree, I consciously modeled my own rhetorical patterns on the highly concrete style of political speech of the Southern Civil Rights workers*" ("Beyond the Cold War: The Education of an American Radical," 4, emphasis added).

97. Hogan, *Many Minds, One Heart*, 7. The 1988 film *Mississippi Burning*, starring Gene Hackman and Willem Dafoe, film depicted the FBI (which in reality often proved indifferent to the safety of civil rights workers) as anti-racist crusaders. For a far more accurate film on Freedom Summer, see *Freedom on My Mind* (California Newsreel, 1994), produced by Connie Field and Marilyn Mulford.

98. Savio interview by Eynon, 43; Savio interview by Schatz, 36.

99. Osman interview.

100. Savio to Cheryl Stevenson, August 4, 1964.

101. Savio to Cheryl Stevenson, July 25, 1964. For Savio the choice of major was difficult, and was linked to a larger identity problem. He was, as Stevenson, recalled, "floundering around trying to figure out where he belonged in life." Coming out of a strong physics background, he was in the process of switching to philosophy, which was his first Berkeley major. According to Stevenson, "this had to do with the fact that he had all these questions about people and ethics,... stuff that was closer to the church, and closer to relationship issues. But at the same time physics offered a refuge for him—and he'd get very excited about abstract ideas that didn't bear much relationship to our lives in any immediate way" (Stevenson interview by author, 3). Choosing academic specialties is rarely easy, especially in the case of someone like Savio, who excelled in many fields. Making the choice all the more agonizing was that it also had psychological implications, since he "identified science and technology with his father," who had longed to be a chemist, and "the humanities with his mother," who had wanted to be an English teacher. His choice of major and later "vocational conflicts had a great deal to do with his feeling that choosing science was to ally with the father and maleness, choosing humanities was to ally with his mother and femaleness" (Lynne Hollander Savio e-mail to author, May 18, 2008).

102. Savio to Cheryl Stevenson, July 25, 1964.

103. Ganz interview, 3–5. Related to these spiritual concerns, Savio in Mississippi was sorting out his philosophical outlook. Pre-Mississippi, he flirted with radical skepticism as an alternative to his earlier religious faith, and was "on a 'doubt all things' trip, in part fed by analytic philosophy. I tended in my worst moments to believe it's all sense data and that's just a patch of purple." But coming into Mississippi, with its clear conflict of good and evil, cured him of such skepticism, bringing him "into contact with some reality…Mississippi was obviously the proof" (Savio, "Thirty Years Later," 64).

104. Savio to Cheryl Stevenson, July 25, and August 22, 1964. Prone as Savio was to depression, Mississippi did not pull him in that direction. The only time he wrote home feeling depressed that summer was when he had to pause from his activism, as he waited to testify against his assailants in Jackson. There his brief feelings of depression were linked to his childhood rather than to his activism, as the cold, aloof University of Mississippi employee whose Jackson home he was staying in reminded him of his father and the tensions that had made his early home life so difficult and unhappy (Savio to Cheryl Stevenson, August 12 and 16, 1964).
It is striking that Mississippi's psychological impact on him was so positive, especially considering that others in this southern crusade came away traumatized by the racist beatings, bombings, church burnings, and murders that summer. SNCC leader John Lewis noted with regret that such violence transformed some volunteers, who "went down there…idealistic…full of hope, and came out hardened…by the hurt and hatred they saw or suffered.…, wounded…emotionally," displaying "symptoms" of "shell-shocked soldiers…clinical signs of depression" (Lewis, *Walking with the Wind*, 267, 273). This contrast may be due to the fact that only weeks after returning from the South, Savio was hurled into a new struggle, the FSM, and so had no time to reflect on any negative emotions from that tense summer; thus he took away mostly fond memories of Freedom Summer's liberating impact.

Chapter 4

1. Clark Kerr, "Fall of 1964 at Berkeley: Confrontation Yields to Reconciliation," in Cohen and Zelnik, eds., *The Free Speech Movement: Reflections on Berkeley in the 1960s*, 365–66. On the Depression-era origins of Berkeley campus restrictions on free speech, see C. Michael Otten, *University Authority and the Student* (Berkeley: University of California Press, 1970), 108–19; Cohen, *When the Old Left Was Young*, 118–33; Minutes of the Academic Senate, August 27, 1934, and *Academic Personnel Manual*, sec. 010, both in UC Berkeley Archives, Bancroft Library.
Ironically, in the context of UC's history, scarred by the anti-radical purge of the McCarthy era—with its anti-Communist loyalty oath that drove away some of its most liberal and radical faculty—Kerr was something of a reformer. As a faculty member he had been critical of the loyalty oath, and as president of UC in 1963 had lifted the university's ban on Communist speakers. But where allowing such speakers on campus at administration-controlled, faculty-policed forums was a moderate reform compatible with Kerr's brand of liberalism, allowing leftist students or nonstudents on their own to organize political actions from campus and to engage in advocacy there seemed simply too radical. "We did not," Kerr explained, "want the University of California to be perceived as a fortress from which students could plan and prepare to

sally forth to attack society." This formulation makes it sound as if Berkeley's student movement in 1964 was attacking "society," when it was assaulting racism in order to make society more democratic. Clark Kerr, *The Gold and the Blue: A Personal Memoir of the University of California, 1949–1967* (Berkeley: University of California Press, 2001–3), 2:133–35, 140.

2. This activity on the Bancroft strip was the successor to the Sather Gate tradition, which denotes the same type of politicking occurring on city property just outside UC's southern gate since the 1930s. As the campus expanded, its southern entrance moved as well, so in the 1960s that entrance was a block south of Sather Gate, at Bancroft and Telegraph Avenue. In both cases there was more political freedom off campus than on, as only on city property had political advocacy been allowed—a sign of the way the UC administration had constricted liberty in the area it controlled. See Kerr, *The Gold and the Blue*, 2:145.

3. In Kerr's view, the decision by Strong and Vice Chancellor Sherriffs to ban advocacy on the Bancroft strip was "the second greatest administrative blunder...in university history," the first being President Sproul's decision in the cold war years to impose an anti-Communist loyalty oath on the faculty. Kerr, after blaming Strong and Sherriffs, took some measure of responsibility for the free speech crisis by confessing that "I compounded Strong's and Sherriffs's blunder by not countermanding it immediately. This was the third greatest error, one I have regretted ever since and always will" (Kerr, *The Gold and the Blue*, 2:161).

4. Savio interview by Cohen and Pickell, 24.

5. Savio interview by Heirich, 65–66.

6. Savio interview by Schatz, 33; Mario Savio "The Activist's Dream," memoir outline [1995]; Savio, "Thirty Years Later," 61–62.

7. Savio interview by Kitchell, 3.

8. Savio, "Thirty Years Later," 65.

9. Savio interview by Eynon, 47.

10. Savio interview by Kitchell, 4. Note, however, that though Savio's reading of the free speech crisis is centered on the rights of students to advocate for the civil rights movement, some conservatives opposed the ban even though they were not boosters of the civil rights movement, out of a combination of the free speech principle and self-interest, since the ban denied speech rights to those from all parts of the political spectrum. Conservative students initially supported the free speech protests, but most backed away once those protests involved civil disobedience.

11. Savio interview by Giles, 7; Savio, "Beyond the Cold War: An Education in Politics," 22.

12. Savio, "Beyond the Cold War: An Education in Politics," 22.

13. Mario Savio, "An End to History," appendix in Hal Draper, *Berkeley: The New Student Revolt* (New York: Grove Press, 1965), 179 (reprinted in part IV of *Freedom's Orator*).

14. Savio, "Beyond the Cold War: The Education of an American Radical," 8.

15. Jack Weinberg, interview by Mark Kitchell, October 10, 1985, transcript in author's possession, 11.

16. Kerr, "Fall of 1964 at Berkeley," 398 n. 38.

17. Savio interview by Cohen and Pickell, 16; Savio, "Thirty Years Later," 66.

18. Savio interview by Cohen and Pickell, 18.

19. Kerr, *The Gold and the Blue*, 2:161, 167–76, 179–83; Edward W. Strong, "Philosopher, Professor, and Berkeley Chancellor, 1961–1965. XIV. Tumult at Berkeley: September–December 1964" (interview by Harriet Nathan, 1988, University History Series, Regional Oral History Office, UC Berkeley), 1–3, 5, 6–7, 9; "Dean of Students Arleigh Williams: The Free Speech Movement, and the Six Years' War, 1964–1970" (interview by Germaine LaBerge, 1988 and 1989, University History Series, Regional Oral History Office, UC Berkeley), 91, 95; Katherine Towle, interview by Max Heirich, June 14, 1965, 1–5, 13, copy in author's possession.

20. Kerr, *The Gold and the Blue*, 2:161, 179–85, 187; Kerr, "Fall of 1964 at Berkeley," 372–75, 391; Clark Kerr, "University of California Crises: Loyalty Oath and Free Speech Movement. II. The Free Speech Movement" (interview by Amelia Fry, 1969, Earl Warren Oral History Project, Regional Oral History Office, UC Berkeley), 1–7; Colvig, *Turning Points and Ironies*, 111; Peter S. Van Houten, "The Changing Relationship Between Berkeley and Its Students, 1945–1970," in Peter S. Van Houten and Edward L. Barrett Jr., *Berkeley and Its Students: Days of Conflict, Years of Change, 1945–1970* (Berkeley: Public Policy Press, 2003), 34–36. But if there was no Knowland call to Kerr, this does not mean that the right-wing Oakland publisher played no role in fomenting the crisis. A student at UC's Regent Scholarship reception in September reported that in response to a question Chancellor Strong stated that "this whole thing [free speech ban] had started because Bill Knowland called the University "(Jo Freeman, interview by Max Heirich, June 1965, transcript in author's possession, 21–22). Yet if this call came to the university, who received it is unclear, and Strong never subsequently confirmed such a call. On Knowland's denials that he made any such calls, see Colvig, *Turning Points and Ironies*, 84.

21. Kerr, *The Gold and the Blue*, 2:187; Kerr, "University of California Crises: Loyalty Oath and Free Speech Movement," 2; Max Heirich, *The Spiral of Conflict: Berkeley 1964* (New York: Columbia University Press, 1971), 92–93.

22. Kerr, *The Gold and the Blue*, 2:187. According to historian W. J. Rorabaugh, evidence surfaced years after the FSM suggesting that legal ownership of the Bancroft strip rested with the city, not UC. But, Rorabaugh shrewdly observed, neither the UC administration nor the students protesters took time to explore the "legal niceties," since this free speech dispute was not "about the law" but was "about power" (Rorabaugh, *Berkeley at War*, 19). Note, however, that the sources Rorabaugh cites (197 n. 24) are at best ambiguous as to whether legal ownership of the strip belonged to the city of Berkeley. UC Vice President Wellman recalled that in 1964 it belonged to UC, while Regent Elinor Raas Heller recalled it belonging to the city. Wellman and Kerr note that while the Regents had voted to deed the strip to the city in 1959, this had never been carried out, and so it was actually UC property. See Kerr, *The Gold and the Blue*, 2:130, 183–84; Harry R. Wellman, "Teaching, Research, and Administration, University of California 1925–1967" (interview by Malca Chall, 1976, Regional Oral History Office, UC Berkeley), 156; Elinor Raas Heller, "A Volunteer in Politics, in Higher Education, and on Governing Boards" (interview by Malca Chall, 1984, Women in Politics Oral History Project, Regional Oral History Office, UC Berkeley), 543.

23. Kerr, *The Gold and the Blue*, 2:187; Alex C. Sherriffs to Clark Kerr, September 15, 1964, and Edward Strong to Clark Kerr, November 4, 1964, both in Chancellor's Papers.

24. Clark Kerr, "The University: Civil Rights and Civic Responsibilities" (Charter Day Address, UC Davis, May 5, 1964), in Clark Kerr, ed., *Documentary Supplement to the Gold and the Blue* (Berkeley: Berkeley Public Policy Press, 2003), 73–74.

25. Kerr, "The University: Civil Rights and Civic Responsibilities," 74–75; Colvig, *Turning Points and Ironies*, 60.

26. Alex C. Sherriffs, "The University of California and the Free Speech Movement: Perspectives from a Faculty Member and Administrator. III. Origins of the Free Speech Movement" (interview by James H Rowland, 1978, Governmental History Documentation Project, Godwin Knight,/Edmund Brown, Sr., Era, University of California), 3–4. Kerr also seems to have set the stage for Strong and Sherriffs's decision in summer 1964 to crack down on student free speech by warning them in March 1964 that Left extremists planned on "creating disturbances" on campus in the coming academic year. See Strong, "Philosopher, Professor, and Berkeley Chancellor, 1961–1965. XIV. Tumult at Berkeley: September–December 1964," 2.

27. Strong, "Philosopher, Professor, and Berkeley Chancellor, 1961–1965. XIV. Tumult at Berkeley: September–December 1964," 6. Kerr later claimed that Strong and Sherriffs distorted his Davis speech, miscasting it as a new policy when actually it dated back to the 1930s and using its bar on campus political advocacy as an "excuse" for their crackdown on the Bancroft-Telegraph free speech area. Actually, neither Strong nor Sherriffs acted as if the Davis speech had articulated a new policy; rather, they invoked that speech because it was the most recent and eloquent defense of the UC policy barring political advocacy. See Kerr, *The Gold and the Blue*, 2:177; Sherriffs, "The University of California and the Free Speech Movement: Perspectives from a Faculty Member and Administrator. III. Origins of the Free Speech Movement," 3–4; Strong, "Philosopher, Professor, and Berkeley Chancellor, 1961–1965. XIV. Tumult at Berkeley: September–December 1964," 1–9.

28. Kerr, *The Gold and the Blue*, 2:177; Cohen and Zelnik, eds., *The Free Speech Movement*, 48 n. 43. A conservative legislator threatened to pass legislation in Sacramento to force UC to punish student protesters who broke the law in their civil rights protest. See Colvig, *Turning Points*, 60.

29. On Kerr's "minute-by-minute command" on the administration's anti-FSM tactics and strategy, see Heller, "A Volunteer in Politics," 544.

30. On the main period of negotiations, see Reginald E. Zelnik, "On the Side of the Angels: The Berkeley Faculty and the FSM," in Cohen and Zelnik, eds., *The Free Speech Movement*, 274–88.

31. Jackie Goldberg, interview by Max Heirich, May 14, 1965, 45–49, transcript in author's possession; Savio interview by Heirich, 66–67; Heirich, *The Spiral of Conflict*, 105; Towle interview, 5–8, 15. Note that SLATE's name arose because in student government elections this student group ran a slate of progressive candidates all of whom opposed racial discrimination in student organizations—a radical departure from the apolitical norm in a student government that had focused on fraternities and football.

32. Savio interview by Heirich, 62; Savio, "Thirty Years Later," 65; Freeman, *At Berkeley in the Sixties*, 155–56; Weinberg interview by author, 5.

33. Goines, *The Free Speech Movement*, 116; Savio interview by Heirich, 63; Mario Savio testimony in FSM trial, *People of the State of California vs. Mario Savio et al.*, nos. C-7468 through C-7547, First Consolidated Trial, May 13, 1965, available online at

http://content.cdlib.org/xtf/search?style=oac-tei&relation=fsm%20–%20leg%20–%20
trial&sort=title&startDoc=21.

34. Savio, "Thirty Years Later," 66; Savio interview by Eynon, 48.

35. Savio, "Thirty Years Later," 66; Savio testimony, May 13, 1965, 35, 38.

36. Savio, "Thirty Years Later," 66; Savio interview by Heirich, 63.

37. Editors of *California Monthly*, "Chronology of Events: Three Months of Crisis,"
in Lipset and Wolin, eds., *The Berkeley Student Revolt*, 103–4; Savio testimony, May 13,
1965, 40–41.

38. Savio interview by Heirich, 67; Heirich, *Spiral of Conflict*, 116; Goines, *The Free
Speech Movement*, 128–29; Savio testimony, May 13, 1965, 46.

39. Editors of *California Monthly*, "Chronology of Events," 106; Savio interview by
Heirich, 77.

40. Ibid.

41. Savio testimony, May 13, 1965, 49.

42. Ibid., 50.

43. Arleigh Williams to Faculty-Student Committee on Student Conduct, October
12, 1964, Chancellor's Papers.

44. Ibid.

45. Heirich, *Spiral of Conflict*, 456–57.

46. Savio interview by Heirich, 22–26, 104.

47. Heirich, *Spiral of Conflict*, 120–27; Goines, *The Free Speech Movement*, 140–47.

48. Savio testimony, May 13, 1965, 53–54. According to Savio's testimony, 409
students signed the petition of complicity.

49. Savio testimony, May 13, 1965, 53–55.

50. Mario Savio, "Commentary on a Memorandum Prepared by Dean Arleigh
Williams Alleging That Certain of My Actions Have Been in Violation of University
Policies on the Use of Facilities" (c. October 1964, Mario Savio disciplinary file,
Chancellor's Papers). Also see Savio testimony, May 13, 1965, 55.

51. Arleigh Williams, "Memorandum to Chancellor E. W. Strong, Re: Individual
Student Violations of the University Policy on the Use of Facilities, October 1, 1964," in
Goines, *The Free Speech Movement*, 145.

52. Savio interview by Heirich, 70.

53. Ibid., 69–70.

54. Williams, "Memorandum to Chancellor E. W. Strong," 145; Savio testimony,
May 13, 1965, 60.

55. Williams, "Memorandum to Chancellor E. W. Strong," 146.

56. Ibid.

57. Savio, "Commentary on a Memorandum Prepared by Dean Arleigh Williams."

58. Weinberg interview by author, 8.

59. Ibid., 51.

60. Heirich, *Spiral of Conflict*, 130.

61. Text of Savio's speech in Goines, *The Free Speech Movement*, 151. Kerr was,
as Berkeley political scientist Michael Rogin put it, "a beautiful target" for Savio
"because of his [Kerr's] notion of the university as basically a [knowledge] factory
that was producing products for industry." Author of *The Uses of the University*, Kerr
was the most eminent champion of the new research-oriented multiversity serving
cold war America's military-industrial complex. He was, in Savio's words, the leading

"ideologist for a new view of the university which we hope we can stop before it gets started," and his educational vision clashed with Savio's idealistic view of knowledge. As Bettina Aptheker, a key FSM leader, explained, "From Mario's point of view knowledge is pure.... But he saw what [under Kerr's vision] the University was doing with knowledge was instrumental ... using it to build bombs or control people.... So he saw it as corruptive." Michael Paul Rogin, interview by Lisa Rubens, February 23, 2000, Berkeley, Free Speech Movement Oral History Project, 9; Savio, "The Berkeley Knowledge Factory," 75; Aptheker interview by author, 23–24.

62. Text of Savio's speech in Goines, *The Free Speech Movement*, 152.

63. Ibid.

64. Ibid., 153.

65. Ibid.

66. Jack Weinberg, interview by Max Heirich, June 11, 1965, 7; Heirich, *Spiral of Conflict*, 122; Savio, "The Berkeley Knowledge Factory," 76; Hal Draper, "The Mind of Clark Kerr," in *Berkeley: The New Student Revolt*, 199–214. Draper, a veteran of the socialist student movement of the 1930s, was a Berkeley librarian in 1964.

67. Text of Mario Savio's September 30 speech, in Heirich, *Spiral of Conflict*, 132–35.

68. Ibid., 133.

69. Ibid., 134–35.

70. Ibid.

71. Ibid.

72. Ibid., 135.

73. Ibid., 136–37.

74. Weinberg interview by author, 22.

75. Ibid., 10.

76. Armand Kuris to Lynne Hollander Savio [December 1996], copy in author's possession.

77. Mario Savio, "The Philosophy of a Young Activist" (speech to the Philosophy Club, Sonoma State University, April 20, 1993), 13–14, transcript in author's possession.

78. Ibid. Savio alluded in this 1993 speech to the special idealism of teens, but he pointed out in his notes for this speech that during the FSM he "did not originate and never subscribed to the proposition that 'You can't trust anyone over 30'" (Savio, notes for "The Philosophy of a Young Activist," copy in author's possession, 4).

79. Savio interview by Eynon, 53. On the critical-mindedness and leadership style that enhanced one's individuality, which Savio admired in SNCC organizers, he told the story of a SNCC workshop he attended, whose focus was nonviolence. The SNCC worker cautioned against preaching nonviolence to the black farmers in Mississippi, even though SNCC was committed to nonviolence: Imagine "that you're in a farmhouse, with a black family, and ... the night riders come. The farmer wants to defend his family, wants to shoot back. You may be non-violent but what will you do? Will you start to make a speech to that farmer telling him that he shouldn't shoot back?" Here the SNCC organizer was not telling "you what to think, but they told you a situation to think about.... You could make up your own mind. They just wanted to be sure that you weren't making up your mind on the basis of having overlooked half the story. I was impressed by that style of leadership ... [and] when I found myself in a leadership position that was the model of leadership ... I had" (Savio interview by Eynon, 52–53).

80. Savio interview by Eynon, 57–58.

81. Ibid., 53.

82. Michael Lerner, "Remembering Mario Savio," *Tikkun*, January/February 1997, 27; Jackie Goldberg, remarks at Mario Savio's funeral, November 9, 1996, 14, transcript in author's possession; Ross Lucas to Michael, December 13, copy in author's possession, 1997; Sara Wickland O'Brien, entry in memorial book from memorial service for Mario Savio, UC Berkeley, December 8, 1996, copy in author's possession; Rev. Patricia Porth Roberts to Anya, December 31, 1996, copy in author's possession.

83. Syd Stapleton, interview by author, Berkeley, October 10, 2004, 6. This concern with ethics was central to Savio's activism. He believed that "politics…ought to be a branch of ethics.…I don't think the deciding question…is one of efficiency; this is a question of ethics" (Savio interview by Kitchell, transcript of tape 1, 2).

84. Savio interview by Kitchell, transcript of tape 3, 2.

85. Savio, "Beyond the Cold War: An Education in Politics," 23.

86. Stapleton interview, 12.

87. Weinberg interview by author, 50; Jack Weinberg interview in Goines, *The Free Speech Movement*, 158.

Chapter 5

1. Kitty Malloy, notes of meeting with Kerr, Strong, Sherriffs, Williams, Towle, Alumni House, September 30, 1964, Chancellor's Papers.

2. Savio interview by Cohen and Pickell, 30.

3. Weinberg interview by Kitchell, 17–23.

4. Savio interview by Heirich, 90.

5. Savio interview by Kitchell, tape 1, 5–6. Savio's removing his shoes so as not to damage the car was symbolic of the blockade's nonviolence. Though the campus police could not complete their arrest because of the blockade, at no time did they feel threatened by the protesters—who were, as one of the officers put it, in a "friendly mood.…It was a very peaceful movement." As the blockade wore on and the police needed to be relieved, they were able to change shifts with no resistance from the crowd. N. H. Dan Cheatham, "An FSM Iconic Event: The Officers' Story," *Chronicle of the University of California*, Spring 2002, 33–34.

6. Savio interview by Heirich, 94–95; Savio interview by Eynon, 59.

7. Savio interview by Cohen and Pickell, 33.

8. Savio interview by Heirich, 50.

9. Mario Savio, notes for memoir, n.d. [c. 1985], copy in author's possession.

10. Savio interview by Kitchell, tape 1, 6.

11. Draper, *Berkeley: The New Student Revolt*, 46.

12. Rogin interview, 9.

13. Savio interview by Heirich, 51.

14. Jackie Goldberg interview by Heirich, 54.

15. Savio interview by Kitchell, tape 1, 6.

16. Text of Savio speech in Heirich, *Spiral of Conflict*, 156.

17. Ibid., 158.

18. Weinberg interview by Kitchell, 23.

19. Savio interview by Giles, 7–8; Savio, "Thirty Years Later," 67.

20. Ganz interview, 3.

21. Weinberg interview by author, 25.

22. Reginald Zelnik, remarks at memorial service for Mario Savio, UC Berkeley, December 8, 1996, 19; Marcus, "On Mario Savio," 567.

23. John Searle interview by author, October 8, 2004, Berkeley, 3.

24. Minutes of meeting with the chancellor, at the request of Charles Powell, ASUC president, with self-stated leader of protest groups, Mario Savio, October 1, 1964, Chancellor's Papers.

25. Ibid.

26. Ibid. This was a reference to the SLATE pamphlet by Brad Cleaveland, "A Letter of Undergraduates," reprinted in Lipset and Wolin, eds., *The Berkeley Student Revolt*, 66–81.

27. Edward Strong, notes of November 10, 1964, phone call from Clark Kerr to Strong, Chancellor's Papers.

28. Lincoln Constance, "Versatile Berkeley Botanist: Plant Taxonomy and University Governance," interview by Ann Lage, Berkeley, 1986, Regional Oral History Office, UC Berkeley, 6; Wofsy, "When the FSM Disturbed the Faculty Peace," 347; Leon Wofsy Oral History, Regional Oral History Office, UC Berkeley, 26.

29. Weinberg interview by author, 21.

30. Ibid., 6.

31. Savio interview by Heirich, 98–99; Goines, *The Free Speech Movement*, 178; Heirich, *The Spiral of Conflict*, 162.

32. Heirich, *The Spiral of Conflict*, 163.

33. Ibid.

34. Savio interview by Kitchell, tape 2, 1.

35. Ibid., tape 3, 1.

36. Ibid., tape 2, 1.

37. Weinberg interview by author, 9, 20–21. Savio's retrospective characterization of himself and his fellow militants as "civil rights hotheads" confirms Weinberg's own recollection of how driven the two of them were on behalf of their cause of free speech/civil rights movement solidarity. See Savio, "The Free Speech Movement and the Rhetoric of the Student Movement," 5.

38. Cohen, "'This Was *Their* Fight,'" 252; Editors of *California Monthly*, "Chronology of Events," 110.

39. Weinberg interview by author, 22.

40. Ibid., 21.

41. Heirich, *The Spiral of Conflict*, 164; Goines, *The Free Speech Movement*, 182–87; Savio interview by Kitchell, tape 2, 1.

42. Heirich, *The Spiral of Conflict*, 168–69; Goines, *The Free Speech Movement*, 192–93.

43. Heirich, *The Spiral of Conflict*, 170–71; Goines, *The Free Speech Movement*, 193.

44. Goines, *The Free Speech Movement*, 193.

45. Ibid., 193–95; Heirich, *The Spiral of Conflict*, 172–75.

46. Savio interview by Heirich, 97.

47. Savio interview by Kitchell, tape 1, 4.

48. Savio interview by Heirich, 107.

49. Ibid.

50. Goines, *The Free Speech Movement*, 214.

51. Savio interview by Heirich, 97.

52. Jackie Goldberg interview by Marston Schultz, July 27, 1965, in Goines, *The Free Speech Movement*, 217; Jackie Goldberg interview by author, October 8. 2004, Berkeley, 3.

53. Jackie Goldberg interview by Mark Kitchell, c. 1984, transcript in author's possession, 7; Jackie Goldberg interview by Heirich, 56–57, transcript in author's possession; Heirich, *The Spiral of Conflict*, 184–85; Jackie Goldberg interview by author, 4–5.

54. Jackie Goldberg interview by Kitchell, 7; Jackie Goldberg interview by Heirich, 56–57; Jackie Goldberg interview by author, 4–5.

55. Jackie Goldberg interview by author, 4–5.

56. Freeman, *At Berkeley in the Sixties*, 164–65.

57. Jackie Goldberg interview by author, 3.

58. Jackie Goldberg interview in Goines, *The Free Speech Movement*, 218.

59. Goines, *The Free Speech Movement*, 220.

60. Savio interview by Heirich, 108, 113.

61. Jackie Goldberg interview by Kitchell, 7.

62. Goines, *The Free Speech Movement*, 220–21.

63. Kerr, *The Gold and the Blue*, 2:197.

64. Savio interview by Heirich, 108; Goines, *The Free Speech Movement*, 217. A copy of the Pact of October 2 with the change in phrasing Goldberg inserted can be found in Freeman, *At Berkeley in the Sixties*, 167.

65. Kerr interview.

66. Freeman, *At Berkeley in the Sixties*, 167.

67. Savio interview by Kitchell, tape 1, 4.

68. Savio interview by Cohen and Pickell, 28.

69. Jackie Goldberg interview by author, 5.

70. Savio interview by Cohen and Pickell, 26.

71. Ibid.

72. Jack Weinberg came to view the Pact of October 2 as a form of recognition similar to that accorded the labor movement when an employer recognizes a union as a bargaining agent for workers. See Weinberg interview by Kitchell, 24–25; Goines, *The Free Speech Movement*, 233.

73. Savio interview by Cohen and Pickell, 29.

74. Goines, *The Free Speech Movement*, 230–32.

75. Ibid., 231.

76. Ibid., 231–32.

77. Ibid., 230–32.

78. Bettina Aptheker, "Remembering Mario Savio," *Tikkun*, January–February 1997, 30.

79. Savio, "The Free Speech Movement and the Rhetoric of the Student Movement," 3.

80. Zelnik remarks at memorial service, 19–20 ; Reginald E. Zelnik, remarks at FSM session at Organization of American Historians convention, April 1997, San Francisco, tape in author's possession.

81. Wendy Lesser, "Elegy for Mario Savio," in Cohen and Zelnik, eds., *The Free Speech Movement*, 563–64.

82. Heirich, *Spiral of Conflict*, 103–24.

83. Zelnik remarks at FSM session ; Reginald Zelnik, e-mail to author, March 17, 2000; Robin Dellabough, "California Q&A: A Conversation with Mario Savio and Bettina Aptheker," *California Monthly*, December 1984, 20; Savio interview by Eynon, 70; Mario Savio, "Beyond the Cold War: An Education in Politics," 31; Savio, notes for speech to Sonoma State University Philosophy Club, April 20, 1993.

Robert Jervis, a UC political science graduate student in 1964, shrewdly observed that "Communists were not the most radical members of the FSM" since "they tended to be pragmatic and usually opposed high-risk moves." The most radical were those like Savio who tended to see "all politics in terms of moral issues. They asked in any situation 'Is a principle being violated?' and not 'What will be the consequence of one type of response as opposed to another?'" This is slightly overstated since Savio, as in the Pact of October 2, did think strategically, and often heeded the advice of the FSM's key tactician, Jack Weinberg. Still, Savio's first inclination in politics was to be guided by moral judgments, not by expediency, as Jervis suggests. Robert Jervis, "The Berkeley Free Speech Conflict in Light of Social Science" (unpublished paper, n.d.), 13.

84. Savio interview by Cohen and Pickell, 16; Savio, "An End to History," 179, 181; Savio, "The Berkeley Knowledge Factory," 76.

85. Weinberg interview by Kitchell, 24–25; Goines, *The Free Speech Movement*, 233.

86. Kerr, *The Gold and the Blue*, 2:198.

Chapter 6

1. Weinberg interview by author, 42.

2. Robert Hurwitt, "How Red Was My Berkeley," *Berkeley Express*, September 15, 1989, 15.

3. Zelnik, "On the Side of the Angels, 265, 322.

4. Savio interview by Eynon, 55–56.

5. Savio interview by Heirich, 24; Kathleen Piper and Jack Radey, "Nuts and Bolts of the FSM" (remarks at FSM fortieth-anniversary commemoration session, Berkeley, October 2004, transcript in author's possession), 1–2, 7–10.

6. Savio interview by Heirich, 24.

7. Ibid., 25.

8. Ibid., 26.

9. Savio interview by Eynon, 53–54; Savio interview by Cohen and Pickell, 5.

10. Savio interview by Cohen and Pickell, 5–6, Savio, "Beyond the Cold War: The Education of an American Radical," 7.

11. Savio interview by Kitchell, tape 3, 2.

12. Weinberg interview by Kitchell, 28.

13. Jackie Goldberg interview by author, 6.

14. Ibid., 7.

15. Aptheker interview by author, 6.

16. Jackie Goldberg interview by author, 6–10, Goines, *The Free Speech Movement*, 240–44.

17. Jackie Goldberg interview by author, 7. On the reasons why student radicals mistrusted the Greek system, see Robert Cohen, "Driving Jim Crow off Frat Row: The Struggle to Desegregate Fraternities and Sororities at the University of California at Berkeley, 1946–1967," National Academy of Education, Palo Alto, 1991, copy in author's possession; Clark Kerr, *The Gold and the Blue*, 2:243; Larry Colton, *Goat Brothers* (New York: Doubleday, 1994), 26–28.

While not explicitly sexist, the displacing of Goldberg by Savio as the movement's spokesperson was a setback for gender equity. Though the movement had women prominent in its leadership, such as Steering Committee members Bettina Aptheker and Suzanne Goldberg, it remained male-dominated—so much so that, as will be discussed in chapter 10, women had difficulty making themselves heard in FSM Executive Committee meetings.

18. Bettina Aptheker, interview by Max Heirich, July 2, 1965, 42, copy of transcript in author's possession.

19. Ibid., 39–40.

20. Aptheker interview by author, 1–3.

21. Freeman, *At Berkeley in the Sixties*, 181. Note that though Freeman's recent memoir argues that Savio and Weinberg controlled the Steering Committee, back in 1965 she claimed that the Steering Committee had "four controllers....Savio, Weinberg, Aptheker, and Stapleton" (Freeman interview, 50).

22. Jack Weinberg interview by author, 25.

23. Ibid., 12.

24. Bettina Aptheker, e-mail to author, April 24, 2008.

25. Weinberg interview by author, 25.

26. Savio interview by Eynon, 61–62.

27. Ibid., 62.

28. Goines, *The Free Speech Movement*, 247–48.

29. Weinberg interview by author, 12. On the roots of this kind of consensus decision-making process in the pacifist movement and SNCC, see Francesca Polletta, *Freedom Is an Endless Meeting: Democracy in American Social Movements* (Chicago: University of Chicago Press, 2002), 42–48, 80–83.

30. Weinberg interview by author, 12.

31. Goldberg, "Mario, Personal and Political," in Cohen and Zelnik, *The Free Speech Movement*, 557–58.

32. Savio interview by Heirich, 69.

33. Ibid.

34. Weinberg interview by author, 55.

35. Ibid., 54.

36. Savio interview by Heirich, 69.

37. Ibid.

38. Ibid.

39. Weinberg interview by author, 53.

40. Clark Kerr letter to the *Daily Californian*, December 1, 1964. Note that though Aptheker's Communist connections were obvious, she did not formally acknowledge her Communist Party membership until the year after the FSM (on November 9, 1965). See Bettina Aptheker, *Intimate Politics: How I Grew Up Red, Fought for Free Speech, and Became a Feminist Rebel* (Emeryville, Calif.: Seal Press, 2006), 164–65.

41. *San Francisco Examiner*, October 3, 1964.

42. Ibid., November 25–27, 1964.

43. W. C. Sullivan to J. F. Bland, December 11, 1964, Re: Mario Savio, Student Demonstrations, University of California at Berkeley, Mario Savio FBI file, 100-443052, obtained under the Freedom of Information Act, copy in author's possession; Seth Rosenfeld, "Mario Savio's FBI Odyssey," *San Francisco Chronicle Magazine*, October 10, 2004, 16–23, 27.

44. Weinberg interview by author, 53; Stapleton interview, 6. For Weinberg's clearest published explanation of his "don't trust anyone over thirty" remark, see Tom Brokaw, *Boom! Voices of the Sixties* (New York: Random House, 2007), 593.

45. Weinberg interview by author, 55.

46. Ibid., 24.

47. *Berkeley Daily Gazette*, November 11, 1964. Attesting to Savio's engagement with philosophical and ethical questions in the FSM semester, he carried a copy of J. L. Austin's *Sense and Sensibilia* in his pocket. This important work of linguistic philosophy was for Savio "a way of escaping from a very intense skepticism." Near the front of the book Savio, as a counter to radical skepticism, wrote one of his favorite quotes—with its powerful ethical imperative—from Pedro Calderón de la Barca's play *Life Is a Dream*: "I am dreaming, and I want to do good. For the good you do is never lost. Not even in dreams" (Savio, "The Philosophy of a Young Activist," 14–16).

48. Weinberg interview by author, 54.

49. Savio interview by Eynon, 63–64.

50. Ibid., 63.

51. A. H. Raskin, "The Berkeley Affair: Mr. Kerr vs. Mario Savio & Co.," *New York Times Magazine*, February 14, 1965, reprinted in Michael V. Miller and Susan Gilmore, eds., *Revolution at Berkeley: The Crisis in American Education* (New York: Dial Press, 1965), 79.

52. Savio interview by Eynon, 65–66.

53. Ibid., 66–67.

54. Ibid., 65; Piper and Radey, "Nuts and Bolts of the FSM," 1–2, 7–10.

55. Savio interview by Eynon, 60–61.

56. Ibid., 61.

57. Ibid., 53–54; 60–64; Savio interview Kitchell, tape 3, 2; Savio, "The Free Speech Movement and the Rhetoric of the Student Movement," 1; Savio, notes for "The Philosophy of a Young Activist."

58. Kitty Malloy, memo for files, October 5, 1964, Chancellor's Papers; Owen Chamberlain to Chancellor Strong, October 5, 1964, Chancellor's Papers; Katherine A. Towle to Mario Savio, October 6, 1964, Chancellor's Papers; Heirich, *Spiral of Conflict*, 218–19.

59. October 5, 1964, FSM rally, transcript, Chancellor's Papers, 8, 10.

60. Ibid., 9–10.

61. Ibid., 8, 12.

62. Ibid., 12.

63. Ibid.

64. Ibid., 12–13.

65. Ibid.

66. Heirich, *The Spiral of Conflict*, 218.

67. Goines, *The Free Speech Movement*, 237.

68. Ibid.

69. October 5, 1964, FSM rally, transcript, 16–19.

70. Ibid., 16.

71. Ibid.

72. Ibid., 16–17.

73. Ibid., 17–19; also see Clark Kerr's news conference following LA Town Hall Speech, partial transcript, n.d, President's Papers, UC Berkeley Archives, Bancroft Library (hereafter President's Papers).

74. Akiko Owen, memo for the files, October 7, 1964, Chancellor's Papers.

75. Savio interview by Heirich, 107, 113; Savio interview by Cohen and Pickell, 26. There were parallels in the civil rights movement on this issue of civility—that politeness and deference to authority helped to maintain white supremacy in the South, and that the struggle for equality demanded defiance of the old order and its repressive code of civility. See William H. Chafe, *Civilities and Civil Rights: Greensboro, North Carolina, and the Black Struggle for Freedom* (New York: Oxford University Press, 1980), 8–10, 42–152.

76. Minutes of October 12, 1964, meeting between the chancellor and the FSM Steering Committee, 10, Chancellor's Papers.

77. Kenneth M. Stampp, "Historian of Slavery, the Civil War, and Reconstruction, University of California, Berkeley, 1946–1983," interview by Ann Lage, Berkeley, June 8, 1996, Regional Oral History Office, UC Berkeley, 453–54, transcript at Bancroft Library, UC Berkeley.

78. Aptheker interview by author, 8.

79. While rejecting the psychodeterminism of Berkeley philosophy professor Lewis Feuer, who in his book *The Conflict of Generations: The Character and Significance of Student Movements* (New York: Basic Books, 1969) interpreted the Berkeley rebellion and all student movements as simply irrational expressions of generational rage, with administrators the surrogate father figures, Savio "always felt that Feuer should be given a little bit more credit" for exploring the role that psychological factors played in youth political protest. Savio "did not reject that [psychological] analysis" of student protest as "a subsidiary thing," which reinforced the political factors motivating student rebels. Lynne Hollander Savio thought it possible that in Savio's case "a certain amount of the passion that motivated him [as a student rebel] was in this personal struggle against his father. But to say that does not eliminate the political" motivations, which were central (Hollander Savio interview, 2, 7).

80. Weinberg interview by Heirich, 33–34.

81. Weinberg interview by Heirich, 109–10; Savio interview by Cohen and Pickell, 26–28; Weinberg interview by Kitchell, 25; Savio, "The Berkeley Knowledge Factory," 75–81; Savio, "Thirty Years Later," 68.

82. *Daily Californian*, October, 8, 1964.

83. Ibid., October 4, 1964.

84. Ibid., October 16, 1964.

85. Captain Woodward's transcript of FSM rally on the steps of Sproul Hall, made at the request of the [UC] president's office, October 16, 1964, 8, University Archives, Bancroft Library, UC Berkeley.

86. Ibid., 1–2.

87. Ibid., 6.

88. Ibid., 7.
89. Ibid., 4, 6–7.
90. Ibid., 7.
91. Ibid., 2.
92. Ibid., 1–8.
93. Weinberg interview by author, 11.
94. Free Speech Movement rally, October 16, 1964, transcript, 3.
95. Ibid., 5.
96. Ibid., 7.
97. Minutes of the Campus Committee on Political Activity, October 21, 24, 28, 29, November 4, 5, and 7, 1964, Free Speech Movement Records, Bancroft Library.
98. The best account of the CCPA hearings is Zelnik, "On the Side of the Angels," 274–88.
99. Weinberg interview by author, 10.
100. Zelnik, "On the Side of the Angels," 284; Goines, *The Free Speech Movement*, 307.
101. Zelnik, "On the Side of the Angels," 282–83.
102. Ibid., 283–84.
103. CCPA minutes, November 7, 1964, 1–12, Free Speech Movement Archives, Bancroft Library, also available via the FSM Digital Archive: http://content.cdlib.org/search?style=oac-tei&relation=fsm+–+places+–+ccpa&sort=title; Weinberg interview by Heirich, 42–45.
104. CCPA minutes, November 7, 1964, 6–7.
105. CCPA minutes, November 7, 1964, 2–4; Weinberg interview by Heirich, 43–44.
106. CCPA minutes, November 7, 1964, 2.
107. Heirich, *Spiral of Conflict*, 224–26, 235.
108. *Berkeley Daily Gazette*, November 7, 1964.
109. Zelnik, "On the Side of the Angels," 285.
110. *Berkeley Daily Gazette*, November 9 and 10, 1964.

Chapter 7

1. Minutes of November 10, 1964, 2 P.M. meeting of Strong, Kerr, Cunningham, Chancellor's Papers. From almost the start of the FSM, Kerr and Strong thought Savio too radical to lead mainstream students. See Memorandum for Files, Conversation Between Alex Sherriffs and Clark Kerr, October 8, 1964, Chancellor's Papers; Memo for the Files, Meeting of Strong, Sherriffs, Searcy, Malloy, and Mauchlan, October 7, 1964, Chancellor's Papers.
2. "Strictly confidential" notes from Marty Lipset, 11:55 a.m., November 11, 1964—by phone to ECB [UC Vice President Earl Bolton], Chancellor's Papers.
3. Minutes of November 10, 1964, 2 P.M. meeting of Strong, Kerr, Cunningham; also see William F. Shepard to Clark Kerr, November 10, 1964, President's Papers.
4. Savio, "Thirty Years Later," 68–69.
5. Freeman, *At Berkeley in the Sixties*, 190–92, Freeman interview by Heirich, 74.
6. Savio, "Thirty Years Later," 68–69.
7. Goines, *The Free Speech Movement*, 303.
8. Ibid., 307, 312–13.

9. Brian Turner, interview by author, October 17, 2004, Silver Springs, Md., tape in author's possession.

10. Freeman interview, 45, 51.

11. Barbara Garson to Rabbit [Marvin Garson], November 1964, http://content. cdlib.org/ark:/13030/kt4b69n6rv/?&query=&brand=oac.

12. Barbara Garson, puppet show script, n.d., Free Speech Movement Papers, Bancroft Library, UC Berkeley. The puppet show was put on by the San Francisco Mime Troupe to an appreciative crowd on Sproul Plaza on the first anniversary of the December 1964 sit-in. It was titled "Mario and the Magician," and also included the playing of a tape of Savio's famous speech from that sit-in. See John Searle to Roger W. Heyns, December 2, 1965, Chancellor's Papers. Garson later authored the best-selling play *Macbird* (1966), which lampooned LBJ.

13. Weinberg interview by author, 13.

14. Savio interview by Heirich, 114–28; Goines, *The Free Speech Movement*, 303–26.

15. Freeman interview, 52.

16. Freeman herself later admitted that she was worried as to how students who had not been to an FSM meeting since its founding would be received, and whether they would even be seated at the meeting (Freeman interview, 70).

17. Weinberg interview by author, 16, 42.

18. Ibid., 42.

19. Ibid., 42–43.

20. Ibid., 42.

21. Freeman discussed her attempt to cut a separate deal with Kerr in the chapter "Secret Negotiations" of her memoir, *At Berkeley in the Sixties*, 190–92. While her memoir is illuminating on other aspects of the FSM crisis, this chapter is misleading on a key point concerning the nature of her negotiations with Kerr. She claims that "Kerr was willing to give us everything we wanted—minimal rules and no restrictions on advocacy—but he would not give in to the FSM and particularly not to Mario Savio" (191). Actually, Freeman was not even asking Kerr to give the FSM "everything we wanted" on the free speech issue, but was asking for what *she* wanted, which was considerably less than the FSM's key free speech demand. Indeed, as Freeman told Max Heirich in 1965, she was seeking a "compromise," which would give in to Kerr on the central FSM demand that political advocacy, including advocacy of civil disobedience (which meant disruptive civil rights sit-ins where laws were broken), not be restricted or lead to punishment by the university. "We proposed," Freeman told Heirich, "that if a group or person advocated an illegal act…such as a sit-in…later found to be conclusively illegal in the courts, and it could be laid—the act could be laid to the advocacy of such an act on campus—then the university could take disciplinary action" (Freeman interview, 74). The FSM opposed giving such disciplinary authority to the university since this would restrict free speech and could inhibit student involvement in the civil rights movement.

22. It is also why the memoirs of both FSM rank-and-filers and leaders reflect such anger with Freeman as "a fink" "trying to sell us out" (Andy Wells and Brian Mulloney, in Goines, *The Free Speech Movement*, 309, 313; Stapleton interview, 3). Friction over Freeman's attempt to cut a separate deal with Kerr has lingered for decades among FSM veterans. See Jack Radey–Jo Freeman e-mail exchange, July 17 and 22, 2004, copies in author's possession.

23. "Strictly confidential" notes from Marty Lipset, 11:55 a.m., November 11, 1964—by phone to ECB [UC Vice President Earl Bolton], Chancellor's Papers; notes of meeting of Strong, Kerr, and Cunningham, November 10, 1964, 2 P.M. Chancellor's Papers; JEJ to Alex [Sheriffs], November 14, 1964, Chancellor's Papers.

24. Goines, *The Free Speech Movement*, 322–26; Heirich, *Spiral of Conflict*, 244–45; Savio interview by Heirich, 118–28.

25. Freeman, *At Berkeley in the Sixties*, 189. Freeman's priority seemed to be to winning a partial victory for free speech, and she had no qualms about bypassing the FSM leadership toward that end, displaying more loyalty to that cause than to the FSM itself, whose militant politics she mistrusted. Thus, in 1965, recounting her secret negotiations, Freeman explained that she told Kerr that "we weren't too worried about whether FSM was undermined as an organization [but] we didn't want to do something that might harm the whole struggle for free speech, and hopelessly split the students at large. And right now, since FSM was the only thing that had the power and the backing to do anything [on behalf of free speech], we weren't going to do anything which might hurt it, unless we substantially got what was needed to preclude the necessity of a movement of this kind" (Freeman interview, 72–73).

26. Freeman interview, 40–42, 50.

27. Ibid., 41.

28. Ibid. Freeman thought that because of its ultramilitance the FSM was "a failure" that fared poorly in attracting community, faculty, and even student support. See Jo Freeman, "A Time for Choosing" (July 1965), 11, copy in author's possession.

29. Freeman interview, 44.

30. Ibid., 73.

31. Ibid., 72–75. Note, however, that only in the Berkeley context could Freeman be considered moderate. She had been active in the Bay Area civil rights movement and was arrested in the Sheraton Palace sit-in. It was her connections to the Democratic Party, Kerr, and anti-FSM faculty, along with her feud with FSM militants, that left her with that label. She later became a prolific feminist scholar.

32. Weinberg interview by author, 15. Weinberg was correct about anti-Communism shaping Lipset's hostile view of the student movement. At a private dinner in the spring semester 1964, historian Lawrence W. Levine found Lipset dismissing the leaders of a local student civil rights protest—probably the Sheraton Palace sit-in—as "Communists" or "Communist dupes," and when Levine rejected this charge, Lipset became enraged (Lawrence W. Levine, interview by Ann Lage, Regional Oral History Office, UC Berkeley, 2004–5, 308). On the history of Shactmanites, see Maurice Isserman, *If I Had a Hammer: The Death of the Old Left and the Birth of the New Left* (New York: Basic Books, 1987), 35–76.

33. Savio interview by Heirich, 118–28.

34. Mario Savio and Suzanne Goldberg, interview by Max Heirich, June 8, 1965, 121, 123, transcript in author's possession.

35. Ibid., 122, 125, 126.

36. Ibid., 124, 127.

37. Ibid., 127.

38. Turner interview, 23.

39. Brian Turner, e-mail to author, August 31, 2004.

40. Freeman interview, 42.

454 Notes to Pages 158–165

42. Ibid., 52; Turner interview, 13.

43. Jack Radey, e-mail to Brian Turner, August 31, 2004, copy in author's possession. A powerful refutation of the moderates' critique comes from Executive Committee member Pat Iyama, who stressed that Ex Com meetings were "very democratic…Everybody could participate…[and] vote…People felt they could influence the decision-making. We weren't just getting orders from on high. We were actually making decisions" (Pat Iyama, interview by Mark Kitchell, c. 1984, 11, copy in author's possession).

44. Turner interview, 23.

45. Freeman interview, 69.

46. Ibid., 91–92. But Savio was not totally consistent in such tolerance. See Freeman interview, 44.

47. Freeman interview, 63–64.

48. Ibid., 65.

49. Minutes of November 10, 1964, 2 P.M. meeting of Strong, Kerr, Cunningham, Chancellor's Papers. Shortly after the FSM, Freeman candidly summarized these moderate misperceptions, writing, "The minority faction of the Executive Committee, to which I usually belonged.…kept trying to maintain that the Administration was somewhat rational and not totally vindictive and their actions continually proved us wrong, our position was continually undermined" (Freeman, "A Time for Choosing," 9).

50. Minutes of November 10, 1964, 2 P.M. meeting of Strong, Kerr, Cunningham, Chancellor's Papers.

51. *Daily Californian*, November 10, 1964.

52. Ibid.

53. *Free Speech Movement Newsletter*, no. 4, November 17, 1964.

54. Ibid.

55. "Chronology of Events: Three Months of Crisis," *California Monthly*, February 1965, 53.

56. Minutes of November 10, 1964, 2 P.M. meeting of Strong, Kerr, Cunningham, Chancellor's Papers.

57. *San Francisco Chronicle*, November 11, 1964.

58. Zelnik, "On the Side of the Angels," 289. The committee did acknowledge that the protesters had violated university regulations, but even this was phrased sympathetically in its conclusion that though the suspended students "were motivated by high principles" this "does not cause the violations to disappear."

59. Kerr, *The Gold and the Blue*, 2:204.

60. *San Francisco Chronicle*, November 26, 1964.

61. Weinberg interview by Kitchell, 30–31.

62. *San Francisco Chronicle*, November 13, 1964.

63. *Berkeley Daily Gazette*, November 20, 1964.

64. Ibid.

65. Savio, "The Berkeley Knowledge Factory," 80.

66. Ibid., 81.

67. Ibid.

68. *San Francisco Chronicle*, November 21, 1964.

69. Ibid.; Heirich, *Spiral of Conflict*, 255–56.

70. Aptheker interview by Heirich, 47.

71. Ibid.

72. Savio interview by Heirich, 134–35.

73. Goines, *The Free Speech Movement*, 343.

74. Aptheker interview by Heirich, 48.

75. Ibid., 47.

76. Michael Rossman, interview by Max Heirich, c. 1965, 92–93, transcript in author's possession.

77. Suzanne Goldberg interview by Heirich, 134–35.

78. Savio interview by Eynon, 55.

79. Aptheker interview by Heirich, 48.

80. Rossman interview by Heirich, 84.

81. The only bitterness at the rally was that sparked by Jo Freeman's speech near the rally's end. She denounced the FSM leadership, charging that the Steering and Executive Committees opted for the sit-in without consulting their constituents, and also claimed that nonradical groups had been excluded from the FSM's decision-making process. These charges elicited little support from the crowd, which was aware that the question of whether to sit in actually had been debated exhaustively, and was in fact still being debated in the plaza. Freeman claimed that all the speakers at the rally had been pro-sit-in, when in fact Weissman and Zelnik had spoken against sitting in and Art Goldberg had charted a middle course. Goldberg spoke directly after Freeman and termed her remarks "completely inaccurate," indignant at what he took to be her implication that "clean" nonradicals opposed the sit-in while "dirty" radicals supported it. Goldberg pointed out that the sit-in opponents included Maoists, while its supporters included conservative Republicans. All the speeches from this November 23 rally can be heard online at the Web site of the UC Berkeley Library Social Activism Sound Recording Project, www.lib.berkeley.edu/MRC/pacificafsm.html.

82. Savio interview by Eynon, 55.

83. Ibid., 55–56.

84. Mario Savio's speech before the "aborted sit-in," November 23, 1964, copy in author's possession, 3.

85. Savio interview by Eynon, 56.

86. Ibid., 55.

87. Savio, speech before the "aborted sit-in," 1.

88. Ibid., 1–2.

89. Ibid., 2.

90. Ibid. Actually, the truth about the administration's relationship to the Heyman Committee was even worse than Savio knew. It was not just that the administration, as Savio put it, "couldn't accept" the committee's findings, but that both Kerr and Strong, anticipating that the committee "may go pretty light" in their punishment for the FSM leaders, privately looked for mechanisms to mete out greater punishment even before the Heyman Committee announced its findings. Kerr and Strong expressed interest in finding other disciplinary committee venues or even bringing criminal charges against these FSMers as an alternative to the leniency they expected from the Heyman Committee. See notes of telephone conversations between Strong and Kerr, October 29 and November 10, 1964, Chancellor's Papers.

91. Savio, speech before the "aborted sit-in," 1.

92. Ibid., 3.

93. Ibid.

94. Ibid.

95. Savio interview by Heirich, 135.

96. Aptheker interview by author, 2.

97. Ibid.

98. Aptheker interview by Heirich, 48.

99. Aptheker interview by author, 2.

100. *San Francisco Chronicle*, November 24, 1964.

101. Savio, speech before the "aborted sit-in," 3; Aptheker interview by Heirich, 49.

102. *San Francisco Chronicle*, November 24, 1964.

103. Savio interview by Heirich, 137.

104. Goines, *The Free Speech Movement*, 345.

105. Rossman interview by Heirich, 91.

106. Aptheker interview by Heirich, 49.

107. Heirich, *Spiral of Conflict*, 265–67; Art Goldberg, interview by Max Heirich, May 18, 1965, 24–25; Jackie Goldberg interview by author, 21.

108. Aptheker interview by Heirich, 49.

109. Weinberg interview by Mark Kitchell, 32.

110. Edward Strong to Mario Savio, November 25, 1964, Mario Savio disciplinary file, Chancellor's Papers. The one act that Savio alone was cited for was for biting Berkeley city police officer Philip E. Mower on the left thigh.

111. Weinberg interview by Mark Kitchell, 32.

112. Jackie Goldberg interview by author, 8.

113. Freeman interview, 88. Freeman endorsed and participated in the FSM's culminating sit-in at Sproul Hall (Freeman, "A Time for Choosing," 12–13). Her perception that the new disciplinary actions violated the Pact of October 2 was widely shared by UC students. But technically the new round of discipline did not violate that pact because though it covered the initial (preblockade) suspensions it did not address the police car blockade itself. So in a technical sense this left the administration free to address the campus rule violations caused by the blockade and not covered by the Heyman Committee report. Such technicalities were, however, meaningless to most students and faculty, and the fact that Kerr and Strong failed to recognize that this would be so was a sign of how tone deaf they had become to campus political reality.

114. Aptheker interview by Heirich, 50.

115. Savio interview by Heirich, 138.

116. Aptheker interview by Heirich, 51.

117. Mario Savio and Suzanne Goldberg to Clark Kerr, December 1, 1964, Chancellor's Papers.

118. Ibid.

119. At first glance it might seem as if the December 1 Savio-Goldberg letter to Kerr made impossible demands and so was simply a provocation, not offering terms Kerr could meet in time to prevent the sit-in on December 2. But three of the five demands, those that Kerr could have met alone—without consulting the regents—were required to meet the twenty-four-hour deadline. The two others required only that he initiate their adoption. See Savio testimony, May 19, 1965, 14.

120. *Berkeley Daily Gazette*, November 30, 1964.

121. Ibid., December 1 and 2, 1964.

122. *San Francisco Chronicle*, December 2, 1964.

123. "Showdown," FSM leaflet, http://content.cdlib.org/ark:/13030/kt6m3nb1bk/ ?&query=&brand=oac.

124. *San Francisco Chronicle*, December 2, 1964.

125. "Showdown."

Chapter 8

1. Weinberg interview by author, 1. Also see Weinberg interview by Heirich, 68–71; Weinberg interview by Kitchell, 32–33.

2. Mario Savio speech, December 2, 1964, transcribed from tape available at www.lib.berkeley.edu/MRC/pacificafsm.html. For the complete version of the speech, see Widmer, ed., *American Speeches*, 616–18. However, this published version has an error in the speech's most famous lines, so for these the reader is referred above to the online recording of the speech. The "bodies upon the gears" speech is reprinted in part IV of *Freedom's Orator*.

3. David Burner, *Making Peace with the '60s* (Princeton: Princeton University Press, 1996), 141.

4. For the linking of Savio to Thoreau, see Rorabaugh, *Berkeley at War*, 31; Jeff Lustig, "The FSM and the Vision of a New Left," in Cohen and Zelnik, eds., *The Free Speech Movement*, 219; John Patrick Diggins, *The Rise and Fall of the American Left* (New York: W. W. Norton, 1992), 18; Henry May, "The Student Movement at Berkeley," 461. May (460–61) also connected Savio to Tolstoy, Gandhi, Whitman, Emerson, existentialism, neo-antinomianism, and romantic anarchism. The Charlie Chaplin connection is found in Mark Hamilton Lytle, *America's Uncivil Wars: The Sixties Era from Elvis to the Fall of Richard Nixon* (New York: Oxford University Press, 2006), 172. Connecting Savio to Martin Luther King Jr. and "Letter from Birmingham Jail" is Burner in *Making Peace with the '60s*, 141. On Savio and C. Wright Mills, see Rossinow, *The Politics of Authenticity*, 50. Connecting Savio to Herbert Marcuse is James J. Farrell, *The Spirit of the Sixties: The Making of Postwar Radicalism* (New York: Routledge, 1997), 160. On Mario and prefigurative utopian politics, see Wini Breines, *Community and Organization in the New Left, 1962–1968: The Great Refusal* (New Brunswick: Rutgers University Press, 1989), 23–29.

5. Weinberg interview by author, 1–2.

6. Ibid., 2.

7. Zelnik remarks at memorial service, 19. The iconoclasm and anger in the "bodies upon the gears" speech was characteristic of the most famous U.S. student movement oratory of its time, including SNCC leader John Lewis's speech at the March on Washington in August 1963 and SDS president Paul Potter's April 1965 speech at the first large anti–Vietnam War march. Lewis and Potter displayed Savioesque anger in the face of racism and war. Their indignation was directed toward powerful liberals whom they deemed unwilling to distinguish themselves from the Right when it counted the most. Where Lewis went after Kennedy for refusing to stand up for civil rights in the face of racist violence, Savio rebuked Kerr for deferring to the big businessmen on the Board of Regents who sought to stifle student civil rights protest. Potter found LBJ guilty of compromising democratic ideals for the sake of a cold

warrior crusade, propping up the "dictator" Diem in the name of "freedom." Beneath the lofty rhetoric of these liberals, Savio, Potter, and Lewis believed, lay something deeply undemocratic: power used for domination, to impose order and maintain the status quo. It was "an autocracy" running the university, Savio had said from the steps of Sproul.

Although all three speeches displayed something of a revolutionary temperament, they avoided Old Left–style rhetoric. Savio and Potter expressed their most radical thoughts metaphorically, with Savio raging against "the machine" and the SDS leader urging that antiwar protesters "name…describe…analyze…understand…and change that system," yet never himself naming "that system" (a system Marxists would simply call capitalism), which led America into oppressive wars. Lewis came the closest of the three to outright revolutionary rhetoric when he called, in the initial version of his speech, for "nonviolent revolution" to "free ourselves of the chains of political and economic slavery." But these words proved too radical for mainstream civil rights leaders, and Lewis—under pressure from those leaders—deleted them from his speech at the March on Washington. All three expressed dissent militantly but in terms that could not be easily dismissed in the way that explicitly anticapitalist discourse was in those cold war years. See Paul Potter, speech at April 17, 1965, antiwar march on Washington, http://sdsrebels.com/potter.htm, 3; Lewis, *Walking with the Wind*, 217–24; Gitlin, *The Sixties*, 185.

8. Searle interview by author, 1. Sociologist Nathan Glazer, a Berkeley faculty critic of the FSM, reacted negatively to Savio's famous speech. See Joseph Dorman, *Arguing the World: The New York Intellectuals in Their Own Words* (New York: Free Press, 2000), 147.

9. While atypical of his FSM oratory, the emotional edge to Savio's remarks and his urging others to challenge authority was by no means unprecedented. He made a similar appeal for students to defy university regulations just before the aborted sit-in on November 23, and he can be seen in a news clip, included in the film *Berkeley in the 60s*, urging students to join in the protests on September 30 against the suspensions of free speech activists.

10. Marty Roysher speech, tape of December 2, 1964 FSM rally, available online at www.lib.berkeley.edu/MRC/pacificafsm.html.

11. Heirich *The Spiral of Conflict*, 270–71.

12. Jeff Goodwin, James M. Jasper, and Francesca Polletta, *Passionate Politics: Emotions and Social Movements* (Chicago: University of Chicago Press, 2001), 13, 16.

13. Marty Roysher and Michael Rossman speeches, tape of December 2, 1964 FSM rally, available online at www.lib.berkeley.edu/MRC/pacificafsm.html.

14. Steve Weissman and Charles Powell speeches, tape of December 2, 1964 FSM rally, available online at www.lib.berkeley.edu/MRC/pacificafsm.html.

15. Savio's December 2, 1964, speech appears on the folk protest album by Ani DiFranco and Utah Phillips, *Fellow Workers* (1999) and on punk rock band Good Riddance's album *Operation Phoenix* (1999). The speech has appeared in other, folk, rock, and ska songs since the sixties by Fear Factory, Me Mom and Morgentaler, From Monument to Masses, the Paper Chase, and Phobia. Clips of the speech have appeared in the feature film *Bobby*, about Robert F. Kennedy and America in the 1960s, in the movie *Half-Nelson* (2006, written by Ryan Fleck and Anna Boden) about a troubled inner-city teacher who sought to school his students in social

criticism, and in *No Direction Home*, Martin Scorsese's documentary on Bob Dylan. The speech even made its way to an imagined future, paraphrased by a rebellious character in the science fiction TV series *Battlestar Galactica* in the final episode of season 2 (2006) The elasticity of Savio's "machine" metaphor was exemplified in a 2002 interview of folksinger Ani Di Franco, who explained that during her concerts she played his speech since it symbolized the freedom that comes from "trying to create an alternative to the destructive Machine, whether it be the music industry or capitalism." Ronald Ehmke, "Ani DiFranco Talks About the Making of Her Album, *So Much Shouting, So Much Laughter*," June 28, 2002, http://www.righteousbabe.com/ani/sms_sml/interview.asp.

16. Aptheker interview by author 9; Bettina Aptheker, e-mail to author, February 17, 2007.

17. "Showdown," December 1–2, 1964, leaflet available at the FSM digital archive, http://bancroft.berkeley.edu/FSM; *San Francisco Chronicle*, December 2, 1964; Michael Rossman speech, tape of December 2, 1964, FSM rally, www.lib.berkeley.edu/MRC/pacificafsm.html. Even ASUC president Charlie Powell used the "machine" metaphor in his anti-sit-in remarks at the December 2 rally (also on the tape of the December 2, 1964, FSM rally).

Savio tended to be careful about citing authors whose ideas and words he borrowed, and earlier in the FSM, when speaking of historical precedents for civil disobedience (from atop the police car as the fraternity crowd heckled him), had mentioned Thoreau. So if he intended to borrow the "machine" image from Thoreau on December 2, he almost certainly would have invoked the name of this prophet of civil disobedience. But even if he was not *consciously* drawing his imagery from Thoreau, it is possible that in explaining the principles justifying the sit-in and defiance of unjust authority he was influenced by this nineteenth-century thinker, since he had read and admired his writings. There are two similarities between the phrasing used by Thoreau in *On Civil Disobedience* and Savio's phrasing on December 2, but these are not even close to being identical. Thoreau had urged that when the machine of government promotes injustice, "let your life be a counter friction to stop the machine." Savio's speech urged that when "the operation of the machine becomes so odious…you've got to make it stop." So both equated stopping a machine with resisting injustice. Thoreau had written that when injustice has "a spring, a pulley, a rope, or a crank, exclusively for itself, then perhaps you may consider whether the remedy [i.e. the use of civil disobedience] will not be worse than the evil." This itemized list bears some resemblance to Savio's images of "gears…wheels…levers…all the apparatus" in the December 2 speech. But Savio used his list in an entirely different way than Thoreau. Where Thoreau's reminds readers to be cautious and discriminating about engaging in civil disobedience, Savio's list was invoked to urge the crowd to commit civil disobedience. This is why his list differs from Thoreau's in having its inanimate object mesh with human resisters; at Sproul, Savio said, "You've got to *put your bodies upon* the gears, *upon* the wheels, *upon* the levers, *upon* all the apparatus" (emphasis added). Yet even with these distinctions there are enough similarities to suggest Thoreau's influence, however unconscious it might have been.

The case for such influence, however, is weakened if one keeps in mind that Savio had used the machine metaphor earlier in the FSM (during the September 30 sit-in) and in ways that were not at all similar to Thoreau. Back in that first sit-in, his use of the machine metaphor was linked to his critique of Clark Kerr's use of an industrial metaphor in *Uses of the University*, where Kerr praised the university for its role in the "knowledge industry." Here Savio was influenced as well by Hal Draper, who in his anti-Kerr polemic derided him for converting the university into a "knowledge factory." Savio on September 30 had spoken of the university as a "machine" that "every now and then doesn't work" because its "parts break down." In this university "machine" the "parts are human beings," and dissidents "really gum up the whole works." So the administration throws the dissenters out, just as a factory owner would "throw the parts out" of a "defective machine." Thus one could just as easily credit Kerr or Draper as Thoreau for setting the stage for Savio's use of the machine metaphor in his December 2 speech. With industrial imagery already in circulation, thanks to Kerr and Draper, it was but a small step for Savio to take from the factory floor the machine as a metaphor for dehumanizing power. Henry David Thoreau, *Civil Disobedience and Other Essays* (New York: Dover Publications, 1993), 8; Hal Draper, "The Mind of Clark Kerr," in *Berkeley: The New Student Revolt*, 203, 205; Mario Savio, September 30 speech, in Goines, *The Free Speech Movement*, 152. It is possible that Draper's use of the "knowledge factory" metaphor was a variation on one of the earliest accounts of the Berkeley New Left, which referred to Berkeley education as an "assembly line from lecture to lecture, from exam to exam…a 'factory'…the River Rouge of the Intellect." David Horowitz, *Student* (New York: Ballantine Books, 1962), 13–15.

18. Michael Rossman speech, December 2, 1964, FSM rally.

19. Ibid.

20. Mario Savio, December 2, 1964, speech, in Widmer, ed., *American Speeches*, 617.

21. Ibid.

22. On the lack of triumphalism in Savio's speech, see Lustig, "The FSM and the Vision of a New Left," 217.

23. Savio, speech of December 2, 1964, 617–18.

24. Ibid., 618.

25. Ibid., 617.

26. Michael Lerner, "Remembering Mario Savio," *Tikkun*, January-February 1997, 27; Jackie Goldberg, remarks at Mario Savio's funeral, November 9, 1996, 14.

27. Jackie Goldberg interview by author, 13. That this speech had such an impact on Goldberg was especially impressive since she and Savio had feuded earlier as he pushed her out of the movement's leadership. Goldberg's line about "that whole business about my feet," telling herself not to go in to Sproul but feeling carried by her feet to go in anyway, was apparently a reference to Julia Vinograd's poem "The Sproul Hall Sit-In for the 30th Anniversary of the Free Speech Movement," which was read at the fortieth-anniversary commemoration of the FSM, shortly before I interviewed Goldberg. The poem began:

I remember telling my legs,
Legs you aren't going into that building, no way,
Stop walking legs, you listen to me.
My legs didn't listen
They walked into Sproul Hall
Carrying me with them.

28. Rossman remarks at memorial service, 15.

29. Cohen, "'This Was *Their* Fight,'" 245.

30. Lawrence W. Levine, "To Act or Not to Act: The Berkeley Faculty and the Free Speech Movement," paper delivered at the annual meeting of the Organization of American Historians, San Jose, California, 2005, 2.

31. Clark Kerr, interview by Robert Cohen and Reginald Zelnik, Berkeley, July 2, 1999, tape in author's possession.

32. Savio, speech of December 2, 1964, 617.

33. Searle interview by author, 1. Savio's oratory had the hybridity it did because, despite its roots in the SNCC/Freedom Summer experience, his speeches both used *and transcended* that early SNCC style. While influenced by that democratic approach to public speaking, with its unadorned narrative and lack of jargon, Savio developed a speaking style more poetic, elaborate, and metaphorical than the oratory he had encountered in Mississippi. During most of Freedom Summer, it was conversation that was central, not speechmaking, since much of the organizing was done door-to-door, person-to-person, and Mississippi was in this respect different from Berkeley in fall 1964, where students were more reliant on rallies and oratory explaining the complex free speech dispute.

Bob Moses was skeptical about speechifying and was known for his pensiveness, his sparse and carefully chosen words, and even his silences, rather than for the kind of soaring oratory that made Savio famous. Moses insisted that not words but action—grassroots organizing—did the most to build effective movements for social change: "'How do you attract the tools you need [for movement building] from among the people?' Well it isn't by getting people who are going to respond to the big speech." Moses "deliberately did not develop" himself "as an orator" because he "had feelings that oratory is not necessarily a way to help people grow." He thought grand oratory had a tendency to promise too much, which was inappropriate in Mississippi "because the problem itself," the racist resistance to change, "was too…immense." In this context it was more important "to understate everything…What you had to show people was that you were actually biting off a small piece of the problem.…In Mississippi, when I talked, I just tried to talk about what it was we were doing" to win the vote and battle discrimination. Charles Payne, "This Transformation of the People: An Interview with Bob Moses," in Steven F. Lawson and Charles Payne, *Debating the Civil Rights Movement 1945–1968* (Lanham, Md.: Rowman and Littlefield, 2006), 175–76.

Thus while Savio shared with Moses a powerful intellect, deep knowledge of philosophy, a highly democratic sensibility, personal courage, and a disdain for political celebrity, he was not—much as he might love to be—simply a white Bob Moses. Out of the foundation that Moses and SNCC helped set for him, Savio developed a style of political oratory that was unique and enduring.

34. Savio, "The Berkeley Knowledge Factory," 77.

35. "The University Has Become a Factory," 100.

36. Savio, "The Berkeley Knowledge Factory," 76.

37. Ibid.; Savio, "An End to History," remarks made in Sproul Hall during the December 2 sit-in, in Hal Draper, *Berkeley: The New Student Revolt*, 179.

38. Savio, "The Berkeley Knowledge Factory," 75.

39. Savio, "An End to History," 181; Savio, "The Berkeley Knowledge Factory," 76.

40. Savio, "The Berkeley Knowledge Factory," 75.

41. Savio, speech of December 2, 1964, 617.

42. Savio, speech of September 30, 151.

43. Savio, speech of December 2, 1964, 617.

44. Ibid., 616.

45. Ibid. At the very time of this FSM rally ASUC senators across the plaza tried to hold a rally of their own against the sit-in. At one point the tape of the FSM rally reflects the amplified speakers at that ASUC event almost drowning out the FSM rally speakers (tape of December 2, 1964 FSM rally, www.lib.berkeley.edu/MRC/pacificafsm .html#onsite).html.

46. Savio, speech of December 2, 1964, 616.

47. Ibid.; *San Francisco Examiner*, November 25–27, 1964.

48. Savio, speech of December 2, 1964, 618.

49. Ibid.

50. Joan Baez remarks, tape of December 2, 1964 FSM rally, http://www.lib. berkeley.edu/MRC/pacificafsm.html#onsite.

51. Mario Savio remarks at the conclusion of the rally, tape of December 2, 1964, FSM rally, www.lib.berkeley.edu/MRC/pacificafsm.html#onsite; *San Francisco Chronicle*, December 3, 1964; *New York Times*, December 3, 1964; *Berkeley Daily Gazette*, December 2–3, 1964.

52. Rossman interview by Heirich, 130.

53. *San Francisco Chronicle*, December 3, 1964.

54. Ibid.; *San Francisco Examiner*, December 3, 1964; *Oakland Tribune*, December 3, 1964; *Berkeley Daily Gazette*, December 2 and 3, 1964; Bettina Aptheker, testimony at FSM trial, May 12, 1965, 67–87, http://content.cdlib.org/xtf/search?style=oac-tei& relation=fsm%20–%20leg%20–%20trial&sort=title&startDoc=21; Mario Savio testimony, May 19, 1965, 44–49.

55. *San Francisco Chronicle*, December 3, 1964.

56. *San Francisco Examiner*, December 3, 1964.

57. Ibid.; *Berkeley Daily Gazette*, December 3, 1964; *San Francisco Chronicle*, December 3, 1964; *New York Times*, December 3, 1964.

58. Savio, "An End to History," 179–82 (reprinted in part IV of *Freedom's Orator*).

59. Ibid., 179.

60. Ibid., 180.

61. Ibid., 180–81.

62. Ibid., 181–82.

63. Ibid., 182.

64. Ibid.

65. Ibid.

66. Doug Rossinow, "Mario Savio and the Politics of Authenticity," in Cohen and Zelnik, eds., *The Free Speech Movement*, 538–45; Savio, "An End to History," 181.

67. Kerr, *The Gold and the Blue*, 2:212.

68. Ibid., 212–13. According to Kerr, Governor Brown told him that Strong had urged him to overrule Kerr and order police to clear the building. But Strong denied that he had done this.

69. Rarick, *California Rising*, 304–6; *San Francisco Examiner*, December 4, 1964.

70. Savio testimony at FSM trial, May 19, 1965, 38–39, 50–52.

71. Ibid., 57.

72. For the most thorough report on arrest figures, see ECB [UC Vice President Earl C. Bolton], "Analysis of Those Arrested in Friday Morning Sit-in," December 4, 1964, President's Papers; *New York Times*, December 4, 1964; Savio testimony, May 19, 1965, 63–64.

73. *New York Times*, December 4, 1964.

74. Ibid., December 3, 1964.

75. Ralph J. Gleason, "The Tragedy at the Greek Theatre," *San Francisco Chronicle*, December 9, 1964. Gleason later became a founder of *Rolling Stone* magazine.

76. Henry May, "The Student Movement at Berkeley: Some Impressions," in Lipset and Wolin, eds., *The Berkeley Student Revolt*, 459.

77. Kerr, *The Gold and the Blue*, 2:152–53.

78. Clark Kerr, *The Uses of the University* (New York: Harper Torch, 1966), 86.

79. Ibid., 88.

80. Ibid., 88, 90–91.

81. Shelia Slaughter and Gary Rhoades, *Academic Capitalism and the New Economy: Markets, State, and Higher Education* (Baltimore: Johns Hopkins University Press, 2004), inside front cover flap. Slaughter and Rhoades argue (17):

Like corporations, colleges and universities have begun to treat knowledge as a raw material....The knowledge is often heavily technologized or digitized. Biotechnology and information technology are key examples and illustrate the importance of universities as knowledge sites. Corporations protect knowledge through patents...[and universities have increasingly adopted such corporate behavior]. Prior to 1981, fewer than 250 patents were issued to universities per year. In 1999 colleges and universities filed 5,545 patents. In 1978, several universities permitted acquisition of equity in companies licensing their technology; by 2000, 70 per cent of a sample of sixty-seven research universities had participated in at least one equity deal. In the past five years (1997–2002), approximately half of the states have adjusted their conflict of interest laws so that universities, as represented by administrators, and faculty as inventors and advisors, can hold equity positions in private corporations even when those corporations do business with universities.

82. David L. Kirp, *Shakespeare, Einstein, and the Bottom Line: The Marketing of Higher Education* (Cambridge, Mass.: Harvard University Press, 2003), 219. The latest controversy over corporatization at UC Berkeley occurred in 2007 as UC contracted with BP Amoco PLC to build a biofuel research center, offering so little consultation with the campus community that the student government and Academic Senate protested. See *Daily Californian*, April 20, 30, May 31, 2007.

83. Savio, speech of December 2, 1964, 617. The FSM's focus was on *gaining* student free speech rights, not *subtracting* from the university its right to continue its connections with the Pentagon. But at the first FSM sit-in Savio argued that a

democratic university would allow students to weigh in on the question of whether UC should continue to do atomic weapons research. Savio and the FSM, by questioning the purposes of higher education and insisting on a student voice in determining those purposes, helped to open the door to the protests that occurred on campuses across the United States in the 1960s concerning universities' connections to the military, ROTC, and defense research. See Immanuel Wallerstein and Paul Starr, eds., *The University Crisis Reader* (New York: Random House, 1971), 185–292.

84. Savio, "Beyond the Cold War: An Education in Politics," 18–19. Even Ronald Reagan used the "knowledge factory" term, though in Reagan's hands it was shorn of its anticapitalist implications and used to lambaste liberal faculty. Nonetheless, Reagan echoed Savio in speaking of "the disappointment and resentment of an entire college generation that finds itself being fed into a knowledge factory with no regard for their individuality, aspirations, or their dreams." Ronald Reagan, speech at the Commonwealth Club, San Francisco, June 13, 1969, in Wallerstein and Starr, eds., *University Crisis Reader*, 130).

85. Savio, speech of September 30, 1964, 151.

86. Lawrence W. Levine, "From the Big Apple to Berkeley: Perspectives of a Junior Faculty Member," in Cohen and Zelnik, eds., *The Free Speech Movement*, 344. Actually Savio had said "real classes" would take place, "something which hasn't occurred at this university in a good long time"—and he was stressing that these would occur during the sit-in.

87. Savio, speech of December 2, 1964, 617–18.

88. Savio interview by Kitchell, tape 2, 2.

89. Zelnik, "On the Side of the Angels," 271–73; Heirich, *Spiral of Conflict*, 218–19.

90. Levine, "To Act or Not to Act," 3.

91. Ibid., 4; Zelnik, "On the Side of the Angels," 278, 297–98; Wofsy, "When the FSM Disturbed the Faculty Peace," 348.

92. Levine, "To Act or Not to Act," 2–5.

93. Ibid., 4–5.

94. Mario Savio to Joe Savio, January 10, 1964, copy in author's possession.

95. Savio, introduction to Hal Draper, *Berkeley: The New Student Revolt*, 4.

96. "The University Has Become a Factory," 100.

97. Ibid.

98. Mario Savio, "Berkeley Fall: The Berkeley Student Rebellion of 1964," in Mario Savio, Raya Dunayevskaya, and Eugene Walker, *The Free Speech Movement and the Negro Revolution* (Detroit: News and Letters, 1965), 17.

99. Carl Schorske, "Intellectual Life, Civil Libertarian Issues, and the Student Movement at the University of California at Berkeley, 1960–1969," interview by Ann Lage, Regional Oral History Office, UC Berkeley, 2000, 51, 53, 102.

100. Levine, "From the Big Apple to Berkeley," 344; Levine, "To Act or Not to Act," 11.

101. Clark Kerr, "Address at Commencement Exercises, Berkeley Campus, 12 July, 1965," FSM Records, University Archives, Bancroft Library.

102. Kerr, *Uses of the University*, 65.

103. Savio, "An End to History," 179–80.

104. Ibid., 181.

105. Kerr, *The Gold and the Blue*, 2:212; Kerr interview by Cohen and Zelnik.

106. Weinberg interview by author, 30.

Chapter 9

1. Savio, "Thirty Years Later," 68–70; Heirich, *The Spiral of Conflict*, 286–87.

2. *San Francisco Chronicle*, December 5, 1964. While the *Chronicle* put the crowd size at 6,000, the *Berkeley Daily Gazette*, which tended to be less overtly hostile to the FSM and more accurate, put the crowd size at 12,000. See *Berkeley Daily Gazette*, December 4, 1964.

3. Zelnik, "On the Side of the Angels," 303.

4. *San Francisco Examiner*, December 4, 1964.

5. Zelnik, "On the Side of the Angels," 306.

6. *San Francisco Examiner*, December 4, 1964.

7. Ibid.; G.C. to Clark Kerr, December 4, 1964, President's Papers; Rorabaugh, *Berkeley at War*, 32.

8. *San Francisco Examiner*, December 4, 1964.

9. Zelnik, "On the Side of the Angels," 306–8; Kerr, *The Gold and the Blue*, 2:213–15.

10. *San Francisco Chronicle*, December 8, 1964.

11. Savio, "Berkeley Knowledge Factory," 78; Savio interview by Heirich, 141–42.

12. Savio, "Berkeley Knowledge Factory," 78; Robert Scalapino, interview by Lisa Rubens, Berkeley Regional Oral History Office, May 17, 2001, 61; John Leggett, interview by Lisa Rubens, Berkeley Regional Oral History Office, January 24, 2001, 70.

13. Goines, *The Free Speech Movement*, 423.

14. *San Francisco Chronicle*, December 9, 1964.

15. Heirich, *The Spiral of Conflict*, 291.

16. *San Francisco Examiner*, December 8, 1964.

17. Kerr, *The Gold and the Blue*, 2:214.

18. Savio interview by Heirich, 143.

19. Aptheker interview by Heirich, 57.

20. Savio interview by Heirich, 143; Savio, "The Berkeley Knowledge Factory," 79.

21. Savio, "Thirty Years Later," 68.

22. Savio interview by Heirich, 143; Aptheker interview by Heirich, 57; Aptheker interview by author, 21.

23. *New York Times*, December 8, 1964.

24. Ibid.; *San Francisco Examiner*, December 8, 1964; *San Francisco Chronicle*, December 8, 1964.

25. News footage of Mario Savio being interviewed at the Greek Theatre following the police attack on him, excerpted in documentary film *Berkeley in the Sixties* by Mark Kitchell; Savio interview by Heirich, 144; Savio interview by Kitchell, tape 2, 1–2; Savio, "Thirty Years Later," 68–69.

26. *New York Times*, December 8, 1964.

27. Kerr, *The Gold and the Blue*, 2:215.

28. *Daily Californian*, December 8, 1964.

29. *New York Times*, December 8, 1964; Aptheker interview by author, 21.

30. *San Francisco Examiner*, December 8, 1964.

31. Kerr, *The Gold and the Blue*, 2:215.

32. *New York Times*, December 8, 1964; *San Francisco Chronicle*, December 8, 1964.

33. Dorothea Lange's remarks were reported to me in July 1999 by Henry Mayer, who was working on a biography of her. One faculty member sympathetic to the FSM

termed Savio's walk to the stage, asserting his right to speak, "a magnificent moment of heroism, personal heroism." Leggett interview, 71.

34. John Searle, interview by Mark Kitchell, take 79, 7, c. 1984, copy of transcript in author's possession This excerpt from the Searle interviews also appears in the film *Berkeley in the Sixties*.

35. Zelnik, "On the Side of the Angels," 313–18.

36. Clark Kerr to Sidney Hook, November 3, 1965, Chancellor's Papers.

37. Savio, "Thirty Years Later," 69; Bettina Aptheker, quoted in Cohen, "The FSM and Beyond," 66.

38. Ibid. On the loyalty oath at UC, see Bob Blauner, *Resisting McCarthyism: To Sign or Not to Sign the California Loyalty Oath* (Palo Alto: Stanford University Press, 2009).

39. Savio, "Thirty Years Later," 69.

40. FSM rally, Sproul Hall steps, December 9, 1964, transcript, Chancellor's Papers, 2; excerpt of Mario Savio's December 9, 1964, speech in documentary film *Berkeley in the Sixties*; Goines, *The Free Speech Movement*, 480.

41. Nathan Glazer, *Remembering the Answers: Essays on the American Student Revolt* (New York: Basic Books, 1970), 184–87; Bloom, *Closing of the American Mind*, 313–35.

42. FSM rally, December 9, 1964, transcript, 1. Savio's idealism about the university and its potential is suggested in the titles he chose for the chapters on the FSM that he was planning to write in his memoir. These were "Free Speech at Last" and "…And a Free University!" Savio, "Beyond the Cold War: The Education of an American Radical," 6.

43. FSM rally, December 9, 1964, transcript, 1–2.

44. *San Francisco Chronicle*, December 10, 1964; Savio, "Berkeley Knowledge Factory," 75–76.

45. FSM rally, December 9, 1964, transcript, 1–2.

46. *San Francisco Chronicle*, December 9 and 10, 1964.

47. James Farmer, remarks at UC Berkeley, December 15, 1964, transcript, President's Papers. On labor, see Draper, *Berkeley: The New Student Revolt*, 107–8; Bettina Aptheker, e-mail to author, April 24, 2008. On Savio and the East Coast and midwestern campus tour by FSM leaders, see Robert Cohen's introduction to Savio, "The Berkeley Knowledge Factory," 71–74. The Vietnam War was mentioned at the FSM's victory rally. See FSM rally, December 9, 1964, transcript, 8.

48. Mervin D. Field, "The UC Student Protests: California Poll," in Lipset and Wolin, eds., *The Berkeley Student Revolt*, 199.

49. Edmund G. Brown to Max Rafferty, February 11, 65, Edmund G. Brown Papers (hereafter EGP), Bancroft Library.

50. Mrs. L. Robles to Edmund G. Brown, December 8, 1964, EGP.

51. World War II veteran to Edmund G. Brown, December 4, 1964, EGP.

52. "Frightened Citizen" to Edmund G. Brown, December 11, 1964, EGP.

53. Josephine Southward to Edmund G. Brown, December 14, 1964, EGP.

54. S. H. Vogel to Edmund G. Brown, December 9, 1964, EGP.

55. M. H. Lund to Pat Brown, December 5, 1964, EGP.

56. "Frightened Citizen" to Edmund G. Brown, December 11, 1964, EGP.

57. Mrs. L. Robles to Edmund G. Brown, December 8, 1964, EGP.

58. Mrs. L. Strome to Edmund G. Brown, December 7, 1964, EGP.

59. John Ellis to Edmund G. Brown, December 7, 1964, EGP.

60. John B. and Helen L. Wilson, telegram to Edmund G. Brown, December 9, 1964, EGP.

61. Mrs. Harry Brown, telegram to Edmund G. Brown, December 8, 1964, EGP.

62. Dr. Lawrence E. White, telegram to Edmund G. Brown, December 8, 1964, EGP.

63. Irene R. Davis, telegram to Edmund G. Brown December 9, 1964, EGP.

64. Strong, "Philosopher, Professor, and Berkeley Chancellor," 11.

65. Searle interview by Kitchell, take 79, 8.

66. Ibid.

67. The day of the final FSM sit-in, Vice Chancellor Alex Sherriffs, in urging Kerr to take a hard line against the protesters, connected student unrest and labor insurgency. He "told Kerr about McNiven's meeting last night with about 200 business men in San Francisco. These men wondered what was wrong with the university administration; if there were strikes against the university, they were concerned about strikes against their businesses." Sherriffs to Kerr—telephone call, December 2, 1964, 11:00 A.M., Chancellor's Papers.

68. Schorske, "Intellectual, Life, Civil Libertarian Issues, and the Student Movement," 91–92, 94.

69. Press release JB-#831, Gov Edmund G. Brown, December 9, 1964; Edmund G. Brown to "Dear Friend" [form letter on FSM crisis, December 1964], EGP; *San Francisco Examiner*, December 4, 1964.

70. Dallek, *The Right Moment: Ronald Reagan's First Victory*, 80–102, 189–96; Rorabaugh, "The FSM, Berkeley Politics, and Ronald Reagan," 511–18.

71. Even sympathetic faculty were critical of the FSM's liberal-bashing tendencies. See Wofsy interview, 2–3. On the Left-liberal relationship nationally, see Michael Kazin, "What Liberals Owe to Radicals," in Neil Jumonville and Kevin Mattson, eds., *Liberalism for a New Century* (Berkeley: University of California Press, 2007), 126–27.

72. It may seem unfair to criticize Savio for not anticipating in 1964 the rise of Ronald Reagan to the governorship in 1966, the backlash politics that carried Richard Nixon to the White House in 1968, and the ascent of the New Right. But it is evident that the liberal "sellout" in Atlantic City and Governor Brown's police invasion of Sproul embittered Savio, and his loathing of the Democratic Party blinded him to the threat from the right. In 1966 Savio underestimated Reaganism as a political force, dismissing the idea "that a Reagan victory" in the California governor's race "will mean the beginning of the dark ages." He thought liberals in the Democratic Party would stymie Reagan even if he did get elected. "The whole system functions in such a way that nothing new really happens. It's designed to keep new things from occurring...to institutionalize the end of all historical change" (Mario Savio, speech at ZTA fraternity, 1966, transcript in author's possession, 3–4). While Democrats in the California legislature did force Reagan to make compromises as governor, his election was a first step on the road to the White House, which ended up moving American politics far to the right and toppling much of the New Deal order. This was arguably the most significant change in American electoral politics in the late twentieth century, and Savio failed to recognize its early manifestations.

73. "1984: Reflections" [on the FSM], *California Monthly*, December 1984, 21.

74. Brinton H. Stone to Vice Chancellor Earl Cheit, December 2, 1996, Chancellor's papers, Bancroft Library Stone, a UC Berkeley placement advisor,

also condemned "professors with romantic ideas of being Liberal heroes," who by allying themselves with the student movement empowered "academic scum." Urging that UC use its "legal talent" to get Savio and these other "Lee Harvey Oswald types" locked up, he slammed liberal professors in anti-Semitic terms. Expressing fear of the university becoming politicized, Stone referenced two of Berkeley's leading liberal Jewish social science faculty, Philip Selznick and Jerome Skolnik, in his comment that UC was "becoming Latin Americanized by beatniks, peaceniks, Selsnicks [sic] or Skolnicks."

75. "1984: Reflections," 17.

76. Dorman, *Arguing the World*, 147. For an elaboration of this argument against the use of civil disobedience on campus, see Glazer, *Remembering the Answers*, 113–30.

77. "1984: Reflections," 21.

78. Ibid.

79. Searle interview by Kitchell, take 79, 7–8.

80. Donald Farish, telephone interview by author, October 25, 2007, 2.

81. Rose Lucas to Michael, December 13, 1996. This letter and all the 1996 memorial correspondence below are from the private collection of Lynne Hollander Savio, copies in author's possession (hereafter LHS).

82. Sheila, message in Mario Savio memorial book, written by attendees of the Savio memorial ceremony, UC Berkeley, December 8, 1996, LHS.

83. Laura Plotkin to Savio family, November 19, 1996, LHS.

84. Rev. Patricia Roberts e-mail to Anya, December 31, 1996, LHS.

85. Adrianne Aron to Daniel Savio, December 15, 1996, LHS. Savio's oratory not only appealed to political novices but also to more committed activists. See Lerner, "Remembering Mario Savio," 27.

86. Kate Coleman, "Mario Savio Remembered," copy in author's possession.

87. Jeff Lustig to Lynne Hollander Savio, November 12, 1996, LHS.

88. Garson, "Mario Savio: Stirring Up the Students," *London Guardian*, November 9, 1996.

89. Moffet B. Hall, message in Savio memorial book, November 1996.

90. Jon Carroll, "A Long Goodbye to Mario Savio," *San Francisco Chronicle*, November 8, 1996.

91. Meg O'Hara, "Reflecting on Mario Savio," *Daily Californian*, December 2, 1996.

92. David McCullough to the family of Mario Savio, November 11, 1996, LHS.

93. Robert Scheer, "The Man Who Stopped the Machine," *Los Angeles Times*, November 12, 1996.

94. David McCullough to the family of Mario Savio, November 11, 1996, LHS.

95. David Wofsy to Lynne Hollander Savio, November 6, 1996, LHS. On other testaments to Savio's impact on sixties activists beyond Berkeley, see Bob Massi to Lynne Hollander Savio, December 3, 1996, LHS; Theodore Kornweibel Jr., "Mario Savio's Moment of Destiny," *San Francisco Chronicle*, November 13, 1996; Bill Banks to Lynne Hollander Savio, December 2, 1996, LHS; Patty Coughlan message in Savio memorial book, December 5, 1996, LHS. For criticism of that influence, see Searle interview by Kitchell, take 79, 8–9.

96. SAC Cincinnati to SAC San Francisco, December 30, 1964, Mario Savio FBI file, 100-5406052, copy in author's possession.

97. David Farber, *The Age of Great Dreams: America in the 1960s* (New York: Hill and Wang, 1994), 3.

98. Barbara Olsen Parker, e-mail to Reginald E. Zelnik, January 12, 1997, copy in author's possession.

99. Feldman-Wood interview, 11–12; Stevenson interview, 4, 8–9.

100. Savio, "Beyond the Cold War: The Education of an American Radical," typed version, 4; Savio, "Beyond the Cold War: An Education in Politics," 22.

101. Savio, "Beyond the Cold War: The Education of an American Radical," typed version, 4–5.

102. Mario Savio to Friends, August 29, 1984, copy in author's possession.

Chapter 10

1. *San Francisco Examiner*, December 10, 1964; *San Francisco Chronicle*, December 10, 1964; *Berkeley Daily Gazette*, December 10, 1964; J. F. Bland to W. C. Sullivan, December 11, 1964, FBI file SF 100-50460, copy in author's possession. For the only complete version of a speech Savio gave on this campus speaking tour, see Savio, "The Berkeley Knowledge Factory," 75–81, and on its historical context, see my introduction to it, ibid., 71–74.

2. Confidential memo on Mario Robert Savio and Suzanne Savio, San Francisco, September 17, 1965, FBI file 100-54060-2764, copy in author's possession.

3. *Daily Californian*, February 5, 1965.

4. *Los Angeles Times*, February 3, 1965.

5. *San Francisco Examiner*, April 2, 1965; *People of the State of California vs. Mario Savio et al.*, nos. C-7468 through C-7547, First Consolidated Trial, May 13, 1965, Reporter's Transcript of Trial Before the Hon. Rupert G. Crittenden, Judge, April 1, 1965, 38–40.

6. Goines, *The Free Speech Movement*, 527, 529.

7. *Daily Californian*, March 3, 1965; *Oakland Tribune*, March 2, 1965.

8. *Berkeley Daily Gazette*, December 19, 1964.

9. This FBI spying on and Red-baiting of Savio and the FSM became public only in 1982 after Berkeley's student newspaper learned of it through FBI documents attained via a Freedom of Information Act request. See *Daily Californian*, May 28, June 1 and 2, 1982; Seth Rosenfeld, "Mario Savio's FBI Odyssey," *San Francisco Chronicle Magazine*, October 10, 2004, 16–23, 27. Savio and other FSMers were spied upon not only by the FBI but also by segregationist intelligence agents of the state of Mississippi. See Jo Freeman, "The Berkeley FSM and the Mississippi Sovereignty Commissions," *Left History*, Spring 2003, 135–44.

10. FBI file 157-258, Berkeley, February 16, 1965 (filing agent's name deleted by FBI censor), copy in author's possession.

11. FBI file 100-54060, San Francisco, May 19, 1965 (filing agent's name deleted by FBI censor), copy in author's possession.

12. Goines, *The Free Speech Movement*, 485–88.

13. Ibid., 487.

14. Heirich, *Spiral of Conflict*, 360–61.

15. Ibid., 365.

16. Goines, *The Free Speech Movement*, 489–90.

17. Ibid., 488–99; "Position of the Free Speech Movement on the Obscenity Cases," March 18, 1965, Chancellor's Papers.

18. Goines, *The Free Speech Movement*, 491.

19. *San Francisco Chronicle*, March 12, 1965. However, even before the "fuck" controversy began, Savio was aware that important free speech principles were violated when authorities sought to bar the use of obscene language in social commentary. The day before the start of that controversy, Savio met with the UC administration urging that Lenny Bruce, the comedian whose use of obscene language in his act had led to his arrest, be allowed to speak on campus. See Neil Smelser to Martin Meyerson, March 3, 15, 1965, Chancellor's Papers. Still, it is striking that in 1965 so much of the Berkeley Left—which proved indifferent to the free speech implications of campus obscenity case—did not connect with the history of free speech in the Bay Area, failing to recognize the way censorship had been used there, under the guise of policing obscenity, against such cultural radicals as Lenny Bruce and Allen Ginsberg. See Ronald K. L. Collins and David M. Skover, *The Trials of Lenny Bruce: The Rise and Fall of an American Icon* (Naperville, Ill.: Sourcebooks, 2002), 37–78. On the evolution of the national obscenity debate later in the sixties, see Kenneth Cmiel, "The Politics of Civility," in David Farber, ed., *The Sixties: From Memory to History* (Chapel Hill: University of North Carolina Press, 1998), 274–82.

20. Heirich, *The Spiral of Conflict*, 368.

21. Mario Savio, remarks at the panel discussion "December 8th and the Present Crisis," March 25, 1965, Berkeley, transcript, copy in author's possession, 3.

22. Ibid., 3–4.

23. Ibid., 4, 6.

24. Ibid., 5.

25. Ibid., 6.

26. Ibid., 7.

27. Rorabaugh, *Berkeley at War*, 39.

28. Heirich, *The Spiral of Conflict*, 374; *San Francisco Chronicle*, April 28, 1965; *San Francisco Examiner*, April 26, 1965.

29. Weinberg interview by author, 35. This failure of much of the Left to defend the obscenity protesters was, according to Weinberg, connected to the sexual puritanism and instrumentalist views on free speech displayed by segments of the campus radical community: "All of those prudes in the Old Left, a lot of people who thought it was wrong.... While the Free Speech Movement and.... the Communist Party wing of the FSM weaved this enormous defense of civil liberties as an abstraction, at least that Communist Party wing of the Free Speech Movement, as far as the people being consistent, I think that maybe Bettina believed the rhetoric, but...this was not a group of civil libertarians. This was a group just as ready to go the other way. They could use civil liberties language when it could meet their needs but they didn't believe it" (Weinberg interview by author, 36).

30. Savio, remarks at the panel discussion "December 8th and the Present Crisis," 7–8.

31. *Daily Californian*, April 8 and 23, 1965. On Strong's resignation, see Kerr, *The Gold and the Blue*, 2:257–58.

32. Mario Savio, farewell speech, April 26, 1965, Sproul Plaza, Berkeley, transcript, copy in author's possession, 5.

33. *San Francisco Examiner*, April 27, 1965.

34. *San Francisco Chronicle*, April 28, 1965.

35. *Berkeley Daily Gazette*, April 27, 1965; *Daily Californian*, April 27 and 28, 1965.

36. Weinberg interview by author, 32–33.

37. *Daily Californian*, April 28, 1965.

38. Savio, farewell speech, 5.

39. Ibid. Savio's self-criticism had considerable merit, for in the waning days of the FSM in 1965 he had become a dominant figure, even in internal decision making. See Weinberg interview by Heirich, 90. The Bonaparte comparison had family roots, as Savio was in that speech thinking of his Fascist grandfather—whom he loved but whose politics were so "wrong-headed…One of his personal heroes was Napoleon Bonaparte, and I had this little particular connection in the back of my mind when" making the resignation speech. "You can't give out all the footnotes when you're making a speech" (Savio interview by Kitchell, tape 3, 2).

40. Savio, farewell speech, 1–4.

41. Ibid.

42. Kerr, *The Gold and the Blue*, 2:260–62. Where Savio differed with Kerr was that Savio's opposition to the regents was grounded not in one action but in many, and that Savio wanted a total change in the way this governing body was structured. Savio would have replaced the business-dominated Board of Regents with "scholars of various kinds. People who have made notable contributions in the arts, music…public health. There should be serious representation of minority groups, [the] working community, racial minorities, serious representation of laborers."("The University Has Become a Factory," 100: Mario Savio, interview by Jack Fincher, 1965, 3–4, transcript in author's possession). Note that Fincher's is the lengthy Savio interview whose excerpts *Life* ran as "The University Has Become a Factory" on February 26, 1965.

43. Savio, farewell speech, 3.

44. Ibid.

45. Savio interview by Fincher, 6.

46. *Daily Californian*, April 28, 1965.

47. Zelnik, "On the Side of the Angels," 264–338.

48. Cohen, "The Many Meanings of the FSM," 32–33; Wofsy, "When the FSM Disturbed the Faculty Peace," 351–52.

49. Savio, farewell speech, 2. For an illuminating discussion of the intellectual implications of Savio's support for the Tussman plan, see David A. Hollinger, "A View from the Margins," in Cohen and Zelnik, eds., *The Free Speech Movement*, 178–82.

50. Savio, farewell speech, 1.

51. Rorabaugh, "The FSM, Berkeley Politics, and Ronald Reagan," 515–16.

52. Savio, farewell speech, 4–5.

53. Ibid.

54. Mario Savio to Joseph and Dora Savio, April 28, 1965, copy in author's possession.

55. Ibid.

56. Earl C. Bolton to Clark Kerr, December 21, 1964, President's Papers; Robert Cohen, "Mario Savio and Berkeley's 'Little Free Speech Movement' of 1966," in Cohen and Zelnik, eds., *The Free Speech Movement*, 449–84.

57. *San Francisco Examiner*, July 15, 1965; *Berkeley Daily Gazette*, July 27, 1965; David Goines, *The Free Speech Movement*, 526–62.

58. *San Francisco Chronicle*, July 27, 1965.

59. Charles De Benedetti, *An American Ordeal: The Antiwar Movement of the Vietnam Era* (Syracuse, N.Y.: Syracuse University Press, 1990), 107–8; *We Accuse*, 1. Note that the Berkeley teach-in, which came two months after the one in Michigan, dwarfed it in terms of its attendance—with Michigan drawing some three thousand and Berkeley five to ten times that number (depending upon whose crowd estimates one uses) See Tom Wells, *The War Within: America's Battle over Vietnam* (New York: Henry Holt, 1994), 24–25. The Berkeley teach-in reflected New Left sexism in that only one of the many speakers was female.

60. Savio, "The Free Speech Movement and the Rhetoric of the Student Movement," 6–7.

61. Ibid., 6.

62. Ibid.; Mario Savio, "All I Really Have Is a Lot of Questions," transcript of Savio's teach-in speech, in *We Accuse*, 31 (this speech is reprinted in part IV of *Freedom's Orator*).

63. Savio, "The Free Speech Movement and the Rhetoric of the Student Movement," 6–7.

64. Savio, "Beyond the Cold War: An Education in Politics," 32–34.

65. Mario Savio, "The New Radicals: An Exchange," *New Politics*, Fall 1965, 13. On Mario's differences with Marxism, also see Jeff Lustig to Mario Savio, December 5, 1994, copy in author's possession.

66. Savio, "The New Radicals: An Exchange," 15.

67. Weinberg interview by author, 3–4.

68. Ibid., 28.

69. Ibid., 28–29.

70. Ibid., 4, 35.

71. Ibid., 29–30.

72. Suzanne Goldberg, "Mario: Personal and Political," 559–60; Mario Savio to Office of the Registrar, December 10, 1965; Mario Savio to the Dean of Arts and Sciences, August 11, 1966, both in Mario Savio disciplinary file, Chancellor's Papers.

73. Cohen, "Mario Savio and Berkeley's 'Little Free Speech Movement' of 1966," 469–71, 481 n. 53–56, 482 n. 57–59.

74. Ibid., 449–76.

75. Savio interview by Cohen and Pickell, 32; Mario Savio, Bettina Aptheker, Dan Rosenthal, and Brian O'Brian [O'Brien], *The Save the Steps Rally, Friday, November 4, 1966: A Complete Transcription of the Speeches* (Berkeley: Academic Publishing, 1966), 6–10.

76. *Save the Steps Rally*, 1–2.

77. Ibid., 3.

78. Weinberg interview by author, 34; Cohen, "Berkeley's 'Little Free Speech Movement,'" 465–68.

79. "Our Traditional Liberties," in Chancellor's Papers; Savio interview by Cohen and Pickell, 32.

80. *Save the Steps Rally*, 7.

81. Ibid., 10.

82. Ibid., 8.

83. Ibid., 9.

84. Cohen, "Berkeley's 'Little Free Speech Movement,'" 465–67, 481 nn. 44–49.

85. Ibid., 468–71, 482 nn. 58–59.

86. Savio publicly opposed the attempt to mobilize students to protest the barring of his readmission, on the grounds that he was "philosophically opposed to student movements on behalf of individual persons" (*Daily Californian*, November 9, 1966).

87. *San Francisco Chronicle*, December 1, 1966; *Berkeley Barb*, December 2, 1966; Ironically, at a time when the UC administration was implementing new rules to limit the political rights of nonstudent protesters on campus, it insisted in the Naval ROTC case that nonstudents—i.e., military recruiters—be allowed to set up a recruitment table while denying this same right to students who wanted to set up an antiwar table in the same building. See Rorabaugh, *Berkeley at War*, 109.

88. Reginald E. Zelnik, e-mail to author, December 19, 1999.

89. David Halberstam, *The Children* (New York: Fawcett, 1998), 357–58.

90. *Los Angeles Times*, July 6, 1969.

91. Ibid.

92. Goldberg, "Mario: Personal and Political," 560–61.

93. Savio, "Thirty Years Later," 59.

94. Mario Savio to Lynne Hollander, December 21, 1968, copy in author's possession.

95. *Daily Californian*, February 14, 1967.

96. Ibid.; Mario Savio, "The Uncertain Future of the Multiversity: A Partisan Scrutiny of Berkeley's Muscatine Report," *Harper's Magazine*, October 1966, 88–94.

97. Savio, "The Uncertain Future of the Multiversity," 88.

98. *Daily Californian*, February 14, 1967, January 23 and 25, 1967. Savio later said he was "ashamed" of his remarks about Kerr both because they were unkind and he had made them without consulting the FSM's Steering Committee. Savio interview by Giles, 5.

99. *Daily Californian*, February 14, January 23 and 25, 1967.

100. *Daily Californian*, February 14, 1967.

101. Robert Scheer, "The Man Who Stopped the Machine," *Los Angeles Times*, November 12, 1996.

102. Stew Albert, "Remembering Mario Savio," *Tikkun*, January-February 1997, 29.

103. Savio, "Beyond the Cold War: The Education of an American Radical," typed version, 5; Savio, "Beyond the Cold War: The Education of an American Radical," 9; Savio, "Beyond the Cold War: An Education in Politics," 25.

104. Savio, "Beyond the Cold War: An Education in Politics," 25.

105. *We Accuse*.

106. Savio, "Beyond the Cold War: Education of an American Radical," typed version, 5.

107. Ibid.

108. Ibid.

109. Savio, "Beyond the Cold War: The Education of an American Radical," 11; Savio, "The Free Speech Movement and the Rhetoric of the Student Movement," 6–8.

110. Savio, "Beyond the Cold War: Education of an American Radical," typed version, 5. On the appeal of Marxism to some on the late-sixties New Left, see Max Elbaum, *Revolution in the Air: Sixties Radicals Turn to Lenin, Mao, and Che* (New York: Verso, 2002), 1–162.

111. Savio, "Beyond the Cold War: Education of an American Radical," typed version, 5.

112. SAC San Francisco to FBI Director, February 13, 1967, FBI file 100-54060.

113. Mario Savio to Lynne Hollander, July 19, 1967, copy in author's possession. The only FSMer to publish an account of his experience serving the prison sentence is Michael Rossman, in *Wedding Within the War* (Garden City, N.Y.: Doubleday, 1971), 169–200.

114. Mario Savio to Lynne Hollander, August 10, 1967, copy in author's possession.

115. Ibid.

116. Ibid.

117. Suzanne Goldberg, interview by Lisa Rubens, July 17, 2000, transcript in author's possession, 29.

118. Ibid., 17.

119. Aptheker interview by author, 15–16. On this Executive Committee sexism, also see Iyama interview, 11.

120. Mario Savio to Lynne Hollander, August 10, 1967.

121. Truston Davis, remarks at Mario Savio's funeral, November 9, 1996, tape in author's possession.

122. *Berkeley Daily Gazette*, March 11 and May 3, 1968; *Berkeley Barb*, April 5–11, 1968; *Hayward Pioneer*, May 14, 1968.

123. Mario Savio to Art Gatti, September 13, 1968, copy in author's possession.

124. Ibid. The McCarthy reference is to the supporters of Eugene McCarthy's antiwar presidential candidacy.

125. Savio, "Beyond the Cold War: The Education of an American Radical," 12.

126. *Berkeley Barb*, March 22, 1968; Joel Wilson, "'Free Huey': The Black Panthers, the Peace and Freedom Party, and the Politics of Race in 1968," Ph.D. dissertation, UC Santa Cruz, 2002, 186–87, 193–94.

127. *Wall Street Journal*, June 4, 1969.

128. Weinberg interview by author, 29.

129. Joel Wilson, "'Free Huey,'" 5.

130. Mario Savio, "Seize the Means of Leisure," *Daily Californian*, July 1, 1969.

131. *Daily Californian*, February 23, 1971.

132. Todd Gitlin, *The Sixties*, 222–438. Savio; "The Activist's Dream," 23.

133. Savio, "The Free Speech Movement and the Rhetoric of the Student Movement," 7.

134. Ibid., 4.

135. Ibid., 7–8. For a similar perspective by another early New Left leader on such late New Left revolutionary fantasies, see Carl Oglesby, *Ravens in the Storm: A Personal History of the 1960s Antiwar Movement* (New York: Scribner, 2008), 215.

136. Savio, "Beyond the Cold War: An Education in Politics," 28.

137. Savio, "The Free Speech Movement and the Rhetoric of the Student Movement," 7.

138. Savio, "Beyond the Cold War: The Education of an American Radical," version II, 11.

139. Ibid.

140. Savio, "Beyond the Cold War: An Education in Politics," 32.

141. Ibid., 33.

142. Ibid., 32–33.

143. Savio, "Beyond the Cold War: The Education of an American Radical," 12. This unwillingness to follow a hypercritical policy on Israel is linked to Savio's fondness

for Judaism, or at least for Jewish friends, teachers, and wives (both of his wives were Jewish), who he felt had helped to liberate him from the intellectual rigidity of his Catholic background. This is what Savio was alluding to when in recalling his intellectual trajectory he mentioned how in moving toward Christianity "Saul became Paul, [while] in some ways I'm going the other way: It's not like the road from Damascus to Jerusalem, more like the road from Rome to Jerusalem" (Savio, "Philosophy of a Young Activist," 1).

Savio continued to be more vigilant in standing up on Jewish human rights issues than many radical Jews. His ethical approach to politics, the background of having had a fascist grandfather and feeling embarrassed by Italy's role in World War II, and being horrified by the Holocaust left Savio with no tolerance for anti-Semitism. This can be seen in an incident that occurred in the 1990s when the Campus Coalitions for Human Rights and Social Responsibility, an organization Savio helped to found, was confronted with an anti-Semitic issue. This was primarily a faculty organization, though it did have student members. It turned out that one of the graduate students in the organization, and who ended up on its Steering Committee, was a Palestinian, who as an undergraduate had been involved in an anti-Semitic incident at San Francisco State, centered on a mural on that campus, which had the star of David dripping blood and dollar signs. When historian Barbara Epstein, a Steering Committee member, checked on this story, she learned from a San Francisco State faculty member who had debated this student that he had displayed anti-Semitic attitudes. Epstein "raised this at a steering committee meeting and the one person who had a really clear perspective on it was Mario. Mario said that if this turned out to be the case and that" this student on the Steering Committee "was anti-Semitic, he had no interest in working with anti-Semites. Everyone else [on the Steering Committee] sort of hemmed and hawed about it. And, of course, the interesting thing was everybody else [on that committee] was Jewish....What I was impressed by was Mario's willingness to take a stand on it when nobody else was willing to address the issue....To Mario politics and ethics/morality were extremely close. There really was no dividing line. I think that for some other faculty there was a greater distance; they were thinking more about the political implications rather than their moral stance on this issue. Whereas for Mario the political issues were there because of moral issues or were one and the same" (Epstein telephone interview, 4–5).

144. Savio, "The Free Speech Movement and Rhetoric of the Student Movement," 6–7.

145. Ibid., 8.

146. Ibid., 6–7.

147. Ibid., 8.

148. Savio, "Beyond the Cold War: The Education of an American Radical," 11.

149. Ibid.

150. Savio, "Beyond the Cold War: An Education in Politics," 32.

151. Ibid., 33.

152. Savio, "Beyond the Cold War: The Education of an American Radical," 10.

153. Savio, "The Free Speech Movement and the Rhetoric of the Student Movement," 7–8.

154. Savio, "Beyond the Cold War: An Education in Politics," 30.

155. Ibid., 34–39. On the unsuccessful attempt from within the CPUSA to challenge Party orthodoxy on Soviet imperialism in Czechoslovakia and on other issues, see

Aptheker, *Intimate Politics*, 214–16; Dorothy Ray Healey and Maurice Isserman, *California Red: A Life in the Communist Party* (Urbana: University of Illinois Press, 1993), 228–35; Peggy Dennis, *The Autobiography of an American Communist: A Personal View of a Political Life* (Westport: Lawrence Hill, 1977), 276–79.

156. Savio, "Beyond the Cold War: An Education in Politics," 34–39.

157. Mario Savio, typescript of his antiwar speech [1969 or 1970], copy in author's possession, 1–14.

158. Savio, "Beyond the Cold War: An Education in Politics," 30, 37, 39, 41; Savio antiwar speech [1969 or 1970], 1–14.

159. Savio, "Beyond the Cold War: An Education in Politics," 41. The scholarship on Nixon and Allende confirms Savio's reading of the Allende tragedy. The Nixon administration policy toward Allende's Chile was among the most glaring examples of the United States subverting democracy abroad to serve U.S. business interests, Washington's cold war ideology, and Machiavellian geopolitics. See John Haslam, *The Nixon Administration and the Death of Allende's Chile* (New York: Verso, 2005); Robert Dallek, *Nixon and Kissinger: Partners in Power* (New York: Harper Collins, 2007), 230–42, 509–15.

160. Savio interview by Kitchell, tape 2, 4.

161. Ibid.

162. Savio, "Beyond the Cold War: The Education of an American Radical," 15.

163. Savio interview by Kitchell, tape 2, 4–5.

164. Ibid., 4. Savio's ambivalence on drugs can be seen in the draft outlines for his autobiography, where he expressed a wariness of drug abuse and drugs as escapism, but also sympathy with the countercultural solidarity that shared use of pot helped to forge. Thus Savio wrote that "the most irresponsible slogan of the era was carried by Timothy Leary: 'Turn on, Tune in, Drop out.'...Yet not all uses of drugs were negative. The joints we passed in counterculture community gatherings helped bond us" (Savio, "Beyond the Cold War: The Education of an American Radical," 16). In a 1966 speech Savio distinguished between persistent and casual drug use, being skeptical of the former (as escapist) and sympathetic with the latter, arguing that as long as it was not abusive, such casual drug use was a form of "pursuit of happiness," which sometimes yielded increasing personal and even political awareness:

Ever since the Beat generation, there has been one strand, one current among students and among the young which has continued into today, which is for saying "Well to hell with politics, it's just a hopeless thing. None of this public life, boy scout helping the lady across the street thing for me." Nowadays in a lot of student communities this is represented by people who are...frequently high on LSD. I'm not speaking against LSD or marijuana, I'm speaking against a certain use of it which does constitute an escape. These people very often could be quite productive contributing members of society if we had a community, but they despair of its formation. There's another group of people who nevertheless, largely come from the white middle class, students who through their own experience with these non-addictive drugs have actually been helped to see their own selves in some detail.... [making] it possible for some people to see a depth of deprivation in themselves which they wouldn't otherwise…[be] able to articulate." (Savio, speech at ZTA fraternity, 12)

Savio's lack of enthusiasm about drugs may also have derived from his negative experience when he was first introduced to marijuana. Michael Rossman, interview by Daniel Savio, May 30, 2006, Berkeley, tape in author's possession.

165. Savio interview by Kitchell, tape 2, 4.–5.

166. Savio, "Beyond the Cold War: The Education of an American Radical," 17. Although Savio was an avid supporter of the women's movement, he only reluctantly went along with abortion rights. He praised the movement's "revolutionary potential" while alluding to his "reluctant and ambivalent acceptance of the women's movement demand for 'reproductive' rights." He termed this his "crypto-Catholic reactions" to the abortion issue. Savio, "Beyond the Cold War: The Education of an American Radical," version II, 14, copy in author's possession.

167. Savio, "Beyond the Cold War: The Education of an American Radical," 17.

168. Ibid., 18; Savio, "Beyond the Cold War: The Education of an American Radical," typed version, 7. Note that the two other Savio outlines for his memoir cited above were handwritten.

169. Savio, "Beyond the Cold War: An Education in Politics," 45.

170. Ibid., 42. Savio's view of the Cold War's persistence and the New Left's inability to halt it should be contrasted with recent historical scholarship, which argues that the global youth protests of the 1960s disrupted the Cold War world order and led to the rise of détente. See Jeremi Suri, *Power and Protest: Global Revolution and the Rise of Détente* (Cambridge, Mass.: Harvard University Press, 2003).

171. Savio, "Beyond the Cold War: The Education of an American Radical," 13.

172. Goldberg, "Mario: Personal and Political," 560–61; Lynne Hollander Savio, e-mail to author, February 25, 2004.

173. Savio "Beyond the Cold War: The Education of an American Radical," 14; Savio, "Beyond the Cold War: An Education in Politics," 46–47.

174. Ibid.

175. Savio, "Beyond the Cold War: An Education in Politics," 46.

176. Reginald Zelnik e-mail to author, January 3, 2004; Lynne Hollander Savio e-mail to author, May 18, 2008.

177. Suzanne Goldberg e-mail to author, March 18, 2009.

178. Savio, "Beyond the Cold War: An Education in Politics," 46.

179. Lynne Hollander Savio, e-mail to author, February 17, 2004.

180. Savio "Beyond the Cold War: The Education of an American Radical," 13. Although his depression disrupted and ultimately ended his Vietnam-era political activism, Savio thought his grim outlook might have sharpened his political analysis, heightening his awareness of the obstacles to change in the Nixon era and keeping him from falling into any of the romantic delusions of those in the New Left who thought a revolutionary crisis was at hand. As Savio put it, "My own unhappiness may actually have helped keep me open to a darker side of the public reality which others were only too pleased to ignore." Savio, "The Education of an American Radical," 14.

Chapter 11

1. Doug Rossinow, "Letting Go: Revisiting the New Left's Demise," in John McMillan and Paul Buhle, eds., *The New Left Revisited* (Philadelphia: Temple University Press, 2003), 241–57; Gitlin, *The Sixties*, 377–438.

2. Mario Savio, "Beyond the Cold War: An Education in Politics," 46–47; Lynne Hollander Savio, e-mail to author, March 6, 2004.

3. Lynne Hollander Savio, e-mails to author, February 16, 17, 25, August 8, 2004; Hollander Savio interview, 2–3.

4. Mario Savio, "3 A.M.," unpublished poem, October 19, 1977, copy in author's possession. Savio's poems are the only introspective writings of his to which I have had access that discuss his life while he was in a mental institution. Since those closest to him during that time have been unwilling to discuss his experiences in this period, I have been forced to keep my account of this part of his life brief and quite incomplete.

5. Mario Savio, "Day Song In Purgatory," unpublished poem, n.d., copy in author's possession; "I believe in the coming of dead flowers," unpublished poem, copy in author's possession.

6. Mario Savio to Art Gatti, March 31 [c. 1972], copy in author's possession.

7. Mario Savio, unpublished poem, March 4, 1978, copy in author's possession.

8. Mario Savio, "Pyulecretude," unpublished poem, December 8, 1977, copy in author's possession.

9. Mario Savio, "Demonstrators," unpublished poem, n.d., copy in author's possession.

10. Lynne Hollander Savio, e-mail to author, February 25, 2004.

11. Lynne Hollander Savio, e-mails to author, February 25, 2004, August 8, 2004, and May 16, 2008; Mario Savio, unpublished poem, July 20, 1978, copy in author's possession.

12. Lynne Hollander Savio, e-mail to author, February 25, 2004.

13. Oliver Johns, telephone interview by author, December 14, 2006, 7.

14. Ibid., 12.

15. Ibid., 2.

16. Oliver Johns, remarks at Mario Savio memorial service, Berkeley 8; Oliver Johns, *Analytical Mechanics for Relativity and Quantum Mechanics* (New York: Oxford University Press, 2005), 169.

17. Johns interview, 1.

18. Ibid., 4.

19. Geoff Marcy, telephone interview by author, December 21, 2006, 4, 10–11.

20. Ibid., 2–3.

21. Ibid., 5.

22. Ibid., 7.

23. Ibid., 9.

24. Ibid., 6.

25. Mario Savio, essay on the Citizens' Party, 1980, copy in author's possession, 1–12.

26. Ibid., 3.

27. Mario Savio, "Public Ownership and Democratic Control of 'Big Oil,'" 1980, copy in author's possession 1.

28. Adam Hochschild, interview by Daniel Savio, June 2, 2007, Berkeley, transcript in author's possession, 2.

29. Savio, essay on the Citizens' Party, 1–3.

30. Ibid., 4, 9.

31. Jerry Fischer, remarks at Mario Savio's funeral, November 9, 1996, 3.

32. Robin Dellabough, "A Conversation with Mario Savio and Bettina Aptheker," 20; Mario Savio, "Beyond the Cold War," *Daily Californian*, October 1, 1984; Savio speech at FSM-20, October 2, 1984, in Cohen, ed., "The FSM and Beyond," 53–55.

33. Savio, "Beyond the Cold War: The Education of an American Radical," typed version, 7.

34. Savio, "Resisting Reaganism and War in Central America," speech at FSM-20, October 2, 1984, 55 (reprinted in part IV of *Freedom's Orator*).

35. Ibid.; *Daily Californian*, October 3, 1984.

36. Savio, "Resisting Reaganism," 54–55.

37. Ibid.; Savio, "Beyond the Cold War," *Daily Californian*, October 1, 1984 (reprinted in part IV of *Freedom's Orator*).

38. Savio, "Resisting Reaganism," 54.

39. Ibid.

40. *Daily Californian*, April 17, 1985; Mario Savio, "April Coalition," speech, April 20, 1985, copy in author's possession; *Daily Californian*, October 2, 1985; Pedro Noguera, "The Berkeley Divestment Movement," speech, February 1, 2007, New York, 8–9, transcript in author's possession.

41. Savio, "The Free Speech Movement and Rhetoric of the Student Movement," 8–10.

42. Savio, notes for Santa Cruz speech, June 17, 1985, copy in author's possession, 7.

43. Lynne Hollander Savio, e-mail to author, January 21, 2005.

44. Mario Savio, "Nicaragua Summer of Peace—Draft Proposal" [1985], copy in author's possession, 1–7.

45. Ibid., 1.

46. Ibid., 4.

47. Ibid., 1.

48. Ibid., 2, 6.

49. Lynne Hollander Savio, e-mail to author, April 7 and May 10, 2008.

50. Savio, Nicaragua Summer of Peace—Draft Proposal, 6. Savio's approach to international conflict, whether in Central America or Europe, was to buy into neither side's propaganda. As he explained in 1985, "We do not by any means need to exchange one set of exaggerated beliefs for another. If the US version of the history of the Cold War is wrong this does not imply that the Russian version is right. Nor do we need to become uncritical agents of the government of Nicaragua (I have never been an uncritical supporter even of myself)." Savio, notes for Santa Cruz speech, 9. Savio felt the need for a new wave of activism in a personal way because of Reagan's hostility to the student and civil rights movements. "Reagan came to political prominence as the avowed enemy of all that the Movement had championed. Indeed, Reagan's campaign for governor cast him as defender of civilized order against the twin assaults of black youth in Los Angeles (Watts [where there was a major race riot in 1965]) and white youth in Berkeley. His present Attorney General Edwin Meese (back in his days as Alameda County Assistant District Attorney) actually helped prepare the case against the FSM's 800 arrestees. Given Meese's current attack on affirmative action and

basic constitutional rights, it is fair to say....that the anti-free speech movement has temporarily triumphed in Washington." Savio, "Beyond the Cold War: Education of an American Radical," 18.

51. Savio, "Resisting Reaganism," 55.

52. Mario Savio, Nicaragua Summer of Peace—Draft Proposal, 6.

53. Mario Savio, "Beyond the Big Chill: Resistance and Survival," speech at Columbia University, November 13, 1984, tape in author's possession.

54. Ibid.

55. Ibid.

56. Lynne Hollander Savio, e-mail to author, January 21, 2005.

57. *New York Times*, March 13, 1983; Art Goldberg, "Right to Heckle," *Nation*, April 1983), 387; "The Mob vs. Kirkpatrick," *Newsweek*, March 23, 1983, 77; *Daily Californian*, February 16, 17, and 22, 1983.

58. Mario Savio, remarks at FSM-20, evening panel, October 2, 1984, tape in author's possession. Savio came to this free speech position after some agonizing—and discussion with Reginald Zelnik, who helped convinced him that on free speech grounds, Kirkpatrick had to be allowed to speak on campus. See Cohen and Zelnik, *The Free Speech Movement*, 476–78.

59. Lynne Hollander Savio, e-mail to author, November 9, 2007.

60. For Mario's Santa Cruz speech, see Savio, "Thirty Years Later," 57–72. The only other 1990s Savio speech that has been published was his 1994 speech reflecting on the FSM's "spiritual values," during FSM-30. See Savio, "Speech for an Anniversary."

61. Savio, "The Second Generation," 1–5, 9–10.

62. Savio, "Thirty Years Later," 69–72; Savio, "Beyond the Cold War," *Daily Californian*, October 2, 1984.

63. Mario Savio, journal from Italy trip [1995]; Lynne Hollander Savio, e-mail to author February 25, 2004.

64. Lynne Hollander Savio, e-mail to author, March 22, 2004.

65. Ibid.

66. Oliver Johns, remarks at memorial service for Mario Savio, UC Berkeley, December 8, 1996, 8.

67. Ibid.

68. Jerry Fischer, remarks at Mario Savio's funeral, November 9, 1996, 3.

69. Lynne Hollander Savio, e-mail to author, February 25, 2004; Elaine Sundberg, remarks at memorial service for Mario Savio, UC Berkeley, December 8, 1996, 9–10; Raskin, "Mario Savio's Second Act: the 1990s," 520–21. Note, however, that Raskin erred in stating that Sundberg, as ILE director, hired Mario. Savio was hired by her predecessor.

70. Raskin, "Mario Savio's Second Act," 523.

71. Mario Savio, "AE (Aristotle-Euler) Diagrams: An Alternative Complete Method for the Categorical Syllogism," *Notre Dame Journal of Formal Logic*, Fall 1998.

72. Raskin, "Mario Savio's Second Act," 522–23; Victor Garlin, interview by author, New York City, December 22, 2006, 4.

73. Raskin, "Mario Savio's Second Act," 521–22; Santa Rosa *Press Democrat*, May 2, 1991; Mario Savio, notes on the "student as Nigger" controversy, [May 1991], copy in author's possession. On Granahan's censorship charge against Savio, also see Andrea Granahan telephone interview by the author, May 16, 2009, tape in author's possession

and Granahan e-mails to author, may 16 and 17, 2009. None of Savio's notes or other writings on this dispute confirms this charge; instead, they suggest that he searched for a way to offer more effective advice and mentorship for its racially insensitive staff.

74. Mario Savio, notes on the "Student as Nigger" controversy [May 1991], copy in author's possession.

75. Mario Savio, draft of letter to *Press Democrat* [May 1991], copy in author's possession.

76. Savio, notes on the "Student as Nigger" controversy; Granahan interview.

77. Savio, draft of letter to *Press Democrat*.

78. Ibid.

79. Ruben Armiñana, telephone interview by author, November 26, 2007, 4.

80. Mario Savio, notes for speeches on Sonoma State differential fee controversy [fall 1996], copy in author's possession, 3.

81. Garlin interview by author, 1, 11.

82. Savio, notes for speeches on Sonoma State differential fee controversy, 3.

83. Elaine Sundberg, remarks at memorial service for Mario Savio, UC Berkeley, December 8, 1996, 10.

84. Victor Garlin, remarks at memorial service for Mario Savio, Sonoma State University, December 1996, transcript in author's possession, 2.

85. Mario Savio to Ruben Armiñana [1993], copy in author's possession; Victor Garlin, interview by Daniel Savio, June 1, 2006, Berkeley, tape in author's possession; Garlin interview by author, 4.

86. Elizabeth Hoffman, "How Mario Savio and Joe Berry Helped CFA Lecturers to Organize," *California Faculty*, Spring 2006, 19.

87. Jack Kurzweil, interview by Daniel Savio, June 20, 2006, Berkeley, tape in author's possession.

88. Savio, notes for speech to Sonoma State University Philosophy Club, April 20, 1993. Savio ran out of time before he could discuss the range of thinkers who had influenced his thinking during the FSM years, but his notes indicated that these included Kant, Kierkegaard, Thomas Aquinas, Jacques Maritain, Emmanuel Mounier, Jean Wahl, G. E. Moore, Gabriel Marcel, Albert Camus, the Catholic Worker Movement, J. L. Austin, Leo Tolstoy, John Austin, Herbert Marcuse, and Pedro Calderón de la Barca.

89. Savio, "The Philosophy of a Young Activist," 1. While selecting the middle initial *E* to honor his mother, Savio also began to use the middle name Elliot (Lynne Hollander Savio, e-mail to author, June 9, 2008).

90. Mario Savio, "A Moment to Move Against Class-Ridden Barbarism," speech at ACLU dinner, Sebastopol, California, February 24, 1995, in author's possession (full text of this speech appears in part IV of *Freedom's Orator*). Recent historical accounts tend to support Savio's critical reading of California's right-wing-dominated voter initiatives during the 1990s. See Robin Dale Jacobson, *The New Nativism: Proposition 187 and the Debate over Immigration* (Minneapolis: University of Minnesota Press, 2008).

91. Mario Savio, "Building a Compassionate Community," speech at FSM-30, version I, transcript in author's possession, 5 (full text of this speech appears in part IV of *Freedom's Orator*).

92. Savio, "A Moment to Move Against Class-Ridden Barbarism."

93. Savio, "Building a Compassionate Community," version II, 3.

94. Ibid., 2.

95. Ibid., 3.

96. Mario Savio, "Their Values and Ours," discussion of "spiritual values," FSM-30, initially published as "Speech for an Anniversary."

97. Ibid., 4–8.

98. Ibid., 7.

99. Ibid.

100. Nadav Savio and Mario Savio, *In Defense of Affirmative Action: The Case Against Proposition 209* (Oakland: Campus Coalitions for Human Rights and Social Justice, 1996), 1 (reprinted in part IV of *Freedom's Orator*); Lynne Hollander Savio, e-mail to author, March 25, 2004.

101. Savio, "Class-Ridden Barbarism," 2–5; Kurzweil interview; Lynne Hollander Savio, e-mail to author, March 25, 2004.

102. Garlin interview by Daniel Savio.

103. Kurzweil interview.

104. Ibid.

105. Jeff Lustig, interview by Daniel Savio, June 11, 2006, Berkeley, tape in author's possession.

106. Santa Rosa *Press Democrat*, February 21, 1995; Savio also gave an interview to another local paper. See Sebastopol *Times and News*, February 22, 1995.

107. Santa Rosa *Press Democrat*, February 21, 1995.

108. Savio, "Class-Ridden Barbarism," 2–3.

109. Ibid., 3.

110. Savio, "Thirty Years Later," speech at UC Santa Cruz, November 15, 1995, 57–58.

111. Ibid., 70–71.

112. Ibid., 58.

113. Ibid., 70–71.

114. Ibid., 71.

115. Ibid., 70.

116. Savio and Savio, *In Defense of Affirmative Action*.

117. Nadav Savio, interview by Daniel Savio, June 1, 2007, San Francisco, transcript in author's possession, 1.

118. Ibid.

119. Mario Savio, "Diversity Is a Responsibility," *Daily Californian*, July 25, 1995.

120. The Campus Coalitions for Human Rights and Social Responsibility did not prove an enduring organization in part because it was linked to the aftermath of the specific ballot initiatives. When outrage cooled over those conservative initiatives on immigrant rights and affirmative action, "nothing came along immediately" that could serve as the "glue to hold the organization together" (Epstein interview, 6).

121. Mario Savio to the editor of Santa Rosa *Press Democrat*, February 25, 1995, copy in author's possession.

122. Todd Gitlin, *The Twilight of Common Dreams: Why America Is Wracked by Culture Wars* (New York: Metropolitan Books, 1995), 126–59.

123. Jacobson, *The New Nativism*, xiv; Elaine Korry, "Black Student Enrollment at UCLA Plunges," National Public Radio, March 29, 2009, http://www.npr.org/templates/story/story.php?storyId=5563891.

Chapter 12

1. Mario Savio, "A Challenge to the Other 'Partners in Excellence,'" *Sonoma State Star*, October 8, 1996; Mario Savio, remarks at Sonoma State University forum on the differential fee referendum, November 1, 1996, tape in author's possession; Mario Savio to Lowell Finley, November 2, 1996, Sonoma State/Differential Dispute, *Hollander v. Munitz*, legal file 690.00, Altshuler, Berzon, Nussbaum, and Rubin, copy in author's possession.

2. Christopher Newfield, *Unmaking the Public University: The Forty-Year Assault on the Middle Class* (Cambridge, Mass.: Harvard University Press, 2008), 1–13.

3. Mario Savio, "A Moment to Move Against Class-Ridden Barbarism," speech at ACLU dinner, February 24, 1995, 4.

4. Ibid.

5. Elaine Sundberg, interview by Daniel Savio, Sebastopol, California, December 29, 2006, tape in author's possession; Garlin interview by author; Lynne Hollander Savio, e-mails to author, March 9, 2004 and November 28, 2007; Raskin, "Mario Savio's Second Act," 527; Armiñana interview, 1.

6. Armiñana interview, 6.

7. Ruben Armiñana, "SSU's Fee Vote: Issue of Quality," Santa Rosa *Press Democrat*, June 5, 1996; Armiñana interview, 2.

8. Mario Savio, notes for speeches on Sonoma State differential fee controversy, 4. President Armiñana and Provost Donald Farish disputed this criticism, claiming that in planning to upgrade SSU they intended to keep the campus as diverse—with as many students of color—as it had been in the past. In 1996 Armiñana contended that minority enrollments had increased during his presidency (SSU fee forum, November 1, 1996, tape in author's possession); Donald Farish, telephone interview by author, October 25, 2007, 7). According to data from SSU's Office of the Provost, Sonoma State's black student population fell from 3.5 percent in 1994 to 1.9 percent in 2005, while the numbers of Chicano students rose from 5.9 percent to 7.3 percent. The biggest change, and the strongest evidence of gentrification, is reflected in the age and class background of SSU students. SSU was once widely accessible to working-class reentry students, who tended to work full-time and to be older than conventional, more affluent college students. The percentage of students ages thirty to thirty-nine attending SSU declined from 14 percent in 1994 to 7.3 percent in 2005, and students forty years of age or older experienced a similar decline, from 15 percent to 8.9 percent of the student body (Office of the Provost, Institutional Research, "Demographics, Fall Semesters 1994–2005," copy in author's possession). Critics of SSU's gentrification charge that under Armiñana's leadership between 1993 and 1999 access declined dramatically, with the number of more affluent freshmen (from families with income levels above $75,000) rising by 57 percent, while low-income freshmen (from families with income levels below $25,000) declined by 47 percent (Peter Phillips, "Gentrification of Sonoma State," October 2000, www.sonoma.edu/senate/Referendum/GentrificationofSonomaState.rtf).

9. Savio, notes for speeches on Sonoma State differential fee controversy, 2. On President Armiñana's advocacy of making SSU "California's public Ivy" League university, see *Sonoma State Star*, September 10, 1996. Former SSU provost Donald Farish argues that the term "public Ivy" was a poor one—and tried but failed to

convince Armiñana not to adopt it—since, in his view, it incorrectly imputed elitist
motivations to the administration's efforts to upgrade the quality and stabilize the
finances and enrollments of SSU. Farish interview, 6–7.

10. *San Francisco Chronicle*, October 31, 1996. Savio thought it absurd to hold that
student fees would add to the fiscal health of a public university: "How does opening
up a new source of income from some students make the legislature increase their
funding [of Sonoma State]? There's no incentive for them to do so."

11. Savio, notes for speeches on Sonoma State differential fee controversy, 1. Also
see Mario Savio, "A Few Reasons for a 'No' Vote on Fee Increase," *Sonoma State Star*,
October 29, 1996; Mario Savio to Lowell Finley, October 25, 1996, n.d., and November 2,
1996, Sonoma State/Differential Dispute, *Hollander v. Munitz*, legal file 690.00,
Altshuler, Berzon, Nussbaum, and Rubin, copies in author's possession.

12. Garlin interview by author, 2. The best sources on the issue of administration
political pressure exerted at SSU on behalf of the fee increases are the sworn affidavits
documenting allegations of such pressure in Sonoma State/Differential Dispute,
Hollander v. Munitz, legal file 690.00, case no. 214974, Altshuler, Berzon, Nussbaum,
and Rubin, Superior Court Pleadings, vol. 1., copy in author's possession. Among the
allegations made in these affidavits were that student employees of the university were
required to attend administration-run pro-fee sessions, campus officials had torn
down anti-fee posters on campus, the student newspaper's faculty advisor forced the
editor to remove from her article discussion of faculty criticism of the fee, and high-
ranking administrators personally rebuked faculty critics of the fees.

13. Sonoma State University, *Voter Pamphlet: Partners for Excellence: Referendum
on Undergraduate Student Fee, November 20 and 21, 1996*, Sonoma State/Differential
Dispute, *Hollander v. Munitz*, legal file 690.00 Altshuler, Berzon, Nussbaum, and
Rubin, copy in author's possession; Mette Adams, remarks at memorial service for
Mario Savio, UC Berkeley, December 8, 1996.

14. Armiñana interview, 3. Note, however, that the issue of bias and administration
heavy-handedness in connection with this voter education pamphlet did not end with
its publication. Bryan Baker, an assistant professor of geography and the only faculty
member whose anti-fee statement appeared in that pamphlet, received an e-mail
from President Armiñana, indicating that he was "worried" about Baker's comments
"in opposition" to the fee. Armiñana's e-mail accused Baker of using "the same logic"
as that employed by right-wing extremists in the "so called 'militias.'" If the leaders
of institutions such as the government and the SSU administration were, Armiñana
wrote, deemed "untrustworthy and liars…then our society is in immediate danger of
collapse into anarchy and chaos." Baker viewed Armiñana's message as suggesting "a
level of defensiveness and an all-or-nothing, you're either for me or against me attitude
that…is inappropriate for an official charged…with the responsibility to engage in a
consultative process…concerning any proposal to create new mandatory fees." Ruben
Armiñana, e-mail to Bryan Baker, October 24, 1996; Bryan Baker affidavit, November 15,
1996, Sonoma State/Differential Dispute, *Hollander v. Munitz*, legal file 690.00, case no.
214974, Altshuler, Berzon, Nussbaum, and Rubin, Superior Court Pleadings, vol. 1, copy
in author's possession, 3.

15. Mette Adams, telephone interview by author, October 30, 2007, 2.

16. Ibid.

17. Garlin remarks at memorial service, 3. Note that former SSU provost Donald
Farish, though unable to recall why the pamphlet ended up being so biased, argues

that the administration made a good-faith effort to run the referendum fairly. He also claims that the SSU's political climate would have precluded the administration from even considering working to run an unfair fee process because the "Sonoma State...faculty...enjoyed being adversarial, and there was a lot of strong union sentiment....So...we couldn't have gotten away with much, independent of Mario....We had to show...we were being fair....We made an honest effort to solicit input into this booklet so we could present both sides....And yeah, there was [a] little fussiness about the balance" (Farish interview, 3).

18. Garlin interview by author, 7.

19. Ibid., 1.

20. Armiñana's partisanship was evident in the contradictory way he discussed the voter pamphlet. He admitted that the process of putting together the pamphlet was flawed, but he also said was not prepared to do anything to offset this, such as delaying the election until a more balanced pamphlet could be sent out to all SSU students. He cast the calls for postponement not as aimed at fairness but as merely a "delaying tactic" by fee opponents. Armiñana interview, 3.

21. Raskin, "Mario Savio's Second Act," 526.

22. Lynne Hollander Savio, e-mails to author, March 9, 2004, and November 28, 2007; Lynne Hollander Savio, testimony, November 12, 1998, State of California Dept. of Industrial Relations, Workers' Compensation Appeals Board Case, *Mario Savio (Deceased) et al. vs. Sonoma State University*, copy in author's possession, 6.

23. Lynne Hollander Savio, e-mails to author, March 9, 2004, and November 28, 2007; Leo Aguilar, remarks at memorial service for Mario Savio, Sonoma State University, 13.

24. *Sonoma State Star*, October 15, 1996.

25. Raskin, "Mario Savio's Second Act," 527; Lynne Hollander Savio, e-mail to author, March 9, 2004.

26. Lynne Hollander Savio, e-mail to author, March 9, 2004.

27. Savio, notes for speeches on Sonoma State differential fee controversy, 5; Mario Savio, notes for first open discussion on the fee issue, 2–3, copies in author's possession, c. September 1996.

28. Savio, notes for speeches on Sonoma State differential fee controversy, 1.

29. Adams remarks at memorial service, 12.

30. Lowell Finley, interview by author, August 25, 2004, Berkeley, 2.

31. Adams interview, 1–2.

32. Ibid.

33. Farish interview, 3, 6.

34. Ibid., 1.

35. Ibid., 2, 7.

36. Ibid., 7.

37. Ibid., 1–2.

38. Ibid., 1.

39. Tape of November 1, 1996, fee forum at Sonoma State University, copy in author's possession; Adams interview, 2.

40. Tape of November 1, 1996 fee forum. Armiñana argues that the memo from the vice president about the freshman seminars was not evidence of pressure being placed on students or faculty to vote for the fee, since he claims that the memo only asked that the fees be discussed, not that they be promoted in the class (Armiñana interview, 4).

But the fact that the administration made such efforts to reach freshmen may itself be evidence of partisanship, since it was assumed by both sides that freshmen would be the most likely to support the fees (since they would be in school the longest and stand the best chance of benefiting from the new spending once the fees kicked in).

41. Tape of November 1, 1996, fee forum.

42. Armiñana interview, 5; Ruben Armiñana, testimony, November 12, 1998, State of California Dept. of Industrial Relations, Workers' Compensation Appeals Board Case, *Mario Savio (Deceased) et al. vs. Sonoma State University*, 26.

43. Lynne Hollander Savio, e-mail to author, March 9, 2004; Hollander Savio testimony, 9; Daniel Hollander Savio, Elaine Sundberg, Susan Kashack, and Victor Garlin, testimony, November 12, 1998, State of California Dept. of Industrial Relations, Workers' Compensation Appeals Board Case, *Mario Savio (Deceased) et al. vs. Sonoma State University*, 10, 12, 15, 17.

44. Adams interview, 2.

45. Ibid. Ironically, Savio came away from the tense forum worried not about his own health but about Armiñana's; he was concerned that the stress of this encounter might cause SSU's president to have a heart attack. See Hollander Savio testimony, 7.

46. Lynne Hollander Savio, e-mails to author, March 9, 2004, and October 18, 2007; Michael Rossman to Friends, November 20, 1996, copy in author's possession.

47. Mario Savio to Lowell Finley, November 2, 1996.

48. Finley interview, 4.

49. Santa Rosa *Press Democrat*, November 19, 1996.

50. Ibid., November 22, 1996.

51. Farish interview, 5.

52. Armiñana interview, 5.

53. Adams interview, 3–4.

54. Zelnik remarks at funeral, 9.

55. Ibid.

56. Rossman remarks at memorial service, 15.

57. Lynne Hollander Savio, e-mails to author, March 9 and 25, 2004.

58. Santa Rosa *Press Democrat*, December 6, 1996; Sonoma State University memorial ceremony for Mario Savio, December 5, 1996, transcript in author's possession, 1–10.

59. Garlin interview by author, 16; Judith Hunt, testimony, November 12, 1998, State of California Dept. of Industrial Relations, Workers' Compensation Appeals Board Case, *Mario Savio (Deceased) et al. vs. Sonoma State University*, 20–21.

60. This idealism was very much on display even in the way Savio wrote his byline in his anti-fee editorials, which he signed "For a Community of Learners from Mario Savio." See *Sonoma State Star*, October 8 and 29, 1996.

61. Farish interview, 5 Actually, Savio was not doing "heavy lifting" at the time of his fatal heart attack. His collapse came when "he was carrying a small amp[lifer]...to the car on the way to taking [his son] Daniel to a party....So it's not like he was overtaxing himself" (Lynne Hollander Savio, e-mail to author, October 18, 2007; Hollander Savio testimony, 7).

62. Farish interview, 5.

63. Lynne Hollander Savio, e-mail to author, May 18, 2008. According to Lynne Hollander Savio (e-mail to author, October 18, 2007):

the workmen's comp claim...was based on the idea that Mario was functioning in his capacity as a faculty member even in opposing the fee increase. He had also reported to me that the forum on the fee increase was extremely upsetting to him (that was the Friday before the weekend he collapsed). Armiñana claimed in court that it was very amicable, but Mario thought otherwise. The referee said the video [of the fee forum] didn't show Mario as upset, but that's what he reported. Following that, he spent the weekend working on the [law] suit [against the fee referendum], and the referee said that suing the university wasn't part of his job description, although he felt the other activities were. In short, if he had collapsed after the forum, I would probably have won the case.

64. Sonoma's student activists saw themselves as defending the tradition of accessible, tuition-free public higher education embodied in California's Master Plan for Higher Education. Though they did not mention Kerr's name, they did invoke the plan—and Kerr was the leader who oversaw its writing and implementation. See Adams interview, 6; John Aubrey Douglas, *The California Idea and American Higher Education: 1850 to the 1960 Master Plan* (Stanford: Stanford University Press, 2000). Savio also invoked the Master Plan in opposing the fee hike; see Garlin testimony, 16.

65. In the decade following Savio's death, however, the Cal State system moved away from the tradition of accessible education that he was trying to preserve. Statewide educational fees, according to Armiñana, "doubled or more in California. The idea of...a free or almost free university really no longer exists except in the ideology of some people" (Armiñana interview, 6).

66. Mette Adams, e-mail to author, November 1, 2007. Also see Matthew Morgan, remarks at memorial service for Mario Savio, Sonoma State University, 8.

67. Roger Kimball, *Tenured Radicals: How Politics Has Corrupted Our Higher Education* (New York: Harper and Row, 1990). For an insightful critique of these polemical attacks on radicalism in American higher education, which were a key part of the "culture wars" of the 1990s, see Lawrence W. Levine, *The Opening of the American Mind: Canons, Culture, and History* (Boston: Beacon Press, 1997), 3–34. Also see Bruce L. R. Smith, Jeremy D. Mayer, and A. Lee Fritschler, *Closed Minds? Politics and Ideology in American Universities* (Washington, D.C.: Brookings Institution Press, 2008).

68. The *New York Times*, for example, made no mention of any of Savio's political activism during his SSU years in its obituary. See *New York Times*, November 8, 1996.

69. On the post-sixties academic Left, see Gosse, *Rethinking the New Left*, 198–200; Jim Downs and Jennifer Manion, eds., *Taking Back the Academy, History of Activism, History as Activism* (New York: Routledge, 2004), 57–208; Doug McAdam, "From Relevance to Irrelevance: The Curious Impact of the Sixties on Public Sociology," in Craig Calhoun, ed., *Sociology in America: A History* (Chicago: University of Chicago Press, 2007), 411–26; Diggins, *The Rise and Fall of the American Left*, 288–98.

70. Savio, "Thirty Years Later," 68–72.

71. Bettina Aptheker, remarks at memorial service for Mario Savio, UC Berkeley, December 8, 1996, 25.

72. Savio interview by Giles, 8. In Cohen and Zelnik, eds., *The Free Speech Movement*, a fuller version of this quotation appears opposite the title page.

73. Searle interview by author, 1.

74. Letter from Mario Savio to Nadav Savio, September 18, 1990, transcript of memorial service for Mario Savio, UC Berkeley, September 18, 1990, 24. Nadav had been in Ecuador as part of his college semester abroad program.

75. Searle interview by author, 7.

76. Ibid., 8.

77. Chang-Lin Tien to Lynne Hollander Savio, December 6, 1996, copy in author's possession.

78. Leon F. Litwack, "On the Dedication of the Mario Savio Steps, University of California at Berkeley, December 3, 1997," copy in author's possession, 2–5. For a slightly abridged version, see Leon Litwack, "Savio Steps," *California Monthly*, February 1998, 8.

79. Mario Savio, notes for a proposal [never submitted] for the Berkeley campus FSM Monument [1990], copy in author's possession, 4–6. The idea of an FSM monument generated political heat when Chancellor Ira Michael Heyman decided that the FSM was too controversial to be so honored. He would allow a monument to free speech but not if it named the Free Speech Movement—so, ironically, artists submitting proposals for a monument to free speech did not have the freedom to speak of the FSM. See Heyman to the Members of the Berkeley Art Project, June 29, 1990, copy in author's possession. A piece of conceptual art honoring free speech but not the FSM was allowed to be permanently displayed on campus.

80. In 2000, thanks to a generous donation by Steven Silberstein, something finally was named on the campus for the Free Speech Movement: a café—which featured historical photos and writings from the FSM—next to Berkeley's undergraduate library. There had been some discussion about naming the café after Savio, but his family and FSM veterans decided to name it after the movement. On the café's opening, see Martin Roysher, "Recollections of the Free Speech Movement," in Cohen and Zelnik, eds., *The Free Speech Movement*, 140.

81. Suzanne Goldberg, remarks at Mario Savio's funeral, November 9, 1996, 20.

82. Aptheker, *Intimate Politics*.

83. Mario Savio, "Beyond the Cold War: An Education in Politics," 22.

84. Savio, "Building a Compassionate Community," 7. Emphasis added.

85. Rossman remarks at memorial service, 16.

86. Nadav Savio interview, 4.

INDEX

Free Speech Movement (*continued*)
    TA and student strike, 157, 163, 177,
        190–91, 194, 198, 208, 210
    rally after arrests, 208–9
    Greek Theatre, 210–14
    December 8 resolutions, 11, 214–15,
        240, 242–43, 247
    victory rally, 216–17, 231
    court trial, 231–32, 241, 243
    obscenity controversy,
        222, 233–36, 239, 241, 470n.19,
        470n.29
    other free speech disputes, 236–37
    Savio resigns, 237–42
    FSM disbands, 238
  anniversaries of. *See* FSM-20; FSM-30
  community feeling in, 96, 100–101, 109,
    179, 193, 270
  egalitarianism in, 192, 221, 313, 320
  explosiveness of, 107–9
  gender bias in, 192–93, 256, 448n.17,
    472n.59
  grassroots activism in, 95–96, 120, 135
  hyperdemocratic ethos of, 7–8, 94–95,
    120, 121, 123–24, 126, 128, 133, 152,
    153–54, 159, 167, 168, 221, 238
  as largest student protest, 2, 3, 116, 198
  legacy of, 221–23, 227–28, 253, 267, 313
  links to civil rights movement, 97, 101,
    139, 144, 194–95, 218, 222, 226, 241,
    329
  moderates in, 151–60, 439n.10, 453n.31,
    454n.49, 455n.81
  monuments and tributes to, 318,
    488n.79–80
  as moral cause, 3, 76–77, 96–97, 104,
    186
  Old Left politics in, 118–19, 124, 130–31,
    141, 155, 156–57, 158–59, 447n.83
  oratory. *See* oratory of Mario Savio
  public disapproval of, 4, 218–22, 419n.14
  solidarity in, 77, 86–87, 96, 100, 120, 154,
    174, 228

  See also Executive Committee of FSM;
    Little Free Speech Movement;
    Steering Committee of FSM; UC
    Berkeley administration; UC
    Berkeley faculty
Free Speech Movement newsletter, 151–52,
  179, 182, 183, 225
Free Student Union, 238
French student rebellion, 263
FSM. *See* Free Speech Movement
FSM-20 (Free Speech Movement 20th
  Anniversary):
  author as an organizer of, 10
  Savio's concerns about, 285–86
  Savio's oratory, 11, 228, 279–80, 282, 316,
    339–45, 346–49
FSM-30 (Free Speech Movement 30th
  Anniversary), 291–92, 316,
  358–66

Gandhi, Mahatma, 179
Ganz, Marshall, 53, 72, 434n.68, 435n.83
Garlin, Victor, 288–89, 301, 302, 310
Garofalo, Reebee, 68
Garson, Barbara, 151–52, 225
Gatti, Art, 38, 258, 272
gay and lesbian movement, 226, 267, 279
gender bias:
  in Freedom Summer work, 434n.61
  in FSM, 192–93, 256, 448n.17, 472n.59
  and Reaganism, 277
  and Savio's educational choices,
    437n.101
  See also feminist movement
Germany, 292
Gingrich, Newt, 290, 296, 311
Ginsberg, Allen, 470n.19
Gitlin, Todd, 8, 9, 10, 259, 298
Glazer, Nathan, 209
Gleason, Ralph J., 199, 211, 463n.75
Glendora, Calif., 38
Goines, David, 151, 153

Pimentel, George, 222
police. *See* law enforcement
police car blockade:
    negotiations in, 104–6, 109–15
    Pact of October 2 ending, 109–16,
        119–20
    as perfect democratic moment, 101–2
    police car as podium, vii, 1, 99–100, 102,
        103, 115–16
    press reaction to, 1–2
    provocation for, 1, 98–99
    Savio's oratory, vii, 1–2, 102–4,
        115–18
    sense of community in, 100–101
political advocacy ban. *See* Free Speech
    Movement
politics. *See* American politics
Potter, Paul, 457n.7
Powell, Charles, 104, 182, 190–91
Powell, Colin, 13, 313
presidential campaign of 1964, 75, 92,
    437n.92
press. *See* media
Press Democrat, 287, 288, 294
Progressive Labor faction, 8
Proposition 187, 290, 291–92, 293, 294,
    298, 300
Proposition 209, 290, 293, 297, 298, 300

Queens College, 37
Queens College Mexican Volunteers, 37
Queens, New York, 6

radicalism. *See* sixties radicalism
Rafferty, Max, 246
Raskin, A.H., 134
Raskin, Jonah, 302
Reagan administration:
    and Central American policy,
        276–82
    education advisor, 80

Reaganism:
    as American imperialism, 277, 278,
        279–80, 282
    as backlash against sixties, 13, 160, 221,
        267, 279, 311, 467n.72
    Savio's critique of, 11, 276–77, 278–84,
        339–45, 346–49
Reagan, Ronald:
    election to governorship, 221,
        467n.72
    election to presidency, 4, 277
    firing of Clark Kerr, 239, 251–52
    New Right politics of, 13, 221, 279, 283,
        316, 479n.50
    on universities as knowledge factories,
        464n.84
Rebuilding a Lost Faith (Stoddard), 28
Reconstruction, 62–63, 64
Red-baiting:
    in civil rights movement, 44, 139
    in Free Speech Movement, 81, 130–31,
        138–39, 155, 182, 191
    by media, 130–31, 217
    of Savio, 44, 430n.60
Red scares, 75
Republican National Convention (1964),
    78, 79, 82
Republican party, 313
Rhoades, Gary, 201
Richmond Housing Authority sit-in, 89
the Right. *See* New Right
Rogin, Michael, 101
Roosevelt, Franklin D., 14, 46
Roseanne (TV show), 295
Rosenthal, Dan, 111, 112
Rossman, Michael:
    December 2 speech, 182, 183–84, 185, 186
    prison sentence, 474n.113
    at Savio's memorial service, 309,
        313, 320
    on Sproul Hall sit-in, 193
    on Steering Committee, 127, 133,
        167, 173